IFIP Advances in Information and Communication Technology

600

Editor-in-Chief

Kai Rannenberg, Goethe University Frankfurt, Germany

IFIP – The International Federation for Information Processing

IFIP was founded in 1960 under the auspices of UNESCO, following the first World Computer Congress held in Paris the previous year. A federation for societies working in information processing, IFIP's aim is two-fold: to support information processing in the countries of its members and to encourage technology transfer to developing nations. As its mission statement clearly states:

IFIP is the global non-profit federation of societies of ICT professionals that aims at achieving a worldwide professional and socially responsible development and application of information and communication technologies.

IFIP is a non-profit-making organization, run almost solely by 2500 volunteers. It operates through a number of technical committees and working groups, which organize events and publications. IFIP's events range from large international open conferences to working conferences and local seminars.

The flagship event is the IFIP World Computer Congress, at which both invited and contributed papers are presented. Contributed papers are rigorously refereed and the rejection rate is high.

As with the Congress, participation in the open conferences is open to all and papers may be invited or submitted. Again, submitted papers are stringently refereed.

The working conferences are structured differently. They are usually run by a working group and attendance is generally smaller and occasionally by invitation only. Their purpose is to create an atmosphere conducive to innovation and development. Refereeing is also rigorous and papers are subjected to extensive group discussion.

Publications arising from IFIP events vary. The papers presented at the IFIP World Computer Congress and at open conferences are published as conference proceedings, while the results of the working conferences are often published as collections of selected and edited papers.

IFIP distinguishes three types of institutional membership: Country Representative Members, Members at Large, and Associate Members. The type of organization that can apply for membership is a wide variety and includes national or international societies of individual computer scientists/ICT professionals, associations or federations of such societies, government institutions/government related organizations, national or international research institutes or consortia, universities, academies of sciences, companies, national or international associations or federations of companies.

More information about this series at http://www.springer.com/series/6102

Michael Goedicke · Erich Neuhold ·
Kai Rannenberg (Eds.)

Advancing Research in Information and Communication Technology

IFIP's Exciting First 60+ Years,
Views from the Technical Committees
and Working Groups

 Springer

Editors
Michael Goedicke
University of Duisburg-Essen
Essen, Germany

Erich Neuhold
University of Vienna
Vienna, Austria

Kai Rannenberg
Goethe University Frankfurt
Frankfurt/Main, Germany

ISSN 1868-4238   ISSN 1868-422X (electronic)
IFIP Advances in Information and Communication Technology
ISSN 2730-5759   ISSN 2730-5767 (electronic)
IFIP AICT Festschrifts
ISBN 978-3-030-81703-9   ISBN 978-3-030-81701-5 (eBook)
https://doi.org/10.1007/978-3-030-81701-5

This Springer imprint is published by the registered company Springer Nature Switzerland AG
The registered company address is: Gewerbestrasse 11, 6330 Cham, Switzerland

Foreword

IFIP — the International Federation for Information Processing —was founded in 1960 following the first World Computer Congress, and under the auspices of UNESCO. Its aim was to support and advance the work of the then-fledgling societies dealing with information processing (which we now refer to as information and communication technology, or ICT) and the nascent computing industry. Computer Science, or Computing as a discipline of science, was also in its infancy.

Today, IFIP is the global federation of ICT societies and associations committed to advancing scientific progress and the professional and socially-responsible application of technology based on scientific progress. IFIP's members are national, regional, and international ICT societies. In turn, their members are ICT scientists, researchers, academics, educators, professionals, practitioners, and policy-makers, who are focused on developing and advancing ICT foundational knowledge and expertise; promoting digital equity; educating and enhancing public understanding of technology and its potential (both for good and, occasionally, ill); and increasing professionalism and professional standards.

Along with its member societies, IFIP is a strong advocate for ICT equality and works closely with UNESCO, the United Nations, ITU, and many other international bodies to promote understanding of issues related to technology. We aim to collaborate on solutions to help in the achievement of the United Nations Sustainable Development Goals (SDGs).

IFIP also seeks to raise awareness and understanding amongst the wider community about where technology is headed, how it can enhance the quality of all our lives, and how to ensure that all people have equal access and equal opportunity.

In both science and research, IFIP is uniquely placed to achieve these outcomes through its global network of 13 Technical Committees and more than 130 Working Groups, which bring together experts in different fields to share and enhance their knowledge, and to focus attention on key areas related to science and technology.

IFIP member societies, and their individual members, have access to the largest network of technical expertise in the world. This enables them to make valuable connections, grow their knowledge and skills, and contribute to the development of global insights and standards for ICT and ICT professionals.

Most of the more than 100 events IFIP organizes every year are based on the work of IFIP Technical Committees and Working Groups and bring together international experts on various ICT-related topics, to share the latest scientific findings, discuss the ICT-related technological and societal developments, and reflect on the latest issues of relevance to the ICT profession.

Given this breadth and depth of competence we welcome the survey of current findings, summary of the state of the art, and discussions in Technical Committees and their Working Groups that are contained in this volume of Advancing ICT Research, and which document the wide range of scientific activities within IFIP. The final chapter of this volume deserves special attention— it is the current Code of Ethics which IFIP has adopted for itself.

Please join us as we celebrate IFIP's 60th anniversary with a range of online and blended events addressing all aspects of ICT and enjoy this volume of ICT achievements.

Mike Hinchey
IFIP President (2016–2022)

Preface

Soon after IFIP was founded, it established Technical Committees (TCs) and related Working Groups (WGs) to foster exchange and development with regard to the scientific and technical aspects of information processing. IFIP TCs are as diverse as the different aspects of information processing, but they share the following aims:

- To establish and maintain liaison with national and international organizations with allied interests and to foster cooperative action, collaborative research, and information exchange.
- To identify subjects and priorities for research, to stimulate theoretical work on fundamental issues and to foster fundamental research which will underpin future development.
- To provide a forum for professionals with a view to promoting the study, collection, exchange, and dissemination of ideas, information, and research findings and thereby to promote the state of the art.
- To seek and use the most effective ways of disseminating information about IFIP's work including the organization of conferences, workshops, and symposia and the timely production of relevant publications.
- To have special regard for the needs of developing countries and to seek practicable ways of working with them.
- To encourage communication and to promote interaction between users, practitioners, and researchers.
- To foster interdisciplinary work and – in particular – to collaborate with other Technical Committees and Working Groups.

Considering these aims and the corresponding activities and competencies of the IFIP TCs, it seems natural that they were invited to contribute high quality ICT Research publications with insights from the breadth of their entire work on a global/worldwide scale. Consequently, the editors of this book were lucky enough to receive 17 contributions from nine TCs and several of their WGs. These contributions describe the scientific, technical, and further work in the TCs and WGs and in many cases also assess the consequences of the work's results. They will help IFIP and their readers to explore the developments of IFIP and the profession now and over the next 60 years. The contributions are arranged per TC and conclude with the chapter on the IFIP code of ethics and conduct as a joint IFIP endeavour and achievement.

The WGs of TC 1 "Foundations of Computer Science" contributed two chapters focussing on complexity and signal flow theory:

- "Hot Current Topics of Descriptional Complexity" reflects the work of WG 1.2 "Descriptional Complexity" aiming for powerful yet operational descriptions of information and the algorithms that process it.
- "A Survey of Compositional Signal Flow Theory" is a joint contribution by WG 1.3 "Foundations of System Specification" and WG 1.8 "Concurrency Theory" and

illustrates the use of special graphical models to advance the description of signal flow graphs and make it easier to understand the corresponding signal flows.

The WGs of TC 2 "Software: Theory and Practice" also contributed two chapters concentrating on essentials of software engineering such as algorithms and data management:

- "Algorithmics" contributed by WG 2.1 "Algorithmic Languages and Calculi" describes the WG's contributions to the rigorous and reliable design of computer programs of all kinds, which basically is "Algorithmics".
- WG 2.6 "Database" contributed "Advances in Data Management in the Big Data Era", sharing its expertise in recent advancements in data integration, metadata management, data quality, and graph management, as well as data stream and fog computing,

TC 3 "Education" contributed the chapter "Computers and education – recognising opportunities and managing challenges". It considers the shifting focus of TC 3's concerns for computing and education over the past 60 years, the reasons for those shifts, and the challenges that educators have faced in developing appropriate uses of computers in their practices. The chapter explores the roles and influences of TC 3 activities, including an overview of important TC 3 visions and declarations that highlighted contemporary and future issues, and the status of an evolving declaration focusing on future sustainability and computing. The chapter concludes with an overview of the impact of TC 3, and signposts next steps in its ongoing journey.

The WGs of TC 5 "Information Technology Applications" provided six chapters showing the importance and diversity of applications of information processing:

- WG 5.4 "Computer Aided Innovation" contributed "Computing Inventive Activities in an Industrial Context – New Scientific Challenges and Orientations". This chapter is based on WG 5.4's activities in studying the computerization innovation in industrial environments and puts them in relation to the rebirth of artificial intelligence and the 4.0 paradigm in manufacturing and industry in general.
- WG 5.5 "Cooperation Infrastructure for Virtual Enterprises and Electronic Business (COVE)" contributed "The Evolution Path to Collaborative Networks 4.0". Hence, this chapter starts with a classification of collaborative networks, continues with a history of four generations of collaborative networks, and leads to a reflection of ongoing developments, trends, challenges, and expectations. It turns out that collaborative networks have been evolving in 24 sub-dimensions. The set of trends and challenges that are mentioned and exemplified in relation to each of the sub-dimensions also constitute the elements of a research agenda for the coming years in this area.
- WG 5.7 "Advances in Production Management Systems" contributed a chapter in line with its name but adding the subtitle "Issues, Trends, and Vision Towards 2030". Based on more than 42 years of experience this chapter reviews past, current, and future issues and trends to establish a coherent vision and research agenda for the WG 5.7 and its international community. The chapter covers a wide range of production aspects and resources required to design, engineer, and manage the next generation of sustainable and smart production systems.

- WG 5.8 "Enterprise Interoperability" contributed a state-of-the-art view on methods and approaches for interoperable enterprise systems. It includes the WG view on the state of the art in enterprise modelling, enterprise engineering, enterprise architectures, enterprise integration, and enterprise interoperability. A brief history of these topics, with special attention to the work developed by WG 5.8 former and current members follows. With respect to application, references to production systems and the manufacturing enterprise are made. The chapter closes with a brief look into very recent developments in the domain of enterprise interoperability.
- WG 5.12 "Architectures for Enterprise Integration" like WG 5.7 combined its chapter's title from its name and a subtitle, in this case "Twenty-five Years of the GERAM Framework". With GERAM being the "Generalised Enterprise Reference Architecture and Methodology" published in 1994, this chapter is about the use of systems thinking and systems theory in enterprise architecture and about how it is possible to reconcile and understand, based on a single overarching framework, the interplay of two major enterprise change endeavours: enterprise engineering (i.e. deliberate change) and evolutionary, organic change. The chapter also demonstrates how such change processes can be illustrated by employing systems thinking to construct dynamic business models. Finally, the chapter attempts to plot the way GERAM, as a framework to think about the creation and evolution of complex socio-technical systems of systems, will continue to contribute to society in the context of future challenges and emerging opportunities.
- WG 5.15 "Information Technology in Disaster Risk Reduction (ITDRR)" contributed "Synthesis of a Composite Imitation Model of the Cognitive Structure of the Ergatic System Operator Based on Conceptual Pattern Technology". To reduce the risk of disasters one wants to support the human operators of ergatic systems and hence study their cognitive structures. Thus, this chapter reports how for the purpose of studying the cognitive structures of human operators of ergatic systems, an IT system has been developed for the conceptual synthesis of relevant simulation models (cognitive structures) based on the use of conceptual modelling.

TC 6 "Communication Systems" and especially WG 6.6 "Management of Networks and Distributed Systems" contributed "Blockchains and Distributed Ledgers Uncovered: Clarifications, Achievements, and Open Issues". WG 6.6 has investigated blockchains in various aspects; hence, this contribution summarizes and clarifies key characteristics of blockchains and the related approach of distributed ledgers. The value of both is outlined in combination with selected and exemplified application domains. In addition, a set of open issues is discussed, as they possibly hinder practical operation, e.g. excessive expectations, missing interoperability, wrong scalability promises, or out-of-scope trust assumptions. Then the state of the art is clarified and current, as well as necessary, research steps to follow are outlined.

TC 7 "System Modelling and Optimization" contributed a historical note on its activities over the last 53 years describing how the eight WGs of TC 7 and the related events evolved and what this means for the future, as modelling and optimization remain important in various applications. Examples are reinforcement learning and quality learning, adequate methods and sufficiently efficient implementations to address large scale data problems, and, most recently, the modelling of pandemics.

TC 8 "Information Systems" contributed "The Future of Information Systems in a Post-COVID World by TC8 (Information Systems)". The article highlights the accomplishments of TC 8 and its working groups over its 50 year history and envisages strategies for the future. It begins with an overall view of the diverse and changing roles of the Information Systems field, then moves forward to foresee environmental sustainability and digital glocalization in a post-COVID-19 world. Next the article describes the achievements of TC 8, the establishment of its ten WGs, and what TC 8 and its WGs have to offer in the future. Lastly, the article identifies the individual working groups of TC 8 to detail their activities as important conduits of research and practice in the field of IS over the past 50 years, then imagine the roles of the TC8 working groups in a post-COVID landscape.

TC 9 "ICT and Society" contributed "The Impact of Human Choice and Computers and Technical Committee 9 on ICTs and Society: A Critical Sociotechnical Tale". This article recounts the history of the Human Choice and Computers (HCC) conference series, and of TC 9 itself. It documents a textual analysis of the proceedings of the HCC conferences and biographical detail concerning the key players involved. It shows that not only has there been a marked focus, over more than four decades, on a critical and sociotechnical approach to understanding the relationship between ICTs and society but that HCC and TC 9 may be regarded as the original and continuing home of the critical academic voice in ICT.

TC 11 "Security and Privacy Protection in Information Processing Systems" contributed "Information Security and Privacy – Challenges and Outlook". This chapter examines the role of TC 11 and its 14 WGs in the ever-changing and evolving domain of fast-developing technologies that are not always matched with a commensurate focus on security and privacy matters. The discussion provides an outline of key issues in information security when viewed from technical, organizational, and human perspectives, which collectively represent the breadth of areas within which TC 11 and its WGs are seeking to make contributions. So, the chapter documents the challenges involved in achieving and maintaining security and privacy, alongside insights into the ways that they are being tackled within IFIP activities.

The concluding chapter of this book is dedicated to the IFIP Code of Ethics and Conduct that the IFIP General Assembly adopted on September 24, 2020. It also includes a section on the creation of this code. This section describes the work on the code that TC 9 had already initiated in 1988 and that involved IFIP as a whole and its member societies. In addition, there is a prologue by the IFIP Task and Finish Group on the development, the nature, the structure, the status, and the benefits of the code. The code itself consists of sections on professional responsibilities, professional leadership principles, and compliance with the code. As such it is offered to member societies and any other interested parties.

Besides giving valuable insights into important and upcoming topics of information processing, all the contributions show the rich diversity of the international work being done in IFIP and how it represents the global research and application of information processing. They also document the essential role of IFIP as a platform for this work.

Especially in these challenging times caused by the COVID-19 pandemic, we are honoured to bring you this collection and express our appreciation to all the contributors who supported making IFIP AICT 600 a success. There is a long list of people who volunteered their time and energy to put together the chapters and who deserve acknowledgement.

We hope you find AICT 600 interesting, stimulating, and inspiring for your future work regardless of the challenging times in which IFIP is celebrating its 60th anniversary.

May 2021

Michael Goedicke
Erich Neuhold
Kai Rannenberg

Contents

TC 6: Communication Systems

TC 7: System Modeling and Optimization

TC 8: Information Systems

TC 9: ICT and Society

TC 11: Security and Privacy Protection in Information Processing Systems

IFIP General

TC 1: Foundations of Computer Science

Part I: Foundations of Computer Science

Hot Current Topics of Descriptional Complexity

Martin Kutrib[1]([✉]), Nelma Moreira[2], Giovanni Pighizzini[3], and Rogério Reis[2]

[1] Institut für Informatik, Universität Giessen, Arndtstr. 2, 35392 Giessen, Germany
kutrib@informatik.uni-giessen.de
[2] CMUP and DCC, Faculdade de Ciências da Universidade do Porto,
Rua do Campo Alegre, 4169-007 Porto, Portugal
{nelma.moreira,rogerio.reis}@fc.up.pt
[3] Dipartimento di Informatica, Università degli Studi di Milano, via Celoria 18,
20133 Milano, Italy
pighizzini@di.unimi.it

Preamble

Descriptional complexity has historically been a multidisciplinary area of study, with contributions from automata theory, computational complexity, cryptography, information theory, probability, statistics, pattern recognition, machine learning, computational learning theory, computer vision, neural networks, formal languages and other fields. Some basic questions are: How succinctly can a descriptional system represent objects (for example, encoded as formal languages) in comparison with other descriptional systems? What is the maximal size trade-off when changing from one system to another, and can it be achieved?

Since the late nineties the scope of the IFIP Working Group 1.02 encompasses all aspects of descriptional complexity, both in theory and application. The formal orientation suggested its establishment under the head of the IFIP Technical Committee TC1 on Foundations of Computer Science.

The topics of the working group include but are not limited to descriptional complexity of formal systems and structures, various measures of descriptional complexity of automata, grammars, languages and of related systems, trade-offs between descriptional complexity and mode of operation, circuit complexity of Boolean functions and related measures, succinctness of description of (finite) objects, descriptional complexity in resource bounded or structure bounded environments, structural complexity, descriptional complexity of formal systems for applications (for example, software reliability, software and hardware testing, modeling of natural languages), descriptional complexity aspects of nature motivated (bio-inspired) architectures and unconventional models of computing.

Furthermore, the Working Group tries to promote interaction and the exchange of information across traditional discipline boundaries and to provide a point of contact for all researchers in all disciplines interested in descriptional complexity and its applications.

© IFIP International Federation for Information Processing 2021
Published by Springer Nature Switzerland AG 2021
M. Goedicke et al. (Eds.): Advancing Research in Information and Communication Technology,
IFIP AICT 600, pp. 3–28, 2021. https://doi.org/10.1007/978-3-030-81701-5_1

Here, we first address the basic ideas and concepts of descriptional complexity from a general abstract perspective. Then we select some recent trends in the area, discuss problems, results, and open questions. In particular, we address operational state complexity, that is, the size impact of decomposing formal systems, a bridge between descriptional and computational complexity, where the size of two-way finite automata is related to the L versus NL problem, the descriptional complexity of so-called limited automata which are Turing machines with rewriting restrictions, and look at parameterized nondeterminism in finite automata (that may change their mind). Then we are interested in the question to what extent the descriptional capacity can be boosted by transductions. Finally, we turn to enumerations and average complexity. The results presented are not proved but we merely draw attention to the overall picture and some of the main ideas involved.

Our tour on the subjects covers some current hot topics in the field of descriptional complexity. It obviously lacks completeness and it reflects our personal view of what constitute some of the most interesting links to descriptional complexity theory. In truth there is much more to the field than can be summarized here.

1   Descriptional Complexity: Idea and Basic Concepts

Since the early days of theoretical computer science the relative succinctness of different representations of (sets of) objects by formal systems have been a subject of intensive research. An obvious choice to encode the objects is by strings over a finite number of different symbols. Then a set of objects is a set of strings. To move closer to a machinery that can be used for the studies, a string is called a word and a set of words is said to be a formal language. A formal language can be described by several means, for example, by automata, grammars, rewriting systems, equation systems, etc. In general, such a descriptional system is a set of finite descriptors for languages. Core questions of descriptional complexity are "How succinctly (related to a size complexity measure) can a system represent a formal language in comparison with other systems?" and "What is the maximum trade-off when the representation is changed from one descriptional system to another, and can this maximum be achieved?"

Descriptional complexity has historically been a multidisciplinary area of study, with contributions from very different areas of computer science such as, for example, automata and formal language theory, computational complexity, cryptography, information theory, etc. The approach to analyze the size of systems as opposed to the computational power seems to originate from Stearns [87] who studied the relative succinctness of regular languages represented by deterministic finite automata and deterministic pushdown automata. In the classification of automata, grammars, and related (formal) systems it turned out that the gain in economy of description heavily depends on the considered systems. For instance, it is well known that nondeterministic finite automata (NFA) can be converted into equivalent deterministic finite automata (DFA) of at most exponential size. The underlying construction is probably one of the best-known results on descriptional complexity: by this so-called powerset construction, each state of the DFA is associated with a subset of NFA states [81]. Moreover, the construction turned out to be optimal. That is, the bound on the number of states necessary for the construction is tight in the sense that for an arbitrary n there is always some n-state NFA which cannot be simulated by any DFA with strictly less than 2^n states [64,68,70]. For deterministic pushdown automata accepting a regular language, we know that they can be converted into equivalent finite automata of at most doubly-exponential size [88]. In the levels of exponentiation this bound is tight. In [68] a double exponential lower bound has been obtained. The precise bound is still an open problem. In contrast, if we replace "deterministic pushdown automata" with "nondeterministic pushdown automata" then we are faced with the phenomenon of non-recursive trade-offs. That is, the maximum size blow-up cannot be bounded by any recursive function. In other words, when the size trade-off from one descriptional system to another is non-recursive, one can choose an arbitrarily large computable function f but the gain in economy of description eventually exceeds f when changing from the former system to the latter. Essentially, this means that the gain in economy of description can be arbitrary and, thus, the achievable benefit in description length is of arbitrary size. This cornerstone of descriptional complexity theory originates from the seminal paper by Meyer and Fischer [68]. Non-recursive trade-offs usually sprout at the wayside of the crossroads of (un)decidability, and in many cases proving such trade-offs apparently requires ingenuity and careful constructions.

Nowadays, descriptional complexity has become a large and widespread area. Classical main branches are, for example, mutual simulations, state complexity of operations, whose systematic study was initiated in [92], magic numbers, a research field initiated in [48], the size impact of adding resources to a system, determinization of nondeterministic finite automata accepting subregular languages [8], transition complexity of NFA [23,33,46,47,63], and non-recursive trade-offs, and many others. Further results and references can be found, for example, in the surveys [32,41,42,57].

In order to be more precise, we now turn to present and discuss the very basics of descriptional complexity.

We denote the set of nonnegative integers by $\mathbb{N}$. Let Σ^* denote the set of all words over a finite alphabet Σ. The *empty word* is denoted by λ, and we set $\Sigma^+ = \Sigma^* - \{\lambda\}$. For the *reversal of a word* w we write w^R and for its *length* we write $|w|$. We use $\subseteq$ for *inclusions* and $\subset$ for *strict inclusions*. In general, the family of all languages accepted by a device of some type X is denoted by $\mathscr{L}(X)$.

Next, we formalize the intuitive notion of a representation or description of formal languages. We say that a *descriptional system* S is a set of encodings of items where each item $D \in S$ *represents* or *describes* a formal language $L(D)$, and the underlying alphabet alph(D) over which D represents a language can be read off from D. In the following, we call the items *descriptors* and identify the encodings of some language representation with the representation itself. The *family of languages represented* (or *described*) by S is $\mathscr{L}(S) = \{ L(D) \mid D \in S \}$.

For every language L, the set $\mathcal{S}(L) = \{\, D \in \mathcal{S} \mid L(D) = L \,\}$ is the set of its descriptors in $\mathcal{S}$.

For example, deterministic finite automata can be encoded over some fixed alphabet such that their input alphabets can be extracted from the encodings. The set of these encodings is a descriptional system $\mathcal{S}$, and $\mathscr{L}(\mathcal{S})$ is the family of regular languages.

A *(size) complexity measure* for a descriptional system $\mathcal{S}$ is a total, computable mapping $c : \mathcal{S} \to \mathbb{N}$. From the viewpoint that a descriptional system is a set of encoding strings, the lengths of the strings are a natural measure for the size. We denote it by length. In fact, we will use length to obtain a rough classification of different complexity measures. We distinguish between measures that (with respect to the size of the underlying alphabet) are related with length by a computable function and measures that are not. If there is a total computable function $g : \mathbb{N} \times \mathbb{N} \to \mathbb{N}$ such that, for all $D \in \mathcal{S}$, $\mathsf{length}(D) \leq g(c(D), |\mathrm{alph}(D)|)$, then c is said to be an *s-measure* (a *size* measure). Since for any coding alphabet there are only finitely many descriptors having at most length $g(c(D), |\mathrm{alph}(D)|)$, over the same alphabet there are only finitely many descriptors in $\mathcal{S}$ having the same size as D. If, in addition, for any alphabet Σ, the set of descriptors in $\mathcal{S}$ describing languages over Σ is recursively enumerable in order of increasing size, then c is said to be an *sn-measure*.

For example, further size complexity measures for nondeterministic finite automata are the *number of states* (state) and the *number of transition* (trans). Clearly, length, state, and trans are sn-measures for finite automata.

Whenever we consider the relative succinctness of two descriptional systems $\mathcal{S}_1$ and $\mathcal{S}_2$, we assume the intersection $\mathscr{L}(\mathcal{S}_1) \cap \mathscr{L}(\mathcal{S}_2)$ to be non-empty. Let $\mathcal{S}_1$ and $\mathcal{S}_2$ be descriptional systems with complexity measures c_1 and c_2, respectively. A total function $f : \mathbb{N} \to \mathbb{N}$, is said to be a *lower bound* for the increase in complexity when changing from a descriptor in $\mathcal{S}_1$ to an equivalent descriptor in $\mathcal{S}_2$, if for infinitely many $D_1 \in \mathcal{S}_1$ with $L(D_1) \in \mathscr{L}(\mathcal{S}_2)$ there exists a *minimal* $D_2 \in \mathcal{S}_2(L(D_1))$ such that $c_2(D_2) \geq f(c_1(D_1))$. A total function $f : \mathbb{N} \to \mathbb{N}$ is an *upper bound* for the increase in complexity when changing from a descriptor in $\mathcal{S}_1$ to an equivalent descriptor in $\mathcal{S}_2$, if for all $D_1 \in \mathcal{S}_1$ with $L(D_1) \in \mathscr{L}(\mathcal{S}_2)$, there exists a $D_2 \in \mathcal{S}_2(L(D_1))$ such that $c_2(D_2) \leq f(c_1(D_1))$. If there is no recursive, that is, computable function serving as upper bound, the *trade-off is said to be non-recursive*.

2   Operational State Complexity

The *(deterministic) state complexity* of a regular language L is the number of states of its minimal complete deterministic finite automaton, and is denoted by $sc(L)$. This is the most well-studied descriptional measure for regular languages, but one may as well consider the minimal number of states or the minimal number of transitions of nondeterministic finite automata, $nsc(L)$ and $tsc(L)$, or even consider the same measures but for incomplete DFAs. Another usual measure is the size of the syntactic monoid (syntactic complexity).

While representational complexity considers the changes of size caused by conversions between different models, the operational complexity considers the size of the model of a language resulting from an operation performed on one or more languages. As an example for the first case we have the determinization: given an n-state NFA for a regular language, the equivalent DFA has at most 2^n states. This, established in 1957 by Rabin and Scott [81], is considered the first result in state complexity.

The *state complexity of an operation* (or *operational state complexity*) on regular languages is the worst-case state complexity of a language resulting from the operation, considered as a function of the state complexities of the operands.

Given a binary operation $\circ$, the $\circ$-*language operation state complexity problem* can be stated as follows:

- given an m-state DFA A_1 and an n-state DFA A_2;
- how many states are sufficient and necessary, in the worst case, to accept the language $L(A_1) \circ L(A_2)$ by a DFA?

This formulation can be generalized for operations with a different number of arguments, other kinds of automata and classes of languages.

An upper bound can be obtained by providing an algorithm that, given DFAs for the operands, constructs a DFA that accepts the resulting language. Most algorithms first construct an NFA and then apply to it the subset construction. The number of states of the resulting DFA is an upper bound for the state complexity of the referred operation.

To show that an upper bound is tight, for each operand a family of languages, indexed by their state complexity, must be given such that the resulting automata achieve that bound. We can call those families *witnesses*.

Table 1. State complexity and nondeterministic state complexity for basic operations on regular and finite languages. The state complexity of the operands is m and n, and k is the alphabet size.

	Regular		Finite	
	sc	nsc	sc	sc
$L_1 \cup L_2$	mn	$m+n+1$	$mn-(m+n)$	$m+n-2$
$L_1 \cap L_2$	mn	mn	$mn-3(m+n)+12$	$O(mn)$
$\overline{L}$	m	2^m	m	$\Theta(k^{\frac{m}{1+\log k}})$
$L_1 L_2$	$m2^n - 2^{n-1}$	$m+n$	$(m-n+3)2^{n-2}$	$m+n-1$
$L^\star$	$2^{m-1}+2^{m-1}$	$m+1$	$2^{m-3}+2^{m-4}$	$m-1$
L^R	2^m	$m+1$	$O(k^{\frac{m}{1+\log k}})$	m

In 1994, Yu, Zhuang and Salomaa [93] studied the state complexity of basic regularity preserving operations such as concatenation, star, reversal, union, and intersection. More than two decades before, in 1970, Maslov [66] had already presented some estimates for union, concatenation, and star, as well as for other regularity preserving operations such as cyclic shift or proportional removals.

In the last decades, a huge amount of results were obtained on this subject. Several lines of research have emerged. One was to consider other operations, such as the "shuffle", or combined operations, such as the "star of union" or the "star-complement-star". The state complexities of most of these combined operations are much lower than the mathematical composition of the state complexities of their component individual operations. Another line of research was to reduce the alphabet size of the witness languages. The range of state complexities that may result from an operation, as opposed to the worst-case value, was studied under the so called *magic number problem*. *Magic numbers* for a given operation (or conversion) are the ones that cannot occur as state complexity values [48]. Many subclasses of regular languages are of special interest, such as, finite, unary, or star-free. For those, and many other, the operational state complexity restricted to a given subclass was studied. Moreover many of the above problems were also considered for nondeterministic state complexity or transition complexity. A list of these recent results as well as details on the witnesses used can be found in the surveys by Gao, Moreira, Reis and Yu [27] and by Brzozowski [13]. Davies's PhD thesis [21] presents detailed proofs of the operational state complexity for some basic operations on regular languages, and provides an excellent introduction to the subject. As an illustration, in Table 1 we present the results for some basic operations on regular and finite languages, both for deterministic and nondeterministic state complexities. From these results it is evident that the complexity of determinization plays a fundamental role in the operational complexity. Given an m-state NFA for a finite language over an alphabet of size k, the equivalent DFA has at most $\Theta(k^{\frac{m}{1+\log k}})$ states, and this bound is tight [83]. Campeanu, Culik and Salomaa [14], presented the first formal study of operational state complexity on finite languages. The state complexity of basic operations on NFA (both for regular and finite languages) were studied by Holzer and Kutrib [40].

A great effort was spent to find witnesses with minimal alphabet size. Many different witnesses were found for the various operations. Symbolic manipulation software is in general used to help to establish witness candidates that after can be formally proved to attain the maximal bounds. However, the reason why a given witness would work for several complexity bounds is not well understood. In 2012, Brzozowski identified a family of languages that witnesses the state complexity of all basic operations on regular languages [12]. Figure 1 presents the minimal DFA for the language family. More importantly, he established conditions for a family of languages to attain those bounds and, in this sense, to be *the most complex regular languages*. A fundamental condition was that, for a language with state complexity m, the size of its syntactic monoid should be m^m, which is the tight upper bound.

This research triggered the development of an algebraic approach to operational descriptional complexity. Given a complete DFA A, each letter corresponds to a transformation on the set of states. One says that the letter acts on the set

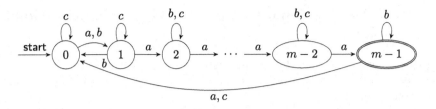

Fig. 1. Brzozowski's "universal" witness.

of states. This notion can be extended to words, and the set of transformations induced by all words, with composition, is a monoid, the transition monoid of A. The syntactic complexity of a regular language is the size of the transition monoid of its minimal DFA (also called the *syntactic monoid*). For instance, in Fig. 1 the letter a performs a cyclic permutation, b a transposition $(0, 1)$ (i.e. interchanges those states and all other are fixed points), and c sends $m - 1$ to 0, keeping unaltered the other states. It can be shown that every transformation of $\{0, \ldots, m - 1\}$ can be represented as the action of a word over $\{a, b, c\}$ [12]. The operational syntactic complexity on regular and subregular languages was extensively studied mainly by Brzozowski and co-authors.

The use of algebraic characterizations in operational state complexity is now a hot topic of research. Bell, Brzozowski, Moreira, and Reis [4] considered the following question: for which pairs of languages (L_m, L'_n) (with state complexities m and n, respectively) does $L_m \circ L'_n$ reach the maximal state complexity mn for every proper binary Boolean operation $\circ$? A sufficient condition (excluding known counterexamples) is that the transition monoids contain the symmetric groups S_m and S_n, respectively. Davies refined those conditions proving that in general (except restricted cases) it is sufficient that the transition monoids contain 2-transitive groups [20, 21].

It is known that a witness with a maximal transition monoid is guaranteed to maximize the state complexity of reversal. This is not the case for other operations. In general it is difficult to know which transformations one needs to associate to each letter on an operand DFA to ensure that the resulting DFA from the operation is, in some sense, maximal. If the alphabet size is not an issue, one can use the one-letter-per-action (OLPA) technique: i.e. the witnesses have one letter for each possible transformation. Sakoda and Sipser used this technique for studying the state complexity of the conversions between one-way and two-way finite automata [82] (see Sect. 3). Although some authors used this technique sparsely in past, only recently it was formalized by Davies [19, 21] and Caron, Hamel-De le Court, Luque and Patrou [15]. Its power, limitations, and which consequences it can have in this topic remains open. Anyhow, deepening the connection between combinatorial and algebraic methods seems fruitful.

3   When Descriptional Complexity Meets Computational Complexity

Usually, when we refer to finite automata, we implicitly assume that we are considering *one-way finite automata*, namely automata that can read the input only from left to right.

The extension to the *two-way* case, namely to automata which are able to move the input head in both directions, is an interesting area, with challenging descriptional complexity problems and important connections with classical computational complexity. Actually, the investigation of complexity questions for one-way and two-way finite automata can be carried out as a part of the area of computational complexity, with classes of problems, reductions, complete problems and, of course, open questions, as emphasized in [49] by Christos Kapoutsis who introduced the name *Minicomplexity* for this area.

Here, we present a short outline on two-way finite automata and on the connections with computational complexity.

First of all, we have to mention that it is well known that the capability of moving the head in both directions does not increase the computational power of finite automata. Two-way finite automata, in both deterministic and non-deterministic versions (2DFA and 2NFA, for short), still characterize the class of regular languages. This result was independently proved in 1959 by Rabin and Scott and by Shepherdson, by showing constructions transforming 2NFAs into equivalent DFAs [81,85]. (An alternative transformation was obtained by Vardi [89].) The increment in the number of states in such transformations is exponential. We will now present a simple example showing that such an increasing cannot be avoided. Before doing that, we mention that in two-way automata we assume that the input is surrounded by two special symbols called the *left* and the *right endmarker*.

For each integer $n > 0$, let us consider the language

$$I_n = (a + b)^* a (a + b)^{n-1} .$$

It is not difficult to see that I_n is recognized by an NFA with $n + 1$ states, while any DFA accepting it requires 2^n states in order to remember, at each step of the computation, the suffix of length n of the input string so far inspected (a formal proof can be done with standard distinguishability arguments). We can easily construct a 2DFA which recognizes I_n by locating the right endmarker and then moving the head to the left to check if the nth symbol from the right is an a. This can be implemented using $n + 2$ states.

A more sophisticated example with similar properties is

$$L_n = (a + b)^* a (a + b)^{n-1} a (a + b)^* ,$$

where we ask that strings contain a pair of a's with $n - 1$ symbols in between. In this case, a 2DFA can check a string w by moving the head from the first symbol of w to the right, up to reach a cell containing a. Then, it moves n more positions to the right. If the reached cell contains another a, then the automaton accepts. Otherwise, it moves the head $n - 1$ cell to the left, reaching the cell to the right of the first a, and it repeats by using the same approach, looking for a cell containing a while moving to the right. Even for L_n we can obtain an NFA and a 2DFA with $O(n)$ states while each DFA requires a number of states exponential in n.[1]

One natural question arising after seeing these two examples is whether or not two-way motion can be used to remove the nondeterminism, without significantly increasing the size of the description. This problem was posed by Sakoda and Sipser in 1978 [82] and, actually, it was formulated by the two following questions:

1. *For every 2NFA M, is there an equivalent 2DFA with only polynomially more states than M?*
2. *For every NFA M, is there an equivalent 2DFA with only polynomially more states than M?*

Sakoda and Sipser conjectured that both questions have negative answers. To support such a conjecture, they presented a complete analogy with the P versus NP problem.

Two years later, Sipser proved exponential separations, under the conditions that the simulating 2DFAs are *sweeping*, namely they can reverse the movement of the input head only at the endmarkers [86]. However, Berman and Micali showed that this does not solve the general problem [5,69].

For several years not so much work has been done around these questions, until the first years of this millennium, when new investigations on two-way automata have been carried out and several new results, solving some special cases, have been obtained. However, it seems that we are still far from a solution for the general case.

Besides the result on sweeping 2DFAs, similar separations have been obtained for the simulation of NFAs and 2NFAs by restricted kinds of 2DFAs, as *oblivious* 2DFAs [45,60], *rotating* automata [54], *few reversal* automata [51]. Exponential separations between these kinds of devices and unrestricted 2DFAs have been also proved, showing that these results do not solve the general problem. For a more detailed overview and further references see [75].

Some results providing polynomial simulations of restricted forms of 2NFAs by (unrestricted) 2DFAs have been obtained by considering the unary case (i.e., the input alphabet contains only one-letter, so this gives a restriction on the class

---

[1] The 2DFA we described for I_n makes use of the endmarkers, while the 2DFA for L_n does not use them. Actually, we could adapt the technique used to recognize L_n in order to obtain a 2DFA with $O(n)$ states accepting I_n, without using the endmarkers. The main difference is that the 2DFA so obtained may need to reverse the direction of its head many times, while the 2DFA we described for I_n makes only one reversal. It seems quite natural to have endmarkers in two-way automata. However, in some works they are presented without endmarkers. This does not change the computational power. The example of I_n shows some differences when we consider size and number of reversals. In general, it has been proved that two-way automata can have different properties with or without endmarkers [90].

of accepted languages) [29], and the case of *outer nondeterministic automata*, which can make nondeterministic choices only when the head visits one of the endmarkers [28].[2]

Recently, a different approach was proposed, trying to obtain polynomial simulations of 2NFAs by some extensions of 2DFAs. In [34] it is presented a polynomial simulation by single-tape deterministic Turing machines working in linear time (by a result by Hennie [38], these machines are no more powerful than finite automata). It will be interesting to continue this approach by considering, for instance, simulations by *deterministic 1-limited automata*. These devices are discussed in the next section.

As already mentioned, Sakoda and Sipser presented an analogy between the above Questions 1. and 2. and the P versus NP question. In particular they defined a notion of reducibility and presented complete problems for the two questions.

Starting from an initial result by Berman and Lingas [6], strong connections have been discovered between the question of Sakoda and Sipser and the open question L versus NL (classes of languages accepted in logarithmic space by deterministic and nondeterministic Turing machines, respectively).

In [30], by considering the unary case, it was proved that L = NL would imply a state polynomial simulation of unary 2NFAs by 2DFAs. So, showing that the simulation of 2NFAs by 2DFAs is not polynomial, already in the restricted case of a unary alphabet, would separate L and NL. We point out that at the moment the best known simulation in the unary case is superpolynomial, but subexponential [29]. This result and that of Berman and Lingas have been generalized by Kapoutisis in [52] and further generalized in [55], by considering the class L/poly of languages accepted by deterministic logspace bounded machines that can access a *polynomial advice*. It was proved the following:

Theorem 1 ([55]). L/poly ⊇ NL *if and only if there is a polynomial simulation of* unary *2NFAs by 2DFAs.*

Actually, further characterizations of L/poly ⊇ NL have been presented in [55]. Among them, it was shown that L/poly ⊇ NL is equivalent to the existence of 2DFAs of size polynomial in h which are able to check accessibility in unary encoded h vertex graphs and to check two-way liveness in h-tall, h-column graphs. Hence, such versions of accessibility and liveness problems are complete for the above Question 1. in the unary case. It was conjectured that these statements are false.

These results show important connections between descriptional complexity of automata and classical computational complexity. As we mentioned at the beginning of the section, following the approach of *minicomplexity*, the investigation on the complexity of finite automata can be carried out in the wider area of

---

[2] Concerning the unary case, the state cost of simulation of *one-way* nondeterministic automata by 2DFAs has been proved to be quadratic [17]. This gives a positive answer to the second question in the unary case.

computational complexity, using the same methods (reductions, complete problems, etc.). We recommend the works [50,53] to appreciate the minicomplexity approach.

4   Turing Machines with Rewriting Restrictions

It is well known that each class of languages in the Chomsky hierarchy has a corresponding family of recognizing devices. By considering for the top level, i.e., Type 0 languages, Turing machines with a read-only input tape and a separate worktape, we easily obtain a hierarchy of machines by restricting the space used on the worktape to be linear in the input length for context-sensitive languages, by accessing it as a pushdown store in the case of context-free languages[3], and by removing the worktape for regular languages.

Having the same computational power of multi-tape machines, single-tape Turing machines are sufficient to characterize the class of Type 0 languages. Furthermore, restricting these devices to use only the portion of the tape which initially contains the input, we obtain *linear bounded* automata, which characterize context-sensitive languages. However, by still considering pushdown automata for the family of context-free languages, we do not obtain a hierarchy of machines.

A less-known characterization of the class of context-free languages in terms of machines was obtained by Hibbard in 1967, in terms of *limited automata*, a class of single-tape nondeterministic Turing machines satisfying the following rewriting restriction: fixed an integer $d \geq 0$, a d-limited automaton (d-LA, for short) can rewrite the contents of each tape cell *only in the first d visits* [39]. Without loss of generality, d-LAs can be restricted to use only the portion of the tape which initially contains the input.

Hibbard proved that for each fixed $d \geq 2$, the class of languages accepted by d-LAs coincides with the class of context-free languages. Since d-LAs are a restriction of linear bounded automata and, clearly, they are extensions of finite automata, using 2-LAs for the class of context-free languages we obtain a single-tape machine hierarchy corresponding to the Chomsky hierarchy.

To give a sake of the way used by limited automata to operate, we describe a simple strategy that can be implemented by a 2-LA in order to recognize the language consisting of all sequences of balanced brackets. An input sequence of brackets can be inspected starting from the leftmost symbol and moving to the right, until reaching the first closing bracket. If the sequence is balanced, then the corresponding opening bracket is necessarily the last bracket before it, that must be of the same type. If so, these two brackets can be overwritten by a special symbol, and the same procedure can be repeated by moving from the position of the just overwritten opening bracket to locate the first closing bracket, overwriting it, then checking if the last bracket before it is of the same type, overwriting it, and so on. When no more closing brackets are left in the

---

[3] It can be easily seen that each context free-language can be accepted by a pushdown automaton which uses an amount of pushdown store which is linear in the input length.

sequence, even none opening bracket should be left. In this case the original sequence was balanced and the machine can accept; in all other cases the machine rejects. If the input sequence is written on a Turing machine tape, one bracket per cell, and the computation starts, as usual, with the head scanning the cell containing the leftmost input symbol, then each cell containing a closing bracket is overwritten only when the head visits it for the first time. Thereafter, the head is moved back to the left to search the corresponding opening bracket, which was already visited one time and which is overwritten when the head visits it for the second time. After these *active visits*, a cell can be visited further many times, but it cannot be overwritten, so it is "frozen". Hence, each tape cell is overwritten at most in the first 2 visits.

In the last years, limited automata have been investigated in a series of papers, with the main focus on their descriptional complexity (for a recent overview see [76]). The costs of the simulations between pushdown automata and 2-LAs have been stated in [78]. These results have been extended to d-LAs, with $d > 2$ in [61]. In [78] it was also proved that *deterministic* 2-LAs (D-2-LAs) are equivalent to deterministic pushdown automata. As proved in [39], the class of languages accepted by deterministic limited automata becomes larger by increasing the number of possible rewritings, i.e., by increasing the value of d we obtain a proper infinite hierarchy of languages accepted by D-d-LAs. However, this hierarchy does not cover all the class of context-free languages.

We now focus on the subfamily of *1-limited automata*, i.e., single-tape machines that can rewrite the contents of any tape cell only in the first visit. This model characterizes regular languages [91], so they are equivalent to finite automata. The cost of the conversions of nondeterministic and deterministic 1-LAs into equivalent finite automata have been studied in [77] and they are summarized in Fig. 2, with some other costs. Some comments on these results:

- The double exponential simulation (a) of 1-LAs by one-way DFAs is obtained by combining the Shepherdson construction for simulating 2NFAs by DFAs with the classical subset construction. The double exponential gap, which cannot be reduced, is due to a double role of the nondeterminism: when a cell is visited for the first time, a symbol is written on it according to a nondeterministic decision; in the next visits to the same cell, the available nondeterministic choices also depend on the symbol which is written in it, namely the symbol written during the first visit.
- The arrow (b) represents the Sakoda and Sipser question, for which an exponential upper bound but only a polynomial lower bound are known.
- Arrow (c) presents a similar question for limited automata, translated of one exponentiation level: by (a) we know that the elimination of the nondeterminism from 1-LAs costs at most a double exponential in size, however the best known lower bound is exponential. It could be interesting to know if there are strict relationships between these two questions, e.g., if an exponential gap from 2NFAs to 2DFAs would imply a double exponential gap from 1-LAs to D-1-LAs and vice versa.

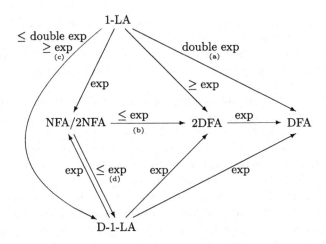

Fig. 2. Costs of some conversions between different kinds of limited automata and finite automata.

- The exponential upper bound in (d) derives from (b). An exponential lower bound will close the Sakoda and Sipser question. So the study of the conversion in (d) can be seen as a "relaxed" version of the Sakoda and Sipser question where nondeterminism is removed by allowing to rewrite tape cells in the first visit.

  We point out that in [34] it was recently obtained a polynomial blowup from 2NFAs to single-tape deterministic machines working in linear time. Since with a polynomial increase in the size, each 1-LA can be converted into an equivalent one working in linear time, also preserving determinism [35], proving that the simulation (d) costs polynomial would improve that result.

In Sect. 3 we have already mentioned the *unary case* and its relevance in the connection with the Sakoda and Sipser question. Several results related to limited automata in the unary case have been obtained in [61,62]. Further results concerning unary 1-LA are presented in [79].

5   Automata that May Change Their Mind

The concept of nondeterministic machines was introduced in the seminal paper of Rabin and Scott [81] on finite automata and their decision problems from 1959. Over the years, nondeterminism turned out to be a very fruitful concept in different areas of computer science like, for example, computability theory, complexity theory, automata theory, formal language theory, etc., to mention only a few.

For finite automata it is folklore that deterministic finite automata (DFA) are as powerful as nondeterministic finite automata (NFA) from a computational capacity point of view. However, from a descriptional complexity point of view

NFAs can offer exponential savings in size compared with DFAs. That is reason enough to consider nondeterminism as a resource of the underlying model and to quantify its usage to some extend. A lot of results on such quantifications are subsumed under the name *limited nondeterminism* in the literature, see, for example, [32] for a survey.

Being interested in the power of the amount of nondeterminism with respect to computations and conciseness it has been newly interpreted in terms of *one-time nondeterministic automata* [44] and its generalization *mind-changing automata* [43]. The idea of mind-changing automata is that at the outset the automaton is partially deterministic. In this way, defined transitions constitute situations for which the automaton already has an opinion (on how to proceed), while undefined transitions constitute situations for which the automaton is still irresolute. Whenever the automaton encounters a situation for which it is irresolute, it can form its opinion by choosing an appropriate transition out of a set of transitions. The chosen transition is then added to the transition function. Finally, whenever the automaton is in a situation for which a transition is defined, it can change its mind and interchange the transition by an alternative matching transition from the set of available transitions. Now, the total number of mind changes is considered as a limited resource.

We illustrate the notion by the following example.

Example 2. Consider the mind-changing finite automaton (MCFA) M depicted in Fig. 3, where the transitions of the initial transition function δ_0 are drawn with solid arrows and that of the initial set of alternative transitions T_0 are depicted with dashed arrows. So, we have $\delta_0(1, a) = \delta_0(1, b) = 1$, $\delta_0(2, a) = \delta_0(2, b) = 3$, and $T_0 = \{(1, a, 2)\}$. The *language accepted* by M with up to $k \geq 0$ mind changes is denoted by $L_k(M)$.

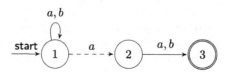

Fig. 3. The MCFA M of Example 2.

Obviously, $L_0(M) = \emptyset$, since the automaton can never change any transition and thus the sole accepting state 3 cannot be reached.

Whenever M decides to make a mind-changing step, that is, exchanging the original transition $(1, a, 1)$ by $(1, a, 2)$ from T_0, then the sole accepting state 3 can be reached from 1 *via* state 2 by reading either aa or ab. Let us see how this works on input $w = baab$. To this end let $\delta' = (\delta_0 \cup \{(1, a, 2)\}) \setminus \{(1, a, 1)\}$ and $T' = (T_0 \cup \{(1, a, 1)\}) \setminus \{(1, a, 2)\}$. Then an accepting computation on input w is

$$(1, baab, \delta_0, T_0) \vdash (1, aab, \delta_0, T_0) \vdash (1, ab, \delta_0, T_0) \vdash (2, b, \delta', T') \vdash (3, \lambda, \delta', T'),$$

where the sole mind-change appeared at the next to last computation step. Yet there is another computation on w which is not accepting, since the mind-change appeared too early and the computation blocks. This non-accepting computation is

$$(1, baab, \delta_0, T_0) \vdash (1, aab, \delta_0, T_0) \vdash (2, ab, \delta', T') \vdash (3, b, \delta', T').$$

It is worth mentioning, that although the underlying automata induced by δ_0 and δ' are both deterministic, there are more than one computation on M, due to the mind-changes. By our example it is not hard to see that

$$L_1(M) = \{\, w \in \{a, b\}^* \mid \text{the next to last letter of } w \text{ is an } a \,\}$$

and moreover $L_k(M) = L_1(M)$, for $k \geq 1$.

In case we consider the MCFA M' with initial transition function δ' and initial set of alternative transitions T', then one observes that

$$L_0(M') = L_1(M') = b^* a (a + b)$$

and $L_k(M') = \{\, w \in \{a, b\}^* \mid \text{the next to last letter of } w \text{ is an } a \,\}$, for $k \geq 2$. ∎

Intuitively, it is clear that the family of languages accepted by MCFAs coincides with the regular languages. Although the concept of mind changes does do not improve the computational power of ordinary finite automata, the question for the descriptional complexity of such devices arises. It turned out that the upper bound on the costs for the simulations of an MCFA M by a DFA depends on the *nondeterministic degree* $d(M)$ of M that is defined as

$$d(M) = \prod_{\substack{(q,a) \in Q \times \Sigma \\ |\delta_0(q,a) \cup \{p \mid (q,a,p) \in T_0\}| \neq 0}} |\delta_0(q, a) \cup \{\, p \mid (q, a, p) \in T_0 \,\}|,$$

where Q is the state set and Σ is the input alphabet.

Theorem 3. *Let M be an n-state MCFA. Then $(k+1) \cdot n \cdot d(M) + 1$ states are sufficient for an NFA to accept the language $L_k(M)$, for every $k \geq 0$.*

From Theorem 3 and the powerset construction on NFAs an upper bound for the simulation by DFAs follows. Note that the DFAs are partial. At least one state can be saved in the exponent.

Corollary 4. *Let $k \geq 0$ be a constant and M be an n-state MCFA with input alphabet Σ. Then, $2^{(k+1) \cdot n \cdot d(M)} + 1$ states are sufficient for a DFA to accept the language $L_k(M)$.*

How about the lower bounds for the simulations? In this connection a special case, that is, an MCFA M that may change its mind only once ($L_1(M)$) on a single transition ($|T_0|$), has been studied in more detail. Even in this special case the MCFA can be more succinct than nondeterministic finite automata.

We consider complete MCFAs, where an MCFA M is said to be *complete* if the underlying initial DFA M' is complete, that is, $|\delta_0(q, a)| = 1$, for every state q and every input symbol a. For $k = 0$ it is obvious that $L_0(M) = L(M')$. Thus, in this case we do not save states when comparing MCFAs and DFAs.

Theorem 5. *Let M be an n-state complete MCFA having $|T_0| = 1$. Then $2^{n+\log n-1}$ states are sufficient and necessary in the worst case for a DFA to accept the language $L_1(M)$.*

An MCFA that witnesses the matching lower bound of Theorem 5 is depicted in Fig. 4.

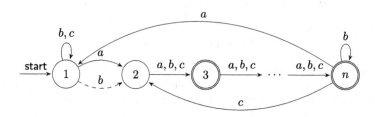

Fig. 4. The n-state complete MCFA M with a singleton set of alternative transitions T_0 witnessing the lower bound of Theorem 5. The transitions from δ_0 are drawn with solid arrows and that of T_0 are depicted with dashed arrows.

The lower bound of Theorem 5 implies that any nondeterministic finite automaton accepting these languages requires at least $n+\log n-1$ states. In other words, there is a sequence of regular languages $(R_n)_{n\geq 3}$ accepted by an n-state complete mind-changing finite automaton with a single alternative transition with at most one mind-change such that any nondeterministic finite automaton accepting R_n requires at least $n + \log n - 1$ states.

At this point one may ask, whether it is possible to generalize Theorem 5 to $k \geq 1$ mind-changing moves in general? Since T_0 is required to be a singleton set, the constraint $k \geq 1$ means that during the computation one can alternate up to k times between two transitions during the computation. Indeed, it is not hard to see that the upper bound construction given in the proof of Theorem 5 for the case $k = 1$ generalizes to arbitrary fixed k with $k \geq 1$.

Theorem 6. *Let M be an n-state complete MCFA having $|T_0| = 1$. Then, for $k \geq 2$, $2^{\log(k+1)\cdot(n-1)+\log n}$ states are sufficient for a DFA to accept the language $L_k(M)$.*

What about the lower bound? Here the situation is much more involved compared to the lower bound construction. At the moment, we can only provide the non-matching lower bound from Theorem 5 for $k \geq 2$, which is somehow trivial. Nevertheless, to improve the upper or the lower bound for the conversion under consideration is left as an open problem.

Finally, it is mentioned that also mind-changing pushdown automata have been considered [43]. While for any (constant) number of mind-changes MCFAs characterize the regular languages, the situation for pushdown automata changes drastically. In fact, for mind-changing pushdown automata, there is an infinite proper hierarchy depending on the number of mind-changes strictly in between the deterministic and arbitrary context-free languages. From the descriptional complexity point of view there are non-recursive trade-offs between all hierarchy levels.

6   Boosting the Descriptional Capacity by Transductions

Finite-state transducers are finite automata with an output and they have been studied at least since 1950s. A typical application of finite-state transducers is, for example, the lexical analysis of computer programs or XML documents. Here, the correct formatting of the input is verified, comments are removed, the correct spelling of the commands is checked, and the sequence of input symbols is translated into a list of tokens. The output produced is subsequently processed by a pushdown automaton that realizes the syntactic analysis. Another example is the use of *cascading* finite-state transducers. Here, one has a finite number of transducers $T_1, T_2, \ldots, T_n$, where the output of T_i is the input for the next transducer T_{i+1}. Such cascades of finite-state transducers have been used, for example, in [26] to extract information from natural language texts. Another example is the Krohn-Rhodes decomposition theorem which shows that every regular language is representable as the cascade of several finite-state transducers, each one having a "simple" algebraic structure [31,36]. Finally, it is shown in [18] that cascades of deterministic pushdown transducers lead to a proper infinite hierarchy in between the deterministic context-free and the deterministic context-sensitive languages with respect to the number of transducers involved. All the examples of cascading transductions so far addressed have in common that the subsequently applied transducers are, at least in principle, different. Another point of view is taken in [7,65], where subsequently applied *identical* transducers are studied. Such *iterated* finite-state transducers are considered as language generating devices starting with some symbol in the initial state of the transducer, iteratively applying in multiple sweeps the transducer to the output produced so far, and eventually halting in an accepting state of the transducer after a last sweep. These iterated finite-state transducers are quite powerful since their nondeterministic version can generate non-recursive languages with only three states. Even in the deterministic case, one state suffices to generate the class of D0L Lindenmayer languages and two states are sufficient to generate languages which are neither context-free nor in 0L. It is worth remarking that an essential feature in these models is that the underlying finite-state transducer is *not length-preserving*. In contrast to all these examples and other works in the literature (see, for example, [74]), where the subsequently applied transducers are in principle different and not necessarily length-preserving, the model of *iterated uniform finite-state transducers* introduced in [58,59] as language accepting devices requires that the same transducer is applied in every sweep and that the transduction is length-preserving.

So, an iterated uniform finite-state transducer is basically a finite-state transducer which processes the input in multiple passes (also sweeps). In the first pass, it reads the input word followed by an endmarker and emits an output word.

In the following passes, it reads the output word of the previous pass and emits a new output word. The number of passes taken, the *sweep complexity*, is given as a function of the length of the input. The transducers to be iterated are length-preserving finite-state transducers, also known as Mealy machines [67].

It is known that at least a logarithmic number of sweeps is necessary to accept non-regular languages. Under a natural constructibility condition it is shown that there exists a proper infinite hierarchy of accepted language families depending on the sweep complexity beyond the logarithm, both in the deterministic (IUFST) and nondeterministic (NIUFST) case [59]. Also, nondeterminism is separated from determinism for all the hierarchy levels.

From the descriptional complexity viewpoint a constant bound on the sweep complexity is of particular interest. So, the succinctness dependent on the constant $k \geq 1$ and in comparison with more traditional models of finite-state automata has been studied in more detail.

Example 7. For $k \geq 1$, the language $E_k = \{a, b\}^* b \{a, b\}^{k-1}$, whose words are characterized by having the letter b at the kth position from the right, is considered. It is well known that any deterministic finite automaton (DFA) needs at least 2^k states to accept E_k.

A k-sweep IUFST T (k-IUFST) can accept E_k with three states only. The basic idea of T's processing is to shift the input word symbol by symbol to the right, whereby an a is inserted at the first position and the last symbol is removed (this takes two states). In this way, in the first $k-1$ sweeps the input is shifted $k-1$ positions to the right. In a final sweep, it is sufficient to check whether the last symbol is a b. The number of the current sweep can be stored as index of the endmarker.   ∎

The example shows that iterated transductions may lead to a drastic decrease of the number of states for accepting regular languages. It may suggest that the descriptional power of k-IUFSTs always outperforms that of DFAs. However, some languages are particularly size-demanding that even iterated transduction cannot reduce the number of states for their recognition. Witnesses for this fact are the unary regular languages $L_p = \{ a^{m \cdot p} \mid m \geq 0 \}$ where p is a prime number. The state-graph of the minimal DFA accepting L_p consists of a simple directed cycle of p states, beginning from and ending into a designated state which is both the initial and the unique accepting state. In fact, this elementary automaton is actually the best we can provide for L_p, regardless the (classical) computational paradigm we may want to adopt: for example, it is known that p states are necessary for accepting L_p on DFAs, NFAs, two-way DFAs, and two-way NFAs. Even on k-IUFSTs the language L_p needs at least p states to be accepted.

Theorem 8. *Let $k \geq 1$. Then p states are necessary and sufficient for a k-IUFST to accept L_p.*

To study the descriptional power of k-sweep iterated uniform finite-state transducer versus classical finite automata, it is helpful to consider first the sweep reduction and determinization.

Theorem 9. *Let $n, k > 0$ be integers. Every n-state k-NIUFST (resp., k-IUFST) can be converted to an equivalent $2n^i$-state $\lceil \frac{k}{i} \rceil$-NIUFST (resp., $\lceil \frac{k}{i} \rceil$-IUFST).*

The sweep reduction can directly be used to transform constant sweep bounded IUFST and NIUFSTs into equivalent DFAs and NFAs.

Corollary 10. *Let $n, k > 0$ be integers. Every n-state k-NIUFST (resp., k-IUFST) can be converted to an equivalent NFA (resp., DFA) with at most $2n^k$ states.*

The result presented in Theorem 9 turned out to be almost optimal in the sense that there are languages witnessing that n^k states are necessary.

Let us discuss in more detail the possibility of trading states for input sweeps and vice versa. Concerning the relation between the necessary number of states and the number of sweeps, we have the following situation: Theorem 8 shows that there are languages for which additional sweeps do not help to decrease the number of states at all. By Corollary 10, any n-state k-IUFST can be converted into an equivalent DFA with at most $2n^k$ states. Conversely, clearly we cannot reduce the number of states below two or three (for non-trivial languages) by increasing the number of sweeps. So, there is an upper bound for the number of sweeps that may help. In other words, for any regular language L we have a fixed sweep range from 1 to some k_L in which we can trade states for sweeps and vice versa.

Theorem 11. *Let $k \geq 2$ and $n \geq 3$ be integers, and T be an n-state k-IUFST such that the minimal DFA for $L(T)$ has $2n^k$ states. Then any $(k-1)$-IUFST for $L(T)$ must have at least $\lceil n^{k/k-1} \rceil$ states.*

Finally, removing the nondeterminism and the sweeps at the same time means to convert a k-NIUFST to a DFA. Conversion to an NFA with subsequent determinization gives the upper bound of 2^{2n^k} states. A lower bound for this size blow-up is derived by considering the witness language

$$E_{n,k} = \{ \, vbw \mid v, w \in \{a, b\}^*, |w| = c \cdot n^k \text{ for } c > 0 \}$$

for any $n, k > 1$.

Theorem 12. *For any integers $m > 1$ and $k > 0$, an m-state k-NIUFST can be converted to an equivalent 2^{2n^k}-state DFA. There is an m-state k-NIUFST which cannot be converted to an equivalent DFA with less than $2^{(m-1)^k}$ states.*

Finally, it should be mentioned that for k-IUFST the commonly considered decision problems have the same computational complexity as for deterministic finite automata, that is, they are NL-complete. When the bound of the sweep complexity is beyond logarithm, typical decision problems become non-semidecidable.

Several possible lines of research on iterated transducers may be tackled. First of all, it would be natural to consider the same decision problems as in the deterministic case as well as the size cost of implementing language operations for nondeterministic transducers. It would also be interesting to study more general forms of iterated transduction where, for example, different transductions can be performed at different sweeps, or where further information, apart from the output, can be passed on from one sweep to the next.

7   Enumerations and Average Complexity

Descriptional complexity, similarly to what happens in computational complexity, is almost always considered for its worst-case. However, in most cases, this worst-case complexity is only achieved for sets of inputs of very small significance. For practical applications, the average-case analysis, where input data is assumed to follow a given probability distribution, can provide much more accurate prediction of the needed computational resources.

The study of complexity results on average can be performed through experimentation, for which well behaved random generators for the computational models, and thus rigorous enumerative descriptions of their classes, are needed. Enumerative formulae and asymptotic estimates for different kinds of finite automata were presented in 1960s and 1970s. For a survey, we refer the reader to Domaratzki [22]. Concerning uniform random generation, first Nicaud [71] presented a random generator for binary accessible nonisomorphic DFAs that was extended to arbitrary alphabets by Champarnaud and Paranthoën [16]. Almeida, Moreira and Reis [1] based on a string representation, gave another enumeration and random generator for the same class of automata, that avoided any ulterior rejection phase. Bassino and Nicaud [3] improving their previous work gave asymptotic estimates on the number of objects of this class of a given size, as well as, presented a random generator based on Boltzmann samplers. Almeida, Moreira and Reis [2] presented a canonical form for minimal acyclic DFAs which allows its exact enumeration, and that was later extended to non-minimal (trim) acyclic DFAs. An exact enumerative formula based on that representation, and using generalized parking functions, was published by Priez [80]. A random generator for accessible acyclic DFAs was developed by Felice and Nicaud [24], but that is feasible only for small sized automata. On this subject, a survey by Nicaud [73] can be consulted for further details. In the case of NFAs the situation is much more challenging. Testing if two NFAs are isomorphic is an hard problem and thus feasible uniform random generators are not expected to be found. Moreover, with high probability, a uniform random NFA is universal, so other distributions should be considered. Restricted subclasses of NFAs adequate for random generation were studied by Héam and Joly [37] and by Ferreira, Moreira and Reis [25].

For regular expressions random generation is easily obtained from any unambiguous context-free grammar that generated them. All random generators listed here aim an uniform distribution of the objects generated. This distribution, although "naturally" chosen as unbiased, was subject of a study of its expressivity by Koechlin, Nicaud and Rotondo [56] showing that, at least for some aspects of the behavior of the regular expressions other distributions should be considered. In particular, those authors studied absorbing patterns in regular expressions with respect to language equivalence. What is implied by their results is that if one uniformly random generates regular expressions one cannot expect to obtain, with a reasonable probability, regular languages outside a constant set of languages. This means that a core set of languages have so many regular expressions representatives that the remaining languages very scarcely appear. Both the experimental studies and the analytic combinatorics studies, mentioned below, aim to the estimation of the relative descriptional complexity of different models as combinatorial objects by themselves, disregarding language equivalence.

Alternative methods to obtain average results in descriptional complexity can be used in order to avoid the experimentation. Because Kolmogorov incompressible objects have a behavior that it is, by definition, indistinguishable from the average, its study should give rise to average complexity results in a very elegant and succinct manner. Nevertheless, and although canonical string representations exist for some of the models and the successful application of these ideas in computational complexity, no results can be here listed using such technique.

An elegant alternative is the framework of analytic combinatorics [84], by relating combinatorial objects to algebraic properties of complex analytic generating functions. In particular, the behavior of these functions around their dominant singularities gives access to the asymptotic form of their (power) series coefficients. In recent years, the average size of different NFA constructions from regular expressions, using the framework of analytic combinatorics was studied. Nicaud [72] showed that, for a uniform distribution, the position automaton has asymptotically and on average linear size w.r.t the size of the expressions. Several other constructions for regular expressions and other kind of expressions were also considered [9,11]. In those studies, whenever explicit expressions for the generating functions were obtained, it was possible to estimate asymptotic average values using relatively standard analytic methods. However, in general, one does not deal with just one combinatorial class, but with an infinite family of combinatorial classes indexed by the size of the alphabet. This raises problems that do not appear in standard combinatorial classes, such as graphs or trees. Moreover, in many cases, having explicit expressions for the generating functions is unmanageable. Then one needs to use generating functions implicitly defined by algebraic curves, and develop a method to extract the required information for the asymptotic estimates. This method allowed to find, for the combinatorial classes considered, the behavior of the generating function without knowing beforehand the explicit value of its singularity. As an example it was possible to study the average behavior of regular expressions in star normal form [10]. The average results obtained so far on the descriptional complexity of conversions of regular expressions to other models have revealed that asymptotic complexities in the worst case when linear are halved on the average case and square-rooted in the other cases (see [11] for a recent list of average case results).

All these studies using the framework of analytic combinatorics are based on the combinatorial class of regular expressions (or some subset of those). It would be very interesting to see if the same approach could be applied to combinatorial classes of other models, like DFAs, and, in particular, if the goal of characterizing the average behavior of determinization of NFAs is attainable with this technique.

References

1. Almeida, M., Moreira, N., Reis, R.: Enumeration and generation with a string automata representation. Theoret. Comput. Sci. **387**(2), 93–102 (2007)
2. Almeida, M., Moreira, N., Reis, R.: Exact generation of minimal acyclic deterministic finite automata. Int. J. Found. Comput. Sci. **19**(4), 751–765 (2008)
3. Bassino, F., Nicaud, C.: Enumeration and random generation of accessible automata. Theoret. Comput. Sci. **381**(1–3), 86–104 (2007)
4. Bell, J., Brzozowski, J., Moreira, N., Reis, R.: Symmetric groups and quotient complexity of Boolean operations. In: Esparza, J., Fraigniaud, P., Husfeldt, T., Koutsoupias, E. (eds.) ICALP 2014. LNCS, vol. 8573, pp. 1–12. Springer, Heidelberg (2014). https://doi.org/10.1007/978-3-662-43951-7_1
5. Berman, P.: A note on sweeping automata. In: de Bakker, J.W., van Leeuwen, J. (eds.) Proceedings 7th ICALP 1980. LNCS, vol. 85, pp. 91–97. Springer (1980). https://doi.org/10.1007/3-540-10003-2_62
6. Berman, P., Lingas, A.: On the complexity of regular languages in terms of finite automata. Technical Report 304, Polish Academy of Sciences (1977)
7. Bordihn, H., Fernau, H., Holzer, M., Manca, V., Martin-Vide, C.: Iterated sequential transducers as language generating devices. Theoret. Comput. Sci. **369**, 67–81 (2006)
8. Bordihn, H., Holzer, M., Kutrib, M.: Determinization of finite automata accepting subregular languages. Theoret. Comput. Sci. **410**, 3209–3222 (2009)
9. Broda, S., Machiavelo, A., Moreira, N., Reis, R.: Average size of automata constructions from regular expressions. Bull. EATCS **116**, 167–192 (2015)
10. Broda, S., Machiavelo, A., Moreira, N., Reis, R.: On average behaviour of regular expressions in strong star normal form. Int. J. Found. Comput. Sci. **30**(6–7), 899–920 (2019)
11. Broda, S., Machiavelo, A., Moreira, N., Reis, R.: Analytic combinatorics and descriptional complexity of regular languages on average. ACM SIGACT News **51**(1), 38–56 (2020)
12. Brzozowski, J.: In search of most complex regular languages. Int. J. Found. Comput. Sci. **24**(6), 691–708 (2013)
13. Brzozowski, J.A.: Towards a theory of complexity of regular languages. J. Autom. Lang. Comb. **23**(1–3), 67–101 (2018)
14. Câmpeanu, C., Culik, K., Salomaa, K., Yu, S.: State complexity of basic operations on finite languages. In: Boldt, O., Jürgensen, H. (eds.) WIA 1999. LNCS, vol. 2214, pp. 60–70. Springer, Heidelberg (2001). https://doi.org/10.1007/3-540-45526-4_6
15. Caron, P., le Court, E.H., Luque, J., Patrou, B.: New tools for state complexity. Discret. Math. Theor. Comput. Sci. 22(1) (2020)
16. Champarnaud, J.M., Paranthoën, T.: Random generation of DFAs. Theoret. Comput. Sci. **330**(2), 221–235 (2005)
17. Chrobak, M.: Finite automata and unary languages. Theoret. Comput. Sci. **47**(3), 149–158 (1986)

18. Citrini, C., Crespi-Reghizzi, S., Mandrioli, D.: On deterministic multi-pass analysis. SIAM J. Comput. **15**, 668–693 (1986)
19. Davies, S.: A general approach to state complexity of operations: formalization and limitations. In: Hoshi, M., Seki, S. (eds.) DLT 2018. LNCS, vol. 11088, pp. 256–268. Springer, Cham (2018). https://doi.org/10.1007/978-3-319-98654-8_21
20. Davies, S.: Primitivity, uniform minimality, and state complexity of Boolean operations. Theory Comput. Syst. **62**(8), 1952–2005 (2018)
21. Davies, S.: Algebraic Approaches to State Complexity of Regular Operations. Ph.D. thesis, University of Waterloo, Ontario, Canada (2019)
22. Domaratzki, M.: Enumeration of formal languages. Bull. EATCS **89**, 113–133 (2006)
23. Domaratzki, M., Salomaa, K.: Lower bounds for the transition complexity of NFAs. In: Královič, R., Urzyczyn, P. (eds.) MFCS 2006. LNCS, vol. 4162, pp. 315–326. Springer, Heidelberg (2006). https://doi.org/10.1007/11821069_28
24. De Felice, S., Nicaud, C.: Random generation of deterministic acyclic automata using the recursive method. In: Bulatov, A.A., Shur, A.M. (eds.) CSR 2013. LNCS, vol. 7913, pp. 88–99. Springer, Heidelberg (2013). https://doi.org/10.1007/978-3-642-38536-0_8
25. Ferreira, M., Moreira, N., Reis, R.: Forward injective finite automata: exact and random generation of nonisomorphic NFAs. In: Konstantinidis, S., Pighizzini, G. (eds.) DCFS 2018. LNCS, vol. 10952, pp. 88–100. Springer, Cham (2018). https://doi.org/10.1007/978-3-319-94631-3_8
26. Friburger, N., Maurel, D.: Finite-state transducer cascades to extract named entities in texts. Theoret. Comput. Sci. **313**, 93–104 (2004)
27. Gao, Y., Moreira, N., Reis, R., Yu, S.: A survey on operational state complexity. J. Autom. Lang. Comb. **21**(4), 251–310 (2017)
28. Geffert, V., Guillon, B., Pighizzini, G.: Two-way automata making choices only at the endmarkers. Inf. Comput. **239**, 71–86 (2014)
29. Geffert, V., Mereghetti, C., Pighizzini, G.: Converting two-way nondeterministic unary automata into simpler automata. Theoret. Comput. Sci. **295**, 189–203 (2003)
30. Geffert, V., Pighizzini, G.: Two-way unary automata versus logarithmic space. Inf. Comput. **209**(7), 1016–1025 (2011)
31. Ginzburg, A.: Algebraic Theory of Automata. Academic Press, Cambridge (1968)
32. Goldstine, J., et al.: Descriptional complexity of machines with limited resources. J. UCS **8**, 193–234 (2002)
33. Gruber, H., Holzer, M.: On the average state and transition complexity of finite languages. Theoret. Comput. Sci. **387**, 155–166 (2007)
34. Guillon, B., Pighizzini, G., Prigioniero, L., Průša, D.: Two-way automata and one-tape machines. In: Hoshi, M., Seki, S. (eds.) DLT 2018. LNCS, vol. 11088, pp. 366–378. Springer, Cham (2018). https://doi.org/10.1007/978-3-319-98654-8_30
35. Guillon, B., Prigioniero, L.: Linear-time limited automata. Theoret. Comput. Sci. **798**, 95–108 (2019)
36. Hartmanis, J., Stearns, R.E.: Algebraic Structure Theory of Sequential Machines. Prentice-Hall, Hoboken (1966)
37. Héam, P.-C., Joly, J.-L.: On the uniform random generation of non deterministic automata up to isomorphism. In: Drewes, F. (ed.) CIAA 2015. LNCS, vol. 9223, pp. 140–152. Springer, Cham (2015). https://doi.org/10.1007/978-3-319-22360-5_12
38. Hennie, F.C.: One-tape, off-line Turing machine computations. Inform. Control **8**(6), 553–578 (1965)
39. Hibbard, T.N.: A generalization of context-free determinism. Inform. Control **11**(1/2), 196–238 (1967)

40. Holzer, M., Kutrib, M.: State complexity of basic operations on nondeterministic finite automata. In: Champarnaud, J.-M., Maurel, D. (eds.) CIAA 2002. LNCS, vol. 2608, pp. 148–157. Springer, Heidelberg (2003). https://doi.org/10.1007/3-540-44977-9_14

41. Holzer, M., Kutrib, M.: Descriptional complexity - an introductory survey. In: Martin-Vide, C. (ed.) Scientific Applications of Language Methods, pp. 1–58. Imperial College Press (2010)

42. Holzer, M., Kutrib, M.: Descriptional and computational complexity of finite automata - a survey. Inform. Comput. **209**, 456–470 (2011)

43. Holzer, M., Kutrib, M.: Automata that may change their mind. In: Freund, R., Hospodár, M., Jirásková, G., Pighizzini, G. (eds.) Non-Classical Models of Automata and Applications (NCMA 2018). books@ocg.at, vol. 332, pp. 83–98. Austrian Computer Society, Vienna (2018)

44. Holzer, M., Kutrib, M.: One-time nondeterministic computations. Int. J. Found. Comput. Sci. **30**, 1069–1089 (2019)

45. Hromkovič, J., Schnitger, G.: Nondeterminism versus determinism for two-way finite automata: generalizations of Sipser's separation. In: Baeten, J.C.M., Lenstra, J.K., Parrow, J., Woeginger, G.J. (eds.) ICALP 2003. LNCS, vol. 2719, pp. 439–451. Springer, Heidelberg (2003). https://doi.org/10.1007/3-540-45061-0_36

46. Hromkovič, J., Schnitger, G.: NFAs with and without ϵ-transitions. In: Caires, L., Italiano, G.F., Monteiro, L., Palamidessi, C., Yung, M. (eds.) ICALP 2005. LNCS, vol. 3580, pp. 385–396. Springer, Heidelberg (2005). https://doi.org/10.1007/11523468_32

47. Hromkovič, J., Seibert, S., Wilke, T.: Translating regular expressions into small ϵ-free nondeterministic finite automata. J. Comput. System Sci. **62**, 565–588 (2001)

48. Iwama, K., Kambayashi, Y., Takaki, K.: Tight bounds on the number of states of DFAs that are equivalent to n-state NFAs. Theoret. Comput. Sci. **237**, 485–494 (2000)

49. Kapoutsis, C.A.: Minicomplexity. In: Kutrib, M., Moreira, N., Reis, R. (eds.) DCFS 2012. LNCS, vol. 7386, pp. 20–42. Springer, Heidelberg (2012). https://doi.org/10.1007/978-3-642-31623-4_2

50. Kapoutsis, C.A.: Minicomplexity. J. Autom. Lang. Comb. **17**(2–4), 205–224 (2012)

51. Kapoutsis, C.A.: Nondeterminism is essential in small two-way finite automata with few reversals. Inf. Comput. **222**, 208–227 (2013)

52. Kapoutsis, C.A.: Two-way automata versus logarithmic space. Theory Comput. Syst. **55**(2), 421–447 (2014)

53. Kapoutsis, C.A.: Minicomplexity - some motivation, some history, and some structure (invited talk extended abstract). In: Catania, B., Královic, R., Nawrocki, J.R., Pighizzini, G. (eds.) SOFSEM 2019. LNCS, vol. 11376, pp. 28–38. Springer (2019)

54. Kapoutsis, C.A., Královic, R., Mömke, T.: Size complexity of rotating and sweeping automata. J. Comput. Syst. Sci. **78**(2), 537–558 (2012)

55. Kapoutsis, C.A., Pighizzini, G.: Two-way automata characterizations of L/poly versus NL. Theory Comput. Syst. **56**(4), 662–685 (2015)

56. Koechlin, F., Nicaud, C., Rotondo, P.: Uniform random expressions lack expressivity. In: Rossmanith, P., Heggernes, P., Katoen, J. (eds.) MFCS 2019. LIPIcs, vol. 138, pp. 51:1–51:14. Schloss Dagstuhl - Leibniz-Zentrum für Informatik (2019)

57. Kutrib, M.: The phenomenon of non-recursive trade-offs. Int. J. Found. Comput. Sci. **16**, 957–973 (2005)

58. Kutrib, M., Malcher, A., Mereghetti, C., Palano, B.: Descriptional complexity of iterated uniform finite-state transducers. In: Hospodár, M., Jirásková, G., Konstantinidis, S. (eds.) DCFS 2019. LNCS, vol. 11612, pp. 223–234. Springer, Cham (2019). https://doi.org/10.1007/978-3-030-23247-4_17

59. Kutrib, M., Malcher, A., Mereghetti, C., Palano, B.: Deterministic and nondeterministic iterated uniform finite-state transducers: computational and descriptional power. In: Anselmo, M., Della Vedova, G., Manea, F., Pauly, A. (eds.) CiE 2020. LNCS, vol. 12098, pp. 87–99. Springer, Cham (2020). https://doi.org/10.1007/978-3-030-51466-2_8

60. Kutrib, M., Malcher, A., Pighizzini, G.: Oblivious two-way finite automata: decidability and complexity. Inf. Comput. **237**, 294–302 (2014)

61. Kutrib, M., Pighizzini, G., Wendlandt, M.: Descriptional complexity of limited automata. Inf. Comput. **259**(2), 259–276 (2018)

62. Kutrib, M., Wendlandt, M.: On simulation cost of unary limited automata. In: Shallit, J., Okhotin, A. (eds.) DCFS 2015. LNCS, vol. 9118, pp. 153–164. Springer, Cham (2015). https://doi.org/10.1007/978-3-319-19225-3_13

63. Lifshits, Y.: A lower bound on the size of ε-free NFA corresponding to a regular expression. Inform. Process. Lett. **85**(6), 293–299 (2003)

64. Lupanov, O.B.: A comparison of two types of finite sources. Problemy Kybernetiki **9**, 321–326 (1963). (in Russian), German translation: Über den Vergleich zweier Typen endlicher Quellen. Probleme der Kybernetik 6 (1966), 328–335

65. Manca, V.: On the generative power of iterated transductions. In: Ito, M., Păun, G., Yu, S. (eds.) Words, Semigroups, and Transductions - Festschrift in Honor of Gabriel Thierrin, pp. 315–327. World Scientific (2001)

66. Maslov, A.N.: Estimates of the number of states of finite automata. Dokllady Akademii Nauk SSSR **194**, 1266–1268 (1970). (in Russian). English translation in Soviet Mathematics Doklady, 11, 1373–1375 (1970)

67. Mealy, G.H.: A method for synthesizing sequential circuits. Bell Syst. Tech. J. **34**, 1045–1079 (1955)

68. Meyer, A.R., Fischer, M.J.: Economy of description by automata, grammars, and formal systems. In: Symposium on Switching and Automata Theory (SWAT 1971), pp. 188–191. IEEE (1971)

69. Micali, S.: Two-way deterministic finite automata are exponentially more succinct than sweeping automata. Inf. Process. Lett. **12**(2), 103–105 (1981)

70. Moore, F.R.: On the bounds for state-set size in the proofs of equivalence between deterministic, nondeterministic, and two-way finite automata. IEEE Trans. Comput. **20**(10), 1211–1214 (1971)

71. Nicaud, C.: Étude du comportement en moyenne des automates finis et des langages rationnels. Ph.D. thesis, Université de Paris 7 (2000)

72. Nicaud, C.: On the average size of Glushkov's automata. In: Dediu, A.H., Ionescu, A.M., Martín-Vide, C. (eds.) LATA 2009. LNCS, vol. 5457, pp. 626–637. Springer, Heidelberg (2009). https://doi.org/10.1007/978-3-642-00982-2_53

73. Nicaud, C.: Random deterministic automata. In: Csuhaj-Varjú, E., Dietzfelbinger, M., Ésik, Z. (eds.) MFCS 2014. LNCS, vol. 8634, pp. 5–23. Springer, Heidelberg (2014). https://doi.org/10.1007/978-3-662-44522-8_2

74. Pierce, A.: Decision Problems on Iterated Length-Preserving Transducers. Bachelor's thesis, SCS Carnegie Mellon University, Pittsburgh (2011)

75. Pighizzini, G.: Two-way finite automata: old and recent results. Fundam. Inform. **126**(2–3), 225–246 (2013)

76. Pighizzini, G.: Limited automata: properties, complexity and variants. In: Hospodár, M., Jirásková, G., Konstantinidis, S. (eds.) DCFS 2019. LNCS, vol. 11612, pp. 57–73. Springer, Cham (2019). https://doi.org/10.1007/978-3-030-23247-4_4
77. Pighizzini, G., Pisoni, A.: Limited automata and regular languages. Int. J. Found. Comput. Sci. **25**(7), 897–916 (2014)
78. Pighizzini, G., Pisoni, A.: Limited automata and context-free languages. Fundam. Inform. **136**(1–2), 157–176 (2015)
79. Pighizzini, G., Prigioniero, L.: Limited automata and unary languages. Inf. Comput. **266**, 60–74 (2019)
80. Priez, J.B.: Enumeration of minimal acyclic automata via generalized parking functions. In: FPSAC 2015. DMTCS, January 2015
81. Rabin, M.O., Scott, D.: Finite automata and their decision problems. IBM J. Res. Dev. **3**, 114–125 (1959)
82. Sakoda, W.J., Sipser, M.: Nondeterminism and the size of two way finite automata. In: Lipton, R.J., Burkhard, W.A., Savitch, W.J., Friedman, E.P., Aho, A.V. (eds.) Proceedings of the 10th Annual ACM Symposium on Theory of Computing, 1–3 May 1978, San Diego, California, USA, pp. 275–286. ACM (1978)
83. Salomaa, K., Yu, S.: NFA to DFA transformation for finite languages over arbitrary alphabets. J. Autom. Lang. Comb. **2**(3), 177–186 (1997)
84. Sedgewick, R., Flajolet, P.: Analysis of Algorithms. Addision-Wesley, Boston (1996)
85. Shepherdson, J.C.: The reduction of two-way automata to one-way automata. IBM J. Res. Dev. **3**(2), 198–200 (1959)
86. Sipser, M.: Lower bounds on the size of sweeping automata. J. Comput. Syst. Sci. **21**(2), 195–202 (1980)
87. Stearns, R.E.: A regularity test for pushdown machines. Inform. Control **11**, 323–340 (1967)
88. Valiant, L.G.: Regularity and related problems for deterministic pushdown automata. J. ACM **22**, 1–10 (1975)
89. Vardi, M.Y.: A note on the reduction of two-way automata to one-way automata. Inf. Process. Lett. **30**(5), 261–264 (1989)
90. Vardi, M.Y.: Endmarkers can make a difference. Inf. Process. Lett. **35**(3), 145–148 (1990)
91. Wagner, K.W., Wechsung, G.: Computational Complexity. D. Reidel Publishing Company, Dordrecht (1986)
92. Yu, S.: State complexity of regular languages. J. Autom. Lang. Comb. **6**, 221–234 (2001)
93. Yu, S., Zhuang, Q., Salomaa, K.: The state complexities of some basic operations on regular languages. Theoret. Comput. Sci. **125**(2), 315–328 (1994)

A Survey of Compositional Signal Flow Theory

Filippo Bonchi[1] ⓘ, Paweł Sobociński[3]([✉]) ⓘ, and Fabio Zanasi[2] ⓘ

[1] Università di Pisa, Pisa, Italy
fibonchi@di.unipi.it
[2] University College London, London, UK
f.zanasi@ucl.ac.uk
[3] Tallinn University of Technology, Tallinn, Estonia
pawel@cs.ioc.ee

Abstract. Signal flow graphs are combinatorial models for linear dynamical systems, playing a foundational role in control theory and engineering. In this survey, we overview a series of works [3,10,11,13,15–18,31,51,63] that develop a compositional theory of these structures, and explore several striking insights emerging from this approach. In particular, the use of *string diagrams*, a categorical syntax for graphical models, allows to switch from the traditional combinatorial treatment of signal flow graphs to an algebraic characterisation. Within this framework, signal flow graphs may then be treated as a fully-fledged (visual) programming language, and equipped with important meta-theoretical properties, such as a complete axiomatisation and a full abstraction theorem. Moreover, the abstract viewpoint offered by string diagrams reveals that the same algebraic structures modelling linear dynamical systems may also be used to interpret diverse kinds of models, such as electrical circuits and Petri nets.

In this respect, our work is a contribution to *compositional network theory* (see e.g., [1,2,4–6,9,12,20,21,23,24,26,28–30,32,37,49,59], ?), an emerging multidisciplinary research programme aiming at a uniform compositional study of different sorts of computational models.

Keywords: Signal flow graphs · Compositional semantics · Category theory · String diagrams

1 String Diagrams as Resource Sensitive Syntax

Traditional syntax is often identified with trees. Terms are generated from a *signature* Σ, which contains *generators* (aka *operations*) $\sigma \in \Sigma$, each with an

P. Sobociński—supported by the ESF funded Estonian IT Academy research measure (project 2014-2020.4.05.19-0001) and the Estonian Research Council grant PRG1210.

M. Goedicke et al. (Eds.): Advancing Research in Information and Communication Technology,
IFIP AICT 600, pp. 29–56, 2021. https://doi.org/10.1007/978-3-030-81701-5_2

arity $ar(\sigma) \in \mathbb{N}$. The arity tells us the number of arguments σ requires. In computer science, syntax is often introduced in as a BNF specification. So, e.g.,:

$$t ::= Var \mid \sigma(t_1, t_2, \ldots, t_n) \quad (\sigma \in \Sigma \wedge ar(\sigma) = n) \tag{1}$$

where Var is a collection of variables. Derivations in (1) are in 1-1 correspondence with those trees where the internal nodes are labelled with $\sigma \in \Sigma$ with $ar(\sigma)$ children, and the leaves are variables and *constants* (arity 0 generators).

The BNF description makes the recursive nature of syntax explicit. The corresponding proof principle is *structural induction* which is extremely useful in programming language theory. Mathematically, these principles stem from the fact that syntax is *free*: it is the initial algebra of a functor $F_{\Sigma, Var} : \mathbf{Set} \to \mathbf{Set}$, or, following Lawvere [43], the *free category* $\mathcal{L}_\Sigma$ *with finite products* on Σ.

The latter description is especially illuminating because it emphasises the central role of finite products, which betrays an underlying assumption about the *cartesianity* of whatever the syntax is meant to express. In particular, variables in scope can be used several times, or not used at all. Thus, the data we operate on is *classical*: it can be copied and discarded at will. Perhaps less obvious is the post-hoc justification of the definition of signature: all operations denote *functions* that have precisely one output. Any operation with two outputs can simply be decomposed into two single-output operations by discarding appropriate outputs. Thus being more liberal with the definition of signature by allowing coarities other than 1 would not increase expressivity.

What is an appropriate notion of syntax when the underlying data is not classical? Or if we want to denote non-functional entities (e.g., relations)? A syntax that is more expressive, in this sense, but retains its recursive specification and the associated principle of structural induction?

The answer is to replace free categories with products with *free props* [41,44].

Definition 1 (Prop). *A prop (**pro**duct and **p**ermutation category) is a symmetric strict monoidal category with set of objects* $\mathbb{N}$, *and the monoidal product on objects is addition:* $m \oplus n := m + n$.

We now give a more concrete description of how terms are constructed. Instead of trees, terms are *string diagrams* [57]: terms built from the generators of Σ, quotiented by topologically intuitive deformations. First, because we are in a resource sensitive setting, we need to be more liberal with our notion of signature.

Definition 2. *A monoidal signature* Σ *is a collection of generators* $\sigma \in \Sigma$, *each with an arity* $ar(\sigma) \in \mathbb{N}$ *and coarity* $coar(\sigma) \in \mathbb{N}$.

Concrete terms can still be given a BNF description, as follows:

$$c ::= \sigma \in \Sigma \mid \tag{2}$$

$$\boxed{} \mid — \mid \times \mid c \oplus c \mid c; c \tag{3}$$

Differently from (1), arities and coarities are not handled in the BNF but with the additional structure of (3) and an associated sorting discipline, shown below. We only consider terms that have a sort, which is unique if it exists.

$$\frac{}{\sigma : (ar(\sigma), coar(\sigma))} \quad \frac{}{\boxed{\;\;}\; : (0,0)} \quad \frac{}{\text{—} : (1,1)} \quad \frac{}{\times : (2,2)} \quad \frac{c : (n,z) \quad d : (z,m)}{c\,;d : (n,m)} \quad \frac{c : (n,m) \quad d : (r,z)}{c\oplus d : (n+r, m+z)}$$

The diagrammatic convention for $\sigma \in \Sigma$ is to draw it as a box with $ar(\sigma)$ "dangling wires" on the left and $coar(\sigma)$ on the right:

$$ar(\sigma) \left\{ \boxed{\;\sigma\;} \right\} coar(\sigma).$$

The intuition for the two operations in (3) is given by their diagrammatic conventions:

$c\,;c'$ is drawn $\boxed{c}\boxed{c'}$ and $c\oplus c'$ is drawn $\begin{smallmatrix}\boxed{c}\\\boxed{c'}\end{smallmatrix}$. The sorting discipline thus keeps track of the "dangling wires" of each term and ensures that the above diagrammatic convention makes sense.

Example 1. Consider a signature for a simple thread coordination language:

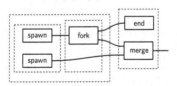

The following is derivable from (2), (3), drawn according to the conventions.

Note that we need to introduce the dotted line boxes in order to identify precisely the term drawn. Indeed the above corresponds to the term

$$((\mathsf{spawn} \oplus \mathsf{spawn})\,; (\mathsf{fork} \oplus \text{—})))\,; (\mathsf{end} \oplus \mathsf{merge})$$

Note that other terms yield the same connectivity, for example:

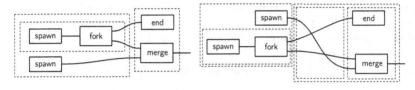

which correspond, respectively, to

$$(\mathsf{spawn}\,; \mathsf{fork}) \oplus \mathsf{spawn})\,; (\mathsf{end} \oplus \mathsf{merge}) \text{ and}$$

(spawn ⊕ (spawn ; fork)) ⊕ ((($\times$ ⊕ —) ; (— ⊕ $\times$)) ; (end ⊕ merge)).

The laws of props identify all and precisely the terms that have the same underlying connectivity. The slogan is "only the topology matters". This means that, in the free prop on Σ, we do not need to blemish our diagrams with dotted-line boxes, and string diagrams unambiguously represent terms (up-to the laws of props). Nevertheless, we have access to the low-level representation given by (2), (3), with the particular choice of representative immaterial.

Moreover, the fact that our diagrams are the arrows of free props means that they behave analogously to classical syntax. Indeed, as we have seen, they have a recursive definition and enjoy an analogous principle of structural induction.

2   The Calculus of Signal Flow Diagrams

The subject of this paper is a specific string diagrammatic syntax, called the *calculus of signal flow diagrams*. We shall see that, as the name suggests, this syntax is adapted to reason algebraically about *signal flow graphs*, a well-known foundational structure in control theory and engineering (see *e.g.*, [45,58]).

Fixed a semiring R, the monoidal signature of the calculus of signal flow diagrams is:

$$\Sigma = \{-\bullet, -\!\!\!\mathsf{C}, -\!\boxed{x}\!-, \,\mathsf{D}\!-, \circ\!-, \bullet\!-, \,\mathsf{D}\!-, -\!\boxed{x}\!-, -\!\!\!\mathsf{C}, -\!\circ\}$$
$$\cup \{-\!\boxed{r}\!-, -\!\boxed{r}\!-\mid r \in \mathsf{R}\,\} \qquad (4)$$

The sorts are apparent from the depictions and given by counting dangling wires on each side. As we shall see, the indeterminate x plays a role akin to that in polynomials. Let Circ be the free prop on (4), as in Sect. 1. We usually refer to the arrows of Circ (i.e., terms obtained from composing generators in (4)) as *circuits*.

While we delay the semantics of the terms of Circ, to Sects. 3 and 4, it is useful to introduce some intuitions for our generators. The five leftmost generators and —$\boxed{r}$— of (4) can be thought of as taking signals—values in R—from the left boundary to the right: thus —C is a *copier*, duplicating the signal arriving on the left; —$\bullet$ accepts any signal on the left and discards it, producing nothing on the right; D— is an *adder* that takes two signals on the left and emits their sum on the right, and $\circ$— constantly emits the signal 0 on the right; —$\boxed{r}$— is an *amplifier*, multiplying the signal on the left by $r \in$ R. Finally, —$\boxed{x}$— is a *delay*, a synchronous one place buffer initialised with 0. The five rightmost generators of (4) and —$\boxed{r}$— are "reflected about the y-axis". Their behaviour is symmetric—here it is helpful to think of signals as flowing from right to left.

Example 2.   Consider the two circuits below.

According to our intuitions, in the left circuit, the signal flows from right to left, while in the other from left to right – indeed, the "cup" ●— ; —◖ and "cap" ◗— ; —● allow us to form a feedback loop. In Sect. 3, we shall provide circuits with a formal semantics. In Example 4 we shall see that the circuits have the same semantics, despite the apparent incompatibility in signal flow direction.

We identify two sub-categories of Circ: $\overrightarrow{\mathsf{Circ}}$ is the free prop on

$$\{ \text{—●}, \text{—◖}, \text{—}\boxed{x}\text{—}, \text{◗—}, \text{◦—} \} \cup \{ \text{—}\boxed{r}\text{—} \mid r \in \mathsf{R} \}$$

and $\overleftarrow{\mathsf{Circ}}$ is the free prop on

$$\{ \text{●—}, \text{◗—}, \text{—}\boxed{x}\text{—}, \text{—◖}, \text{—◦} \} \cup \{ \text{—}\boxed{r}\text{—} \mid r \in \mathsf{R} \}$$

The notation recalls the intuition that for circuits in $\overrightarrow{\mathsf{Circ}}$, the signal flows from left to right, and in $\overleftarrow{\mathsf{Circ}}$ from right to left. Clearly $\overleftarrow{\mathsf{Circ}}$ is isomorphic to the opposite category of $\overrightarrow{\mathsf{Circ}}$: $\overleftarrow{\mathsf{Circ}}$ circuits can be seen as reflections of $\overrightarrow{\mathsf{Circ}}$ circuits.

2.1   Feedback and Classical Signal Flow Diagrams

Beyond $\overrightarrow{\mathsf{Circ}}$ and $\overleftarrow{\mathsf{Circ}}$, we identify a class of circuits that adheres closely to the orthodox notion of signal flow graph [45], albeit without directed wires. Here, the signal can flow from left to right, as in $\overrightarrow{\mathsf{Circ}}$, but with the possibility of *feedbacks*, provided that these pass through at least one delay. This amounts to defining, for all n, m, a map $\mathsf{Tr}(\cdot)\colon \mathsf{Circ}[n+1, m+1] \to \mathsf{Circ}[n, m]$ taking $c\colon n+1 \to m+1$ to the n-to-m circuit below:

$$\begin{array}{c} \vdots \; \boxed{\;c\;} \boxed{x} \; \vdots \end{array} \tag{5}$$

Intuitively, $\mathsf{Tr}(\cdot)$ adds to c a feedback loop from its topmost right to its topmost left port. We can now formally define classical signal flow graphs as the (symmetric monoidal) sub-category SF of Circ inductively given as follows:

(i) if $c \in \overrightarrow{\mathsf{Circ}}[n, m]$, then $c \in \mathsf{SF}[n, m]$
(ii) if $c \in \mathsf{SF}[n+1, m+1]$, then $\mathsf{Tr}(c) \in \mathsf{SF}[n, m]$
(iii) if $c_1 \in \mathsf{SF}[n, z]$ and $c_2 \in \mathsf{SF}[z, m]$, then $c_1 \; ; \; c_2 \in \mathsf{SF}[n, m]$
(iv) if $c_1 \in \mathsf{SF}[n, m]$ and $c_2 \in \mathsf{SF}[r, z]$, then $c_1 \oplus c_2 \in \mathsf{SF}[n+r, m+z]$.

Equivalently, SF is the smallest sub-category of Circ that contains $\overrightarrow{\mathsf{Circ}}$ and is closed under Tr. For instance, the right circuit of Example 2 is in SF.

Remark 1. The reader may have recognised in (5) the structure of a *trace* [38]. In fact, there is a tradition of modelling systems with feedback in terms of traced monoidal categories [34]. The algebraic core of these structures has also been studied in the context of iteration theories [8] and Stefanescu's network algebra [60]. Concerning the more specific setting of signal flow graphs, previous categorical approaches have been mostly based on coalgebra theory [7,46,55]. A distinguishing feature of the string diagrammatic approach presented here (originated in [15], and then independently proposed in [3]) is the adoption of a more abstract framework, Circ, featuring more circuit diagrams than just classical signal flow graphs (which form a subcategory SF). As we will see in Sects. 4 and 5, the increased generality comes at the price of making the operational analysis subtler. The payoff is a more elementary syntax (4), not featuring any primitive for recursion, and the possibility of a neat axiomatisation (Sect. 3.1) in terms of well-known algebraic structures such as bimonoids and Frobenius monoids.

3   Denotational Semantics

Here we equip circuits with a *denotational semantics*, assigning to each an element of an appropriate mathematical universe.

Since each generator of (4) has a clear flow directionality, it may be tempting to interpret them as *functions*, mapping inputs to outputs. However, when "incompatible" connectors are combined, functional interpretations often become untenable. For instance, there is no clear way of understanding ●— ; —◀ as a function. It can, however, be interpreted as a *relation* that constrains the observable behaviours: for example, in this particular case, the constraint is that at any point in time the *same* value is observed on both ports.

The semantics of a circuit $c \in \mathsf{Circ}[n, m]$ is thus some relation R. A pair $(u, v) \in R$ is *evidence of a possible execution*. The specific nature of u and v changes according to the semantic model chosen, but the idea is that in the execution evidenced by (u, v), u and v are vectors of observations, with u accounting for what is observed on the left ports and v for what is observed on the right ports. Such relations naturally organise themselves as arrows of a prop.

Definition 3 (Rel$_X$). *Given a set X of observations, Rel_X is the prop with arrows $m \to n$ the relations $R \subseteq X^m \times X^n$. The monoidal product is given by cartesian product, and composition of $R : m_1 \to m_2$ and $S : m_2 \to m_3$ is:*

$$\{(u, v) \mid u \in \mathsf{R}^{m_1}, v \in \mathsf{R}^{m_3} \text{ and there is } w \in \mathsf{R}^{m_2} \text{ with } (u, w) \in R \text{ and } (w, v) \in S\}$$

Since the syntax (4) is parametrised over a semiring R, and the interpretation of the white generators $\{ \mathrel{\rhd}\!-, \circ\!-, -\!\mathrel{\lhd}, -\!\circ \}$ is addition, it is natural to consider observations at each port as elements of R, which provides the bare-bone algebraic structure (addition and multiplication) of signals. As alluded to previously, different choices of R allow us to change the semantic model of a circuit. For the remainder of this section we assume that the semiring of signals R is a field k.

The denotational semantics assigns to a circuit c, the relation of *trajectories* that correspond to all possible executions of c. There are, again, different choices for what one may consider as an "execution", giving us one additional dimension of semantic models. The two cases mainly studied in the literature are: *finite-in-the-past, infinite-in-the-future* executions—equivalent to assuming executions start with 0-initialised registers—and *bi-infinite* trajectories, equivalent to (additionally) considering executions where registers can hold arbitrary initial values at all times. We will make these observations more precise in Remark 5, having introduced formal operational semantics of circuits.

The set of *finite-in-the-past, infinite-in-the-future* trajectories is the field $k((x))$ of *Laurent series* over k. Indeed, a Laurent series σ can be understood as a *stream*, i.e., an infinite sequence of k-elements

$$\sigma_{-2}\ \sigma_{-1}\ \underline{\sigma_0}\ \sigma_1\ \sigma_2\ \ldots\ \sigma_n\ \ldots$$

where σ_i intuitively represents a discrete unit of signal appearing at one of the circuit ports at a certain moment in time. We underline the *initial* moment of time: thus, in the above, the behaviour σ_0 is observed at time 0. Thus a Laurent series may have possibly infinitely many non-zero observations in the future (σ_1, σ_2, etc.), but only finitely many in the past (σ_{-1} and σ_{-2}). An equivalent way of seeing Laurent series is as formal sums $\sigma = \sum_{i=d}^{\infty} \sigma_i x^i$, where $d \in \mathbb{Z}$ indexes the first non-zero element appearing in σ. In this way, Laurent series can be manipulated (added, multiplied) as polynomials. In fact, Laurent series are well-known to be the field of fractions of the ring $k[[x]]$ of formal power series.

The set of *bi-infinite* trajectories is $k^{\mathbb{Z}}$, i.e., the set of functions from the set of integers $\mathbb{Z}$ to k. The algebraic structure common to both $k((x))$ and $k^{\mathbb{Z}}$ is that they are $k[x, x^{-1}]$ modules: roughly speaking, this amounts to saying that:

– trajectories are time-independent: they can be moved one place forward in time (captured as the action of multiplying by x) and moved one place back in time (the action of multiplying by x^{-1});
– trajectories are linear: the always 0 sequence is a trajectory and trajectories are closed under pointwise addition.

We can define the denotational semantics in a trajectory-agnostic way:

Definition 4. *Let* Traj $\in \{ k((x)), k^{\mathbb{Z}} \}$. *The prop morphism* $[\![\cdot]\!]\colon$ Circ $\to$ Rel$_{\mathsf{Traj}}$ *is inductively defined on circuits as follows. For the generators in* (4)

$$\begin{aligned}
&\prec\!\!\!\bullet \longmapsto \left\{ \left(\sigma, \begin{pmatrix} \sigma \\ \sigma \end{pmatrix}\right) \mid \sigma \in \mathsf{Traj} \right\} &\quad& \succ\!\!\!\bullet \longmapsto \left\{ \left(\begin{pmatrix} \sigma \\ \tau \end{pmatrix}, \sigma + \tau\right) \mid \sigma, \tau \in \mathsf{Traj} \right\}\\
&\longrightarrow\!\!\bullet \longmapsto \{(\sigma, \bullet) \mid \sigma \in \mathsf{Traj}\} &\quad& \circ\!\!- \longmapsto \{(\bullet, 0)\}\\
&\boxed{r}\!\!- \longmapsto \{(\sigma, \sigma \cdot r) \mid \sigma \in \mathsf{Traj}\} &\quad& \boxed{x}\!\!- \longmapsto \{(\sigma, \sigma \cdot x) \mid \sigma \in \mathsf{Traj}\}
\end{aligned}$$

where $\bullet$ *is the only element of* $k((x))^0$. *The semantics of the reflected generators is symmetric, e.g.,* $\bullet\!\!-$ *is mapped to* $\{(\sigma, \bullet) \mid p \in k((x))\}$.

For space reasons, we refer the reader to [31] (and Remark 3 below) for more details on the semantics in terms of bi-infinite trajectories. Henceforth, we shall fix the choice of Laurent series $k((x))$ as the trajectories of choice.

Example 3. In Example 2, we presented the circuit c_2 as the composition of four sequential chunks. Their denotational semantics, following Definition 4, is below.

$$[\![(\bullet\!\!-\ ;\ -\!\!\blacktriangleleft\!\!\bigcirc) \oplus -\!\!\!\!-]\!] = \{ (\sigma_1, \begin{pmatrix} \tau_1 \\ \tau_1 \\ \sigma_1 \end{pmatrix}) \mid \sigma_1, \tau_1 \in \mathsf{k}((x)) \}$$

$$[\![-\!\!\!\!- \oplus (\bigcirc\!\!\!-\ ;\ -\!\!\blacktriangleleft\!\!\bigcirc)]\!] = \{ (\begin{pmatrix} \tau_2 \\ \sigma_2 \\ \rho_2 \end{pmatrix}, \begin{pmatrix} \tau_2 \\ \sigma_2 + \rho_2 \\ \sigma_2 + \rho_2 \end{pmatrix}) \mid \sigma_2, \tau_2, \rho_2 \in \mathsf{k}((x)) \}$$

$$[\![(-\!\!\!\!- \oplus -\!\!\boxed{x}\!\!-) \oplus -\!\!\!\!-]\!] = \{ (\begin{pmatrix} \tau_3 \\ \sigma_3 \\ \rho_3 \end{pmatrix}, \begin{pmatrix} \tau_3 \\ x \cdot \sigma_3 \\ \rho_3 \end{pmatrix}) \mid \sigma_3, \tau_3, \rho_3 \in \mathsf{k}((x)) \}$$

$$[\![(\bigcirc\!\!\blacktriangleright\ ;\ -\!\!\bullet) \oplus -\!\!\!\!-]\!] = \{ (\begin{pmatrix} \tau_4 \\ \tau_4 \\ \sigma_4 \end{pmatrix}, \sigma_4) \mid \sigma_4, \tau_4 \in \mathsf{k}((x)) \}$$

The composition in $\mathsf{Rel}_{\mathsf{k}((x))}$ of the four linear relations above is

$$\{ (\sigma_1, \sigma_4) \mid \text{there exist } \sigma_2, \sigma_3, \tau_1, \dots, \tau_4, \rho_2, \rho_3 \text{ s.t. } \begin{cases} \tau_1 = \tau_2 = \sigma_2 = \tau_3 = \tau_4, \\ \sigma_2 + \rho_2 = \sigma_3, \ x \cdot \sigma_3 = \tau_4 \\ \sigma_1 = \rho_2, \ \sigma_2 + \rho_2 = \rho_3 = \sigma_4 \end{cases} \}$$

By simple algebraic manipulations one can check that the above systems of equations has a unique solution given by $\sigma_4 = \frac{1}{1-x}\sigma_1$. Since $[\![\cdot]\!]$ is a prop morphism and c_2 is the composition of the four chunks above, we obtain

$$[\![c_2]\!] = \{ (\sigma_1, \frac{1}{1-x} \cdot \sigma_1) \mid \sigma_1 \in \mathsf{k}((x)) \}.$$

This relation contains all pairs of streams that can occur on the left and on the right ports of c_2. For instance if $\underline{1}, 0, 0 \dots$ is on the left, $\underline{1}, 1, 1 \dots$ is on the right.

For the other circuit of Example 2, namely c_1, it is immediate to see that

$$[\![c_1]\!] = \{ ((1-x) \cdot \sigma_1, \sigma_1) \mid \sigma_1 \in \mathsf{k}((x)) \}$$

which is the same relation as $[\![c_2]\!]$. In Example 4, we will prove the equivalence of the two circuits using equational reasoning, justified in the next section.

3.1 Interacting Hopf Algebras: The Equational Theory of Circuits

As witnessed by Example 3, different circuits (as morphisms of Circ) may have the same denotational semantics. It is thus natural to ask whether there is an equational theory which *axiomatises* denotational equality, i.e., it makes two circuits equal precisely when they denote the same relation. In fact, an equational theory exists, and it is remarkably modular.

The results in this section rely on various "polynomial-like" concepts: the ring of polynomials $\mathsf{k}[x]$, its field of fractions $\mathsf{k}(x)$, the ring $\mathsf{k}\langle x \rangle$ of *rational* fractions of polynomials, formal power series $\mathsf{k}[[x]]$, and its field of fractions, the field of Laurent series $\mathsf{k}((x))$. We give a summary in Table 1. Note that polynomials $p \in \mathsf{k}[x]$ are expressible in our syntax (4): for example, the polynomial $1 + x + 2x^2$ is captured by the following diagram:

Table 1. Rings and fields over a field k (k_i and l_j range over k).

k[x]	ring of polynomials	$\sum_0^n k_i x^i$ for some $n \in \mathbb{N}$
k(x)	field of polynomial fractions	$\frac{p}{q}$ for $p, q \in$ k[x] with $q \neq 0$
k⟨x⟩	ring of rationals	$\frac{\sum_0^n k_i x^i}{\sum_0^m l_j x^j}$ with $l_0 \neq 0$
k[[x]]	ring of formal power series	$\sum_0^\infty k_i x^i$
k((x))	field of Laurent series	$\sum_d^\infty k_i x^i$ for some $d \in \mathbb{Z}$

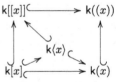

The equational theory, given in Fig. 1, is comprised of the following 'blocks':

- In the first block, both the black and white structures form commutative monoids and comonoids, capturing properties of addition and copying.
- In the second block, the white monoid and black comonoid interact as a bimonoid. Bimonoids are one of two canonical ways that monoids and comonoids interact, as shown in [41].
- In the third and fourth block, both the black and the white monoid/comonoid pair form an extraspecial Frobenius monoid. The Frobenius equations (fr 1) and (fr 2) are a famous algebraic pattern which establishes a bridge between algebraic and topological phenomena, see [22, 24, 40]. The "extraspecial" refers to the last two equations on each line, two additional equations, the *special* equation (•-sp, ○-sp) and the *bone* equation (•-bo, ○-sp). The Frobenius equations, together with the special equation, are the other canonical pattern of interaction between monoids and comonoids identified in [41]. Together with the bone equation, the set of four equations characterises *corelations*, see [19, 25, 64].
- The equations in the fifth block are parametrised over $p \in$ k[x] and describe commutativity of —$\boxed{p}$— with respect to the other operations, as well as multiplication and addition of scalars.
- The sixth block describes the interpretation of —$\boxed{p}$— as division by p, and shows how fractions are expressible in the circuit syntax.
- Finally, the last block expresses the possibility of changing the colour of "feedback loops", modulo the insertion of the scalar -1. In fact, it can be shown that these loops define a *compact closed structure* [39] on the category of circuits.

Remark 2. The axioms in Fig. 1 are refereed to as the theory of *Interacting Hopf Algebras* (𝕀ℍ). The name hints at the modular nature of the theory: the Frobenius monoid equations (fourth block), the fractions equations (sixth block) and the feedback equations (last block) can be seen as the result of combining the two Hopf algebras (the remaining blocks) via distributive laws of props [18, 63]. In fact, 𝕀ℍ is modular at multiple levels: Hopf algebras themselves can be factorised in terms of distributive laws between monoids and comonoids [18, 63]. Another interesting observation is that the black (copying) and the white

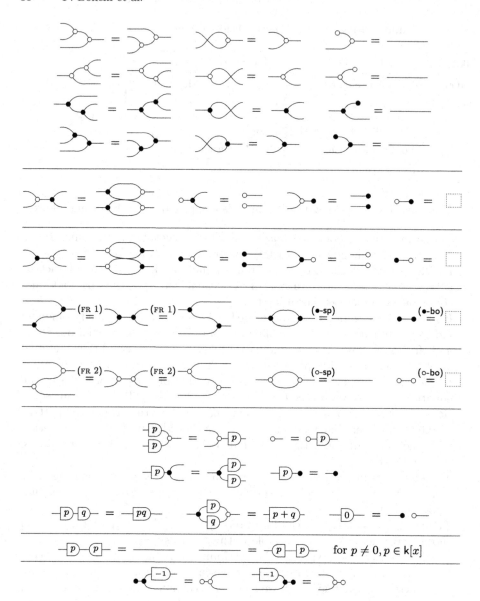

Fig. 1. Axioms of Interacting Hopf Algebras ($\mathbb{IH}$).

structure (addition) are totally symmetric, in the sense that $\mathbb{IH}$ is invariant wrt colour swapping. The symmetry between the two colours is broken only by the 2-categorical structure of $\mathbb{IH}$, see [12].

The theory $\mathbb{IH}$ is *sound and complete* for denotational equivalence of circuits.

Theorem 1. *For all circuits c, d in* Circ, $[\![c]\!] = [\![d]\!]$ *iff* $c \overset{\text{IH}}{=} d$.

The proof of this result relies on the modular structure of IH: exploiting Lack's theory for composing props [41], completeness results for the sub-theories (*cf.* Theorem 3 below) are "put together" to achieve completeness for the whole IH, see [18,63]. Also note that the same completeness theorem was independently obtained by Baez and Erbele [3] relying on a normal form argument.

Remark 3. It is worth mentioning that the denotational semantics in terms of bi-infinite trajectories $k^{\mathbb{Z}}$ (see Definition 4 and above) also enjoys a completeness results, in terms of an equational theory which is very close to IH. Most notably, the axiomatisation of bi-infinite trajectories lacks the axiom $-\boxed{p}-\boxed{p}\!- \;=\; \text{———}$, which is replaced by a weaker version. See [31] for the full details.

Example 4. In Example 3, we have shown that the circuits c_1 and c_2 of Example 2 denotes the same relation. This equivalence can be proved by equational reasoning in IH, as the following derivation demonstrates:

Theorem 1 gives a partial account of Circ expressivity. Indeed, it states that $[\![\cdot]\!]\colon$ Circ $\to$ Rel$_{k((x))}$ is *faithful*, but what about *fullness*? In other words, what property characterises the image of $[\![\cdot]\!]$? It turns out these are precisely the relations that are vector spaces over the field $k(x)$ of polynomial fractions. Formally stated, this is Theorem 2 below, but first we recall two necessary concepts.

Definition 5 (LinRel$_k$, Matk)**.** *Given a field* k,

– LinRel$_k$ *is the sub-prop of* Rel$_k$ *(Definition 3) with arrows those relations that are linear, namely an arrow $n \to m$ is a sub vector-space of k^{n+m}.*
– MatR *is the sub-prop of* LinRel$_k$ *with arrows being just linear maps, namely an arrow $n \to m$ is a $m \times n$-matrix over* k.

Writing IH for the quotient of Circ by $\overset{\text{IH}}{=}$, we may now state that

Theorem 2. *There is an isomorphisms of props between* IH *and* LinRel$_{k(x)}$.

In other words, Theorem 2 says that the denotational semantics factors as

$$
\begin{array}{ccc}
\text{Circ} & \xrightarrow{\;[\cdot]\;} & \text{Rel}_{k((x))} \\
\downarrow & & \uparrow \\
\text{IH} & \xrightarrow{\;\cong\;} & \text{LinRel}_{k(x)}
\end{array}
$$

We can provide similar results for the subprops of Circ introduced in Sect. 2. We write HA, HA^{op} and SF respectively for $\overrightarrow{\text{Circ}}$, $\overleftarrow{\text{Circ}}$ and SF quotiented by $\overset{\text{IH}}{=}$.

Theorem 3. *There are isomorphisms of props between:*

1. HA *and* $\mathsf{Matk}[x]$;
2. HA^{op} *and* $\mathsf{Matk}[x]^{op}$;
3. SF *and* $\mathsf{Matk}\langle x \rangle$.

Remark 4 (Kleene theorem). The last point of Theorem 3 can be thought as an analogue of Kleene's theorem for regular languages: it provides a syntactic characterisation of the *rational* behaviours. The relations denoted by SF are particularly well behaved functions, since they do not actually require the full generality of Laurent series: any rational polynomial generates a finite power series, without the need for a "finite past." The correspondence between (orthodox) signal-flow diagrams and rational matrices is well-known (see e.g., [54]): here we give a categorical, string-diagrammatic, account of this characterisation where notions of "input", "output" and direction of flow are derivative.

We also mention that point 1 of Theorem 3 seems to be a folklore result, ubiquitously appearing in different flavours [36,41,42,48,52,63].

4   Operational Semantics

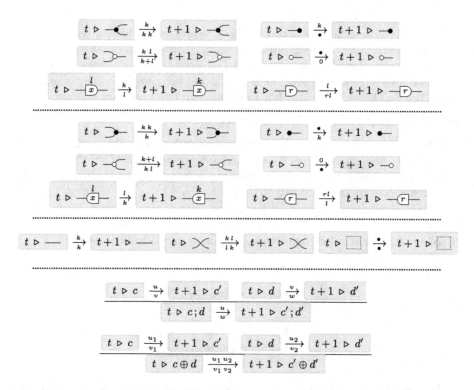

Fig. 2. Structural rules for operational semantics, with $p \in \mathbb{Z}$, k, l ranging over k and u, v, w vectors of elements of k of the appropriate size. The only vector of k^0 is written as $\bullet$ (as in Definition 4), while a vector $(k_1 \ldots k_n)^T \in \mathsf{k}^n$ as $k_1 \ldots k_n$.

As for programming languages, denotational semantics is just one way of giving formal meaning to circuit syntax. In this section we take a different perspective, and regard circuits as state-based machines, the step-by-step execution of which is the *operational semantics.*

The atomic components of the operational semantics will be transitions of shape $t \triangleright c \xrightarrow{\;v\;}{\scriptstyle w} t' \triangleright c'$. Here c and c' are *states*, that is, circuits augmented with information about which values $k \in \mathsf{k}$ are stored in each register ($-\boxed{x}-$ and $-\boxed{x}-$) at that computation step. States are decorated with runtime contexts: t and t' are integers that—intuitively—indicate the time when the transition happens.[1] Finally, the labels v and w are the values (k-vectors) observed respectively on the left and on the right interfaces of c, when transitioning to c'.

Example 5. For a concrete example, recall the circuit c_2 (Example 2). As shown in Example 3, the relation $[\![c_2]\!]$ pairs $\underline{1}, 0, 0, \dots$ with $\underline{1}, 1, 1, \dots$. In the operational semantics, this is broken down into step-by-step observations, as follows:

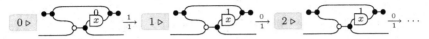

At each step, the register $-\boxed{x}-$ is annotated with its current value. One reads above trace as saying that, at time 0, value 1 is read both on the left and on the right; at time 1, value 0 is read on the left, and 1 on the right, and so on.

In the example above, the register is initialised at 0. We will assume this through the whole paper, as made explicit by the following definition.

Definition 6. *Let $c\colon n \to m$ be a circuit in* Circ. *The initial state c_0 of c is the one where all the registers store* 0. *A* computation *of c starting at time $t \leq 0$ is a (possibly infinite) sequence of transitions*

$$t \triangleright c_0 \xrightarrow[\;w_t\;]{\;v_t\;} t+1 \triangleright c_1 \xrightarrow[\;w_{t+1}\;]{\;v_{t+1}\;} t+2 \triangleright c_2 \xrightarrow[\;w_{t+2}\;]{\;v_{t+2}\;} \dots \qquad (6)$$

It is important to remark that the rules in Fig. 2 define the valid transitions for any circuit, inductively on the syntax of Circ. The definitions for the generators reflect the intuition of Sect. 2; for instance, $-\blacktriangleleft$ acts as a *copier*, because when k is observed on the left then two copies of k are observed on the right. Also, all the generators are stateless except for the registers $-\boxed{x}-$ and $-\boxed{x}-$. For $-\boxed{x}-$, the idea is that whenever it receives a value k on the left, it releases the currently stored value l on the right, and k becomes the newly stored value. Symmetrically, in the definition for $-\boxed{x}-$ (and, more generally, any generator of $\overleftarrow{\mathsf{Circ}}$) it is helpful to think of signals as coming from the right, and exiting from the left.

This description hints at a potential issue. On the one hand, the purpose of providing an operational semantics is to describe step-by-step evolution of circuits as executable machines. On the other hand, we allow for the composition

---

[1] Note that, being an integer, time may be negative—as we shall see in Example 6, some executions must start in the past.

of circuits, such as those of $\vec{\mathsf{Circ}}$ and of $\overleftarrow{\mathsf{Circ}}$, in which signals intuitively flow in different directions. What is the computational meaning of such composites?

As seen in Example 5, sometimes it is possible to construct computationally meaningful circuits with a mix of $\vec{\mathsf{Circ}}$- and $\overleftarrow{\mathsf{Circ}}$-components: c_2 has a clear left-to-right directionality, as the $\overleftarrow{\mathsf{Circ}}$-components (•— and ⟩—) only contribute to a feedback loop. Other circuits exhibit a more puzzling behaviour, for example:

Example 6. In —ⓍⱵⓍ—, both interfaces seem to act as outputs. The equational theory $\mathbb{IH}$ equates it with ——, and thus they have the same denotational semantics. However, their operational behaviour is subtly different. Indeed, whereas for any sequence $a_i \in \mathsf{k}$, —— admits the computation

$$0 \triangleright \quad —— \quad \xrightarrow[a_0]{a_0} \quad 1 \triangleright \quad —— \quad \xrightarrow[a_1]{a_1} \quad 2 \triangleright \quad —— \quad \xrightarrow[a_2]{a_2} \quad \cdots \tag{7}$$

The circuit —ⓍⱵⓍ— admits a similar computation, but we must begin at time $t = -1$ in order to first "load" the registers with a_0:

$$-1 \triangleright \; -\boxed{x}\!\!-\!\!\boxed{x}- \overset{0 \; 0}{\xrightarrow{\;0\;}} \; 0 \triangleright \; -\boxed{x}\!\!-\!\!\boxed{x}- \overset{a_0 \; a_0}{\xrightarrow{\;a_0\;}} \; 1 \triangleright \; -\boxed{x}\!\!-\!\!\boxed{x}- \overset{a_1 \; a_1}{\xrightarrow{\;a_1\;}} \; \cdots \tag{8}$$

The circuit —ⓍⒼⓍⱵ, which again is equal to —— in $\mathbb{IH}$, has yet a different operational behaviour. Although every computation of —— can be reproduced, —ⓍⒼⓍⱵ admits additional, problematic computations. Indeed, consider

$$0 \triangleright \; -\boxed{x}\!\!-\!\!\boxed{x}\!\!- \overset{0 \; 0}{\xrightarrow{\;0\;}} 1 \triangleright \; -\boxed{x}\!\!-\!\!\boxed{x}\!\!- \overset{0 \; 1}{} \tag{9}$$

at which point no further transition is possible—the circuit can deadlock.

At a deeper level, Example 6 demonstrates that the operational semantics is not meant to be executable for all circuits: the rule for sequential composition implicitly quantifies existentially on the middle value v, resulting in potentially unbounded non-determinism. Reaching a satisfactory understanding of this phenomenon is the subject of the next section. As a preliminary observation, it is worth observing that, if one restricts to *infinite* computations, then the mismatch outlined in Example 6 disappears, and we have a perfect correspondence between operational and denotational equivalence.

In order to state this result, we introduce a preliminary notion. As customary in control theory, we consider *trajectories*: traces that possibly start in the past.

Definition 7. *To any infinite computation as in (6) we can associate a $\mathbb{Z}$-indexed sequence $\sigma : \mathbb{Z} \to \mathsf{k}^n \times \mathsf{k}^m$, called a* trajectory, *as follows:*

$$\sigma(i) = \begin{cases} (u_i, v_i) & \text{if } i \geq t, \\ (0,0) & \text{otherwise.} \end{cases} \tag{10}$$

Note that σ is finite in the past, i.e., for which $\exists j \in \mathbb{Z}$ such that $\sigma(i) = (0,0)$ for $i \leq j$.

We call operational semantics *the set $\langle c \rangle$ of trajectories given by the infinite computations of c.*

Remark 5. We purposefully used the same term "trajectories" as in the denotational semantics: indeed, there is a close connection between computations that start in an initial state and Laurent series, which we encountered in Sect. 3. Indeed the sequence of observations at any port is clearly a Laurent series – any computation can be trivially (i.e., with 0 observations) continued infinitely into the past, as reflected by (10) in Definition 6. One could generalise the notion of computation so that one would not need to start in the initialised state: in that case, the corresponding notion of trajectory 10 could be a bona-fide bi-infinite sequence, i.e., with σ possibly infinite in the past. See [30, 31] for more details.

Theorem 4 (Operational-Denotational correspondence). *For all circuits c, d of* Circ, $\langle c \rangle = \langle d \rangle$ *if and only if* $[\![c]\!] = [\![d]\!]$.

Example 7. Consider (7) and (8) in Example 6. According to (10) both are translated into the trajectory σ mapping $i \geq 0$ to (a_i, a_i) and $i < 0$ into $(0, 0)$. More generally, it holds that $\langle$ —— $\rangle = \langle$ —$\boxed{x}$—$\boxed{x}$—$\rangle$. Note the two circuits would be distinguished when looking at their finite traces— compare (7) with (8). However, by Theorem 4, $\langle$ —— $\rangle = \langle$ —$\boxed{x}$—$\boxed{x}$—$\rangle$ also holds. Indeed, problematic computations, like (9), are all finite and, by definition, do not give rise to any trajectory.

5   Realisability

In light of Example 6, one may ask how common deadlock situations (as the one in (9)) and computations that need to start in the past (as in (8)) are. It turns out these issues are avoided when considering the operational semantics of the sub-class SF of circuits that adhere to the classical notion of signal flow graphs.

Lemma 1. *Let c be a circuit diagram in* SF.

1. *There are no deadlocks - for every $t \in \mathbb{Z}$ and state c_t, there exists a transition*

$$t \triangleright c_t \xrightarrow[w_t]{v_t} t+1 \triangleright c_{t+1} \,.$$

2. *Every computation with only trivial observations in the past can be started at time 0. That is, for any $k \in \mathbb{N}$, if*

$$-k \triangleright c_0 \xrightarrow[0]{0} -k+1 \triangleright c_1 \xrightarrow[0]{0} \cdots \xrightarrow[0]{0} 0 \triangleright c_k \xrightarrow[w_k]{v_k} 0 \triangleright c_{k+1} \xrightarrow[w_{k+1}]{v_{k+1}} \cdots$$

then also

$$0 \triangleright c_0 \xrightarrow[w_k]{v_k} 1 \triangleright c_{k+1} \xrightarrow[w_{k+1}]{v_{k+1}} 2 \triangleright c_{k+2} \xrightarrow[w_{k+2}]{v_{k+2}} \cdots$$

The key insight behind this result is that, in SF, the existential quantification in sequential circuit composition becomes deterministic, subject to a choice of inputs at each step of evaluation. Therefore, circuits in SF provide a proper operational realisation of the relation behaviour that they denote. What can we say about the other behaviours denoted in Circ? Can they be executed somehow? Do they have a proper operational realisation?

Below we shall see that the answer to the last questions is positive, in fact, within the equational theory of $\mathbb{IH}$, Circ is nothing but a "jumbled up" version of SF: more precisely, while every circuit in SF has inputs on the left and outputs on the right, for every circuit in Circ there is a way of partitioning its left and right ports into "inputs" and "outputs", in the sense that appropriate rewiring yields an $\mathbb{IH}$-equal circuit in SF.

We begin by giving a precise definition of what we mean by "jumbling up" the wires of a circuit. First, for each $n, m \in \mathbb{N}$, we define circuits $\eta_n : n \to 1{+}1{+}n$ and $\epsilon_m : 1 + 1 + m \to m$ in Circ as illustrated below.

$$\eta_n := \boxed{\quad n \quad} \qquad \epsilon_m := \boxed{\quad m \quad}$$

Next, we define the families of operators $\mathsf{L}_{n,m} : \mathsf{Circ}[n{+}1, m] \to \mathsf{Circ}[n, 1{+}m]$ and $\mathsf{R}_{n,m} : \mathsf{Circ}[n, 1{+}m] \to \mathsf{Circ}[1{+}n, m]$ as follows: for any circuit $c \in \mathsf{Circ}[n{+}1, m]$,

$$\mathsf{L}_{n,m}(c) = \eta_n \,;\, (id_1 \oplus c) \qquad \left(\boxed{\; n \; \boxed{c} \; m \;} \right)$$

and, for any circuit $d \in \mathsf{Circ}[n, m + 1]$

$$\mathsf{R}_{n,m}(d) = (id_1 \oplus d) \,;\, \epsilon_m. \qquad \left(\boxed{\; n \; \boxed{d} \; m \;} \right)$$

Definition 8. *A circuit $c_2 \in \mathsf{Circ}[n_2, m_2]$ is a* rewiring *of $c_1 \in \mathsf{Circ}[n_1, m_1]$ when c_2 can be obtained from c_1 by a combination of the following operations:*

(i) application of $\mathsf{L}_{n,m}$, for some n and m,
(ii) application of $\mathsf{R}_{n,m}$, for some n and m,
(iii) post-composition with a permutation,
(iv) pre-composition with a permutation.

Permutations are needed to rewire an arbitrary—i.e., not merely the first— port on each of the boundaries. For instance, they allow to rewire the second port on the right as the third on the left in the circuit $c: 2 \to 2$ below:

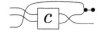

At the semantics level, a rewiring denotes an isomorphisms between a subspace of type $k(x)^n \times k(x)^m$ and one of type $k(x)^i \times k(x)^j$ where $n{+}m = i{+}j$. For instance, for any circuit c, $[\![c]\!] \subseteq k(x)^{n+1} \times k(x)^m$ is isomorphic to $[\![\mathsf{L}_{n,m}(c)]\!] \subseteq k(x)^n \times k(x)^{m+1}$ as a subspace of $k(x)^{n+m+1}$.

Theorem 5 (Realisability). *For every circuit $c \in$ Circ, there exists $d \in$ SF such that c is $\mathbb{IH}$-equivalent to some rewiring of d.*

The above theorem guarantees that an input-output partition of the ports of any circuit in Circ always exists. Note that such a partition is not unique, as illustrated by the following example.

Example 8. The circuit c_1 of Example 2 is equivalent to the rewiring of two different signal flow graphs, illustrated below.

Indeed the rightmost circuit above is c_2 of Example 2 which is $\mathbb{IH}$-equivalent to c_1. The leftmost circuit is $R_{0,1}(L_{0,1}(c_1)\,;\,\times)$. Intuitively, the rightmost circuit above corresponds to choosing the leftmost port of c_1 to be the input and the rightmost to be the output; in the rightmost diagram we do the opposite the choice: the leftmost port of c_1 is the output and the rightmost is the input.

5.1   Compositionality vs Directionality of Signal Flow

The fact that the input-output partition is not unique corresponds to the fact in some circuits there is more than one way of orienting flow. This allows us to crystallise what we consider to be a central methodological contribution of the compositional approach: since it is only by forgetting the input-output distinction that the algebra $\mathbb{IH}$ of signal flow is revealed, and signal flow graphs can be given a compositional semantics. The notions of input and output cannot, therefore, be considered as primitive; they are, rather, derived notions. This is different from classical approaches – for example Mason [45] emphasises inputs, outputs and flow directional as a central feature:

> "flow graphs differ from electrical network graphs in that their branches are directed. In accounting for branch directions it is necessary to take an entirely different line of approach..."

The compositional approach is therefore closely connected to the approach of Willems [61] and *behavioural control theory*, which emphasises a relational treatment of observable behaviour. Willems himself railed [62] against including the notions of inputs, outputs and directionality in fundamental mathematical descriptions of interconnected systems:

> "Adding a signal flow direction is often a figment of one's imagination, and when something is not real, it will turn out to be cumbersome sooner or later. [...] The input/output framework is totally inappropriate for dealing with all but the most special system interconnections. [Inputs/outputs] often needlessly complicates matters, mathematically and conceptually."

Inputs, outputs and flow directionality *are* crucial for when one wants to an implementation of a behaviour—i.e., an executable circuit—as clarified at the beginning of this section. Since any circuit in Circ denotes the same relation as a rewiring of a signal flow graph, then all the denoted behaviours can be properly realised. This explains the name "Realisability" for Theorem 5.

Circuits, their algebraic theory, and their compositional semantics can thus be considered a bona fide process algebra of signal flow, and serve both as a language for *specifications* and for (executable) *implementations*. In fact, the language lends itself to formal methods techniques such as *refinement*, see [10].

6   The Affine Extensions

Engineers usually do not distinguish between linear and *affine* systems, as the numerical methods to study the two are substantially the same. From our perspective however, such distinction is important since, in order to express affine behaviours, we need to extend the calculus of signal flow graphs, as well as the main results illustrated so far. Such extension turns out be extremely interesting because on the one hand, it enables the modelling of systems with richer patterns of behaviour, like current and voltage sources in Sect. 7 or mutual exclusion in Sect. 8; on the other hand, it allows to define *contextual equivalence* and turn Theorem 4 in a proper *full abstraction result* (Theorem 8).

As usual, we start with the syntax. The syntactic prop ACirc is obtained by extending the grammar in (4) with an extra constants, $\vdash$, having 0 interfaces on the left and 1 on the right.

The denotational semantics $[\![\cdot]\!]$: ACirc $\to$ Rel$_{k((x))}$ extends Definition 4 with

$$\vdash \longmapsto \{(\bullet, 1)\}.$$

where $1 \in k((x))$ denotes the Laurent series $0, \underline{1}, 0, 0, \ldots$ Thus, intuitively, $\vdash$ emits such streams on the right port.

For the equational theory, we need to identify which axioms govern the behaviour of the extra connector $\vdash$. It turns out [13] that following three equations suffice.

(11)

The first two say that $\vdash$ can be deleted and copied by the comonoid structure, just like $\circ\!\!-$. The third equation is justified by the possibility of expressing the empty set, by, for example,

$$[\![\vdash\!\circ]\!] = \{(\bullet, 1)\} ; \{(0, \bullet)\} = \varnothing.$$
(12)

Since for any R and S in Rel$_{k((x))}$, $\varnothing \oplus R = \varnothing \oplus S = \varnothing$, composing or taking the monoidal product of $\varnothing$ with any relation results in $\varnothing$; $\varnothing$ is thus analogous to logical false. Indeed we can use equation $(\varnothing)$ to derive the following lemma.

Lemma 2. *For any two circuit $c, d: k \to l$ of ACirc,*

In the above lemma and hereafter, $\overset{\text{oIIH}}{=}$ stands for the smallest congruence on circuits in ACirc containing the axioms in Fig. 1 and those in (11). Moreover, we call AIH the quotient of ACirc by $\overset{\text{oIIH}}{=}$.

Theorem 6. *For all circuits c, d in* ACirc, $[\![c]\!] = [\![d]\!]$ *iff* $c \overset{\text{oIIH}}{=} d$.

To characterise the expressivity of ACirc, we need to introduce *affine* relations [13].

Definition 9 ($\mathsf{ARel_R}$). *Let R be a semiring. For $R, S \subseteq \mathsf{R}^n$, their Minkowski sum is defined as $R + S = \{u + v \mid u \in R \text{ and } v \in R\}$. A set $R \subseteq \mathsf{R}^n$ is said to be an affine subspace if there exist finite $B, D \subseteq \mathsf{R}^n$ such that $R = \bigcup_{v \in B} \{\{v\} + \langle D \rangle\}$. Elements of B are called* base points *and those of D the* directions.*

A R-affine relation $R \colon n \to n$ is an affine subspace $R \subseteq \mathsf{R}^n \times \mathsf{R}^m$. The prop $\mathsf{ARel_R}$ is the sub-prop of $\mathsf{Rel_R}$ (Definition 3) with arrows being affine relations.

When R is a field, the above definition simplifies: an affine subspace of R^n is a subset $R \subseteq \mathsf{R}^n$ which is either empty or there exists a vector $u \in \mathsf{R}^n$ and a linear subspace L of R^n such that $R = u + L \;\rightleftharpoons\; \{u + v \mid v \in L\}$. When R is the field of fraction of polynomials, $\mathsf{k}(x)$, $\mathsf{ARel}_{\mathsf{k}(x)}$ exactly characterises the expressivity of ACirc.

Theorem 7. *There is an isomorphisms of PROPs between* AIH *and* $\mathsf{ARel}_{\mathsf{k}(x)}$.

The proof of this result uses a normal form argument, building on the characterisation of Theorem 2 [13].

6.1   Full Abstraction

A first payoff of the affine extension is the possibility of formulating a notion of *contextual equivalence* for circuit diagrams, and consequently a *full abstraction* result.

To this aim, first we extend the operational semantics to the syntax ACirc. This amounts to augmenting the rules in Fig. 2 with

$$0 \triangleright {\vdash} \;\; \overset{\bullet}{\underset{1}{\rightarrow}} \;\; 1 \triangleright {\vdash} \qquad\qquad t \triangleright {\vdash} \;\; \overset{\bullet}{\underset{0}{\rightarrow}} \;\; t+1 \triangleright {\vdash} \qquad (t \neq 0)$$

The behaviour of the affine generator ${\vdash}$ depends on the time: when $t = 0$, it emits 1 o the right, otherwise it emits 0. It is easy to see that $\langle{\vdash}\rangle$ contains only the trajectory (see Definition 7) mapping time 0 into $(\bullet, 1)$ and all the other times $t \in \mathbb{Z}$ into $(\bullet, 0)$. The operational behaviour of ${\dashv}$ is symmetrical. Observe that the behaviour of all other generators in Fig. 2 is time-independent.

Example 9. Recall from (12) that $[\![{\vdash}\!\circ]\!] = \emptyset$. The same happens with the operational semantics: ${\vdash}\!\circ$ has no possible transition at $t = 0$, since at that time ${\vdash}$ must emit a 1 and $\!\circ$ can only synchronise on a 0. Instead, the circuit $\square$ can always perform an infinite computation $t \triangleright \square \overset{\bullet}{\underset{\bullet}{\rightarrow}} t+1 \triangleright \square \overset{\bullet}{\underset{\bullet}{\rightarrow}} \cdots$, for any $t \leq 0$. It is worth observing that for all c, $\square \oplus c$ can perform the same computations of c, while ${\vdash}\!\circ \oplus c$ cannot ever make a transition at time 0.

Roughly speaking, the computations of ⊢o and ⊡ mirror images of the two possible denotations: there are only two $0 \to 0$ arrows in $\mathsf{Rel}_{k((x))}$: the empty relation and the identity one. The former intuitively corresponds to logical false, as we said earlier; the second to logical truth.

Definition 10. *For a circuit* $c \in \mathsf{ACirc}[0,0]$ *we write* $c \uparrow$ *if* c *can perform an infinite computation and* $c \not\uparrow$ *otherwise. For instance* ⊡ $\uparrow$, *while* ⊢o $\not\uparrow$.

We take the predicate $\uparrow$ as our basic operational observation. To be able to make observations about arbitrary circuits we need to introduce an appropriate notion of context. Roughly speaking, contexts for us are circuits in $\mathsf{ACirc}[0,0]$ with a hole into which we can plug another circuit. Since ours is a variable-free presentation, "dangling wires" assume the role of free variables [33]: restricting to contexts in $\mathsf{ACirc}[0,0]$ is therefore analogous to considering *ground* contexts—i.e., contexts with no free variables—a standard concept of programming language theory. For more details on contexts, we refer the reader to [14].

With this setup, given a circuit $c \in \mathsf{ACirc}[n,m]$, we can insert it into a context $C[-]$ and observe the possible outcome: either $C[c] \uparrow$ or $C[c] \not\uparrow$. This naturally leads us to contextual equivalence and the formulation of full abstraction.

Definition 11. *Given* $c, d \in \mathsf{ACirc}[n,m]$, *we say that they are* contextually equivalent, *written* $c \equiv d$, *if for all contexts* $C[-]$,

$$C[c] \uparrow \quad \textit{iff} \quad C[d] \uparrow .$$

Theorem 8 (Full abstraction). $c \equiv d$ *iff* $c \overset{\text{oⅢH}}{=} d$.

Example 10. Recall from Example 6, the circuits — and —⊡-⊡—. Take the context $C[-] = c_\sigma ; - ; c_\tau$ for $c_\sigma \in \mathsf{ACirc}[0,1]$ and $c_\tau \in \mathsf{ACirc}[1,0]$. Assume that c_σ and c_τ have a single infinite computation. Call σ and τ the corresponding trajectories. If $\sigma = \tau$, both $C[\text{—}]$ and $C[\text{—}⊡\text{-}⊡\text{—}]$ would be able to perform an infinite computation. Instead if $\sigma \neq \tau$, none of them would perform any infinite computation: — would stop at time t, for t the first moment such that $\sigma(t) \neq \tau(t)$, while $C[\text{—}⊡\text{-}⊡\text{—}]$ would stop at time $t+1$.

Now take as context $C[-] = \bullet\text{—} ; - ; \text{—}\bullet$. In contrast to c_σ and c_τ, $\bullet\text{—}$ and $\text{—}\bullet$ can perform more than one single computation: at any time they can nondeterministically emit any value. Thus every computation of $C[\text{—}] = ax/bone-black.tikz$ can *always* be extended to an infinite one, forcing synchronisation of $\bullet\text{—}$ and $\text{—}\bullet$ at each step. For $C[\text{—}⊡\text{-}⊡\text{—}] = \bullet\text{—}⊡\text{-}⊡\text{—}\bullet$, $\bullet\text{—}$ and $\text{—}\bullet$ may emit different values at time t, but the computation will get stuck at $t+1$. However, our definition of $\uparrow$ only cares about whether $C[\text{—}⊡\text{-}⊡\text{—}]$ *can* perform an infinite computation. Indeed it can, as long as $\bullet\text{—}$ and $\text{—}\bullet$ consistently emit the same value at each time step.

If we think of contexts as tests, and say that a circuit c passes test $C[-]$ if $C[c]$ perform an infinite computation, then our notion of contextual equivalence is *may-testing* equivalence [27]. From this perspective, —— and —$\boxed{x}$-$\boxed{x}$— are not *must equivalent*, since the former must pass the test ●— ; — ; —● while —$\boxed{x}$-$\boxed{x}$— may not.

It is worth to remark here that the distinction between may and must testing cease to make sense for circuits equipped with a proper flow directionality and thus a deterministic, input-output, behaviour. It is indeed possible to have for ACirc a weaker form of Realisability (Theorem 5) that we avoid to illustrate in this survey. We refer the interested reader to Sects. 5 and 6 of [14].

7   Electrical Circuits

A main advantage of adopting an abstract and very elementary circuit syntax is that signal flow graphs become just one of the computational models that can be studied therein. In this section, we will focus on electrical circuits, showing how they can be modelled within ACirc. In the next section, we will sketch how yet a different model, Petri nets, can be given a similar account.

Elementary electrical engineering focusses on open linear circuit analysis. Such circuits may include voltage ($\overset{k}{\ominus}$) and current sources ($\overset{k}{\ominus}$), resistors ($\overset{k}{\text{-WW-}}$), inductors ($\overset{k}{\text{-mm-}}$), capacitors ($\overset{k}{\text{-||-}}$), junctions (filled nodes) and open terminals (unfilled nodes). An example is illustrated below.

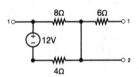

We may encode these systems syntactically as the morphisms of a prop ECirc, freely generated by the signature

$$\Sigma = \{ \dashv\negmedspace\boxed{} \,, \; —● \,, \; \boxed{}\negmedspace\vdash \,, \; ●— \} \cup \{ \overset{k}{\text{-WW-}} \,, \; \overset{k}{\text{-mm-}} \,, \; \overset{k}{\text{-||-}} \,, \; \overset{k}{\ominus} \,, \; \overset{k}{\ominus} \mid k \in R_+ \} \quad (13)$$

where the parameter k ranges over the non-negative reals. Arrows $m \to n$ of ECirc represent open linear electrical circuits with m open terminals on the left and n open terminals on the right.

Next, we provide an encoding of electrical circuits into circuit diagrams. This amounts to define a function $\mathfrak{I}(-)$ that translates arrows in ECirc$[n, m]$ into arrows ACirc$[2n, 2m]$. The 2 is needed because each electrical wire carries 2 quantities (current and voltage) and thus its represented by two wires in ACirc. For each generator in Σ, Fig. 3 provides its translation into a circuit of ACirc. The translation for arbitrary circuits follows inductively by the one of generators.

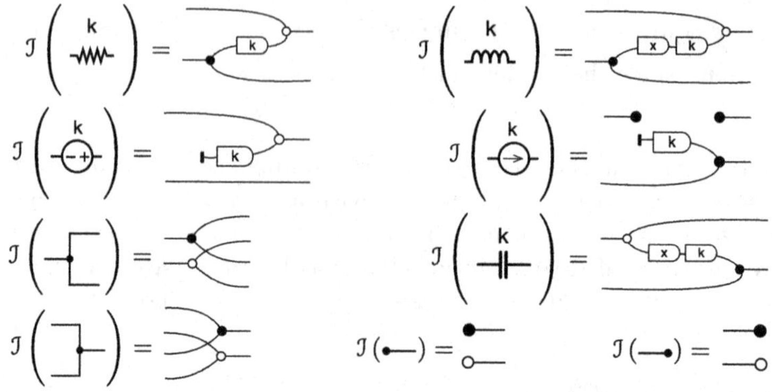

Fig. 3. Compositional encoding of open electrical circuits.

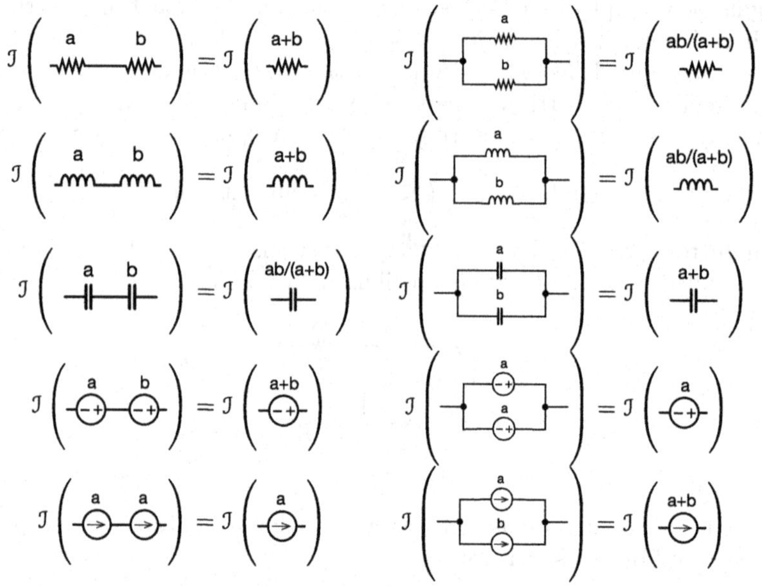

Fig. 4. Properties of resitors, inductors, capacitors, voltage and current sources in sequence (left) and parallel (right)

Figure 4 illustrates some well-known properties of electric components in series and parallel. The main payoff of working in ACirc is that now these properties can be now proved equationally by using the theory AIH. For instance, the equivalence in the first row of the second column (resistors in parallel) can be proved as follows.

$$\mathfrak{I}\left(-\!\!\!\!\begin{array}{c} a \\ \text{-WW-} \\ b \\ \text{-WW-} \end{array}\!\!\!\!-\right) = \quad = \quad$$

$$= \quad = \mathfrak{I}\left(\begin{array}{c} ab/(a+b) \\ \text{-WW-} \end{array}\right)$$

Remark 6. The circuit ⟨ $\boxed{a}$ / $\boxed{b}$ ⟩, which appears in the last step above, means $\frac{1}{\frac{1}{a}+\frac{1}{b}} = \frac{ab}{a+b}$ when both $a \neq 0$ and $b \neq 0$. Note, however, that it is more general than the traditional $\frac{ab}{a+b}$, e.g., it is well-defined even when both $a = b = 0$. In that case, parallel zero resistors reduce, as expected, to a wire:

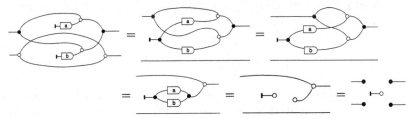

Similarly, the expression behaves as expected if one substitutes *infinite* resistances, which in graphical linear algebra is "1/0", i.e., —○ ●—. The same holds for inductors in series and capacitors in parallel.

Remark 7. Observe that in in the rightmost column of the fourth row of Fig. 4, the two parallel voltage source must have the same voltage a. Indeed, in engineering literature, parallel voltage sources of different voltages are disallowed. It is nonetheless interesting to see what happens in the semantics.

This, as we have seen, is the way of expressing the empty relation in the affine calculus. The same holds for current source in series (first column, last row).

Remark 8. For more details about the encoding of electrical circuits in affine circuit diagrams, the reader may refer to [13]. A similar semantics was given by Baez and Coya [26,37], building on the work of Baez, Erbele and Fong [3,6], and Rosebrugh, Sabadini and Walters [53]. However, such works only consider *passive* linear circuits, namely circuits without voltage and current sources.

8   From Control Theory to Concurrency

We have shown that the calculus of signal flow diagrams admits an axiomatisation of a significant family of behaviours (linear dynamical systems), capturing a well-known pre-existing combinatorial model (signal flow graphs). The approach is compositional, allowing for the syntactic representation of open systems and emphasising their algebraic properties, but at the same time is graphical, emphasising their connection topology and combinatorial properties.

Historically, putting different emphasis on these aspects has led to different research threads in the analysis of *concurrent systems*. On the one hand, we have the algebraic approach put forward by *process calculi* [35,47,56]. On the other hand, there is the tradition of graphical models of concurrent behaviour, such as *Petri nets* (see e.g., [50]).

It thus seems that the calculus signal flow diagrams may act as a middle ground between the perspectives offered by process calculi and by graphical models. This led us [11] to analyse concurrent systems with the same diagrammatic approach used for the analysis of linear behaviour in signal flow theory.

What is most striking is that, passing from linear to concurrent behaviour, the setup may remain essentially unaltered: one can use the same generators of the syntax (4), and the only significant change is modelling their behaviour via a different set of signals, passing from a field k to the semiring of natural numbers $\mathbb{N}$.

In order to explain this point, we illustrate two examples from [13] and [11].

$$c_1 := \qquad\qquad\qquad c_2 := \qquad\qquad\qquad\qquad (14)$$

In the (affine) calculus of signal flow diagrams, the behaviour of c_1 is not particularly interesting. It is the relation

$$\{(\bullet, \begin{pmatrix} \sigma \\ \tau \end{pmatrix}) \mid \sigma + \tau = 1\}$$

where σ and τ are arbitrary trajectories over a field k. Switching the signal space from k to $\mathbb{N}$, gives us something much more relevant, namely *mutual exclusion*: the circuits has only two possible behaviours:

$$\{(\bullet, \begin{pmatrix} 1 \\ 0 \end{pmatrix}), (\bullet, \begin{pmatrix} 0 \\ 1 \end{pmatrix})\}.$$

Indeed there are only those two possible solutions to the equation $\sigma + \tau = 1$ when σ and τ are trajectories over $\mathbb{N}$. The fact that signals are in $\mathbb{N}$, and thus cannot be negative, allows us to interpret them as *resources*: they can be shared and consumed and their absence may inhibit certain behaviours.

This become even more clear when considering the circuit c_2. Its behaviour as signal flow diagram is trivial: it is the full relation ●— ●—, relating any input to any output. To see this it is convenient to think operationally: assume some value $s \in$ k is currently in the register. Now, given input k on the left, in order to output k' on the right, one just needs to find k'' such that $k' + k'' = s$, which is always possible by taking $k'' = s - k'$.

Note that this is not the case, when k', k'', s range over $\mathbb{N}$: the output k' should be *smaller* than the content of the register s. If one interprets these quantities as *tokens*, the circuit c_2 is exactly a *place* of a Petri nets: from a place containing s tokens can be taken a number of tokens $k' \leq s$ and can be inserted an arbitrary number of tokens k. After these operations, the place would contain $k + (s - k')$, i.e., $k + k''$, tokens.

These observations have been crystallised in the *resources calculus* [11,51]: the syntax is the same as for the calculus of signal flow diagrams, but the signal universe is fixed to be $\mathbb{N}$. This switch forces to move from *linear* to *additive* relations and, consequently, to change the axiomatisation [11]. In [13], it is shown that the algebra of stateless connectors [20] can be easily encoded into the (affine extension) of the resource calculus. An extended study of Petri nets within the resource calculus is illustrated in [11]. This provides an insightful understanding as Petri nets as linear dynamical systems (but over $\mathbb{N}$) as well as an elegant compositional operational semantics. The denotational semantics instead appears to be challenging and surely deserves further investigations.

9   This Research and IFIP AICT 600 - IFIP 60 year Festivity Issue

The research described in this paper intersects with the interests of two TC1 working groups: *IFIP-WG 1.3 Foundations of System Specification* and *IFIP-WG 1.8 Concurrency Theory*. It also touches on TC2 topics, being relevant to *IFIP-WG 2.2 Formal Description of Programming Concepts*. First, signal flow graphs are a simple, yet pervasive, model of computation. The 2-dimensional approach described here is flexible enough to enable the string diagrammatic syntax to express both formal specifications as well as implementations. The axiomatic characterisation means that the former can be transformed in a principled way to the latter. Further, the operational semantics we give is a kind of concurrent process algebra, and—in the affine extension—we explore ramifications for the study of the semantics of Petri nets, a classical model of concurrency. Finally, the emphasis on the interaction between denotational and operational approaches—with a focus on *compositionality*—emerged from the study of formal programming language semantics but is becoming ever more important in Theoretical Computer Science.

References

1. Abramsky, S., Coecke, B.: A categorical semantics of quantum protocols. In: 2004 Proceedings of the 19th Annual IEEE Symposium on Logic in Computer Science (LICS), pp. 415–425. IEEE (2004)

2. Backens, M.: The zx-calculus is complete for stabilizer quantum mechanics. New J. Phys. **16**(9), 093021 (2014)
3. Baez, J., Erbele, J.: Categories in control. Theor. Appl. Categ. **30**, 836–881 (2015)
4. Baez, J., Fong, B., Pollard, B.: A compositional framework for Markov processes. J. Math. Phys. **57**, 033301 (2016)
5. Baez, J.C.: Network theory (2014). http://math.ucr.edu/home/baez/networks/. Accessed 15 Apr 2014
6. Baez, J.C., Fong, B.: A compositional framework for passive linear networks. arXiv preprint arXiv:1504.05625 (2015)
7. Basold, H., Bonsangue, M., Hansen, H.H., Rutten, J.: (Co)Algebraic characterizations of signal flow graphs. In: van Breugel, F., Kashefi, E., Palamidessi, C., Rutten, J. (eds.) Horizons of the Mind. A Tribute to Prakash Panangaden. LNCS, vol. 8464, pp. 124–145. Springer, Cham (2014). https://doi.org/10.1007/978-3-319-06880-0_6
8. Bloom, S.L., Ésik, Z., Zsuzsa, B.: Iteration Theories: The Equational Logic of Iterative Processes. Springer, Heidelberg (1993). https://doi.org/10.1007/978-3-642-78034-9
9. Bonchi, F., Gadducci, F., Kissinger, A., Sobocinski, P., Zanasi, F.: Rewriting modulo symmetric monoidal structure. CoRR abs/1602.06771 (2016)
10. Bonchi, F., Holland, J., Pavlovic, D., Sobociński, P.: Refinement for signal flow graphs. In: 28th International Conference on Concurrency Theory, CONCUR 2017, 5–8 September 2017, Berlin, Germany, pp. 24:1–24:16 (2017). https://doi.org/10.4230/LIPIcs.CONCUR.2017.24
11. Bonchi, F., Holland, J., Piedeleu, R., Sobociński, P., Zanasi, F.: Diagrammatic algebra: from linear to concurrent systems. In: Proceedings of the 46th ACM SIGPLAN Symposium on Principles of Programming Languages (POPL), vol. 3, pp. 1–28 (2019)
12. Bonchi, F., Pavlovic, D., Sobocinski, P.: Functorial semantics for relational theories. arXiv preprint arXiv:1711.08699 (2017)
13. Bonchi, F., Piedeleu, R., Sobociński, P., Zanasi, F.: Graphical affine algebra. In: Proceedings of the 34th Annual ACM/IEEE Symposium on Logic in Computer Science (LICS), pp. 1–12 (2019)
14. Bonchi, F., Piedeleu, R., Sobociński, P., Zanasi, F.: Contextual equivalence for signal flow graphs. In: FoSSaCS 2020. LNCS, vol. 12077, pp. 77–96. Springer, Cham (2020). https://doi.org/10.1007/978-3-030-45231-5_5
15. Bonchi, F., Sobociński, P., Zanasi, F.: A categorical semantics of signal flow graphs. In: Baldan, P., Gorla, D. (eds.) CONCUR 2014. LNCS, vol. 8704, pp. 435–450. Springer, Heidelberg (2014). https://doi.org/10.1007/978-3-662-44584-6_30
16. Bonchi, F., Sobociński, P., Zanasi, F.: Full abstraction for signal flow graphs. In: Proceedings of the 42nd Annual ACM SIGPLAN Symposium on Principles of Programming Languages (POPL), pp. 515–526 (2015)
17. Bonchi, F., Sobociński, P., Zanasi, F.: The calculus of signal flow diagrams I: linear relations on streams. Inf. Comput. **252**, 2–29 (2017)
18. Bonchi, F., Sobociński, P., Zanasi, F.: Interacting Hopf algebras. J. Pure Appl. Algebra **221**(1), 144–184 (2017)
19. Bruni, R., Gadducci, F.: Some algebraic laws for spans (and their connections with multi-relations). In: RelMiS 2001. Elsevier (2001)
20. Bruni, R., Lanese, I., Montanari, U.: A basic algebra of stateless connectors. Theoret. Comput. Sci. **366**(1–2), 98–120 (2006)

21. Bruni, R., Melgratti, H., Montanari, U.: Connector Algebras, Petri Nets, and BIP. In: Clarke, E., Virbitskaite, I., Voronkov, A. (eds.) PSI 2011. LNCS, vol. 7162, pp. 19–38. Springer, Heidelberg (2012). https://doi.org/10.1007/978-3-642-29709-0_2

22. Carboni, A., Walters, R.F.C.: Cartesian bicategories I. J. Pure Appl. Algebra **49**, 11–32 (1987)

23. Coecke, B., Duncan, R.: Interacting quantum observables. In: Proceedings of the 35th International Colloquium on Automata, Languages and Programming (ICALP), Part II, pp. 298–310 (2008)

24. Coecke, B., Kissinger, A.: Picturing Quantum Processes - A First Course in Quantum Theory and Diagrammatic Reasoning. Cambridge University Press (2017)

25. Coya, B., Fong, B.: Corelations are the prop for extraspecial commutative Frobenius monoids. Theor. Appl. Categor. **32**(11), 380–395 (2017)

26. Coya, B.: Circuits, Bond Graphs, and Signal-Flow Diagrams: A Categorical Perspective. Ph.D. thesis, University of California Riverside (2018)

27. De Nicola, R., Hennessy, M.C.: Testing equivalences for processes. Theor. Comput. Sci. **34**(1–2), 83–133 (1984)

28. Dixon, L., Kissinger, A.: Open-graphs and monoidal theories. Math. Struct. Comput. Sci. **23**(2), 308–359 (2013)

29. Fong, B.: Causal Theories: A Categorical Perspective on Bayesian Networks. Master's thesis, University of Oxford (2012). arxiv.org/abs/1301.6201

30. Fong, B.: The Algebra of Open and Interconnected Systems. Ph.D. thesis. University of Oxford (2016)

31. Fong, B., Rapisarda, P., Sobociński, P.: A categorical approach to open and interconnected dynamical systems. In: LICS 2016 (2016)

32. Ghica, D.R., Jung, A.: Categorical semantics of digital circuits. In: Proceedings of the 16th Conference on Formal Methods in Computer-Aided Design (FMCAD), pp. 41–48 (2016)

33. Ghica, D.R., Lopez, A.: A structural and nominal syntax for diagrams. In: Proceedings 14th International Conference on Quantum Physics and Logic (QPL), pp. 71–83 (2017)

34. Hasegawa, M.: Recursion from cyclic sharing: traced monoidal categories and models of cyclic lambda calculi. In: de Groote, P., Roger Hindley, J. (eds.) TLCA 1997. LNCS, vol. 1210, pp. 196–213. Springer, Heidelberg (1997). https://doi.org/10.1007/3-540-62688-3_37

35. Hoare, C.A.R.: Communicating Sequential Processes. Prentice Hall (1985)

36. Hyland, M., Power, J.: Symmetric monoidal sketches. In: Proceedings of the 2nd International ACM SIGPLAN Conference on on Principles and Practice of Declarative Programming, pp. 280–288. ACM (2000). https://doi.org/10.1145/351268.351299

37. Baez, J.C., Brandon Coya, F.R.: Props in network theory. CoRR abs/1707.08321 (2017). http://arxiv.org/abs/1707.08321

38. Joyal, A., Street, R., Verity, D.: Traced monoidal categories. Math. Proc. Cambridge Philos. Soc. **119**(3), 447–468 (1996)

39. Kelly, G.M., Laplaza, M.L.: Coherence for compact closed categories. J. Pure Appl. Algebra **19**, 193–213 (1980)

40. Kock, J.: Frobenius Algebras and 2D Topological Quantum Field Theories. Cambridge University Press (2003)

41. Lack, S.: Composing PROPs. Theor. Appl. Categ. **13**(9), 147–163 (2004)

42. Lafont, Y.: Towards an algebraic theory of Boolean circuits. J. Pure Appl. Algebra **184**(2–3), 257–310 (2003)

43. Lawvere, W.F.: Functorial Semantics of Algebraic Theories. Ph.D. thesis (2004)
44. Mac Lane, S.: Categorical algebra. Bull. Am. Math. Soc. **71**, 40–106 (1965)
45. Mason, S.J.: Feedback Theory: I. Some Properties of Signal Flow Graphs. MIT Research Laboratory of Electronics (1953)
46. Milius, S.: A sound and complete calculus for finite stream circuits. In: Proceedings of the 2010 25th Annual IEEE Symposium on Logic in Computer Science (LICS), pp. 421–430 (2010)
47. Milner, R.: A Calculus of Communicating Systems. Springer, New York (1982). https://doi.org/10.1007/3-540-10235-3
48. Mimram, S.: The structure of first-order causality. Math. Struct. Comput. Sci. **21**, 65–110 (2011)
49. Pavlovic, D.: Monoidal computer I: basic computability by string diagrams. Inf. Comput. **226**, 94–116 (2013)
50. Peterson, J.L.: Petri Nets. ACM Comput. Surv. **9**(3), 223–252 (1977)
51. Piedeleu, R.: Picturing Resources in Concurrency. Ph.D. thesis, University of Oxford (2018)
52. Pirashvili, T.: On the PROP corresponding to bialgebras. Cah. Top. Géom. Diff, Cat XLIII (2002)
53. Rosebrugh, R., Sabadini, N., Walters, R.F.C.: Generic commutative separable algebras and cospans of graphs. Theor. Appl. Categ. **17**(6), 164–177 (2005)
54. Rutten, J.J.M.M.: A tutorial on coinductive stream calculus and signal flow graphs. Theoret. Comput. Sci. **343**(3), 443–481 (2005)
55. Rutten, J.J.M.M.: Rational streams coalgebraically. Logic. Meth. Comput. Sci. **4**(3), 1–22 (2008)
56. Sangiorgi, D., Walker, D.: PI-Calculus: A Theory of Mobile Processes. Cambridge University Press, New York (2001)
57. Selinger, P.: A survey of graphical languages for monoidal categories. In: Coecke, B. (eds.) New Structures for Physics. Lecture Notes in Physics, vol. 813. Springer, Heidelberg (2010) . https://doi.org/10.1007/978-3-642-12821-9_4
58. Shannon, C.E.: The theory and design of linear differential equation machines. Technical report, National Defence Research Council (1942)
59. Stefanescu, G.: Network Algebra. Discrete Mathematics and Theoretical Computer Science. Springer, London (2000). https://doi.org/10.1007/978-1-4471-0479-7
60. Stefanescu, G.: Network Algebra. Springer, London (2000). https://doi.org/10.1007/978-1-4471-0479-7
61. Willems, J.C.: The behavioural approach to open and interconnected systems. IEEE Control Syst. Mag. **27**, 46–99 (2007)
62. Willems, J.: Linear systems in discrete time. In: van den Hof, P.M.J., C.S., Heuberger, P. (eds.) Festschrift on the Occasion of the Retirement of Okko Bosgra, pp. 3–12 (2009)
63. Zanasi, F.: Interacting Hopf Algebras: the theory of linear systems. Ph.D. thesis, Ecole Normale Supérieure de Lyon (2015)
64. Zanasi, F.: The algebra of partial equivalence relations. Electron. Notes Theoret. Comput. Sci. **325**, 313–333 (2016)

TC 2: Software: Theory and Practice

Algorithmics

Richard Bird[1], Jeremy Gibbons[1], Ralf Hinze[2], Peter Höfner[3], Johan Jeuring[4], Lambert Meertens[1], Bernhard Möller[5], Carroll Morgan[6(✉)], Tom Schrijvers[7], Wouter Swierstra[4], and Nicolas Wu[8]

[1] University of Oxford, Oxford, UK
{bird,jeremy.gibbons}@cs.ox.ac.uk, lambert@kestrel.edu
[2] Technische Universität Kaiserslautern, Kaiserslautern, Germany
ralf-hinze@cs.uni-kl.de
[3] Australian National University, Canberra, Australia
peter.hoefner@anu.edu.au
[4] Utrecht University, Utrecht, Netherlands
{j.t.jeuring,w.s.swierstra}@uu.nl
[5] Universität Augsburg, Augsburg, Germany
bernhard.moeller@informatik.uni-augsburg.de
[6] University of New South Wales and Data61 (CSIRO), Sydney, Australia
carroll.morgan@unsw.edu.au
[7] KU Lueven, Lueven, Belgium
tom.schrijvers@cs.kuleuven.be
[8] Imperial College London, London, England
n.wu@imperial.ac.uk

Abstract. *Algorithmics* is the study and practice of taking a high-level description of a program's purpose and, from it, producing an executable program of acceptable efficiency. Each step in that process is justified by rigorous, careful reasoning at the moment it is taken; and the repertoire of steps allowed by that rigour, at each stage, guides the development of the algorithm itself.

IFIP's Working Group 2.1 [i] has always been concerned with Algorithmics: both the design of its notations and the laws that enable its calculations. ALGOL 60 had already shown that orthogonality, simplicity and rigour in a programming language improves the quality of its programs.

Our Group's title "Algorithmic Languages and Calculi" describes our activities: the discovery of precise but more general rules of calculational reasoning for the many new styles of programming that have developed over the 60 years since IFIP's founding. As our contribution to the birthday celebrations, we outline how we have tried to contribute during those decades to the rigorous and reliable design of computer programs of all kinds—to *Algorithmics*. (Roman-numbered references like [i] in this abstract refer to details given in Sect. 10.)

Keywords: Working groups · Algorithmic programming · Calculi

© IFIP International Federation for Information Processing 2021
Published by Springer Nature Switzerland AG 2021
M. Goedicke et al. (Eds.): Advancing Research in Information and Communication Technology,
IFIP AICT 600, pp. 59–98, 2021. https://doi.org/10.1007/978-3-030-81701-5_3

1   Introduction

WG2.1 is one of the the first Working Groups of IFIP, and the oldest extant: it was founded at the request of TC2, which had begun its own very first meeting only two days before [ii]. Initially the "IFIP Working Group 2.1 on ALGOL", it is now known as the

IFIP Working Group 2.1 on Algorithmic Languages and Calculi.   [iii]

The Group has always focused on methods for systematic program construction; and our goal is to make the methods steadily more powerful and more general. For example, the formalisation of the inductive assertion method [iv] led to a logical method based on pre- and postconditions [v], and then to a strongly calculational goal-directed method [vi]. Generalising programs to special cases of specifications [vii] led to the *Mathematics of Program Construction*. And a program-algebraic approach evolved from that: the "Laws of Programming" [viii].

Mathematics (of program construction or otherwise) can be carried out with pencil and paper. For programs, however, there are more significant advantages in automation than for mathematics generally; thus the Group has always paid attention to program transformation systems [ix]—but their design should be based on the 'by hand' calculations that preceded them.

Language design, including the advancement of ALGOL, remained a main interest for many years, focussing for a period specifically on a more advanced language called "Abstracto". Abstracto generalised what 'programming' languages actually *should* be: rather than just for programming or writing executable code, they should also be able to describe algorithms in an abstract way. They should allow expressing (initially vague) ideas about an algorithm's high-level structure and, after transformations adding details, reach a level from which the final step to 'real' programming-language code is simple enough to minimise the risk of transcription errors. In sum, Abstracto was supposed to support and codify our *Algorithmics* activity: but our activity itself outgrew that.

ALGOL 60 and 68 were languages more oriented to programmers' thoughts than to computers' hardware. In their 'successor' Abstracto, we wanted [xi]

...a programming language some of whose features we know:

1. It is very high level, whatever that means.   (1)
2. It is suitable for expressing initial thoughts on construction of a program.
3. It need not be (and probably is not) executable...

Abstracto was to be an *algorithmic language*: one for describing the algorithmic steps in a computation, not just the input-output relation or similar behavioural specification. But it was still intended to be a 'tool of thought', rather than primarily an implementation language.

But the Abstracto approach was *itself* soon abstracted by abandoning the imperative ALGOL-like language structures, switching to a more functional presentation [xii] in which there was an algebra of programs *themselves*, rather than say an algebra of statements *about* programs. The framework for this became known as the "Bird–Meertens Formalism", a very concise notation in which algorithmic strategies can be expressed and transformed (Sect. 2). That exposed many general algorithmic patterns and calculational laws about them that had, until then, been obscured by the earlier imperative control structures.

A similar abstracting approach was applied to *data* structures in the form of a hierarchy –the Boom hierarchy– leading from sets through multisets (bags) and lists to (binary) trees [xiii] (Subsect. 2.3, Sect. 3). The insight was that all these structures had a common pattern of constructors (an empty structure, a singleton constructor, and a binary combiner). They were distinguished from each other not by the signatures of their operations, but rather by the algebraic laws imposed on the constructors: the fewer laws, the more structure in the generated elements.

A further abstraction was to allow the constructors to vary, i.e. to have an even more general approach in which one could say rigorously "Sum the integers in a structure, no matter what its shape." and then reason effectively about it, for example that "Square all the integers in a structure, and then add them up." is the same as "Sum the squares of all the integers in that structure." This led to *generic* programming (Sect. 3). Genericity was achieved by using *elementary* concepts from algebra and category theory — functors, initial and final algebras, and the various kinds of morphisms on them [xiv] (Sect. 4). Programs taking advantage of this are called "polytypic", i.e. allowing many kinds of type structures, in the same way that polymorphic programs allow many kinds of type values within a single class of structures.

Unfortunately, the kind of specification that most polytypic languages support in their type signatures is very limited. Type theory [xv] however showed how any specification expressible in predicate logic could serve as the *type* of a program. That enables programmers to capture arbitrary invariants and specifications of their programs, such as *balanced* trees or *sorted* lists, simply as part of the program's type. Since types are checked at compile-time, any type-correct program will never violate those specifications at runtime. This is supported by *dependently typed* programming languages (Sect. 5).

Besides the activities around data structures there was also a branch of work dealing with the task of mimicking imperative structures, as, e.g., necessary to describe interaction with the environment, in a purely functional context. *Monads, applicative functors*, and *algebraic effects* have provided a mathematically solid account that could be formulated in a way that allowed program-algebraic calculation after all (Sect. 6).

The investigations into data structures and generic algorithms on them were mainly carried out around (quotients of) tree-like structures. However, there are numerous more general (graph-like) structures which are not easily represented in that framework. As these should be approachable by calculations as well, our activities have therefore also dealt with relational or relationally based structures, which is their natural mathematical representation. Abstracting relations to algebraic structures such as Kleene algebras provides notions well suited for

$$*(y{\neq}0 \;\to\; z,x,y := z',x',y' \mid z',x',y' : \\ z{\cdot}x^y = x^Y \;\&\; y{\neq}0 \supset z'{\cdot}x'^{y'}{=}x^Y \;\&\; y'{<}y).$$

$$*(y{\neq}0 \;\to\; z,x,y := z',x',y' \mid z',x',y',r : \\ z' = z{\cdot}x^r \;\&\; x' = x{\cdot}x \;\&\; y{=}2y'{+}r \;\&\; \\ (r{=}0 \;\vee\; r{=}1)).$$

Fig. 1. Abstracto 84 [xx]

describing not only data structures but also control structures of various kinds (Sect. 7). This approach also links nicely to the predicate transformer approaches [vi] and the "Laws of Programming" [viii].

Systematic program construction benefits greatly from program construction systems — tools to support the work of the program constructor. This work involves reasoning about programs, which can be shallow and tedious; automated tools are less error-prone than humans at such activities. Moreover, programs are usually much longer than formal expressions in other contexts, such as in traditional mathematics; so tool support is also a convenience. Finally, a system can record the development history, producing automatically the software documentation that allows a replay, upon a change of specification, or an audit if something goes wrong. The Group has always worked on design and engineering of transformation systems in parallel with the work on the underlying transformation calculi; our survey therefore concludes with a more detailed account of corresponding tool support (Sect. 8).

Generally, the Group's pattern has always been to expand the concepts that enable rigorous construction of correct programs, then streamline their application, and finally simplify their presentation. And then... expand again.

As the trajectory in this section has described (with the benefit of hindsight) the Group has always had diverse interests that arise from our program-calculational 'mindset' applied to other computer-science interest areas and even real-world contemporary problems [xvi].

2 From ALGOL, via Abstracto... to Squiggol

2.1 *Abstracto*: the first move towards algorithmics

After the completion of the *Revised Report on ALGOL 68* [xix], the Group set up a *Future Work* subcommittee to decide how to progress. This subcommittee in turn organised two public conferences on *New Directions in Algorithmic Languages* [xi], after which the Group focussed again on specific topics. The Chair highlighted two foci: programming languages for beginners [xvii], and "Abstracto". The first led to the development of the beginner's language ABC and hence eventually to Python [xviii]; the other was *Abstracto*, and was

> ... not a specification language as such since it is still concerned with how to do things and not just what is to be done, but [allowing] the expression of the 'how' in the simplest and most abstract possible way. [xi]

A representative example of Abstracto is shown in Fig. 1. It is part of the development of a 'fast exponentiation' algorithm: given natural numbers X and

```
                                        input dm, mr;
                                        slm := 0;
                                        for m ∈ dm do
                                          alm := −∞;
      input dm, mr;                       for i ∈ mr[m] do
      gdb := 0;                             if i·age > alm then
      for m ∈ dm do                           lm, alm := i, i·age
        gdb := gdb ∪ mr[m]                  endif
      endfor;                             endfor;
      aoi := −∞;              ⟹          slm := slm ∪ {lm}
      for i ∈ gdb do                    endfor;
        if i·age > aoi then             aoi := −∞;
          oi, aoi := i, i·age           for i ∈ slm do
        endif                             if i·age > aoi then
      endfor;                               oi, aoi := i, i·age
      output oi.                           endif
                                        endfor;
                                        output oi.
```

Fig. 2. The oldest inhabitant, in Abstracto [136]

Y, compute $z = X^Y$ using only $O(\log_2 Y)$ iterations. The program on the left shows a 'while' loop, with invariant $z \times x^y = X^Y$, variant y, and guard $y \neq 0$. The program on the right factors out $r = y \bmod 2$, refining the nondeterminism in the first program to a deterministic loop. Thus our vision for Abstracto was as a kind of 'refinement calculus' for imperative programs [xxi].

2.2 The Bird–Meertens Formalism (BMF): A Higher-Level Approach

Although the Abstracto approach was successful, in the sense that it could be used to solve the various challenge problems that the Group worked on, after some time it was realised that the transformation steps needed were too low level — and so a key insight was to lift the reasoning to a higher level [xxii], namely to abandon the imperative ALGOL-like style and the corresponding refinement-oriented approach of Abstracto, and to switch instead to a more algebraic, functional presentation.

It made a big difference. Consider for example the two programs in Fig. 2 [xx], where the problem is to find the (assumed unique) oldest inhabitant of the Netherlands. The data is given by a collection dm of Dutch municipalities, and an array $mr[-]$ of municipal registers of individuals, one register per municipality. The program on the left combines all the municipal registers into one national register; the program on the right finds the oldest inhabitant of each municipality, and then findest the oldest among those 'local Methuselahs'. Provided that no municipality is uninhabited, the two programs have equivalent behaviour. However, one cannot reasonably expect that precise transformation, from the one to the other, to be present in any catalogue of transformations. Instead, the

$$
\begin{aligned}
mss \;=\; & \text{definition} \\
& \uparrow/ \cdot +/* \cdot segs \\
=\; & \text{definition of } segs \\
& \uparrow/ \cdot +/* \cdot +\!\!+/ \cdot tails * \cdot inits \\
=\; & \text{map and reduce promotion} \\
& \uparrow/ \cdot (\uparrow/ \cdot +/* \cdot tails) * \cdot inits \\
=\; & \text{Horner's rule with } a \circledast b = (a + b) \uparrow 0 \\
& \uparrow/ \cdot \circledast \!\!\not/_0 * \cdot inits \\
=\; & \text{accumulation lemma} \\
& \uparrow/ \cdot \circledast \!\!\not\!\!/_0
\end{aligned}
$$

Fig. 3. The maximum segment sum problem [xxiv]

development should proceed by a series of *simpler* steps that, because of their simplicity, can feasibly be collected in a smaller and more manageable catalogue of general-purpose transformations.

The equivalent higher-level transformation is this one: [xxii]

$$\uparrow_{age}/ +/mr \cdot dm \;=\; \uparrow_{age}/(\uparrow_{age}/mr) \cdot dm$$

Its left-hand side takes the oldest in the union of the registers of each of the municipalities, and the right-hand side takes the oldest among those local Methuselahs. The "$\oplus/$" reduces a collection using binary operator $\oplus$; the "$+$" is binary union; the "$\uparrow_f$" chooses which of two arguments has the greater f-value; the "$g*$" maps function g over a collection; and finally, function composition is indicated by juxtaposition. The functional presentation is clearly an order of magnitude shorter than the Abstracto one. It is also easier to see what form the small general-purpose trans-

Let us calculate!

formation steps should take—simple equations such as "reduce promotion" $(\oplus/ +/ = \oplus/ \oplus/*)$ and "map fusion" $(f* g* = (f \, g)*)$ [xxiii]. The notation evolved further through the 1980s [xxiv], and came to be known as "Squiggol". It was later given the more respectable name "Bird–Meertens Formalism" [xxv], and inspired the Group's further efforts in rigorous, concise program development.

Another example of concise calculation is given in Fig. 3.

2.3   The Boom Hierarchy of Data Structures

The operators and transformation rules of Squiggol/BMF apply equally to lists, bags, and sets. And those three datatypes are conceptually linked by their common signature of constructors (an empty structure, a singleton constructor, and a binary combination) but satisfying different laws (associativity, commutativity, and idempotence of the binary combination, with the empty structure as a unit). Moreover, the core operations (maps, filters, and reductions) are homomorphisms over this algebraic structure.

Crucially, each datatype is the *free algebra* on that common signature, with a given set of equations, generated from a domain of individual elements; that is, there exists a *unique* homomorphism from the datatype to any other algebra of the same kind. For example, writing "[ ]" for the empty structure, "[x]" for a singleton, "$+\!\!\!+$" for the binary combination, and given a binary operator $\oplus$ with unit e, the three equations

$$
\begin{aligned}
\oplus/[\,] &= e \\
\oplus/[a] &= a \\
\oplus/(x +\!\!\!+ y) &= \oplus/x \oplus \oplus/y
\end{aligned}
$$

determine the reduction operator $\oplus/$ uniquely: provided that $\oplus$ is associative, these three equations have as their unique solution the aggregation function from lists. But if we add the assumption that $\oplus$ is also commutative, then there is a unique function from bags; and if we add idempotence, then there is a unique function from sets.

If out of curiosity we assert *no* equations of the binary operator alone, only that the empty structure is its unit, then we obtain a fourth member of the family, a peculiar sort of binary tree. The four members form a hierarchy, by adding the three equations one by one to this tree type. The resulting hierarchy of data structures was called the "Boom" hierarchy [xiii]. Its connections to the Eindhoven quantifier notation [xxvi] greatly simplified the body of operators and laws needed for a useful theory.

3   Generic Programming: Function Follows Form

The Boom hierarchy is an example of how we can use algebras and homomorphisms to describe a collection of datatypes, together with a number of basic operations on those datatypes. In the case of the Boom hierarchy, the constructors of the algebra are fixed, and the laws the operators satisfy vary. Another axis along which we can abstract is the *constructors* of a datatype: we realised that concepts from category theory can be used to describe a large collection of datatypes as initial algebras or final coalgebras of a functor [xiv]. The action of the initial algebra represents the constructors of the datatype it models. And it has the attractive property that any homomorphism on the functor algebra induces a unique function from the initial algebra. Such a function was called a *catamorphism* [xxvii]. A catamorphism captures the canonical recursive form on a datatype represented by an initial algebra. In the functional programming world, a catamorphism is called a fold, and in object-oriented programming languages the concept corresponds closely to visitors. Typical examples are functions like map, applying an argument function to all elements in a value of a datatype, and size, returning the number of elements in a value of a (container) datatype. Catamorphisms satisfy a nice fusion property, which is the basis of many laws in programming calculi. This work started a line of research

```
flatten  :: Regular d => d a -> [a]
flatten  =   cata fl

polytypic fl :: f a [a] -> [a] =
  case f of
    g + h -> either fl fl
    g * h -> \(x,y) -> fl x ++ fl y
    ()      -> \x -> []
    Par    -> \x -> [x]
    Rec    -> \x -> x
    d @ g -> concat . flatten . pmap fl
    Con t -> \x -> []

data Either a b  =  Left a | Right b
```

Fig. 4. A PolyP program to flatten a container to a list [xxix]

on *datatype-generic programming* [xxviii], capturing various forms of recursion as morphisms, more about which in Sect. 4.

The program calculus thus developed could be used to calculate solutions to many software problems. As a spin-off, the theory described programs that could be implemented in a standard, but different, way on datatypes that can be described as initial functor-algebras. No general-purpose programming language supported such typed, generic functions, so these functions had to be implemented over and again for different datatypes.

Using the structure of polynomial functors, the language PolyP was designed that extended the lazy, higher-order functional programming language Haskell [xxix]. In PolyP, a generic function is defined by means of induction on the structure of functors. Using this programming language it was possible to define not only the recursive combinators from the program calculus, such as folds and unfolds, but also to write generic programs for unification, term rewriting, pattern matching, etc. Figure 4 shows an example of a polytypic program.

PolyP supported the definition of generic functions on datatypes that can be described as initial functor-algebras but do not involve mutual recursion. While sufficient for proof-of-concept demonstration purposes, this last restriction was a severe limitation on practical applicability. Generic programming is particularly attractive in situations with large datatypes, such as the abstract syntax of programming languages, and such datatypes are usually mutually recursive. Generic Haskell was developed to support generic functions on sets of mutually recursive datatypes [xxx]. Generic functions defined in Generic Haskell can be applied to values of almost any datatype definable in Haskell. Figure 5 shows how a generic equality function is implemented in Generic Haskell.

The approach of defining generic functions in Generic Haskell can also be used to define type-indexed (or generic) datatypes. A type-indexed datatype is a data type that is constructed in a generic way from an argument data type. For example, in the case of digital searching, we have to define a search tree type

$$
\begin{aligned}
&\textbf{type } \mathsf{Eq}\{\!\!\{\star\}\!\!\} \; t && = t \to t \to \mathsf{Bool} \\
&\textbf{type } \mathsf{Eq}\{\!\!\{\kappa \to \nu\}\!\!\} \; t && = \forall a \,.\, \mathsf{Eq}\{\!\!\{\kappa\}\!\!\} \; a \to \mathsf{Eq}\{\!\!\{\nu\}\!\!\} \; (t \; a)
\end{aligned}
$$

$$
\begin{aligned}
&eq\{\!\![t :: \kappa]\!\!\} && :: \mathsf{Eq}\{\!\!\{\kappa\}\!\!\} \; t \\
&eq\{\!\![\mathsf{Char}]\!\!\} && = eqChar \\
&eq\{\!\![\mathsf{Int}]\!\!\} && = eqInt \\
&eq\{\!\![\mathsf{Unit}]\!\!\} \; Unit \; Unit && = True \\
&eq\{\!\![:+:]\!\!\} \; eqa \; eqb \; (Inl \; a) \; (Inl \; a') && = eqa \; a \; a' \\
&eq\{\!\![:+:]\!\!\} \; eqa \; eqb \; (Inl \; a) \; (Inr \; b') && = False \\
&eq\{\!\![:+:]\!\!\} \; eqa \; eqb \; (Inr \; b) \; (Inl \; a') && = False \\
&eq\{\!\![:+:]\!\!\} \; eqa \; eqb \; (Inr \; b) \; (Inr \; b') && = eqb \; b \; b' \\
&eq\{\!\![:*:]\!\!\} \; eqa \; eqb \; (a :*: b) \; (a' :*: b') && = eqa \; a \; a' \wedge eqb \; b \; b'
\end{aligned}
$$

Fig. 5. A generic Haskell program for equality [xxx]

by induction on the structure of the type of search keys. Generic Haskell also supports the possibility of defining type-indexed datatypes [xxxi]. The functional programming language Haskell now supports a light-weight variant of type-indexed datatypes through type families.

The fixed-point structure of datatypes is lost in Generic Haskell, however, and with it the capability of defining the generic fold function. It was then discovered how to obtain a fixed-point representation of possibly mutually recursive datatypes, bringing the generic fold function back into the fold [xxxii]. Thus we can define the fold function for the abstract syntax of a programming language, bringing generic programming within reach of compiler writers.

Meanwhile, Haskell –or, more precisely, compilers supporting various Haskell extensions– evolved considerably since PolyP and Generic Haskell were developed. With respect to types, GHC, the Glasgow Haskell Compiler, now supports multiple-parameter type classes, generalised algebraic datatypes (GADTs), type families, etc. Using these extensions, it is now possible to define generic functions in Haskell itself, using a library for generic programming. Since 2000, tens of such libraries have been developed world-wide [xxxiii]. Since –from a generic programming perspective– the expressiveness of these libraries is almost the same as the special-purpose language extensions, and since such libraries are much easier to develop, maintain, and ship, these libraries make generic programming more generally available. Indeed, these libraries have found their way to a wider audience: for example, Scrap Your Boilerplate has been downloaded almost 300,000 times, and Generic Deriving almost 100,000 times [xxxiii].

4   Morphisms: Suddenly They Are Everywhere

In Sect. 3 we identified catamorphisms as a canonical recursive form on a datatype represented by an initial algebra: in functional-programming parlance, a *fold*. From there, however, further work [xxxiv] led to a rich research agenda concerned with capturing the pattern of many other useful recursive functions that did not quite fit that scheme, that were not *quite* 'catamorphic'. Indeed, it gave rise to a whole zoo of morphisms: *mutu*morphisms, *zygo*morphisms, *histo*morphisms, generalised folds, and generic accumulations [xxxv]. Just as with catamorphisms, those recursion schemes attracted attention because they made termination or progress manifest (no need to prove or check it) and they enjoyed many useful and general calculational properties — which would otherwise have to be established afresh for each new application.

4.1   Diversification

Where while-loops are governed by a predicate on the current state, and for loops by an incrementing counter, structured recursion schemes such as catamorphisms take a more restricted approach where it is the structure of the input data itself that controls the flow of execution ("function follows form").

As a simple example, consider how a list of integers is summed: a catamorphism simply recurses over the structure of the list. No for-loop index variable, and no predicate: when the list is empty the sum is zero, and when the list contains at least one number it should be added to the sum of the residual list. While-loops could easily encode such tasks, but their extra expressive power is also their weakness: we know that it is not always tractable to analyse loops in general. With catamorphisms, the analysis is much simpler — the recursion scheme is simply induction over a datatype.

The analogy with induction goes further. Number theorists have long studied computable functions on natural numbers, and an important class are the primitive recursive functions, which provide the recursive step with the original argument as well as the result of recursing on that argument. Such functions are an instance of the *paramorphism* [xxxvi], which is an interchangeable variation on the catamorphism.

Further still, an attractive variant of induction is *strong* induction, where the inductive step can rely on all the previous steps. Its parallel as a recursion scheme is the *histomorphism* and, just as strong induction and induction are interchangeable, histomorphisms are encodable as catamorphisms. The utility of these schemes –the point of it all– is however to make it convenient to describe programs that would otherwise be difficult to express, and to derive others from them. In the case of histomorphisms (strong recursion), for example, it is the essence of simple dynamic programming programs such as the knapsack problem, or counting the number of possible bracketings, that was captured. More complex dynamic programming problems, such as the multiplication of a chain of matrices, requires a slightly more nuanced recursion scheme, the *dynamorphism*, where an intermediate data structure is generated.

We recall that the exploitation of various forms of duality revolutionalised the field of physics; algorithmics similarly benefits from an important form of input-output duality. Each recursion scheme features a dual scheme: while one focuses on consuming the input, the other emphasizes producing the output. To illustrate, consider how insertion sort deconstructs a list by extracting numbers one at a time (input), inserting them appropriately into a sorted list (output).

Whereas the deconstruction of the original list is another catamorphism, the construction of the sorted list exemplifies an *anamorphism*—it is the dual situation. Thus expressing insertion sort in terms of recursion schemes allows us to dualize the algorithm to obtain another sorting algorithm *for free*: selection sort. This works by constructing a sorted list (an anamorphism), and at each step performs a selection that deconstructs the unsorted list to extract the smallest element (a paramorphism).

Another way to understand a catamorphism is that it applies a strategy that takes subsolutions and conquers them (with a so-called *algebra*) to provide a final solution. Dually, an anamorphism applies a strategy that takes a problem and splits it up into subproblems (with a so-called *coalgebra*). Those can be understood as the two components of a divide-and-conquer strategy, and the combination is known as a *hylomorphism*, depicted in the diagram below:

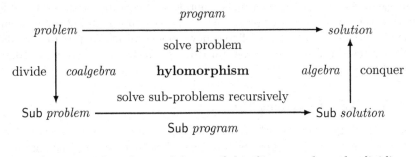

Catamorphisms are then the special case of this diagram where the dividing step simply *deconstructs* a data structure, and anamorphisms the special case where the conquering step *constructs* a data structure.

4.2 Unification

The multitude of generalisations of catamorphisms and their duals is bewildering.

Many of them were defined as adaptations of catamorphisms, but in most cases showing that those corresponded directly to catamorphisms required careful calculation. And with so many different variations, a natural question is whether there is some underlying commonality that unifies them all. Indeed there is.

The unification was achieved by borrowing some slightly more sophisticated machinery from category theory. A first attempt was to use comonads, which allow access to contextual information [xxxvii], to organise the structure of recursive calls. Another attempt used adjunctions instead as the common thread [xxxviii]. That resulted in so-called "adjoint" folds, which show how a catamorphism in one category can give rise to a different recursion scheme in another. Although the two methods were initially thought to be disjoint, later work revealed recursion schemes from comonads to be a special case of adjoint folds with an appropriate distributive law.

Each of these two unifications of recursion schemes treated generalizations of catamorphisms separately to their dual counterparts of anamorphisms. But both are special cases of hylomorphisms; and so the next step was to generalise *all* inductive and coinductive recursion schemes within the single unifying theme of *conjugate hylomorphisms* — or 'the mother of all recursion schemes'. Naturally, the Group named it the *mamamorphism*. This time, the more sophisticated categorical techniques were used to extend the work on adjoint folds with conjugate distributive laws to connect pairs of adjunctions.

All in all, the unifying work on recursion schemes benefitted greatly from the unifying power of category theory — which is what category theory is for.

5   Dependent Types: Types You Can Depend on

Datatype-generic programming explores how to define functions and datatypes by induction over the structure of algebraic types. This line of research within the Group sparked further interest in the exploration of how to use static type information in the construction of programs. In particular, emerging programming languages with *dependent types* offered new opportunities for program verification, program transformation, program calculation and type-directed program development.

5.1   What Are Dependent Types?

The idea of programming with dependent types dates back at least as far as the 1970's, when it became increasingly clear that there was a deep connection between constructive mathematics and computer programming [xxxix]. In the late 20th century, a number of new programming languages emerged, exploring these ideas [xl]. Those languages, and their implementations, enabled the further exploration of the possibilities that statically typed languages with dependent types offered. Each of them adopted the *Curry-Howard correspondence* [xli], connecting programming languages and mathematical logic, as the guiding principle of *program language design*. The terms of each language correspond to both programs and proofs; a type can equally well be read as a specification or a proposition. To ensure the logic underlying a language's type system is *sound*, all functions must be total, disallowing partial incomplete pattern matching and diverging functions. The benefit of this disciplined approach to software development is that these languages provide a unified setting for both programming and program verification. Given the strong traditions of program calculation and functional programming within the Group, for instance, using the Bird–Meertens Formalism to perform equational reasoning about Haskell programs, there was a clear interest in these new languages. Furthermore, the richer language of algebraic data types offered the ability to enforce invariants during a program's construction.

5.2   Dependent Types

At the beginning of the 21st century, the relation between dependently typed programming and datatype generic programming was clearly emerging [xlii] leading to several influential PhD theses on this topic. The interest in dependent types from members of the Group dates back to the late 80's [xliii].

The new languages based on type theory reinvigorated some of the past research that members of the Group have done on the derivation of correct programs. Following the Agda tutorial at Meeting #63 [xliv], the work on relational program calculation, for example, was shown to be possible within dependently typed languages. Similarly, the refinement calculus, used to derive a program from its specification, could be embedded in a proof assistant, enabling pen and paper proofs to be machine-checked. Program calculation in the style of Dijkstra using predicate transformer semantics could be modelled using type theory, rather than the traditional impredicative set theory. Types and proof assistants based on type theory became a central tool in the calculation of correct programs [xlv].

At that point, an influx of new members broadened the Group's interest to novel application areas for dependently typed programming [xlvi], such as scientific computation, decision problems, and even the study of climate change. Combinator parsing, previously studied in the context of functional programming (see Subsect. 6.2), was implemented in a total language with dependent types [xlvii].

The new languages with dependent types also enabled new opportunities to exploit static type information to guide program development [xlviii] — in the same spirit as the research on datatype generic programming. Types can be read as a (partial) specification. The discovery of a type-correct program can arise from a dialogue with the type checker, helping establish a program's correctness as it is written. There are numerous domain-specific languages and data types designed to enforce certain correctness properties by construction.

Dependently typed programming languages marry constructive logic and programming in a manner unfamiliar to most programmers. To ensure that the type system is sound, all programs must be total. Yet any mainstream language relies on numerous *effects*, such as general recursion, mutable state, concurrency, or exceptions, each of which break the promise of totality. To address this, there has been a line of research on how to incorporate effects in dependently typed program languages [xlix]. This, in turn, led to renewed interest from the Group on how to program safely and robustly in the presence of arbitary side-effects in any language, resulting in the study of *algebraic effects* (see Sect. 6).

6 Computational Effects: Beyond the Functional

When the Group switched to a purely functional presentation of programs [xxii], that is from Abstracto to Squiggol (Sect. 2), at first this also meant doing away with a group of programming-language features known collectively as "effects".

6.1 Effects and Monads

Effects cover all behavioural aspects of a computational function that go beyond the input-output behaviour of mathematical functions. It includes interaction of a program with its environment (the file system and operating system, other processes, human operators, distant servers, ...), mechanisms for structuring the internal control flow (partiality and exceptions, backtracking, nondeterminism and probability, delimited control, ...), and implicit dataflows (mutable state and global variables).

While some of these effects are indeed symptoms of a low-level imperative encoding, such as local mutable state, others are essential in real-world programs that interact with the environment. And they can be important for structuring programs compositionally: examples are exceptions and backtracking.

Fortunately, it turned out that useful effects need not be abandoned in a purely functional setting [l]—the 'doing away with' was only temporary. Effects can after all be modelled with pure functions. Here are some examples:

$$a \to b$$ a pure function
$$a \to 1 + b$$ a partial function
$$a \to e + b$$ a function with exceptions e
$$a \to b^+$$ a nondeterministic function
$$a \to b^*$$ ... which might also fail
$$a \to b \times o^*$$ a function that sends o's to its environment
$$a \to \mu x.((i \to x) + b)$$ a function that reads i's from its environment
$$a \to (s \to (b \times s))$$ a function with implicit state s
$$\vdots$$

(where b^+ denotes non-empty sequences of b's, and b^* possibly empty sequences).

It turned out that all those different types of functions with effects are 'Kleisli' arrows for appropriately structured *monads* [li]. The utility of the monad was that it handled calculation, in particular composition, of the types above in a single unified way. Whereas two functions of types $a \to b$ and $b \to c$ are easily composed to make a single function of type $a \to c$, it is not clear at first how to compose $a \to e+b$ and $b \to e+c$ to $a \to e+c$, or for that matter $a \to b^+$ and $b \to c^+$ to $a \to c^+$. And even when the (in retrospect) obvious definitions are adopted, one for each, the challenge is then to see those definitions as instances of a single generalised composition. That's what Kleisli composition achieves.

6.2 Functions Too Weak, Monads Too Strong: Applicative Functors? Just Right

Once monads had brought effects back in the purview of purely functional reasoning, the Group turned its attention to reasoning about such programs—'effectful' programs. One fruitful example has been the study of *recursive descent parsers* [lii]. They lend themselves to a combinator style of programming. Moreover, the combinators fall neatly out of the observation that the datatype of parsers that return a parsed value is another monad, a combination of implicit state and nondeterminism with failure: the Kleisli arrows are of the form

$$a \to (\Sigma^* \to (b \times \Sigma^*)^*)$$

where the alphabet of symbols is Σ or, in verse [liii],

A parser for things
is a function from strings
to lists of pairs
of things and strings.

But the monadic presentation makes static analysis difficult: the interface allows earlier inputs to determine the parser used for later inputs, which is both more expressive than necessary (because few applications require such configurable syntax) and too expressive to analyse (because the later parser is not statically available). A weaker interface for effects turns out to be nearly as expressive, and much more amenable to analysis. The essence of this weaker interface was abstracted as an 'applicative functor', and has served as the foundation of significant subsequent work [liv].

6.3 Algebraic Effects and Handlers

But how to reason about effectful programs, such as applicative parsers, nondeterministic functions, and programs that perform I/O? A first step is to treat the effectful operations as an abstract datatype, provide a purely functional specification of that data abstraction, prove the program correct with respect to the algebraic specification, but run the program against the 'real' implementation that incurs actual effects such as I/O. In fact, one could consider the algebraic specification as the interface in the first place, and incorporate its axioms into traditional equational reasoning; it is then the responsibility of the implementer of the effect to satisfy the axioms. This approach is cleanly formalized in the notion of *algebraic effects and handlers*, whereby a pure functional program assembles a term describing the effects to be performed, and a complementary environment *handles* the term, by analogy with handling an exception [lv]. In fact, that term is a value of a type captured as the *free monad* on the signature of the effect operations, a datatype-generic notion (see Sect. 3).

7 Lifting the Game: A Purely Algebraic View of Algorithms and Languages

The systematic construction of algorithms –or, more generally, of computer programs– needs languages that are precise, effective, and that allow calculational reasoning. Previous sections showed how the Group discovered the striking similarities between derivations from quite different areas, such as path problems and regular languages [lvi]. Using algebra in its purest form, i.e. starting with a collection of postulated axioms and carrying out (program) derivations based on those laws alone, therefore enables an extremely abstract treatment: those derivations are then valid in *any* programming model that satisfies the axioms.

Calculi based on the algebra of binary relations [lvii] were prime candidates for that, since they allow a natural treatment of directed graphs—and they abstract and unify data structures (e.g. trees), transition systems and many more concepts.

	semiring (program interpretation)		relation algebra
+	(nondeterministic) choice	∪	union
·	sequential composition	;	relational composition
≤	refinement	⊆	subset
0	abort	∅	empty relation
1	skip	I	identity relation

Fig. 6. Operators of semirings and relation algebras

Also, relations are intimately connected with predicates and hence can be used to describe (by pre- and postconditions) and calculate input-output behaviour. In particular, they cover principles of algorithm design such as dynamic programming, greedy algorithms etc. [lvi]

Relation Algebras make relations, i.e. sets of argument-value pairs, 'first-class citizens' by viewing them as algebraic elements subject to operators that treat them as a whole without looking at their internal structure. The 'point-free' approach that this enables often admits considerable concision. The basic relational operators (Fig. 6, right) are simply set union, intersection and complement, supplemented by sequential composition.

Although a relation-algebraic approach already allows the unified treatment of different instances of graph problems [lviii], replacing sets of pairs (single relations) by other entities yields further models of the same algebraic signature, known as *(idempotent) semirings*. Figure 6 (left) shows the operators common to semirings.

And those structures have applications in programming languages, algorithms, logic and software engineering:

- *Classical logic* is a well known simple semiring, in which choice corresponds to disjunction, composition to conjunction, 0 to false and 1 to true. To subsume classical logic fully, however, one requires negation — i.e. a Boolean algebra.
- When elements of a semiring are interpreted as (arbitrary) *programs*, the basic operators represent nondetermistic choice and sequential composition; 0 corresponds to the program abort and 1 to skip. Equations such as $1 \cdot x = x = x \cdot 1$ and $0 \cdot x = 0 = x \cdot 0$ form the basis of algebraic reasoning, including program transformations. The equations describe the facts that any program x composed with skip is identical to the program itself, and that any program composed with abort is identical to abort. This allows the expression of programs and specifications in the same framework. A program P satisfies a specification S if $P \leq S$, where $\leq$ expresses refinement, which is the canonical order available in every idempotent semiring. (In other styles of program calculation, that would be written $S \sqsubseteq P$.) This simple formulation of program correctness enables a wide range of methods for calculational program derivation and program verification [lix].
- Using partial maps as algebraic elements allows treating data structures with pointers. This usage was inspired by Squiggol (Sect. 2) [lx].

- When the underlying structure reflects the memory cells (heaps), the algebraic framework provides an abstract version of separation logic [lxi].
- When the algebraic elements are interpreted as sets of sets or sets of lists it is possible to derive aspects of feature-oriented software development, including the formal characterisation of product families and of feature interactions [lxii].
- Graphs are often equipped with edge labels representing weights, capacities or probabilities; likewise automata and labelled transition systems carry extra edge information in addition to source and target. Those can be treated by generalising Boolean matrices to matrices over other algebras. For classical graph algorithms, such as shortest-path algorithms, the max-plus algebra and the min-plus algebra are useful as underlying structure—here, min/max play the roles of (biased) choice, and plus is the operator for sequential composition (that is, adding path lengths/costs).
- Probabilistic aspects can be represented by matrices with real values between 0 and 1, and fit into the very same algebraic framework. Applications include calculational derivations of fuzzy algorithms.
- Fundamental concepts of programming-language semantics, including concurrent programs and termination, can be handled algebraically as well. Beyond the areas mentioned above, the Group has also applied this algebra in several areas, included object-oriented programming, data processing, game analysis and routing in mobile networks [lxii].

But semirings can be extended: and those extensions are used to capture additional concepts from data structures, program logics and program transformation. Here are some examples.

Kleene algebras, generalising the algebra of regular expressions, offer the additional operator $\_^*$ of arbitrary finite iteration. Algebraically, the loop while p do x becomes $(p \cdot x)^* \cdot \neg p$, which is the least fixed-point of the function λy. if p then $x \cdot y$ else skip [lxiii].

Here p is a specific element, called a *test*, representing a predicate on the state space. The set of tests offers a negation operator $\neg$ and hence forms a Boolean algebra [lxiv]. In the interpretation where algebraic elements are programs, a test p corresponds to an assert statement. For tests p, q and program element x the inequation $p \cdot x \leq x \cdot q$ algebraically expresses the Hoare triple $\{p\}x\{q\}$ [lxi].

Furthermore, in certain Kleene algebras, known as *quantales*, the principle of fixed-point fusion [lxv] is a theorem, i.e. it can be derived from the axioms. This illustrates once again the powers of 'algebraic unification'. Fusion, shown in Sects. 2 and 3 to be an extremely practical law for transforming functional programs, is now available for many other kinds of program too. Examples include merging of programs with the same loop structure, or 'deforestation', i.e. avoiding the generation of a large intermediate data structure that afterwards is 'consumed' again, in favour of 'generation and consumption on the fly'. This is also known as "virtual" data structures [lxvi].

Omega algebras [lxvii], which offer an operator $\_^\omega$ for infinite iteration, allow the description and analysis of systems or programs with potentially never-ending behaviour, such as operating systems.

In algebras with finite and infinite behaviour, some algebraic laws of sequential composition need to be adapted by separating the finite and the infinite traces of a program x into the disjoint sets $\text{fin}\, x$ and $\text{inf}\, x$. While the above law $x \cdot 1 = x$ still holds for all elements, the property $x \cdot 0 = 0$ no longer holds when x contains infinite traces; it weakens to $(\text{fin}\, x) \cdot 0 = 0$. The intuitive explanation is that infinite traces do not terminate, and therefore a possible successor, including abort, can never be 'executed'. Therefore the while-loop now has the more general behaviour

$$(p \cdot x)^* \cdot \neg p \quad = \quad (p \cdot \text{fin}\, x)^* \cdot (\neg p + p \cdot \text{inf}\, x) \quad ,$$

which means that after a finitely many finite traces from x the loop either terminates by not satisfying the test p any longer, or an infinite trace from x takes over, leading to overall non-termination. When x is purely finite, i.e., satisfies $\text{inf}\, x = 0$, this reduces to the expression given previously.

Like the operators of semirings, the operators of finite and infinite iterations (and many of their combinations) satisfy a common set of laws, and thus algebra helps to unify their treatment including the derivation of program transformations and refinement theorems. Applications range from termination in classical programs, via protocols, to dynamic and hybrid systems [lxvii].

Omega algebras are also used to develop a unified framework for various logics, including the temporal logics LTL, CTL and CTL*, neighbourhood logic and separation logic [lxi].

To sum up: algebraic characterisations have helped to express (and prove) new notions and results and to unify concepts and identify the above-mentioned similarities. The Group has developed a coherent view on algorithms and languages from an algebraic perspective, and applies the same algebraic techniques to tackle modern technology, including the analysis of protocols and quantum computing. All the algebras in question provide a first-order equational calculus, which makes them ideal to be supported by *automated theorem provers* and *interactive proof assistants* [lxviii] [xliv]. As a consequence, they are well suited for developing tools that support program derivations and refinement in a (semi-)automated style.

8 System Support: the Right Tool for the Job

Calculational program construction derives a program from a formal specification by manageable, controlled steps that *–because* they are calculated– guarantee that the final product meets its initial specification. As we have seen, this methodology has been practised by many Group members, and many others too [lxix]. And it applies to many programming styles, including both functional and imperative. For the former one uses mostly equational reasoning, applying the defining equations of functions together with laws of the underlying data structures. For the latter, inequations deploying a refinement relation are common [lxx]. A frequent synonym for "calculation rules" is "transformation rules".

A breakthrough occurred when the Group raised the level of reasoning (Sect. 2): from manipulations of imperative code (Abstracto) to algebraic abstractions of functional control patterns (Squiggol). This made it possible to compact derivations of several pages in traditional approaches down to one page or even less. A similar observation concerns the general theme of 'algebraicisation' (see Sect. 7).

8.1   System Support

Of course, calculational program construction can be done with pencil and paper, and initially it should be so: that encourages a simplicity and elegance in its methods. Ultimately, if the method proves to be useful, there are a number of good reasons for introducing system support:

- By its very nature, program transformation leads to frequent rewritings of program fragments; such clerical work should be automatic. And, by *its* very nature, a system does this mechanical activity better than a human can.
- The system can record the applicability conditions and help in reducing them to simpler forms, ideally all the way to "true".
- And, as mentioned in Sect. 1, the system can construct a *development history*, again a clerical task. This history serves as detailed software documentation, since it reflects every design decision that enters into the final program. Thus, if a line of development turns out to be a blind alley, the history can be used for backtracking to try out alternative design decisions. Moreover, it is the key aid to software maintenance: when the specification has to be modified (because of new requirements), one can try to 'replay' a recorded development accordingly.

Thus the Group gave considerable attention to program transformation systems [ix] once the methods they automated were sufficiently mature. In the remainder of this section we take a brief look at one of them: it touches on several areas within the Group, and several Group members were involved in it and in follow-on projects.

8.2   An Example: The Project CIP

The project CIP (*Computer-aided, Intuition-guided Programming*) at TU Munich ran roughly through the period 1977–1990.

The Wide-Spectrum Language CIP-L. The CIP approach was based on a particular 'life cycle of transformational program development', roughly characterised by the following levels [lxxi]:

1. formal problem specification (usually descriptive, not (yet) executable, possibly non-deterministic);

2. recursive functional program;
3. efficiency-improved functional program;
4. deterministic, tail-recursive solution;
5. efficient procedural or machine-oriented program.

However, not all of these levels need occur: a development may start below Level 1 and end above Level 5; and it may skip some of the intermediate levels.

The language CIP-L was however especially designed to cover all five levels [lxxii]. Since transformations usually do not change a program as a whole, only small portions of it, it was mandatory to design one integrated wide-spectrum language rather separate languages for each level. In particular, the language included assertion constructs at all levels, thus allowing the incorporation of pre- and postconditions uniformly for functions and statements — so it is also connected to the refinement calculi that were developed around the same time [lxx]. CIP-L was partly inspired by Abstracto (Subsect. 2.1); in a sense, it tried to present a model of a possible concrete instance of Abstracto.

The Transformation System CIP-S. The purpose of CIP-S was the transformational development of programs and program schemes. In addition to bookkeeping tasks, that included the manipulation of concrete programs, the derivation of new transformation rules within the system, and support for the verification of side conditions of transformation rules [lxxiii].

In keeping with the overall CIP methodology, the kernel of the system was itself formally specified: starting from that specification, all routines were developed to Pascal-level CIP-L using an earlier prototype system. The results were embedded into an appropriate user environment, yielding a first operational version of CIP-S around 1990. In conjunction with a compiler for a substantial executable subset of CIP-L, the CIP-S system has been successfully used in education. The transformational approach was continued by the Group.

Experiences. There is an extensive body of case studies using the CIP methodology. They concern mostly small and medium-sized algorithms, e.g., sorting and parsing [lxxiv]. The formal development of CIP-S itself showed that the method is suitable for larger software projects too.

9   Summary; but No Conclusion

This is not a 'conclusion'. And this article is not a history. It is a description of a *goal*, a justification of its importance, and a summary of the trajectory that has led, and still leads, to progress towards that goal. And what we especially enjoy about that trajectory we have followed, right from the start 60 years ago, is that it has always been the same one:

Let us calculate!   (Sect. 2 p6)

Why is that goal so important?

Writing programs using a careful process of walk-throughs and reviews is (alone) not enough; "growing" programs [lxxv] in a top-down way is (alone) not enough; proving your program correct afterwards is (alone) not enough. We have always believed that maintaining correctness from the very top, and then 'all the way down' is what we all should be aiming for.

But will we ever get there? *No, we will not.*

During the 1970's, an array-out-of-bounds error in a high-level program would typically lead to a core dump, an inch-high stack of paper that was examined at just one spot, an "Ah, yes!" and then the whole thing just thrown away. Thirty years of progress brought us to 'Interactive Development Environments' and the internet, where sometimes the programmer was not even sure *where* the just-corrected version of a program had been 'deployed', nor exactly *whether* it contained the fix (because of caching). Error messages from a remote server in some far-away city flicked up out of the window, too quickly to be read, and could not be scrolled back. And twenty more years bring us up-to-date, with 'intelligent' aquarium thermometers that can be hacked from half a world away and used to raid a company's private database. *Plus ça change...*

The one constant through all of this is *people*, their tolerance for impediments to getting their work done and their perseverance in spite of them. The technology we are trying to control, to approach rigorously, is always sitting on that boundary, just beyond our reach: we will never calculate far enough.

Thus, however good we become at calculating, and convincing others to do so, there will always be economic forces that promote and propagate computer applications that we *cannot* develop by careful walk-throughs, or grow top-down, or prove correct... or calculate. This 'catching up' factor is what drives all the IFIP working groups — we constantly extend our methods improve the impact of computers generally, to make them safer and increase their reliability, as their use becomes ever more ambitious and spreads ever more widely.

We are not so much 'pushing' as 'being pulled'. There is the excitement.

10   Detailed Attributions and Citations

[i] **Contributors** —
All of the members members of WG2.1, past and present, deserve credit for what is reported here. Among those who provided actual text were Richard Bird, Jeremy Gibbons, Ralf Hinze, Peter Höfner, Johan Jeuring, Lambert Meertens, Bernhard Möller, Carroll Morgan, Tom Schrijvers, Wouter Swierstra and Nicolas Wu.

Carroll Morgan was Group Chair at the time of writing, and is the corresponding author.

[ii] **The founding of IFIP** —
It was established on 23 March 1962 [26, 158].

[iii] **Change of name** —
At Meeting #39 in Chamrousse in January 1989, Formal Resolution 2 was to recommend to TC2 that the Group's name be changed to "WG2.1 on

ALGOL: Algorithmic Languages and Calculi". But TC2 rejected the recommendation, as reported at Meeting #40. At Meeting #41 in Burton in May 1990, it was reported that TC2 suggested instead simply "Algorithmic Languages and Calculi", and this suggestion was accepted by the Group. TC2 approved the change, which was reported at Meeting #42 in Louvain-la-Neuve in January 1991.

[iv] **Assigning meanings to programs** —
This was Floyd's association of predicates with flowchart arcs [70].

[v] **An axiomatic basis for computer programming** —
This was Hoare's logic for partial correctness [95].

[vi] **A Discipline of Programming** —
This was Dijkstra's calculus of weakest preconditions [65].

[vii] **Predicative programming** —
This generalisation was the work of Hoare and Hehner [87,88,96].

[viii] **Laws of Programming** —
This work was presented by a number of authors, including Hoare, at Oxford's Programming Research Group [97].

[ix] **Program-transformation systems** —
Systems designed and implemented by Group members include the Argonne TAMPR (Transformation-Assisted Multiple Program Realization) System [41–43], ARIES (Acquisition of Requirements and Incremental Evolution of Specifications) [113], (R)APTS (Rutgers Abstract Program Transformation System) [162], KIDS (Kestrel Interactive Development System) [185], POPART (Producer of Parsers And Related Tools) [201,202], ZAP [67,68], and the Munich CIP (Computer-aided, Intuition-guided Programming) project [21,23,149]. Comparisons of various transformation systems are presented in [69,170].

[x] **The name "Abstracto"** —
The lecturer who made that remark was Leo Geurts [73, p57]; he added that "in abstracto" was Dutch [sic!] for "in the abstract".

[xi] **Criteria for Abstracto** —
These criteria for Abstracto were proposed by Robert Dewar, who was the Group's chairman at the time [64]. His letter was written in July 1977 [64], in advance of Meeting #23 of the Group in Oxford in December of that year. The *New Directions in Algorithmic Languages* conferences were in 1975 and 1976, the work of a subcommittee chaired by Robert Dewar and with proceedings [181,182] edited by Stephen Schuman.

[xii] **Abstracting Abstracto** —
This landmark step was suggested and developed by Richard Bird and Lambert Meertens.

[xiii] **The Boom Hierarchy** —
The Boom hierarchy was introduced by Hendrik Boom [38], and thus namesd "Boom" (by others) — another pun, since Hendrik is Dutch, and "boom" is Dutch for tree. Backhouse [11] presents a detailed study of the Boom Hierarchy, and compares it to the quantifier notation introduced by Edsger Dijkstra and colleagues at Eindhoven.

[xiv] **The appeal to category theory** —
The introduction of concepts from category theory was due to Grant Malcolm [126], based on the work of Hagino [86].

[xv] **The connection between type structure and data structure** —
This observation was made by Martin Löf [130], and later by many others, including by Roland Backhouse in his work on type theory [13].

[xvi] **The Group's diverse interests** —
Our methods have been applied to separation logic [56], pointer structures [34,142], database queries [79,146], geographic information systems [145], climate change [39,108,110], scientific computation [109], planning [36] and logistics [172], and domain-specific languages for parsing/pretty printing/program calculation.

[xvii] **Beginner's programming languages** —
Beginner's programming languages designed and implemented by Group members include Peter King's *MABEL*, Kees Koster's *ELAN*, and Lambert Meertens' *ABC* [74].

[xviii] **Inspiration for Python** —
ABC's influence on Python [176] can be seen at Guido van Rossum's biographical page, and at the ABC and Python pages on Wikipedia:
https://gvanrossum.github.io/bio.html
https://en.wikipedia.org/wiki/ABC_(programming_language)
https://en.wikipedia.org/wiki/Python_(programming_language)

[xix] **Revised Report on ALGOL 68** —
ALGOL 68 was designed by WG2.1 at the direction of TC2. On December 20, 1968, the language was formally adopted by the Group, and subsequently approved for publication by the General Assembly of IFIP.

[xx] **Example of Abstracto** —
This example is from Lambert Meertens [135].

[xxi] **Refinement calculus** —
The 'Abstracto vision' was Lambert Meertens'. It was developed in much greater depth by Ralph Back (independently) [9,10] and, later, by Carroll Morgan [151,152]. When Morgan asked Meertens why he had not pursued the refinement calculus further, Meertens' reply was "It didn't work."

[xxii] **Higher-level reasoning** —
Meertens became disillusioned with Abstracto's low-level transformations, as described in [137]. It was Richard Bird who provided the key insight needed to lift the reasoning to a higher level [30]. Examples are given in [136].

[xxiii] **Program transformations** —
These examples, and many others, were described by Bird [30].

[xxiv] **Evolving notation** —
Bird took the work forwards through the 1980's, notably in a series of tutorial papers [31–33] produced in quick succession; an example, the calculation for the Maximum Segment Sum problem, is shown in Fig. 3.

[xxv] **The names "Squiggol" and "BMF"** —
Meertens recalls that Robert Dewar passed a note to him with the single word "Squigol" on it, making a pun with language names such as ALGOL, COBOL, and SNOBOL [138]. The first appearance of the name in the minutes is for Meeting #35 in Sausalito in December 1985. However, it has come to be written "Squiggol", perhaps to emphasise that the pronunciation should be ˈskwɪgɒl ("qui") rather than ˈskwaɪgɒl ("quae"). Later, at a meeting of the STOP project in Nijmegen in 1988, Doaitse Swierstra coined the more sober name "Bird–Meertens Formalism" (BMF), making a different pun with "Backus–Naur Form" (BNF).

[xxvi] **The Eindhoven quantifier notation** —
The Eindhoven quantifier notation rationalised the notation for binding a variable, determining its range and forming elements from it [11,153]. In the conventional $\sum_{n=0}^{N} n^2$ for example, the n below the $\sum$ is a binding occurrence; but the n in n^2 is bound; and the n^2 forms elements from that bound variable. The 0 and the N determine the range of n, and the $\sum$ itself gives the 'quantifier', the operation (usually associative and commutative) carried out on the elements. In the Eindhoven notation that would be written in the order quantifier, bound variable(s), range, element-former. The whole expression is *always* enclosed by binding-scope delimiters — so the example above might be written $(+n : 0 \le n \le N : n^2)$.
The advantage of using the Eindhoven notation is that uniform calculational laws apply to the manipulation of those expressions, and they greatly reduce the risk of error.

[xxvii] **Catamorphisms** —
Meertens coined the term catamorphism for the unique function induced by a homomorphism from the initial algebra, in a working document presented at Meeting #38 in Rome (1988).

[xxviii] **Datatype-generic programming** —
The term 'datatype-generic programming' was coined by Roland Backhouse and Jeremy Gibbons for a project that ran 2003–2006 [14]; the point was to distinguish from the different use of the term 'generic programming' in languages like C++, where it essentially means parametric polymorphism. Within the context of the Group, 'datatype-generic programming' has come to mean parametrization by a functor, as with catamorphisms, and plain 'generic programming' to mean functions defined more specifically over the sum-of-products structure of a polynomial functor, as with PolyP and Generic Haskell.

[xxix] **Polytypic programming languages and PolyP —**
The language PolyP, an extension of the lazy, higher-order functional programming language Haskell [173], was designed by Jansson and Jeuring at Chalmers, Gothenburg [111]. The development of PolyP and its applications was discussed at Meeting #49 in Rancho Santa Fe (1996), Meeting #51 in Oxford (1998), and Meeting #53 in Potsdam (1999).

[xxx] **Generic datatypes with mutual recursion —**
The theory to make Generic Haskell possible was developed by Hinze, a first-time observer in Potsdam (1999). He presented his theory at Meeting #54 in Blackheath (2000) [91]. To support generic functions on sets of mutually recursive datatypes, Hinze, Jeuring, and Löh developed Generic Haskell from 2000 onwards [94,119]. Various aspects of Generic Haskell were discussed also at Meeting #59 in Nottingham in 2004.

[xxxi] **Type-indexed datatypes —**
Type-indexed datatypes were introduced by Hinze et al. [94]. The type families extension of Haskell is based on the work of Chakravarty et al. [50].

[xxxii] **Fixed-point representation of mutually recursive datatypes —**
Rodriguez and others developed MultiRec [178], a generic programming library that uses a fixed-point representation of possibly mutually recursive datatypes.

[xxxiii] **Generic programming libraries —**
For an early comparison of generic programming libraries, see Rodriguez et al. [177]. An early variant of Scrap Your Boilerplate [118] was discussed at Meeting #56 on Ameland, The Netherlands (2001). Generic Deriving [122] was discussed at Meeting #70 in Ulm.

[xxxiv] **Catamorphisms —**
This work was done mainly by Grant Malcolm [126].

[xxxv] **A zoo of morphisms —**
There were mutumorphisms [71], which are pairs of mutually recursive functions; zygomorphisms [125], which consist of a main recursive function and an auxiliary one on which it depends; histomorphisms [195], in which the body has access to the recursive images of all subterms, not just the immediate ones; so-called generalised folds [28], which use polymorphic recursion to handle nested datatypes; and then there were generic accumulations [163], which keep intermediate results in additional paramters for later stages in the computation.

[xxxvi] **Paramorphism —**
This was introduced by Lambert Meertens at Meeting #41 in Burton, UK (1990) [139].

[xxxvii] **Recursion schemes from comonads —**
This appeared in Uustalu et al [197]. Comonads capture the general idea of 'evaluation in context' [196], and this scheme makes contextual information available to the body of the recursion. It was used to subsume both zygomorphisms and histomorphisms.

[xxxviii] **Adjoint folds** —
This was done by Hinze [92]. Using adjunctions as the common thread, adjoint folds arise by inserting a left adjoint functor into the recursive characterisation, thereby adapting the form of the recursion; they subsume paramorphisms, accumulating folds, mutumorphisms (and hence zygomorphisms), and generalised folds. Later, it was observed that adjoint folds could be used to subsume recursion schemes from comonads by Hinze and Wu [93].

[xxxix] **Constructive mathematics and computer programming** —
The connection between constructive mathematics and computer programming was pioneered by the Swedish philosopher and logician Per Martin-Löf [130].

[xl] **Programming languages implementing dependent types** —
Programming languages with dependent types include ALF [124], Cayenne [7], ATS [203], Epigram [132], Agda [159] and Idris [44].

[xli] **Curry-Howard correspondence** —
The Curry-Howard correspondence describes how the typing rules of the lambda calculus are in one-to-one correspondence with the natural deduction rules in logic. Wadler [200] gives a historic overview of this idea, aimed at a more general audience.

[xlii] **Generic programming in dependently typed languages** —
The idea of using dependent types to define an explicit *universe* of types was one of the early applications of dependently typed programming [4, 27]. Since then, there have been several PhD theses exploring this idea further [53,57,115,123,155,159]

[xliii] **WG2.1 and dependent types** —
Backhouse started exploring type theory in the mid 1980's [13]. At Meeting #42, Nordström was invited as an observer and talked about the work on ALF. Throughout the early 21st century, observers and members were frequently active in the area of type theory or generic programming, including McBride, Löh, Jansson, Swierstra, Dagand, McKinna and many others.

[xliv] **Algebra of programming in Agda** —
Patrik Jansson gave a first tutorial on the dependently typed programming language Agda at Meeting #63 in Kyoto in 2007. This lead to an exploration of how to mechanize the kind of program that was previously carried out on paper [156].

[xlv] **Program calculation and type theory** —
As type theory is a language for describing both proofs and programs, it is no surprise that it provides the ideal setting for formalizing the program calculation techniques that members of the Group pioneered [3, 190,192].

[xlvi] **Applications of dependent types** —
As languages with dependent types matured, various researchers started exploring novel and unexpected applications in a variety of domains [40, 58,109,110].

[xlvii] **Dependently typed combinator parsing** —
This was for example investigated by Nils Danielsson [58].

[xlviii] **Dependent types and program development** —
Many modern dependently typed programming languages are equipped
with some sort of IDE. Once the type signature of a method has been
fixed, the programmer can interactively find a suitable definition. There
are numerous examples of how a powerful type signature can give strong
guarantees about a data structure's invariants [131], the correctness of a
domain-specific language [59], or type preservation of a compiler [134].

[xlix] **Dependent types and effects** —
There is a large body of work studying how to incorporate side-effects
in dependently typed programming languages. This can be done by constructing denotational models [189, 191], by adding new effectful primitives to the type theory [157], or by giving an algebraic account of the
properties that laws that effects satisfy [45, 77].

[l] **Monads** —
This insight was made by Eugenio Moggi while studying semantics of
programming languages [141].

[li] **Kleisli arrows** —
Mike Spivey adopted this notion of monads for writing purely functional
programs with exceptions [186]; Phil Wadler generalized it to other
effects, and popularized it as the main abstraction for dealing with
effects in Haskell [198, 199].

[lii] **Parser combinators** —
The combinator style of parsing is due to William Burge [48]. The
monadic presentation was popularized by Graham Hutton and Erik
Meijer [107], and a dependently typed version presented by Nils Danielsson [xlvii].

[liii] **Parsers in verse** —
The verse characterization of the parser type is due Fritz Ruehr [179].

[liv] **Applicative functors** —
The applicative interface for parsers was invented by Doaitse Swierstra [188]. This and other applications inspired Conor McBride and
Ross Paterson to identify the abstraction of *applicative functors* (also
called "strong lax-monoidal functors" or "idioms") [133]. Like monads,
applicative functors have turned out to have unforeseen applications,
such as in datatype traversals [29, 78] and distributed computing [75].

[lv] **Algebraic effects** —
Purely functional specifications of effects were studied by Wouter Swierstra in his PhD thesis [189, 191]. The axioms of an algebraic specification
can be applied to equational reasoning involving either combinators or
the imperative-flavoured comprehension notation provided for example
by Haskell's **do** notation [77]. Algebraic effects and handlers were introduced by Gordon Plotkin then explored more fully in Matija Pretnar's
PhD thesis [175], and are now the subject of much active work in the
Group and beyond.

[lvi] **Applications of relation algebra —**
Roland Backhouse and B.A. Carré discovered similarities between an
algebra for path problems and the algebra of regular languages [15].
Tony Hoare and others developed algebraic laws of programming, insisting that "specifications obey all the laws of the calculus of relations"
[97]. Richard Bird and Oege de Moor used relations for the calculational
derivation of programs covering principles of algorithm design such as
dynamic programming, greedy algorithms, exhaustive search and divide
and conquer [35].

[lvii] **Algebra of binary relations —**
Calculi based on the algebra of binary relations were developed by
George Boole, Charles Peirce, Ernst Schröder, Augustus De Morgan
and Alfred Tarski [171, 180, 194].

[lviii] **Graph algorithms —**
Walter Guttmann, for example, showed that the same correctness proof
shows that well-known algorithms solve the minimum weight spanning
tree problem, the minimum bottleneck spanning tree problem and similar optimisation problems with different aggregation functions [84].
Algebraic versions of Dijkstra's shortest path algorithm and the one
by Floyd/Warshall are applications of these algorithms to structures
different from graphs, pinpointing the mathematical requirements on
the underlying cost algebra that ensure their correctness [102]. Roland
Backhouse and colleagues are currently writing a book on algorithmic
graph theory presented relationally [18].

[lix] **Program analysis —**
Program analysis using an algebraic style of reasoning has always been
a core activity of the Group; for examples see [62, 63, 66].

[lx] **Pointer structures —**
Bernhard Möller and Richard Bird researched representations of data
structures in general, and pointer structures in particular [34, 142].

[lxi] **Algebraic logics —**
An important step to an algebraic form of program logic was taken
by Hoare and his colleagues [97]. More recently, the central aspects of
Separation Logic [160, 161] were treated algebraically [54–56].
Next to programming semantics, the infinite iteration operator can be
applied to model various logics. The temporal logics LTL, CTL and
CTL* have been in [60, 114, 150]. There were studies on logics for hybrid
systems [100, 101] and Neighbourhood Logic [99].

[lxii] **Further applications of the algebraic approach —**
The Group discovered countless areas in computer science where semirings are the underlying structure. Applications reach from, fundamental concepts of programming language semantics, including concurrent
programs [98] and termination [16, 61, 66, 90] via games [12, 17, 183] and
data processing [174], to multi-agent systems [144] and quantum computing [193].
Beyond that, matrix-style reasoning has applications in object-oriented

programming [121] and feature-oriented software development, including aspects of product families [106] and of feature interactions [20].

[lxiii] **Algebraic semantics of the while loop** —
The fixed-point characterisation of while loops goes back to Andrzej Blikle and David Park [37,164]. Dexter Kozen transferred the concept into the setting of Kleene algebras [116].

[lxiv] **Algebras with tests** —
Test elements form a Boolean subalgebra. It represents an algebraic version of the usual assertion logics like the Hoare calculus [117,147]. There is a direct link to weakest (liberal) preconditions [35,148].

[lxv] **Fixed-point fusion** —
Fixed-point fusion is a consequence of the fixed-point semantics of recursion [1,140].

[lxvi] **Virtual data structures** —
These were described by Doaitse Swierstra and Oege de Moor [187].

[lxvii] **Omega algebras** —
The omega operator was introduce by Cohen [51]; Möller performed a systematic study of its foundations [143].
Guttmann used it for analysing executions of lazy and strict computations [82]. Infinite traces, also called *streams*, have many applications including the modelling protocols [142], as well as dynamic and hybrid systems [100,183,184] . The corresponding algebras can also be used to formally reason about (non)termination in classical programs [104].

[lxviii] **Tool-Support for algebraic reasoning** —
Peter Höfner and Georg Struth proved countless theorems of all these algebras in automated theorem provers, such as Prover9 [103,105]. Walter Guttmann, Peter Höfner, Georg Struth and others used the interactive proof assistant Isabelle/HOL to implement the algebras, the concrete models, as well as many program derivations, e.g. [5,6,80,83].

[lxix] **Program transformation** —
In the functional realm, fundamental ideas in program transformation were introduced by Cooper [52] and subsequently developed by others, in particular Burstall and Darlington [49]. Later activities occurred within the ISI project [19,120] and at Kestrel Institute [81]. In the realm of artificial intelligence there were ideas in the field of automated programming (e.g., the DEDALUS system [127] and its successor [128,129]).

[lxx] **Refinement calculi** —
Imperative programming calculi based on refinement include those of Dijkstra [65], Back [8], Hoare [96,97], Hehner [87–89], Morris [154], and Morgan [151,152].

[lxxi] **Transformational development** —
For background on the 'life cycle of transformational program development', see Broy [2]. The five levels of the 'wide spectrum' are due to Partsch [168].

[lxxii] **The language CIP-L** —
The language CIP-L is described in detail in the first of two volumes about the CIP project as a whole [24]. For some of the motivation, see Bauer [22] and Broy and Pepper [47].

[lxxiii] **The system CIP-S** —
The specification of the CIP-S system can be found in the second volume about the CIP project [25]. The more interesting parts of the formal development of the system, together with the transformation rules used, can also be found there. Successors to CIP-S were developed by Partsch [169] and Guttmann *et al.* [85].

[lxxiv] **Experiences with CIP** —
Smaller CIP case studies include sorting [46,165] and parsing [166–168]. As noted above, the CIP-S system itself [25] constitutes a larger case study.

[lxxv] **Programs should be grown** —
Fred Brooks wrote "Some years ago Harlan Mills proposed that any software system should be grown by incremental development." [72]

Acknowledgements. Section 2 is based on a paper more specifically about the evolution of the Bird–Meertens Formalism [76], Sect. 3 partly based on a paper about the contributions to generic programming of the Software Technology group at Utrecht University [112], and Sect. 4 partly based on a paper about the unification of recursion schemes [93].

References

1. Aarts, C., et al.: Fixed-point calculus. Inf. Process. Lett. **53**(3), 131–136 (1995)
2. Agresti, W.M.: What are the new paradigms? In: Agresti, W.M. (ed.) New Paradigms for Software Development. IEEE Computer Society Press (1986)
3. Alpuim, J., Swierstra, W.: Embedding the refinement calculus in Coq. Sci. Comput. Program. **164**, 37–48 (2018)
4. Altenkirch, T., Mcbride, C.: Generic programming within dependently typed programming. In: Gibbons, J., Jeuring, J. (eds.) Generic Programming. ITIFIP, vol. 115, pp. 1–20. Springer, Boston, MA (2003). https://doi.org/10.1007/978-0-387-35672-3_1
5. Armstrong, A., Struth, G., Weber, T.: Kleene algebra. Archive of Formal Proofs (2013). http://isa-afp.org/entries/Kleene_Algebra.html
6. Armstrong, A., Foster, S., Struth, G., Weber, T.: Relation algebra. Archive of Formal Proofs (2014). http://isa-afp.org/entries/Relation_Algebra.html
7. Augustsson, L.: Cayenne - a language with dependent types. In: International Conference on Functional Programming, ICFP 1998, pp. 239–250 (1998)
8. Back, R.J.: On the correctness of refinement steps in program development. PhD thesis. Report A-1978-4, Department of Computer Science, University of Helsinki (1978)
9. Back, R.J.: On correct refinement of programs. J. Comput. Syst. Sci. **23**(1), 49–68 (1981). https://doi.org/10.1016/0022-0000(81)90005-2

10. Back, R.J., von Wright, J.: Refinement Calculus: A Systematic Introduction. Graduate Texts in Computer Science, Springer (1998). https://doi.org/10.1007/978-1-4612-1674-2_4

11. Backhouse, R.: An exploration of the Bird-Meertens formalism. Technical report CS 8810, Department of Computer Science, Groningen University (1988)

12. Backhouse, R., Michaelis, D.: Fixed-point characterisation of winning strategies in impartial games. In: Berghammer, R., Möller, B., Struth, G. (eds.) Relational and Kleene-Algebraic Methods in Computer Science. Lecture Notes in Computer Science, vol. 3051, pp. 34–47. Springer (2004)

13. Backhouse, R., Chisholm, P., Malcolm, G., Saaman, E.: Do-it-yourself type theory. Formal Aspects Comput. **1**(1), 19–84 (1989)

14. Backhouse, R., Gibbons, J., Hinze, R., Jeuring, J. (eds.): Spring School on Datatype-Generic Programming, Lecture Notes in Computer Science, vol. 4719. Springer-Verlag (2007). https://doi.org/10.1007/978-3-540-76786-2

15. Backhouse, R.C., Carré, B.A.: Regular algebra applied to path-finding problems. IMA J. Appl. Math. **15**(2), 161–186 (1975). https://doi.org/10.1093/imamat/15.2.161

16. Backhouse, R.C., Doornbos, H.: Datatype-generic termination proofs. Theor. Comput. Syst. **43**(3–4), 362–393 (2008). https://doi.org/10.1007/s00224-007-9056-z

17. Backhouse, R.C., Chen, W., Ferreira, J.F.: The algorithmics of solitaire-like games. Sci. Comput. Program. **78**(11), 2029–2046 (2013). https://doi.org/10.1016/j.scico.2012.07.007

18. Backhouse, R.C., Doornbos, H., Glück, R., van der Woude, J.: Elements of algorithmic graph theory: an exercise in point-free reasoning, (working document) (2019)

19. Balzer, R., Goldman, N., Wile, D.: On the transformational implementation approach to programming. In: Yeh, R.T., Ramamoorthy, C.V. (eds.) International Conference on Software Engineering, IEEE Computer Society, pp. 337–344 (1976)

20. Batory, D.S., Höfner, P., Kim, J.: Feature interactions, products, and composition. In: Denney, E., Schultz, U.P. (eds.) Generative Programming and Component Engineering. ACM, pp. 13–22 (2011). https://doi.org/10.1145/2047862.2047867

21. Bauer, F.L.: Programming as an evolutionary process. In: Yeh, R.T., Ramamoorthy, C. (eds.) International Conference on Software Engineering, IEEE Computer Society, pp. 223–234 (1976)

22. Bauer, F.L.: From specifications to machine code: Program construction through formal reasoning. In: Ohno, Y., Basili, V., Enomoto, H., Kobayashi, K., Yeh, R.T. (eds.) International Conference on Software Engineering, IEEE Computer Society, pp. 84–91 (1982)

23. Bauer, F.L., Wössner, H.: Algorithmic Language and Program Development. Texts and Monographs in Computer Science. Springer (1982). https://doi.org/10.1007/978-3-642-61807-9

24. Bauer, F.L., et al.: The Munich Project CIP, Volume I: The Wide Spectrum Language CIP-L. Lecture Notes in Computer Science, vol. 183. Springer (1985). https://doi.org/10.1007/3-540-15187-7

25. Bauer, F.L., et al.: The Munich Project CIP, Volume II: The Program Transformation System CIP-S, Lecture Notes in Computer Science, vol. 292. Springer-Verlag, Berlin (1987). https://doi.org/10.1007/3-540-18779-0

26. Bemer, R.: A politico-social history of ALGOL. In: Annual Review of Automatic Programming 5, pp. 151–237. Pergamon Press, Oxford (1969)

27. Benke, M., Dybjer, P., Jansson, P.: Universes for generic programs and proofs in dependent type theory. Nordic J. Comput. **10**(4), 265–289 (2003)
28. Bird, R., Paterson, R.: Generalised folds for nested datatypes. Formal Aspects Comput. **11**(2), 200–222 (1999). https://doi.org/10.1007/s001650050047
29. Bird, R., Gibbons, J., Mehner, S., Voigtländer, J., Schrijvers, T.: Understanding idiomatic traversals backwards and forwards. In: Haskell Symposium. ACM (2013). https://doi.org/10.1145/25037782503781 (2013)
30. Bird, R.S.: Some notational suggestions for transformational programming. Working Paper NIJ-3, IFIP WG2.1, also Technical Report RCS 144, Department of Computer Science, University of Reading (1981)
31. Bird, R.S.: An introduction to the theory of lists. Monograph PRG-56, Programming Research Group, University of Oxford (1986)
32. Bird, R.S.: A calculus of functions for program derivation. Monograph PRG-64, Programming Research Group, University of Oxford (1987)
33. Bird, R.S.: Lectures on constructive functional programming. Monograph PRG-69, Programming Research Group, University of Oxford (1988)
34. Bird, R.S.: Unfolding pointer algorithms. J. Funct. Program. **11**(3), 347–358 (2001). https://doi.org/10.1017/S0956796801003914
35. Bird, R.S., de Moor, O.: Algebra of Programming. Prentice Hall International Series in Computer Science. Prentice Hall, Hoboken (1997)
36. Blaine, L., Gilham, L., Liu, J., Smith, D.R., Westfold, S.J.: Planware: domain-specific synthesis of high-performance schedulers. In: Automated Software Engineering, IEEE Computer Society, p. 270 (1998). https://doi.org/10.1109/ASE.1998.732672
37. Blikle, A.: Iterative systems: An algebraic approach. Bulletin de l'Académie Polonaise des Sciences, Série des sciences mathématiques, astronomiques et physiques XX(1) (1972)
38. Boom, H.: Further thoughts on Abstracto. Working Paper ELC-9, IFIP WG2.1 (1981)
39. Botta, N., Jansson, P., Ionescu, C.: Contributions to a computational theory of policy advice and avoidability. J. Funct. Programm. **27**, e23 (2017). https://doi.org/10.1017/S0956796817000156
40. Botta, N., Jansson, P., Ionescu, C., Christiansen, D.R., Brady, E.: Sequential decision problems, dependent types and generic solutions. Logical Meth. Comput. Sci. **13**(1) (2017). https://doi.org/10.23638/LMCS-13(1:7)2017
41. Boyle, J., Harmer, T.J., Winter, V.L.: The TAMPR program transformation system: simplifying the development of numerical software. In: Arge, E., Bruaset, A.M., Langtangen, H.P. (eds,) Modern Software Tools for Scientific Computing, Birkhäuser, pp. 353–372 (1996). https://doi.org/10.1007/978-1-4612-1986-6_17
42. Boyle, J.M.: An introduction to Transformation-Assisted Multiple Program Realization (TAMPR) system. In: Bunch, J.R. (ed.) Cooperative Development of Mathematical Software, Department of Mathematics, University of California, San Diego (1976)
43. Boyle, J.M., Dritz, K.W.: An automated programming system to facilitate the development of quality mathematical software. In: Rosenfeld, J. (ed.) IFIP Congress, North-Holland, pp. 542–546 (1974)
44. Brady, E.: Idris, a general-purpose dependently typed programming language: design and implementation. J. Funct. Program. **23**(5), 552–593 (2013)
45. Brady, E.: Programming and reasoning with algebraic effects and dependent types. In: International Conference on Functional Programming, pp. 133–144 (2013)

46. Broy, M.: Program construction by transformations: a family tree of sorting programs. In: Biermann, A., Guiho, G. (eds.) Computer Program Synthesis Methodologies, NATO Advanced Study Institutes Series, vol. 95. Springer (1983). https://doi.org/10.1007/978-94-009-7019-9_1

47. Broy, M., Pepper, P.: On the coherence of programming language and programming methodology. In: Bormann, (ed.) IFIP Working Conference on Programming Languages and System Design, North-Holland, pp. 41–53 (1983)

48. Burge, W.H.: Recursive Programming Techniques. Addison-Wesley, Boston (1975)

49. Burstall, R.M., Darlington, J.: A transformation system for developing recursive programs. J. ACM **24**(1), 44–67 (1977)

50. Chakravarty, M.M.T., Keller, G., Jones, S.L.P., Marlow, S.: Associated types with class. In: Palsberg, J., Abadi, M. (eds.) Principles of Programming Languages. ACM, pp. 1–13 (2005). https://doi.org/10.1145/1040305.1040306

51. Cohen, E.: Separation and reduction. In: Backhouse, R., Oliveira, J.N. (eds.) MPC 2000. LNCS, vol. 1837, pp. 45–59. Springer, Heidelberg (2000). https://doi.org/10.1007/10722010_4

52. Cooper, D.: The equivalence of certain computations. Comput. J. **9**, 45–52 (1966)

53. Dagand, P.E., et al.: A cosmology of datatypes: Reusability and dependent types. Ph.D. thesis, University of Strathclyde (2013)

54. Dang, H., Möller, B.: Concurrency and local reasoning under reverse exchange. Sci. Comput. Programm. **85**, Part B, 204–223 (2013)

55. Dang, H., Möller, B.: Extended transitive separation logic. J. Logical Algebraic Meth. Programm. **84**(3), 303–325 (2015). https://doi.org/10.1016/j.jlamp.2014.12.002

56. Dang, H., Höfner, P., Möller, B.: Algebraic separation logic. J. Logic Algebraic Programm. **80**(6), 221–247 (2011). https://doi.org/10.1016/j.jlap.2011.04.003

57. Danielsson, N.A.: Functional program correctness through types. Ph.D. thesis, Chalmers University of Technology and Gothenburg University (2007)

58. Danielsson, N.A.: Total parser combinators. In: International Conference on Functional Programming, pp. 285–296 (2010)

59. Danielsson, N.A.: Correct-by-construction pretty-printing. In: Workshop on Dependently-Typed Programming, pp. 1–12 (2013)

60. Desharnais, J., Möller, B.: Non-associative Kleene algebra and temporal logics. In: Höfner, P., Pous, D., Struth, G. (eds.) Relational and Algebraic Methods in Computer Science. Lecture Notes in Computer Science, vol. 10226, pp. 93–108 (2017). https://doi.org/10.1007/978-3-319-57418-9_6

61. Desharnais, J., Möller, B., Struth, G.: Termination in modal Kleene algebra. In: Mayr, E.W., Mitchell, J.C., Lévy, J.J. (eds.) Exploring New Frontiers of Theoretical Informatics, pp. 647–660, Kluwer (2004)

62. Desharnais, J., Möller, B., Struth, G.: Kleene algebra with domain. ACM Trans. Comput. Log. **7**(4), 798–833 (2006)

63. Desharnais, J., Möller, B., Tchier, F.: Kleene under a modal demonic star. J. Logic Algebraic Programm. **66**(2), 127–160 (2006). https://doi.org/10.1016/j.jlap.2005.04.006

64. Dewar, R.: Letter to members of IFIP WG2.1 (1977). http://ershov-arc.iis.nsk.su/archive/eaindex.asp?did=29067

65. Dijkstra, E.W.: A Discipline of Programming. Prentice Hall, Hoboken (1976)

66. Doornbos, H., Backhouse, R.C.: Algebra of program termination. In: Backhouse, R.C., Crole, R.L., Gibbons, J. (eds.) Algebraic and Coalgebraic Methods in the

Mathematics of Program Construction, Lecture Notes in Computer Science, vol. 2297, pp. 203–236. Springer (2000). https://doi.org/10.1007/3-540-47797-7_6

67. Feather, M.S.: A system for developing programs by transformation. Ph.D thesis, University of Edinburgh, UK (1979). http://hdl.handle.net/1842/7296

68. Feather, M.S.: A system for assisting program transformation. ACM Trans. Programm. Lang. **4**(1), 1–20 (1982). https://doi.org/10.1145/357153.357154

69. Feather, M.S.: A survey and classification of some program transformation approaches and techniques. In: Meertens, L. (ed.) Program Specification and Transformation, North-Holland, pp. 165–195 (1987)

70. Floyd, R.W.: Assigning meaning to programs. In: Schwartz, J.T. (ed.) Mathematical Aspects of Computer Science, American Mathematical Society, Proceedings of Symposia in Applied Mathematics, vol. 19, pp. 19–32 (1967)

71. Fokkinga, M.: Tupling and mutumorphisms. The Squiggolist **1**(4), 81–82 (1990)

72. Brooks, J.F.: The Mythical Man-Month. Addison-Wesley, Boston (1975)

73. Geurts, L., Meertens, L.: Remarks on Abstracto. Algol. Bull. **42**, 56–63 (1978)

74. Geurts, L., Meertens, L., Pemberton, S.: The ABC Programmer's Handbook. Prentice-Hall, Hoboken, iSBN 0-13-000027-2 (1990)

75. Gibbons, J.: Free delivery (functional pearl). In: Haskell Symposium, pp. 45–50 (2016). https://doi.org/10.1145/2976002.2976005

76. Gibbons, J.: The school of Squiggol: A history of the Bird-Meertens formalism. In: Astarte, T. (ed.) Workshop on the History of Formal Methods. Springer-Verlag, Lecture Notes in Computer Science (2020). (to appear)

77. Gibbons, J., Hinze, R.: Just do it: Simple monadic equational reasoning. In: International Conference on Functional Programming, pp. 2–14 (2011). https://doi.org/10.1145/2034773.2034777

78. Gibbons, J., dos Santos Oliveira, B.C.: The essence of the iterator pattern. J. Funct. Programm. **19**(3,4), 377–402 (2009). https://doi.org/10.1017/S0956796809007291

79. Gibbons, J., Henglein, F., Hinze, R., Wu, N.: Relational algebra by way of adjunctions. Proc. ACM Programm. Lang. **2**(ICFP), 86:1–86:28 (2018). https://doi.org/10.1145/3236781

80. Gomes, V.B.F., Guttmann, W., Höfner, P., Struth, G., Weber, T.: Kleene algebras with domain. Archive of Formal Proofs (2016). http://isa-afp.org/entries/KAD.html

81. Green, C., et al.: Research on knowledge-based programming and algorithm design. Technical report Kes.U.81.2, Kestrel Institute (1981, revised 1982) (1981)

82. Guttmann, W.: Infinite executions of lazy and strict computations. J. Logical Algebraic Meth. Programm. **84**(3), 326–340 (2015). https://doi.org/10.1016/j.jlamp.2014.08.001

83. Guttmann, W.: Stone algebras. Archive of Formal Proofs (2016). http://isa-afp.org/entries/Stone_Algebras.html

84. Guttmann, W.: An algebraic framework for minimum spanning tree problems. Theoret. Comput. Sci. **744**, 37–55 (2018)

85. Guttmann, W., Partsch, H., Schulte, W., Vullinghs, T.: Tool support for the interactive derivation of formally correct functional programs. J. Univ. Comput. Sci. **9**(2), 173 (2003). https://doi.org/10.3217/jucs-009-02-0173

86. Hagino, T.: A categorical programming language. Ph.D thesis, University of Edinburgh, UK (1987)

87. Hehner, E.C.R.: Predicative programming, part I. Commun. ACM **27**(2), 134–143 (1984). https://doi.org/10.1145/69610.357988

88. Hehner, E.C.R.: Predicative programming, part II. Commun. ACM **27**(2), 144–151 (1984). https://doi.org/10.1145/69610.357990

89. Hehner, E.C.R.: A Practical Theory of Programming. Springer (1993). https://doi.org/10.1007/978-1-4419-8596-5_7

90. Hehner, E.C.R.: Specifications, programs, and total correctness. Sci. Comput. Program. **34**(3), 191–205 (1999). https://doi.org/10.1016/S0167-6423(98)00027-6

91. Hinze, R.: Polytypic values possess polykinded types. Sci. Comput. Program. **43**(2–3), 129–159 (2002)

92. Hinze, R.: Adjoint folds and unfolds–an extended study. Sci. Comput. Program. **78**(11), 2108–2159 (2013). https://doi.org/10.1016/j.scico.2012.07.011

93. Hinze, R., Wu, N.: Unifying structured recursion schemes: an extended study. J. Funct. Program. **26**, 47 (2016)

94. Hinze, R., Jeuring, J., Löh, A.: Type-indexed data types. Sci. Comput. Program. **51**(1–2), 117–151 (2004)

95. Hoare, C.A.R.: An axiomatic basis for computer programming. Commun. ACM **12**(10), 576–580 (1969). https://doi.org/10.1145/363235.363259

96. Hoare, C.A.R.: Programs are predicates. Philosophical Transactions of the Royal Society of London (A 312), 475–489 (1984)

97. Hoare, C.A.R., et al.: Laws of programming. Commun. ACM **30**(8), 672–686 (1987). https://doi.org/10.1145/27651.27653

98. Hoare, T., Möller, B., Struth, G., Wehrman, I.: Concurrent Kleene algebra and its foundations. J. Logic Algebraic Programm. **80**(6), 266–296 (2011). https://doi.org/10.1016/j.jlap.2011.04.005

99. Höfner, P., Möller, B.: Algebraic neighbourhood logic. J. Logic Algebraic Programm. **76**, 35–59 (2008)

100. Höfner, P., Möller, B.: An algebra of hybrid systems. J. Logic Algebraic Programm. **78**, 74–97 (2009). https://doi.org/10.1016/j.jlap.2008.08.005

101. Höfner, P., Möller, B.: Fixing Zeno gaps. Theoret. Comput. Sci. **412**(28), 3303–3322 (2011). https://doi.org/10.1016/j.tcs.2011.03.018

102. Höfner, P., Möller, B.: Dijkstra, Floyd and Warshall meet Kleene. Formal Aspects Comput. **24**(4–6), 459–476 (2012). https://doi.org/10.1007/s00165-012-0245-4

103. Höfner, P., Struth, G.: Automated reasoning in Kleene algebra. In: Pfenning, F. (ed.) CADE 2007. LNCS (LNAI), vol. 4603, pp. 279–294. Springer, Heidelberg (2007). https://doi.org/10.1007/978-3-540-73595-3_19

104. Höfner, P., Struth, G.: Non-termination in idempotent semirings. In: Berghammer, R., Möller, B., Struth, G. (eds.) RelMiCS 2008. LNCS, vol. 4988, pp. 206–220. Springer, Heidelberg (2008). https://doi.org/10.1007/978-3-540-78913-0_16

105. Höfner, P., Struth, G.: On automating the calculus of relations. In: Armando, A., Baumgartner, P., Dowek, G. (eds.) IJCAR 2008. LNCS (LNAI), vol. 5195, pp. 50–66. Springer, Heidelberg (2008). https://doi.org/10.1007/978-3-540-71070-7_5

106. Höfner, P., Khédri, R., Möller, B.: Supplementing product families with behaviour. Softw. Inform. **5**(1–2), 245–266 (2011)

107. Hutton, G., Meijer, E.: Monadic parsing in Haskell. J. Funct. Program. **8**(4), 437–444 (1998). https://doi.org/10.1017/S0956796898003050

108. Ionescu, C.: Vulnerability modelling with functional programming and dependent types. Math. Struct. Comput. Sci. **26**(1), 114–128 (2016). https://doi.org/10.1017/S0960129514000139

109. Ionescu, C., Jansson, P.: Dependently-typed programming in scientific computing. In: Hinze, R. (ed.) IFL 2012. LNCS, vol. 8241, pp. 140–156. Springer, Heidelberg (2013). https://doi.org/10.1007/978-3-642-41582-1_9

110. Ionescu, C., Jansson, P.: Testing versus proving in climate impact research. In: TYPES 2011, Schloss Dagstuhl-Leibniz-Zentrum für Informatik, Dagstuhl, Germany, Leibniz International Proceedings in Informatics (LIPIcs), vol. 19, pp. 41–54 (2013). https://doi.org/10.4230/LIPIcs.TYPES.2011.41

111. Jansson, P., Jeuring, J.: PolyP – a polytypic programming language extension. In: Principles of Programming Languages, pp. 470–482 (1997)

112. Jeuring, J., Meertens, L.: Geniaal programmeren-generic programming at Utrecht-. In: et al. HB (ed.) Fascination for computation, 25 jaar opleiding informatica, Department of Information and Computing Sciences, Utrecht University, pp. 75–88 (2009)

113. Johnson, W.L., Feather, M.S., Harris, D.R.: The KBSA requirements/specifications facet: ARIES. In: Knowledge-Based Software Engineering, IEEE Computer Society, pp. 48–56 (1991). https://doi.org/10.1109/KBSE.1991.638020

114. von Karger, B., Berghammer, R.: A relational model for temporal logic. Logic J. IGPL **6**, 157–173 (1998)

115. Ko, H.S.: Analysis and synthesis of inductive families. DPhil thesis, Oxford University, UK (2014)

116. Kozen, D.: Kleene algebra with tests. ACM Trans. Program. Lang. Syst. **19**(3), 427–443 (1997)

117. Kozen, D.: On Hoare logic and Kleene algebra with tests. ACM Trans. Comput. Log. **1**(1), 60–76 (2000)

118. Lämmel, R., Jones, S.P.: Scrap your boilerplate: a practical design pattern for generic programming. In: Types in Language Design and Implementation, pp. 26–37 (2003)

119. Löh, A., Clarke, D., Jeuring, J.: Dependency-style generic Haskell. In: Shivers, O. (ed.) International Conference on Functional Programming. ACM Press, pp. 141–152 (2003)

120. London, P., Feather, M.: Implementing specification freedoms. Sci. Comput. Program. **2**(2), 91–131 (1982)

121. Macedo, H., Oliveira, J.N.: A linear algebra approach to OLAP. Formal Aspects Comput. **27**(2), 283–307 (2015). https://doi.org/10.1007/s00165-014-0316-9

122. Magalhães, J.P., Dijkstra, A., Jeuring, J., Löh, A.: A generic deriving mechanism for Haskell. In: Haskell Symposium, pp. 37–48 (2010)

123. Magalhães, J.P.R.: Less is more: generic programming theory and practice. PhD thesis, Utrecht University, Netherlands (2012)

124. Magnusson, L., Nordström, B.: The ALF proof editor and its proof engine. In: Barendregt, H., Nipkow, T. (eds.) TYPES 1993. LNCS, vol. 806, pp. 213–237. Springer, Heidelberg (1994). https://doi.org/10.1007/3-540-58085-9_78

125. Malcolm, G.: Algebraic data types and program transformation. PhD thesis, University of Groningen (1990)

126. Malcolm, G.: Data structures and program transformation. Sci. Comput. Program. **14**, 255–279 (1990)

127. Manna, Z., Waldinger, R.J.: Synthesis: dreams → programs. IEEE Trans. Software Eng. **5**(4), 294–328 (1979). https://doi.org/10.1109/TSE.1979.234198

128. Manna, Z., Waldinger, R.J.: A deductive approach to program synthesis. ACM Trans. Program. Lang. Syst. **2**(1), 90–121 (1980). https://doi.org/10.1145/357084.357090

129. Manna, Z., Waldinger, R.J.: The Deductive Foundations of Computer Programming. Addison-Wesley, Boston (1993)

130. Martin-Löf, P.: Constructive mathematics and computer programming. In: Studies in Logic and the Foundations of Mathematics, vol. 104, Elsevier, pp. 153–175 (1982)
131. McBride, C.: How to keep your neighbours in order. In: International Conference on Functional Programming, Association for Computing Machinery, New York, NY, USA, ICFP 2014, pp. 297–309 (2014). https://doi.org/10.1145/2628136. 2628163
132. McBride, C., McKinna, J.: The view from the left. J. Funct. Program. **14**(1), 69–111 (2004)
133. McBride, C., Paterson, R.: Applicative programming with effects. J. Funct. Program. **18**(1), 1–13 (2008). https://doi.org/10.1017/S0956796807006326
134. McKinna, J., Wright, J.: A type-correct, stack-safe, provably correct, expression compiler in Epigram, unpublished draft (2006)
135. Meertens, L.: Abstracto 84: The next generation. In: Proceedings of the 1979 Annual Conference. ACM, pp. 33–39 (1979)
136. Meertens, L.: Algorithmics: Towards programming as a mathematical activity. In: de Bakker, J.W., Hazewinkel, M., Lenstra, J.K. (eds.) Proceedings of the CWI Symposium on Mathematics and Computer Science, North-Holland, pp. 289–334 (1986). https://ir.cwi.nl/pub/20634
137. Meertens, L.: An Abstracto reader prepared for IFIP WG 2.1. Technical report CS-N8702, CWI, Amsterdam (1987)
138. Meertens, L.: Squiggol versus Squigol, private email to JG (2019)
139. Meertens, L.G.L.T.: Paramorphisms. Formal Aspects Comput. **4**(5), 413–424 (1992)
140. Meijer, E., Fokkinga, M.M., Paterson, R.: Functional programming with bananas, lenses, envelopes and barbed wire. In: Hughes, J. (ed.) Functional Programming Languages and Computer Architecture. Lecture Notes in Computer Science, vol. 523. Springer, pp. 124–144 (1991). https://doi.org/10.1007/3540543961_7
141. Moggi, E.: Notions of computation and monads. Inf. Comput. **93**(1), 55–92 (1991)
142. Möller, B.: Calculating with pointer structures. In: IFIP TC2/WG 2.1 Working Conference on Algorithmic Languages and Calculi, pp. 24–48. Chapman & Hall (1997)
143. Möller, B.: Kleene getting lazy. Sci. Comput. Program. **65**, 195–214 (2007)
144. Möller, B.: Modal knowledge and game semirings. Comput. J. **56**(1), 53–69 (2013). https://doi.org/10.1093/comjnl/bxs140
145. Möller, B.: Geographic wayfinders and space-time algebra. J. Logical Algebraic Meth. Programm. **104**, 274–302 (2019). https://doi.org/10.1016/j.jlamp.2019.02. 003
146. Möller, B., Roocks, P.: An algebra of database preferences. J. Logical Algebraic Meth. Programm. **84**(3), 456–481 (2015). https://doi.org/10.1016/j.jlamp.2015. 01.001
147. Möller, B., Struth, G.: Modal Kleene algebra and partial correctness. In: Rattray, C., Maharaj, S., Shankland, C. (eds.) AMAST 2004. LNCS, vol. 3116, pp. 379–393. Springer, Heidelberg (2004). https://doi.org/10.1007/978-3-540-27815-3_30
148. Möller, B., Struth, G.: wp Is wlp. In: MacCaull, W., Winter, W., Düntsch, I. (eds.) Relational Methods in Computer Science. Lecture Notes in Computer Science, vol. 3929, pp. 200–211. Springer (2005). https://doi.org/10.1007/11734673_16
149. Möller, B., Partsch, H., Pepper, P.: Programming with transformations: an overview of the Munich CIP project (1983)

150. Möller, B., Höfner, P., Struth, G.: Quantales and temporal logics. In: Johnson, M., Vene, V. (eds.) AMAST 2006. LNCS, vol. 4019, pp. 263–277. Springer, Heidelberg (2006). https://doi.org/10.1007/11784180_21

151. Morgan, C.: The specification statement. ACM Trans. Program. Lang. Syst. 10(3), 403–419 (1988). https://doi.org/10.1145/44501.44503

152. Morgan, C.: Programming from Specifications. Prentice Hall, Hoboken (1990)

153. Morgan, C.: An old new notation for elementary probability theory. Sci. Comput. Program. 85, 115–136 (2014). https://doi.org/10.1016/j.scico.2013.09.003. special Issue on Mathematics of Program Construction 2012

154. Morris, J.M.: A theoretical basis for stepwise refinement and the programming calculus. Sci. Comput. Program. 9(3), 287–306 (1987)

155. Morris, P.W.: Constructing universes for generic programming. PhD thesis, University of Nottingham, UK (2007)

156. Mu, S.C., Ko, H.S., Jansson, P.: Algebra of programming in Agda: dependent types for relational program derivation. J. Funct. Program. 19(5), 545–579 (2009)

157. Nanevski, A., Morrisett, G., Birkedal, L.: Polymorphism and separation in Hoare type theory. In: International Conference on Functional Programming, pp. 62–73 (2006)

158. Naur, P.: The IFIP working group on ALGOL. ALGOL Bull. (Issue 15), 52 (1962)

159. Norell, U.: Towards a practical programming language based on dependent type theory. PhD thesis, Chalmers University of Technology (2007)

160. O'Hearn, P.: Resources, concurrency, and local reasoning. Theoret. Comput. Sci. 375, 271–307 (2007)

161. O'Hearn, P., Reynolds, J., Yang, H.: Local reasoning about programs that alter data structures. In: Fribourg, L. (ed.) CSL 2001. LNCS, vol. 2142, pp. 1–19. Springer, Heidelberg (2001). https://doi.org/10.1007/3-540-44802-0_1

162. Paige, R.: Transformational programming – Applications to algorithms and systems. In: Wright, J.R., Landweber, L., Demers, A.J., Teitelbaum, T. (eds.) Principles of Programming Languages. ACM, pp. 73–87 (1983). https://doi.org/10.1145/567067.567076

163. Pardo, A.: Generic accumulations. In: Gibbons, J., Jeuring, J. (eds.) Generic Programming: IFIP TC2/WG2.1 Working Conference on Generic Programming. Kluwer Academic Publishers, International Federation for Information Processing, vol. 115, pp. 49–78 (2002)

164. Park, D.: On the semantics of fair parallelism. In: Bjøorner, D. (ed.) Abstract Software Specifications. LNCS, vol. 86, pp. 504–526. Springer, Heidelberg (1980). https://doi.org/10.1007/3-540-10007-5_47

165. Partsch, H.: An exercise in the transformational derivation of an efficient program by joing development of control and data structure. Sci. Comput. Program. 3(1), 1–35 (1983). https://doi.org/10.1016/0167-6423(83)90002-3

166. Partsch, H.: Structuring transformational developments: a case study based on Earley's recognizer. Sci. Comput. Program. 4(1), 17–44 (1984). https://doi.org/10.1016/0167-6423(84)90010-8

167. Partsch, H.: Transformational derivation of parsing algorithms executable on parallel architectures. In: Ammann. U. (ed.) Programmiersprachen und Programmentwicklung, Informatik-Fachberichte, vol. 77, pp. 41–57. Springer (1984). https://doi.org/10.1007/978-3-642-69393-9_3

168. Partsch, H.: Transformational program development in a particular program domain. Sci. Comput. Program. 7(2), 99–241 (1986). https://doi.org/10.1016/0167-6423(86)90008-0

169. Partsch, H.: Specification and Transformation of Programs – A Formal Approach to Software Development. Texts and Monographs in Computer Science. Springer (1990). https://doi.org/10.1007/978-3-642-61512-2

170. Partsch, H., Steinbrüggen, R.: Program transformation systems. ACM Comput. Surv. **15**(3), 199–236 (1983)

171. Peirce, C.S.: Description of a notation for the logic of relatives, resulting from an amplification of the conceptions of Boole's calculus of logic. Memoirs Am. Acad. Arts Sci. **9**, 317–378 (1870)

172. Pepper, P., Smith, D.R.: A high-level derivation of global search algorithms (with constraint propagation). Sci. Comput. Program. **28**(2–3), 247–271 (1997). https://doi.org/10.1016/S0167-6423(96)00023-8

173. Jones, S.P., et al.: Haskell 98, Language and Libraries. The Revised Report. Cambridge University Press, a special issue of the Journal of Functional Programming (2003)

174. Pontes, R., Matos, M., Oliveira, J.N., Pereira, J.O.: Implementing a linear algebra approach to data processing. In: Cunha, J., Fernandes, J.P., Lämmel, R., Saraiva, J., Zaytsev, V. (eds.) GTTSE 2015. LNCS, vol. 10223, pp. 215–222. Springer, Cham (2017). https://doi.org/10.1007/978-3-319-60074-1_9

175. Pretnar, M.: The logic and handling of algebraic effects. PhD thesis, School of Informatics, University of Edinburgh (2010)

176. Python Software Foundation: Python website (1997). https://www.python.org/

177. Yakushev, A.R., Jeuring, J., Jansson, P., Gerdes, A., Kiselyov, O., Oliveira, B.C.D.S.: Comparing libraries for generic programming in Haskell. In: Haskell Symposium, pp. 111–122 (2008)

178. Yakushev, A.R., Holdermans, S., Löh, A., Jeuring, J.: Generic programming with fixed points for mutually recursive datatypes. In: Hutton, G., Tolmach, A.P. (eds.) International Conference on Functional Programming, pp. 233–244 (2009)

179. Ruehr, F.: Dr Seuss on parser monads (2001). https://willamette.edu/~fruehr/haskell/seuss.html

180. Schröder, E.: Vorlesungen über die Algebra der Logik, vol 3. Taubner (1895)

181. Schuman, S.A. (ed.): New Directions in Algorithmic Languages, Prepared for IFIP Working Group 2.1 on Algol, Institut de Recherche d'Informatique et d'Automatique (1975)

182. Schuman, S.A. (ed.): New Directions in Algorithmic Languages, Prepared for IFIP Working Group 2.1 on Algol, Institut de Recherche d'Informatique et d'Automatique (1976)

183. Sintzoff, M.: On the design of correct and optimal dynamical systems and games. Inf. Process. Lett. **88**(1–2), 59–65 (2003). https://doi.org/10.1016/S0020-0190(03)00387-9

184. Sintzoff, M.: Synthesis of optimal control policies for some infinite-state transition systems. In: Audebaud, P., Paulin-Mohring, C. (eds.) MPC 2008. LNCS, vol. 5133, pp. 336–359. Springer, Heidelberg (2008). https://doi.org/10.1007/978-3-540-70594-9_18

185. Smith, D.R.: KIDS: a semiautomatic program development system. IEEE Trans. Softw. Eng. **16**(9), 1024–1043 (1990). https://doi.org/10.1109/32.58788

186. Spivey, J.M.: A functional theory of exceptions. Sci. Comput. Program. **14**(1), 25–42 (1990). https://doi.org/10.1016/0167-6423(90)90056-J

187. Swierstra, S.D., de Moor, O.: Virtual data structures. In: Möller, B., Partsch, H., Schuman, S. (eds.) Formal Program Development. LNCS, vol. 755, pp. 355–371. Springer, Heidelberg (1993). https://doi.org/10.1007/3-540-57499-9_26

188. Swierstra, S.D., Duponcheel, L.: Deterministic, error-correcting combinator parsers. In: Launchbury, J., Meijer, E., Sheard, T. (eds.) AFP 1996. LNCS, vol. 1129, pp. 184–207. Springer, Heidelberg (1996). https://doi.org/10.1007/3-540-61628-4_7

189. Swierstra, W.: A functional specification of effects. PhD thesis, University of Nottingham (2008)

190. Swierstra, W., Alpuim, J.: From proposition to program. In: Kiselyov, O., King, A. (eds.) FLOPS 2016. LNCS, vol. 9613, pp. 29–44. Springer, Cham (2016). https://doi.org/10.1007/978-3-319-29604-3_3

191. Swierstra, W., Altenkirch, T.: Beauty in the beast. In: Haskell Workshop, pp. 25–36 (2007). http://doi.acm.org/10.1145/1291201.1291206

192. Swierstra, W., Baanen, T.: A predicate transformer semantics for effects (functional pearl). Proc. ACM Programm. Lang. **3**(ICFP), 1–26 (2019)

193. Tafliovich, A., Hehner, E.C.R.: Quantum predicative programming. In: Uustalu, T. (ed.) MPC 2006. LNCS, vol. 4014, pp. 433–454. Springer, Heidelberg (2006). https://doi.org/10.1007/11783596_25

194. Tarski, A.: On the calculus of relations. J. Symb. Log. **6**(3), 73–89 (1941). https://doi.org/10.2307/2268577

195. Uustalu, T., Vene, V.: Primitive (co)recursion and course-of-value (co)iteration, categorically. Informatica **10**(1), 5–26 (1999)

196. Uustalu, T., Vene, V.: Comonadic notions of computation. Electron. Notes Theoer. Comput. Sci. **203**(5), 263–284 (2008). https://doi.org/10.1016/j.entcs.2008.05.029

197. Uustalu, T., Vene, V., Pardo, A.: Recursion schemes from comonads. Nordic J. Comput. **8**(3), 366–390 (2001)

198. Wadler, P.: Comprehending monads. In: LISP and Functional Programming. ACM, pp. 61–78 (1990). https://doi.org/10.1145/91556.91592

199. Wadler, P.: The essence of functional programming. In: Principles of Programming Languages. ACM, pp. 1–14 (1992). https://doi.org/10.1145/143165.143169

200. Wadler, P.: Propositions as types. Commun. ACM **58**(12), 75–84 (2015)

201. Wile, D.: POPART: producer of parsers and related tools: System builder's manual. USC/ISI Information Science Institute, University of Southern California, Technical report (1981)

202. Wile, D.: Program developments as formal objects. USC/ISI Information Science Institute, University of Southern California, Technical report (1981)

203. Xi, H., Pfenning, F.: Dependent types in practical programming. In: Principles of Programming Languages, pp. 214–227 (1999)

Advances in Data Management
in the Big Data Era

Antonia Azzini[1], Sylvio Barbon Jr.[7], Valerio Bellandi[2], Tiziana Catarci[5],
Paolo Ceravolo[2], Philippe Cudré-Mauroux[9], Samira Maghool[2],
Jaroslav Pokorny[8], Monica Scannapieco[6], Florence Sedes[4],
Gabriel Marques Tavares[2], and Robert Wrembel[3(✉)]

[1] Consortium for the Technology Transfer, C2T, Milan, Italy
antonia.azzini@consorzioc2t.it
[2] Università Degli Studi di Milano, Milan, Italy
{valerio.bellandi,paolo.ceravolo,samira.maghool,gabriel.tavares}@unimi.it
[3] Poznan University of Technology, Poznan, Poland
robert.wrembel@cs.put.poznan.pl
[4] IRIT, University Toulouse 3 Paul Sabatier, Toulouse, France
sedes@irit.fr
[5] SAPIENZA Università di Roma, Rome, Italy
catarci@diag.uniroma1.it
[6] Istituto Nazionale di Statistica (Istat), Rome, Italy
scannapi@istat.it
[7] Londrina State University (UEL), Londrina, Brazil
barbon@uel.br
[8] Charles University, Prague, Czech Republic
pokorny@ksi.mff.cuni.cz
[9] eXascale Infolab, University of Fribourg, Fribourg, Switzerland
pcm@csail.mit.edu, pcm@unifr.ch

Abstract. Highly-heterogeneous and fast-arriving large amounts of
data, otherwise said *Big Data*, induced the development of novel *Data
Management* technologies. In this paper, the members of the IFIP Working Group 2.6 share their expertise in some of these technologies, focusing on: recent advancements in data integration, metadata management,
data quality, graph management, as well as data stream and fog computing are discussed.

Keywords: Data integration · Metadata · Data quality · Knowledge
graphs · Data streams · Fog computing

1 Introduction

Data proliferation has been a reality for years and it is now considered the norm.
Data of *multiple structures* and *large volumes* are produced at a *substantial speed*,
challenging our ability to appropriately maintain and consume it. These three

© IFIP International Federation for Information Processing 2021
Published by Springer Nature Switzerland AG 2021
M. Goedicke et al. (Eds.): Advancing Research in Information and Communication Technology,
IFIP AICT 600, pp. 99–126, 2021. https://doi.org/10.1007/978-3-030-81701-5_4

characteristics are commonly known as the 3Vs (*Variety, Volume,* and *Velocity*) and describe the essential features of the so-called Big Data ecosystem [51]. The data types being produced and processed range from numbers, timestamps, short and large texts to time series, images, graphs, sounds, and videos, i.e., from fully structured to unstructured. The complexity of Big Data induced intensive research towards the development of new (or revisited) data models, data processing paradigms, and data processing architectures.

This complexity, in conjunction with the lack of standards for representing their components, computations, and processes, has made the design of data-intensive applications a failure-prone and resource-intensive activity. One of the reasons behind it can be identified in a lack of sound modeling practices. Indeed, multiple components and procedures must be coordinated to ensure a high level of data quality and accessibility for the application layers, e.g. data analytics and reporting. We believe that a major challenge of Big Data research requires - even more than developing new analytics - devising innovative data management techniques capable to deliver functional and non-functional properties like, among others: data quality, data integration, metadata discovery, reconciliation and augmentation, explainable analytics, data flow compliance or optimization.

Data Management research can address such challenges according to the FAIR principles. The goal is generating Findable, Accessible, Interoperable, and Reusable data. Methods, principles, and perspectives developed by the Data Management and Data Semantics community can significantly contribute to this goal. Solutions for integrating and querying schema-less data, for example, have received much attention. Standards for metadata management have been proposed to improve data integration among silos and to make data more discoverable and accessible through heterogeneous infrastructures. A further level of application of Data Management principles into Big Data technologies involves consistently distributing data processing across networks of interrelated data sources (sensors and data-flows), ensuring data quality and effective inference. The strong relationship between data quality and analytics also takes on research aimed at integrating Knowledge Graphs with advanced analytics powered by Machine Learning and Artificial Intelligence. Despite intensive research on data management techniques for Big Data (see [116] for more detail), unsolved issues and challenges persist. It motivated the members of the IFIP Working Group 2.6 (WG2.6): Databases[1] to further investigate the challenges and to publish a manifesto paper on Big Data Semantics [20]. The *Manifesto* revealed the limits of current technologies and identified concrete open problems. The WG2.6 *Manifesto* is not the only activity of the Working Group. WG2.6 ensues its tradition of promoting novel research areas in Data Semantics by means of research papers [2,22,48,67,93,94] and by organizing international research events. Since 2011, WG2.6 runs annually its main research event, i.e., International Symposium on Data-driven Process Discovery and Analysis (SIMPDA)[2]. In 2018 the

---

[1] https://www.ifip.org/bulletin/bulltcs/memtc02.htm.
[2] https://dblp.org/db/conf/simpda/index.html.

group initiated an international workshop on Semantics in Big Data Management (SemBDM).

Following the aforementioned WG2.6 *Manifesto*, in this summary paper, we overview current advances on the most significant topics presented in [116]), in the expertise area of the members of the WG 2.6. The topics include: leveraging knowledge graphs in the data integration process - Sect. 2, metadata discovery and management - Sect. 3, data quality - Sect. 4, data integration architectures - Sect. 5, graphs embedding - Sect. 6, processing and analyses of data stream in fog computing - Sect. 7, functional integration of relational and NoSQL databases - Sect. 8. Final remarks are reported in Sect. 9.

2 Knowledge Graphs for Data Integration

Knowledge Graphs have become one of the key instruments to integrate heterogeneous data. They provide declarative and extensible mechanisms to relate arbitrary concepts and data through flexible graphs that can be leveraged by downstream processes such as entity search [80] or ontology-based access to distributed information [27].

Integrating enterprise data into a given Knowledge Graph used to be a highly complex, manual and time-consuming task. Yet, several recent efforts streamlined this process to make it more amenable to large companies by introducing scalable and efficient pipelines [53,71,88]. The *XI Pipeline* [24] is a recent proposal in that context, which provides an end-to-end solution to semi-automatically map existing content onto a Knowledge Graph. We briefly discuss this pipeline below in Sect. 2.1—as an example of a state-of-the-art process to integrate data leveraging knowledge graphs—before delving into some of its applications in Sect. 2.2.

2.1 The XI Pipeline

An overview the XI Pipeline used to integrate heterogeneous contents leveraging a Knowledge Graph is given in Fig. 1. This pipeline focuses on semi-automatically integrating unstructured or semi-structured documents, as they are often considered the most challenging types of data to integrate, and as end-to-end techniques to integrate strictly structured data abound [75,87]. The Knowledge Graph underpinning the integration process should be given a priori, and can be built by crowdsourcing, by sampling from existing graphs, or through a manual process. The integration process starts with semi-structured or unstructured data given as input (left-hand side of Fig. 1) and goes through a series of steps, succinctly described below, to integrate the content by creating a set of new nodes and edges in the Knowledge Graph as output (right-hand side of Fig. 1).

Named Entity Recognition (NER) is the first step in the pipeline. NER is commonly used to integrate semi-structured or unstructured content, and tries to identify all *mentions* of entities of interest (e.g., locations, objects, persons or

Fig. 1. The XI pipeline goes through a series of five steps to integrate semi-structured or unstructured content leveraging a knowledge graph

concepts) from the input content. This is typically achieved through Information Retrieval techniques using inverted indices over the Knowledge Graph to identify all relevant entities from the input content by leveraging ad-hoc object retrieval [105] as well as Big Data and statistical techniques [81].

Entity Linking naturally follows NER by linking the entities identified in the input to their correct counterpart in the Knowledge Graph. Various matching algorithms can be used in that sense, which can be complemented by crowdsourcing and human-in-the-loop approaches [29] for best results.

Type Ranking assumes that each entity in the Knowledge Graph is associated with a series of *types*. However, the types associated to a given entity in the graph are typically not all relevant to the *mention* of that entity as found in the input data. The XI Pipeline introduces the task of ranking entity types given their mentions in the input data [102] by leveraging features from both the underlying type hierarchy as well as from the (textual) context surrounding the mention [103]. The result of this process is a ranking of fine-grained types associated to each entity mention, which is invaluable when tackling downstream steps such as Co-Reference Resolution or Relation Extraction (see below).

Co-Reference Resolution identifies noun phrases (e.g., "the Swiss champion" or "the former president") from the input content that cannot be resolved by simple Entity Linking techniques. Such phrases are then automatically disambiguated and mapped onto entities in the Knowledge Graph by leveraging type information and the their context [82].

Relation Extraction finally attempts to identify *relationships* between pairs of entities appearing in the input content. The XI Pipeline resorts to Distant Supervision [91] in that context, leveraging a new neural architecture (the Aggregated Piecewise Convolutional Neural Network [90]) to solve this task effectively.

The outcome of the process described above is a set of nodes and links connecting mentions from the input data to entities and relations in the Knowledge Graph. As a result, the Knowledge Graph can then be used as a central gateway (i.e., as a *mediation layer*) to retrieve all heterogeneous pieces of data related to a given entity, type, relation or query.

2.2   Applications

Knowledge Graph integration can be used to solve many integration tasks in practice. The XI Pipeline, for instance, was successfully deployed in three very different scenarios:

- it was used to integrate research articles into a Knowledge Graph [1], in order to power pub/sub notifications related to specific research concepts, as well as research papers recommendations;
- it was also used to integrate and query series of heterogeneous tweets [104], which are otherwise very difficult to handle given their very short and noisy nature;
- finally, a particular instance of this pipeline was used in a large enterprise setting in order to integrate large-scale log data [65] and power a variety of applications ranging from job auditing and compliance to automated service level objectives, or extraction of recurring tasks and global job ranking.

3   Metadata Management: The Potential of Context

Metadata are simply defined as data about data [50] or information about information[3]. They are provided to help in the interpretation or exploitation of the data of interest, describing, locating, and enabling to retrieve them efficiently. Generally elicited from the contents themselves, they can be obtained from the context to enrich the value of a dataset. Indeed, metadata makes data sets understandable by both humans and machines, enabling interoperability, between systems with different hardware and software platforms, data structures, and interfaces, with minimal loss of data and semantics [25]. Fostering searchability metadata facilitates the integration of legacy resource and organizational silos or isolated applications. Metadata can help to comply with security and privacy requirements. Indeed, the core data remaining safe and protected, only metadata are transmitted across the network. Searchable data also helps to minimize data transfer paving the way to *sustainability*.

3.1   From Multimedia Contents to Metadata Management: The Example of Social Interaction Analysis

Multimedia contents have to be acquired and stored in real-time and in different locations. In order to efficiently retrieve the desired information, centralized metadata abstract, i.e., a concise version of the whole metadata, that locates some multimedia contents on remote servers, can be computed. The originality of this abstract is to be automatically built based on the extracted metadata. In [57] we presented a method to implement this approach in an industrial context and illustrated our framework with current Semantic Web technologies, such as RDF and SPARQL for representing and querying semantic metadata. Some experimental results, provided in order to show the benefits of indexing and retrieving multimedia contents without centralizing multimedia contents or their associated metadata, proved the efficiency of such a metadata abstract.

The metadata extraction is the most resource-consuming process in the management of multimedia collections. This raises the problem of the efficient

---

[3] https://csrc.nist.gov/glossary/term/metadata.

management of these large data volumes while minimizing resource consumption. User's constant interactions with multimedia contents and metadata complicate this management process. Issues about metadata management have been fixed by integrating "extra" information enrichment at different levels, each one relying on a layer. The metadata model matches the most widely used metadata standards, flexible and extensible in structure and vocabulary. In a multimedia management system, the indexing process is the most resource-consuming, through algorithms that extract metadata, whereas, in conventional systems, indexing implements a fixed set of indexing algorithms, without considering the resource consumption and user's changing needs. The user's needs are specified in his queries. In order to limit the metadata volume and on the other to reduce the resource consumption, we propose to split the indexing process into two phases: first time, at the contents acquisition time (i.e., implicit indexation), and, a second time, if necessary, at the query execution time (i.e., explicit indexation), the indexing algorithms being dynamically determined according to the required metadata.

Figure 2 shows an architecture for a framework based on a *holistic approach* that integrates multimodal heterogeneous cues and contextual information (complementary "exogenous" data) in a dynamic and optional way according to their availability or not. Such an approach allows the analysis of multi "signals" in parallel (where humans are able only to focus on one). This analysis can be further enriched from data related to the context of the scene (location, date, type of music, event description, etc.) or related to individuals (name, age, gender, data extracted from their social networks, etc.). The contextual information enriches the modeling of extracted metadata and gives them a more "semantic" dimension. Managing this heterogeneity is an essential step for implementing a holistic approach.

The automation of social interaction capturing and observation using nonintrusive devices without predefined scenarios introduces various issues we mentioned above namely (i) privacy and security, (ii) heterogeneity, and (iii) volume.

The proposed approach manages heterogeneous cues coming from different modalities as multi-layer sources (visual signals, voice signals, contextual information) at different time scales and different combinations between layers. The approach has been designed to operate without the need for intrusive devices, in order to ensure the capture of real behaviors and achieve the naturalistic observation. We have deployed the project on OVALIE platform which aims to study eating behaviors in different real-life contexts. To handle the high variety of the social cues, we propose a comprehensive (meta)data model for the visual nonverbal cues [83]. This model consists of four groups of entities: (i) acquisition group to store the used sensors' metadata (e.g., owner details, model number, transmission mode, data format, etc.); (ii) experiment group used to store the experiment's description including title, data, responsible person, and location, also the list of algorithms that are used to extract the social cues; (iii) video group used to store metadata related to the recorded video such as segments start/end timestamps, and frames information; and (iv) features group

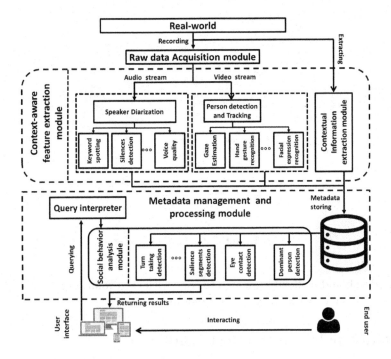

Fig. 2. Social interaction analysis framework architecture

to store the extracted social cues for each detected person in a given conceptual frame (conceptual frame is multiple frames that have a common timestamp and have to be analyzed together) as shown in the second figure. This generic data model shows the relationships between experiment, acquisition, video, and feature groups of entities, which are color-coded as green, orange, yellow, and gray in Fig. 3.

3.2   Internet of Things and Metadata for Trust Metrics

Internet of Things (IoT) is characterized by a high heterogeneity at different levels, and we mentioned how metadata models match this heterogeneity : (i) from the device level, a set of heterogeneous devices with dissimilar capabilities from computational and communication standpoints. Identifying, addressing, naming, and managing such devices in a standardized way is the first challenge. (ii) from a network-centric perspective, communication and interaction through various networks using different communication protocols (iii) from a data-centric vision, IoT is about exchanging massive amounts of data. It is essential to provide data with standardized formats, models and semantic descriptions, to support automated reasoning. As we said, optimization of energy and network bandwidth usage becomes an issue. As a matter of sustainability, metadata models allow for extensions and different types of metadata in different domains: the meta-

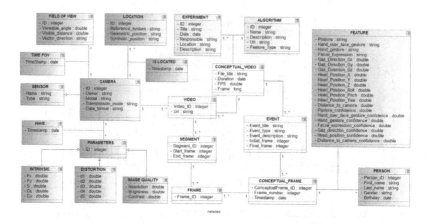

Fig. 3. Metadata meta modeling

data model should be flexible enough to cope with the evolutionary applications, devices, and needs, with energy-aware requirements.

4 Data Quality in the Post-truth Era

When people think about *data quality*, they often reduce it just to *accuracy*, e.g., the city name "Chicago" misspelled as "Chcago". However, data quality is more than simply accuracy: other significant dimensions such as completeness, consistency, and currency are necessary in order to fully characterize it. [9] provides a deep overview of which dimensions define data quality and describes several historical approaches to data quality characterization such as [112].

4.1 From Data Quality to Information Quality: An Increased Complexity of Quality Characterization

Most of the efforts paid to define data quality are related to structured data. However, a vast amount of realities is instead represented by types of information that are not structured data: a photo of a landscape, a map and a descriptive text in a travel guide, newspaper articles, satellite imagery etc. Dimensions for structured data are closely related to inner characteristic and properties of the underlying data model. An example is given by the different types of completeness, defined with and without the open world assumption for the different types of structures of the relational model, namely the tuple, the column, the table, and the set of tables [85].

When dealing with data types beyond structured data, it becomes necessary to define new dimensions for data quality, and, it becomes then more suitable to talk about *information* quality rather than *data* quality. With information quality, quality characterization starts to be dependent on the specific data type, e.g. quality dimensions characterizing images, such as sharpness and noise, are very different from quality dimensions characterizing maps, such as topological consistency and positional accuracy.

In addition to the dependency on data types, information quality can have some relevant domain specialization. For instance, textual data describing laws can be characterized by dimensions such as conciseness and unambiguity, while textual data of novels can be characterized by cohesion and coherence [9].

4.2   Information Quality in Modern Society

We are living in a datafied society [66], where there is a relevant paradigm shift: from "primarily designed" data that were modeled and stored within information systems with a defined semantics, to "secondary produced" data, i.e. data resulting from interactions with devices or passively produced by systems, like sensors data and Web logs. These data are collectively referred to as Big Data: in addition to the 3Vs characterizing Big Data, a fourth V is particularly important i.e. *Veracity*. Veracity directly refers to information quality problems: with the huge volume of generated data, the fast velocity of arriving data, and the large variety of heterogeneous data, the quality of Big Data is far from being perfect [18]. A notable example of the need for assessing Veracity is the fake news phenomenon, causing the spreading of misinformation across social media users [44]. A further example is provided by information available on the Web, for which the issue of assessing veracity is particularly important. In [62], for instance, several sources providing the same information in two domains on the Web, namely Stocks and Flights, are compared to discover inconsistencies and inaccuracies and hence point to the "true" data. As another example, in [34], an approach for assessing the veracity of linked data is presented with a proposal of a fact-checking framework for data modeled as RDF triples.

Quality of today information also includes a new relevant dimension, namely *data fairness*. Fairness can be defined in terms of lack of discrimination, i.e. treating someone differently. It is possible to distinguish between two categories of fairness: individual fairness, for which similar predictions are given to similar individuals and group fairness (also known as statistical fairness), for which different groups are treated equally independently of a particular race, gender, or sexual orientation [31]. A very famous example of group unfairness is the COM-PAS algorithm used by the Department of Corrections in Wisconsin, New York and Florida that has led to harsher sentencing toward African Americans [7]. In order to achieve fairness, it is important to deal with bias in data, algorithmic and user evaluation. In [68], several examples of different types of bias impacting on fairness are provided, including social bias, e.g. if a review is influenced by different scores provided by other reviewers and there is hence a social influence experienced, or cause-effect bias, which can happen as a result of the fallacy that correlation implies causation. Notably, there are several cases of population bias for instance in the health domain, where the fallacy of predictions can be particularly serious. A notable field for data fairness is in relation to learning algorithms (data analytics and Machine Learning - ML) that base their predictions on training data and improve them with the growth of such data. In

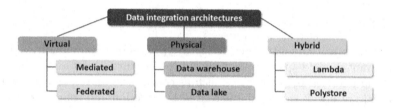

Fig. 4. The taxonomy of data integration architectures

a typical project, the creation and curation of training data sets is largely a human-based activity and involves several people: domain experts, data scientists, machine learning experts, etc. In other words, data-related human design decisions affect learning outcomes throughout the entire process pipeline, even if at a certain point these decisions seem to disappear in the black-box "magic" approach of ML algorithms. On the other hand, it is now gaining attention the fact that humans typically suffer from conscious and unconscious biases, and current historical data used in training set very often incorporate such biases, so perpetuating and amplifying existing inequalities and unfair choices. It is a still open problem to figure out concrete solutions on how to discover and eliminate unintended unfair biases from the training data sets and/or to create "by design" data sets that are natively "fair".

5 Data Integration Architectures for Standard and Big Data

Large companies typically store their data in heterogeneous storage systems, ranging from files to fully functional databases, further called *data storage systems* (DSSs). Querying such DSSs in an integrated way is challenging as the systems typically support different ways of querying, use different data models and schemas (even if designed in the same data model, e.g., relational). For more than 50 years researchers worldwide have dealt with this problem and have proposed a few data integration architectures. Their achievements are outlined in this section.

5.1 Data Integration Taxonomy

The taxonomy of Data Integration (DI) architectures is shown in Fig. 4. Three main categories are distinguished, namely: *virtual, materialized,* and *hybrid*. In the *virtual* architecture, data are stored in their original DSSs and are accessed on the fly, via an integration layer. In the *physical* architecture, data are ingested from DSSs and stored locally (materialized) in advance in an integration system. The *hybrid* architecture combines the functionality of the two aforementioned DI architectures, i.e., some data are integrated and accessed on the fly, whereas other data are pre-integrated and materialized.

5.2   Virtual Integration

Two types of *virtual* architectures have been proposed, i.e., *federated* [12,32] and *mediated* [115]. Their main feature is that data are integrated on the fly via an intermediate layer located between the user and DSSs. This layer is responsible for: (1) transforming source data models into the common one, typically the relational one, (2) decomposing user queries into sub-queries and routing them into appropriate DSSs, (3) transforming the sub-queries into executable snippets on each DSS, (4) transforming and integrating results of the sub-queries.

The main difference between the *federated* and *mediated* architecture is that the first one is used to integrate databases and it uses more components in the intermediate layer (e.g., a transforming processor, a component schema, a filtering processor, and an export schema). The *mediated* architecture is applied to integrating also other DSSs than databases. It uses two main components as the integration layer, i.e., a wrapper and a mediator.

5.3   Physical Integration

Two types of such architectures, accepted as de-facto industry standard, have been proposed, i.e., a *data warehouse* (DW) [49,106] and a *data lake* (DL).

In the DW architecture, the integration is implemented by means of the Extract-Transform-Load (ETL) layer where the so-called ETL processes (work-flows) are run. They are responsible for: (1) ingesting data from data sources, (2) transforming heterogeneous data into a common data model and schema, (3) cleaning, normalizing, and eliminating data duplicates, (4) loading data into a central repository - a data warehouse.

The widespread of Big Data induced another architecture - a Data Lake, used to implement a staging area. The DL is a repository that stores a vast amount of heterogeneous data ingested in their original formats [84,100]. Then, the content of a DL processed by ETL processes to build cleaned, homogenized, and integrated data repositories. To this end, rich and well-organized metadata annotations are needed to provide a precise description of data [70]. Typical storage for DLs is based on Hadoop, Azure, or Amazon S3.

5.4   Hybrid Integration

For storing Big Data, alternative data stores have been developed, including key-value, column family, document, and graph stores, commonly referred to as NoSQL stores. Multiple systems produce data at much larger speed than before - we refer to such systems as streaming data sources (e.g., sensors, medical monitors) [52]. The variety of data formats and speed of data production by DSSs, makes the data integration process very challenging. To ease this process, two novel data integration architectures have been developed recently, i.e., the *polystore* and the *lambda* architecture.

The Polystore Architecture. Figure 5 shows a general architecture of a poly-store. Heterogeneous DSSs (denoted as *DS1*, ..., *DS4*) are connected to the *integration middleware* via dedicated interfaces (drivers) (denoted as *Interface1*, ..., *Interface4*). They offer the functionality of wrappers (as in the mediated architecture). The *integration middleware* makes available all these DSs for querying via a common schema. This middleware offers functionality similar to a *mediator*. These features make the polystore a virtual DI architecture. Typical types of DSs integrated into the polystore architecture include: relational, array, key-value, graph, stream, DFS [96].

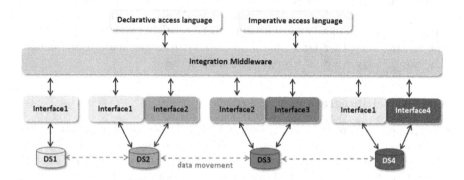

Fig. 5. An overview of the *polystore* architecture

Three features distinguish polystores from other architectures. First, the *integration middleware* allows to query DSs using different languages, typically a declarative one (SQL-like) and an imperative one. Second, data sets can be relocated from one DSS into another, to improve the performance of queries. Technically speaking, data sets can be either copied (replicated) or moved into a DSS where a given query will be executed faster. For example, let us assume that *DS1* is a relational database and *Interface1* exposes a relational data model and SQL; *DS2* is a key-value store and *Interface2* exposes a procedural interface for searching. Notice that *DS2* can also be accessed via *Interface1*. If an SQL query is executed on both *DS1* and *DS2* via *Interface1*, the global optimizer may decide to move or copy data from *DS2* into *DS1*. This feature makes the polystore a materialized DI architecture, therefore classified as a hybrid DI architecture. Third, a given DS may be queried via more than one interface and thus, provide data in different data models.

Examples of polystores include among others: BigDAWG [30], Polypheny-DB [109], CloudMdsQL [55], Estocada [5,14] (an overview of such systems is available in [96]).

The Lambda Architecture. The lambda architecture combines an architecture for collecting data in a batch mode (cf. the batch layer in Fig. 6) and collecting fast arriving data (cf. the real-time layer in Fig. 6) [92]. The purpose of lambda is to be able to combine slowly arriving data with fast arriving data for analysis. The bath layer can be instantiated by a standard DW architecture, whereas the real-time layer can be instantiated by a standard stream processing architecture. Both layers are integrated using the serving layer, typically implemented by means of materialized and virtual views.

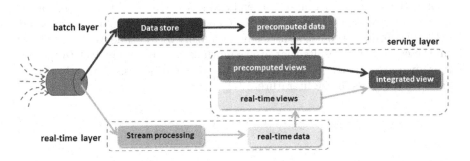

Fig. 6. An overview of the *Lambda* architecture

Typical components used in this architecture include: (1) in the batch layer - relational DBMSs or NoSQL DSSs, (2) in the real-time layer - Kafka, Kafka Streams, Spark, and Cassandra.

To sum up, the data integration architectures developed for Big Data extend the ones developed earlier for standard DSSs. Despite substantial research and technological advancements in this field, there still exist multiple unsolved problems. Some of the problems include (1) development of metadata standards for interoperable data DI architectures (in the spirit of [52]), (2) query optimization techniques in the highly heterogeneous and distributed architecture, composed of various data models, physical storage models, and hardware (in the spirit of [38]), (3) performance optimization of data integration processes (in the spirit of [3,89].

6   Graph Embeddings

Data Graphs, consisting in networks of nodes and relationships, are largely adopted in support of distributed and modular data modeling and data analytics procedures. Learning and predicting new links in social media [35], protein-protein interaction [101], distributed monitoring of business process [60] distributed ledgers [56] are among examples of applications leveraging on graph data models.

A limit of data graphs is that the information they carry cannot be readily applied in Machine Learning (ML) due to a mismatch at the representation level. While ML typically works with feature vectors, where a single instance is described by a flat set of features, data graphs link the features related to a data instance using a network of interconnected nodes. Graph embedding helps in handling this mismatch by transforming nodes, edges, and their features into a vector space while partially preserving properties of their original graph structure. The general goal is that nodes connected in the graph are kept closer in the embedding space but task dependent transformation strategies are studied to meet the requirements of different ML algorithms. Three common steps are needed in defining an embedding procedure: (i) define an encoding procedure mapping the nodes of a graph into embeddings, (ii) define a decoding procedure to extract node properties from the embeddings (i.e. node neighborhood or labels) (iii) optimize the decoding results, typically by multiple iterations, to get from the embeddings results that are as much as possible equivalent to those of the original graph. Figure 7 schematizes this idea and represents the three most mentioned methods in the literature.

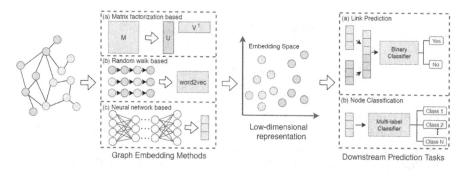

Fig. 7. A schematic comparison of three proposed algorithms in graph embedding adapted from [120] page 2

Matrix Factorization-Based Algorithms. These algorithms focus on factorizing the matrix representation of nodes relations in order to obtain the embedding. For some property matrices, the factorization problem is abstracted in eigenvalue decomposition (e.g. Laplacian matrix [6]) while for unstructured matrices the goal is solving an optimization problem (e.g. gradient descent methods). For example, SocDim [98] factorizes the modularity matrix and the normalized Laplacian matrix; NEU [119] factorizes similarity matrices that encode an higher order of the adjacency matrix, Laplacian Eigenmaps [10] adopt pairwise similarity and imposed a quadratic penalty function, MDS [47] adopt the Euclidean distance between two feature vectors as pairwise similarity. Other proposals [108,114] aim to learn pairwise distances by semidefinite programming procedures. For preserving high-order proximity, HOPE [72] factorizes several matrices based on different similarity measures while GraRep [16] factorizes a matrix that is related to the k-step transition probability matrix. Multiple objective functions can be adopted in order to compensate the advantages/disadvantages of different techniques [4,15].

Random Walk-Based Algorithm. The idea is to encode the coordinates such that the similarity of two nodes in the embedding space equals the probability that the two nodes co-occur on a random walk over the network. Deepwalk [73] and Node2vec [42] are two popular random walk strategies while the former uses a deterministic approach and the latter a probabilistic one. Other techniques run random walks on modified versions of the original network. Walklets [74] modify the random walk strategy used in DeepWalk by skipping over some nodes in the graph. LINE [97], to embed larger information, optimizes a designed objective function based on 1-hop and 2-hop random walk probabilities that preserves both the local and global network structures.

Neural Network-Based Algorithms. This approach uses neural network to construct deep encoders, i.e. the output space is non-orthogonal to the input space. For example, SDNE [111] and DNGR [17] use deep autoencoder. Different approaches that adopt convolutional neural network differ in the way of formulating convolution-like operations on graphs [13, 28, 45, 86]. GCNs [54] learns how to propagate information across the graph to compute node features and generate node embeddings based on local network neighborhoods. GraphSAGE [43] uses graph convolutional networks to generalized neighborhood aggregation. It is worth noting that all these deep encoders can be combined with similarity functions obtained by random walk methods.

Hybrid Methods. Sometimes multiple methods are combined. In [121] the authors leverage the heterogeneous information in a Knowledge Graph (KG) to improve recommendation performance using TransR [64] for network embedding, and autoencoders for textual and visual information. KR-EAR [63] constructs a relational triple encoder (TransE [113], TransR [11]) to embed the correlations between entities and relations, and an attributional triple encoder to embed the correlations between entities and attributes. TransE and TransH models build the embeddings by putting both entities and relations within the same semantic space while TransR build the embeddings putting entities and relations in separate spaces.

The Explainability Challenge. Graph embeddings represents a powerful tool for conciliating the representational power of data graphs with the powerful analytics of ML. This approach has been however criticized for creating an additional level of complexity that isolates the input and the output data by a black-box procedure that hamper the explainability of ML results. The community is then trying to get explainable ML methods. A promising approach is linking the layers of a neural network with symbols of a *lingua franca* [37]. In this context, Knowledge Graphs could play a crucial role in supporting explainability especially with embeddings methods that exploit the layer of the neural network for generating the vector space. In a neural network architecture where input features, hidden layers, computational units, and predicted output are mapped to the entities of a KGs, results could be easily translated in terms of these entities. Whilst most of the existing methods in KG embeddings such as TransE, TransH, and TransR, are not explainable by design, an increasing number of recent studies concentrating on transparent explainable models [8, 33, 95, 117].

7   Data Stream Processing and Analytics in Fog Computing

The advent and development of the Internet of Things (IoT) encompasses that everything can connect to the Internet, generating data streams from the events recorded by sensors and probes. Data stream processing imposes specific constraints on data management [39]. If the conventional processing model clearly differentiates between data storage and data processing stages, handling data streams implies processing in real-time weakening the role of central data storage and data management procedures. The needs covered by *Data Management* are however still in place with data streams, or even emphasized. Heterogeneous and decentralized sources require *data integration, noise filtering, concept drift detection, uncertainty,* and *data quality management* [99]. That is to say, data management is not canceled, but it is simply decentralized as it has to follow data at the production and transmission levels. The *Fog Computing* paradigm represents, in this sense, an important advancement for the Cloud Computing solutions often coupled with data stream processing.

7.1   Recent Advances in Stream Processing Algorithms

Great work has been done to address the challenges of data stream processing by designing innovative algorithms and data analytics procedures. We present the most relevant contributions in the area by distinguishing three families of algorithms based on the main goal they address. In particular, we have highly accurate solutions, lightweight algorithms, and robust methods.

Highly Accurate Solutions. Considering the requirement of high predictive performance and the huge volume of data provided by IoT ecosystems, Deep Learning (DL) solutions arise as a suitable processing tool. DL architectures such as Convolutional Neural Networks (CNNs), Recurrent Neural Networks (RNNs), and Long Short Term Memory (LSTM) can learn hidden features from the raw and noisy data [69]. Some recent frameworks support the vastest DL modeling, e.g., ADLStream [58] demonstrated superior predictive performance than traditional statistical temporal series approaches and most well-known stream mining algorithms.

Lightweight Algorithms. A restricted computational cost scenario composed of lightweight devices demands reducing memory costs. In this category, we group the algorithms capable of reaching a competitive predictive performance with low memory cost without compromising processing time. An example is the Strict Very Fast Decision Tree [23], an algorithm that minimizes tree growth, substantially reducing memory usage, leading to being used as a base learning into ensemble solutions.

Robust Methods. Concept drifts detection, novelty pattern recognition, and forget outdated concepts are requirements for building a robust data stream method. In this category, concept drift detectors embedded into ensemble methods have been stood out. This sophisticated combination takes advantage of non-parametric drift detection methods based on Hoeffding's bounds [36], for triggering model updating. Ensembles are highly predictive and effective methods for mitigating concept drift, paving the way for hybrid architecture for supporting robust classification procedures with non-stationary data streams.

7.2   The Fog Computing Paradigm

If the IoT requires that objects can continuously communicate [61], to ensure timely data processing there is a need to continuously reconfigure the computational resources used for processing data streams [46]. Up to now, mostly cloud-based computational resources have been utilized for this. However, cloud data centers are usually located far away from IoT sources, which leads to an increase in latency since data needs to be sent from the data sources to the cloud and back. Today a new emerging architectural paradigm is changing this processing model. *Fog Computing* is a cloud technology in which terminal-generated data does not load directly into the cloud, but is instead pre-processed by decentralized mini data centers [26]. The concept involves a network structure extending from the network's outer perimeter in which data generated by IoT devices is sent to the public cloud central data endpoint or to a private data processing center (private cloud). With the advent of Fog Computing, it is possible to perform data processing and data management in the cloud as well as at the edge of the network, i.e., exploiting the computational resources offered by networked devices (Fig. 8). To better understand how to extend this idea can be applied we need to review the stages composing data stream processing pipelines. In fact, we can model a classical data streaming pipeline into three main stages [20].

Data Preparation. This stage relates the cleaning and transforming raw data prior to processing and analysis. It is an important step and often involves reformatting data, making corrections to data, and combining multiple source sets to enrich data. Data preparation is often a lengthy undertaking for data professionals or business users, but it is essential as a prerequisite to put data in context, turn it into insights, and eliminate bias resulting from poor data quality. For example, the data preparation process usually includes standardizing data formats, enriching source data, removing outliers, and/or transform the data format [21,107].

Data Analytics. This stage aim at extracting knowledge from the data acquired by the sensors. *Descriptive Analytics* allows representing the facts recorded. *Predictive Analytics* allows performing data analysis in order to draw predictions on future outcomes. *Prescriptive Analytics* combines data analysis with the ability to take and manage decision-making procedures. Prescriptive Analytics provides strategic indications or operational solutions based on both Descriptive Analysis and Predictive Analysis [19].

Visualization and Reporting. This stage aims at presenting the information carried by data, using visual elements like charts, graphs, and maps. Data visu-

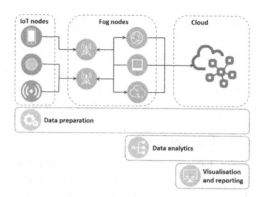

Fig. 8. Fog computing and its relationship with data processing stages

alization tools provide an accessible way to see and understand trends, outliers, and patterns in data [118]. In the world of Big Data and IoT, data visualization tools and technologies are a key factors to analyze massive amounts of information and to make data-driven decisions.

Data Stream Pipelines in the Fog. A key design decision to be taken in modeling data stream processing and analytics is how distributing these stages in the edge area (in the "Fog"). As a consequence, it becomes crucial to understand how data management affects the results of complex and distributed processing analytics. Further work is then required to understand the implications of unifying and interconnecting decentralized procedures with their possibly conflicting requirements and boosting effects. For example, several filtering or aggregations can be applied directly in the edge area. Figure 8 illustrates this concept by showing that some data processing stages can be applied directly to the IoT or Fog nodes. Data Preparation applies to the IoT, Fog, or Cloud layers. Data Analytics applies to the Fog and Cloud layers, while Data Visualization and Reporting apply to the Cloud layer only.

8   Integration of Relational and NoSQL Databases Functionally

Relational and NoSQL databases (DBs) contained in one integrated architecture require an infrastructure involving data and software of both transactional and analytical types (cf. Sect. 5). A particular case of integration of relational and NoSQL DBs concerns graph DBs and document DBs using JSON format. One tendency is to use multi-level modeling approaches involving both relational and NoSQL architectures enabling their simple integration [78].

Today, NoSQL DBs are considered in contrast to traditional RDBMSs products. On the other hand, yet other modeling approaches are possible, e.g., a functional approach. We can mention Gremlin - a functional graph query language that provides traversal operators/functions chained together to form path-like expressions. Gremlin is supported by many GDBMSs. Significant works using a functional approach to data management are contained in [41].

The main aim of the section is to use a functional approach introduced in [76] to modeling both relations and data structures occurring in NoSQL DBs. For graphs, we will use a *(labelled) property multigraph model*. Both nodes and edges are defined by a unique identifier (Id). Properties are simply single-valued attributes. A property graph is represented by a set of typed partial functions. The functions considered will be of two kinds: single-valued and multi-valued. Regardless of the fact that the graphs are considered schema-less in NoSQL DBs, we will use graph DB schemas. The associated model of JSON data based on JSON Schema can deal with data also as functions. The relations in a relational DB can be considered also as typed functions. Some possibilities for integration on the level of a common query language are presented and discussed.

For graph querying in today's practice, we can consider GDBMS Neo4j and its popular query language Cypher. For relational DBMSs, of course, we assume SQL. Querying JSON documents can be done, e.g., with as in the most popular document store MongoDB. Then, a typed lambda calculus, i.e., the language of lambda terms (*LT language*), can be used as a data manipulation language. More integration details can be found in [79].

8.1   Functional Approach to Data Modeling and Querying

The functional approach used here is based on a typing system. For our purposes, we use elementary types and a number of structured types. Typed functions appropriate to modeling real data objects are attributes viewed as empirical typed functions that are described by an expression of a natural language [76]. To propose them means that we construct a conceptual or DB schema.

We assume the existence of some (*elementary*) *types* $S_1,...,S_k$ ($k \geq 1$) constituting a *base* **B**. Always *Bool* ϵ **B**. It allows to model sets (resp. relationships) as unary (resp. n-ary) characteristic functions. Table 1 presents basic structured types for typing objects in relational, graph, and JSON data model, respectively.

Table 1. Types used in relational, graph, and document data models

Type name	Type structure	Relational model	Graph model	Document model
Functional	$(S{:}R_1,\ldots,R_n)$	Yes, n$\geq$1, S=Bool	Yes, n=1	Yes, n=1
Tuple	$(R_1,\ldots,R_m)$	No	Yes, S is a tuple, m$\geq$1	No
Set	$\{R_1,\ldots,R_m\}$	No	No	Yes, n$\geq$1
Array	$[R_1,\ldots,R_m]$	No	No	Yes, n$\geq$1

Supposing, e.g., entity types *Movie* and *User*, then the expression "the movies rated by a user" denotes a ((*Bool:Movie*):*User*)-object, i.e. a (partial) function f:*User* $\rightarrow$ (*Bool:Movie*). At the schema level we write *Rates*/((*Bool:Movie*):*User*). GDBMSs can use attributes of types $(R_1{:}R_2)$ and ((*Bool:R$_1$*):*R$_2$*), respectively, where R_1 and R_2 are entity types. Properties require to use tuple types, e.g., *Movie/((Title, Director):Movie)*. A relational DB can contain *Actors/(Bool: Name, Title, Role)*.

Logical connectives, quantifiers and predicates are also typed functions, e.g., **and**/(*Bool:Bool,Bool*), + is (*Number: Number, Number*)-object. The aggregation function $COUNT_R$ is of type (*Number:(Bool:R)*). A manipulation language for functions – *LT language*, uses terms based on *applications, lambda abstractions, tuples*, and *components of tuples*. Document DBs use also terms like *set elements, arrays*, and *elements of array*. Typically, lambda abstractions serve as a tool for expressing queries, i.e., they provide answers – typically relations. The query "Give a set of couples associating to each film directed by Burton the number of actors who acted in it" can be expressed but the term

$$\lambda\ t,\ p\ (p = COUNT(\lambda\ a\ \exists\ t,\ r\ Actor(a,t,r)\ \textbf{and}\ \exists m\ Movie(m)(t,\text{'Burton'})\ ))$$

A more advanced approach enables to construct more complicated data structures, i.e., new graphs or documents [77]. JSON types can be extended to regular expressions.

8.2   Integration of Relational, Graph, and Document Databases

For example, [40] offers three ways of integration of relational and NoSQL DBs: *native, hybrid*, and *reducing to one option, either relational or NoSQL*. In [68], possible approaches are categorized as a *polyglot persistence, multi-model approach*, and *schema and data conversion*. We use the multi-model approach, particularly *multi-level modelling* with a *special abstract model*. Obviously, there are more approaches, e.g., *NoSQL-on-RDBMS, SQL-on-Hadoop*, and *ontology integration* [79]. The approaches are mutually related and rather describe particular cases with given NoSQL/relational DBs than more exactly specified categories.

A multi-model approach reminds a more user-friendly solution of heterogeneous DB integration as it was known in the context of heterogeneous relational DBs in the past. Here, we suppose that different DB models are behind participating DBs. An alternative for data processing with relational and NoSQL data in one infrastructure uses common design methods based on a modification of the traditional 3-level ANSI/SPARC approach. This multi-level modeling is most relevant for our multi-model approach.

One sub-approach of the multi-model approach is a *hybrid approach*, e.g. [110]. In this case, the query is executed on more data sources, relational and some NoSQL, but the additional layer is used to enable data integration. For example, a generalizable SQL query interface for both relational and NoSQL systems called Unity is described in [59]. Unity is an integration and virtualization system as it allows SQL queries that span multiple sources and uses its internal query engine to perform joins across sources.

In our case, LT queries sent to the integrated system are translated into queries compatible with the RDBMS (e.g., SQL) and GDBMS (e.g., Cypher), or JSON document store (e.g. MongoDB), respectively.

9   Conclusion

A widespread of huge data volumes of arbitrary structures encouraged new data management techniques for data processing. In this summary paper, we overviewed current advances in some of these techniques, being in the expertise of the members of the IFIP Working Group 2.6: Databases. Despite traditional *Data Management* has been considered inappropriate to the data processing techniques used in the Big Data ecosystem the current advancements make clear important challenges emerging in this area need to embrace a Data Management perspective.

Data integration typically requires a mediation layer to integrate heterogeneous content. In this article, we saw how *Knowledge Graphs* can be used as such a layer to integrate Big Data, using pipelines to automatically identify and relate pieces of data from the input content and map them onto entities and relations in a Knowledge Graph. The resulting integrated Knowledge Graph can then be used as a global abstraction to efficiently and effectively search, query or manipulate all heterogeneous sources centrally.

Initially designed for summarizing, describing, enriching (un)structured (big) data collections, *Metadata* help from now on to comply with larger requirements to adapt to new environments such as IoT, social interactions analysis, cybersecurity, and other. Indeed, the data itself remaining safe and protected, only metadata are transmitted and exchanged. Minimizing data transfer, exploiting, and improving data locality is a crucial concern, paving the way to *sustainability*: metadata models allow for flexibility and context-awareness in any domain and at various levels, with privacy, security and energy-aware requirements.

Quality of today information also includes a new relevant dimension, namely *Data Fairness*. Fairness can be defined in terms of lack of discrimination, i.e. treating someone differently. In order to achieve fairness, it is important to deal with bias in data, algorithmic and user evaluation.

In order to address *Big Data Management*, standard data integration architectures turned out to be inadequate, mainly because of their inability to store and process efficiently large volumes of complex data, novel data integration architectures have been developed. The two most successful ones include a polystore and lambda. Nonetheless, they have not provided solutions to all problems. Still open research and technological problems for such architectures include the development of metadata standards, query optimization techniques, and performance optimization of data integration processes.

Graph embeddings represents a powerful tool for conciliating the representational power of data graphs with the powerful analytics of ML. This approach has been however criticized for creating an additional level of complexity that isolates the input and the output data by a black-box procedure that hamper the explainability of ML results. A promising approach is linking the layers of a neural network with symbols of a *lingua franca* [37]. In this context, Knowledge Graphs could play a crucial role in supporting explainability especially with embeddings methods that exploit the layer of the neural network for generating the vector space.

Fog Computing is a cloud technology in which terminal-generated data does not load directly into the cloud, but is instead pre-processed by decentralized mini data centers. With the advent of Fog Computing, it is possible to perform data processing and data management in the cloud as well as at the edge of the network. As a consequence, it becomes crucial to understand how data management affects the results of complex and distributed processing analytics.

The integration of *relational and NoSQL databases* can be done in many different ways. We used an architecture using a multi-model and multilevel approach with a special abstract model based on typed functional objects. Then a typed lambda calculus can be used as a powerful tool for querying in such integrated database architecture.

References

1. Aberer, K., Boyarsky, A., Cudré-Mauroux, P., Demartini, G., Ruchayskiy, O.: Sciencewise: a web-based interactive semantic platform for scientific collaboration. In: International Semantic Web Conference (ISWC) (2011)
2. Aberer, K., et al.: Emergent semantics principles and issues. In: Lee, Y.J., Li, J., Whang, K.-Y., Lee, D. (eds.) DASFAA 2004. LNCS, vol. 2973, pp. 25–38. Springer, Heidelberg (2004). https://doi.org/10.1007/978-3-540-24571-1_2
3. Ali, S.M.F., Wrembel, R.: Towards a cost model to optimize user-defined functions in an ETL workflow based on user-defined performance metrics. In: European Conference on Advances in Databases and Information Systems (ADBIS), pp. 441–456 (2019)
4. Allab, K., Labiod, L., Nadif, M.: A semi-NMF-PCA unified framework for data clustering. IEEE Trans. Knowl. Data Eng. (TKDE) **29**(1), 2–16 (2016)
5. Alotaibi, R., Bursztyn, D., Deutsch, A., Manolescu, I., Zampetakis, S.: Towards scalable hybrid stores: constraint-based rewriting to the rescue. In: International Conference on Management of Data (SIGMOD), pp. 1660–1677 (2019)
6. Anderson, W.N., Jr., Morley, T.D.: Eigenvalues of the Laplacian of a graph. Linear Multilinear Algebra **18**(2), 141–145 (1985)
7. Angwin, J., Larson, J., Mattu, S., Kirchner, L.: Machine bias. ProPublica (2016)
8. Barbieri, N., Bonchi, F., Manco, G.: Who to follow and why: link prediction with explanations. In: ACM SIGKDD International Conference on Knowledge Discovery and Data Mining (KDD), pp. 1266–1275 (2014)
9. Batini, C., Scannapieco, M.: Data and Information Quality. DSA, Springer, Cham (2016). https://doi.org/10.1007/978-3-319-24106-7
10. Belkin, M., Niyogi, P.: Laplacian eigenmaps and spectral techniques for embedding and clustering. In: Advances in Neural Information Processing Systems, pp. 585–591 (2002)
11. Bordes, A., Usunier, N., Garcia-Duran, A., Weston, J., Yakhnenko, O.: Translating embeddings for modeling multi-relational data. In: Conference on Advances in Neural Information Processing Systems (NIPS), pp. 2787–2795 (2013)
12. Bouguettaya, A., Benatallah, B., Elmargamid, A.: Interconnecting Heterogeneous Information Systems. Kluwer (1998)
13. Bruna, J., Zaremba, W., Szlam, A., LeCun, Y.: Spectral networks and locally connected networks on graphs. arXiv:1312.6203 (2013)

14. Bugiotti, F., Bursztyn, D., Deutsch, A., Manolescu, I., Zampetakis, S.: Flexible hybrid stores: constraint-based rewriting to the rescue. In: IEEE International Conference on Data Engineering (ICDE), pp. 1394–1397 (2016)
15. Cai, D., He, X., Han, J.: Spectral regression: a unified subspace learning framework for content-based image retrieval. In: ACM Multimedia, pp. 403–412 (2007)
16. Cao, S., Lu, W., Xu, Q.: GraRep: Learning graph representations with global structural information. In: International Conference on Information and Knowledge Management (CIKM), pp. 891–900 (2015)
17. Cao, S., Lu, W., Xu, Q.: Deep neural networks for learning graph representations. In: AAAI Conference on Artificial Intelligence (2016)
18. Catarci, T., Scannapieco, M., Console, M., Demetrescu, C.: My (fair) big data. In: IEEE International Conference on Big Data, pp. 2974–2979 (2017)
19. Ceravolo, P., Zavatarelli, F.: Knowledge acquisition in process intelligence. In: International Conference on Information and Communication Technology Research (ICTRC), pp. 218–221 (2015)
20. Ceravolo, P., et al.: Big data semantics. J. Data Seman. **7**(2), 65–85 (2018)
21. Ceravolo, P., Damiani, E., Torabi, M., Barbon, S.: Toward a new generation of log pre-processing methods for process mining. In: Carmona, J., Engels, G., Kumar, A. (eds.) BPM 2017. LNBIP, vol. 297, pp. 55–70. Springer, Cham (2017). https://doi.org/10.1007/978-3-319-65015-9_4
22. Ceravolo, P., Guetl, C., Rinderle-Ma, S. (eds.): SIMPDA 2016. LNBIP, vol. 307. Springer, Cham (2018). https://doi.org/10.1007/978-3-319-74161-1
23. da Costa, V.G.T., de Leon Ferreira, A.C.P., Junior, S.B., et al.: Strict very fast decision tree: a memory conservative algorithm for data stream mining. Pattern Recogn. Lett. **116**, 22–28 (2018)
24. Cudré-Mauroux, P.: Leveraging knowledge graphs for big data integration: the XI pipeline. Seman. Web **11**(1), 13–17 (2020)
25. Damiani, E., Ardagna, C., Ceravolo, P., Scarabottolo, N.: Toward model-based big data-as-a-service: the TOREADOR approach. In: Kirikova, M., Nørvåg, K., Papadopoulos, G.A. (eds.) ADBIS 2017. LNCS, vol. 10509, pp. 3–9. Springer, Cham (2017). https://doi.org/10.1007/978-3-319-66917-5_1
26. Dastjerdi, A.V., Buyya, R.: Fog computing: helping the internet of things realize its potential. IEEE Comput. **49**(8), 112–116 (2016)
27. Decker, S., Erdmann, M., Fensel, D., Studer, R.: ONTOBROKER: ontology based access to distributed and semi-structured information. In: Meersman, R., Tari, Z., Stevens, S. (eds.) Database Semantics. ITIFIP, vol. 11, pp. 351–369. Springer, Boston (1999). https://doi.org/10.1007/978-0-387-35561-0_20
28. Defferrard, M., Bresson, X., Vandergheynst, P.: Convolutional neural networks on graphs with fast localized spectral filtering. In: Conference on Advances in Neural Information Processing Systems (NIPS), pp. 3844–3852 (2016)
29. Demartini, G., Difallah, D.E., Cudré-Mauroux, P.: Large-scale linked data integration using probabilistic reasoning and crowdsourcing. VLDB J. **22**(5), 665–687 (2013)
30. Duggan, J., et al.: The BigDAWG polystore system. SIGMOD Rec. **44**(2), 11–16 (2015)
31. Dwork, C., Hardt, M., Pitassi, T., Reingold, O., Zemel, R.S.: Fairness through awareness. In: Innovations in Theoretical Computer Science, pp. 214–226 (2012)
32. Elmagarmid, A., Rusinkiewicz, M., Sheth, A. (eds.): Management of Heterogeneous and Autonomous Database Systems. Morgan Kaufmann (1999)

33. van Engelen, J.E., Boekhout, H.D., Takes, F.W.: Explainable and efficient link prediction in real-world network data. In: Boström, H., Knobbe, A., Soares, C., Papapetrou, P. (eds.) IDA 2016. LNCS, vol. 9897, pp. 295–307. Springer, Cham (2016). https://doi.org/10.1007/978-3-319-46349-0_26

34. Esteves, D., Rula, A., Reddy, A.J., Lehmann, J.: Toward veracity assessment in RDF knowledge bases: an exploratory analysis. J. Data Inf. Qual. 9(3), 16:1–16:26 (2018)

35. Freeman, L.C.: Visualizing social networks. J. Soc. Struct. 1(1), 4 (2000)

36. Frías-Blanco, I., del Campo-Ávila, J., Ramos-Jimenez, G., Morales-Bueno, R., Ortiz-Díaz, A., Caballero-Mota, Y.: Online and non-parametric drift detection methods based on Hoeffding's bounds. IEEE Trans. Knowl. Data Eng. (TKDE) 27(3), 810–823 (2014)

37. Futia, G., Vetrò, A.: On the integration of knowledge graphs into deep learning models for a more comprehensible AI? Three challenges for future research. Information 11(2), 122 (2020)

38. Gadepally, V., et al.: The BigDAWG polystore system and architecture. In: IEEE High Performance Extreme Computing Conference (HPEC), pp. 1–6 (2016)

39. Gama, J., Gaber, M.M.: Learning from Data Streams: Processing Techniques in Sensor Networks. Springer, Berlin (2007). https://doi.org/10.1007/3-540-73679-4

40. Gaspar, D., Coric, I. (eds.): Bridging relational and NoSQL databases. In: IGI (2017)

41. Gray, P., Kerschberg, L., King, P., Poulovassilje, A. (eds.): The Functional Approach to Data Management, Modeling, Analyzing and Integrating Heterogeneous Data. Springer, Berlin (2004). https://doi.org/10.1007/978-3-662-05372-0

42. Grover, A., Leskovec, J.: Node2vec: scalable feature learning for networks. In: ACM SIGKDD International Conference on Knowledge Discovery and Data Mining (KDD), pp. 855–864 (2016)

43. Hamilton, W., Ying, Z., Leskovec, J.: Inductive representation learning on large graphs. In: Conference on Advances in Neural Information Processing Systems (NIPS), pp. 1024–1034 (2017)

44. Hassan, N., Li, C., Yang, J., Yu, C.: Introduction to the special issue on combating digital misinformation and disinformation. J. Data Inf. Qual. 11(3), 9:1–9:3 (2019)

45. Henaff, M., Bruna, J., LeCun, Y.: Deep convolutional networks on graph-structured data. arXiv:1506.05163 (2015)

46. Hießl, T., Hochreiner, C., Schulte, S.: Towards a framework for data stream processing in the fog. Informatik Spektrum 42(4), 256–265 (2019). https://doi.org/10.1007/s00287-019-01192-z

47. Hofmann, T., Buhmann, J.: Multidimensional scaling and data clustering. In: Advances in Neural Information Processing Systems, pp. 459–466 (1995)

48. Hsiao, D.K., Neuhold, E.J., Sacks-Davis, R.: IFIP TC2 WG2.6 Database Semantics Conference on Interoperable Database Systems. Elsevier (2014)

49. Jarke, M., Lenzerini, M., Vassiliou, Y., Vassiliadis, P.: Fundamentals of Data Warehouses. Springer, Berlin (2003). https://doi.org/10.1007/978-3-662-05153-5

50. Jeffery, K.G.: Metadata: the future of information systems. State of the art and research themes, information systems engineering (2000)

51. Jin, X., Wah, B.W., Cheng, X., Wang, Y.: Significance and challenges of big data research. Big Data Res. 2(2), 59–64 (2015)

52. Jovanovic, P., Romero, O., Simitsis, A., Abelló, A.: Incremental consolidation of data-intensive multi-flows. IEEE Trans. Knowl. Data Eng. (TKDE) 28(5), 1203–1216 (2016)

53. Jozashoori, S., Vidal, M.: Mapsdi: a scaled-up semantic data integration framework for knowledge graph creation. In: International Conference on the Move to Meaningful Internet Systems (OTM), LNCS, vol. 11877, pp. 58–75 (2019)
54. Kipf, T.N., Welling, M.: Semi-supervised classification with graph convolutional networks. arXiv:1609.02907 (2016)
55. Kolev, B., Bondiombouy, C., Valduriez, P., Jiménez-Peris, R., Pau, R., Pereira, J.: The CloudMdsQL multistore system. In: International Conference on Management of Data (SIGMOD), pp. 2113–2116 (2016)
56. Kuo, T.T., Kim, H.E., Ohno-Machado, L.: Blockchain distributed ledger technologies for biomedical and health care applications. J. Am. Med. Inform. Assoc. **24**(6), 1211–1220 (2017)
57. Laborie, S., Manzat, A.M., Sèdes, F.: Managing and querying efficiently distributed semantic multimedia metadata collections. IEEE MultiMedia **16**(4), 12–20 (2009)
58. Lara-Benítez, P., Carranza-García, M., García-Gutiérrez, J., Riquelme, J.C.: Asynchronous dual-pipeline deep learning framework for online data stream classification. Integr. Comput. Aided Eng. **1**(2), 1–19 (2020)
59. Lawrence, R.: Integration and virtualization of relational SQL and NoSQL systems including MySQL and MongoDB. In: IEEE International Conference on Computational Science and Computational Intelligence (CSCI), pp. 285–219 (2014)
60. Leida, M., Ceravolo, P., Damiani, E., Asal, R., Colombo, M.: Dynamic access control to semantics-aware streamed process logs. J. Data Seman. **8**(3), 203–218 (2019)
61. Li, S., Da Xu, L., Zhao, S.: 5G internet of things: a survey. J. Ind. Inf. Integr. **10**, 1–9 (2018)
62. Li, X., Dong, X.L., Lyons, K., Meng, W., Srivastava, D.: Truth finding on the deep web: is the problem solved? VLDB Endowment **6**(2), 97–108 (2012)
63. Lin, Y., Liu, Z., Sun, M.: Knowledge representation learning with entities, attributes and relations. Ethnicity **1**, 41–52 (2016)
64. Lin, Y., Liu, Z., Sun, M., Liu, Y., Zhu, X.: Learning entity and relation embeddings for knowledge graph completion. In: AAAI Conference on Artificial Intelligence (2015)
65. Mavlyutov, R., Curino, C., Asipov, B., Cudré-Mauroux, P.: Dependency-driven analytics: a compass for uncharted data oceans. In: Conference on Innovative Data Systems Research (CIDR) (2017)
66. Mayer-Schonberger, V., Cukier, K.: Big Data: A Revolution That Will Transform How We Live, Work, and Think. John Murray (2013)
67. Meersman, R., Tari, Z., Stevens, S. (eds.): Database Semantics. ITIFIP, vol. 11. Springer, Boston (1999). https://doi.org/10.1007/978-0-387-35561-0
68. Mehrabi, N., Morstatter, F., Saxena, N., Lerman, K., Galstyan, A.: A survey on bias and fairness in machine learning. CoRR abs/1908.09635 (2019)
69. Mohammadi, M., Al-Fuqaha, A., Sorour, S., Guizani, M.: Deep learning for IoT big data and streaming analytics: a survey. IEEE Commun. Surv. Tutorials **20**(4), 2923–2960 (2018)
70. Nadal, S., et al.: A software reference architecture for semantic-aware big data systems. Inf. Softw. Technol. (IST) **90**, 75–92 (2017)
71. Noy, N.F., Gao, Y., Jain, A., Narayanan, A., Patterson, A., Taylor, J.: Industry-scale knowledge graphs: lessons and challenges. Commun. ACM **62**(8), 36–43 (2019)

72. Ou, M., Cui, P., Pei, J., Zhang, Z., Zhu, W.: Asymmetric transitivity preserving graph embedding. In: ACM SIGKDD International Conference on Knowledge Discovery and Data Mining (KDD), pp. 1105–1114 (2016)
73. Perozzi, B., Al-Rfou, R., Skiena, S.: Deepwalk: online learning of social representations. In: ACM SIGKDD International Conference on Knowledge Discovery and Data Mining (KDD), pp. 701–710 (2014)
74. Perozzi, B., Kulkarni, V., Chen, H., Skiena, S.: Don't walk, skip! online learning of multi-scale network embeddings. In: International Conference on Advances in Social Networks Analysis and Mining (ASONAM), pp. 258–265 (2017)
75. Poggi, A., Rodriguez-Muro, M., Ruzzi, M.: Ontology-based database access with DIG-Mastro and the OBDA plugin for protégé. In: OWLED Workshop on OWL (2008)
76. Pokorný, J.: Database semantics in heterogeneous environment. In: Seminar on Current Trends in Theory and Practice of Informatics (SOFSEM), pp. 125–142 (1996)
77. Pokorný, J.: Functional querying in graph databases. Vietnam J. Comput. Sci. 5(2), 95–105 (2017)
78. Pokorný, J.: Integration of relational and NoSQL databases. In: Asian Conference on Intelligent Information and Database Systems (ACIIDS), pp. 35–45 (2018)
79. Pokorný, J.: Integration of relational and graph databases functionally. Found. Comput. Decis. Sci. 44(4), 427–441 (2019)
80. Pound, J., Mika, P., Zaragoza, H.: Ad-hoc object retrieval in the web of data. In: International Conference on World Wide Web (WWW), pp. 771–780 (2010)
81. Prokofyev, R., Demartini, G., Cudré-Mauroux, P.: Effective named entity recognition for idiosyncratic web collections. In: International Conference on World Wide Web (WWW), pp. 397–408 (2014)
82. Prokofyev, R., Tonon, A., Luggen, M., Vouilloz, L., Difallah, D.E., Cudré-Mauroux, P.: SANAPHOR: ontology-based coreference resolution. In: Arenas, M., et al. (eds.) ISWC 2015. LNCS, vol. 9366, pp. 458–473. Springer, Cham (2015). https://doi.org/10.1007/978-3-319-25007-6_27
83. Qodseya, M.: Visual non-verbal social cues data modeling. In: Woo, C., Lu, J., Li, Z., Ling, T.W., Li, G., Lee, M.L. (eds.) ER 2018. LNCS, vol. 11158, pp. 82–87. Springer, Cham (2018). https://doi.org/10.1007/978-3-030-01391-2_16
84. Russom, P.: Data lakes: purposes, practices, patterns, and platforms. TDWI white paper (2017)
85. Scannapieco, M., Batini, C.: Completeness in the relational model: a comprehensive framework. In: International Conference on Information Quality (ICIQ), pp. 333–345 (2004)
86. Scarselli, F., Gori, M., Tsoi, A.C., Hagenbuchner, M., Monfardini, G.: The graph neural network model. IEEE Trans. Neural Netw. 20(1), 61–80 (2008)
87. Sequeda, J.F., Miranker, D.P.: A pay-as-you-go methodology for ontology-based data access. IEEE Internet Comput. 21(2), 92–96 (2017)
88. Sequeda, J.F., Briggs, W.J., Miranker, D.P., Heideman, W.P.: A pay-as-you-go methodology to design and build enterprise knowledge graphs from relational databases. In: Ghidini, C., et al. (eds.) ISWC 2019. LNCS, vol. 11779, pp. 526–545. Springer, Cham (2019). https://doi.org/10.1007/978-3-030-30796-7_32
89. Simitsis, A., Vassiliadis, P., Sellis, T.K.: State-space optimization of ETL workflows. IEEE Trans. Knowl. Data Eng. (TKDE) 17(10), 1404–1419 (2005)
90. Smirnova, A., Audiffren, J., Cudre-Mauroux, P.: APCNN: tackling class imbalance in relation extraction through aggregated piecewise convolutional neural networks. In: Swiss Conference on Data Science (SDS), pp. 63–68 (2019)

91. Smirnova, A., Cudré-Mauroux, P.: Relation extraction using distant supervision: a survey. ACM Comput. Surv. **51**(5), 106:1–106:35 (2018)
92. Souza, A.: Lambda architecture - how to build a big data pipeline (2019). https://towardsdatascience.com
93. Spaccapietra, S., Maryanski, F. (eds.): Data Mining and Reverse Engineering. ITIFIP, Springer, Boston (1998). https://doi.org/10.1007/978-0-387-35300-5
94. Stanchev, P.L., Smeulders, A.W., Groen, F.C.: An approach to image indexing of documents. In: IFIP TC2/WG 2.6 Working Conference on Visual Database Systems, pp. 63–77 (1991)
95. Subramanian, A., Pruthi, D., Jhamtani, H., Berg-Kirkpatrick, T., Hovy, E.: Spine: sparse interpretable neural embeddings. In: AAAI Conference on Artificial Intelligence (2018)
96. Tan, R., Chirkova, R., Gadepally, V., Mattson, T.G.: Enabling query processing across heterogeneous data models: a survey. In: IEEE International Conference on Big Data, pp. 3211–3220 (2017)
97. Tang, J., Qu, M., Wang, M., Zhang, M., Yan, J., Mei, Q.: Line: large-scale information network embedding. In: International Conference on World Wide Web (WWW), pp. 1067–1077 (2015)
98. Tang, L., Liu, H.: Leveraging social media networks for classification. Data Min. Knowl. Disc. **23**(3), 447–478 (2011)
99. Tennant, M., Stahl, F., Rana, O., Gomes, J.B.: Scalable real-time classification of data streams with concept drift. Future Gener. Comput. Syst. **75**, 187–199 (2017)
100. Terrizzano, I., Schwarz, P., Roth, M., Colino, J.E.: Data wrangling: the challenging journey from the wild to the lake. In: Conference on Innovative Data Systems Research (CIDR) (2015)
101. Theocharidis, A., Van Dongen, S., Enright, A.J., Freeman, T.C.: Network visualization and analysis of gene expression data using BioLayout express 3D. Nature Protocols **4**(10), 1535 (2009)
102. Tonon, A., Catasta, M., Demartini, G., Cudré-Mauroux, P., Aberer, K.: *TRank*: ranking entity types using the web of data. In: Alani, H., et al. (eds.) ISWC 2013. LNCS, vol. 8218, pp. 640–656. Springer, Heidelberg (2013). https://doi.org/10.1007/978-3-642-41335-3_40
103. Tonon, A., Catasta, M., Prokofyev, R., Demartini, G., Aberer, K., Cudre-Mauroux, P.: Contextualized ranking of entity types based on knowledge graphs. J. Web Seman. **37–38**, 170–183 (2016)
104. Tonon, A., Cudré-Mauroux, P., Blarer, A., Lenders, V., Motik, B.: ArmaTweet: detecting events by semantic tweet analysis. In: Blomqvist, E., Maynard, D., Gangemi, A., Hoekstra, R., Hitzler, P., Hartig, O. (eds.) ESWC 2017. LNCS, vol. 10250, pp. 138–153. Springer, Cham (2017). https://doi.org/10.1007/978-3-319-58451-5_10
105. Tonon, A., Demartini, G., Cudré-Mauroux, P.: Combining inverted indices and structured search for ad-hoc object retrieval. In: Conference on Research and Development in Information Retrieval, pp. 125–134 (2012)
106. Vaisman, A.A., Zimányi, E.: Data Warehouse Systems - Design and Implementation. Data-Centric Systems and Applications, Springer, Berlin (2014)
107. Valencia-Parra, Á., Varela-Vaca, Á.J., López, M.T.G., Ceravolo, P.: CHAMALEON: framework to improve data wrangling with complex data. In: International Conference on Information Systems (ICIS) (2019)
108. Vandenberghe, L., Boyd, S.: Semidefinite programming. SIAM Rev. **38**(1), 49–95 (1996)

109. Vogt, M., Stiemer, A., Schuldt, H.: Polypheny-DB: towards a distributed and self-adaptive polystore. In: IEEE International Conference on Big Data, pp. 3364–3373 (2018)
110. Vyawahare, H., Karde, P.P., Thakare, V.: A hybrid database approach using graph and relational database. In: IEEE International Conference on Research in Intelligent and Computing in Engineering (RICE), pp. 1–4 (2018)
111. Wang, D., Cui, P., Zhu, W.: Structural deep network embedding. In: ACM SIGKDD International Conference on Knowledge Discovery and Data Mining (KDD), pp. 1225–1234 (2016)
112. Wang, R.Y., Strong, D.M.: Beyond accuracy: what data quality means to data consumers. J. Manage. Inf. Syst. **12**(4), 5–33 (1996)
113. Wang, Z., Zhang, J., Feng, J., Chen, Z.: Knowledge graph embedding by translating on hyperplanes. In: AAAI Conference on Artificial Intelligence (2014)
114. Weinberger, K.Q., Sha, F., Saul, L.K.: Learning a kernel matrix for nonlinear dimensionality reduction. In: International Conference on Machine Learning (ICML), p. 106 (2004)
115. Wiederhold, G.: Mediators in the architecture of future information systems. IEEE Comput. **25**(3), 38–49 (1992)
116. Wrembel, R., Abelló, A., Song, I.: DOLAP data warehouse research over two decades: trends and challenges. Inf. Syst. **85**, 44–47 (2019)
117. Xie, Q., Ma, X., Dai, Z., Hovy, E.: An interpretable knowledge transfer model for knowledge base completion. arXiv:1704.05908 (2017)
118. Yamamoto, S., Mori, H. (eds.): HIMI 2018. LNCS, vol. 10905. Springer, Cham (2018). https://doi.org/10.1007/978-3-319-92046-7
119. Yang, C., Sun, M., Liu, Z., Tu, C.: Fast network embedding enhancement via high order proximity approximation. In: International Joint Conference on Artificial Intelligence (IJCAI), pp. 3894–3900 (2017)
120. Yue, X., et al.: Graph embedding on biomedical networks: methods, applications and evaluations. Bioinformatics **36**(4), 1241–1251 (2020)
121. Zhang, F., Yuan, N.J., Lian, D., Xie, X., Ma, W.Y.: Collaborative knowledge base embedding for recommender systems. In: ACM SIGKDD International Conference on Knowledge Discovery and Data Mining (KDD), pp. 353–362 (2016)

TC 3: Education

Computers and Education – Recognising Opportunities and Managing Challenges
IFIP TC3 – Technical Committee on Education

Don Passey[1]([✉]) [iD], Torsten Brinda[2], Bernard Cornu[3], Jaana Holvikivi[4] [iD],
Cathy Lewin[5] [iD], Johannes Magenheim[6] [iD], Raymond Morel[7], Javier Osorio[8] [iD],
Arthur Tatnall[9] [iD], Barrie Thompson[10], and Mary Webb[11] [iD]

[1] Chair of TC3, National Representative of the UK, Department of Educational Research,
Lancaster University, Lancaster LA1 4YD, UK
d.passey@lancaster.ac.uk
[2] Chair of TC3 WG3.1, University of Duisburg-Essen, Essen, Germany
torsten.brinda@uni-due.de
[3] Past chair of TC3, University of Grenoble, CNED, Poitiers, France
[4] Chair of TC3 WG3.4, Helsinki Metropolia University of Applied Sciences, Helsinki, Finland
[5] Chair of TC3 WG3.3, Manchester Metropolitan University, Manchester, UK
C.Lewin@mmu.ac.uk
[6] National Representative of Germany, University of Paderborn, Paderborn, Germany
jsm@uni-paderborn.de
[7] National Representative of Switzerland, University of Geneva, Geneva, Switzerland
[8] Chair of TC3 WG3.7, University of Las Palmas de Gran Canaria, Las Palmas, Spain
javier.osorio@ulpgc.es
[9] Editor-in-chief of EAIT, Victoria University, Melbourne, Australia
Arthur.Tatnall@vu.edu.au
[10] Past chair of TC3 WG3.4, University of Sunderland, Sunderland, UK
[11] Chair of the TC3 Task Force on the Computing Curriculum, King's College, London, UK
mary.webb@kcl.ac.uk

Abstract. IFIP's Technical Committee 3 (TC3) is dedicated to concerns about uses of computing and digital technologies in education. TC3 covers the interests of those who are concerned with policy, practice and research in the fields of digital technologies and computing used for educational purposes, whether for management, teaching or learning, and whether by teachers, learners, parents, policy makers, developers, or the wider adult population involved in lifelong learning. This chapter considers the shifting focus of IFIP TC3's concerns for computing and education over the past 60 years, the reasons for those shifts, and the challenges that educators have faced in developing appropriate uses of computers in their practices. The chapter explores the roles and influences of TC3 conferences, its academic journal, its working groups, and its current task force. Separate sections provide an overview of important TC3 visions and declarations that have

All present and past members of IFIP TC3 and its WGs are recognised in the work presented in this chapter. Specific contributions to this text were provided by the authors listed.

© IFIP International Federation for Information Processing 2021
Published by Springer Nature Switzerland AG 2021
M. Goedicke et al. (Eds.): Advancing Research in Information and Communication Technology,
IFIP AICT 600, pp. 129–152, 2021. https://doi.org/10.1007/978-3-030-81701-5_5

highlighted contemporary and future issues, and the status of an evolving declaration focusing on future sustainability and computing. The chapter concludes with an overview of the impact of TC3, and signposts next steps in its ongoing journey.

Keywords: Educational technologies · Education and technologies · Digital technologies and education · Information technologies · Communication technologies · Educational technologies and research · Educational technologies and pedagogical practices · Educational technologies and policy · Educational management and technologies · Professional development and educational technologies

1   The Shifting Focus of IFIP TC3's Concerns - Education for, with, and through Computing

It has not always been agreed that computing should be linked to education, or in what ways. Authors from a range of countries [1] describe how, in the 1980s, a range of national initiatives focused on early computers being made available to educational institutions (schools, colleges and universities) to provide for 'learning about computers'. This focus through early initiatives was succeeded in many countries by the wider integration of subsequent models of computers into educational institutions but more focused on 'learning with computers' [2]. As time has progressed, arguments have become stronger for links between the disciplines of computing and other subjects, and whilst there are already a number of important ways in which computing and education are linked, more are emerging as time goes forward. Recently, many countries have introduced computing curricula into schools [3] that focus more on, again, 'learning about computers' and 'learning to program computers'; however, with the vastly increased computer facilities now available in educational institutions, this focus has been supplemented with 'learning with computers', and importantly, 'learning to be productive with computers' [4]. IFIP TC3 has been involved in not just monitoring these shifts of focus, which have occurred just as much in higher, vocational and adult lifelong learning settings as in schools, but on actively supporting its members and wider international participants in gaining awareness and direction in using computers for educational purposes in their individual contexts.

This chapter explores the shifting focus of IFIP TC3's concerns for computing and education over the past 60 years. In the following section, Sect. 2, reasons for those shifts and the emerging challenges that educators have faced in developing appropriate uses of computers in their practices will be discussed in more detail. Section 3 describes the important roles and influences of TC3 conferences, and how these have not only mirrored contemporary concerns for computing and education, but have also pointed to future issues and benefits. In Sect. 4, TC3's academic journal is discussed; this journal has played a major role in dissemination not only of the work of TC3 members and its groups, but also in the context of a wider related academic literature. In Sects. 5, 6, 7 and 8, the important contributions of TC3's four working groups (WGs) are detailed, showing how each group focuses on a core area of interest. Section 9 details the work of the current TC3 task force on the computing curriculum, and Sect. 10 includes separate sub-sections that each provide an overview of salient TC3 visions and declarations, all arising from deliberations and outcomes of major TC3 conferences and highlighting contemporary and future issues; in the last sub-section, the status of the currently evolving declaration focusing on future sustainability and computing is described. The chapter concludes with Sect. 11, which provides an overview of the impact of TC3 over the last 60 years, and indicates next steps in its ongoing journey.

2 Challenges in Developing Awareness and Practices of Computer Uses in Education

In terms of enhancing awareness and understanding of how computers can be effectively used to support educational practices and policy, IFIP TC3 has undoubtedly faced the same form of challenges in finding ways forward that other organisations and institutions have sought to address over the past 60 years. Enabling educators and those in education to be aware of the potential, benefits and issues arising when using computers in educational practice has been an ongoing concern for members of TC3. Part of the challenge of introducing and integrating computing (a term used in this chapter to refer to the technological dimensions of digital activity and use, and the writing of programs) into educational practice has been concerned with the nature of the subject of computing itself. Computer science (a term used in this chapter to refer to the study of the principles and uses of digital technologies) has been strongly identified as a science and technology discipline, whereas education (and many specific subject areas within it) has been identified as a social science or humanities discipline. This form of identification has led many teachers and educators to question the roles and abilities of computers to support specific disciplines or subject areas, through pedagogical processes. In itself, this disciplinary difference does not lead to a natural rift between the subjects, but the difference does mean that those who broach that rift may come from quite different disciplinary backgrounds. Whilst computer science has been regarded or perceived as a discipline that has tended to rely in the past upon positivistic or quantitative approaches to its development and research, education has emerged as a discipline that was initially influenced by positivistic approaches, but has latterly become more influenced by post-positivistic, interpretivistic, and critical constructivist approaches. These disciplinary differences and the implied, evolving and emerging approaches have been paralleled by different ways that education has been seen in relation to computer science.

Initially, for TC3 and a number of countries who took up a policy or initiatives on computers and education at an early stage, education was seen as a way to teach and learn about computers, computing and computer science. A shift over the next 10 or more years was then towards education being seen as ways to teach and learn with computing and digital devices and resources. More recently, the shift has been towards teaching informatics or computer science, and most recently, there has been an emergence resulting in education being concerned with ways to teach and learn to influence computer science practice and development. Over the same time period, computer science itself has shifted in its concerns for development, research and evidence that are increasingly socially related, concerned with the ways that its outcomes can be used, how they influence and can be integrated with social practices. While computer science artefacts were often initially concerned with actions outside human behaviour and consciousness (although they have increasingly influenced them), the trends now are concerned more with their integration with human behaviour and consciousness. These shifts have resulted in a greater focus over time on inter- and multi-disciplinarity for those concerned with development and research into computing and digital technology destined for educational purposes. This has resulted in an increasing reliance and need for computing and technology expertise to be matched and supported by social science and humanities expertise.

The trends that we see today are already enabling uses of computing and digital technologies to provide wider access to education and learning, to provide widening opportunities for management of education, teaching and learning, and to enhance practices for teachers, learners, developers and policy makers. In this chapter, we show how TC3 has continued to focus on key challenges and issues in these evolving contexts, how it has sought to identify ways in which computing and digital technologies can be used most effectively for educational purposes, and how TC3 has played its part, and continues to play its part, in that journey.

3   Involving and Influencing – TC3 Conferences and Their Focus

TC3 has run international conferences for many years. Conference titles and focus have been pertinent to the contemporary issues of their time. The shift in titles and focus over the last 50 years has been important in terms of maintaining an up-to-date perspective but also to highlight future possibilities; in this respect, the shift highlights key issues and challenges that have emerged and are emerging.

TC3 and its Working Groups (WGs), through their many international conferences over the years, have led to the sharing and wider dissemination through presentation and publication of many leading-edge, accepted papers in proceedings and in books. In the case of some conferences, the papers have appeared in university publications, but in most cases, they have been published in book form by international publishing houses including Chapman & Hall, Kluwer and Springer. In recent years, most have been published by Springer, and the papers accepted have been double-blind peer reviewed before a selection is made of the most pertinent and leading articles. For post-conference publications, authors of accepted articles are given opportunity to improve their papers following discussion within the conferences, giving opportunity to take advantage of additional and important contemporary leading perspectives.

TC3 has run a range of different conferences, but the flagship conferences for TC3 have been World Conferences on Computers in Education (WCCEs). Since 1970, eleven of these conferences have been run. Whilst the first conference (Amsterdam, The Netherlands, 1970) focused on conceptions of computer education [5], the second conference (Marseille, France, 1975) focused more on how computers could be integrated and used in education by teachers [6]. A greater focus was placed on learners at a later stage, in 1995 (Birmingham, United Kingdom) [7] for example, while concerns for how computers could support education worldwide has been a focus since 2013 (Torun, Poland) [8]. The most recent WCCE (Dublin, Ireland) has focused on the wider range of users

– learners, teachers, developers, researchers and policy makers - with an increasing concern for those users with specific educational needs or in disadvantaged situations [9].

TC3 has additionally run streams within the wider IFIP World Computer Congress (WCC) conferences. Since 2002, four of these TC3 streams have been run. On each occasion, specific topics have been explored: the development of TelE learning in 2002 [10], the building of the information society in 2004 [11], learning to live in a knowledge society in 2008 [12], and the key competencies needed for living in a knowledge society in 2010 [13].

Within TC3, individual WGs, or WGs working collaboratively, have also run their own conferences. The conferences for current WGs are reviewed in later sections of this chapter, which focus on emerging concerns and themes of those WGs. One conference of note, run by a WG that no longer exists, focused on the online or distance provision of education using technologies as early as 2003 [14]. This highlights how TC3 has identified and often led on discussions and sharing of perspectives that can contribute to a wider understanding of how computers can be used in different and emerging educational practices. From the titles and themes across these conferences, it is clear to see that the interests and focus of TC3 have shifted in line with contemporary concerns. Across the timeline, this can be summarised as follows:

- 1970 – an initial focus on computer education (teaching and learning the subject of computing, about and with computers), followed within five years with a focus on computers in education (teaching and learning in other subjects, using computers)
- 1980 – the focus is on the increasing range of subjects where computers could be used in teaching and learning, the developing and emerging forms of digital technologies such as videodisks, and the impact of uses of computers and digital technologies on teaching and learning
- 1990 – the focus is more on the learner, and how computers and digital technologies are enabling learning, widening approaches to learning, and impacts from digital multi-media resources
- 2000 – the focus is on the widening impact of computers and digital technologies on society as a whole, on approaches to education that are linked to a knowledge society, and addressing and developing lifelong learning needs and approaches
- 2010 – the focus is more on the possibilities arising from communication, how computers and digital resources enable widening interaction, communication and collaboration, and impacts on conceptions of education and social and socio-cultural learning approaches
- 2020 – the focus is more on the possibilities arising from features of computer science and digital resources that support the individual, the individual with specific educational needs, and the role of individuals in being enabled to be producers as well as consumers, linked to greater focus on the teaching and learning of informatics and computer science

4   The TC3 Academic Journal, its Articles and Their Focus

While conferences have provided opportunities for researchers, practitioners and policy makers to share and discuss their findings and challenges, TC3 has also been instrumental in supporting a wider sharing through an academic journal route. Education and Information Technologies (EAIT) is the official journal of TC3, published by Springer. The EAIT journal has played a vitally important role in enabling key research to be channelled and disseminated. The focus and range of articles over time portrays elements that researchers have regarded as challenges or problems to be solved or shared, so having a view across the period of the journal offers another important perspective of how the field of computers and education has shifted and continues to develop.

EAIT covers the complex relationships between information and communication technologies and education, from the micro-concerns of specific applications or instances of use in classrooms to the macro-concerns of national policies and major projects; from classes of five-year-old children to adults in tertiary institutions; from teachers and administrators to researchers and designers; from institutions to open, distance and lifelong learning. The journal's breadth of coverage allows EAIT to examine fundamental issues at all levels, discuss specific instances and cases, draw inferences and probe theory, while being embedded in the research and practice of professionals.

EAIT was first published in 1996. EAIT has unquestionably grown over the years. While early volumes had four issues per year, the later volumes (in 2019, for example) had six issues, with a total of 184 articles, selected from 708 submissions. Springer publishes all accepted articles as *Online First Articles* before they are assigned to an issue. In 2019, there were 313,606 EAIT article downloads from the website. EAIT has been edited by a succession of international editors, and currently, the editor-in-chief is supported by three associate editors, and an active international editorial board of 29 members, from: Australia, New Zealand, the United Kingdom (UK), the United States of America (USA), Germany, Israel, South Africa, Greece, Finland, Switzerland, Bahrain, Hong Kong, France and The Netherlands. EAIT has become a truly international journal, with articles received in Volume 24 (2019) from authors in: Australia, Bahrain, Belgium, Canada, China, Colombia, Croatia, Cyprus, Egypt, Estonia, Fiji, Finland, France, Germany, Ghana, Greece, India, Indonesia, Iran, Ireland, Israel, Japan, Kazakhstan, Kuwait, Libya, Malaysia, Morocco, Nicaragua, Nigeria, Northern Ireland, Norway, Oman, Pakistan, Poland, Russia, Rwanda, Serbia, South Africa, South Korea, Spain, Sweden, Tanzania, Thailand, Tunisia, Turkey, the UK, Ukraine, the United Arab Emirates and the USA.

An idea of how research interest and attention on specific topics in the field of education and information technologies has changed over the years can be gained by exploring the titles of articles from several volumes across the journal's history. The topics also reveal how certain topics have remained the same over the years, while specific technology attention has often changed. So, for example, whilst one article [15] offered a framework for teaching a specific topic area, *the social and ethical impact of computing*, more recently, such frameworks have been offered on specific topics concerned with computing and computer science education. Studies that have explored uses of computers from teacher and teaching perspectives have remained over time (such as Chitiyo [16], and Voogt, Knezek and Roblin [17], as have studies that have explored learner experiences (such as Dillon [18], and Tiernan [19]). The need for connection between developers and practitioners has also been highlighted over time (such as Hinostroza, Rehbein, Mellar and Preston [20], and Rennstich [21]). Concerns for reconceptualisation of educational policy and practice have also regularly arisen; for example, the need to explore lifelong learning dimensions [22], and the need to review copyright regulations in a digital context [23]. Papers have also not always indicated positive outcomes for uses of computers in education; for example, papers that indicate the rejection of uses of integrated learning systems [24], and social media [25]. Most recently, topics have highlighted emerging technologies for education, such as the use of immersive virtual reality [26] and machine learning applications [27]. Special issues of the journal again show topics that have persisted, while others arise from the development of emerging technologies and the functionalities that they offer for education. A continuing concern has been the role that research plays in identifying the value and benefits of computers in education; for example, a focus on evaluation [28], on factors that are important [29], and on how students, computers and learning are connected [30]. The application and integration of technologies into educational practice has also been a theme that has persisted over time; for example, the topic of secondary informatics education [31], integrating mobile and panoramic video into education [32], and developing computing in the curriculum [33]. Uses of emerging technologies have been represented as they have emerged; for example, virtual realities [34], uses of serious games to support learning [35], and teaching and learning with social network sites [36].

5   WG3.1 – Informatics and Digital Technologies in School Education - Emerging Themes

WG3.1 was established in 1966, focusing on "Informatics and Information and Communication Technologies (ICT) in Secondary Education". In 2014, the WG was merged with WG3.5 (which focused on "Primary Education"), creating a WG that covered "Informatics and Digital Technologies in School Education". The current aims of WG3.1 have been reflected in recent IFIP TC3 conferences, providing international perspectives on the debate of developing and integrating informatics education (where the term informatics is used in some countries that is in this chapter the equivalent of the term computer science used in other countries) at all school levels. Such perspectives have included those from research activities as well as those from best practice experience, promoting acquisition and updating of appropriate knowledge and expertise for any whose teaching environment requires contact with computer-based systems. Such knowledge and experience considers the nature, content and method of delivery of school education, both within informatics (computer science) and digital technologies (digital humanities, and media literacy). The overall aims of WG3.1 are to enable learners to become discerning digital citizens who are able to act in a complex and digitalised world.

Current themes within the work of WG3.1 cover: early childhood and school education, including related informal learning contexts; computing education and digital literacy; the integration of digital technologies in education; the professional development of teachers; and the provision of pre-service and in-service teacher education. This range of work aims to enable educators to use and contribute to the development of digital educational resources, including professional learning networks.

WG3.1 has been involved in a number of conferences in recent years, organised with other WGs. The aims and focus of WG3.1, as discussed above, are clearly demonstrated by the themes of a number of recent conferences. These include: empowering teaching for digital equity and agency [37]; empowering learners for life in the digital age [38]; a new culture of learning: computing and next generations [39]; key competencies in informatics and ICT [40]; ICT and learning in the Net Generation [41]; and ICT and the teacher of the future [42]. Over the years, there has been an increasing interest in the role of communications technologies, informatics and computer science, interconnectivity and international perspectives, social and special educational needs, and digital equity and agency.

6   WG3.3 – Research into Educational Applications of Information Technologies - Emerging Themes

This WG provides a forum to identify issues and priorities for research into educational applications of information technologies and to map research policies arising from the differing approaches and cultural contexts in IFIP member countries. It aims to: identify research needs and topics in the field of education; improve research approaches and methods; synthesise research on major topics in the field; and disseminate research, in partnership with educational research communities. The group, with members from over 40 different countries, has many interests that relate to national issues and recent educational technology trends such as bring-your-own-devices (BYOD), artificial intelligence and the computer science curriculum. These themes relate to policy makers' interests in harnessing educational technologies to address national and international concerns such as improving attainment, supporting inclusive pedagogies, and skilling the workforce to meet the demands for digital expertise.

WG3.3 has a close working relationship with EDUsummIT, with representation in 11 of the 13 thematic working groups at the most recent EDUsummIT event in 2019. This international summit covered topics such as machine learning, learning analytics, and research approaches for educational technology, curriculum and knowledge building [43]. Other topics of research interest that group members currently study include mobile learning, computational thinking, teacher education and professional development, and cultural differences in the conceptualisation and delivery of ICT and computer science curricula. The growing interest in computer science and digital skills over the last decade led to the creation of a specific task force on the computer science/informatics curriculum, established in 2014.

Research from WG3.3 is well represented in many TC3 conferences, providing state-of-the-art findings that are accessible to other researchers, as well as policy makers and practitioners. Particular themes that have been supported by research papers from WG3.3 include: learners and learning contexts - new alignments for the digital age [44]; empowering learners for life in the digital age [38]; rethinking learning in a digital age [45]; mobile learning [46]; technology enhanced quality learning for all [47]; and addressing educational challenges - the role of ICT [48]. These themes indicate the important focus that has been and continues to be an ongoing concern of WG3.3, in monitoring the uses, outcomes and impacts of educational technologies on learning and learners.

7 WG3.4 – Professional and Vocational Education in ICT - Emerging Themes

WG3.4 was founded in 1971, and is focused on higher, professional and vocational education in ICT – education leading towards careers or professional development in some form of computing. The membership of WG3.4 comprises academics (in fields of computer science, information systems, etc.), ICT trainers and ICT practitioners from all over the world. Members' interests range from the use of computer-mediated education, the on-going professional education of both ICT and non-ICT professionals, the activities of national ICT professional bodies, the delivery of effective ICT vocational education to post-secondary learners and the integration of ICT into other tertiary curricula.

WG3.4's goal is to promote the acquisition and updating of appropriate ICT knowledge and expertise by all. Its aim is to consider the nature, content and method of delivery of professional and vocational education within the ICT sector, which will enable learners to achieve their employment expectations, and to foster lifelong learning in the contemporary and evolving networked environment.

Regarding professional education within ICT, of particular note was the production in 1998 by a small working group of WG3.4 members of the document entitled "Harmonisation of Professional Standards" (an Appendix in Thompson [49]). At IFIP's World Computer Congress held in Beijing in August 2000, the harmonisation project was re-considered, and over the next 5 years a significant number of international activities were undertaken to promote the IFIP harmonisation document and evaluate its relevance to the discipline of software engineering. These activities were reported at the IFIP TC3 WCCE in 2005 and summarised in a paper presented at the IFIP 19th World Computer Congress [49].

Regarding wider educational issues, WG3.4 has, since 1993, run nine working conferences, either as a single WG or jointly with other group(s), which have reflected particular contemporary interests at those times. The themes of those conferences have covered: software engineering education [50]; software quality and productivity [51]; the place of information technology in management and business education [52]; educating professionals for network-centric organisations [53]; e-training practices for professional organisations [54]; information and communication technologies and real-life learning [55]; education, training and lifelong learning [56]; open and social technologies for networked learning [57]; key competencies in ICT and informatics [40]; and sustainable ICT, education and learning [58]. Members of the group had a major input to IFIP sub-conferences held at the World Summit on the Information Society (WSIS) 2003 addressing education and the knowledge society [59], and at the IFIP World Computer Congress 2006 addressing education for the 21st century [60].

The emphasis of the work of WG3.4 over this period has shifted from technical, managerial, and business education towards issues related to networked and mobile learning and sustainable development goals. WG3.4 is keeping abreast of the application of latest methods and technologies in ICT learning, both in the Global South and the Global North. WG3.4 aims at encouraging mobile and creative solutions to the challenges of lifelong learning through research and knowledge sharing.

8   WG3.7 – Information Technology in Educational Management (ITEM) - Emerging Themes

The origins of WG3.7 go back to 1994. That year, an international working conference on information technology in educational management was organised in Jerusalem, Israel by WG3.4. An outcome of the conference was to establish WG3.7. The meeting brought together an important number of researchers and practitioners concerned with what could be the best practices to enhance educational management with the support of information technology. At that time, personal computing had experienced a widespread acceptance and the continuous development of communications foretold how information and communications technologies would have a large impact on all aspects of education, including that of management and administration of educational centres. The participants in the first meeting agreed that much was still to be done in this field, and jointly proposed to seek to create a new working group under the umbrella of TC3. Two years later, in 1996, the group was officially acknowledged by IFIP as WG3.7, with a chair elected by members in 1998. The first international conference on information technology in educational management organised by the newly constituted WG3.7 was held in Hong Kong, China in 1996.

The main aim of WG3.7 is to promote effective and efficient use of ICT within management, policies, development of and planning of educational institutions. The scope of WG3.7 is focused across the whole range of educational institutions concerned with education, from kindergartens to higher education, adult education, and those in professional development and training settings at a local, regional, national or international level.

Since 1994, 11 conferences have been organised exclusively by WG3.7, held on six continents (excepting Antarctica). WG3.7 has also participated in international conferences organised by other WGs. The topics of these conferences indicate emerging concerns of this WG: information technology in educational management [61]; information technology in educational management for schools of the future [62]; the integration of information for educational management [63]; pathways to institutional improvement with information technology in educational management [64]; information technology and educational management in the knowledge society [65]; knowledge management for educational innovation [66]; information technology and managing quality education [67]; and stakeholders and information technology in education [68].

More than 250 papers related to information technology in educational management have been published by WG3.7 members across the 1994–2020 period. Main themes have evolved over the years, as technology has developed and new issues in education and in educational management have arisen. The topic that has received most attention is assimilation and integration of IT into educational management. Other emerging themes over the years have been those of strategies to integrate IT into educational management and IT applications in educational management. Recently, several members of WG3.7

have participated in the publication of the *Encyclopedia of Education and Information Technologies* [69], a huge knowledge repository covering many aspects of the interaction between education and information technologies, including IT in kindergartens, primary and secondary schools, universities, training colleges, industry training, distance education and further education.

Interests in overcoming problems derived from adapting a new and changing technology such as IT to educational management has set the standards for WG3.7's ITEM research during the more than 25 years of its existence. Nevertheless, it is recognised that ahead is a task of continuing to complete a compact body of knowledge and adapting to new challenges as a result of the ever-changing educational and technological arena.

9   TC3 Task Force - Deeper Understanding of the Roles of Computer Science and Informatics

A TC3 Task Force is intended to focus attention on emerging developments in education that are fuelled by technological or societal need. The TC3 Task Force on the Computing Curriculum was established in July 2014 in response to calls for change in computer science and informatics curricula in many countries. The Task Force researched key issues and considerations for the curriculum and made recommendations for curriculum design and implementation. This work was summarised in 2016 in a short report, while more recently, the Task Force's work has focused on advances in conceptualising, developing, and assessing computational thinking and analysing how developments in artificial intelligence and machine learning need to be addressed within the curriculum.

At the outset of the work of the Task Force, a series of reviews and reports from different countries identified a need for major reform of the curriculum for computing, computer science, information and communications technology (ICT) or informatics - depending on the terminology used in each country (for example, [70–73]). These reports and papers emphasised a refocusing of computing/ICT education to incorporate computer science as the underlying subject discipline. In some countries where curricula had often previously contained strong computer science, it was argued that they had become weakened and often refocused on educating young people as *users* of new technologies rather than *creators*. In some countries, such as Israel and Cyprus, computer science had been retained since its emergence in the 1980s, but rationales for its presence in curricula and curricula themselves were nevertheless under scrutiny [74, 75].

The major rationales for including computer science in the K-12 curriculum put forward in reports from many countries were economic, social and cultural [76]. The economic rationale rested on the need for a country to produce computer scientists to sustain a competitive edge in a world driven by technology, but also on the requirement for professionals in all industries to have sufficient understanding of computer science in order to deploy technology to support innovation and development. The social rationale emphasised the value in society of active creators and producers rather than passive consumers of technology. Such capability empowers people to lead, create and innovate within society and in curriculum terms, so that this knowledge is part of the "powerful knowledge" [77] needed to enable people to choose their role in society. The curriculum rationale rested on enabling people to be drivers of cultural change rather than having change imposed by technological developments.

Many educators have identified the importance of people studying elements of computer science in order to support their learning of other subjects - in particular, being able to engage in "computational thinking" and other forms of thinking promoted by engaging in computer science, such as systems thinking, as well as developing understanding about the capabilities and potential of new technologies. This new thinking and understanding is not digital literacy (whose importance was already well-established), but a set of skills, understanding and thinking that can be developed by engaging with and understanding computer science, understanding how computers work and designing and creating computer-based solutions, including through programming. Considerations for developing curricula leads to implications for teacher professional development [78]. Broader recommendations for addressing key challenges for curriculum change in relation to computer science have been developed by the Task Force [75], further developed in relation to a wider range of country contexts in a report arising from a meeting between the Task Force and UNESCO [79]. Key recommendations were to adopt a globally agreed statement of computer science/informatics as a discipline in its own right, to articulate the nature, importance and relevance of computer science/informatics to society and education, and to disseminate and communicate a clear rationale to different stakeholders about the need to have computer science/informatics as a distinct subject in school curricula. Recommendations for policy and practice were to promote computational thinking through the means of a computer science/informatics curriculum which aims at making computational thinking commonplace, to design computer science/informatics curricula based on a content analysis, and then continue to research students' learning as well as the effects of different pedagogical approaches, and to identify clear learning outcomes, assessments and standards for computer science/informatics. Important caveats were to encourage more computer science/informatics graduates to become teachers and provide professional development for existing teachers, and to identify and allocate resources for teaching computer science/informatics.

More recently, the Task Force has focused on how developments in machine learning need to be accommodated in curricula for computer science/informatics. The implications of such developments are relevant more broadly across the curriculum, and members of the Task Force have contributed to an international discussion and report [80]. A key recommendation of this report, in relation to curricula for computer science/informatics, was to ensure that all students develop a strong background in machine learning. It was argued that in order to develop their conceptual understanding of how machine learning works, students must have opportunities to use and apply machine learning and to create their own examples. Furthermore, as a powerful tool that may not be used to its full potential, a need for students to understand how machine learning can be used to identify and solve real-world problems was recommended.

Currently, while many countries have made major changes to their curricula for computer science/informatics, others are still in the process of change. Implementing such curricula is still a major challenge for many countries. Rapid technological developments, especially in machine learning and quantum computing, mean that ongoing curriculum change continues to be inevitable.

10   Education and Computing - Visions and Declarations

TC3 has generated a number of visions and declarations over the years, arising from an analysis of outcomes from conferences, often WCCEs. Key declarations and visions were the Stellenbosch Declaration (arising from WCCE 2005), the Bento Gonçalves Declaration (arising from WCCE 2009), the Torun Vision (arising from WCCE 2013), the Dublin Declaration (arising from WCCE 2017), and the latest is the Zanzibar Declaration (arising from SUZA 2019). The identification of key themes and trends from these previous WCCEs and their declarations led in all cases to the production of a series of recommendations and actions, for policy, practice and research. The Stellenbosch Declaration called for actions to support digital solidarity, learners and lifelong learning, teachers and decision-making strategies, networking, and research. The Bento Gonçalves Declaration called for actions to support the learner and teacher through curriculum initiatives, to develop research, learning environments, professionalism, and collaborative communities. The Torun Vision set out two key challenges for the future. The first was to move from consuming to innovating; to create, conceptualise and produce using programming and computer science (CS), as well as using information and communication technology (ICT) applications. The second was to deploy digital technologies to better support different interactions with different stakeholders, according to technologies selected and used (such as those with online or haptic features), accommodating institutional diversities, gender, cultural, native language, cognitive and social backgrounds. The Dublin Declaration followed this vision, and provided recommendations and actions to take these key needs forward. The latest declaration, the Zanzibar Declaration, highlights the need to consider sustainable education in the context of emerging technologies.

The Stellenbosch and Dublin Declarations resulted from formal processes undertaken within respective WCCE conferences, and the Zanzibar Declaration is a current initiative instigated across TC3. As these Declarations are key documents in identifying contemporary issues of their times, they will be discussed in more detail in the sub-sections following.

10.1   The Stellenbosch Declaration

In 2005, TC3 held its WCCE in South Africa. The theme was *"40 years of computers in education: what works?"* Seven hundred delegates from more than 30 countries from six continents gathered for 4 days. Having many of the main actors of ICT in education in the world was a unique opportunity, not only to listen to each other's presentations, but to engage them to think and produce together and then to deliver an "address to the world". Consequently, all delegates were asked to contribute to a common reflection about education in the next decade. Each speaker was asked to provide one key idea, recommendation or suggestion. In each conference session, the chairperson was asked to provide three ideas, suggestions or recommendations as an output of that session. All delegates were also asked to contribute with one idea. The main aim was to generate a wide view about the "hot topics", what was being done around the world about ICT and education, at the research level, as well as in teaching and learning practice. Every day, a committee gathered and studied the contributions. At the end of the conference, a text, synthesising the contributions, was presented to the audience and adopted as the Stellenbosch Declaration. A researcher studied the Declaration and the way it was produced: "The IFIP Stellenbosch Declaration: Browsing the researchers' and practitioners' core ideas on ICT in education" [81].

The preamble of the Declaration stated that:

> *We, the members of the group, hope that this Stellenbosch Declaration will improve the integration of ICT in Education as a resource for both better teaching and learning and as a preparation of citizens for the Knowledge Society. We address this to all stakeholders in ICT in Education: teachers, practitioners, researchers, academics, managers, decision-makers and policy-makers, in order to increase the access to Education for everyone around the World. [...] As educators, we know that information and knowledge are not the same. We want not only an Information Society, but also a Knowledge Society in which Knowledge can be shared and distributed all around the world, enabling all children and all people to access Knowledge and to benefit from being educated.*

The Declaration addressed six topics: digital solidarity; learners and lifelong learning; decision-making strategies; networking; research; and teachers. For each of these topics, the Declaration made a statement and proposed some recommendations, at the societal level, at the learning and teaching level, and at the technological and infrastructure level. An annex to the Declaration offered a list of 107 possible actions, chosen from among the suggestions offered by the participants.

The Declaration was translated into many languages and was published in many journals. Fifteen years later, reading again the Declaration shows that even if the world has changed, the core issues and the main recommendations remain totally accurate. While a lot of progress has been made since, many questions are still open.

10.2 The Dublin Declaration

Twelve years later in 2017, the Dublin Declaration stated that in terms of computing, computer education and uses of technologies for teaching and learning, these were considered to be at a pivotal point of change. It was clear from evidence in the WCCE 2017 presentations that international, national and local computer and educational technology strategies, policies and curricula were shifting. Earlier and ongoing outcomes from the activities of important initiatives such as the European Computer Driving Licence (ECDL) clearly contributed to the then current state of play with regard to user practices and uses of ICT. The then current status of computer access and uses across countries, and the identification of key underlying development needs, was clearly shown by widespread monitoring of international and national comparison data, for example, from the Programme for International Student Assessment (PISA) results run by the Organisation for Economic Cooperation and Development (OECD) and from the International Association for the Evaluation of Educational Achievement's (IEA) International Computer and Information Literacy Study (ICILS) focusing on computer and information literacy. Given the wide evidence base at that time, it was clear that learners of all ages and levels could benefit from and should be enabled to develop opportunities that such technologies offer, not only for their individual futures but also for the future of our wider communities and society as a whole. However, it was highlighted that young people need to have sufficient opportunities to be creators and not just consumers of ICT. The theme of WCCE 2017 reflected a focal concern - to seek ways to assure the inclusiveness of technologies to support education, teaching and learning for all social groups. It was clear that teaching about computing should not replace the use of ICT to enhance learning across the curriculum, but that the balance between computing and ICT to enhance learning across the curriculum should be fully considered and accommodated. Importantly also, the balance between educational activities that involve non-computer use as well as computer use was an issue that needed wider consideration, as communities and societies moved towards increased digital ubiquity.

Recommendations put forward in the Dublin Declaration in 2017 are still pertinent today. Those recommendations covered a number of specific areas. For future direction with computer science education, it was recommended, for example, an entitlement for young people to be educated in computing, incorporating computer science and computational thinking as the underlying academic discipline, as well as digital literacy – as all young people have a right to become creators and not only consumers of ICT for their future. Importantly, to support these young people, there is a need to create more and well-trained computer science teachers.

It was recommended that, to address the gap between developing and developed countries in the use of ICT in education, there should be a focus on new pedagogical opportunities offered by mobile learning applications and their adoption in the education field. From an infrastructure perspective, it was recommended that infrastructure challenges should neither be considered as a matter of funding nor as a technocratic approach; school administrators and parents should be included in developing creative support and maintenance, as part of a wider holistic approach to development. To support this approach, there should be co-operation with countries with a high degree of ICT development in education, to share their experience in IT usage/skills in the educational domain.

To support inclusiveness and student engagement, recommendation was made to encourage schools to implement problems and ideas from real life and from students' out-of-school interests, activities and hobbies, to allow children to enjoy solving them in a challenging way, even in their free time. Some caution was also recommended, to develop emotional intelligence of our students, as this is often a missing component of all virtual learning environments and other digital resources. A goal should be to pay closer attention to implementing this aspect into pedagogies that involve educational software.

Importantly, to support teacher education and continuing professional development, recommendations were made to develop educators who can teach computational thinking rather than just teaching programming from standard lesson plans and textbooks, and to build further capacity in digitally-literate teachers in every discipline. The approach recommended was to provide professional development for teachers, which should be problem-based and adopt project-based approaches supported by and supplemented with communities of practice, as these latter facilities provide enormous potential for effective professional development. It was recommended that teachers should become more aware of the importance of learning analytics as potential instruments to improve learning processes, but considering the need for such data to provide useful and important feedback to improve educators' work. To support teacher professional development, international groups can promote ways of developing communities of research-active teachers to develop and disseminate their own evidence of the impact of ICT on teaching and learning.

To develop appropriate game-based learning and gamification, a recommendation was made to promote further research to set the basis of a comprehensive framework to support game-based teaching and learning at all levels of education. The need was recognised to train pre-service and in-service teachers in the use of game-based learning approaches.

To move towards e-evaluation, recommendations were made to consider stealth assessment as an approach to formative (rather than summative) assessment that is seamless - woven deep into the fabric of the activity such as a game and not taking away the 'fun of learning'. Further, it was recommended that the assessment approach from research be examined, to see how it can be taken into mainstream learning, and to study the rapid rise in e-examinations, for authentic assessment that matches modern workplace practices and many student learning experiences.

It was considered that, for any of the recommendations above (and others in the full Declaration) to be taken forward, there needed to be greater levels of international cooperation and collaboration between researchers and practitioners, through appropriate research processes, from design to dissemination. In addition, research approaches in this field should continue to integrate and combine the expertise of education, psychology, sociology, computer science and economics to provide robust, well-rounded, critical perspectives to ensure the most appropriate outcomes to drive the future of education forward. High-quality interdisciplinary research was felt to be needed to establish a strong and informative evidence base before adopting large-scale implementation and investments in educational technology initiatives. For implementation, an evidence base should be established to assess the impact and integration of technology in the classroom through a synergy between quantitative and qualitative methods, where studies are framed in appropriate theoretical terms, with consistency between theoretical position, design, methodology, data collection and analysis. Conceptions of research, policy and practice should be revisited in this field in this context. While teachers need to be considered to be producers of knowledge, maintaining the variety of uses for learners of all ages, identifying outcomes that relate to contexts, and measuring impacts where purpose and future developments are fully considered, were identified as all essential elements that need to be integrated into contemporary and future research, policy, teacher education, teaching and learning practices in this field.

10.3   Issues that We Face Internationally - the Zanzibar Declaration - Sustainable Education in the Digital Age

Looking outwardly and internationally, the perturbations, changes, and problems observed during the last decades reveal that we are certainly not living anymore in a static, but in a dynamic, world. Numerous disruptions in many domains have arisen, and the relationship between ICT and education has continued to receive increasing attention in many countries and regions. The importance of the relationship between ICT and education is also reflected in the current (2020) Coronavirus (COVID-19) pandemic crisis; home office and e-learning have become part of everyday life for many employees and students in 2020, and ICT-supported communication is becoming an essential part of social life.

For the educational field, it is possible to identify specific changes that have arisen over the past decade, such as modifications in pedagogy, demands from societies, and the emergence of new technologies. Thinking about what requirements will arise in the future in different areas of ICT and education, what strategies will be appropriate for research, development, and practice? What kind of information and knowledge do politicians, stakeholder researchers, and practitioners need to base their decisions and work on?

In the April 2019 annual general meeting, TC3 initiated a Declaration on "Sustainable Education in View of Rapid Emerging Technologies in the Digital Age". This Declaration describes future challenges and proposes approaches to their resolution. The Declaration followed discussions and presentations at an international conference (SUZA 2019, April 25–27, on Sustainable ICT, Education and Learning, run in Zanzibar, Tanzania). This Declaration is now in the process of being formulated and detailed. In this sub-section, an overview of the intended process and outcomes is outlined, to indicate key focal topics that TC3 is highlighting.

In developing the Zanzibar Declaration, TC3 draws on the many years of experience and relevant resolutions of international organisations (e.g. the World Summit of the Information Societies (WSIS), the United Nations Educational, Scientific and Cultural Organization (UNESCO), the International Telecommunications Union (ITU), and the World Intellectual Property Organization (WIPO)). Through the experience and exchange of views with experts from these organisations and through additional relevant meetings, it was important to incorporate substantive positions of various stakeholders from different countries within IFIP in this Declaration. To be able to consider as many local contexts and experiences as possible, as many IFIP experts and practitioners as possible are given the opportunity to contribute their ideas to the document. In this way, the various experiences regarding current technological ICT developments and the resulting demands on education in different national contexts can be taken into account. As this will be a dynamic process, collected contributions and data will be supplemented and updated from time to time. In this respect, the outcomes will represent a current status and describe different development paths towards an end status in different countries.

Whilst the Zanzibar Declaration is a work-in-progress, details of the current process and procedures to take this initiative forward are offered here. This will provide an idea of the range of current concerns that TC3 is exploring from an international perspective, relating to the future of computing and education. A matrix to provide an orientation through identified key contemporary topics has been developed (see Fig. 1). This matrix contains, in the left-hand column, emerging ICT technologies (T1 to T16), and in the top two right-hand rows, the possible social impacts of different applications in areas of societies (S1 to S11). Educational requirements resulting from the relationship between the technologies and the social impacts in specific contexts need to be appropriately considered and addressed. Possible contributions to the Declaration can be made by respondents; contributions can be assigned to a specific cell in the matrix, preferably addressing in the response all three components (technology, social impacts, and educational requirements). Both positive and negative aspects of the respective topic should be included, so that each contribution in a cell of the grid can be referenced, and indeed based, on everyday practice.

Création : 2019-05-16, par RMO Révision : 2019-07-03, par JSI Version : 02	S1 (Cyber)Security	S2 Privacy	S3 Social / Surveillance	S4 Decent work	S5 Health Care	S6 e-government / e-administration e-law	S7 environment / ecology / sustainability	S8 ethics / deontology / governance / code of conduct	S9 mobility	S10 Digital equity	S11 Gender Equity
T1 IoT - Internet of Things	MLM		JSI					JSI			
T2 Quantum Computing											
T3 Communication (eg 5G)					FIA				FIA		ISM
T4 Implication of Big Data											
T5 Blockchain											
T6 3D / 4D Printing											
T7 VR virtual reality - AR Augmented Reality					KNS						
T8 Autonomous Systems	MLM							GDU	GDU		
T9 Cloud Computing											
T10 Humanoids								GDU		GDU	
T11 Transhumanism			FIA								
T12 Nano Technologies											
T13 Technologies of Recognition (tracking)	MLM										
T14 Future Technologies										RMO	
T15 AI (artificial intelligence) activities			JSI		KNS			RMO GDU	GDU		
T16 Robotics			FIA		FIA						

Fig. 1. Orientation matrix of key themes relating to sustainable and future education with computing.

As an example of a possible contribution, for T8 Autonomous System with S9 Mobility, it would be possible to consider from a perspective that is *Positive*: Autonomous Systems will change public and private transportation; they may lead to reduction of traffic and emission of carbon dioxide; they will speed up transport and better tailor it to individual needs. From a *Negative* perspective: there is high expenditure on technical infrastructure; responsibility shifts from humans to algorithms; ethically difficult conflict situations can arise; the wealth of data generated could be used for social surveillance; destruction of workplaces (reducing onsite work) is considered possible. From an educational requirements (ER) perspective: IT basic understandings of autonomous systems should be integrated into curricula in an appropriate form and with suitable tools at different age levels (for example, algorithms, robots, autonomous vehicles constructed by students, (visual) programming language), and contextualised social impact should be considered using story-telling examples (e.g. jobs of taxi drivers).

The view on this topic (T8/S9) would possibly look quite different from the perspective of another country, a developing country, for example. When exploring the details in the matrix, it is, therefore, essential to consider the context-specific conditions in the examples, as these may reveal diversities between different locations, different cultural traditions, and institutional conditions. It will also be possible to view perspectives through the impact of a specific ICT technology on societies by selecting a row and addressing different areas of application. It will be possible to freely add any combination of technology or social impacts not contained in the matrix, and to describe a corresponding example.

It might be that entries will not be completed for all fields of the matrix, but, conversely, there could be accumulations and clustering of content in and around some cells. Thus, a heat map with example clusters on future relevant challenges could be created, which could then be addressed more fully in the Zanzibar Declaration. In addition, a collection of context-specific examples of the social impacts of future ICT technologies and a consideration of their resulting educational challenges could be created in this way.

Members of an initial working group have made first entries in some of the cells of the matrix (see the 3-letter abbreviations in Fig. 1). From these, it was found that a high degree of diversity arose when looking at specific topics. When the content of the matrix is further completed, the concept and the results of the initiative will be evaluated and presented at future conferences and meetings of TC3. It is planned that these events will include the (postponed) WSIS Forum 2020 and the next WCCE. WSIS is a natural platform to exchange perspectives gained on all the topics linked to this initiative with policy makers, politicians and other stakeholders. Each year, in Geneva, Switzerland, the WSIS Forum takes place with some 3,000 participants, supported by key international organisations. One of the key outcomes of the WSIS events has been the adoption of an agreed document entitled 'Sustainable Development Goals (SDG)'. As WSIS states:

The 2030 Agenda for Sustainable Development, adopted by all United Nations Member States in 2015, provides a shared blueprint for peace and prosperity for people and the planet, now and into the future. At its heart are the 17 Sustainable Development Goals (SDGs), which are an urgent call for action by all countries - developed and developing - in a global partnership. They recognize that ending poverty and other deprivations must go hand-in-hand with strategies that improve health and education, reduce inequality, and spur economic growth – all while tackling climate change and working to preserve our oceans and forests [82].

Having worked for four years with these guidelines, considering the local charitable aims of the SDGs, it has become evident that in the 17 SDGs three of these are prerequisites to meet real-world challenges of future 'Information and Knowledge Societies'. These three are concerned with: Education (SDG 4); Security (mainly addressed in SDGs 11, 16); and Ethics, Governance, and Code of Conduct (mainly addressed in SDGs 11, 16). Effectively, without those three together, it is considered that there is limited chance to realise socially just and environmentally friendly 'Information and Knowledge Societies'. Thus, education is one of the central fields and needs of activities of the United Nations and the WSIS Forum, and the three SDGs are inherently related to the topic of the Zanzibar Declaration that TC3 will develop to support its members and wider communities worldwide.

11   The Impact We Have Had – and Where We Go from Here

The work of TC3 over the years has had impact on research, policy and practice as well as more directly on IFIP and TC3 members. Impact on research is clear – the number and range of conferences, published books and academic papers through its journal EAIT are all a testament to the deep and broad contributions TC3 has made to the field.

Citations and downloads, references and identification of future work, have all been strong indicators of the impacts on research in this field. TC3 has also been instrumental in running doctoral consortia that have been associated with conferences, supporting young researchers in developing their practice and contacts.

Impact on policy is also clear. Members of TC3 and its WGs have often been key stakeholders at policy level, either directly working in policy roles, or advising key stakeholders in ministries and governments. In this respect, members of TC3 have contributed to government and ministry policy discussions and decisions in countries including Botswana, Denmark, France, Italy, Israel, Lithuania, Norway, Poland, Switzerland, and the UK. Policy support through TC3 work at institutional levels should also not be ignored here. Members of TC3 have often been in key positions within their own institutions, whether that be at school, college or university level. In all of these policy cases, those individuals have been supported through insights they have gained from TC3 conferences and meetings. In some cases, international collaboration has additionally resulted at policy level.

Impact on practitioners is also apparent. There have been a range of educational practitioners that have been members of TC3 and its WGs. In many cases, conferences have been supplemented with workshops, specifically designed to support and inform teachers, school leaders and school administrators. Feedback from these workshops has been positive, and it is clear that TC3 and WG members have been active in disseminating their expertise and experience at much wider international levels through routes such as these.

TC3 has continued a tradition of offering opportunity for discussion and sharing of expertise and experience – across the domains of research, policy and practice. In its current and future work, TC3 will continue to focus on three important areas of concern:

- Monitoring and assessing the potential of emerging new technologies, as their development will certainly not cease in the immediate future, and their application to education will need to be continually and carefully considered.
- International sharing and contextual discussion will support a wider application of new technologies to education, through an ongoing appropriate relationship between research, practice and policy.
- The application of new technologies to support social and individual diversity and needs will continue to be considered in the context of individual and community needs.

TC3 has a continuing major role to play in the future. It can be argued that, in view of contemporary challenges and contexts, there has never been a more important time for sharing, for exploring ways and means to enable and empower further the important working arenas of different stakeholders. Through implementing fundamental research, policy and practice, we may allow the fields of education and computing to come together to support our future (in the arena of what is now being termed 'digital education').

References

1. Tatnall, A., Davey, B. (eds.): Reflections on the History of Computers in Education. IAICT, vol. 424. Springer, Heidelberg (2014). https://doi.org/10.1007/978-3-642-55119-2
2. Passey, D.: Early uses of computers in schools in the United Kingdom: shaping factors and influencing directions. In: Tatnall, A., Davey, B. (eds.) Reflections on the History of Computers in Education. IAICT, vol. 424, pp. 131–149. Springer, Heidelberg (2014). https://doi.org/10.1007/978-3-642-55119-2_9
3. Passey, D.: Computer science (CS) in the compulsory education curriculum: implications for future research. Educ. Inf. Technol. **22**(2), 421–443 (2017)
4. Passey, D., Shonfeld, M., Appleby, L., Judge, M., Saito, T., Smits, A.: Digital agency - empowering equity in and through education. Technol. Knowl. Learn. **23**(3), 425–439 (2018)
5. Scheepmaker, B., Zinn, K. (eds.): World Conference on Computer Education. North Holland, Amsterdam, The Netherlands (1970)
6. Lecarme, O., Lewis, R. (eds.): Computers in education. In: Proceedings of the IFIP 2nd World Conference. North Holland, Amsterdam, The Netherlands (1975)
7. Tinsley, D., Van Weert, T. (eds.): Liberating the Learner. Chapman & Hall, London (1995)
8. Reynolds, N., Webb, M. (eds.): Learning While We Are Connected. Nicholaus Copernicus University Press, Torun, Poland (2013)
9. Tatnall, A., Webb, M. (eds.): WCCE 2017. IAICT, vol. 515. Springer, Cham (2017). https://doi.org/10.1007/978-3-319-74310-3
10. Passey, D., Kendall, M. (eds.): TelE-Learning – The Challenge for the Third Millennium. Kluwer, Alphen aan den Rijn, The Netherlands (2002)
11. Jacquart, R. (ed.): Building the Information Society. Kluwer, Alphen aan den Rijn, The Netherlands (2004)
12. Kendall, M., Samways, B. (eds.): Learning to Live in the Knowledge Society. ITIFIP, vol. 281. Springer, Boston, MA (2008). https://doi.org/10.1007/978-0-387-09729-9
13. Reynolds, N., Turcsányi-Szabó, M. (eds.): KCKS 2010. IAICT, vol. 324. Springer, Heidelberg (2010). https://doi.org/10.1007/978-3-642-15378-5
14. Davies, G., Stacey, E. (eds.): Quality Education at a Distance. Kluwer, Alphen aan den Rijn, The Netherlands (2003)
15. Martin, C.D., Huff, C., Gotterbarn, D., Miller, K.: A framework for implementing and teaching the social and ethical impact of computing. Educ. Inf. Technol. **1**, 101–122 (1996)
16. Chitiyo, R.: The conceptualization of instructional technology by teacher educators in Zimbabwe. Educ. Inf. Technol. **15**, 109–124 (2010)
17. Voogt, J., Knezek, G., Roblin, N.P.: Educational challenges in a digitally networked world. Educ. Inf. Technol. **20**, 619–623 (2015)
18. Dillon, J.: Young people, creativity and new technologies: the challenge of digital arts. Educ. Inf. Technol. **5**, 63–65 (2000)
19. Tiernan, P.: A study of the use of Twitter by students for lecture engagement and discussion. Educ. Inf. Technol. **19**(4), 673–690 (2013). https://doi.org/10.1007/s10639-012-9246-4
20. Hinostroza, E., Rehbein, L.E., Mellar, H., Preston, C.: Developing educational software: a professional tool perspective. Educ. Inf. Technol. **5**, 103–117 (2000)
21. Rennstich, J.K.: Creative online collaboration: a special challenge for co-creation. Educ. Inf. Technol. **24**(2), 1835–1836 (2019). https://doi.org/10.1007/s10639-019-09875-6
22. Kendall, M.: Lifelong learning really matters for elementary education in the 21st century. Educ. Inf. Technol. **10**, 289–296 (2005)
23. McGrail, J.P., McGrail, E.: Overwrought copyright: why copyright law from the analog age does not work in the digital age's society and classroom. Educ. Inf. Technol. **15**, 69–85 (2010)

24. Jervis, A., Gkolia, C.: "The machine stops": one school's rejection of integrated learning systems. Educ. Inf. Technol. **10**, 305–321 (2005)
25. Hutchens, J.S., Hayes, T.: In your facebook: examining facebook usage as misbehaviour on perceived teacher credibility. Educ. Inf. Technol. **19**, 5–20 (2014)
26. Lorenzo, G., Lledó, A., Arráez-Vera, G., Lorenzo-Lledó, A.: The application of immersive virtual reality for students with ASD: a review between 1990–2017. Educ. Inf. Technol. **24**(1), 127–151 (2018). https://doi.org/10.1007/s10639-018-9766-7
27. Qazdar, A., Er-Raha, B., Cherkaoui, C., Mammass, D.: A machine learning algorithm framework for predicting students' performance: a case study of baccalaureate students in Morocco. Educ. Inf. Technol. **24**, 3577–3589 (2019)
28. Marshall, G.: Guest editorial. Educ. Inf. Technol. **4**, 214–220 (1999)
29. Somekh, B.: Learning for the twenty-first century: what really matters? Educ. Inf. Technol. **10**(3) (2005)
30. Hu, C.: Students, computers and learning: where is the connection? Educ. Inf. Technol. **22**(6), 2665–2670 (2017). https://doi.org/10.1007/s10639-017-9670-6
31. Schubert, S., Taylor, H.: Secondary informatics education. Educ. Inf. Technol. **9**(2) (2004)
32. Multisilta, J.: Mobile and panoramic video in education. Educ. Inf. Technol. **19**, 565–567 (2014)
33. Brodnik, A., Lewin, C.: A new culture of learning: developing computing in the curriculum and advancing digital pedagogy. Educ. Inf. Technol. **22**, 417–420 (2017)
34. Selwood, I., Mikropoulos, T., Whitelock, D.: Virtual reality. Educ. Inf. Technol. **5**, 233–236 (2000)
35. Cruz, S., Carvalho, A.A.A., Araújo, I.: A game for learning history on mobile devices. Educ. Inf. Technol. **22**(2), 515–531 (2016). https://doi.org/10.1007/s10639-016-9491-z
36. Forkosh-Baruch, A., Hershkovitz, A., Greenhow, C.: Teachers and learning with social network sites. Educ. Inf. Technol. **22**, 599–603 (2017)
37. Brinda, T., Passey, D., Keane, T. (eds.): OCCE 2020. IAICT, vol. 595. Springer, Cham (2020). https://doi.org/10.1007/978-3-030-59847-1
38. Passey, D., Bottino, R., Lewin, C., Sanchez, E. (eds.): OCCE 2018. IAICT, vol. 524. Springer, Cham (2019). https://doi.org/10.1007/978-3-030-23513-0
39. Brodnik, A., Lewin, C. (eds.): A New Culture of Learning: Computing and Next Generations (NCLCom). Vilnius University Press, Vilnius, Lithuania (2015)
40. Passey, D., Tatnall, A. (eds.): ITEM 2014. IAICT, vol. 444. Springer, Heidelberg (2014). https://doi.org/10.1007/978-3-662-45770-2
41. Schubert, S., Davies, G., Stacey, E. (eds.): LYICT 2008: ICT and Learning in the Net Generation. Open University Malaysia, Kuala Lumpur, Malaysia (2008)
42. Dowling, C., Lai, K.-W. (eds.): ICT and the Teacher of the Future. Kluwer, Alphen aan den Rijn, The Netherlands (2003)
43. Webb, M.E., et al.: Challenges for IT-enabled formative assessment of complex 21st century skills. Technol. Knowl. Learn. **23**(3), 441–456 (2018). https://doi.org/10.1007/s10758-018-9379-7
44. Fisser, P., Phillips, M. (eds.): Learners and Learning Contexts: New Alignments for the Digital Age (EDUsummIT 2019), 29 September – 2 October 2019, Quebec City, Canada. https://edusummit2019.fse.ulaval.ca/files/edusummit2019_ebook.pdf. Accessed 13 May 2020
45. Lai, K.-W., Voogt, J., Knezek, G. (eds.): Rethinking Learning in a Digital Age (EDUsummit 2017), 18–20 September, Borovets, Bulgaria. https://eprints.lancs.ac.uk/id/eprint/89048/1/EDUSummIT_2017_eBook_final.pdf, Accessed 13 May 2020
46. Carvalho, A.A.: Using mobile devices and online tools to promote students' learning. In: Tatnall, A., Mavengere, N. (eds.) SUZA 2019. IAICT, vol. 564, pp. 7–15. Springer, Cham (2019). https://doi.org/10.1007/978-3-030-28764-1_2

47. Lai, K.-W. (ed.): Technology Enhanced Quality Learning for All (EDUsummIT 2015), 14–15 September, Bangkok, Thailand. http://www2.curtin.edu.au/edusummit/local/docs/edusummit2015-ebook.pdf. Accessed 13 May 2020
48. Manchester Metropolitan University (ed.): Addressing Educational Challenges: The Role of ICT. Manchester Metropolitan University, Manchester (2012)
49. Thompson, J.B.: Education and software engineering. In: Impagliazzo, J. (ed.) History of Computing and Education 2 (HCE2). IAICT, vol. 215, pp. 93–105. Springer, New York (2006). https://doi.org/10.1007/978-0-387-34741-7_6
50. Barta, B.-Z., Hung, S.L., Cox, K.R. (eds.): Software Engineering Education. North-Holland, Amsterdam, The Netherlands (1993)
51. Lee, M., Barta, M.-Z., Juliff, P. (eds.): Software Quality and Productivity: Theory, Practice, Education and Training. Chapman & Hall, London (1995)
52. Barta, B.-Z., Tatnall, A., Juliff, P. (eds.): The Place of Information Technology in Management and Business Education. ITIFIP, Springer, Boston, MA (1997). https://doi.org/10.1007/978-0-387-35089-9
53. Juliff, P., Kado, T., Barta, B.-Z. (eds.): Educating Professionals for Network-Centric Organisations. ITIFIP, vol. 17. Springer, Boston, MA (1999). https://doi.org/10.1007/978-0-387-35393-7
54. Nicholson, P., Thompson, J.B., Ruohonen, M., Multisilta, J. (eds.): E-Training Practices for Professional Organisations. Springer, Heidelberg, Germany (2003)
55. van Weert, T., Tatnall, A. (eds.): Information and Communication Technologies and Real-Life Learning. ITIFIP, vol. 182. Springer, Boston, MA (2005). https://doi.org/10.1007/b136546
56. Tatnall, A., Thompson, J.B., Edwards, H.M. (eds.): Education, Training and Lifelong Learning. International Federation for Information Processing, Laxenburg, Austria (2007).
57. Ley, T., Ruohonen, M., Laanpere, M., Tatnall, A. (eds.): OST 2012. IAICT, vol. 395. Springer, Heidelberg (2013). https://doi.org/10.1007/978-3-642-37285-8
58. Tatnall, A., Mavengere, N. (eds.): SUZA 2019. IAICT, vol. 564. Springer, Cham (2019). https://doi.org/10.1007/978-3-030-28764-1
59. Van Weert, T. (ed.): Education and the Knowledge Society: Information Technology Supporting Human Development. Kluwer Academic Publications, Boston, MA (2005)
60. Kumar, D., Turner, J. (eds.): Education for the 21st Century — Impact of ICT and Digital Resources. IIFIP, vol. 210. Springer, Boston, MA (2006). https://doi.org/10.1007/978-0-387-34731-8
61. Barta, B.-Z., Telem, M., Gev, Y. (eds.): Information Technology in Educational Management. IAICT, Springer, Boston, MA (1995). https://doi.org/10.1007/978-0-387-34839-1
62. Fung, A.C.W., Visscher, A.J., Barta, B.-Z., Teather, D.C.B. (eds.): Information Technology in Educational Management for the Schools of the Future. ITIFIP, Springer, Boston, MA (1997). https://doi.org/10.1007/978-0-387-35090-5
63. Fung, A.C.W., Visscher, A.J., Wild, P., Selwood, I. (eds.): The Integration of Information for Educational Management. Felicity Press, Maine, USA (1998)
64. Nolan, C.J.P., Fung, A., Brown, M. (eds.): Pathways to Institutional Improvement with Information Technology in Educational Management. Kluwer, Alphen aan den Rijn, The Netherlands (2000)
65. Tatnall, A., Osorio, J., Visscher, A. (eds.): ITEM 2004. IIFIP, vol. 170. Springer, Boston, MA (2005). https://doi.org/10.1007/b104289
66. Tatnall, A., Okamoto, T., Visscher, A. (eds.): ITEM 2006. IIFIP, vol. 230. Springer, Boston, MA (2007). https://doi.org/10.1007/978-0-387-69312-5
67. Tatnall, A., Kereteletswe, O.C., Visscher, A. (eds.): ITEM 2010. IAICT, vol. 348. Springer, Heidelberg (2011). https://doi.org/10.1007/978-3-642-19715-4
68. Brinda, T., Mavengere, N., Haukijärvi, I., Lewin, C., Passey, D. (eds.): SaITE 2016. IAICT, vol. 493. Springer, Cham (2016). https://doi.org/10.1007/978-3-319-54687-2

69. Tatnall, A. (ed.): Encyclopedia of Education and Information Technologies. Springer, Cham (2020). https://doi.org/10.1007/978-3-030-10576-1

70. The Royal Society: Shut down or restart? The way forward for computing in UK schools. http://royalsociety.org/uploadedFiles/Royal_Society_Content/education/policy/computing-in-schools/2012-01-12-Computing-in-Schools.pdf. Accessed 13 May 2020

71. Wilson, C., Sudol, L.A., Stephenson, C., Stehlik, M.: Running on empty: the failure to teach K-12 computer science in the digital age. ACM, New York, NY (2010)

72. Joint Informatics Europe, ACM Europe Working Group on Informatics Education: Informatics education: Europe cannot afford to miss the boat: report of the joint Informatics Europe & ACM Europe Working Group on Informatics Education. http://www.informatics-europe.org/images/documents/informatics-education-europe-report.pd. Accessed 13 May 2020

73. Bell, T., Andreae, P., Robins, A.: Computer science in NZ high schools: the first year of the new standards. Paper presented at the 43rd ACM Technical Symposium on Computer Science Education, Raleigh, NC (2012)

74. Hazzan, O., Gal-Ezer, J., Blum, L.: A model for high school computer science education: the four key elements that make it! SIGCSE Bull. **40**(1), 281–285 (2008)

75. Webb, M., et al.: Computer science in K-12 school curricula of the 21st century: why, what and when? Educ. Inf. Technol. **22**(2), 445–468 (2016). https://doi.org/10.1007/s10639-016-9493-x

76. Fluck, A., et al.: Arguing for computer science in the school curriculum. Educ. Technol. Soc. **19**(3), 38–46 (2016)

77. Young, M.: Overcoming the crisis in curriculum theory: a knowledge-based approach. J. Curric. Stud. **45**(2), 101–118 (2013)

78. Angeli, C., et al.: A K-6 computational thinking curriculum framework: implications for teacher knowledge. Educ. Technol. Soc. **19**(3), 47–57 (2016)

79. IFIP TC3 Curriculum Task Force: Coding, Programming and the Changing Curriculum for Computing in Schools: Report of UNESCO/IFIP TC3 Meeting at OCCE – Wednesday 27th of June 2018, Linz, Austria. https://www.ifip-tc3.org/publications/. Accessed 13 May 2020

80. Thematic Working Group 4: State of the art in thinking about machine learning: implications for education. In: Fisser, P., Phillips, M. (eds.) Learners and Learning Contexts: New Alignments for the Digital Age (EDUsummIT 2019), 29 Sept–2 Oct 2019, Quebec City, Canada (2020). https://edusummit2019.fse.ulaval.ca/files/edusummit2019_ebook.pdf. Accessed 13 May 2020

81. Ollagnier-Beldame, M.: The IFIP Stellenbosch declaration: browsing the researchers' and practitioners' core ideas on ICT in education. Paper presented at the IFIP Conference, June 2006, Alesund, Norway (2006)

82. United Nations General Assembly: Transforming our world: the 2030 agenda for sustainable development. https://www.un.org/ga/search/view_doc.asp?symbol=A/RES/70/1& Lang=E. Accessed 13 May 2020

TC 5: Information Technology Applications

Computing Inventive Activities in an Industrial Context New Scientific Challenges and Orientations

Denis Cavallucci[1]([⊠]) and Cecilia Zanni-Merk[2]

[1] INSA Strasbourg, ICube Laboratory, 67000 Strasbourg, France
denis.cavallucci@insa-strasbourg.fr
[2] Normandie Université, INSA Rouen, LITIS, 76000 Rouen, France
cecilia.zanni-merk@insa-rouen.fr

Abstract. In light of the increasing computerization of the world, the innovation activity in the industrial context seems to be lacking of tools to improve its performance. Since 2004, the 5.4 working group has been devoted to studying the computerization of this activity in industrial environments, coming up against, throughout its history, the underlying complexity of tackling a theme that is eminently complex because it is multidisciplinary and often in competition with human creative reasoning. However, the rebirth of artificial intelligence and the 4.0 paradigm are now pushing us to reconsider our research axes, as well as the scope of action in which our research must be situated. This article proposes an analysis that aims to refocus our research around a more realistic topic, more in tune with today's world, in line with our understanding of the issues in which our contribution can be deployed and on which scientific foundations.

Keywords: Computer-Aided Innovation · Inventive problem solving · Applied artificial intelligence · R&D 4.0

1 Introduction: The New Challenges Around the Activity of Innovation in the Context of Industry

1.1 Digitization of the Business World

As regularly in its history, a company has to renew itself or risk disappearing. With each technological or societal upheaval, a radical change followed by a necessary adaptation often takes place under the constraint of discomfort and the uncertainty that this causes regarding its survival in the short or medium term. Currently, and for less than a decade, the paradigm of digitization has posed itself to the company with its share of difficulties and the realization that while all companies in all industrial sectors have undertaken these changes, none can escape them.

Whether it is called "Industry 4.0", "Industry of the Future" or "Factory of the Future", this paradigm can be understood as a necessary evolution on how digitalization

M. Goedicke et al. (Eds.): Advancing Research in Information and Communication Technology,
IFIP AICT 600, pp. 155–169, 2021. https://doi.org/10.1007/978-3-030-81701-5_6

and so-called "intelligent" management of the physical operations of the company are carried out. It is therefore natural that workshops, assembly lines, quality departments and shipping were the sectors of the company that were the first to be affected by this change. Today, with sensors (IoT), robots, locating effectors, immaterial devices sending and receiving digital signals from parts, machines, tools, etc., the company's operations are dependent on the versatility of customer orders.

There is, however, one department of the company that has been carrying out this digital transformation for decades: it is Research and Development. The role of the R&D in a company is thus and for a long time, assisted by tools of modelling, calculations, simulation and informational management of its piloting (of its information systems). It then seems logical, in schematizing this situation, to perceive that the physical means are catching up with the intellectual means in the company. However, the connection is not being made and we are still far from a total and digital continuum from customer demand to delivery. Our observations of this continuum reveal a missing link, a gap in computerization on the "intelligent" nature of creative and inventive thinking in R&D. Indeed, while the CAD, calculation or even the recent CAI tools that our group considers as research objects, none of them have taken on the heavy task of operating artificially creative reasoning. Probably because this scientific "leap" is frightening to a society that sometimes stands in the face of unbridled innovation that it perceives as negative for the future of humanity.

The challenge posed by the computerization of creative reasoning is therefore legitimately questionable. If this last bastion of the role of the human being in business gives way, would it not be the advent of an endless creative loop driven solely by the consumer appetite of a society that is bulimic of novelty?

Our choice on this aspect is to move forward while avoiding the thorny pitfall of creativity by approaching this theme through a first link: the (inventive) resolution of problems. If the disciplinary field of Problem Solving is no longer debatable, it is to establish a digression towards "inventive" problem solving, which by definition only deals with what goes beyond the boundaries of the field where the problem arises, to extend to a field that is implicitly distant and unknown at the start of the solving process.

To sum up, we are now moving towards the search for algorithmic forms of knowledge processing to intelligently accompany the reasoning behind the resolution of problems in the design of technical systems, of any size and any level of complexity, from the domain where the problem arises to any other domain likely to contribute to its resolution.

1.2 The Second Life of AI and Its Promises

The intelligent nature of the algorithms that populate today's processors owes much of their effectiveness to the renewal of Artificial Intelligence. Indeed, the oldest among us probably remember that many attempts have been made to bury Artificial Intelligence because of its inability to compete with the incredible capabilities of human reasoning. Yet over the decades, AI research has grown, the information processing capacity of processors has increased almost exponentially, and the advent of the cloud and a space populated by available and limitless knowledge has now opened new perspectives to the world of research and more broadly to society at large. Today, there is no large company, state or nation that does not define itself through the challenges and prospects that AI offers for its future. It must therefore be noted that all the disciplinary variations of AI, its associated techniques, and its often free and open-source tools, are generating an increase in research in this field, which means that it is now up to everyone to appropriate them and use them to reach the "intelligent" stage of a tool, a method, an algorithm, a technical system or a company.

The 4.0 paradigm fits particularly well with the progress of AI since computerization generates omnipresent information flows in the company that are just waiting to be better managed and optimized. In this context, our inventive problem-solving activity can only be conceived by evolving from a formally described state (see our previous work on ontologies) to an intelligent form where AI techniques contribute to reproducing human inventive reasoning to better assist navigation in the near-infinite ocean of knowledge.

1.3   Genesis of the Activity of the Computer-Aided Innovation Group

When our group clustered into a SIG (Special Interest Group) in 2004 under the impetus of Professor Noel Leon together with Professor Gaetano Cascini, we felt it was necessary to understand how the advent of a new generation of tools called CAI would penetrate the industrial world and what research would be necessary to accompany these new tools. A few commercial leaders of the time, such as Invention Machine or Ideation, were then facing each other in a field almost devoid of tools, where only CAD tools reigned supreme. The arrival on the scene of a major CAD player (Dassault Système) and his interest in linking CAD and CAI by joining forces with Invention Machine was to some extent the starter of our group's adventure.

Subsequently, the formulation of our objectives and their scientific orientations would allow us to build a small community that was constantly questioning its role in the computerization of Innovation. Through its collections of articles and its scientific productions, the WGCAI has contributed to questioning various disciplinary fields of science such as engineering sciences, information sciences or management sciences.

However, it has to be said that what was already being debated in the early days is still being debated, and it is still legitimate to question the extent of our contributions to the views of the small size of our group. Are we contributors to a pipeline called Innovation? Or doesn't the assertive industrial and engineering inventiveness of our group and its members require us to work in a more targeted spectrum of innovation, the inventive activity, upstream of it? If we look back at the arguments of the debates at the time, we find the decisive element that made us call ourselves "innovation": we had to extend the spectrum of potential research because it was in its infancy and we did not know at the time whether it would contribute more upstream than downstream of innovation.

Today, the observation made in the first two paragraphs of this article shows that even the narrower field of invention poses a set of challenges that is sufficiently broad for a group like ours, composed essentially of scientists from the engineering sciences, to find a favourable ground for the deployment of its research.

1.4 Towards New Directions and a New Scope of Research

We are therefore facing a new life cycle for our group and the trends that are emerging on its reorientation are of 3 orders:

A refocusing of our scope of action on invention, upstream of a broader innovation process to which we contribute, but focusing on the formalism of its inventive phases. Such phases range from the management of tacit or explicit knowledge, resulting from the fruit of experience, or observed from reliable sources made available, to the production of inventive ideas or concepts when these are outside the scope of what is known in a given field; to reducing the uncertainty of the technical feasibility of these ideas by a formal description, pre-dimensioning, calculation, optimization, a digital or physical prototype allowing the downstream phases of the innovation process to be initiated.

A particular effort will be placed on the role of artificial intelligence techniques in the evolution of our information processing algorithms. This is to improve the parameters for evaluating the accomplishment of invention tasks in terms of completeness, speed and timeliness of information, whether it comes from expert questioning, texts, images, videos, audio transcription, sensors or IoT.

The digitization paradigm of society, and particularly of enterprises, will be at the heart of our concerns. Here we intend to work on aligning our tools with existing tools in the context of the Factory of the Future, especially when these are included in the scope of R&D decisions.

2 At the Origins of Group 5.4 is the TRIZ Theory, Its Incipient Computerization and Its Academic Research

2.1 Some Failures for the Computerization of TRIZ

Let us go back to the origins of our group: the arrival on the international scene of TRIZ-based digital innovation assistance tools. If we look at the headlines of some newspapers of the time, we can read "the tool of the 21st century", certainly in a journalistic style, but the exaggeration of this title reflects the hopes that industrialists placed in a tool (Invention Machine). Two decades later, the conclusion is clear: no tool that claims to be from TRIZ has made a breakthrough in the international industrial scene. No digital tool has supplanted an expert approach led by a human. There are even relatively few TRIZ experts who are willing to work with a digital tool. Our reading of this situation reveals 3 reasons that could partly explain this failure.

The first is that the inventive activity underlying TRIZ is an intimately human activity and that the human cognitive mechanism associated with its creativity is not yet sufficiently challenged by digital intelligence. Even though computations and databases have long since overtaken humans, creative thinking involves the billions of neural connections between synapses in the brain. The act of expanding into timely connections that produce the unexpected is therefore even more intellectually prolific than artificially so. Nevertheless, in the context of finding a solution to a problem and in the perspective of sharing knowledge across disciplines in industry and basic science, digital assistance makes sense and opens up important perspectives.

The second is that the foundations on which TRIZ was born are empirical. Altshuller was an electrical engineer and although he was a visionary, he did not provide the scientific basis for his theory that would have made it more formally usable by others. His method of construction was centralized and based on pedagogical and circumstantial exploitation: does the approach bring a plus in a person's ability to go beyond what they would have produced without the method? This not very robust way of developing a body of knowledge has long been a brake on the evolution of TRIZ in the various learned societies that have long seen TRIZ as a tool rather than as a disciplinary field opening up new perspectives. Information science has thus so far shown little interest in TRIZ, as the mechanisms underlying the theory appear to be rather obscure and not very formal.

Finally, the third reason is linked to the versatility and impatience of the expectations of users of IT tools. All attempts to computerize the TRIZ have come up against what a user expects from such tools: a quick answer and a reduced time to ask a question. However, the existing tools that make use of TRIZ all implicitly require a compilation of the knowledge needed to characterize the initial situation. And since they have not been automated to any great extent, these phases are carried out by the users themselves.

We are therefore faced with the need to automate a maximum of human mental tasks of two distinct orders, formulating and solving:

- **Formulate**: seek information that characterises the problems. It is then necessary to classify this information in data silos after a preliminary interpretation in harmony with a formal ontology that codifies how we have to differentiate what is useful, superfluous, false or indispensable for creative thinking. But how can we approach this aspect of the problem without thinking about the time-consuming side of this activity? One of the reasons why TRIZ is not widely used in industrial circles is the time-consuming side of its use, especially in the analysis of the initial situation.
- **Solve**: starting from a problem formulated canonically, extend the search for information likely to solve it beyond the perimeter of knowledge of the field where the problem arises. But starting from the postulate that human knowledge in all fields is almost infinite, a relevant search that breaks with human intuition poses a set of research problems that we intend to address.

This constitutes a new line of research that is on the borderline between artificial intelligence and engineering. To be successful, this research must involve researchers in information science and engineering science. The challenge is to be able to imitate the inventor's reasoning by teaching the machine to reason like an inventor. If we envisage supervised learning in this framework, it is, therefore, a few thousand humanly constructed expert cases that must be grasped by annotating texts that contain accounts of inventive situations to find a posteriori the cognitive mechanism that occurred during the inventor's creative reasoning in the sense of the TRIZ theory. Thus, if we can find in recent writings the tacit expression of inventive principles inherent to the inventors;' thinking. We could then in real-time associate any new information, as soon as it appears publicly on the Internet, with a TRIZian mechanism automating the relationship between a problem model and a solution model. The user in an invention situation would thus be augmented in his reflections by new (recent) knowledge that is distant from his field of origin, such as to trigger the inventive mechanism that Altshuller studied and depicted in his work with the TRIZ theory.

Finding information, whether by questioning experts or reading texts is, therefore, a time-consuming step in the computerization of TRIZ, which relegates it to the rank of an improved notebook. This is demonstrated by the success of the simplification tools which, by a simple query in the form of a word or an expression, gives access to databases whose content is then more or less skillfully filtered.

The 4 types of texts which constitute for us privileged targets where the expert, scientific and technical knowledge likely to assist the inventive act resides are patents, scientific articles published in international journals and scientific news sites of a journalistic nature.

- **Patents** contain (according to the EPO) 80% of mankind's technical knowledge, even if no proof has ever been provided for this assertion, we can nevertheless reasonably believe that patents contain a large part of the written traces of human inventiveness. It remains for us to free ourselves from their intrinsic legal character by classifying those parts of their content that are likely to populate the ontology of Inventive Design and thus feed a database structured to feed the scheme of inventive thinking.
- **International journal articles** have the advantage of being peer-reviewed and therefore constitute first-rate information with credible content and written according to a certain framework. By targeting certain journals where inventive information from a variety of industrial fields is located, we have a second choice textual target.
- Then **journalistic-style websites** where news related to the invention are updated on a much more regular basis are also a good target. The versatile nature of scientific and technical information means that the emergence of novelty is both rapid (inventive novelties every second) and ephemeral (constantly renewed). The journalistic style (as opposed to the legal style) is deliberately made explicit so that it can be quickly assimilated by as many people as possible. Its syntactic forms are therefore particularly simple and its computer processing is equally simple.
- Finally, we will place in a separate category the **Wikipedia site** which alone contains a large part of the knowledge of humanity. If we limit the parts of Wikipedia dedicated to fundamental scientific knowledge, we have here information of a different nature since it displays very little recent news but rather records fundamental knowledge of all kinds.

In these four bases, we, therefore, have a combination of places where textual information resides that can feed representations of problems as well as elements that can be used to solve them.

To conclude this chapter, if TRIZ computerization is to have any chance of successfully serving society, it will have to automate human reasoning beyond what it is capable of producing without computing. There is therefore a place for machine learning, and the role of deep learning in this quest seems obvious. As our group is setting the limits of industrial use of such tools in the context of the intellectual demands made by research and development departments, we legitimately believe that such research, in this precise context, is in the process of blossoming and spreading in industry.

2.2 The Presence of TRIZ in International Publications

Earlier, we have already discussed the complicated relationship between TRIZ and scientific publications. The very first publications in quantity on the subject of TRIZ came from a site born in 1994: the TRIZ Journal. This site was not peer-reviewed, the articles were not peer-reviewed, and the scientific rigour of the writing and selection was questionable. It is also noted that the first thesis on the subject appeared in 1999 and that therefore the official scientific research on the subject of TRIZ was at first very empirical and based on a literature that was not easily accessible. It was therefore only in the mid-1990s that publications appeared in indexed journals on the subject of TRIZ, and it was a long time before some journals did not find, in the simple presence of the keyword TRIZ in a proposal, a reason for rejection. The beginning of 2010 marks an important turning point in the acceptance of TRIZ as a research topic in its own right. The ETRIA association and its scientific committee annually publishes a collection of contributions from the main laboratories that research the subject. The contributions are often taken up and published in about fifty journals indexed in ISI or Scopus. Over the past 10 years, more than 250 scientific articles have appeared each year in journals on the subject. It is therefore difficult today to contest the legitimacy of research associated with TRIZ in scientific circles.

2.3 Towards a New Discipline to Support the Digitization of Inventive Activity

But let us look ahead with the data mentioned in the previous paragraphs. We have a set of scientific communities from engineering and information sciences that contribute annually to the progress of digitization of inventive activity in the context of the industry. We also have scientific tools that today are major issues for society, such as deep learning and supervised learning. More broadly, the involvement of Artificial Intelligence in research applied to the context of industry and more specifically its R&D. We are working in a new paradigm and the industry of the future is driven by a desire to intelligently digitize its functioning at all levels.

Computer-Aided Invention is thus becoming a new disciplinary field, in which computational systems have their place. They extend from the identification, monitoring and collection of knowledge in all its forms and of a nature to feed inventive thinking, to its processing, its use in the context of invention support, and end with the formalization of new concepts whose proof of feasibility is advanced to a point that allows the use of optimization techniques to move forward robustly in the innovation pipeline. The particular considerations of the alignment of a new information system in the information pipeline of a company are also studied so that bridges are possible between inventive design and routine and computational design. As is the subject of the role that a continuous flow of digital inventive concepts could play in the decision-making aspects of steering a 4.0 company.

3 New Research Frontiers for Group 5.4

During the last years, we have observed a certain shift in the kind of aspects considered while talking innovation. The new topics that are more and more present include theoretical issues about innovation and creative design, sustainability and smart industry.

We choose here to present a small subset of the last works of the members of WG5.4, pioneers of this innovation paradigm shift.

3.1 Theoretical Issues About Innovation and Creative Design

The theoretical issues that have been addressed during the last years include the study of the trade-off between optimisation and invention and the capitalisation of experience in inventive design but also pedagogical issues associated with creativity and inventiveness or the proposal of new paradigms for innovation.

Some authors have worked on the existing synergies between the design optimization process and the TRIZ model of contradictions, by using experimental or simulation data to automatically extract systems of contradictions [Chi18]. The same authors have proposed different ways to formulate innovation directions, from simulation to contradictions [Dub17].

Concerning the capitalisation of experience in innovation, several different approaches have been published. Most of them are based on the use of case-based reasoning, and we can mention one of the first works in this area by [Hou15] where the similarities and differences between the TRIZ theory and case-based reasoning are outlined. We can also mention the works of [Liu20a], who propose a novel approach of clustering of similar design cases, using fuzzy relational analysis, case-based reasoning and the C-K theory. Other approaches in this area involve the use of other technologies for experience capitalisation, such as in [Zha18], that highlights that using classical TRIZ tools to solve a specific problem requires additional knowledge such as the expert's accumulated know-how in their problem-solving practice (i.e. experience). To facilitate the use of experience, this proposal explores a new inventive problem-solving approach based on experience capitalization (Fig. 1). We can also mention the works of [Zan19] that present a survey on the use of the KREM model. The KREM (Knowledge, Rules, Experience, Meta-Knowledge) model permits the capitalisation of experience in smart systems and was successfully applied in different industrial cases (Fig. 2).

The last element of this section concerns the proposal of new invention paradigms or pedagogical aspects. The first structuring works of [Cav11] justified the emergence of new tools allowing computer-aided artefact creation, that are the base of the works of WG 5.4. It is also worth mentioning the works of [Liu19] who proposed mixed approaches with radical innovation and knowledge-based innovation and a radicality evaluation method, obtained by a regression process on two well-known radicality computing formulas, through a statistical analysis of some known design cases. On their side [Wan20] propose a quantitative model of low-end disruptive innovation (interesting because of its simplicity, low cost, ease of use, and high maintained reliability and efficiency of the existing product) based on the OTSM-TRIZ model.

Finally, some other authors have been working on the possibility of teaching innovative design in engineering schools, knowing that new engineers need to be at the cutting edge of technology in all areas. The authors of [Cav13] present some experiments led by them, based on the postulate that any innovation-oriented approach requires that the bases of any design action need to contain new rules of inventiveness where creativity and problem-solving have priority. Also in this pedagogical context, computer tools have their place and need to be developed beyond classical ideas collecting boxes, whether

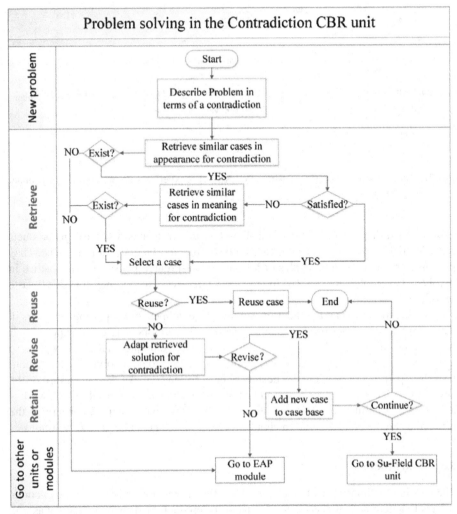

Fig. 1. Joint use of Case-Based Reasoning (CBR) and TRIZ to improve the use of experience in inventive studies

they are physical or digital, extended within a small group of persons or open to variable extents.

3.2 Sustainability

In this section, it is worth mentioning the last works of one of our members (and the associated research group), that has been working on sustainability and environmental issues for several years now.

One of the areas is waste disposal, whose methods and technologies are characterised by slow evolution. In [Rus19], the authors present a proposal of using pyrolysis for waste disposal. Pyrolysis can bring great benefits, in economic and environmental terms, when

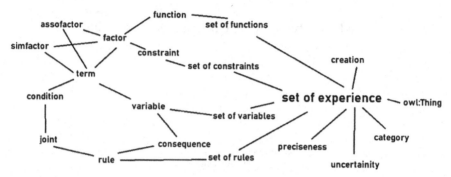

Fig. 2. Capitalization of experience using a SOEKS (set of experience knowledge structure) under its ontology representation

used for waste disposal because instead of just burning waste, it is possible to get products for industrial use, such as reaction gases and oils that have a high calorific value. They present some successful examples of how an Italian-French industrial group, active in pyrolysis has implemented TRIZ to develop a large-scale technology for urban waste recycling.

Another important area is the proposal of eco-guidelines for supporting designers in developing new greener products and processes. The authors of [Rus20] support their work on one of the most known systematic innovation techniques, TRIZ. They propose a rigorous ontology indicating how to apply a specific problem-solving strategy onto a specific part of the problem the designers face, trying to make the user aware of the environmental consequences of the choice of design changes. The result of this work is a set of 59 guidelines that are presented along how they were adapted concerning the original technique, and the reason about why they should generate greener solutions.

3.3   Smart Industry

The concept of Smart Industry (or Industry 4.0 or even Industry of the Future) corresponds to a new way of organizing the means of production. This new industry asserts itself as the convergence of the virtual world, digital design, management (operations, finance and marketing) with the products and objects of the real world. In these new smart factories, human beings, machines and resources communicate with each other naturally taking advantage of new technologies such as the Internet of Things and Services, the Cyber-Physical Systems, the Cloud Manufacturing or the Additive Manufacturing, among others.

Some authors have taken an interest in additive manufacturing as an integral part of modern manufacturing because of its unique capabilities in various application domains, and in particular in a specific case of design, namely design for additive manufacturing (DfAM). [Ren20] propose a design framework for additive manufacturing through the integration of axiomatic design and TRIZ. This integrated approach is effective because the axiomatic design approach can be used to systematically define and analyze a design

problem, while the TRIZ problem-solving approach combined with an additive manufacturing database of existing pieces can be used as an idea generation tool to generate
innovative solutions for the design problem.

In another area associated with Smart Industry, the automation in different manufacturing processes has triggered the use of intelligent condition monitoring systems,
which are crucial for improving productivity and the availability of production systems. To develop such an intelligent system, [Cao19] has proposed an ontology as a
base to develop an innovative intelligent condition monitoring system (Fig. 3). More
recent works of the same group [Cao20] complete the previous works and propose the
joint use of machine learning and deductive semantic technologies for that innovative
development.

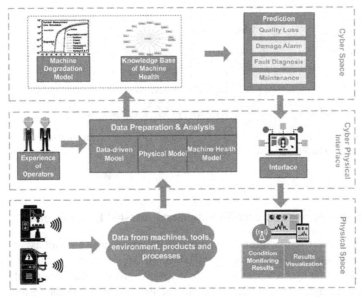

Fig. 3. The proposed framework for an intelligent condition monitoring system based on a cyber-
physical approach

Other members of WG5.4 have been working on cognitive vision systems due to their
potential to revolutionize human life as they are designed to work under complex scenes,
adapting to a range of unforeseen situations, changing accordingly to new scenarios and
exhibiting prospective behaviour. The combination of these properties aims to mimic
human capabilities and create more intelligent and efficient environments. Contextual
information plays an important role when the objective is to reason such as humans do,
as it can make the difference between achieving a weak, generalized set of outputs and
a clear, target and confident understanding of a given situation. Nevertheless, dealing
with contextual information remains a challenge in cognitive systems applications due
to the complexity of reasoning about it in real-time in a flexible but yet efficient way. The
authors of [Sil20] propose an enrichment of a cognitive system with contextual information coming from different sensors and the use of stream reasoning to integrate/process

all these data in real-time and provide a better understanding of the situation in analysis, therefore improving decision-making (Fig. 4).

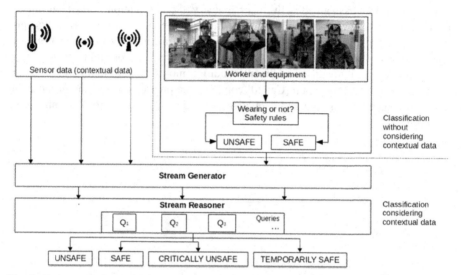

Fig. 4. Framework for enriching a cognitive system with contextual information coming from different sensors processed by stream reasoners

3.4 AI-Based Semi-automated Invention and Assisted Brainstorming

AI-based computer tools within the context of invention raise another axis of research which is more methodological and practical. In this research, one of the WG5.4 teams wonders about the systematization of the inventive process and in particular to what extent certain stages can pass from man to machine, including in the formulation and resolution phases.

Some authors argue that a possible intermediate path lies in reversing the classical process of constructing a problem graph to go step by step in 4 steps towards a list of solution concepts [Mas20] (Fig. 5).

This approach aims to get straight to the point of the problem to the contradiction by feeding on real-time information from semantic extractions from current scientific texts.

In this research, the authors start from the fact that the minimum necessary in the analysis of a problem requires at least one partial solution and two antagonistic problems. This subset must be qualified by one parameter of action and two parameters of evaluation to clarify the contradiction underlying this portion of the graph within a larger problem. From a contradiction to the inventory of the elements of information likely to solve it also implies a large part of automation and exploration of knowledge bases artificially exploited to provoke the creative act. If the solution concept is distant from the expected objective, it is a direct return to a new exercise of formulation-contradiction-resolution

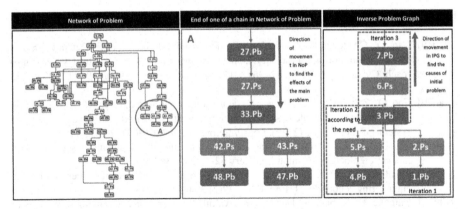

Fig. 5. Network of Problem and its difference with Inverse Problem Graph

which is proposed and so on until the objective is reached. Through this approach, the team tends towards a high level of assistance to the inventive act, making it much faster without sacrificing the inventive relevance of the results.

4 Conclusions

As evoked in the introduction, the new developments in artificial intelligence and the 4.0 paradigm push the WG5.4 to reconsider the research lines and the perimeter where these new directions need to take place. Following this idea, collaborations with other WG in TC5 or with other TCs need to be developed. In particular, natural synergies with other groups of TC5 appear, mainly with *WG5.1 Global product development for the whole life-cycle*, *WG5.7 Advances in production management systems* and *WG5.11 Computers and environment*, because these groups work closely to the new topics that emerged in WG5.4.

But, if we analyse in detail the research works that are the main focus of WG 5.4 today, it is clear that natural synergies appear also with TC12 Artificial Intelligence. The topics addressed by its workgroups (knowledge representation, reasoning and management, machine learning and data mining, collective and computational intelligence) are the ones that appear in the new research lines of WG5.4, as analysed in Sect. 3.

In the years to come, we intend to change the life cycle of our group. Our intentions clearly raise the question of a name change, the expression Computer Aided Innovation seems to be beyond our possibilities, on the other hand, we feel much closer to inventive activity than to the entire continuum that separates an initial problem situation from a market success. One of our past publications talked about the innovation pipeline, and it is quite true that only a very broad multidisciplinary scientific activity could address such a field in its entirety. In view of the size of our group and the scientific fields covered by our members. It is therefore more than a contribution to the upstream inventive phases of the innovation pipeline that needs to be discussed, with particular attention to the role played by the combination of information sciences and engineering sciences in formalizing inventive activities.

References

[Cao19] Cao, Q., Giustozzi, F., Zanni-Merk, C., de Bertrand de Beuvron, F., Reich, C.: Smart condition monitoring for Industry 4.0 manufacturing processes: an ontology based approach. Cybern. Syst. **50**(2), 82–96 (2019). https://doi.org/10.1080/01969722.2019.156 5118

[Cao20] Cao, Q., Zanni-Merk, C., Samet, A., de Bertrand de Beuvron, F., Reich, C.: Using rule quality measures for rule base refinement in knowledge-based predictive maintenance systems. Cybern. Syst. (2020). https://doi.org/10.1080/01969722.2019.1705550

[Cav11] Cavallucci, D.: A research agenda for computing developments associated with innovation pipelines. Comput. Industry **62**(4), 377–383 (2011)

[Cav13] Cavallucci, D., Oget, D.: On the efficiency of teaching TRIZ: experiences in a French engineering school. Int. J. Eng. Educ. **29**(2) 304–317 (2013)

[Chi18] Chibane, H., Dubois, S., De Guio, R.: Automatic extraction and ranking of systems of contradictions out of a design of experiments. In: Cavallucci, D., De Guio, R., Koziołek, S. (eds.) TFC 2018. IAICT, vol. 541, pp. 276–289. Springer, Cham (2018). https://doi.org/10.1007/978-3-030-02456-7_23

[Dub17] Dubois, S., Chibane, H., De Guio, R., et al.: From simulation to contradictions, different ways to formulate innovation directions. In: ETRIA TRIZ Future Conference 2017, Lappeenranta, Finland (2017)

[Hou15] Houssin, R., Renaud, J., Coulibaly, A.: TRIZ theory and case based reasoning: synergies and oppositions. Int. J. Interact. Des. Manuf. IJIDEM **9**(3), 177–183 (2015)

[Liu19] Liu, W., Tan, R., Cao, G., Zhang, Z., Huang, S., Liu, L.: A proposed radicality evaluation method for design ideas at conceptual design stage. Comput. Ind. Eng. **132**, 141–152 (2019) https://doi.org/10.1016/j.cie.2019.04.027

[Liu20a] Liu, W., Tan, R., Cao, G., Yu, F., Li, H.: Creative design through knowledge clustering and case-based reasoning. Eng. Comput. **36**(2), 527–541 (2019). https://doi.org/10.1007/s00366-019-00712-5

[Liu20b] Liu, L., Li, Y., Xiong, Y., Cavallucci, D.: A new function-based patent knowledge retrieval tool for conceptual design of innovative products. Comput. Ind. **115**, 103154 (2020)

[Mas20] Hanifi, M., Chibane, H., Houssin, R., Cavallucci, D.: A method to formulate problem in initial analysis of inventive design. In: Nyffenegger, F., Ríos, J., Rivest, L., Bouras, A. (eds.) PLM 2020. IAICT, vol. 594, pp. 311–323. Springer, Cham (2020). https://doi.org/10.1007/978-3-030-62807-9_25

[Ren20] Renjith, S.C., Park, K., Okudan Kremer, G.E.: A design framework for additive manufacturing: integration of additive manufacturing capabilities in the early design process. Int. J. Precis. Eng. Manuf. **21**(2), 329–345 (2019). https://doi.org/10.1007/s12541-019-00253-3

[Rus19] Russo, D., Peri, P., Spreafico, C.: TRIZ applied to waste pyrolysis project in morocco. In: Benmoussa, R., De Guio, R., Dubois, S., Koziołek, S. (eds.) TFC 2019. IAICT, vol. 572, pp. 295–304. Springer, Cham (2019). https://doi.org/10.1007/978-3-030-32497-1_24

[Rus20] Russo, D., Spreafico, C.: TRIZ-based guidelines for eco-improvement. Sustainability **12**(8), 3412 (2020)

[Sil20] Silva, C., de Oliveira, F., Giustozzi, C.-M., Sanin, C., Szczerbicki, E.: Stream reasoning to improve decision-making in cognitive systems. Cybern. Syst. **51**(2), 214–231 (2020). https://doi.org/10.1080/01969722.2019.1705553

[Wan20] Wang, Y., Peng, Q., Tan, R., Sun, J.: Implementation of low-end disruptive innovation based on OTSM-TRIZ. Comput. Aided Des. Appl. **17**, 993–1006 (2020). https://doi.org/10.14733/cadaps.2020.993-1006

[Zan19] Zanni-Merk, C., Szczerbicki, E.: Building collective intelligence through experience: a survey on the use of the KREM model. J. Intell. Fuzzy Syst. vol. Pre-press, pp. 1–13, 11 July 2019. Pre-press

[Zha18] Zhang, P., Essaid, A., Zanni-Merk, C., Cavallucci, D., Ghabri, S.: Experience capitalization to support decision making in inventive problem solving, Comput. Ind. **101**, 25–40 (2018). https://doi.org/10.1016/j.compind.2018.06.001

The Evolution Path to Collaborative Networks 4.0

Luis M. Camarinha-Matos[1]([✉]) [ID] and Hamideh Afsarmanesh[2] [ID]

[1] School Science and Technology, NOVA University of Lisbon and CTS-UNINOVA,
Campus de Caparica, 2829-516 Caparica, Portugal
`cam@uninova.pt`
[2] University of Amsterdam, Amsterdam, The Netherlands
`h.afsarmanesh@uva.nl`

Abstract. The last two decades have witnessed considerable boost in emergence of a networked society, reflecting the increasing growth in hyper-connectivity among the organizations, people, smart machines, and intelligent systems. This trend was enabled by advances in ICT and more specifically in computer networking. In this context, new forms of coworking and collaboration in networks, composed of distributed, autonomous, and heterogeneous entities have emerged, which first led to the formation of Collaborative Networks (CN) as a new discipline, and then followed by series of milestones leading to its gradual evolution.

Nowadays CNs play a key role in the ongoing process of digital transformation in industry and services. Although it is relatively young, a number of "generations" can be identified through the last decades for the CN discipline. We are now at the beginning of what can be identified as the Collaborative Networks 4.0, characterized by features such as: hybridization in CNs, collaboration between humans and intelligent autonomous systems, collaborative distributed cognitive systems, reflecting on collaborative accountability, handling ethics and coping with risks and disruptions faced in CNs, managing large amounts of collaborative data, monetization of collaboration, creating a collaboration culture, supporting collaboration creativity, handling mass collaboration, and supporting collaborative value creation through new business models, among others.

The IFIP WG 5.5, through its annual conference the PRO-VE, which is now in its 21st edition, has played a determinant role, along these two decades. It has contributed to shaping, promoting, and extending the CN research and development community and its practices; thus, consolidating this area, and identifying and introducing new directions and preserving it as an active research agenda.

Keywords: Collaborative networks · Virtual organizations · Virtual enterprises · Digital transformation · Business ecosystems

1 Introduction

Along the last few decades there has been a noticeable increase in networking, which has enabled a big increase in collaboration activities supported by computer networks. From

© IFIP International Federation for Information Processing 2021
Published by Springer Nature Switzerland AG 2021
M. Goedicke et al. (Eds.): Advancing Research in Information and Communication Technology,
IFIP AICT 600, pp. 170–193, 2021. https://doi.org/10.1007/978-3-030-81701-5_7

an initial focus on collaboration among humans or organizations, the scope has been expanding to include collaboration with and among smart machines and systems. This trend results from a progressive integration of the physical and cyber worlds, namely Cyber-Physical Systems/Internet of Things (CPS/IoT), leading to what can be called a hyper connected world. Complementarily, more and more systems, devices and machines embed higher levels of intelligence, reflecting higher levels of autonomy [1].

Besides the technological drive, the collaboration trend has also been motivated by a number of other factors such as the need to strive in turbulent and even disruptive scenarios, increase in global competition, stronger environmental concerns, push for tailored and one-of-a-kind small products by customers, and tougher quality requirements, as well as the consumer demographic shifts, etc. [2–4].

Understanding and supporting collaboration activities requires contributions from multiple disciplines and areas, including computer science and engineering, industrial engineering, electrical engineering, management, economics, sociology, law, ethics, and even natural ecosystems and biology, etc. Although the subject has attracted considerable attention in different research communities, realizing the need to study and adopt all these contributions has caused a confluence towards developing an interdisciplinary perspective of the area. As such, during the last decades, the collaborative networks (CN) area has emerged and evolved as an established scientific discipline, whose first manifesto can be traced back to 2004/2005 [5, 6].

In parallel with research and development initiatives, a large number of application cases have emerged and become operational in virtually all sectors of the society. Often new experiments on collaboration have emerged even before the publication of their scientific basis is out. This has been induced and motivated by the possibilities offered by new technology and new market needs. Applications of collaborative networks in industry represent one of the largest groups, starting with the evolution of traditional supply chains to more dynamic value chains and global supply networks, including extended enterprises, virtual enterprises, business ecosystems, etc. [7]. This trend can be seen in manufacturing, namely in the so-called Industry 4.0 [8–11], but also in construction, agribusiness, energy, and many other areas. The same has emerged in the area of services, with integrated multi-supplier business and software services in a large variety of sectors including commerce, tourism, insurance, healthcare, elderly care, education, and journalism, among others. Similarly, in the governmental sector for providing better services to citizens, through the integration of service offerings from different governmental organizations. We can also observe the emergence of public-private-social networks to address major societal problems which cannot be solved by any single organization.

In times of global crises, such as the case of COVID-19 pandemic, what becomes particularly noticeable is the high number of collaborative networks emerging worldwide. In different sectors such initiatives may use different terminologies, but a set of common underlying principles can be identified to be shared by all of them, showing that the CNs are nowadays widespread to all sectors of activity in the society.

This chapter aims to give an overview of the various types of CNs, a summary of current developments in the area, and a panorama of their evolution, and emerging directions and challenges.

2   A Classification of Collaborative Networks

There are currently many "manifestations" of collaborative networks in multiple sectors. Nevertheless, all these cases show diverse characteristics e.g., in terms of their structure, duration, purpose, internal agreements, external liabilities, and membership regulations, among many others. In order to facilitate understanding the specific characteristics of each case it is relevant to establish a taxonomy of collaborative networks.

A frequently used taxonomy (Fig. 1) was originally proposed in [12] and has been updated in more recent publications [7, 11, 13]. At its upper level, this taxonomy introduces two main classes:

- *Collaborative Networked Organizations* (CNOs) – to include all cases for which an organizational structure for the set of network members is designed and specified explicitly.
- *Ad-hoc collaborative networks* – to include those manifestations of CNs that emerge in a quasi-spontaneous way, without predefined organizational structure.

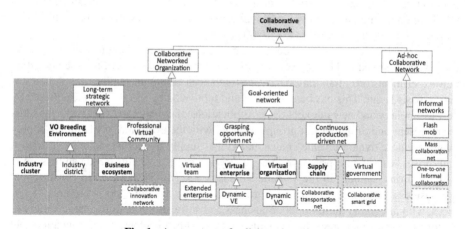

Fig. 1. A taxonomy of collaborative networks

CNOs include two main sub-classes:

- *Long-term strategic networks* – these are associations of entities, usually established with a very long duration in mind, and whose main objective is to help their members prepare for effectively working together whenever relevant new collaboration opportunities arise. In other words, these associations aim to facilitate the rapid and agile formation of goal-oriented networks in response to new opportunities. In order to accomplish such preparedness for collaboration, the involved entities invest in establishing common or interoperable ICT infrastructures/platforms, agree on common business principles, define rules for sharing and working methods, and providing high level of mutual awareness about the competencies and resources of the members, accompanied by trust building processes, etc.

- *Goal-oriented networks* – these are typically established within and through long-term strategic networks, in order for its involved entities to jointly achieve a given goal, such as realizing a specific project, developing a (complex) product, or providing a service, etc.

According to this taxonomy, the long-term strategic networks are further divided into *Virtual organizations Breeding Environments* (VBEs) [14] and *Professional Virtual Communities* (PVCs), depending on whether the main membership type is respectively organizations/enterprises or people (e.g., free-lancers). Today, some variants of VBEs include *Industry Clusters, Industrial Districts Business Ecosystems*, etc. As exceptions, there are some cases of networks that might be considered as both sub-class of the VBE and the PVC, e.g., *Collaborative Innovation networks*.

Goal-oriented Networks include the cases of (i) response to a single opportunity (*Grasping opportunity driven network*), which involves a temporary association of entities that join capabilities and resources to better satisfy the opportunity and that dissolve after the goal is achieved (typically project-oriented); and (ii) continuous production of a product or delivery of services (*Continuous production driven network*). Examples of case (i) include *virtual enterprise* (VE), *virtual organization* (VO), and *extended enterprise*, among others. Examples of case (ii) include *supply chains*, collaborative *virtual government*, etc.

Ad-hoc Collaborative Networks, which often rely on new mobile communication facilities and social networks and are characterized by some kind of "spontaneous emergence" without an apparent (strong) organizational structure. Some of these cases are triggered by some social event or sudden need, or even by human socialization needs. Under this class we can include, for instance, flash mobs, mass collaboration, informal networks, etc.

Considering that CNs are still young phenomena, many new forms are still emerging, namely induced by new technologies. As such, a taxonomy of CNs needs to remain open and subject to continuous expansion and evolution. The presented taxonomy has been used by the research community as a "working taxonomy". It was however defined at the early stage of this area, and it might be natural for other taxonomies to be proposed as new collaboration experiments pop-up once it becomes difficult to link them to the current classes. Furthermore, other taxonomies might also appear as a result of using different classification perspectives. For instance, in [15] Durugbu suggests a classification that uses mainly the same sub-classes but at the upper level they are organized in three different main groups: (1) Organization-driven, including VBEs and dynamic VOs; (2) Business-driven, including Extended Enterprise and Virtual Enterprise; (3) Professional-driven, including PVCs, eScience, and Virtual Labs. Then the class VO is defined as a member of the three groups.

We might also observe in time some transformation of classes. For instance, some ad-hoc cases, with a long duration, are likely to become organized and thus moved to the class of CNOs. That is the situation we observe for some cases of mass collaboration, such as in the Open source and Wikipedia development communities, which have evolved to a more structured cases and could better be classified as a sub-class of continuous production driven network.

3   Generations of Collaborative Networks

Collaborative Networks have been playing a key role in the ongoing process of digital transformation in industry and services. Despite CNs being a relatively young discipline, various development stages or as recently called "development generations" can be identified for it (Fig. 2). These stages/generations can be labelled as follows:

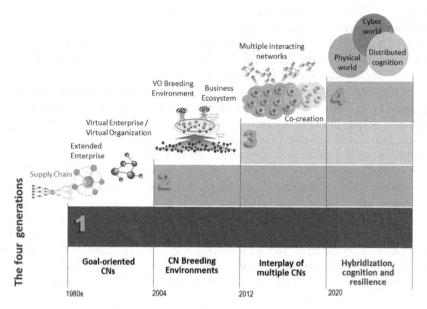

Fig. 2. Collaborative networks generations

- **Collaborative Networks 1.0** – corresponding to the early stage of the CNs, which was mostly focused on goal-oriented networks and that has covered the beginning manifestations of dynamic supply chains, extended enterprises, virtual enterprises, and virtual organizations.
- **Collaborative Networks 2.0** – mainly characterized by the introduction of the notion of VO breeding environment as a strategic network, encompassing business ecosystems, industry clusters, industrial districts, and professional virtual communities as sub-classes.
- **Collaborative Networks 3.0** – focused on addressing the interplay among multiple CNs, including hybrid value systems networks, co-creation and open innovation networks, and narrowing down on issues of multiple levels of membership, inheritance and transition between CNs, multi-supplier "servitization", etc.

At present however, we are entering a new stage of the CNs, whose precise characteristics are still not completely clear, but can so far be tentatively specified as follows:

- **Collaborative Networks 4.0** – primarily capturing: hybridization and collaboration between humans and intelligent autonomous systems, while addressing innovation in handling and support for distributed cognitive systems, reflection on accountability, ethics, coping with risks and disruptions, handling large amounts of data, monetizing collaboration, creation of collaboration culture, collaboration creativity, mass collaboration, collaborative value creation, and defining new business models among others.

In terms of research and development most ongoing challenges are in fact related to this generation.

The IFIP WG 5.5, as reflected in its annual conference PRO-VE (Working Conference on Virtual Enterprises), has played a determinant role, along the last two decades, in formation and shaping of the related research community and its practices, consolidating the area, and pointing to new research and development directions, thus keeping an active research agenda (Fig. 3) [16]. Further to knowledge sharing and promoting a multi-disciplinary convergence, the PRO-VE series acquired a crucial role in the identification of needs, setting the trends, building a research community, and contributing to education.

4   Ongoing Developments, Trends, Challenges and Expectations

Research and development in CNs in the last decades covered a wide spectrum of activities from which a large number of achievements can be pointed out, including development of concepts, models, methods and tools, and their application to a variety of cases. Figure 4 gives a brief high-level view of the main branches of developments on these past works.

More recent and ongoing works involve a greater convergence of knowledge areas and technologies, in line and to some extent influenced by current trends in digital transformation and Industry 4.0 movement [11], eventually leading to a new generation of CNs.

In order to present the leading-edge areas of developments and trends that have revolutionized the CN, as well as the main challenges and expectations which these have raised, we introduce three main categories for the research work in CN. These include addressing: (i) CN's scope, membership, organization, and governance, (ii) CN's support platforms, tools, and infrastructures, and (iii) CN's collaboration culture, strategies, and business models. Furthermore, for each of these categories, we provide a cross section among the sub-dimensions of the category against their related emerging trends and raised challenges. As such, Sects. 4.1 to 4.3 represent each category and provide a set of significant examples within each of their respective cross section tables.

4.1   Evolution in Scope, Membership, Organization and Governance

While earlier works on CN were focused on networks of organizations or people, the same concepts are being extended to other types of collaborative networks. In Fig. 5, the main sub-dimensions of the evolution introduced in this area are mentioned, and

Fig. 3. The role of IFIP WG5.5 and PRO-VE in shaping the collaborative networks area

for each sub-dimension, their recent trends as well as their main raised challenges are exemplified. A summary of our introduced aspects related to each sub-dimension is also described below.

a) *Evolution in scope*

CN concepts are penetrating the area of Cyber-Physical Systems/Internet of Things (CPS/IoT). Previous works on such systems were mostly focused on issues of integration and interoperability, safe communications, control, and energy management.

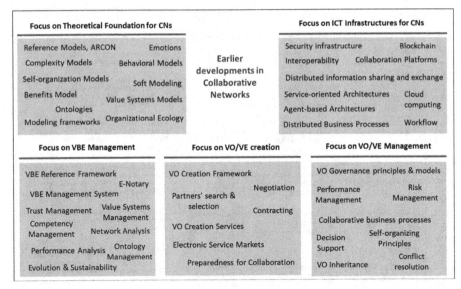

Fig. 4. Some earlier developments in Collaborative Networks

As systems grow in complexity, becoming systems-of-systems (SoS), and involve very large numbers of interconnected components, collaborative networks also offer a new perspective on how to organize and manage them.

Examples include the emerging notion of Collaborative CPS [17], and new approaches to integrated systems-of-systems [18, 19]. In fact, some earlier ideas in this direction can be traced back to [20] which adopted the notions of VO and VBE to materialize agility and reconfigurability of the shop floor, but the approach is attracting more attention recently, as more and more sub-systems embed high levels of intelligence and autonomy [21].

b) *Evolution towards hybridization*

Collaboration between humans and machines gained a new boost with recent developments in collaborative robotics [22] and facilitated by new interfacing and sensing technologies. But nowadays, more extended scenarios are envisioned, involving collaboration among multiple humans and machines/sub-systems [11], taking advantage of the best capabilities of each. In fact, this idea revisits the notion of "balanced automation systems" [23, 24], which can get new realization through advanced digital twins.

Complementarily, understanding CNs as socio-technical systems allows to borrow concepts from social sciences to better model social interactions among network members. One example is reflected in addressing the notion of emotion in CNs [25], which opens new directions for effective governance of networks.

c) *Seeking inspiration from collaboration cases in Nature*

Nature offers a large display of collaboration cases, which appear to have a high degree of sustainability and optimization [13]. These cases have been studied in various disciplines including ecology, biology, zoology, etc., from which we can

Sub-dimension	Recent and ongoing trends	Some emerging challenges
a. Evolution of scope	• Starting to address collaboration among components in complex CPS & SoS • Starting to address collaboration in digital twins	• Identify liability & responsibility borders • Further embed collaboration in digital twins • Transition from control-orientation to collaboration-orientation
b. Hybridization	• Human-Machine collaboration (e.g. collaborative robotics) • Understanding CNs as socio-technical systems • Early models of emotions in CNs	• Explore affective computing & emotions in CNs • Extend Machine-Machine collaboration • Extend human-digital twin concept to enhance H-M collaboration
c. Inspiration in Nature	• Ecosystem metaphor applied to businesses • Stigmergy and self-organization • Identification of structures, behavioral models & enhancement mechanisms	• Better understand collaboration mechanisms and principles • Replicate effective mechanisms and organizational structures from Nature
d. Multi-level networks	• Hyper-connectivity • Co-existence of formal and informal networks • Hybrid value systems	• Support inter-dependence of co-existing CNs • Develop governance for interacting networks • Better understand self-organization, co-evolution, power dynamics, value systems
e. CN Identification and differentiation	• Identification and differentiation of CNs from co-working situations analysis • Identification of collaborative behaviors	• Concisely specify collaborative behaviors • Identify and characterize emerging collaboration forms
f. Resilience & antifragility	• Identification of capabilities and strategies to support resilience and antifragility • CN developments in disaster management	• Find strategies & implementation approaches to enhance resilience and antifragility • Develop new relevant assessment indicators for resilience and antifragility
g. Collaboration – Competition	• Characterization of *coopetitive* environment • Positioning the *coopetitive* notion in CNs	• Better understand interactions collaboration – competition • Develop new collaborative behavior models • Incentives and expectations management
h. Sustainability	• CNs as an enabler of sustainability • Green collaborative networks • CNs in circular economy • Sustaining the collaboration	• Progress from enterprise-centric to ecosystem-oriented perspective • Align developments with standards & UN Agenda 2030 • Seek synergies with social innovation actions

Side label: Evolution in scope, membership, organization and governance

Fig. 5. Overview of evolution in scope, membership, organization and governance

get new knowledge on effective collaboration mechanisms, roles, behavior, and organizational structures.

One of the most popular classes of collaborative networks, the business ecosystems, are in fact inspired on natural ecosystems [26, 27]. Stigmergy is another example of mechanism that has been adopted namely in mass collaboration [11, 28].

d) *Evolution towards multi-level networks*

With the increasing hyper-connectivity among organizations, people, machines, and smart systems, typically multiple networks co-exist and interact. These networks have different durations, can be at different stages of their life cycle, and often share some members and resources. Some of these networks are formal and regulated by contracts, while others are informal and led by social interactions. Frequently these networks comprise members with very different value systems. As such, it is important to understand their complexity, support the interplay among these networks [29], and devise appropriate governance and analysis methods applicable to them. One example can be found in [30], where multiple virtual organizations play a role along the life cycle of a complex product such as a solar power plant.

e) *Identification and differentiation of CNs*

With the diversification in interconnection and socialization mechanisms, new forms of collaboration have emerged. In this context it is important to devise approaches and mechanisms to identify (make visible) and characterize emerging CNs. Examples in this direction include [31] focused on recognition and modeling of collaborative situations, and [32], which addresses the agile operation of small collaborative teams in the context knowledge organizations.

f) *Evolution towards resilient and antifragile CNs*

Society and its organizations face increasing number of disruptive events, which appear with increasing frequency with potentially large impacts. Such extreme events can be caused by economic crises, pandemic situations, climate change, political instability, terrorism, demographic and immigration shifts, changes in regulations, or high dependency on advanced complex technologies, among others. From industry point of view, these can easily disrupt the global supply chains as well as the local business ecosystems. In order to cope with such events, CNs need to develop high resilience, i.e., the capability to absorb shocks and recover [33], and antifragility, i.e. the capability to not only absorb shocks, but to enhance and become better afterwards [34].

An overview of mechanisms and capabilities to build resilience and antifragility in collaborative business ecosystems can be found in [4]. Other examples include [35], which addresses resilience in service-oriented architectures for virtual enterprises, and [36] that proposes a method for formalization and evaluation of resilience in collaborative networks. Regarding antifragility, an example work is [37], which addresses edge-attack and local edge-repair response mechanisms in complex networks.

g) *Interactions collaboration – competition*

The combination of collaboration and competition that often, while in an apparent paradox, take place within the same environment, led to the term "coopetition" and is attracting increasing attention [38].

Characterization of *coopetitive* environments and a better understanding of the behavior of their involved actors can help devising more effective governance for CNs. Complementarily, proper incentives policies and expectations management need to be better developed [13, 39].

h) *Increased focus on sustainability*

CNs have been always pointed out as a core enabler for preserving sustainability [40], and mainly in the sense that resolving the involved challenges in the market and society require collaboration among multiple stakeholders. In this direction, more recently, a number of works introduced the two notions of green virtual enterprise and green VO breeding environment and have further addressed the relation between these two concepts and the circular economy [41–43].

Complementarily, the issue of sustainability of the collaboration itself is addressed in [44] for the context of collaborative business ecosystems. Furthermore, various initiatives are looking into the role that can be played by CNs in the fulfillment of the set of objectives set in the UN Agenda 2030 for Sustainable Development [45].

4.2 Evolution in Support Platforms, Tools, and Infrastructures

The information and communication technologies have always constituted a core enabler for collaborative networks. Therefore, advances in these technologies naturally impact the evolution of CNs, as highlighted in Fig. 6, through a set of main sub-dimensions.

In relation to each sub-dimension, the recent set of trends as well as the main raised challenges are then exemplified and briefly described below.

Sub-dimension	Recent and ongoing trends	Some emerging challenges
a. Collaboration platforms	• New collaboration platforms extending document management systems & enterprise portal technologies • Cloud support to collaboration platforms	• Develop collaboration environments coping with high connectivity • Integrate Intelligence, IoT, Big data, decision support, intelligent assistants, mass collaboration support
b. Enhanced human-system interaction	• Increasing use of simulation, virtual and augmented reality • Improved user experience / intimacy • Applying some aspects of gaming	• Explore more "natural" forms of interaction between humans and systems / machines • Develop collaboration-oriented avatars, new levels of tele-presence / remote interaction and gaming
c. Improved service specification	• Strong trend towards servitization & service-enhanced products • Service-Dominant Logic concept • Multi-supplier service composition	• Enhance mechanisms for service discovery, selection, composition and evolution • Support nomadic and ad-hoc collaboration • Support collaborative service design and on-the-fly orchestration
d. Cyber-security and risks	• Safe communications, access rights, non-repudiation • Digital institutions (e.g. e-Notary) • Early blockchain application in CNs	• Find new ways of managing cyber-risks, risk propagation and counter-attack strategies • Further distributed ledger technologies in CNs • Design new electronic institutions
e. Dealing with data-rich contexts	• Cloud repositories and further application of data analytics and machine learning • Handling increased ubiquity of sensors	• Adopt proper data analytics & machine learning tools • Handle data to enhance traceability and transparency along value chains • Face uncertainty, fake data, and data quality
f. Smartness and sensing	• New levels of context awareness • Smart products and stigmergic collaboration • Sensing, smart, and sustainable (S3) concept	• Leverage adoption of AI / Machine Learning in CNs • Support adaptation to rapidly changing environments
g. Cognitive networks	• Early adoption of cognitive engineering tools in CNs	• Develop cognitive collaborative networks & distributed cognition with evolving capabilities
h. Linked data and ontologies	• Interlinking of data and widely varied knowledge sources • Common ontologies for VBEs	• Experiment and assess open linked data in CNs • Collaborative interlinking, evolution, and refinement of ontologies

(Left margin label: Evolution in support platforms, tools and infrastructures)

Fig. 6. Overview of evolution in support platforms, tools, and infrastructures

a) *Towards a new generation of collaboration platforms*
   New collaboration platforms, mainly focused on collaboration among humans, are primarily resulted from progressive evolution and convergence between document management systems and enterprise portal technologies. Additionally, cloud computing provided these platforms with more elastic resources management and remote access, which is crucial for geographically distributed systems such as the CNs [46]. The combination of various other technologies, including the big data, sensing, IoT, and the AI/ML, offer new possibilities for richer collaboration environments, featuring real-time context awareness, decision-support and intelligent assistance, data handling, analysis and visualization, and data services [47, 48].

b) *Enhancement of human-system interaction*
   The increasing adoption of augmented and virtual reality, simulation, and the so-called "natural user interfaces" allows for better human-machine interaction and system interface. The development of collaboration-oriented avatars [49, 50] adoption of gaming mechanisms, and remote interaction with resources also contribute

to improving the user experience and establishing more effective interaction among network members.

c) *Improved service specification*

There is a strong trend towards "servitization" as reflected in the notions of service-enhanced products [51], product-service systems [52, 53], smart product, and service-dominant logic [54–56].

In recent times, there has been a special focus on the provision of integrated services and combining multi-supplier contributions, which implicitly requires addressing the collaborative networks for service provision [57]. Other directions include development of novel mechanisms for service discovery, service selection, service composition [58], and service evolution in order to adapt to the evolving user requirements as well as the technology evolution [57]. Collaborative design of services, complemented with the "de-construction"/transformation of traditional software systems into collections of services [59], is another trend that attracts research work.

d) *Improved handling of cyber-security and communication risks*

Dealing with cyber-security has been a continuous concern since the early stages of the CN discipline [60]. Various mechanisms for safe communications, access rights management, non-repudiation, authentication, etc. have been addressed. Complementarily, some experiments on electronic institutions were carried out [106]. One example is the electronic notary as an additional facility to support VO creation in VBEs, and as a tool supporting in VBE/business ecosystems management [62].

Further trends include approaches to preclude risk propagation and exploitation of distributed ledger technologies, such as the block-chain [48, 63, 64].

e) *Dealing with data-rich contexts*

The hyper-connectivity among organizations, people, devices, and systems, combined with increased usage of sensors, is leading to data-rich environments which enable better and timely decision-making, and development of new services. In this context, new challenges emerge regarding the adoption of proper data storage, visualization and analytics tools, and applicable machine learning techniques [11, 47]. One relevant point to mention here is the possibility for increased traceability and transparency of the contributors along the value chains [11]. But this new context also poses new challenges regarding data privacy, data ownership, quality of data, fake data identification and handling, and how to cope with uncertainty that may rise in the CNs [47, 65, 66].

f) *Increased smartness and sensing*

Ubiquitous sensing allows for higher levels of context awareness which combined with progressive adoption of AI and ML leads to increasing the smartness, autonomy and self-adaptability capabilities of the infrastructures, systems, and machines. Such contexts support the design of "sensing, smart and sustainable (S3)" networks [67, 68] and thus resulting CNs that feature distributed intelligence. Some examples of applying these ideas to the design of novel collaborative platforms in manufacturing and smart products can be found in [9, 69].

g) *Towards cognitive networks*

An additional level of integration of AI and machine learning elements in CN infrastructures and tools is emerging by the first attempts to embed cognitive engineering tools in such systems. One example is [70], which envisages cognitive-based collaborative networks to support mobile health services. In [71] the Cognitive Model of Creativity is explored to bring computational creativity to manufacturing networks. Another example [72] attempts to deploy cognitive capabilities in a CN for the delivery of public services.

These early examples illustrate a trend that may bring CNs to a form of collective intelligence or distributed cognition.

h) *Exploring linked data and ontologies*

In a hyperconnected world heterogeneous data and knowledge sources abound. The development of new methods to interlink and explore those sources, namely open ones, can enhance collaboration among members of CNs and open the opportunity for creation of new services. Additionally, the interlinking existing ontologies defined by different members in the CN, as well as collaborative refinement and evolution of the shared ontologies for the CN, is also important to facilitate common understanding.

As an example, in [73] linked data methods are used as the bases for development of advanced collaboration spaces. Another example [74] addresses collaborative editing of linked data. An early example of research and development for engineering and evolution of VBE ontology can be found in [75]. Another example [76] discusses extensions of a standard ontology for robotics and automation (CORA) for collaborative robotics and collaboration between humans and cyber-physical systems. A method for ontology evolution is illustrated in [61].

4.3   Evolution in Collaboration Culture, Strategies and Business Models

The third complementary area of evolutions in CNs focuses more on the soft issues related to this paradigm. In Fig. 7, a set of main sub-dimensions for the evolution introduced in this area are mentioned, and for each sub-dimension their recent trends as well as their main raised challenges are exemplified. A summary of our introduced aspects related to each sub-dimension is also described further below.

a) *New collaborative business models*

The ongoing digital transformation processes and the associated convergence of multiple technologies induce new collaborative business models and value co-creation approaches. This trend is reflected in the emergence of concepts such as co-creation, co-innovation, customer intimacy, *glocal* enterprise, shared economy, *servitization*, and hybrid value chains, among others [11, 78–80].

The continued emergence of new collaboration forms raises the challenge of keeping a radar on such new business models, assessing lessons learned, and further modeling and structuring the involved mechanisms [81].

b) *Further addressing of trust, collaboration benefits and risks*

Trust management has been a classical topic in CN research. Various issues have been addressed, such as rational trust modeling, assessment, and management [82], trust monitoring [83], evaluation of the social dimension of trust [84], etc. With the emergence of new collaboration forms it also becomes important to pursue new approaches for trust management in relation to new business models.

Sub-dimension	Recent and ongoing trends	Some emerging challenges
a. **New collaborative business models**	• New studies on business models for CNs • Emerging collaborative value creation forms	• Keep a radar on emerging collaborative business models and assess learned lessons • Further develop collaborative business models • New value co-creation models & mechanisms
b. **Trust, benefits, risks**	• Some models of trust in CNs • Preliminary identification and analysis of risks and benefits in CNs	• Develop generalized risk management approaches for CNs • Model uncertainty and its propagation in CNs • Develop new trust management methods associated to new business models
c. **Open innovation**	• User / customer involvement approaches • Data mining in characterization of open innovation	• Further characterization of open innovation organization and governance • Develop novel models of intellectual property management for innovation in networks
d. **Monetization of collaboration**	• Identification of benefits of collaboration • Early models of collaboration benefits distribution	• Develop appropriate indicators & metrics for value of collaboration • Study effect of indicators on CN behavior • Devise effective ways for benefits distribution
e. **Collaboration culture & awareness**	• New graduate level courses on CNs at MSc and PhD levels • Developing proof of concept demonstration projects in various domains	• Further education and dissemination • Create a culture of collaboration & reduce uncertainty around collaboration • Establish further education curricula on CNs
f. **Expanding portfolio of applications**	• Some published collections of CNs cases • Recent expansion of CNs to less explored domains – energy, healthcare, agribusiness, smart cities, etc.	• Expand portfolio of success stories and demonstrations of collaboration • Normalize description of CN cases
g. **Multi-disciplinarity & inter-disciplinarity**	• CNs discipline is the result of inter-disciplinary effort • Effectively supporting the ubiquity of CNs in all multi- and inter- disciplinary aspects	• Re-enforce multi-disciplinarity and inter-disciplinarity • Seek synergies from diversity of knowledge sources and actors
h. **Responsibility, ethics, compliance**	• Extend early CN legal frameworks • Early specification of the notion of responsibility borders	• Develop new regulatory framework coping with responsibility sharing, ethics and compliance • Redesign strategies to interact with surrounding environment

(Left vertical label: Evolution in collaboration culture, strategies, and business models)

Fig. 7. Overview of evolution in collaboration culture, strategies and business models

The benefits of collaboration are often mentioned in the CN literature. However, there is little work on methods to make a fair distribution of benefits among the CN members. Some early examples include methods based on the Shappley value [85, 86], and a proposal for modeling the "social contributed benefits" and "external (received) benefits", together with a list of their relevant metrics [87]. Nevertheless, further developments of models for fair benefits distribution are still lacking.

Risks of collaboration is another issue that has been intuitively discussed and for which some methods have been proposed addressing the risk analysis and propagation, risk identification, and risk assessment and reduction [88–92]. Yet, a more generalized risk management approach for CNs is still needed, namely in order to cope with new the forms of CNs, and the complexity of multi-level networks.

c) *Evolution in collaboration for open innovation*

Collaboration for the purpose of innovation in an open setting has been another active research topic [92–94]. A comprehensive analysis of interactions between the two areas of collaborative networks and innovation/open innovation is provided in [95].

Customer involvement in CNs, and namely in co-creation/co-innovation processes, has been particularly focused on in recent years [30, 93, 96, 97].

Despite of these recent developments, further characterization of the open innovation processes, and their organization and governance, together with novel approaches to handle the rights to intellectual property in this context, remain open challenges.

d) *Towards monetization of collaboration*

Collaborative work adds certain overhead to the activities of its involved actors, e.g., the communication, reporting, and information exchange costs, the additional needed process formalization efforts, and the conflict resolution, among others. At the same time, various benefits generated through collaboration are difficult to measure and thus may easily be overlooked, e.g., the access to new knowledge, triggering innovative ideas, increased prestige, higher reputation, achieving diversity, as well as improving the potential of risk taking, acquisition of additional competencies, and agility, among others.

It is, therefore, important to devise ways of making collaboration benefits more explicit and measurable. Some earlier attempts in this direction can be found in [85] and [87] which address the modeling of collaboration benefits and identifying its main relevant indicators. Nevertheless, further work is still needed to appropriately define these indicators and introduce metrics for measuring the value of collaboration [11], in other words, to "monetize collaboration". Furthermore, it is also important to study the effect of such indicators on the behavior of the CN members [44].

e) *Creation of collaboration culture and awareness*

The effectiveness of collaboration does not depend solely on technological solutions. Considering the socio-technical nature of the CNs, it is fundamental to increase the general awareness about the main issues in CNs and to promote formal education on this discipline. Various universities have launched graduate courses related to the CN subject at MSc/MBA and PhD levels. One of the first reported examples can be found in [98] and a preliminary proposal for a reference curriculum for CN education is provided in [99]. But further education curricula need to still be established [11] and sharing of experiences and educational resources needs to be promoted.

f) *Expanding the portfolio of application domains*

As part of a wider knowledge dissemination and awareness creation efforts for CNs, it is important to organize and make available collections of (real) case studies of CN applications. One example of such collection is available in [100], but an expansion of this portfolio would be highly beneficial for CN researchers, practitioners, and educators.

In recent years we have noticed a growing expansion of CNs to less explored domains, such as energy [101], health and elderly care [57], agribusiness [102], smart cities [47], etc. In order to facilitate the understanding and sharing of experiences across sectors, it is also important to reach some normalization on the description of the case studies.

g) *Re-enforcing multi-disciplinary/inter-disciplinary approaches*

The CN discipline itself is the result of an inter-disciplinary convergence [5, 6]. With the expansion of CN application to diverse domains and the involvement of new players as the result of ongoing digital transformation process [11], it is necessary to re-enforce the CN's multi-disciplinary and inter-disciplinary dialog, seeking synergies from diverse knowledge areas. Besides the traditional areas of technology and the social sciences involved in the CNs, it is increasingly important to also extend this dialog to natural sciences that study collaboration forms in Nature [13].

h) *Progressing on responsibility, ethics, and compliance*

Legal frameworks for regulating the creation and operation of several classes of CNs have been so far discussed, e.g., in [103–105], and various countries already have specific laws addressing both the "long-term strategic networks" and the "goal-oriented networks".

With the increase in hyper-connectivity as well as in the intelligence/autonomy of machines and systems, it is necessary to further invest on regulatory frameworks coping with issues of responsibility, ethics, and compliance [11] among all entities involved in the CNs. For instance, in [106] there is some discussion on liability and "responsibility borders" in the case of multi-supplier systems-of-systems, but these issues need further developments as we move towards hybridization of CNs.

5   Conclusions

Currently, research and development on collaborative networks are growing in a pervasive manner, as manifested in covering a large number of collaboration forms and CN applications in multiple sectors of the society. Induced by new possibilities offered by advances in information and communication technologies, and motivated by the current digital transformation movement, it is likely that various other new forms of CN will also appear in the coming years. As such, it is important to the CN taxonomy is open, in order to properly allow positioning various types of CNs in relation to one another.

Along the last 2–3 decades, R&D in this area has co-evolved in parallel to the evolutions in ICT developments, the new market, and the societal needs, thus introducing a number of significant leaps in this area. In analogy with the industrial revolutions and the ongoing Industry 4.0 trends, four "generations of CNs" can also be identified. The currently emerging 4th generation is still in its early stages. Nevertheless, it can already be roughly characterized by various dimensions as well as the trends and challenges that once achieved, will boost the CN 4.0. As such, in this chapter an extensive list of trends and challenges is identified, which are organized along three main dimensions of: (1) Evolution in scope, memberships, organization and governance, (2) Evolution in support platforms, tools and infrastructures, and (3) Evolution in collaboration culture, strategies, and business models. The set of trends and challenges that are mentioned and exemplified in relation to each of the above dimensions and their sub-dimensions, also constitute the elements of a research agenda for the coming years in this area.

Acknowledgements. This work was developed in collaboration with the SOCOLNET scientific network and its ARCON-ACM initiative. Partial support also from the Center of Technology and Systems – UNINOVA, and the Portuguese FCT Foundation (project UIDB/00066/2020), and the European Commission (project DiGiFoF).

References

1. Monostori, L.: Cyber-physical production systems: roots expectations and R&D challenges. Procedia CIRP **17**, 9–13 (2014). https://doi.org/10.1016/j.procir.2014.03.115
2. Camarinha-Matos, L.M.: Collaborative networks: a mechanism for enterprise agility and resilience. In: Mertins, K., Bénaben, F., Poler, R., Bourrières, J.-P. (eds.) Enterprise Interoperability VI. PIC, vol. 7, pp. 3–11. Springer, Cham (2014). https://doi.org/10.1007/978-3-319-04948-9_1
3. Romero, D., Molina, A.: Collaborative networked organisations and customer communities: value co-creation and co-innovation in the networking era. Prod. Plan. Control **22**(5–6), 447–472 (2011). https://doi.org/10.1080/09537287.2010.536619
4. Ramezani, J., Camarinha-Matos, L.M.: Approaches for resilience and antifragility in collaborative business ecosystems. Technol. Forecast. Soc. Change **151**, 119846 (2020). https://doi.org/10.1016/j.techfore.2019.119846
5. Camarinha-Matos, L.M., Afsarmanesh, H.: The emerging discipline of collaborative networks. In: Camarinha-Matos, L.M. (ed.) PRO-VE 2004. IIFIP, vol. 149, pp. 3–16. Springer, Boston, MA (2004). https://doi.org/10.1007/1-4020-8139-1_1
6. Camarinha-Matos, L.M., Afsarmanesh, H.: Collaborative networks: a new scientific discipline. J. Intell. Manuf. **16**(4–5), 439–452 (2005)
7. Camarinha-Matos, L.M., Afsarmanesh, H., Galeano, N., Molina, A.: Collaborative networked organizations - concepts and practice in manufacturing enterprises. J. Comput. Industr. Eng. **57**, 46–60 (2009). https://doi.org/10.1016/j.cie.2008.11.024
8. Bartodziej, C.J.: The Concept Industry 4.0 - An Empirical Analysis of Technologies and Applications in Production Logistics. Springer Gabler, Wiesbaden (2017). https://doi.org/10.1007/978-3-658-16502-4
9. Kang, H.S., et al.: Smart manufacturing: past research, present findings, and future directions. Int. J. Precis. Eng. Manuf. -Green Tech. **3**(1), 111–128 (2016)
10. Hermann, M., Pentek, T., Otto, B.: Design principles for Industrie 4.0 scenarios. In: 2016 49th Hawaii International Conference on System Sciences (HICSS), Koloa, pp. 3928–3937. IEEE Xplore (2016). https://doi.org/10.1109/HICSS.2016.488
11. Camarinha-Matos, L.M., Fornasiero, R., Ramezani, J., Ferrada, F.: Collaborative networks: a pillar of digital transformation. Appl. Sci. **9**(24), 5431 (2019). https://doi.org/10.3390/app9245431
12. Camarinha-Matos, L.M., Afsarmanesh, H.: Collaborative networks. In: Wang, K., Kovacs, G.L., Wozny, M., Fang, M. (eds.) PROLAMAT 2006. IIFIP, vol. 207, pp. 26–40. Springer, Boston, MA (2006). https://doi.org/10.1007/0-387-34403-9_4
13. Camarinha-Matos, L.M., Afsarmanesh, H.: Roots of collaboration: nature-inspired solutions for collaborative networks. IEEE Access **6**, 30829–30843 (2018). https://doi.org/10.1109/ACCESS.2018.2845119
14. Afsarmanesh, H., Camarinha-Matos, L.M., Msanjila, S.S.: Models, methodologies, and tools supporting establishment and management of second-generation VBEs. IEEE Trans. Syst. Man Cybern. C. **41**(5), 692–710 (2011)
15. Durugbo, C.: Collaborative networks: a systematic review and multi-level framework. Int. J. Prod. Res. **54**, 3749–3776 (2016). https://doi.org/10.1080/00207543.2015.1122249
16. Camarinha-Matos, L.M.: Collaborative networks in industry and the role of PRO-VE. Int. J. Prod. Manage. Eng. **2**(2), 53–56 (2014)
17. Nazarenko, A.A., Camarinha-Matos, L.M.: Basis for an approach to design collaborative cyber-physical systems. In: Camarinha-Matos, L.M., Almeida, R., Oliveira, J. (eds.) DoCEIS 2019. IAICT, vol. 553, pp. 193–205. Springer, Cham (2019). https://doi.org/10.1007/978-3-030-17771-3_16

18. Osório, A.L., Belloum, A., Afsarmanesh, H., Camarinha-Matos, L.M.: Agnostic informatics system of systems: the open ISoS services framework. In: Camarinha-Matos, L.M., Afsarmanesh, H., Fornasiero, R. (eds.) PRO-VE 2017. IAICT, vol. 506, pp. 407–420. Springer, Cham (2017). https://doi.org/10.1007/978-3-319-65151-4_37
19. Osório, A.L., Camarinha-Matos, L.M., Dias, T., Tavares, J.: Adaptive integration of IoT with informatics systems for collaborative industry: the SITL-IoT case. In: Camarinha-Matos, L.M., Afsarmanesh, H., Antonelli, D. (eds.) PRO-VE 2019. IAICT, vol. 568, pp. 43–54. Springer, Cham (2019). https://doi.org/10.1007/978-3-030-28464-0_5
20. Barata, J., Camarinha-Matos, L.M.: Coalitions of manufacturing components for shop floor agility - the CoBASA architecture. Int. J. Network. Virtual Organ. 2(1), 50 (2003). https://doi.org/10.1504/IJNVO.2003.003518
21. Borangiu, T., Trentesaux, D., Thomas, A., Leitão, P., Barata, J.: Digital transformation of manufacturing through cloud services and resource virtualization. Comput. Ind. 108, 150–162 (2019). https://doi.org/10.1016/j.compind.2019.01.006
22. Goldberg, K.: Robots and the return to collaborative intelligence. Nat. Mach. Intell. 1(1), 2–4 (2019). https://doi.org/10.1038/s42256-018-0008-x
23. Camarinha-Matos, L.M., Rabelo, R., Osório, L.: Balanced automation. In: Tzafestas, S.G. (ed.) Computer-Assisted Management and Control of Manufacturing Systems, pp. 376–414. Springer , London (1997). https://doi.org/10.1007/978-1-4471-0959-4_14
24. Romero, D., Noran, O., Stahre, J., Bernus, P., Fast-Berglund, Å.: Towards a human-centred reference architecture for next generation balanced automation systems: human-automation symbiosis. In: Umeda, S., Nakano, M., Mizuyama, H., Hibino, H., Kiritsis, D., von Cieminski, G. (eds.) APMS 2015. IAICT, vol. 460, pp. 556–566. Springer, Cham (2015). https://doi.org/10.1007/978-3-319-22759-7_64
25. Ferrada, F., Camarinha-Matos, L.M.: A modelling framework for collaborative network emotions. Enterp. Inf. Syst. 13(7–8), 1164–1194 (2019). https://doi.org/10.1080/17517575.2019.1633583
26. Moore, J.F.: The Death of Competition: Leadership and Strategy in the Age of Business Ecosystems. Harper Collins Publishers (1996)
27. Graça, P., Camarinha-Matos, L.M.: Performance indicators for collaborative business ecosystems literature review and trends. Technol. Forecast. Soc. Change 116, 237–255 (2017). https://doi.org/10.1016/j.techfore.2016.10.012
28. Zamiri, M., Camarinha-Matos, L.M.: Mass collaboration and learning: opportunities, challenges, and influential factors. Appl. Sci. 9(13), 2620 (2019). https://doi.org/10.3390/app9132620
29. Camarinha-Matos, L.M., Ferrada, F., Oliveira, A.I.: Interplay of collaborative networks in product servicing. In: Camarinha-Matos, L.M., Scherer, R.J. (eds.) PRO-VE 2013. IAICT, vol. 408, pp. 51–60. Springer, Heidelberg (2013). https://doi.org/10.1007/978-3-642-405 43-3_6
30. Camarinha-Matos, L.M., Oliveira, A.I., Ferrada, F., Sobotka, P., Vataščinová, A., Thamburaj, V.: Collaborative enterprise networks for solar energy. In: Proceedings of ICCCT'15 - IEEE International conference on Computing and Communications Technologies, Chennai, pp. 93–98, 26–27 February 2015. https://doi.org/10.1109/ICCCT2.2015.7292726
31. Gou, J., Liu, Q., Mu, W., Ying, W., Afsarmanesh, H., Benaben, F.: A digital-enabled framework for intelligent collaboration in small teams. In: Camarinha-Matos, L.M., Afsarmanesh, H., Antonelli, D. (eds.) PRO-VE 2019. IAICT, vol. 568, pp. 193–202. Springer, Cham (2019). https://doi.org/10.1007/978-3-030-28464-0_18
32. Liu, Q., Gou, J., Camarinha-Matos, L.M.: Towards agile operation for small teams in knowledge intensive organizations: a collaboration framework. In: Camarinha-Matos, L.M., Afsarmanesh, H., Ortiz, A. (eds.) PRO-VE 2020. IAICT, vol. 598, pp. 263–272. Springer, Cham (2020). https://doi.org/10.1007/978-3-030-62412-5_22

33. Chroust, G., Aumayr, G.: Resilience 2.0: computer-aided disaster management. J. Syst. Sci. Syst. Eng. **26**(3), 321–335 (2017). https://doi.org/10.1007/s11518-017-5335-7

34. Taleb, N.N.: Antifragile: Things that Gain from Disorder. Random House Publishing Group, New York (2012)

35. Bezerra, R.O., Rabelo, R.J., Cancian, M.H.: Supporting SOA resilience in virtual enterprises. In: Camarinha-Matos, L.M., Afsarmanesh, H., Rezgui, Y. (eds.) PRO-VE 2018. IAICT, vol. 534, pp. 111–123. Springer, Cham (2018). https://doi.org/10.1007/978-3-319-99127-6_10

36. Moradi, B., Daclin, N., Chapurlat, V.: Formalization and evaluation of non-functional requirements: application to resilience. In: Camarinha-Matos, L.M., Afsarmanesh, H., Rezgui, Y. (eds.) PRO-VE 2018. IAICT, vol. 534, pp. 124–131. Springer, Cham (2018). https://doi.org/10.1007/978-3-319-99127-6_11

37. Topîrceanu, A., Udrescu, M., Mărculescu, R.: Complex networks antifragility under sustained edge attack-repair mechanisms. In: Masuda, N., Goh, K.-I., Jia, T., Yamanoi, J., Sayama, H. (eds.) NetSci-X 2020. SPC, pp. 185–199. Springer, Cham (2020). https://doi.org/10.1007/978-3-030-38965-9_13

38. Ritala, P., Golnam, A., Wegmann, A.: Coopetition-based business models: the case of Amazon.com. Ind. Mark. Manage. **43**(2), 236–249 (2014). https://doi.org/10.1016/j.indmarman.2013.11.005

39. Levesque, V.R., Calhoun, A.J.K., Bell, K.P., Johnson, T.R.: Turning contention into collaboration: engaging power, trust, and learning in collaborative networks. Soc. Nat. Resour. **30**(2), 245–260 (2017). https://doi.org/10.1080/08941920.2016.1180726

40. Camarinha-Matos, L.M., Afsarmanesh, H., Boucher, X.: The role of collaborative networks in sustainability. In: Camarinha-Matos, L.M., Boucher, X., Afsarmanesh, H. (eds.) PRO-VE 2010. IAICT, vol. 336, pp. 1–16. Springer, Heidelberg (2010). https://doi.org/10.1007/978-3-642-15961-9_1

41. Romero, D., Molina, A.: Green virtual enterprise breeding environment reference framework. In: Camarinha-Matos, L.M., Pereira-Klen, A., Afsarmanesh, H. (eds.) PRO-VE 2011. IAICT, vol. 362, pp. 545–555. Springer, Heidelberg (2011). https://doi.org/10.1007/978-3-642-23330-2_59

42. Romero, D., Noran, O.: Green virtual enterprises and their breeding environments: engineering their sustainability as systems of systems for the circular economy. IFAC-PapersOnLine **48**(3), 2258–2265 (2015). https://doi.org/10.1016/j.ifacol.2015.06.424

43. Romero, D., Nora, O.: Towards green sensing virtual enterprises: interconnected sensing enterprises, intelligent assets and smart products in the cyber-physical circular economy. IFAC-PapersOnline **50**(1), 11719–11724 (2017). https://doi.org/10.1016/j.ifacol.2017.08.1944

44. Graça, P., Camarinha-Matos, L.M.: A model of evolution of a collaborative business ecosystem influenced by performance indicators. In: Camarinha-Matos, L.M., Afsarmanesh, H., Antonelli, D. (eds.) PRO-VE 2019. IAICT, vol. 568, pp. 245–258. Springer, Cham (2019). https://doi.org/10.1007/978-3-030-28464-0_22

45. United Nations; Transforming our world: The 2030 Agenda for Sustainable Development. UN Report A/RES/70/1. https://sustainabledevelopment.un.org/post2015/transformingourworld. Accessed 4 Aug 2020

46. Camarinha-Matos, L.M., Juan-Verdejo, A., Alexakis, S., Bär, H., Surajbali, B.: Cloud-based collaboration spaces for enterprise networks. In: Proceedings of ICCCT 2015 - IEEE International conference on Computing and Communications Technologies, Chennai, pp. 185–190, 26–27 February 2015. https://doi.org/10.1109/ICCCT2.2015.7292743

47. Petersen, S.A., Pourzolfaghar, Z., Alloush, I., Ahlers, D., Krogstie, J., Helfert, M.: Value-added services, virtual enterprises and data spaces inspired enterprise architecture for smart cities. In: Camarinha-Matos, L.M., Afsarmanesh, H., Antonelli, D. (eds.) PRO-VE 2019. IAICT, vol. 568, pp. 393–402. Springer, Cham (2019). https://doi.org/10.1007/978-3-030-28464-0_34

48. Ojo, A.: Next generation government - hyperconnected, smart and augmented. In: Camarinha-Matos, L.M., Afsarmanesh, H., Antonelli, D. (eds.) PRO-VE 2019. IAICT, vol. 568, pp. 285–294. Springer, Cham (2019). https://doi.org/10.1007/978-3-030-28464-0_25

49. Szybicki, D., Kurc, K., Gierlak, P., Burghardt, A., Muszyńska, M., Uliasz, M.: Application of virtual reality in designing and programming of robotic stations. In: Camarinha-Matos, L.M., Afsarmanesh, H., Antonelli, D. (eds.) PRO-VE 2019. IAICT, vol. 568, pp. 585–593. Springer, Cham (2019). https://doi.org/10.1007/978-3-030-28464-0_51

50. Rabelo, R.J., Zambiasi, S.P., Romero, D.: Collaborative softbots: enhancing operational excellence in systems of cyber-physical systems. In: Camarinha-Matos, L.M., Afsarmanesh, H., Antonelli, D. (eds.) PRO-VE 2019. IAICT, vol. 568, pp. 55–68. Springer, Cham (2019). https://doi.org/10.1007/978-3-030-28464-0_6

51. Camarinha-Matos, L.M., Oliveira, A.I., Ferrada, F.: Supporting collaborative networks for complex service-enhanced products. In: Camarinha-Matos, L.M., Bénaben, F., Picard, W. (eds.) PRO-VE 2015. IAICT, vol. 463, pp. 181–192. Springer, Cham (2015). https://doi.org/10.1007/978-3-319-24141-8_16

52. Boucher, X.: Economic and organizational transition towards product/service systems: the case of French SMEs. In: Camarinha-Matos, L.M., Xu, L., Afsarmanesh, H. (eds.) PRO-VE 2012. IAICT, vol. 380, pp. 26–34. Springer, Heidelberg (2012). https://doi.org/10.1007/978-3-642-32775-9_3

53. Sklyar, A., Kowalkowski, C., Sörhammar, D., Tronvoll, B.: Resource integration through digitalisation: a service ecosystem perspective. J. Mark. Manage. 35(11–12), 1–18 (2019). https://doi.org/10.1080/0267257X.2019.1600572

54. Lusch, R.F.; Vargo, S.L.: The Service-Dominant Logic of Marketing: Dialog, Debate, and Directions. Routledge (2014)

55. Turetken, O., Grefen, P.: Designing service-dominant business models. In: Proceedings of the 25th European Conference on Information Systems (ECIS), Guimarães, pp. 2218–2233, 5–10 June 2017

56. Lüftenegger, E., Comuzzi, M., Grefen, P.: The service-dominant ecosystem: mapping a service dominant strategy to a product-service ecosystem. In: Camarinha-Matos, L.M., Scherer, R.J. (eds.) PRO-VE 2013. IAICT, vol. 408, pp. 22–30. Springer, Heidelberg (2013). https://doi.org/10.1007/978-3-642-40543-3_3

57. Baldissera, T.A., Camarinha-Matos, L.M.: SCoPE: service composition and personalization environment. Appl. Sci. 8(11), 2297 (2018). https://doi.org/10.3390/app8112297

58. Afsarmanesh, H., Sargolzaei, M., Shadi, M.: Semi-automated software service integration in virtual organisations. Enterp. Inf. Syst. 9(5–6), 528–555 (2015). https://doi.org/10.1080/17517575.2014.928953

59. Baek, J.S., Kim, S., Pahk, Y., Manzini, E.: A sociotechnical framework for the design of collaborative services. Des. Stud. 55, 54–78 (2018). https://doi.org/10.1016/j.destud.2017.01.001

60. Osório, A.L., Antunes, C., Barata, M.M.: The PRODNET communication infrastructure. In: Camarinha-Matos, L.M., Afsarmanesh, H. (eds.) PRO-VE 1999. ITIFIP, vol. 27, pp. 167–186. Springer, Boston (1999). https://doi.org/10.1007/978-0-387-35577-1_11

61. Cao, T., Mu, W., Montarnal, A., Barthe-Delanoë, A.-M.: A method of ontology evolution and concept evaluation based on knowledge discovery in the heavy haul railway risk system. In: Camarinha-Matos, L.M., Afsarmanesh, H., Antonelli, D. (eds.) PRO-VE 2019. IAICT, vol. 568, pp. 220–233. Springer, Cham (2019). https://doi.org/10.1007/978-3-030-28464-0_20

62. Oliveira, A.I., Camarinha-Matos, L.M.: Negotiation and contracting in collaborative networks. In: Camarinha-Matos, L.M., Pereira, P., Ribeiro, L. (eds.) DoCEIS 2010. IAICT, vol. 314, pp. 83–92. Springer, Heidelberg (2010). https://doi.org/10.1007/978-3-642-11628-5_9

63. Schaffers, H.: The relevance of blockchain for collaborative networked organizations. In: Camarinha-Matos, L.M., Afsarmanesh, H., Rezgui, Y. (eds.) PRO-VE 2018. IAICT, vol. 534, pp. 3–17. Springer, Cham (2018). https://doi.org/10.1007/978-3-319-99127-6_1

64. Silva, H.D., Soares, A.L., Bettoni, A., Francesco, A.B., Albertario, S.: A digital platform architecture to support multi-dimensional surplus capacity sharing. In: Camarinha-Matos, L.M., Afsarmanesh, H., Antonelli, D. (eds.) PRO-VE 2019. IAICT, vol. 568, pp. 323–334. Springer, Cham (2019). https://doi.org/10.1007/978-3-030-28464-0_28

65. Mäki, M., Alamäki, A.: Data privacy concerns throughout the customer journey and different service industries. In: Camarinha-Matos, L.M., Afsarmanesh, H., Antonelli, D. (eds.) PRO-VE 2019. IAICT, vol. 568, pp. 516–526. Springer, Cham (2019). https://doi.org/10.1007/978-3-030-28464-0_45

66. Schuh, G., Hoffmann, J., Bleider, M., Zeller, V.: Assessment of IS integration efforts to implement the internet of production reference architecture. In: Camarinha-Matos, L.M., Afsarmanesh, H., Rezgui, Y. (eds.) PRO-VE 2018. IAICT, vol. 534, pp. 325–333. Springer, Cham (2018). https://doi.org/10.1007/978-3-319-99127-6_28

67. Chavarría-Barrientos, D., Camarinha-Matos, L.M., Molina, A.: Achieving the sensing, smart and sustainable "everything." In: Camarinha-Matos, L.M., Afsarmanesh, H., Fornasiero, R. (eds.) PRO-VE 2017. IAICT, vol. 506, pp. 575–588. Springer, Cham (2017). https://doi.org/10.1007/978-3-319-65151-4_51

68. Chavarría-Barrientos, D., Batres, R., Wright, P.K., Molina, A.: A methodology to create a sensing, smart and sustainable manufacturing enterprise. Int. J. Prod. Res. **56**(1–2), 584–603 (2018). https://doi.org/10.1080/00207543.2017.1386333

69. Mladineo, M., Celar, S., Celent, L., Crnjac, M.: Selecting manufacturing partners in push and pull-type smart collaborative networks. Adv. Eng. Inform. **38**, 291–305 (2018). https://doi.org/10.1016/j.aei.2018.08.001

70. Macedo, P., Madeira, R.N., Camarinha-Matos, L.M.: Cognitive services for collaborative mHealth: the onparkinson case study. In: Camarinha-Matos, L.M., Afsarmanesh, H., Rezgui, Y. (eds.) PRO-VE 2018. IAICT, vol. 534, pp. 442–453. Springer, Cham (2018). https://doi.org/10.1007/978-3-319-99127-6_38

71. Nikghadam-Hojjati, S., Barata, J.: Computational creativity to design cyber-physical systems in industry 4.0. In: Camarinha-Matos, L.M., Afsarmanesh, H., Antonelli, D. (eds.) PRO-VE 2019. IAICT, vol. 568, pp. 29–40. Springer, Cham (2019). https://doi.org/10.1007/978-3-030-28464-0_4

72. Salem, S., Ojo, A., Estevez, E., Fillottrani, P.R.: Towards a cognitive linked public service cloud. In: Camarinha-Matos, L.M., Afsarmanesh, H., Rezgui, Y. (eds.) PRO-VE 2018. IAICT, vol. 534, pp. 430–441. Springer, Cham (2018). https://doi.org/10.1007/978-3-319-99127-6_37

73. Sousa, C., Pereira, C.: Sharing through collaborative spaces: enhancing collaborative networks interoperability. In: Camarinha-Matos, L.M., Afsarmanesh, H. (eds.) PRO-VE 2014. IAICT, vol. 434, pp. 481–488. Springer, Heidelberg (2014). https://doi.org/10.1007/978-3-662-44745-1_48

74. Zarzour, H., Al-Ayyoub, M., Jararweh, Y.: Towards social collaborative editing of distributed linked data. In: 9th International Conference on Information and Communication Systems (ICICS), Irbid, pp. 90–95 (2018). https://doi.org/10.1109/IACS.2018.8355447

75. Afsarmanesh, H., Ermilova, E.: The management of ontologies in the VO breeding environments domain. Int. J. Serv. Oper. Manage. 6(3), 257 (2010). https://doi.org/10.1504/IJSOM.2010.031954

76. Antonelli, D., Bruno, G.: Ontology-based framework to design a collaborative human-robotic workcell. In: Camarinha-Matos, L.M., Afsarmanesh, H., Fornasiero, R. (eds.) PRO-VE 2017. IAICT, vol. 506, pp. 167–174. Springer, Cham (2017). https://doi.org/10.1007/978-3-319-65151-4_16

77. Man, A.-P., Luvison, D.: Collaborative business models: aligning and operationalizing alliances. Bus. Horiz. 62(4), 473–482 (2019). https://doi.org/10.1016/j.bushor.2019.02.004

78. Laukkanen, M., Tura, N.: The potential of sharing economy business models for sustainable value creation. J. Cleaner Prod. 253, 120004 (2020). https://doi.org/10.1016/j.jclepro.2020.120004

79. Kohtamäki, M., Parida, V., Oghazi, P., Gebauer, H., Baines, T.: Digital servitization business models in ecosystems: a theory of the firm. J. Bus. Res. 104, 380–392 (2019). https://doi.org/10.1016/j.jbusres.2019.06.027

80. Valkokari, K., Rantala, T., Alamäki, A., Palomäki, K.: Business impacts of technology disruption - a design science approach to cognitive systems' adoption within collaborative networks. In: Camarinha-Matos, L.M., Afsarmanesh, H., Rezgui, Y. (eds.) PRO-VE 2018. IAICT, vol. 534, pp. 337–348. Springer, Cham (2018). https://doi.org/10.1007/978-3-319-99127-6_29

81. Msanjila, S., Afsarmanesh, H.: FETR: a framework to establish trust relationships among organizations in VBEs. J. Intell. Manuf. 21(3), 251–265 (2010). https://doi.org/10.1007/s10845-008-0178-1

82. Abreu, A., Requeijo, J., Calado, J.M.F., Dias, A.: Control charts to support trust monitoring in dynamic logistics networks. In: Camarinha-Matos, L.M., Afsarmanesh, H., Rezgui, Y. (eds.) PRO-VE 2018. IAICT, vol. 534, pp. 499–511. Springer, Cham (2018). https://doi.org/10.1007/978-3-319-99127-6_43

83. Andrade-Garda, J., et al.: A metrology-based approach for measuring the social dimension of cognitive trust in collaborative networks. Cogn. Technol. Work 22(2), 235–248 (2018). https://doi.org/10.1007/s10111-018-0483-1

84. Abreu A., Camarinha-Matos L.M.: Fair distribution of collaboration benefits. In: Encyclopedia of Networked and Virtual Organizations, IGI Global (2008). https://doi.org/10.4018/978-1-59904-885-7.ch079

85. Wang, Y., Ma, X., Li, Z., Liu, Y., Xu, M., Wang, Y.: Profit distribution in collaborative multiple centers vehicle routing problem. J. Clean. Prod. 144, 203–219 (2017). https://doi.org/10.1016/j.jclepro.2017.01.001

86. Abreu, A., Camarinha-Matos, L.M.: A benefit analysis model for collaborative networks. In: Camarinha-Matos, L.M., Afsarmanesh, H. (eds.) Collaborative Networks: Reference Modeling, pp. 253–276. Springer US, Boston (2008). https://doi.org/10.1007/978-0-387-79426-6_18

87. Jamshidi, A., Abbasgholizadeh Rahimi, S., Ait-kadi, D., Ruiz, A.: A new decision support tool for dynamic risks analysis in collaborative networks. In: Camarinha-Matos, L.M., Bénaben, F., Picard, W. (eds.) PRO-VE 2015. IAICT, vol. 463, pp. 53–62. Springer, Cham (2015). https://doi.org/10.1007/978-3-319-24141-8_5

88. Wulan, M., Petrovic, D.: A fuzzy logic based system for risk analysis and evaluation within enterprise collaborations. Comput. Ind. 63(8), 739–748 (2012). https://doi.org/10.1016/j.compind.2012.08.012

89. Li, J., Bénaben, F., Gou, J., Mu, W.: A proposal for risk identification approach in collaborative networks considering susceptibility to danger. In: Camarinha-Matos, L.M., Afsarmanesh, H., Rezgui, Y. (eds.) PRO-VE 2018. IAICT, vol. 534, pp. 74–84. Springer, Cham (2018). https://doi.org/10.1007/978-3-319-99127-6_7

90. Oliveira, A.I., Camarinha-Matos, L.M.: Negotiation support and risk reduction in collaborative networks. In: Camarinha-Matos, L.M., Tomic, S., Graça, P. (eds.) DoCEIS 2013. IAICT, vol. 394, pp. 15–24. Springer, Heidelberg (2013). https://doi.org/10.1007/978-3-642-37291-9_2

91. Rosas, J., Macedo, P., Tenera, A., Abreu, A., Urze, P.: Risk assessment in open innovation networks. In: Camarinha-Matos, L.M., Bénaben, F., Picard, W. (eds.) PRO-VE 2015. IAICT, vol. 463, pp. 27–38. Springer, Cham (2015). https://doi.org/10.1007/978-3-319-24141-8_3

92. Villa, A., Taurino, T.: Crowd engineering: manage crowd contributions for design and manufacture of innovative products. In: Camarinha-Matos, L.M., Afsarmanesh, H., Antonelli, D. (eds.) PRO-VE 2019. IAICT, vol. 568, pp. 93–102. Springer, Cham (2019). https://doi.org/10.1007/978-3-030-28464-0_9

93. Urze, P., Rosas, J., Tenera, A., Camarinha-Matos, L.M.: Open innovation practitioners mindset on risk. In: Camarinha-Matos, L.M., Afsarmanesh, H., Antonelli, D. (eds.) PRO-VE 2019. IAICT, vol. 568, pp. 103–114. Springer, Cham (2019). https://doi.org/10.1007/978-3-030-28464-0_10

94. Appio, F.P., Martini, A., Massa, S., Testa, S.: Collaborative network of firms: antecedents and state-of-the-art properties. Int. J. Prod. Res. **55**(7), 2121–2134 (2017). https://doi.org/10.1080/00207543.2016.1262083

95. Vilas-Boas, J., Mirnoori, V., Razy, A., Silva, A.: Outlining a new collaborative business model as a result of the green building information modelling impact in the AEC supply chain. In: Camarinha-Matos, L.M., Afsarmanesh, H., Antonelli, D. (eds.) PRO-VE 2019. IAICT, vol. 568, pp. 405–417. Springer, Cham (2019). https://doi.org/10.1007/978-3-030-28464-0_35

96. Fragidis, G.: The user perspective on service ecosystems: key concepts and models. In: Camarinha-Matos, L.M., Afsarmanesh, H., Fornasiero, R. (eds.) PRO-VE 2017. IAICT, vol. 506, pp. 368–380. Springer, Cham (2017). https://doi.org/10.1007/978-3-319-65151-4_34

97. Camarinha-Matos, L.M., Cardoso, T.: Education on virtual organizations: an experience at UNL. In: Camarinha-Matos, L.M. (ed.) PRO-VE 2004. IIFIP, vol. 149, pp. 579–588. Springer, Boston, MA (2004). https://doi.org/10.1007/1-4020-8139-1_61

98. Camarinha-Matos, L.M., Afsarmanesh, H., Cardoso, T., Klen, E.: A reference curriculum for education in collaborative networks. In: Camarinha-Matos, L.M., Afsarmanesh, H., Ollus, M. (eds.) Methods and Tools for Collaborative Networked Organizations, pp. 491–511. Springer US, Boston, MA (2008). https://doi.org/10.1007/978-0-387-79424-2_20

99. Romero, D., Rabelo, R.J., Molina, A.: Collaborative networks as modern industrial organisations: real case studies. Int. J. Comput. Integr. Manuf. **26**(1–2), 1–2 (2013). https://doi.org/10.1080/0951192X.2013.745348

100. Adu-Kankam, K.O., Camarinha-Matos, L.M.: Towards collaborative, virtual power plants: trends and convergence. Sustain. Energy Grids Netw. **16**, 217–230 (2018). https://doi.org/10.1016/j.segan.2018.08.003

101. Esteso, A., Alemany, M.M.E., Ortiz, A.: Conceptual framework for managing uncertainty in a collaborative agri-food supply chain context. In: Camarinha-Matos, L.M., Afsarmanesh, H., Fornasiero, R. (eds.) PRO-VE 2017. IAICT, vol. 506, pp. 715–724. Springer, Cham (2017). https://doi.org/10.1007/978-3-319-65151-4_64

102. Weitzenboeck, E.M.: Building a legal framework for a virtual organisation in the maritime domain: the Marvin experience. In: Proceedings of 7th International Conference on Concurrent Enterprising, Bremen, pp. 27–29, June 2001. https://pdfs.semanticscholar.org/3483/5b3c20b010d7eac64a82f574f3d5e1fc4164.pdf

103. Shelbourn, M., Hassan, T., Carter, C.: Legal and contractual framework for the VO. In: Camarinha-Matos, L.M., Afsarmanesh, H., Ollus, M. (eds.) Virtual Organizations, pp. 167–176. Kluwer Academic Publishers, Boston (2005). https://doi.org/10.1007/0-387-23757-7_11

104. Cevenini, C.: Legal issues of virtual organizations. In: Encyclopedia of Information Science and Technology, IGI Global (2009). https://doi.org/10.4018/978-1-60566-026-4.ch383

105. Osório, A.L., Camarinha-Matos, L.M., Afsarmanesh, H., Belloum, A.: Liability in collaborative maintenance of critical system of systems. In: Camarinha-Matos, L.M., Afsarmanesh, H., Ortiz, A. (eds.) PRO-VE 2020. IAICT, vol. 598, pp. 191–202. Springer, Cham (2020). https://doi.org/10.1007/978-3-030-62412-5_16

106. Cardoso, H.L., Oliveira, E.: Virtual enterprise normative framework within electronic institutions. In: Gleizes, M.-P., Omicini, A., Zambonelli, F. (eds.) ESAW 2004. LNCS (LNAI), vol. 3451, pp. 14–32. Springer, Heidelberg (2005). https://doi.org/10.1007/11423355_2

Advances in Production Management Systems: Issues, Trends, and Vision Towards 2030

David Romero[1(✉)], Gregor Von Cieminski[2], Thorsten Wuest[3], Paolo Gaiardelli[4], Ilkyeong Moon[5], Giuditta Pezzotta[4], Stefan Wiesner[6], Marco Macchi[7], Jannicke Baalsrud Hauge[6], Irene Roda[7], Daryl Powell[8], Torbjørn Netland[9], Boonserm (Serm) Kulvatunyou[10], Nick Szirbik[11], Christoph Roser[12], Erlend Alfnes[13], and Martin Rudberg[14]

[1] Tecnológico de Monterrey, Monterrey, Mexico
david.romero.diaz@gmail.com
[2] ZF Friedrichshafen AG, Friedrichshafen, Germany
gregor.cieminski@zf.com
[3] West Virginia University, Morgantown, USA
thwuest@mail.wvu.edu
[4] University of Bergamo, Bergamo, Italy
{paolo.gaiardelli,giuditta.pezzotta}@unibg.it
[5] Seoul National University, Seoul, South Korea
ikmoon@snu.ac.kr
[6] Bremer Institut für Produktion und Logistik GmbH, University of Bremen, Bremen, Germany
{wie,baa}@biba.uni-bremen.de
[7] Politecnico di Milano, Milan, Italy
{marco.macchi,irene.roda}@polimi.it
[8] SINTEF, Trondheim, Norway
daryl.powell@sintef.no
[9] ETH Zurich, Zurich, Switzerland
tnetland@ethz.ch
[10] National Institute of Standards and Technology (NIST), Gaithersburg, USA
serm@nist.gov
[11] University of Groningen, Groningen, The Netherlands
[12] Karlsruhe University of Applied Sciences, Karlsruhe, Germany
christoph.roser@hs-karlsruhe.de
[13] Norwegian University of Science and Technology (NTNU), Trondheim, Norway
erlend.alfnes@ntnu.no
[14] Linköping University, Linköping, Sweden
martin.rudberg@liu.se

Abstract. Since its inception in 1978, the IFIP Working Group (WG) 5.7 on Advances in Production Management Systems (APMS) has played an active role in the fields of production and production management. The Working Group has focused on the conception, development, strategies, frameworks, architectures, processes, methods, and tools needed for the advancement of both fields. The associated standards created by the IFIP WG5.7 have always been impacted by

© IFIP International Federation for Information Processing 2021
Published by Springer Nature Switzerland AG 2021
M. Goedicke et al. (Eds.): Advancing Research in Information and Communication Technology,
IFIP AICT 600, pp. 194–221, 2021. https://doi.org/10.1007/978-3-030-81701-5_8

the latest developments of scientific rigour, academic research, and industrial practices. The most recent of those developments involves the Fourth Industrial Revolution, which is having remarkable (r)evolutionary and disruptive changes in both the fields and the standards. These changes are triggered by the fusion of advanced operational and informational technologies, innovative operating and business models, as well as social and environmental pressures for more sustainable production systems. This chapter reviews past, current, and future issues and trends to establish a coherent vision and research agenda for the IFIP WG5.7 and its international community. The chapter covers a wide range of production aspects and resources required to design, engineer, and manage the next generation of sustainable and smart production systems.

Keywords: Production management · Cyber-physical production systems · Smart manufacturing · Industry 4.0 · Operator 4.0 · Product-service systems · Product lifecycle · Lean manufacturing · Servitization · Gamification · Customization

1   Introduction

Current social, environmental, economic, and technological "trends" will shape the evolution of new production environments towards 2030 [1, 2]. These trends are impacting not only traditional, discrete manufacturing but also "edge" manufacturing such as farming, food, and biopharma among others. This book chapter identifies those trends. Their impacts on production managers, and the help they need for them to remain competitive in 2030 and beyond. To do so, we investigated for developing a coherent vision and research agenda for production and production management based on information gathered from industry whitepapers, forward-looking manufacturing studies (e.g. The WMF Report [2]) and extensive discussions in the IFIP WG5.7 community.

This chapter is structured as follows: First, we take a brief look at the IFIP WG5.7 today and introduce our vision for 2030. Second, we introduce *Seven Grand Challenges* that pertain to the group's focal research areas. We discuss each grand challenge and reflect on how the IFIP WG5.7 will address it. Each challenge's discussion is structured by first providing a brief overview of its current status, followed by introducing relevant enabling technologies, before elaborating on the related IFIP WG5.7 Special Interest Group (SIG) efforts to address it, to finally presenting a research agenda and future outlook. The last two sections of this chapter include the barriers and enablers for addressing the presented grand challenges and concluding remarks.

2   IFIP WG 5.7 – Advances in Production Management Systems

The aim of IFIP Working Group 5.7 on Advances in Production Management Systems[1] is to globally promote and facilitate the advancement of knowledge, theory, technology, and industrial practice in the field of sustainable and smart production management systems. The IFIP WG5.7 emphasizes a collaborative culture that nurtures state-of-the-art research, which is motivated by current industrial needs, academic excellence, and

---

[1] https://www.ifipwg57.org/.

scientific rigour. Its R&D contributions and best practices are disseminated globally to both academics and practitioners through the annual flagship *APMS – International Conference*[2], the flagship journal *Production Planning & Control (PPC)*, as well as workshops and additional activities organised by *Special Interest Groups (SIGs)*.

The goals of IFIP WG5.7 are to define the next generation production systems and provide methods and algorithms to implement those systems. Achieving those goals requires an interdisciplinary approach that includes topics such as (i) the advancement of, and the integration of, both operational and informational technologies, (ii) the new, Industry 4.0-infused, innovative, business model development methods, (iii) the future role of the ingenuity of humans and their interactions with both of the above, and (iv) the new requirements of the human workforce as part of future manufacturing settings. Successfully addressing these four topics can be achieved only by the continuous development and refinement of an "industry-based," research agenda. An agenda that focuses on improving the industry's best practices in, and stimulating young researchers seeking careers in, production management.

2.1 A Production and Production Management Vision Towards 2030

Our shared IFIP WG5.7 vision is: "*As elements of production systems continue to be more connected across the layers of operations from shop-floor to supply chain, by 2030 production managers will become the orchestrators of the ever more complex and collaborative Human Cyber-Physical Production Systems (HCPPSs)*". Such advanced HCPPSs will be characterized by their dynamic "self-awareness" of the physical world, and their intelligent decisions in the cognitive world. Decisions that must achieve a balance between engineering, societal, environmental, and economic objectives.

In the future, more and more of those decisions will (i) be based on several existing and emerging AI technologies and (ii) rely on a vast amount of real-time, digitally connected information, and (iii) use the stored knowledge inferred and deduced from that information. To make those decisions more "intelligent", these CPPS will need to be highly configurable in both the physical and cognitive worlds. This is the only way, in our view, that future, customized products can be produced with similar or even improved cost, quality, lead-time, and safety. For these improvements to become a reality, "interoperability" will be a key issue.

The subsequent sections of the chapter show that (i) a significant amount of conceptual work on CPPSs has been completed, and (ii) a large range of enabling technologies are readily available for implementation. At the same time, the *Grand Challenges* that lie ahead will require new concepts, methods, algorithms, and technologies. The *Grand Challenges* and their implications on production management are reflective of the changes in both individuals customer expectations, and global supply networks [3]. Each *Grand Challenge,* which was derived from numerous industry reports, is interdisciplinary in nature and domain agnostic. These reports present examples of successful implementations of advanced digital technologies in production, maintenance, and logistics operations. Such industrial examples showcase the potential inherent in aggressively exploring new opportunities to expand technology applications and human ingenuity.

---

[2] https://www.apms-conference.org/.

The fact that smart technologies play an important role in our daily life, as private consumers, is a cause for optimism. Today, office staff and operators of production companies are very familiar with digital technology on a personal level. This will naturally expand to the work environment and become second nature in the next decade. Manufacturing will look very different from today's dark, dirty, dangerous myth.

3   Grand Challenges for Production and Production Management

To date, seven "Grand Challenges" – sometimes called fundamental goals – have been identified. The *Seven Grand Challenges* are:

1. Agile Product Customization Processes
2. Proactive and Socially Intelligent Products and Assets
3. Data-Driven Operations Management
4. Digital Lean Manufacturing Systems
5. Human Cyber-Physical Production Systems
6. Immersive Learning and Virtual Training Environments
7. Servitization of Manufacturing

3.1   Grand Challenge 1: Agile Product Customization Processes

Grand Challenge 1 is to develop *agile product customization processes* with particular attention on (i) "pure-personalized products", known as Engineer-to-Order (ETO) solutions, and (ii) "mass-customized products", which fall under the category of Make-to-Order (MTO) or Build-to-Order (BTO) solutions. If successful, these solutions will help achieve the Industry 4.0 vision of small-batches and item-level productions (i.e. batch-size-1) using agile engineering and production systems. Systems that enable efficient mass-customization and pure-personalization through customer- and product-specific coordination across the entire life cycle [4–6].

3.1.1   Current Status

There is an increasing market demand for mass-customized, personalized products.

Mass-customization requires the alignment of engineering and production activities. Typically, this alignment is achieved by implementing modularity, product platforms, and other techniques that manage both the increase in the number of designs and the decrease in lead times and costs [7]. Most mass-customization research focuses on how mass-producers can increase product variety and customization while maintaining high efficiency [5].

As a result, manufacturers are moving away from Make-to-Stock (MTS) strategies and shifting to Make-to-Order (MTO), routinely called "Engineer-to-Order (ETO)", fulfilment strategies. These strategies are not new [8]. In this context, highly customized engineering and production systems in ETO environments have been characterized traditionally by mostly manual work, poor data availability, and value creation performed by suppliers. In a recent paper, however, the authors strongly argued that these strategies increase both the complexity of, and the uncertainty in, modern, production systems [5].

To utilize these modern systems effectively, *ETO* manufacturers need a different viewpoint than the one described above. That viewpoint involves two activities. First, shifting the "time-of-differentiation" closer to the "time-of-delivery" by more closely linking engineering and production. The linking is done using both standardization and modularization [9]. Second, addressing the lack of contemporary research associated with the new *ETO perspective* on "efficient mass-customization processes" [6]. Those processes start from design and engineering and run through production and inspection.

3.1.2   Enabling Technologies

Some *technologies* that companies could use to enable efficient customisation are:

- *Configure, Price, Quote (CPQ) Software* – as an enabler of sales of customized products in minutes, allowing real-time responses to customer inquiries.
- *Knowledge-Based Engineering (KBE) Systems* – as computer systems that capture and reuse engineering knowledge to automate CAD-based engineering design and simulation activities, allowing an automated engineering process from sales to the programming of robots and machines.
- *Software Connectivity* – as an interoperability solution for real-time, reliable data/information integration among supporting systems including ERP, CRM, Pricing, MES, PLM, CAD/CAM, SCM, and Service.
- *3D Information Models and Visualization Tools* – as enablers for real-time planning, monitoring, and evaluating manufacturing processes, site layout, and material handling for large complex products (e.g. Building Information Models (BIM)).
- *Augmented Reality (AR)* – as a simplifier of complex assembly and installation procedures for engineers and manufacturers by first replacing static, work-instruction documents with AR solutions and then giving engineers the ability to provide operators with instant direction and image/voice instructions.
- *Smart Scheduling Techniques* – as techniques focusing on the use of cyber-physical systems that generate flexible and efficient production schedules on the fly. Such smart techniques can be used for (i) resource-constrained, multi-project scheduling, (ii) rescheduling in the face of unforeseen events at the shop floor, and (iii) time and pricing determination in tendering (see [10]).
- *Internet of Things (IoT)* – as an enabler for tracking customers' products or assets (i.e., equipment) and predicting what they need in advance. IoT can also help in reinventing site management since it is possible to know where both the locations of every tool, part, and soon-to-be-free site areas.
- *Autonomous and Collaborative Robots* – as robots/cobots that can load and unload resources; start, stop, load, and unload machines; and enable a more automated workflow in production systems supporting customized products.
- *Additive Manufacturing (AM)* – as a facilitator of the integration of engineering and production processes with fast feed-forward and feedback information going between the two processes. AM can also increase the options when choosing an efficient customization process in ETO operations.
- *Digital Twins and CAD Parametric Design* – as facilitators of the integration of design, engineering, and production processes with the data captured by sensors and other

reality-capture methodologies (e.g. point clouds) that can create model-based parametric designs. Furthermore, when including a digital twin of the production line, real-time 3D-dimensional concurrent engineering (3DCE) information should be integrated into that digital twin. That information includes models of both the product the processes.

- *Machine Learning and Artificial Intelligence (AI)* – as solvers of constraint-based problems such as improving production efficiency while defining the best possible workflows for producing highly configurable, customized products.

3.1.3 IFIP WG5.7 SIG – Operations Management in ETO Manufacturing

Engineer-to-Order (ETO) is a manufacturing approach where design and engineering are included in the normal activities associated with the order fulfilment process. ETO is used when engineering specifications of products or services are not known in detail upon receipt of the customer order. This situation is common in mechanical industries, the construction sector, shipbuilding, offshore supplier industries, and other types of project-based manufacturing industries. These industries are typically facing several, unique challenges as the products are often one-of-a-kind and/or highly customized.

The IFIP WG5.7 SIG on "Operations Management in ETO Manufacturing" welcomes research contributions and industrial best practices on Operations Management (OM). These contributions can enable more effective use of ETO manufacturing strategies, Industry 4.0 technologies, Supply Chain Management (SCM) practices, lean operations, production planning and control techniques, production strategies, and product platforms.

3.1.4 Research Agenda and Future Outlook

The following *trends* are of importance when developing methods and algorithms that will lead to more efficient ways to design and engineer mass-customized and pure-personalized products [6]:

- *Increasing Complexity* – as products continue to increase the number of digital components and modules, the intensity and types of their interactions will also increase. As a result, the complexity of the final products will also increase. Moreover, from a production perspective, dealing with such complexity requires an appropriate balance between modular and flexible composition and the agile engineering needed to implement that composition in the real world. Finding the right balance is essential to quickly respond to mass-and-personalized customizations.
- *Increasing Competition* – as competition increases over time, cost reductions in engineering, innovative methods, and software tools (e.g. model-based engineering, virtual prototyping, digital mock-ups) will be required to improve the way engineering projects are executed.
- *Digitalization and Industry 4.0* – as "time-to-market" pressures continue to increase, agile product development processes will make more and more use of advanced digital information, AI tools, and Industry 4.0 technologies to support the visualization of engineering data, and the automation of engineering processes and decisions.

- *Glocalization* – as "being global and acting local" becomes the new mantra for having a competitive advantage when it comes to responsiveness and specialization, new strategies will be needed (i) to achieve better market proximity to customers and suppliers, and (ii) for rationalizing new designs and structures for the value chain.

3.2   Grand Challenge 2: Proactive and Socially Intelligent Products and Assets

Grand Challenge 2 is to design and engineer *proactive and socially intelligent products and assets* that (i) meet the requirements of circular lifecycle management options and (ii) use collaborative, multi-agent, cyber-physical, production-management approaches. In this sense, *proactive intelligent products or assets* refer to those smart, connected entities capable of using Just-In-Time (JIT) information to anticipate and automate relevant tasks for themselves or their operators or users [11]. Whereas *socially intelligent products or assets* refer to those smart, connected entities capable of (i) sharing status information, context-aware capabilities, and cooperative initiatives, and (ii) cooperating via a social network to achieve a common or compatible goal [12]. Therefore, *circular lifecycle management of products or assets* refers to a strategy focused on gathering and analysing the data of a product or asset from the perspective of enabling and supporting its circular systems [13–15]. Moreover, *collaborative multi-agent production management approaches* represent a "production control strategy" where production resources, as assets of the production system, are understood as collaborative agents. These agents share a common or compatible goal to manufacture a product within a certain quality, time, and cost constraints [16].

Overall, the goal of this grand challenge is to achieve optimal, system-level performance by making a product or an asset more reliable and productive – for itself, for its operator or user, and for the network of "things" to which it may belong. Several authors have looked at different performance metrics. Guillén et al. [17] and Cho et al. [18] focused on predictive maintenance and quality control; Psarommatis et al. [19, 20] focused on impact analysis at the factory level. Roda and Macchi [21, 22], Roda et al. [23], and Polenghi et al. [24] focused on risk-oriented, strategic, decision-support systems. Moreover, the data needed to estimate these performance metrics should be transformed and integrated to make available information and/or knowledge relevant for more sustainable products and assets [25, 26].

3.2.1   Current Status

From an evolutionary perspective, mechatronic products and assets have evolved into smart, connected entities embedded with sensors, actuators, processors, and software. Their connectivity allows data to be exchanged with their environment, manufacturer, operator or user, as well as with other products or assets and systems. In this context, the next evolutionary stage will require the development of improved cybersecurity, connectivity, interoperability, and data analytics. Also, the current capabilities of product and asset lifecycle management systems need to be extended to deal with the multitude of these connected entities.

3.2.2 Enabling Technologies

Some *enabling technologies* that companies could incorporate into their proactive and socially intelligent products or assets are:

- *Smart Sensors* – as the "eyes-and-ears" that IoT/IIoT devices provide to their applications through novel telemetry systems that monitor their mechanisms and environment.
- *Machine-to-Machine (M2M) and Human-Machine Interfaces (HMIs)* – as the automation of communications and data exchange among networked devices and between the operator and the system, enabling the IIoT.
- *Edge Computing* – as the local data processing power that is closer to the source of the data for faster response time, increased reliability, and cybersecurity.
- *Cloud Computing* – as the global, data-processing power that analyses data from anywhere. It includes additional "data-driven services" for production systems and supply chains.
- *Machine Learning* – as the operational data analytics approach to descriptive, diagnostic, predictive, and prescriptive equipment behaviour for higher levels of reliability and efficiency.
- *5G-Connectivity* – as a more reliable wireless connection offering high-speed (>1 Gbps), low-power, and low-latency (<1 ms) for the IoT/IIoT world(s).
- *Industrial Ontologies*[3] – as integrated data models of products, processes, and production systems for semantic interoperability, knowledge sharing and reuse across the lifecycle of products or assets.
- *Cybersecurity Standards*[4] – as protection from malicious intrusions aimed at modifying the intended behaviour of a smart, connected product or an asset.
- *Circular Technologies*[5] – as resource-efficient, production technologies aimed at minimising waste and emissions, and maintaining the value of products and resources for as long as possible so that circular products and their raw materials can be recycled and recreated in a circular production system.

3.2.3 IFIP WG5.7 SIG – Product and Asset Lifecycle Management

The IFIP WG5.7 SIG on "Product and Asset Lifecycle Management" (PALM) promotes collaborative research and networking activities among researchers and practitioners with a shared interest in the key aspects of product and asset lifecycle management within advanced production systems. The "lifecycle" is the cornerstone based on which the SIG explores innovative ways for the development, coordination, and control of activities undertaken on products and assets. In particular, the SIG encourages research exploring how to design, engineer, implement, and improve collaborative, multi-agent systems. Systems that manage the circular lifecycle of products and assets with particular emphasis on production aspects of that lifecycle.

---

[3] https://www.industrialontologies.org/.

[4] https://www.nist.gov/cyberframework/.

[5] https://www.ellenmacarthurfoundation.org/.

The purposes of the SIG are (i) to identify and share best practices in order to consolidate the knowledge in the field, (ii) to explore the existing gaps in practice and theory in order to identify new research paths, and (iii) to establish interdisciplinary collaborations in international projects and research activities. To achieve these purposes, the SIG is interested in merging academic rigour with practical applications. Suggested topics include (i) the effective management and use of data, information, and knowledge across the different lifecycles, (ii) closing the loops of information as well as knowledge sharing and reuse required by product/asset-related decisions, (iii) the adoption of Zero Defect Manufacturing (ZDM), and Prognostics and Health Management (PHM) strategies to support the optimization of performances along the lifecycle, (iv) the adoption of "intelligent" products and assets for a smart lifecycle management, (v) using the (Industrial) Internet of Things (IIoT), Big Data, Predictive Analytics, Semantic Technologies, as well as advanced Human-Machine Interfaces (HMIs) in order to build an Industry 4.0-infused innovative lifecycle management.

3.2.4   Research Agenda and Future Outlook

Some *emerging paradigms* enabled by proactive and socially intelligent products and assets are:

- *Zero Defect Manufacturing (ZDM)* – as potential quality problems are detected in products and corrected either in a machine or a process before those problems happen [19, 20]. As these machines and processes become more intelligent, detecting in real-time will require the abilities to harvest all relevant data and to use advanced analytics to investigate that data.
- *Prognostics and Health Management (PHM) Systems* – as advanced systems and approaches to predictive maintenance with overall benefits along with asset lifecycle phases [17, 18, 27–29]. Such systems typically include capabilities such as fault detection, fault isolation and identification, and fault prognosis abilities. These capabilities will rely on intelligent assets to provide actionable, real-time data and historical information as needed.
- *Cyber-Physical Product Lifecycle Management (CP-PLM)* – as intelligent products/assets become "cyber-physical", new data-driven and circular, value-added services for augmenting and extending a product lifecycle will become possible [30].
- *Digital Twinning (DT)* – as intelligent products and assets acquire their digital twins, they will be able to use advanced simulations and other prediction models to proactively identify and correct software and hardware performance issues [30–32].

3.3   Grand Challenge 3: Data-Driven Operations Management

Grand Challenge 3 is to develop *data-driven, operations-management* approaches for production planning, control, and management. A *data-driven approach* uses data, intuition, or personal experience – rather than first principles – for decision-making at both shop-floor and the supply-chain levels [33]. This paradigm change is closely associated with the rise of *smart manufacturing systems* [34, 35] because they have an increasing degree of automated, real-time, monitoring, control, and decision-making.

The scope of Operations Management (OM) has been extended from just the local management of processes involved in the creation and delivery of goods to the cloud and other global services that provide that management. This extension is due to the progression of mass-produced products to highly personalized products that are capable of using those services.

Such capabilities increase the "complexity" of OM [33, 36]. According to those authors, new decentralized capabilities are required to handle this complexity, including digitally enabled tools like advanced data analytics supporting human decisions. To predict changes and adapt dynamically, decentralized, value-creation activities will require a decentralized exchange and processing of "smart data[6]" as well. Diverse, data repositories must be included in that smart data.

The grand challenge then in *data-driven operations management* extends into several dimensions, horizontally across the supply chain, vertically through the manufacturing system, and along the life cycle of the product [37]. The goal for this grand challenge is to evolve to a data-driven decision-making culture in OM. A culture that focuses on tasks like processes planning and scheduling, layout planning, part/family formation, production ramp-up, quality management, and production logistics.

3.3.1 Current Status

The proliferation of data-driven operations management tools is hindered by uncertainties regarding their potential and their ROI [38]. Furthermore, interoperability issues prevent a seamless integration of operations across the entire supply chain [39]. However, data gathered in processes like design, engineering, production, inspection, maintenance, and after-services is increasingly used to support the management of operations [40]. The connection of previously independent data sources, together with the increasing availability of new data sources, makes data quality an issue. The data must now be monitored to strengthen trust and support the human operator.

3.3.2 Enabling Technologies

Some *enabling technologies* that companies could use to create data-driven systems are:

- *Machine Learning and Artificial Intelligence (AI)* – as automatic reasoning methods to support the analysis of available manufacturing data to help OM to assess the current status of and predict the future status of any operation [41].
- *Machine Vision Systems* – as computer systems supporting the visualization of complex manufacturing information, becoming in this way the vehicle to communicate data analytics results to stakeholders for OM [42]. Moreover, because of the different requirements for data visualization, sophisticated visualization solutions must be capable of breaking down abstract sensor-based data and provide value-added, applicable information [43].

---

[6] *Smart Data* is defined as high-quality, accurate, up-to-date, and contextualized data targeted to assist specific business needs such as supporting a more confident AI and human decision-making.

- *Data Flow and Standards* – as interoperable data flows will be needed to enable data-driven OM. Data will need to originate from each intelligent process and asset. From them, the data flows to other collaborating, intelligent processes and assets. Hence, data-flow standards can facilitate such collaborations [44]. Open-source, big-data-management systems promise to enable the same kinds of collaborations – even among SMEs [45].

3.3.3 IFIP WG5.7 SIG – Smart Manufacturing Systems and CP Production Systems

The IFIP WG5.7 SIG on "Smart Manufacturing Systems and Cyber-Physical Production Systems" comprises science and industry experts dedicated to facilitating the penetration of smart technologies into manufacturing systems, factories, and supply chains. This dedication has resulted in research and networking activities on models, methods, and tools across the lifecycle of these systems. The research scope of the SIG comprises agile, development methods and approaches to choose, prioritize, and integrate smart technologies. The SIG encourages new ideas related to that scope such as smart manufacturing characterization, maturity analysis, interoperability, industrial ontologies, smart data, OM, and HMI. These ideas can help (i) align technology with performance goals, (ii) create new visions for current smart systems based on smart products and services. Thus, the SIG aims to analyse the state-of-the-art in the above topics, as well as to provide guidance for basic and applied research. Research that can close the existing gaps in the theory and practice through both international and interdisciplinary collaborations.

3.3.4 Research Agenda and Outlook

Some *emerging paradigms* enabled by data-driven operations management approaches are:

- *Data-driven Decision-Making Culture* – as the proactive use of available data and (big) data analytics tools in OM to enable human decisions makers to act on a reliable basis [26].
- *Industrial Data Space*[7]– as a reliable and secure platform for data exchange and trade. This platform leverages existing standards and technologies, as well as accepted governance models for the Data Economy [46].
- *Data-driven Optimized Industrial Value Networks* – as (big) data analytics will achieve an inter-organisational optimisation of the supply chain, dynamically adapting to individual customer requirements [47, 48].
- *Model-based and Ontology-based Data and Knowledge Interoperability* – as model-based standards will make data from the transactional data exchange more interoperable. Ontology-based standards will make heterogeneous data more understandable by computers in a coherent manner [49]. More and more of the data needed to build these models and ontologies will be tracked and interpreted automatically by a computer. Therefore, the cost and speed associated with automatically and correctly integrating and understanding that data must be considered.

---

[7] https://www.internationaldataspaces.org/.

• *Integration of AI Approaches with Knowledge-Bases* – as AI tools are becoming the new approach to data-driven decision-making in OM. There will be a need to integrate these AI tools with existing, traditional, and tacit OM knowledge bases. "Integration" will increase the trustworthiness and performance of such fuzzy, decision-making approaches [50].

3.4   Grand Challenge 4: Digital Lean Manufacturing Systems

Grand Challenge 4 is to update, develop, and demonstrate new lean concepts, methods, and tools that can enable the necessary transformation [51] of traditional production systems towards *Digital Lean Manufacturing (DLM) Systems* [35, 52]. Such a transformation should maintain the current people-centric view of traditional, lean, production systems. Additionally, this transformation must now include the "digital" dimension, preferably by using Industry 4.0 technologies as "enablers" as the foundation for these new DLM systems. In such systems, business processes will be strategically (re-)engineered using the *lean thinking* principles – value, value stream, flow, pull, and perfection [53] – when adopting digital technologies [35, 54]. The goal for this grand challenge is to develop and deploy *digital lean solutions* that contribute towards establishing a cyber-physical, waste-free Industry 4.0 [35, 54].

3.4.1   Current Status

There is a link between the methods-driven approaches to *lean production* and the technology-driven approaches envisioned by Industry 4.0 [51]. There have been many unsuccessful attempts to build this link and implement such a transformation. Hence, production managers must understand that digital technologies (i) will not simply render current lean practices unnecessary, and (ii) cannot be successfully adopted without proper lean methods. Both are complementary and necessary for the development of DLM systems [35, 51]. In this sense, DLM promises (i) to further facilitate the application of lean practices, and (ii) to enhance their scope and direction [35, 52].

Moreover, current production managers must not underestimate the people-centric view of both approaches, that view stresses the fundamental importance of *leadership and learning*, as well as the adoption of a *long-term perspective* for succeeding with a digital (lean) transformation [51, 55]. As part of that perspective, future production managers will need an awareness of both the old, the new, and the emerging Industry 4.0 technologies.

3.4.2   Concepts and Enabling Technologies

Some *concepts* and *enabling technologies* that promise to enhance the future capabilities of manufacturing companies that apply a "digital lean thinking" are:

• *Concepts:*

  o *Digital Waste* – as lean managers go beyond the identification and reduction or elimination of waste (Muda) in the physical world, DLM recognises the existence of "digital waste" as part of the new cyber-physical production environments. Digital waste comes in two forms: (i) as missing digital opportunities to unlock the power of existing data and (ii) as a result of over-digitalization and/or poor information management [35, 54].

- *Methods and Tools:*

  o *Digital Quality Management System* – as real-time monitoring and status reporting of intelligent assets will become a reality. Proactive alerting of potential deviations from quality standards, even before they materialize, will be needed. Alerting will improve both in-process control and, as a result, product quality [35, 56].
  o *Digital Kanban Systems* – as digital technologies will enable smart 'pull' signalling systems to operate in real-time at the shop floor. The "Just-In-Time" movement of materials and electronic information, which will be even more "responsive" to the actual demand instead of forecasts. This responsiveness will help to eliminate overproduction [35].
  o *Jidoka 4.0 Systems* – as novel, human-machine, cooperation systems will be characterized by cyber-physical-social interactions, knowledge exchange, and reciprocal learning. These smart capabilities go beyond "error catching" to facilitate mutual, human-machine learning for quality improvement [35, 57].
  o *Heijunka 4.0 Systems* – as all production resources will be connected in future in IIoT environments, the support of truly holistic production scheduling or re-scheduling approaches will become possible in real-time using just-in-sequence logic [35].

3.4.3   IFIP WG5.7 SIG – The Future of Lean Thinking and Practice

The IFIP WG5.7 SIG on "The Future of Lean Thinking and Practice" seeks to deepen the academic foundations of lean by promoting collaborative research on future and emerging trends in lean production systems. The SIG is composed of researchers and practitioners who are committed to contributing to our understanding of how to reduce waste, unevenness and overburden along the entire value stream. Group members are also encouraged to improve and advance this exciting research field by investigating areas such as lean management, lean production, lean shop-floor control, lean and green, lean services, digital lean manufacturing systems, and lean digital transformations.

The purposes of the SIG are to consolidate state-of-the-art knowledge in the lean-production field, explore gaps in theory and practice, to identify new research paths, and to establish further collaboration in international projects and research activities. The SIG places an emphasis on research that merges academic rigour with practical applications. The objectives of the SIG are (i) to create a platform for exchanging ideas and learning; (ii) to organize Gemba walks and industrial best practice visits for its members; (iii) to organize special sessions/tracks at APMS conferences; (iv) to create special issues in leading international journals; and (v) to publish joint position papers among the SIG members.

3.4.4   Research Agenda and Future Outlook

The emerging paradigm of *digital lean manufacturing* aims to become an extension of the lean philosophy, now considering the cyber-physical nature of production (systems) and operations management, incorporating "digital tools" as an integral part of lean transformations in pursuit of new digital levers to realize safer working environments with higher productivity levels, higher quality, improved delivery performance, optimized resource-usage, and increased production throughput [35].

3.5   Grand Challenge 5: Human Cyber-Physical Production Systems

Grand Challenge 5 is to design, engineer, and implement *Human Cyber-Physical Production Systems (H-CPPSs)* as symbiotic, human-automation, work systems. Such systems emphasize and keep the human-in-the-loop and can get the best of humans and machines capabilities, as production resources that can achieve new production efficiency levels neither can achieve on their own [58, 59]. The goal for this grand challenge is to achieve socially sustainable, cyber-physical production systems, which includes a new generation of operators named "Operators 4.0". The new operators will have new roles and execute new tasks. They will work in environments where humans, machines, and software systems cooperate in real-time to support manufacturing and service operations [59, 60].

In this context, an *Operator 4.0* is defined as a smart and skilled operator who can perform cooperative work in unison with software, hardware (including social robots), as well as isolated work aided using wearable technologies such as smart glasses, helmets, headsets, watches, handhelds, and exoskeletons [58, 59].

Furthermore, the *Operator 4.0 vision* aims for factories of the (near-)future that accommodate workers with different skills, capabilities, and preferences towards the social sustainability of manufacturing [61, 62]. This vision proposes the adoption of human-centred design approaches aimed at demonstrating the social and productivity benefits of "balanced automation systems" [61, 63].

3.5.1   Current Status

According to present research [61, 62, 64], the *Operator 4.0 vision* explores newly available technological means for supporting and aiding the work of the operators in smart production environments. Three types of work aid are being discussed: assisted work, collaborative work, and augmented work. *Assisted Work* is where the operators perform the key tasks and make the key decisions; but, a wearable device, a cobot (collaborative robot), or an AI application (i.e. intelligent personal assistants) executes the repetitive and standardized tasks. In assisted work, operators can reduce their cognitive and physical workload. *Collaborative Work* is where the operators work side-by-side with cobots (collaborative robots) and AIs (e.g. virtual assistants and chatbots). Each worker type performs the tasks it is best at executing and supports other workers as needed. Lastly, *Augmented Work* is where operators use technology (i.e. enterprise wearable devices) to extend their physical, sensorial, and cognitive capabilities [58, 59].

3.5.2   Enabling Technologies

Some *enabling technologies* for "The Operator 4.0" are [59, 65]:

- *Exoskeletons* – as light, wearables suits powered by a system of electric motors, pneumatics, levers, hydraulics, or a combination of these technologies to add strength and endurance to operators movements.
- *Augmented Reality (AR)* – as a digital-assistance technology enriching the real-world factory environment with relevant information for the operator. This information can be overlaid in real-time in the operator's field of view. The resulting "hands-free" information transfer from the digital world to the physical world will reduce human errors.
- *Virtual Reality* – as a multi-purpose, immersive, interactive multimedia, and computer-simulated reality for the operator to explore in a risk-free environment and to see the likely outcomes of decisions in real-time.
- *Wearable Trackers* – as wearable, smart sensors designed to measure location, activity, stress, heart rate, and other health-related metrics. Metrics that support the occupational health and safety of the operator.
- *Intelligent Personal Assistants* – as AI-based chatbots supporting the operator when interfacing with smart machines and robots, computers, databases, and other information systems. These chatbots can support the operator in the execution of different tasks using human-like communication and interaction.
- *Collaborative Robots (Cobots)* – as robots designed to work alongside and in direct cooperation with, but without compromising the safety of, the operator. Cobots can support the operator in performing (i) repetitive, non-ergonomic, and dangerous tasks, and (ii) more precise or force-requiring operations.
- *Enterprise Social Networks* – as mobile and social collaborative methods to connect (smart) operators on the shop floor with other smart factory resources such as smart operators, machines, robots, computers, and software systems.
- *Big Data Analytics* – as a variety of tools for discovering useful information and predicting relevant events from collected data. Those tools support the operator in monitoring, controlling, and optimizing the performance of a cyber-physical production system.

3.5.3   IFIP WG5.7 SIG – Smart Manufacturing Systems and CP Production Systems

The IFIP WG5.7 SIG on "Smart Manufacturing Systems and Cyber-Physical Production Systems" has been recently putting special attention to the emerging Human-Machine Interfaces (HMIs) with physical and cognitive systems. These HMIs are contributing to more inclusive, human-centred, cyber-physical production systems. The SIG encourages the *Operator 4.0 vision* of human + technology rather than human vs. technology for the factories of the future.

3.5.4   Research Agenda and Future Outlook

Current and further research efforts for materializing the *Operator 4.0* vision include:

- *Modelling the Human-in-the-Loop* [60, 66]:

  o *Human-in-the-Loop (HITL)* – as our understanding of the spectrum of the activities involving humans and other processes and assets deepens, new techniques will be needed to derive models of human behaviours and to determine how to incorporate those models into the formal methodology of feedback control to leverage both human and machine intelligence.

- *Collaborative and Aiding Systems Engineering* [59, 63–65]:

  o *Physical Systems* – as smart automation, collaborative robots, and enterprise wearables will be further developed to (i) safely and ergonomically interact with humans, (ii) decrease their physical efforts, (iii) increase their comfort during their work, and (iv) aid in their occupational health and performance.
  o *Sensorial Systems* – as multi-sensor network systems that combine human senses with smart sensors (e.g., infrared-, olfactory-, microphone-, visual-, location-, wearable sensors, etc.) will soon become a reality. Data from these networks can be used for discovering and predicting events, capturing voices and noises, machine vision systems, image processing, mapping and location, etc. In this sense, special care is being put into avoiding the overwhelming human senses.
  o *Joint Cognitive Systems* – as systems that comprise human, OR, AI, and other cognitive capabilities creating a form of highly cooperative intelligence for complex decision-making. In this case, special attention is being put into cognitive ergonomics for proper "cognitive" human-AI interfacing design [67].

3.6 Grand Challenge 6: Immersive Learning and Virtual Training Environments

Grand Challenge 6 focuses on developing *immersive learning and virtual training environments* for the current and future workforce development (see [68]). *Immersive learning* places individuals in an interactive and engaging learning environment, either physically or virtually. This environment can replicate possible situations to teach particular skills or techniques. Teaching can be based on using simulations, game-based learning, Augmented Reality (AR) or Virtual Reality (VR) [69–74]. *Virtual training,* on the other hand, is a training method where individuals perform certain tasks repeatedly by executing them in a VR environment. This method induces the transfer of procedural knowledge and technical skills [75].

There are two goals for this grand challenge. The first is to address the demand from companies for industry-ready engineering graduates who can contribute quickly to their business. The second is to provide workers with the effective means for skill(s) upgrading, re-skilling, and acquisition of new (digital) skills to maintain their employability, and enterprise competitiveness [76, 77].

3.6.1 Current Status

Overall, employers from manufacturing industries are continually concerned about the declining supply of skilled labour and the number of basic training employees needed to make up for the shortcomings of education systems [78, 79]. Furthermore, in today's industry, training programmes continue to be inefficient since they require employees to divert time and resources away from production. So, the research question that arises from both situations is how new, digital technologies can contribute to (i) speed up the learning curves of new hires, and (ii) allow retraining without the current huge effort and disruption to the ongoing production?

3.6.2   Enabling Technologies

Some *enabling technologies* that higher-educational institutions and companies could incorporate into their learning and training programmes are:

- *Simulations* – as learning tools that can take control of a character that is expected to perform a certain task correctly in a controllable, virtual, learning environment that facilitates repetition and retention.
- *Virtual Reality (VR)* – as VR technologies can take advantage of the previously learned knowledge from several simulated situations to ensure a deeper level of understanding of how to perform assigned tasks, especially dangerous tasks where learning rules and regulations may not be enough.
- *Augmented Reality (AR)* – as AR offers an immersive, guided, training platform in a quasi-virtual environment by overlaying digital instructions onto the real world.
- *Game-based Learning* – as "games" create an engaging learning environment where the learners perform certain tasks by following predetermined rules and gain rewards for doing things correctly. Also, competition between learners can accelerate learning.
- *Gemba Walks* – as the learner to "go-and-see" the task (in a real industrial environment), understand it, ask questions, and learn.

3.6.3   IFIP WG5.7 SIG – Serious Games in Production Management Environments

The IFIP WG5.7 SIG on "Serious Games in Production Management Environments" focuses on the convergence of three relevant developments within the advances in production management systems: Industry 4.0, Gamification, and Mixed Reality (MR) (i.e. AR/VR variations) [80–82]. The SIG purposes are (i) to identify the state-of-the-art of this convergence from conceptual, practical, and technological points of view, (ii) to recognize the trends, gaps, and opportunities supported gamification as an exploration of new solutions emerging from this convergence, and (iii) to establish collaborations between the interested international researchers and practitioners.

The SIG predicts that the evolution and synergetic interactions of these three developments will produce new paradigms in teaching and research. Moreover, they will provide answers to questions related to how knowledge is generated and used within the disciplines of industrial engineering, industrial management, and operations management. The SIG envisages the emergence of advanced/complex, virtual-learning environments combined with "interactive" and "collaborative" educational processes. The SIG also foresees the development and adoption of novel technologies via gaming and AR/VR/MR. Pioneering research projects will use the practice of AR/VR/MR.

3.6.4 Research Agenda and Future Outlook

Looking into the near future, some learning and training *emerging paradigms* are:

- *Personalized Learning and Training* – as multiple generations will coexist at the workplace, personalized learning and training will be required according to job requirements, learning preferences, and pre-existing workers' knowledge.
- *Lifelong Learning and Training* – as the only thing we know about the future is that it will be "different", the workforce will need to continuously adapt to changing technologies and organisational structures.
- *Accelerated Learning and Training* – as the pace of knowledge change accelerates, keeping skills up to date will require new methods and technology means for accelerated learning and training processes.

3.7 Grand Challenge 7: Servitization of Manufacturing

Grand Challenge 7 is to support the *servitization of manufacturing*. The significance of the *servitization* phenomenon has been developed over the last decades It has been underlined by a perceptible upsurge of relevant studies [83–85]. Different schools of thought, related to a multitude of disciplines, have tried to investigate its various facets, often embracing different genesis, motivations, cultural, and methodological approaches [86–88].

Servitization is an evolutionary journey that will completely change the traditional product-based, business models. That change will result in a new approach promoting the "performance" associated with a product use [87]. Such a change foresees the provision of the so-called *Product-Service System (PSS)* – as a system of products, services, networks of players, and supporting infrastructure. This new system, which will have a lower environmental impact than traditional businesses, will continuously strive to be competitive and to satisfy customer needs [89].

Recent research has underlined that the dynamics behind such a journey cannot be understood without considering the role of technological innovation in product, process, and service entities [90, 91]. The reasons behind this are a growing interest in the development of what is being referred to as "digital servitization" [88, 90, 92], which concerns with the numerous operational, marketing, and business benefits that can be obtained through the integration of technology into PSSs [40, 92–94].

However, there is little understanding of (i) how and to what extent such integration is steered and fostered by technological development, and (ii) where technology could act as an enabler, a mediator, or a facilitator [96]. While most studies have been developed around applications and benefits of technologically based PSSs taking a strategic perspective, only a few works have sought to understand day-by-day actions that have to be addressed to accomplish an effective digital servitization transformation [97].

Hence, the development of frameworks, methods, and approaches addressing what (i.e. content), where, when (i.e. context), how, and to what extent (i.e. process) technological innovation supports the operational adaptation needed for "servitization" strategies to emerge as mandatory. In this perspective, this grand challenge refers to the design, engineering, management, and delivery of the next generation of technologically enabled

Product-Service Systems (PSSs). Systems that are equipped with the ability to collect and record a large quantity of data about how the products are used and how their associated services are delivered. Specifically, this grand challenge concerns a complete rethinking of current operational processes, organization structures, skills and competencies, management approaches, communication tools, as well as measurement and control systems. At the same time, new methods and tools to review, design, develop, visualize, operationalize, manage, and evaluate smart PSSs are needed to enable companies to create smart, integrated, robust, and flexible solutions. Solutions that can deliver the maximum value across the diverse needs and desires of a varied and global set of customers.

3.7.1 Current Status

Notwithstanding the significant advantages featured in the literature, most organizations that have set out on a servitization journey have found the transition quite problematic [98]. Developing new, client, value propositions; re-designing operations and value chains; increasing the competencies, expertise and skills of people; as well as increasing systems-integration capabilities. These are just some of the research topics being explored over the years to identify effective and efficient servitization journey [92, 98–103].

Recently, interest in the topic has increased with the introduction of new technologies. These technologies make it possible to amplify the availability and intensity of information and to speed up the collection and processing of data. It is in this sense, that Rust [104] said: "the service revolution and the information revolution are two sides of the same coin".

In this context, the next evolutionary stage will require a further understanding of the impact that the new digital technologies would have on the operational management of PSSs. It will be essential to comprehend the extent to which technological innovation will influence relationships among all the actors within the PSS ecosystem to design, engineer and operationalize effective and efficient technologically enabled PSSs.

3.7.2 Enabling Technologies

Some *enabling technologies* that companies could use to create technologically enabled PSSs [90]:

- *Internet of Things (IoT)* – as a new channel for the delivery and provisioning of new services to smart, connected products and assets.
- *Big Data Analytics* – as insights about the interactions between human, human-assisted, or automated service-delivery processes. Such insights can ultimately improve the customer experience.
- *Augmented/Virtual Reality (AR/VR)* – as enabling means to improve customer support agents training, enrich services tangibility, and thus customer experience.
- *Cloud Computing* – as "elastic resources" that can offer at each point in time the needed computing resources to match the current service demand as closely as possible.
- *Horizontal and Vertical Integration* – as a way to improve the delivery and quality of services by enriching the value creation capabilities of a service value chain.

- *Simulations* – as support to evaluate the designs of new product-service solutions.
- *Machine Learning and Artificial Intelligence (AI)* – as enabling means to improve the availability of customer service and support and for supporting decision-making processes along the service delivery process.

3.7.3 IFIP WG5.7 SIG – Service Systems Design, Engineering and Management

The IFIP WG5.7 SIG on "Service Systems Design, Engineering and Management" promotes collaborative research on future and emerging innovative ideas and networking activities related to new models, methods and tools to support service systems along their lifecycle. The purposes of the SIG include (i) to identify and share best practices in order to consolidate the knowledge in the field, (ii) to explore the existing gaps in practice and theory to identify new research paths, and (iii) to establish collaborations in international projects and research activities.

The SIG is composed of researchers and practitioners who are committed to improving and advancing the investigation of Service Systems. In particular, the SIG is focused on exploring how these service systems are developing in several industries including the manufacturing industry (i.e. Product-Service Systems (PSSs)) and several service-oriented industries (i.e. healthcare, finance, entertainment, logistics). The SIG's research answers question about how to design, engineer and manage these domain-specific systems. Moreover, due to the Fourth Industrial Revolution, that research is also answering questions about how new digital technologies can be applied to rethink operations management approaches, processes, structures, skills, competencies, control, communication, and performance.

3.7.4 Research Agenda and Future Outlook

Some *emerging topics* characterizing future research at the ecosystem and company level are:

- *Ecosystem Collaboration* – as a collaborative form needed to use the evolving technological capabilities to improve both value creation and the interactions needed for that creation. To support such collaborations, new models and tools that monitor activities and support decision-making will be needed.
- *Risk and Revenue Sharing Mechanisms* – as new kind of collaboration-based ecosystems emerge, new methods and tools enabling risk and revenue sharing mechanisms will be needed in value co-creation schemas.
- *Data Sharing and Security* – as new forms of these collaborations appear; additional research will be needed to understand how they operate. That research will depend upon information sharing and will feature a high degree of uncertainty and risk. Moreover, since data sharing involves internal data privacy and security, future research will also focus on understanding the factors that foster or inhibit data sharing in the emerging Data Economy.
- *Decision-Making* – as digital-technology adoption increases, the need to monitor and analyse the whole lifecycle of both products and assets will arise. Addressing that need will be fundamental to support decision-making across that lifecycle. Decisions

that will be made in the new product-service systems. Decisions that, more and more, will be made by data-driven and AI tools.

- *Interoperability Standards* – as technology interoperability is required to realize the new collaborative and product-service systems. Consequently, there is an essential need to spur additional research on the topic of standards. Explorative research, for example, in the available ISO global community could be a starting point to address this issue.

4   Discussion: Barriers and Enablers Towards Production 2030

In this section, we consider barriers and enablers from four, sustainability perspectives: social, environmental, economic, and technological.

From a social sustainability perspective, creating an adequate, safe, inclusive, and attractive work environment will be required to build the proposed "human cyber-physical production systems" [58, 63]. In such systems, humans constitute the most flexible production resource; and, they are the root source of competitive advantage in a smart enterprise. The advantage comes from their creativity, ingenuity, and innovation capabilities. Furthermore, a "socially sustainable workforce" will require continuous and multi-faceted learning and training strategies. As noted in Romero and Stahre [105], in "immersive learning and virtual training environments", humans must be able to (i) cope with the accelerated rate of skills obsolescence, and (ii) sustain their competitiveness in the labour market.

From an environmental sustainability perspective, current "green" products and production systems will soon become "circular" products and production systems. These new systems will be capable of (i) minimising waste and emissions, (ii) making the most of any resource present in the production system, (iii) becoming restorative or regenerative industrial systems. To have these capabilities, it will be necessary to design and engineer new "proactive and socially intelligent products and assets" so that they can close all information loops. Loops that are needed for their proper maintenance, repair, reuse, remanufacturing, refurbishing, and recycling [11, 30, 106]. Moreover, the emergence of "digital lean manufacturing systems" [35, 52] will contribute towards establishing a cyber-physical waste-free Industry 4.0 by making physical and digital production processes resource-efficient.

From an economic sustainability perspective, new business models such as the "servitization of manufacturing" [88] will need to decouple the economic development from resources depletion. Additionally, those models must be able to meet customers' demands for mass-customized and pure-personalized products and services using "agile product customization processes" [5, 6].

Lastly, from a technological sustainability perspective, technological innovation and new digital technologies will enable novel "data-driven operations management" approaches. Approaches that advanced, production management systems can use to control and optimize products and assets behaviours, improve customer value, and enable new business models [33, 37].

5   Conclusions

"Production in 2030 will be sustainable, dynamic, and competitive". For achieving such a bold vision, future production managers will require the integration of information, technology, and human ingenuity. This integration will promote the rapid evolution of manufacturing, service, and logistics systems towards sustainable and human-inclusive cyber-physical production systems.

Policymakers, governments, and funding agencies are making funding available for research and technology development to address the *Grand Challenges* globally. At the same time, academia and industry need to collaborate closely and as equal partners on implementing the vision of Production 2030. Given the interdisciplinary nature of the *Seven Grand challenges* put forth in this chapter, we need to come together and put aside animosities to work towards the joint goal. This is not a localized development but a global one. The World will look very different in 2030, and if the sketched-out innovation is successful – and remains agile and adaptive – the World will be a more sustainable place with manufacturing being a driving factor for this positive change.

Acknowledgements and Disclaimer. The co-authors would like to acknowledge the contributions of the IFIP WG5.7 members to the definition of these "Seven Grand Challenges" for Production and Production Management towards 2030. Any mention of commercial products is for information only; it does not imply recommendation or endorsement by the IFIP WG5.7 or NIST.

References

1. World Economic Forum: (2020). https://www.weforum.org/platforms/shaping-the-future-of-production
2. Taisch, M., et al.: World manufacturing forum report – recommendations for the future of manufacturing. World Manufacturing Forum (2018)
3. Sinha, A., Bernardes, E., Calderon, R., Wuest, T.: Digital Supply Networks. McGraw-Hill, New York (2020)
4. Rudberg, M., Wikner, J.: Mass customization in terms of the customer order decoupling point. Prod. Plan. Control **15**(4), 445–458 (2004)
5. Duchi, A., Tamburini, F., Parisi, D., Maghazei, O., Schönsleben, P.: From ETO to mass customization: a two-horizon ETO enabling process. In: Bellemare, J., Carrier, S., Nielsen, K., Piller, F.T. (eds.) Managing Complexity. SPBE, pp. 99–113. Springer, Cham (2017). https://doi.org/10.1007/978-3-319-29058-4_8
6. Vellmar, J., Gepp, M., Schertl, A.: The future of engineering – scenarios of the future way of working in the engineer-to-order business. In: Proceedings of the Annual IEEE International Systems Conference, pp. 1–5 (2017)
7. Bonev, M.: Enabling mass customization in engineer-to-order industries: a multiple case study analysis on concepts, methods and tools. Ph.D. thesis, DTU (2015)
8. Wikner, J., Rudberg, M.: Integrating production and engineering perspectives on the customer order decoupling point. Int. J. Oper. Prod. Manag. **25**(7), 623–641 (2005)
9. Cannas, V.G.: Engineering and production alignment in engineer-to-order supply chains. Ph.D. thesis, Politecnico di Milano (2019)
10. Rossit, D.A., Tohmé, F., Frutos, M.: Industry 4.0: smart scheduling. Int. J. Prod. Res. **57**(12), 3802–3813 (2019)

11. Wuest, T., Schmidt, T., Wei, W., Romero, D.: Towards (pro-)active intelligent products. Int. J. Prod. Lifecycle Manag. **11**(2), 154–189 (2018)
12. Li, H., Palau, A.S., Parlikad, A.K.: A social network of collaborating industrial assets. Proc. Inst. Mech. Eng. Part O: J. Risk Reliab. **232**(4), 389–400 (2018)
13. Kiritsis, D.: Closed-loop PLM for intelligent products in the era of the Internet of Things. Comput. Aided Des. **43**(5), 479–501 (2011)
14. de Oliveira, S.F., Soares, A.L.: A PLM vision for circular economy. In: Camarinha-Matos, L.M., Afsarmanesh, H., Fornasiero, R. (eds.) PRO-VE 2017. IFIP, AICT, vol. 506, pp. 591–602. Springer, Cham (2017). https://doi.org/10.1007/978-3-319-65151-4_52
15. Macchi, M., Roda, I., Toffoli, L.: Remaining useful life estimation for informed end of life management of industrial assets: a conceptual model. In: Moon, I., Lee, G.M., Park, J., Kiritsis, D., von Cieminski, G. (eds.) APMS 2018. IFIP, AICT, vol. 536, pp. 335–342. Springer, Cham (2018). https://doi.org/10.1007/978-3-319-99707-0_42
16. Scholz-Reiter, B., Görges, M., Philipp, T.: Autonomously controlled production systems – influence of autonomous control level on logistic performance. CIRP Ann. **58**(1), 395–398 (2009)
17. Guillén, A.J., Crespo, A., Macchi, M., Gómez, J.: On the role of prognostics and health management in advanced maintenance systems. Prod. Plan. Control Manag. Oper. **27**(12), 991–1004 (2016)
18. Cho, S., et al.: A hybrid machine learning approach for predictive maintenance in smart factories of the future. In: Moon, I., Lee, G.M., Park, J., Kiritsis, D., von Cieminski, G. (eds.) APMS 2018. IFIP, AICT, vol. 536, pp. 311–317. Springer, Cham (2018). https://doi. org/10.1007/978-3-319-99707-0_39
19. Psarommatis, F., Kiritsis, D.: Identification of the inspection specifications for achieving zero defect manufacturing. In: Ameri, F., Stecke, K.E., von Cieminski, G., Kiritsis, D. (eds.) APMS 2019. IFIP, AICT, vol. 566, pp. 267–273. Springer, Cham (2019). https://doi.org/10. 1007/978-3-030-30000-5_34
20. Psarommatis, F., May, G., Dreyfus, P.-A., Kiritsis, D.: Zero defect manufacturing: state-of-the-art review, shortcomings and future directions in research. Int. J. Prod. Res. **58**(1), 1–17 (2020)
21. Roda, I., Macchi, M.: A framework to embed asset management in production companies. Proc. Inst. Mech. Eng. Part O: J. Risk Reliab. **232**(4), 368–378 (2018)
22. Roda, I., Macchi, M.: Factory-level performance evaluation of buffered multi-state production systems. J. Manuf. Syst. **50**, 226–235 (2019)
23. Roda, I., Arena, S., Macchi, M., Orrù, P.F.: Total cost of ownership driven methodology for predictive maintenance implementation in industrial plants. In: Ameri, F., Stecke, K.E., von Cieminski, G., Kiritsis, D. (eds.) APMS 2019. IFIP, AICT, vol. 566, pp. 315–322. Springer, Cham (2019). https://doi.org/10.1007/978-3-030-30000-5_40
24. Polenghi, A., Roda, I., Macchi, M., Trucco, P.: Risk sources affecting the asset management decision-making process in manufacturing: a systematic review of the literature. In: Ameri, F., Stecke, K.E., von Cieminski, G., Kiritsis, D. (eds.) APMS 2019. IFIP, AICT, vol. 566, pp. 274–282. Springer, Cham (2019). https://doi.org/10.1007/978-3-030-30000-5_35
25. Nezami, Z., Zamanifar, K., Arena, D., Kiritsis, D.: Ontology-based resource allocation for Internet of Things. In: Ameri, F., Stecke, K.E., von Cieminski, G., Kiritsis, D. (eds.) APMS 2019. IFIP, AICT, vol. 566, pp. 323–330. Springer, Cham (2019). https://doi.org/10.1007/ 978-3-030-30000-5_41
26. Polenghi, A., Roda, I., Macchi, M., Pozzetti, A.: Conceptual framework for a data model to support asset management decision-making process. In: Ameri, F., Stecke, K.E., von Cieminski, G., Kiritsis, D. (eds.) APMS 2019. IFIP, AICT, vol. 566, pp. 283–290. Springer, Cham (2019). https://doi.org/10.1007/978-3-030-30000-5_36

27. Lee, J., Ni, J., Djurdjanovic, D., Qiu, H., Liao, H.: Intelligent prognostics tools and E-maintenance. Comput. Ind. **57**(6), 476–489 (2006)
28. Sun, B., Zeng, S., Kang, R., Pecht, M.G.: Benefits and challenges of system prognostics. IEEE Trans. Reliab. **61**(2), 323–335 (2012)
29. Fumagalli, L., Cattaneo, L., Roda, I., Macchi, M., Rondi, M.: Data-driven CBM tool for risk-informed decision-making in an electric arc furnace. Int. J. Adv. Manufact. Technol. **105**(1–4), 595–608 (2019)
30. Romero, D., Wuest, T., Harik, R., Thoben, K.-D.: Towards a cyber-physical PLM environment: the role of digital product models, intelligent products, digital twins, product avatars and digital shadow. In: Proceedings of the 21st IFAC World Congress (2020)
31. Negri, E., Fumagalli, L., Macchi, M.: A review of the roles of digital twin in CPS-based production systems. Proc. Manufact. **11**, 939–948 (2017)
32. Ashtari Talkhestani, B., et al.: An architecture of an intelligent digital twin in a cyber-physical production system. Automatisierungstechnik **67**(9), 762–782 (2019)
33. Gölzer, P., Fritzsche, A.: Data-driven operations management: organisational implications of the digital transformation in industrial practice. Prod. Plan. Control **28**(16), 1332–1343 (2017)
34. Mittal, S., Khan, M.A., Romero, D., Wuest, T.: Smart manufacturing: characteristics, technologies and enabling factors. J. Eng. Manuf. **233**(5), 342–1361 (2017)
35. Romero, D., Gaiardelli, P., Powell, D., Wuest, T., Thürer, M.: Digital lean cyber-physical production systems: the emergence of digital lean manufacturing and the significance of digital waste. In: Moon, I., Lee, G.M., Park, J., Kiritsis, D., von Cieminski, G. (eds.) APMS 2018. IFIP, AICT, vol. 535, pp. 11–20. Springer, Cham (2018). https://doi.org/10.1007/978-3-319-99704-9_2
36. Christensen, B., Andersen, A.-L., Medini, K., Brunoe, T.D.: Reconfigurable manufacturing: a case-study of reconfigurability potentials in the manufacturing of capital goods. In: Ameri, F., Stecke, K.E., von Cieminski, G., Kiritsis, D. (eds.) APMS 2019. IFIP, AICT, vol. 566, pp. 366–374. Springer, Cham (2019). https://doi.org/10.1007/978-3-030-30000-5_46
37. Medini, K., Andersen, A.L., Wuest, T., Christensen, B., et al.: Highlights in customer-driven operations management research. Proc. CIRP **86**, 12–19 (2019)
38. Wiesner, S., Gaiardelli, P., Gritti, N., Oberti, G.: Maturity models for digitalization in manufacturing – applicability for SMEs. In: Moon, I., Lee, G.M., Park, J., Kiritsis, D., von Cieminski, G. (eds.) APMS 2018. IFIP, AICT, vol. 536, pp. 81–88. Springer, Cham (2018). https://doi.org/10.1007/978-3-319-99707-0_11
39. Kulvatunyou, B., Ivezic, N., Morris, K., Frechette, S.: Drilling-down on smart manufacturing-enabling composable apps. Manufact. Lett. **10**, 14–17 (2016)
40. Freitag, M., Wiesner, S.: Smart service lifecycle management: a framework and use case. In: Moon, I., Lee, G.M., Park, J., Kiritsis, D., von Cieminski, G. (eds.) APMS 2018. IFIP, AICT, vol. 536, pp. 97–104. Springer, Cham (2018). https://doi.org/10.1007/978-3-319-99707-0_13
41. Alvela Nieto, M.T., Nabati, E.G., Bode, D., Redecker, M.A., Decker, A., Thoben, K.-D.: Enabling energy efficiency in manufacturing environments through deep learning approaches: lessons learned. In: Ameri, F., Stecke, K.E., von Cieminski, G., Kiritsis, D. (eds.) APMS 2019. IFIP, AICT, vol. 567, pp. 567–574. Springer, Cham (2019). https://doi.org/10.1007/978-3-030-29996-5_65
42. Hwang, D., Noh, S.D.: 3D visualization system of manufacturing big data and simulation results of production for an automotive parts supplier. In: Ameri, F., Stecke, K.E., von Cieminski, G., Kiritsis, D. (eds.) APMS 2019. IFIP, AICT, vol. 567, pp. 381–386. Springer, Cham (2019). https://doi.org/10.1007/978-3-030-29996-5_44
43. Thoben, K.D., Wiesner, S., Wuest, T.: "Industrie 4.0" and smart manufacturing – a review of research issues and application examples. Int. J. Autom. Technol. **11**(1), 4–16 (2017)

44. Kulvatunyou, B., Oh, H., Ivezic, N., Nieman, S.T.: Standards-based semantic integration of manufacturing information: past, present, and future. J. Manuf. Syst. **52**, 184–197 (2019)
45. Sahal, R., Breslin, J.G., Ali, M.I.: Big data and stream processing platforms for Industry 4.0 requirements mapping for a predictive maintenance use case. J. Manuf. Syst. **54**, 138–151 (2020)
46. Otto, B., Hompel, M., Wrobel, S.: International data spaces. In: Neugebauer, Reimund (ed.) Digital Transformation, pp. 109–128. Springer, Heidelberg (2019). https://doi.org/10.1007/978-3-662-58134-6_8
47. Schuh, G., Prote, J.-P., Fränken, B., Dany, S., Gützlaff, A.: Reduction of decision complexity as an enabler for continuous production network design. In: Moon, I., Lee, G.M., Park, J., Kiritsis, D., von Cieminski, G. (eds.) APMS 2018. IFIP, AICT, vol. 535, pp. 246–253. Springer, Cham (2018). https://doi.org/10.1007/978-3-319-99704-9_30
48. Tien, K.-W., Kulvatunyou, B., Jung, K., Prabhu, V.: An investigation to manufacturing analytical services composition using the analytical target cascading method. In: Nääs, I., et al. (eds.) APMS 2016. IFIP, AICT, vol. 488, pp. 469–477. Springer, Cham (2016). https://doi.org/10.1007/978-3-319-51133-7_56
49. Kulvatunyou, B., Wallace, E., Kiritsis, D., Smith, B., Will, C.: The industrial ontologies foundry proof-of-concept project. In: Moon, I., Lee, G.M., Park, J., Kiritsis, D., von Cieminski, G. (eds.) APMS 2018. IFIP, AICT, vol. 536, pp. 402–409. Springer, Cham (2018). https://doi.org/10.1007/978-3-319-99707-0_50
50. Brundage, M.P., Kulvatunyou, B., Ademujimi, T., Rakshith, B.: Smart manufacturing through a framework for a knowledge-based diagnosis system. In: Proceedings of the ASME 12th International Manufacturing Science and Engineering Conference (2017)
51. Romero, D., Flores, M., Herrera, M., Resendez, H.: Five management pillars for digital transformation integrating the lean thinking philosophy. In: Proceedings of the 25th International ICE-Conference on Engineering, Technology and Innovation, pp. 1–8 (2019)
52. Powell, D., Romero, D., Gaiardelli, P., Cimini, C., Cavalieri, S.: Towards digital lean cyber-physical production systems: Industry 4.0 technologies as enablers of leaner production. In: Moon, I., Lee, G.M., Park, J., Kiritsis, D., von Cieminski, G. (eds.) APMS 2018. IFIP, AICT, vol. 536, pp. 353–362. Springer, Cham (2018). https://doi.org/10.1007/978-3-319-99707-0_44
53. Womack, J.P., Jones, D.T.: Lean Thinking: Banish Waste and Create Wealth in your Corporation. Simon & Schuster, New York (1996)
54. Romero, D., Gaiardelli, P., Thürer, M., Powell, D., Wuest, T.: Cyber-physical waste identification and elimination strategies in the digital lean manufacturing world. In: Ameri, F., Stecke, K.E., von Cieminski, G., Kiritsis, D. (eds.) APMS 2019. IFIP, AICT, vol. 566, pp. 37–45. Springer, Cham (2019). https://doi.org/10.1007/978-3-030-30000-5_5
55. Netland, T.H., Powell, D.J. (eds.): The Routledge Companion to Lean Management, 1st edn. Routledge, London (2016)
56. Romero, D., Gaiardelli, P., Powell, D., Wuest, T., Thürer, M.: Total quality management and quality circles in the digital lean manufacturing world. In: Ameri, F., Stecke, K.E., von Cieminski, G., Kiritsis, D. (eds.) APMS 2019. IFIP, AICT, vol. 566, pp. 3–11. Springer, Cham (2019). https://doi.org/10.1007/978-3-030-30000-5_1
57. Romero, D., Gaiardelli, P., Powell, D., Wuest, T., Thürer, M.: Rethinking Jidoka systems under automation and learning perspectives in the digital lean manufacturing world. IFAC Pap. Online **52**(13), 899–903 (2019)
58. Romero, D., Bernus, P., Noran, O., Stahre, J., Fast-Berglund, Å.: The Operator 4.0: human cyber-physical systems and adaptive automation towards human-automation symbiosis work systems. In: Nääs, I., et al. (eds.) APMS 2016. IFIP, AICT, vol. 488, pp. 677–686. Springer, Cham (2016). https://doi.org/10.1007/978-3-319-51133-7_80

59. Romero, D., et al.: Towards an Operator 4.0 typology: a human-centric perspective on the fourth industrial revolution technologies. In: Proceedings of the International Conference on Computers and Industrial Engineering (2016)

60. Romero, D., Wuest, T., Stahre, J., Gorecky, D.: Social factory architecture: social networking services and production scenarios through the social Internet of Things, services and people for the social Operator 4.0. In: Lödding, H., Riedel, R., Thoben, K.-D., von Cieminski, G., Kiritsis, D. (eds.) APMS 2017. IFIP, AICT, vol. 513, pp. 265–273. Springer, Cham (2017). https://doi.org/10.1007/978-3-319-66923-6_31

61. Romero, D., Stahre, J., Taisch, M.: The Operator 4.0: towards socially sustainable factories of the future. Comput. Ind. Eng. **139**, 106128 (2020)

62. Kaasinen, E., et al.: Empowering and engaging industrial workers with Operator 4.0 solutions. Comput. Ind. Eng. **139**, 105678 (2020)

63. Romero, D., Noran, O., Stahre, J., Bernus, P., Fast-Berglund, Å.: Towards a human-centred reference architecture for next generation balanced automation systems: human-automation symbiosis. In: Umeda, S., Nakano, M., Mizuyama, H., Hibino, H., Kiritsis, D., von Cieminski, G. (eds.) APMS 2015. IFIP, AICT, vol. 460, pp. 556–566. Springer, Cham (2015). https://doi.org/10.1007/978-3-319-22759-7_64

64. Rauch, E., Linder, C., Dallasega, P.: Anthropocentric perspective of production before and within Industry 4.0. Comput. Ind. Eng. **139**, 105644 (2020)

65. Ruppert, T., Jaskó, S., Holczinger, T., Abonyi, J.: Enabling technologies for Operator 4.0: a survey. Appl. Sci. **8**(9), 1650 (2018)

66. Munir, S., Stankovic, J.A., et al.: Cyber-physical system challenges for human-in-the-loop control. In: Proceedings of the 8th International Workshop on Feedback Computing, vol. 4, pp. 1–4 (2013)

67. Jones, A.T., Romero, D., Wuest, T.: Modeling agents as joint cognitive systems in smart manufacturing systems. Manuf. Lett. **17**, 6–8 (2018)

68. Herrington, J., et al.: Immersive learning technologies: realism and online authentic learning. J. Comput. High. Educ. **19**(1), 80–99 (2007)

69. Baalsrud Hauge, J.M., Pourabdollahian, B., Riedel, J.C.K.H.: The use of serious games in the education of engineers. In: Emmanouilidis, C., Taisch, M., Kiritsis, D. (eds.) APMS 2012. IFIP, AICT, vol. 397, pp. 622–629. Springer, Heidelberg (2013). https://doi.org/10.1007/978-3-642-40352-1_78

70. Pourabdollahian Tehran, B., Oliveira, M.F., Taisch, M., Baalsrud Hauge, J., Riedel, J.C.K.H.: Status and trends of serious game application in engineering and manufacturing education. In: Meijer, S.A., Smeds, R. (eds.) ISAGA 2013. LNCS, vol. 8264, pp. 77–84. Springer, Cham (2014). https://doi.org/10.1007/978-3-319-04954-0_10

71. Dempsey, M., Riedel, R., Kelly, M.: Serious play as a method for process design. In: Grabot, B., Vallespir, B., Gomes, S., Bouras, A., Kiritsis, D. (eds.) APMS 2014. IFIP, AICT, vol. 438, pp. 395–402. Springer, Heidelberg (2014). https://doi.org/10.1007/978-3-662-44739-0_48

72. Garbaya, S., et al.: Sensorial virtualization: coupling gaming and virtual environment. J. Adv. Distrib. Learn. Technol. **2**(5), 16–30 (2014)

73. Stefan, I.A., et al.: Using serious games and simulations for teaching co-operative decision-making. Proc. Comput. Sci. **162**, 745–753 (2019)

74. Hallinger, P., et al.: A bibliometric review of research on simulations and serious games used in educating for sustainability, 1997–2019. Clean. Prod. **256**, 120358 (2020)

75. Ordaz, N., Romero, D., Gorecky, D., Siller, H.R.: Serious games and virtual simulator for automotive manufacturing education and training. Proc. Comput. Sci. **75**, 267–274 (2015)

76. Cerinšek, G., et al.: Recommendations to leverage game-based learning to attract young talent to manufacturing education. In: Alcañiz, M., Göbel, S., Ma, M., Fradinho Oliveira, M., Baalsrud Hauge, J., Marsh, T. (eds.) JCSG 2017. LNCS, vol. 10622, pp. 187–202. Springer, Cham (2017). https://doi.org/10.1007/978-3-319-70111-0_18

77. Vergnano, A., Berselli, G., Pellicciari, M.: Interactive simulation-based-training tools for manufacturing systems operators: an industrial case study. Int. J. Interact. Des. Manuf. **11**, 785–797 (2017)

78. Hořejší, P., Vyšata, J., Rohlíková, L., Polcar, J., Gregor, M.: Serious games in mechanical engineering education. In: Visvizi, A., Lytras, M.D. (eds.) RIIFORUM 2019. SPC, pp. 55–63. Springer, Cham (2019). https://doi.org/10.1007/978-3-030-30809-4_6

79. Taisch, M., et al.: World manufacturing forum report – skills for the future of manufacturing. In: World Manufacturing Forum (2019)

80. Erol, S., Jäger, A., Hold, P., et al.: Tangible Industry 4.0: a scenario-based approach to learning for the future of production. Proc. CIRP **54**, 13–18 (2016)

81. Hantono, B.S., et al.: Meta-review of augmented reality in education. In: Proceedings of the International Conference on Information Technology and Electrical Engineering, pp. 312–315 (2018)

82. Wolf, T.: Intensifying user loyalty through service gamification: motivational experiences and their impact on hedonic and utilitarian value. In: Proceedings of the 40th International Conference in Information Systems (2019)

83. Smith, N., Wuest, T.: Identifying key aspects of success for product service systems. In: Lödding, H., Riedel, R., Thoben, K.-D., von Cieminski, G., Kiritsis, D. (eds.) APMS 2017. IFIP, AICT, vol. 513, pp. 231–238. Springer, Cham (2017). https://doi.org/10.1007/978-3-319-66923-6_27

84. Cavalieri, S., Ouertani, Z.M., Zhibin, J., Rondini, A.: Service transformation in industrial companies. Prod. Res. **56**(8), 2099–2101 (2018)

85. Marjanovic, U., Lalic, B., Majstorovic, V., Medic, N., Prester, J., Palcic, I.: How to increase share of product-related services in revenue? Strategy towards servitization. In: Moon, I., Lee, G.M., Park, J., Kiritsis, D., von Cieminski, G. (eds.) APMS 2018. IFIP, AICT, vol. 536, pp. 57–64. Springer, Cham (2018). https://doi.org/10.1007/978-3-319-99707-0_8

86. Cavalieri, S., Pezzotta, G., Yoshiki, S.: Product-service system engineering: from theory to industrial applications. Comput. Ind. **63**(4), 275–277 (2012)

87. Gaiardelli, P., Martinez, V., Cavalieri, S.: The strategic transition to services: a dominant logic perspective and its implications for operations. Prod. Plan. Control **26**(14–15), 1165–1170 (2015)

88. Baines, T., Bigdeli, A.Z., Bustinza, O.F., Shi, V.G., Baldwin, J., Ridgway, K.: Servitization: revisiting the state-of-the-art and research priorities. Int. Oper. Prod. Manag. **37**(2), 256–278 (2017)

89. Goedkoop, M.J., et al.: Product Service Systems: Ecological and Economic Basics (1999)

90. Romero, D., Gaiardelli, P., Pezzotta, G., Cavalieri, S.: The impact of digital technologies on services characteristics: towards digital servitization. In: Ameri, F., Stecke, K.E., von Cieminski, G., Kiritsis, D. (eds.) APMS 2019. IFIP, AICT, vol. 566, pp. 493–501. Springer, Cham (2019). https://doi.org/10.1007/978-3-030-30000-5_61

91. Marjanovic, U., Rakic, S., Lalic, B.: Digital servitization: the next "Big Thing" in manufacturing industries. In: Ameri, F., Stecke, K.E., von Cieminski, G., Kiritsis, D. (eds.) APMS 2019. IFIP, AICT, vol. 566, pp. 510–517. Springer, Cham (2019). https://doi.org/10.1007/978-3-030-30000-5_63

92. Boucher, X., Medini, K., Coba, C.M.: Framework to model PSS collaborative value networks and assess uncertainty of their economic models. In: Camarinha-Matos, L.M., Afsarmanesh, H., Antonelli, D. (eds.) PRO-VE 2019. IFIP, AICT, vol. 568, pp. 541–551. Springer, Cham (2019). https://doi.org/10.1007/978-3-030-28464-0_47

93. Wiesner, S., Hauge, J.B., Sonntag, P., Thoben, K.-D.: Applicability of agile methods for dynamic requirements in smart PSS development. In: Ameri, F., Stecke, K.E., von Cieminski, G., Kiritsis, D. (eds.) APMS 2019. IFIP, AICT, vol. 566, pp. 666–673. Springer, Cham (2019). https://doi.org/10.1007/978-3-030-30000-5_81

94. Moser, B., Kampker, A., Jussen, P., Frank, J.: Organization of sales for smart product service systems. In: Ameri, F., Stecke, K.E., von Cieminski, G., Kiritsis, D. (eds.) APMS 2019. IFIP, AICT, vol. 566, pp. 518–526. Springer, Cham (2019). https://doi.org/10.1007/978-3-030-30000-5_64

95. Sala, R., Pezzotta, G., Pirola, F., Huang, G.Q.: Decision-support system-based service delivery in the product-service system context: literature review and gap analysis. Proc. CIRP **83**, 126–131 (2019)

96. Sala, R., Zanetti, V., Pezzotta, G., Cavalieri, S.: The role of technology in designing and delivering product-service systems. In: Proceedings of the IEEE Conference, Funchal, Portugal (2017)

97. Baines, T., Shi, V.G.: Delphi study to explore the adoption of servitization in UK companies. Prod. Plan. Control **26**(14–15), 1171–1187 (2015)

98. Kowalkowski, C., Gebauer, H., et al.: Servitization and deservitization: overview, concepts, and definitions. Ind. Mark. Manag. **60**, 4–10 (2017)

99. Wiesner, S., Westphal, I., Hirsch, M., Thoben, K.-D.: Manufacturing service ecosystems. In: Emmanouilidis, C., Taisch, M., Kiritsis, D. (eds.) APMS 2012. IFIP, AICT, vol. 398, pp. 305–312. Springer, Heidelberg (2013). https://doi.org/10.1007/978-3-642-40361-3_39

100. Pirola, F., Pezzotta, G., Andreini, D., Galmozzi, C., Savoia, A., Pinto, R.: Understanding customer needs to engineer product-service systems. In: Grabot, B., Vallespir, B., Gomes, S., Bouras, A., Kiritsis, D. (eds.) APMS 2014. IFIP, AICT, vol. 439, pp. 683–690. Springer, Heidelberg (2014). https://doi.org/10.1007/978-3-662-44736-9_83

101. Rondini, A., Tornese, F., Gnoni, M., Pezzotta, G., Pinto, R.: Business process simulation for the design of sustainable product service systems (PSS). In: Umeda, S., Nakano, M., Mizuyama, H., Hibino, H., Kiritsis, D., von Cieminski, G. (eds.) APMS 2015. IFIP, AICT, vol. 460, pp. 646–653. Springer, Cham (2015). https://doi.org/10.1007/978-3-319-22759-7_74

102. Alexopoulos, K., Koukas, S., Boli, N., Mourtzis, D.: Resource planning for the installation of industrial product service systems. In: Lödding, H., Riedel, R., Thoben, K.-D., von Cieminski, G., Kiritsis, D. (eds.) APMS 2017. IFIP, AICT, vol. 514, pp. 205–213. Springer, Cham (2017). https://doi.org/10.1007/978-3-319-66926-7_24

103. Orellano, M., Medini, K., Lambey-Checchin, C., Norese, M.-F., Neubert, G.: A multi-criteria approach to collaborative product-service systems design. In: Ameri, F., Stecke, K.E., von Cieminski, G., Kiritsis, D. (eds.) APMS 2019. IFIP, AICT, vol. 567, pp. 481–489. Springer, Cham (2019). https://doi.org/10.1007/978-3-030-29996-5_56

104. Rust, R.T.: If everything is service, why is this happening now, and what difference does it make? Invited commentaries on evolving to a new dominant logic for marketing. J. Mark. **68**(1), 18–27 (2004)

105. Romero, D., Stahre, J.: Social sustainability of future manufacturing – challenges and strategies: an essay. In the world manufacturing forum report – skills for the future of manufacturing. In: World Manufacturing Forum (2019)

106. Khan, M., Mittal, S., West, S., Wuest, T.: Review on upgradability – a product lifetime extension strategy in the context of product-service systems. Clean. Prod. **204**, 1154–1168 (2018)

An IFIP WG5.8 State-of-the-Art View on Methods and Approaches for Interoperable Enterprise Systems

Georg Weichhart[1]([⊠]) [iD], Yves Ducq[2] [iD], and Guy Doumeingts[3]

[1] PROFACTOR GmbH, Steyr, Austria
georg.weichhart@profactor.at
[2] University of Bordeaux, Bordeaux, France
yves.ducq@u-bordeaux.fr
[3] Interop-Vlab, Brussels, Belgium
guy.doumeingts@interop-vlab.eu, guy.doumeingts@u-bordeaux.fr

Abstract. IFIP's workgroup 5.8 on Enterprise Interoperability was founded in 2008. In this paper we provide a workgroup point of view on the state of the art in Enterprise Modelling, Enterprise Engineering, Enterprise Architectures, Enterprise Integration, Enterprise Interoperability. We present an overview of the state-of-the-art from the WG5.8's research point of view. A brief history of these topics, with special attention to the work developed by IFIP WG5.8 former and current members is given. With respect to application, references to production systems and the manufacturing enterprise will be made. This article closes with a brief look into very recent developments in the domain of Enterprise Interoperability.

Keywords: Enterprise Interoperability · Enterprise Integration · Enterprise Architecture · Enterprise Engineering

1 Introduction

Over the last decades, enterprises have to improve their performance to compete on a global scale. Improvements are required along multiple dimensions as capabilities of organizational learning, financial short- and long-term perspectives, human resource development, etc. [1]. From a manufacturing enterprise point of view, products and processes and their relations are highly relevant. For this paper the manufacturing domain serves as the prime example, due to the high level of automation, the great potential provided by *Enterprise Interoperability* research can be made visible. In manufacturing there are three dimensions for improvement of relevance. The efficiency dimension requires to take a close look at the used production resources to minimize the amount of resources consumed (and hence reduce also costs). To get the desired quality of the product, the production process needs to be effective to meet the desired quality range. Flexibility, a newer dimension, requires the enterprise to adapt to changing demands and/or other events like supply chain disturbances. This later dimension has evolved in

M. Goedicke et al. (Eds.): Advancing Research in Information and Communication Technology,
IFIP AICT 600, pp. 222–244, 2021. https://doi.org/10.1007/978-3-030-81701-5_9

the manufacturing industry in recent years where product variants have increased, with the vision to have the fully customized product, and where processes are continuously reconfigured [2].

The requirements cannot be considered independently, flexibility of production systems needs to be increased, while the same level of quality and costs has to be maintained [3]. The enterprise and its employees need to continuously learn, improve and the production system has to adapt [4]. Adaptivity is a system's capability to reorganize itself, when coping with changing situations or with disturbances. In addition to this, the production processes and the product type are getting more complex [5]. A system is complex when many hard to understand factors are defining the system. Hard to understand, means that the relationship between factors is nonlinear, hard to observe and/or very dynamic [6]. This complexity is grounded not only in new technologies, but also in the system's ability to evolve and adapt [7].

To support the enterprise system to adapt, handle complexity and still have efficient and effective processes, we describe approaches in the following, which support modelling, engineering, and evolution of enterprise systems.

The following section describes the enterprise as a complex adaptive system. This is followed by an overview on enterprise modelling and enterprise architecting. Enterprise Architectures are described as a special form of enterprise modelling/engineering which supports Enterprise Integration and Enterprise Interoperability. These topics are discussed in later sections.

2 Complex Adaptive Enterprise Systems

For being able to address the enterprise as a system, we take a look at Systems Theory and General Systems Theory (GST) [8]. GST aims at the identification of general principles that are valid across heterogeneous types of systems. GST facilitates the communication between different scientific disciplines through abstraction. The essential concepts of a discipline are described as systems. This abstraction allows scientists of other disciplines to use elements and insights described by systems from other domains [9].

A system is an integrated unit which can be decomposed into a set of tightly connected units. Each unit provides a function which contributes to the overall goal (purpose) of the system. The units and the system do have interfaces that separates them from their environment. A system is independent and autonomous within its environment. In contrast to that, do functional units need the system and the other units.

A system shows a behavior and has a state. It therefore has a history. Sometimes a system contains other systems. In this view, multiple systems form a system-of-systems [10]. The systems in a system-of-systems are independent and hence there is a loose coupling between systems in a system-of-system.

Sometimes systems are described as active units, named agents. Such agents are independent and autonomous - like all systems. Agents convey a notion of intelligence and (pro-) active behavior [11, 12]. Such agent-based systems are called Complex Adaptive Systems, where special attention is placed on the dynamics and time-dependent behavior of the overall system [13, 14].

The interaction of systems in a system-of-systems can be described on multiple levels of granularity. The environment within which the technical systems are found are the services and functions executed. The environment within which these services and functions are executed is the enterprise. The environment within which the enterprise system exists are legal, social and economic constraints and requirements [15].

Taking a look at enterprises these can be described as information processing systems [16]. Figure 1 shows different levels in an enterprise system where different human and artificial agents are communicating. Information needs to be conveyed, understood, decisions are influenced by the information and finally actions are triggered by participants of any communication.

The bottom most level addresses the physical transport of information. The next two levels are about having structures that can be read by all participants. Semantics discusses the interpretation of information by different agents. Pragmatics is about actions triggered by the communication. Executed actions need to be compatible within the social world.

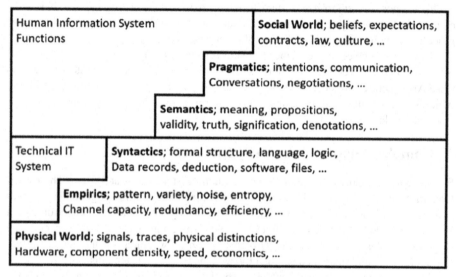

Fig. 1. Organizational semiotics: Stamper's semiotic ladder [16]

Enterprises and Networks of Enterprises can also be described as Complex Adaptive Systems [17, 18]. (Human/Artificial) Agents are interacting with the Enterprise System. There is no organization as such that exercises control, but the agents. However, some agents will have more power than others.

The agents act self-controlled and self-organize as a group establishing the enterprise. Interactions are local between a few agents. In these interactions the agents may be taking a higher system state into account (i.e. an Enterprise-global state). Nevertheless, the overall behavior of the enterprise emerges from these interactions [19].

In any social system, agents' behaviors influence their environment and the environment influences the agents' behaviors [20]. This can be seen when agents learn from each other. Learning and improvement of agents' behaviors are results of self-organization of individual agents and of groups of agents.

To be able to address complex situations, which includes learning, models are helpful. For Enterprises several approaches to Enterprise Modeling and Enterprise Engineering exist, which are discussed in the next section.

3   Enterprise Modelling and Enterprise Engineering

Modelling is a process where abstract representations of the world are developed. Process of abstraction is guided by the goal for which the model is constructed. Semantic models of the enterprise or parts of the enterprise and its functions help to cope with the complexity of the overall system [21]. Models may be used for knowledge management supporting communication between agents. Collaborative learning is supported by collaborative modelling [22, 23]. Models may also be used for control and decision making. The interactive possibilities for groups to evolve models supports evolution of the common understanding of the group [24].

Enterprise Models, by definition, capture what is seen by the modelling agents as important aspects relevant to reach the goal of the model. There is no widely accepted definition of enterprise modelling [25]. On an informal level enterprise modelling is a set of activities that deal with externalizing knowledge about organizational structures and behaviors of an overall enterprise or parts of it.

Typical applications of enterprise modelling are [25]:

- Documentation of Enterprise Systems: Such documentations support analysis, understanding, and sharing of knowledge related to the enterprise.
- Planning and Management of change: Models are built to document the current situation (as-is) or a vision of a future situation (to-be). This supports the transition and management of change.
- Designing and (Re-)Engineering of Enterprise Systems: Following the model-driven engineering approach [26] detailed specifications of the enterprise can be used also for automation e.g. of business processes.
- Performance Analysis: The as-is or to-be performance of an enterprise can be provided. A very abstract model are performance measurement systems which provide a set of dimensions of performance indicators. Very concrete models are simulation models, which allow to evaluate dynamic aspects of enterprise systems in different situations.
- Enterprise Systems Integration: Enterprise models support the integration of enterprise information systems.

For Enterprise Modelling, the following principles have been identified for the modelling process, capturing a large and complex system-of-systems like the enterprise [21]:

- **Principle #1 – Plural nature of enterprise models:** Complexity and size of enterprise systems imposes the need for multiple models and renders a single large model of the enterprise unfeasible. It is simply not possible to construct a model from a single point of view.

- **Principle #2 – Concept of modelling views:** Every model has to support different points of views. The concept of views reduces the complexity, and lets users focus on individual aspects of the model per view. In the domain of enterprise modelling essential views are listed below. However, this is not an exclusive list but rather highlights important views that can be found in multiple approaches (cf. [27–31]).

  o Function View: functionality provided by processes describing the contributions of agents and the behavior of the enterprise
  o Information View: this shows the data, information and knowledge flows and also contains who has access to what.
  o Resource View: this view includes the human and artificial agents and passive objects (like materials) that are required for the execution of tasks within the processes
  o Organization View: this describes roles and responsibilities and rights to access resources

- **Principle #3 – Coverage of the three fundamental types of flows:** Enterprise models do not only capture structural relationships; it must be possible to include dynamic aspects (i.e. flows). Flows are relevant to enterprises in general and to manufacturing enterprises in particular are:

  o Material flow (physical systems flow; this includes power or cooling fluids; any physical resource that is required to perform an activity)
  o Information flow (data, information, knowledge and decisions)
  o Control flow (workflow, processes).

- **Principle #4 – Concept of modelling levels:** Such mechanism also supports management of the complexity of enterprise models. Examples for different levels of abstraction are: the requirements, design and implementation levels of CIMOSA [27, 32] and ARIS [28], conceptual, organizational and physical levels of GRAI-GIM [31, 33].

Enterprise Engineering is grounded in Enterprise Modelling and in addition to the above, this aims at providing concise models. While there is no common agreed upon definition, Enterprise Engineering can be described as follows:

"Enterprise engineering: define, structure, design and implement enterprise operations as communication networks of business processes, which comprise all their related business knowledge, operational information, resources and organisation relations." p. 85 [27].

Three generic goals to Enterprise Engineering have been identified [34]:

- Intellectual manageability: Support the construction and operation of enterprises to work with the above described complexity. Support for managing change and evolution of enterprises is needed.
- Organizational concinnity: Establish a theory and method that supports to address all relevant aspects to be able to operate the enterprise as a coherent and consistent whole.

- Social devotion: Enterprise Engineering aims at the including employees. Humans are important for all aspects of the enterprise, in particular for aspects of dynamics, complexity and uncertainty. Enterprise Engineering aims at empowering humans to gain knowledge.

Enterprise Engineering approaches support analysis, synthesis, decision making, explanation and prediction [34]. The approaches that support the basis for development and design of systems are related and support enterprise architecture engineering. This design aspect of Enterprise Engineering (and Enterprise Modelling) is based on general systems theory (GST) [9] and design science [35]. Selected enterprise architecture frameworks are discussed in the next section.

4   Enterprise Architecture Frameworks

Architectures are models that provide a coarse-grained structure. Like architectures of buildings, these provide rooms and interfaces between rooms (doors). A building's architecture does not prescribe how the rooms are decorated. However, already functionality is assigned to particular rooms like kitchen, bathroom, etc.

Another type of architecture are software architectures: "Software architecture is the principled study of the overall structure of software systems, especially the relations among subsystems and components. From its roots in qualitative descriptions of useful system organizations, software architecture has matured to encompass broad explorations of notations, tools, and analysis techniques ... it now offers concrete guidance for complex software design and development. Software architecture research overlaps and interacts with work on software families, component-based reuse, software design, specific classes of components (e.g., COM), product line, and program analysis." p. 257 [36].

Enterprise Architecture applies the above described aspects to enterprise systems. Enterprise Architectures aim at supporting modelling uniform representations and supporting knowledge transfers and integration/interoperability of different domains across the enterprise [30]. With Enterprise Architectures, often an information system centric perspective is taken, but Enterprise Architectures are used to model many different parts of organizations including: organizational structures and processes, information applications, and software and hardware infrastructure [37].

An example of an information system centric architecture modelling standard, is ARIS (Architecture of Integrated Information Systems) [28]. It provides different views to ensure the enterprise information system meets its requirements. These views are shown in the following image.

The Organization view allows to model the structure of a company, including human resources, machines, hardware and their relationships. The Data view provides information about events generating data and business objects and the relationship. The function view shows activities, groupings and the relationship. The main view is the control view where business processes are modelled which integrate objects form all other views. All the views have three levels of abstraction. The finest granular level is the implementation level, using software [28] (Fig. 2).

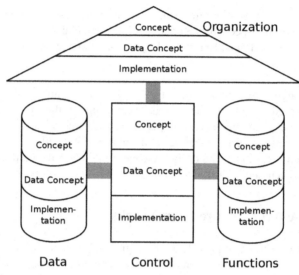

Fig. 2. ARIS house (https://en.wikipedia.org/wiki/Architecture_of_Integrated_Information_S ystems)

ArchiMate® is an enterprise architecture modelling language that also puts emphasis on information systems but follows a service-oriented approach [37]. ArchiMate® is a "visual language with a set of default iconography for describing, analyzing, and communicating many concerns of Enterprise Architectures as they change over time" [38]. ArchiMate® is a registered trademark of The Open Group. The current version of the ArchiMate Core language consists of four layers and three aspects as shown in Fig. 3.

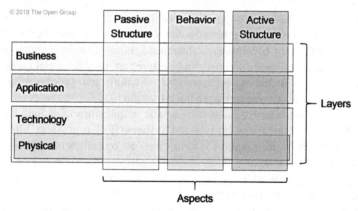

Fig. 3. ArchiMate® Core framework [38].

The business layer describes roles and business processes that need support by software services. These services and software modules that provide the services are described on the application layer. The software modules need infrastructure services (like database services) that are described on the technology layer (which includes physical aspects like servers). Passive structures are for example data structures (application layer) and business objects (business layer). Behavioral elements are business processes and application functions. Active structures are business roles and application components [38].

TOGAF® is also a registered Trademark of the Open Group. The TOGAF® standard describes an Enterprise Architecture framework that "provides the methods and tools for assisting in the acceptance, production, use, and maintenance of an Enterprise Architecture. It is based on an iterative process model supported by best practices and a re-usable set of existing architecture assets." [39]. It guides the Enterprise Architect by providing an Architecture Development Method (ADM). The method "includes establishing an architecture framework, developing architecture content, transitioning, and governing the realization of architectures. All of these activities are carried out within an iterative cycle of continuous architecture definition and realization that allows organizations to transform their enterprises in a controlled manner in response to business goals and opportunities." (Section 2.4) [39].

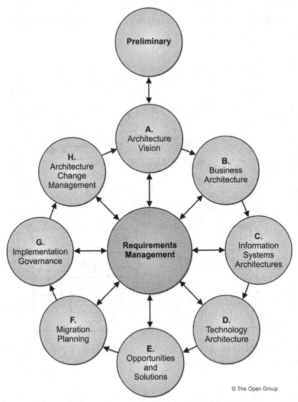

Fig. 4. TOGAF® phases [39]

TOGAF® supports the following phases for architecture development and change (see Fig. 4).

It also addresses the business architecture which could be described in the ArchiMate® business layer. Software Applications are supported in the information system architecture. And the models of the ArchiMate® technology layer can be of use in the technology architecture phase. More phases support the change and evolutions of architectures.

Several Enterprise Architecture Frameworks have been developed for the manufacturing domain. Here, a major driving force for modelling and architecting of large and complex systems has been Computer-Integrated Manufacturing (CIM). The developed frameworks have general applicability to many domains.

The CIMOSA Framework (Computer Integrated Manufacturing Open System Architecture) has been created to support the Enterprise Integration of machines, computers and people [27, 32]. CIMOSA is one of the frameworks (obviously) grounded in the manufacturing domain. The framework provides a process-oriented modelling concept. It allows to model both, the process functionality and the process behavior. Evolutionary Enterprise Modelling and individual enterprise domains (DM) are possible. CIMOSA separates functionality (EA: Enterprise Activity) from the behavior (BRS: Behavioral Rule Set). One might be changed without the other. This allows to break large processes down into smaller processes, ending in networks of EAs which are connected by the BRS [27] (Fig. 5).

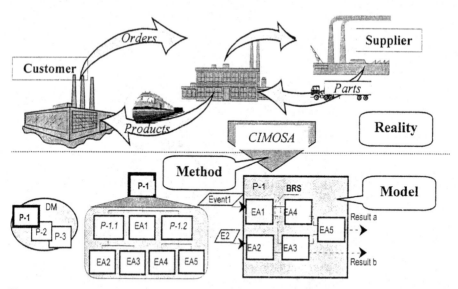

Fig. 5. CIMOSA modelling concepts (DM: Domains; EA: Enterprise Activity; BRS: Behavioral Rule Set; P-x: Processes; E: Event) [27]

Another approach routed in Computer Integrated Manufacturing (CIM) is GRAI (Graph with Results and Activities Interrelated) and GIM (GRAI Integrated Methodology [31, 40] (see also Fig. 6).

The GRAI Model supports three systems that can be found in any enterprise. The physical system, the information system and the decision system. It provides a reference architecture and modelling approach which addresses three aspects: Modelling Views, Life-Cycles of systems, and multiple levels of abstraction. It also provides the GIM structured approach, which aims at guiding the analysis and the design of (manufacturing) facilities during three phases: the analysis phase, the user-oriented design phase and the technical-oriented design phase [41]. GIM supports also the analysis of decision systems of flexible manufacturing and CIM systems from a production management perspective [31, 40].

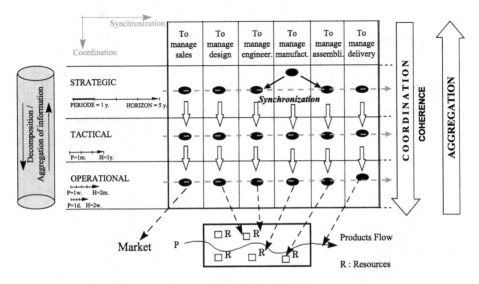

Fig. 6. The GRAI model [31]

GERAM[1] (Generalized Enterprise Reference Architecture and Methodology) has been created by a Task Force formed by IFIP WG 5.12 (International Federation for Information Processing - Workgroup - Architectures for Enterprise Integration) and by IFAC TC 5.3 (International Federation of Automatic Control - Technical Committee - (now named) Integration and Interoperability of Enterprise Systems) [29]. The Task Force brought together different Architecture Frameworks taking important aspects from each. The approach evolved into the standard ISO15704, "Requirements for Generalized Enterprise Reference Architectures and Methodologies" [42]. The standard's mandatory section lists requirements for any enterprise reference architecture, and GERAM is a public appendix to the standard, exemplifying how to fulfil them [29].

One of GERAM's key contribution is its definition of a concise set of concepts for combining and using these for evaluation of architecture frameworks to understand their completeness with respect to scope and complexity [29]. Figure 7 shows the framework components that form this standard.

---

[1] http://www.ict.griffith.edu.au/~bernus/taskforce/geram/versions/geram1-6-3/v1.6.3.html.

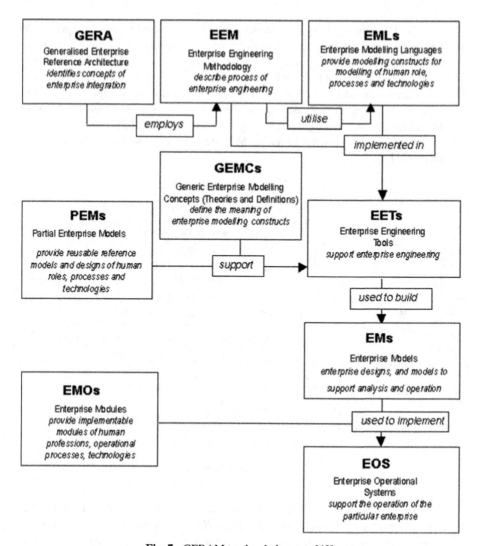

Fig. 7. GERAM top level elements [43]

GERA (Generalized Enterprise Reference Architecture), which is the most important component, holds the basic concepts that are to be used in enterprise engineering and integration. This includes enterprise entities, life-cycles, life histories of enterprise entities, etc. [43].

The Model Driven System Engineering Architecture (MDSEA) follows the Model Driven Architecture (MDA) as defined and adopted by the Object Management Group [44]. MDSEA was developed by EU Project "Manufacturing Service Ecosystem" (MSEE), supporting the transition of enterprises from product manufacturing to product-service production [25, 45]. The MDA approach is adapted to be suitable for a broader modelling domain like product-service supply networks consisting of multiple enterprises.

Figure 8 shows the abstract architecture applying MDSEA levels to the supply network building of services of virtual enterprises.

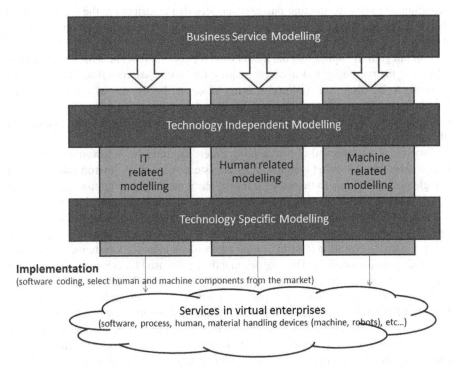

Fig. 8. MDSEA abstract architecture [46]

Business Service Modelling provides technology independent high-level models of provided services and links between enterprises. Here models are used to bridge the gap between knowledge of domain experts and the technical knowledge on lower levels. The Technology Independent Model provides detailed specifications with respect to the concepts related to the information systems, organization and human and physical means for a service system. It is still independent from the technology used for implementation. At the Technology Specific Model level (as the name suggests) the model specifies a particular type of technology used for implementation. The level of detail must be high enough to be able to realize or buy a specific solution.

As already mentioned above, enterprise modelling, enterprise engineer, enterprise architecting support the integration of enterprise systems. In the following section we will take a closer look at theories and approaches of Enterprise Integration and Enterprise Interoperability.

5 Integration and Interoperability of Enterprise Systems

Enterprise Integration is an approach for ensuring the interaction of systems to ensure that a common objective is achieved [47, 48]. This interaction can happen on different levels: Data exchange with integrated technical formats, information models describing a common ontology, interacting business services that contribute to the same business objective, business processes that need to be integrated so the workflows have seamless interfaces.

Full integration implies that the model used for communication is the same as internally used for reasoning and decision making for more loose coupling Interoperability needs to be discussed. Enterprise Integration can be defined as follows: "Enterprise integration: provide the right information at the right place and at the right time and thereby enable communication between people, machines and computers and their efficient cooperation and coordination" p. 85 [27].

Enterprise Interoperability is extending Enterprise Integration towards the requirement to have loose coupled systems, or even systems-of-system. Interoperability is not a single goal that needs to be reached. It also has a process connotation because - due to the independence of systems in a system-of-systems - it is assumed that sub-systems will evolve and interoperability needs to be monitored and re-established as soon as it is lost [33, 49]. In a system-of-systems the systems are not connected in a static manner. In contrast to that, integration is a (final) state where all elements of a system can exchange and understand information. This implies that the model used for communication is also integrated on a semantic and a pragmatic level by the involved elements [18].

The Framework for Enterprise Interoperability (FEI) is an approach developed by the GRAI Research Group (today GR Productique) at University of Bordeaux.

FEI aims at structuring basic Enterprise Interoperability concepts and issues. The framework has three basic dimensions: (i) Interoperability concerns that define the content of interoperation that may take place at various levels of the enterprise (data, service, process, business) (ii) Interoperability barriers that identify various obstacles to interoperability in three categories (conceptual, technological, organizational), (iii) Interoperability approaches that represent the different ways in which barriers can be removed (integrated, unified, and federated). The intersection of an interoperability barrier, an interoperability concern and an interoperability approach is the set of solutions to the breakdown of that interoperability barrier existing for the particular concern and using the selected approach (Fig. 9).

In the ATHENA project different levels (already indicated above) have been identified [33, 51, 52]. To all levels, all barriers identified above are relevant. Similar to above, selected examples are given.

- **Data:** Data models and programming interfaces are the finest granular level of detail. Exemplary organizational barriers are access rights, and privacy issues.
- **Services:** This level addresses business services providing functions. Barriers include incompatibilities in the granularity of a service offered or management rights for services that lead to interoperability issues.

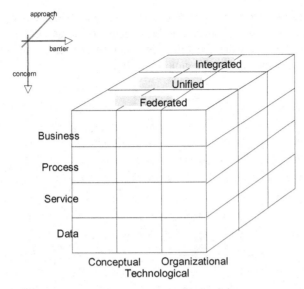

Fig. 9. Framework for Enterprise Interoperability [33, 50]

- **Processes:** Process models define the behavior of organizations and are subject to interoperability barriers like different coverages of overlapping processes; technological issues of workflow systems; incompatible processes of collaborating organizational units.
- **Business:** Conceptual barriers concern the strategy of different collaborating enterprises; or the degree of computerization of units; Legal aspects of organizations can also be an issue.

The above dimensions "barriers" and "concerns" represent the problem space. Solutions are discussed along a third dimension. The tightest level of interoperability is integration. Here the same model is shared between different systems. Hence modifications require all systems to be modified. To increase the loose coupling, interacting systems can agree on a unifying layer. That layer defines the interaction and data on a higher level of abstraction. That layer is known by all systems but not used system-internally.

The degree of increased "looseness" is a federated approach to interoperability where interoperability is negotiated at runtime. Here infrastructure is needed to support that negotiation. For example, management systems to monitor and manage the discovery of services.

Going beyond a federated approach to interoperability means compatibility. However, this marks systems that are not collaborating, but are only not-disturbing each other.

A different framework to interoperability is the European Interoperability Framework [53]. This approach has roots in European, Governmental, Organizational Interoperability. As such it has a legal level, which can be interpreted similar to the "social" level of Stamper's semiotic ladder [16]. The legal level represents (explicit) social norms (laws) to which any enterprise operation must be interoperable. In democratic societies, laws represent explicit social demands and requirements of the society.

In contrast to the framework above there is no conceptual barrier but rather a semantic level, which basically addresses the same need (Fig. 10).

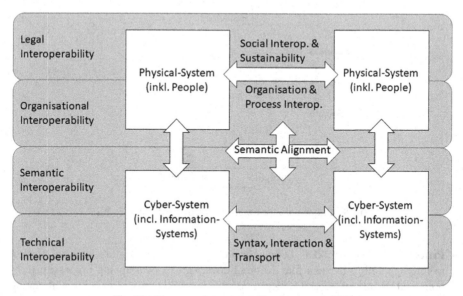

Fig. 10. European Interoperability framework [54]

Several approaches exist on the different layers. On technical level several standards exit supporting connectivity. For example, in manufacturing, OPC-UA is an approach that supports access to remote machine data and the execution of programs [55]. OPC-UA also supports interoperability with the information model [56]. When combined with the Automation ML Standard [57] it supports heterogeneity and variability [58, 59].

Approaches that target the semantic aspects are often based on ontologies. The Ontology of Enterprise Interoperability (OoEI) [49] is such an approach. It formalizes the enterprise as a system and provides a number of concepts for modelling interoperability of enterprise systems. Core concepts of the OoEI are built on top of General Systems Theory [9]. It allows to describe relationships between systems.

In order to address the enterprise as a complex adaptive system (CAS), the OoEI has been extended towards an Ontology of Enterprise Interoperability extended for CAS ($OoEI^{CAS}$) [60]. This approach also makes a move away from the ontological approach towards a Domain Specific Language (DSL). It captures the systemic core of the OoEI and represents it as data structure in $OoEI^{CAS}$. In this approach the actor-model is used to provide a means to implement agents [61, 62]. Using this approach allows to capture active organizational systems and their interaction. The Domain Specific Language (DSL) is implemented in the functional programming language SCALA [63].

An approach that is focusing on the organizational level is MISE (V1 and V2), which provides methodological and tool support for emerging collaborative situations in production systems [64, 65]. It supports dynamic collaborations of networked organizations which are seen as complex adaptive systems. MISE has a business level where the collaborative situation of multiple enterprises is modelled. The technical level provides a workflow model. MISE has services that support the deployment, orchestration and runtime. An agility infrastructure supports adaptation and evolution of models at different levels. It is based on the view of the enterprise as a complex adaptive system [64].

The Liquid Sensing Enterprise (LSE) [66] and the S^3Enterprise (Sensing, Smart and Sustainable Enterprise) [46] also have as a basic assumption that the enterprise system is a complex adaptive system. From an implementation perspective the LSE builds on the High-Level Architecture (HLA) simulation standard for supporting dynamics and interaction. The S^3Enterprise Approach sees a strong need for an enterprise operating system (EOS) that supports a unified information flow between the sensors and the smart algorithms for decision making and the human decision makers as well.

The Enterprise Operating Systems (EOS) [67, 68] addresses the need for support of integration of heterogeneous enterprise software applications, which is a complex, costly and time-consuming task, especially for SMEs. An "EOS can be defined as a set of IT services supporting execution, control and monitoring of enterprise operations by means of message exchange among enterprise resources, model enactment and interoperability capabilities" p. 2716 [68].

The basic conceptual building blocks are shown in the next graphic. As can be seen the EOS combines several existing functionalities in an overarching system, similar to operating systems of computers.

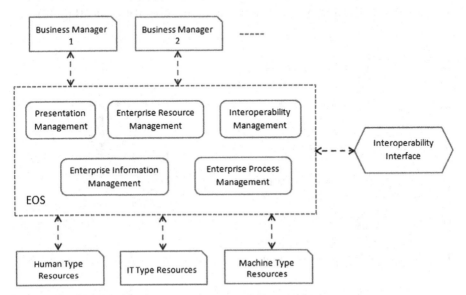

Fig. 11. Enterprise operating system building blocks [68]

A current implementation of the EOS exists based on the High-Level Architecture (HLA) [67]. Nevertheless, the conceptual approach is technology independent.

The EOS does provide key steps towards manufacturing systems of the future, enabling real-time enterprise operations monitoring and control. The EOS approach does include and is in line with IIoT (Industrial Internet of Things) and CPPS (Cyber-Physical Production System) principles (Fig. 11).

6 Towards Interoperability of Cyber-Physical Production Systems (CPPS)

In the most recent years of IFIP WG5.8 "Enterprise Interoperability" members have been starting towards extending the research to include the CPS (Cyber-Physical Systems), CPPS (Cyber-Physical Production Systems) and IIoT (Industrial Internet of Things) [26, 46, 69].

A Cyber-Physical System is a system, which includes a physical and a cyber part. Only both combined bring the required functionality. Such systems have sensors and actors that provide this interaction between both worlds. In addition to this, the software often supports the networking of such systems. Multiple such systems form in the manufacturing domain Cyber-Physical Production Systems [70–72].

In manufacturing one of the main challenges of a modular and agile CPPS is, to disintegrate the current architecture called Automation Pyramid and modularize manufacturing systems. This leads to a situation where modules provide their functionality to many different systems. However, the original pyramid architecture is in place due to different timing constraints and planning horizons that the systems have on the different levels. Unfortunately, that hierarchical organization has been shown to be very rigid. The new CP(P)S type of organization addresses the missing adaptability (Fig. 12).

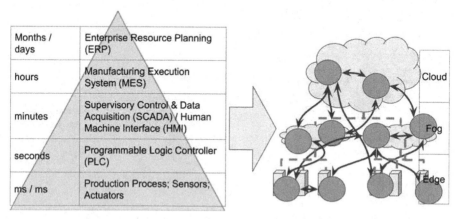

Fig. 12. Automation pyramid architecture evolving into a CPPS architecture (based on [73])

The CPPS perspective provides new challenges which require addressing the enterprise from the physical parts over sensors and data streams to an adaptive and modular network of systems. One of the challenges is the need for new planning and engineering approaches that address Systems-of-Systems, Agent-based Systems and/or Cyber-Physical Production Systems [74, 75].

The Model Driven System Engineering Architecture (MDSEA) and its extension to interoperability concerns called MDISE (Model Driven Interoperability System Engineering) framework are currently extended towards CPS as well [26].

A second fundamental challenge that needs to be solved to enable CP(P)S to provide its full potential is interoperability of such systems [54]. A proper interoperability environment needs to be researched to enable the modular and adaptive nature of a CPPS. Otherwise, the CPSs will be hardwired and the modularization will be more overhead than advantage. This challenge is addressed in the vision of the EOS [46, 68].

7 Conclusions

This article gives an overview of essential developments that have been driven by members of the IFIP WG5.8, even before the founding of this group in 2008. The authors are founding members of IFIP WG5.8. Guy Doumeingts has been the first chair of the workgroup. Yves Ducq served on the board since the beginning of the workgroup and is currently treasurer. Georg Weichhart is WG chair since 2019.

In this article we have reported on several approaches and future challenges in the research field of Enterprise Interoperability and its neighboring fields.

The work developed in WG 5.8 originated in the work of INTEROP Network of Excellence and ATHENA Integrated Project. The work on Enterprise Interoperability is also supported by INTEROP-VLab that was created after the INTEROP NoE ended.

The main methodological principles are to use Enterprise Modelling, Enterprise Architecture and Ontologies to solve problems of interoperability for enterprise applications.

Some of the work mentioned in this article is coming from national and European projects that were carried out from the starting of WG 5.8.

For instance, the first interoperability framework that was developed in the frame of the IDEAS European project was improved in INTEROP-NoE (Network of Excellence) to provide Framework for Enterprise Interoperability (FEI). Another example, concerning Enterprise Modelling for Enterprise Engineering, is the development of a Model Driven Service Engineering Architecture (MDSEA) within the frame of MSEE (Manufacturing SErvice Ecosytem), a European Project supported by the European Commission.

So, the philosophy of the WG 5.8 is to continue to contribute to the development of interoperability topics with sharing the work done by all the partners through their own and common project and to share their experience and application case studies. Of course, some of the WG5.8 members being also members of INTEROP-VLab, which plays a main role to drive the development of this topic at the European and international levels.

In a most recent development, IFIP WG5.8 "Enterprise Interoperability" (see also http://www.ifip-ei.org) has teamed up with IFAC TC5.3 "Integration and Interoperability of Enterprise Systems" (see also http://www.ifac-tc53.org), forming a joint task force to work on new methods and approaches of modelling and architecting for interoperable

Cyber-Physical Systems [76]. This will support to drive the research on both CPS and Enterprise Interoperability.

Acknowledgement. This work has been supported by Pro^{2}Future (FFG under contract No. 854184). Pro^{2}Future is funded within the Austrian COMET Program (under the auspices of the Federal Ministry for Climate Action, Environment, Energy, Mobility, Innovation and Technology (BMK), the Federal Ministry for Digital and Economic Affairs (BMDW)) and of the Provinces of Upper Austria and Styria. COMET is managed by the Austrian Research Promotion Agency FFG. It has also received support by the European Union and the State of Upper Austria within the strategic program Innovative Upper Austria 2020, projects: "Smart Factory Lab" and "DigiManu".

References

1. Weichhart, G., Feiner, T., Stary, C.: Implementing organisational interoperability – the SUd-dEN approach. Comput. Ind. **61**, 152–160 (2010). https://doi.org/10.1016/j.compind.2009.10.011
2. Napoleone, A., Pozzetti, A., Macchi, M.: A framework to manage reconfigurability in manufacturing. Int. J. Prod. Res. **56**, 3815–3837 (2018). https://doi.org/10.1080/00207543.2018.1437286
3. Kusiak, A.: Fundamentals of smart manufacturing: a multi-thread perspective. Annu. Rev. Control **47**, 214–220 (2019). https://doi.org/10.1016/j.arcontrol.2019.02.001
4. Mehandjiev, N., Grefen, P. (eds.): Dynamic Business Process Formation for Instant Virtual Enterprises. Springer, London (2010). https://doi.org/10.1007/978-1-84882-691-5
5. Napoleone, A., Macchi, M., Pozzetti, A.: A review on the characteristics of cyber-physical systems for the future smart factories. J. Manuf. Syst. **54**, 305–335 (2020). https://doi.org/10.1016/j.jmsy.2020.01.007
6. Norman, G.: Chaos, complexity and complicatedness: lessons from rocket science. Med. Educ. **45**, 549–559 (2011). https://doi.org/10.1111/j.1365-2923.2011.03945.x
7. Holland, J.H.: Hidden Order: How Adaptation Builds Complexity. Basic Books, New York (1996)
8. von Bertalanffy, L.: An outline of general system theory. Br. J. Philos. Sci. **1**, 134–165 (1950)
9. von Bertalanffy, L.: General System Theory - Foundations, Development Applications. George Braziller, New York (1969)
10. Boardman, J., Sauser, B.: System of systems - the meaning of of. In: Proceedings of the 2006 IEEE/SMC International Conference on System of Systems Engineering, pp. 1–6 (2006). https://doi.org/10.1109/SYSOSE.2006.1652284.
11. Leitão, P., Vrba, P.: Recent developments and future trends of industrial agents. In: Mařík, V., Vrba, P., Leitão, P. (eds.) HoloMAS 2011. LNCS (LNAI), vol. 6867, pp. 15–28. Springer, Heidelberg (2011). https://doi.org/10.1007/978-3-642-23181-0_2
12. Wooldridge, M.J., Jennings, N.R.: Intelligent agents: theory and practice. Knowl. Eng. Rev. **10**, 115–152 (1995)
13. Mitchell, M.: Complexity: A Guided Tour. Oxford University Press, Oxford (2009)
14. Waldrop, M.M.: Complexity: The Emerging Science at the Edge of Order and Chaos. Simon & Schuster, New York (1992)
15. European Commission: New European Interoperability Framework (2017)
16. Stamper, R., Liu, K., Hafkamp, M., Ades, Y.: Understanding the roles of signs and norms in organizations - a semiotic approach to information systems design. Behav. Inf. Technol. **19**, 15–27 (2000). https://doi.org/10.1080/014492900118768

17. Anderson, P.: Complexity theory and organization science. Organ. Sci. **10**, 216–232 (1999)
18. Weichhart, G.: Requirements for supporting enterprise interoperability in dynamic environments. In: Mertins, K., Bénaben, F., Poler, R., Bourrières, J.-P. (eds.) Enterprise Interoperability VI. PIC, vol. 7, pp. 479–488. Springer, Cham (2014). https://doi.org/10.1007/978-3-319-04948-9_40
19. Weichhart, G.: Supporting interoperability for chaotic and complex adaptive enterprise systems. In: Demey, Y.T., Panetto, H. (eds.) OTM 2013. LNCS, vol. 8186, pp. 86–92. Springer, Heidelberg (2013). https://doi.org/10.1007/978-3-642-41033-8_14
20. Bandura, A.: Social cognitive theory of self-regulation. Organ. Behav. Hum. Decis. Process. **50**, 248–287 (1991)
21. Weichhart, G., Stary, C., Vernadat, F.: Enterprise modelling for interoperable and knowledge-based enterprises. Int. J. Prod. Res. **56**, 2818–2840 (2018). https://doi.org/10.1080/00207543.2017.1406673
22. Oppl, S., Stary, C.: Facilitating shared understanding of work situations using a tangible tabletop interface. Behav. Inf. Technol. **33**, 619–635 (2014). https://doi.org/10.1080/0144929X.2013.833293
23. Oppl, S.: Supporting the collaborative construction of a shared understanding about work with a guided conceptual modeling technique. Group Decis. Negot. **26**(2), 247–283 (2016). https://doi.org/10.1007/s10726-016-9485-7
24. Weichhart, G.: Supporting the evolution and interoperability of organisational models with e-learning technologies. Annu. Rev. Control **39**, 118–127 (2015). https://doi.org/10.1016/j.arcontrol.2015.03.011
25. Vernadat, F.: Enterprise modelling: research review and outlook. Comput. Ind. **122**, 103265 (2020). https://doi.org/10.1016/j.compind.2020.103265
26. Zacharewicz, G., Daclin, N., Doumeingts, G., Haidar, H.: Model driven interoperability for system engineering. Modelling **1**, 94–121 (2020). https://doi.org/10.3390/modelling1020007
27. Kosanke, K., Vernadat, F., Zelm, M.: CIMOSA: enterprise engineering and integration. Comput. Ind. **40**, 83–97 (1999). https://doi.org/10.1016/S0166-3615(99)00016-0
28. IDS Scheer AG: Handbuch zur ARIS-Methode - Version 5. Saarbrücken (2000)
29. Bernus, P., Noran, O., Molina, A.: Enterprise architecture: twenty years of the GERAM framework. Annu. Rev. Control **39**, 83–93 (2015). https://doi.org/10.1016/j.arcontrol.2015.03.008
30. Jonkers, H., Lankhorst, M.M., Quartel, D.A.C., Proper, E., Iacob, M.-E.: ArchiMate(R) for integrated modelling throughout the architecture development and implementation cycle. In: Proceedings of the 2011 IEEE 13th Conference on Commerce and Enterprise Computing (CEC), pp. 294–301 (2011). https://doi.org/10.1109/CEC.2011.52
31. Vallespir, B., Merle, C., Doumeingts, G.: The GRAI integrated method: a technico- economical methodology to design manufacturing systems. IFAC Proc. **25**, 73–78 (1992). https://doi.org/10.1016/S1474-6670(17)52231-4
32. Kosanke, K.: CIMOSA — overview and status. Comput. Ind. **27**, 101–109 (1995). https://doi.org/10.1016/0166-3615(95)00016-9
33. Ducq, Y., Chen, D., Doumeingts, G.: A contribution of system theory to sustainable enterprise interoperability science base. Comput. Ind. **63**, 844–857 (2012). https://doi.org/10.1016/j.compind.2012.08.005
34. Dietz, J.L.G., et al.: The discipline of enterprise engineering. Int. J. Organ. Des. Eng. **3**, 86–114 (2013). https://doi.org/10.1504/IJODE.2013.053669
35. Simon, H.A.: The Sciences of the Artificial. MIT Press, Cambridge (1981)
36. Shaw, M.: The coming-of-age of software architecture research. In: Proceedings of the 23rd International Conference on Software Engineering, ICSE 2001, pp. 656–664 (2001)
37. Iacob, M.E., Jonkers, H., Lankhorst, M., Proper, H., Quartel, D.: ArchiMate 2.0 Specification. The Open Group (2012)

38. The Open Group: ArchiMate Specification (2019)
39. The Open Group: TOGAF Standard (2018)
40. Chen, D., Vallespir, B., Doumeingts, G.: GRAI integrated methodology and its mapping onto generic enterprise reference architecture and methodology. Comput. Ind. **33**, 387–394 (1997)
41. Chen, D., Doumeingts, G., Vallespir, B.: GIM (GRAI Integrated Methodology) and its mapping onto GERAM. IFAC Proc. **29**, 648–653 (1996). https://doi.org/10.1016/S1474-667 0(17)57734-4
42. ISO/TC 184/SC 5: ISO 15704:2019 Enterprise modelling and architecture - requirements for enterprise-referencing architectures and methodologies. International Organization for Standardization (ISO) TC 184/SC 5 Interoperability, Integration, and Architectures for Enterprise Systems and Automation Applications (2019)
43. IFIP-IFAC Task Force: GERAM: Generalised Enterprise Reference Architecture and Methodology (GERAM EA Framework v.1.6.3) (2019). http://www.ict.griffith.edu.au/~bernus/taskfo rce/index.html. Accessed 5 Nov 2019
44. Object Management Group (OMG): Model Driven Architecture (MDA) Guide rev. 2.0. Object Management Group (2014)
45. Bazoun, H., Zacharewicz, G., Ducq, Y., Boyé, H.: SLMToolBox: an implementation of MDSEA for servitisation and enterprise interoperability. In: Mertins, K., Bénaben, F., Poler, R., Bourrières, J.-P. (eds.) Enterprise Interoperability VI. PIC, vol. 7, pp. 101–111. Springer, Cham (2014). https://doi.org/10.1007/978-3-319-04948-9_9
46. Weichhart, G., Molina, A., Chen, D., Whitman, L., Vernadat, F.: Challenges and current developments for sensing, smart and sustainable enterprise systems. Comput. Ind. **79**, 34–46 (2016). https://doi.org/10.1016/j.compind.2015.07.002
47. Morel, G., Panetto, H., Mayer, F., Auzelle, J.-P.: System of enterprise-systems integration issues: an engineering perspective. In: IFAC (ed.) IFAC Conference on Cost Effective Automation in Networked Product Development and Manufacturing, IFAC-CEA 2007. Elsevier, Monterrey (2007)
48. Panetto, H., Jardim-Goncalves, R., Molina, A.: Enterprise integration and networking: theory and practice. Annu. Rev. Control **36**, 284–290 (2012). https://doi.org/10.1016/j.arcontrol. 2012.09.009
49. Naudet, Y., Latour, T., Guédria, W., Chen, D.: Towards a systemic formalisation of interoperability. Comput. Ind. **61**, 176–185 (2010). https://doi.org/10.1016/j.compind.2009. 10.014
50. Chen, D.: Framework for enterprise interoperability. In: Congrès International de Génie Industriel (CIGI 2009) (2009)
51. Berre, A.-J., et al.: The ATHENA interoperability framework. In: Enterprise Interoperability II, pp. 569–580. Springer, London (2007). https://doi.org/10.1007/978-1-84628-858-6_62
52. Chen, D., Doumeingts, G., Vernadat, F.B.: Architectures for enterprise integration and interoperability: past, present and future. Comput. Ind. **59**, 647–659 (2008). https://doi.org/10. 1016/j.compind.2007.12.016
53. Kouroubali, A., Katehakis, D.G.: The new European interoperability framework as a facilitator of digital transformation for citizen empowerment. J. Biomed. Inform. **94**, 103166 (2019). https://doi.org/10.1016/j.jbi.2019.103166
54. Panetto, H., Iung, B., Ivanov, D., Weichhart, G., Wang, X.: Challenges for the cyber-physical manufacturing enterprises of the future. Annu. Rev. Control **47**, 200–213 (2019). https://doi. org/10.1016/j.arcontrol.2019.02.002
55. Mahnke, W., Leitner, S.-H., Damm, M.: OPC Unified Architecture. Springer, Heidelberg (2009). https://doi.org/10.1007/978-3-540-68899-0_1
56. Pauker, F., Frühwirth, T., Kittl, B., Kastner, W.: A systematic approach to OPC UA information model design. Proc. CIRP **57**, 321–326 (2016). https://doi.org/10.1016/j.procir.2016.11.056

57. Lüder, A., Hundt, L., Keibel, A.: Description of manufacturing processes using AutomationML. In: 2010 IEEE 15th Conference on Emerging Technologies and Factory Automation (ETFA 2010), pp. 1–8 (2010)

58. Schleipen, M., Gilani, S.-S., Bischoff, T., Pfrommer, J.: OPC UA & Industrie 4.0 - enabling technology with high diversity and variability. Proc. CIRP **57**, 315–320 (2016). https://doi.org/10.1016/j.procir.2016.11.055

59. Henssen, R., Schleipen, M.: Interoperability between OPC UA and AutomationML. Proc. CIRP **25**, 297–304 (2014)

60. Weichhart, G., Guédria, W., Naudet, Y.: Supporting interoperability in complex adaptive enterprise systems: a domain specific language approach. Data Knowl. Eng. **105**, 90–106 (2016). https://doi.org/10.1016/j.datak.2016.04.001

61. Hewitt, C.: Viewing control structures as patterns of passing messages. Artif. Intell. **8**, 323–364 (1977). https://doi.org/10.1016/0004-3702(77)90033-9

62. Agha, G.A.: Actors: A Model of Concurrent Computation in Distributed Systems (June). http://oai.dtic.mil/oai/oai?verb=getRecord&metadataPrefix=html&identifier=ADA157917

63. Bonér, J., Klang, V., Kuhn, R., Nordwal, P., Antonsson, B., Varga, E.: Akka Scala Documentation. Typesafe Inc., San Francisco (2014)

64. Bénaben, F., Mu, W., Boissel-Dallier, N., Barthe-Delanoe, A.-M., Zribi, S., Pingaud, H.: Supporting interoperability of collaborative networks through engineering of a service-based Mediation Information System (MISE 2.0). Enterp. Inf. Syst. **9**, 556–582 (2015). https://doi.org/10.1080/17517575.2014.928949

65. Bénaben, F., Boissel-Dallier, N., Pingaud, H., Lorre, J.-P.: Semantic issues in model-driven management of information system interoperability. Int. J. Comput. Integr. Manuf. **26**, 1042–1053 (2012). https://doi.org/10.1080/0951192X.2012.684712

66. Agostinho, C., Jardim-Goncalves, R.: Sustaining interoperability of networked liquid-sensing enterprises: a complex systems perspective. Annu. Rev. Control **39**, 128–143 (2015). https://doi.org/10.1016/j.arcontrol.2015.03.012

67. Youssef, J., Zacharewicz, G.: Enterprise Operating System (EOS) in action: distributed simulation of enterprise activities and operations. In: Proceedings of the 2019 Winter Simulation Conference (WSC), pp. 90–104 (2019). https://doi.org/10.1109/WSC40007.2019.9004958

68. Youssef, J.R., Zacharewicz, G., Chen, D., Vernadat, F.: EOS: enterprise operating systems. Int. J. Prod. Res. **56**, 2714–2732 (2017). https://doi.org/10.1080/00207543.2017.1378957

69. Ferreira, J., et al.: Empowering SMEs with cyber-physical production systems: from modelling a polishing process of cutlery production to CPPS experimentation. In: Jardim-Goncalves, R., Sgurev, V., Jotsov, V., Kacprzyk, J. (eds.) Intelligent Systems: Theory, Research and Innovation in Applications. SCI, vol. 864, pp. 139–177. Springer, Cham (2020). https://doi.org/10.1007/978-3-030-38704-4_7

70. Monostori, L.: Cyber-physical production systems: roots, expectations and R&D challenges. Proc. CIRP **17**, 9–13 (2014). https://doi.org/10.1016/j.procir.2014.03.115

71. Monostori, L., et al.: Cyber-physical systems in manufacturing. CIRP Ann. **65**, 621–641 (2016). https://doi.org/10.1016/j.cirp.2016.06.005

72. Weichhart, G., Panetto, H., Molina, A.: Interoperability in the cyber-physical manufacturing enterprise. Annu. Rev. Control (2021). https://doi.org/10.1016/j.arcontrol.2021.03.006

73. VDI/VDE-Gesellschaft Mess- und Automatisierungstechnik: Cyber-Physical Systems: Chancen und Nutzen aus Sicht der Automation. VDI/VDE-Gesellschaft Mess- und Automatisierungstechnik (2013)

74. Weichhart, G., Fast-Berglund, Å., Romero, D., Pichler, A.: An agent- and role-based planning approach for flexible automation of advanced production systems. In: 2018 International Conference on Intelligent Systems (IS), pp. 391–399 (2018). https://doi.org/10.1109/IS.2018.8710546

75. Weichhart, G., Reiser, M., Stary, C.: Task-based design of cyber-physical systems – meeting representational requirements with S-BPM. In: Freitag, M., Kinra, A., Kotzab, H., Kreowski, H.-J., Thoben, K.-D. (eds.) S-BPM ONE 2020. CCIS, vol. 1278, pp. 63–73. Springer, Cham (2020). https://doi.org/10.1007/978-3-030-64351-5_5

76. Weichhart, G., Panetto, H., Guédria, W., Bhullard, G., Moalla, N.: Pathways to CP (P) S modelling & architecting. In: Proceedings of the 10th International Conference on Interoperability for Enterprise Systems and Applications (I-ESA 2020) (2020)

IFIP WG5.12 Architectures for Enterprise Integration: Twenty-Five Years of the GERAM Framework

Peter Bernus[1](✉), Richard Martin[2], Ovidiu Noran[1], and Arturo Molina[3]

[1] Griffith University, Brisbane, Australia
{P.Bernus,O.Noran}@griffith.edu.au
[2] Tinwisle Corp., Bloomington, IN, USA
richardm@tinwisle.com
[3] Tecnológico de Monterrey, México, D.F., Mexico
armolina@tec.mx

Abstract. Apart from the 25-year anniversary in 2019 of the first publication of the GERAM Enterprise Architecture Framework, the timeliness of this paper lies in the new interest in the use of systems theory in Enterprise Architecture (EA), and consequently, 'light-weight' architecture frameworks (AFs). Thus, this paper is about the use of systems thinking and systems theory in EA and about how it is possible to reconcile and understand, based on a single overarching framework, the interplay of two major enterprise change endeavours: enterprise engineering (i.e. deliberate change) and evolutionary, organic change. The paper also demonstrates how such change processes can be illustrated by employing systems thinking to construct dynamic business models; the evolution of these concepts is exemplified using past applications in networked enterprise building, and more recent proposals in environmental-, disaster- and healthcare management. Finally, the paper attempts to plot the way GERAM, as a framework to think about the creation and evolution of complex socio-technical systems of systems, will continue to contribute to society in the context of future challenges and emerging opportunities.

Keywords: Enterprise integration · Enterprise architecture · Enterprise modelling · Reference architecture · Systems engineering · Complex systems

1 Introduction: The History of GERAM

1.1 The Origins

The late 1970s and early 1980s saw a great effort in the manufacturing industry to design and build highly automated, computer-controlled systems of unprecedented complexity. The scope spanned from numerically-controlled machine tools and computer-aided design of parts and process planning, to complete factory automation featuring

---

This paper is an extended version of [1] and [2] to reflect the evolution of the GERAM framework between 2015 and 2019.

© IFIP International Federation for Information Processing 2021
Published by Springer Nature Switzerland AG 2021
M. Goedicke et al. (Eds.): Advancing Research in Information and Communication Technology,
IFIP AICT 600, pp. 245–268, 2021. https://doi.org/10.1007/978-3-030-81701-5_10

workshop- and factory level control, scheduling and planning (including production planning and material requirements planning). As a result, the computer-integrated manufacturing (CIM, or 'enterprise integration' (EI)) movement has steadily evolved, increasingly demanding methods and tools to integrate the information and material flow throughout the enterprise.

In 1990, on recommendation by Jim Nevins (a former architect of the Apollo Guidance Computer, and Deputy Director of MIT Charles Stark Draper Lab), the International Federation for Information Processing (IFIP) and the International Federation for Automation and Control (IFAC) established a joint Task Force (TF) with the mandate to review existing architecting approaches to EI and to make recommendations to the industrial and research community. At that time, the IFIP constituent of the Task Force was operating under IFIP TC5 (Technical Committee on Computer Applications in Technology), and the IFAC constituent under TC-MI (Technical Coordinating Committee for Manufacturing and Instrumentation).

The TF included representatives from the industrial and research communities, with most participants having a mixture of research, engineering, industrial management, and consultancy backgrounds. The TF was first chaired by Ted Williams (Director, Purdue Laboratory for Applied Industrial Control) from 1992 to 1996 and later by Peter Bernus (Griffith University) from 1996 until 2002, until the TF completed its mandate. After 2002, the TF's legacy was inherited by IFIP WG5.12 ('Architectures for Enterprise Integration') and IFAC TC5.3 ('Enterprise Integration and Networking'). The TF reviewed several approaches developed for designing CIM systems and classified them into two categories as outlined in Sect. 1.2 [4, 5].

1.2   From Type I to Type II Architectures and Their Generalisation

The *first approach* was based on generic models, or designs, (called 'architectures') that could subsequently be implemented as information systems (IS) products (or product families) incorporating most or all information-processing tasks in the enterprise. These models typically covered the management and control system of the manufacturing enterprise, although the information flow implemented by the management and control system is necessarily a mirror of the material flow in the manufacturing enterprise. At the time, these models were called by the TF 'Reference Architectures of type I'. Such architectures appealed to vendors because the models produced allowed the definition of a stable set of software products.

The resulting implementations were called Enterprise Resource Planning (ERP) systems. In addition, a number of CIM system-specific Reference Models were developed, attempting to systematise the CIM systems' 'functional building blocks' (such as planning, scheduling and control system modules), thus giving rise to the set of products called 'Manufacturing Execution Systems' (MES). While on the higher levels of management & control there is a high level of uniformity among various enterprises and industries, the lower levels, close to the manufacturing process show great variety, dictated by the manufacturing technology and equipment at hand.

Unfortunately, even on the higher levels of control, the number of competing models ('Reference Architectures of type I') reviewed by the TF was in the order of several dozens (in the middle of 1990s), and neither of these achieved an industry-wide accep-tance, or standard status. It is only recently that international standards were developed for the interface between ERP and Manufacturing Execution Systems (MES), such as the IEC 62264 set of standards for enterprise-control system integration [6].

The second approach developed was based on the recognition that similarly to many engineering disciplines (chemical, manufacturing, software, civil, and systems-), enter-prise engineering should also be based on a so-called 'life-cycle' approach. Accord-ingly, to design an integrated enterprise, the enterprise creation activities (and associ-ated methodologies) should extend over the entire life of the enterprise – i.e., from its inception to its decommissioning. Several such architectures were developed by groups, some with manufacturing and control systems- and some with information systems (IS) background.

Therefore, the TF recommendation was that methodologies for designing and cre-ating CIM systems should be based on architectures with a life cycle approach. These architectures were called by the TF 'Reference Architectures of type II'.

In particular, the TF identified three such architectures: CIMOSA (CIM Open Sys-tems Architecture) [7] GRAI-GIM (Graphs with Results and Activities Interrelated) [8] and PERA (Purdue Enterprise Reference Architecture) [9], and recognised that these three had mutually complementary and useful characteristics. After deliberations, it was proposed that instead of trying to select and recommend a 'single best' reference architecture, the TF would serve the EI community better if it generalised its findings and codified these as requirements that any reference architecture should satisfy. Thus, authors of various proposed approaches could use these requirements constructively to evolve their own reference architectures.

Based on this idea, Bernus and Nemes in 1994 [10, 11] developed the first such gen-eralisation, which was adopted by the Task Force and called the 'Generalised Enterprise Reference Architecture and Methodology' (GERAM). The first comprehensive report was published in several articles and a monograph [4, 5]. The TF decided to base its further work on this proposal and bring the specification of GERAM to its completion.

1.3 From GERAM to ISO15704 – 'Requirements for Enterprise-Referencing Architectures and Methodologies'

The TF realised that it must form links with appropriate standardisation bodies, and thus became a category 'A' liaison to ISO TC184/SC5/WG1 (called 'Industrial Automa-tion Systems & Integration/Architecture, Communications, and Integration Frame-works/Modelling and Architecture'). Workgroup (WG)1 was keen to develop standards in the area and endeavoured to formulate the GERAM requirements as an ISO standard.

Between 1995 and 1999 the TF held the majority of its meetings jointly with ISO TC184/ SC5/WG1, chaired by Jim Nell of the US National Institute of Standards and Technology (NIST). The task standing before the TF was twofold: (1) complete the definition of GERAM, and (2) develop an ISO standard specifying the requirements that an (any) Enterprise Reference Architecture must satisfy. The result was GERAM 1.6.3, released in 1999 and ISO 15704:2000 [14] called "Requirements for Generalised Enterprise Reference Architectures and Methodologies" developed on this basis (three years later GERAM 1.6.3 was later also published as a book chapter [15], thereby remaining in the public domain. The mandatory section of ISO 15704 lists requirements that any enterprise reference architecture must satisfy, while the GERAM document is a public appendix to the standard, exemplifying how to fulfil them.

In subsequent years, the same ISO committee extended ISO 15704 with additional views (decisional and economic), and also released ISO 19439:2006 [16], an ISO standard version of the GERA modelling framework (MF) that is part of GERAM.

Between 2015 and 2019, the work to update GERAM arrived at the current version 'GERAM-ISO' (as part of ISO 15704:2019 [17]), which incorporates time-tested provisions of GERAM into the normative requirements of ISO 15704, and this was carried out by ISO TC184/SC5/WG1 lead by Richard Martin, and contributions from IFIP WG5.12 members.

1.4   Other Relevant Developments in the Field of EA

During the same period, the information systems (IS), software engineering, and systems engineering (SysEng) communities saw a number of similar efforts. Thus, for example, the IS community widely publicised the Zachman Framework [18] that initially targeted the enterprise IS, but was subsequently extended in an attempt to model the entire enterprise's architecture.

The evolved Zachman framework had a similar aim to the enterprise reference architectures of type II – although the stakeholder-role related 'rows' in the framework only corresponded to life cycle activities because life cycle abstraction levels were typically of concern to different stakeholders. Later there were several adaptations of the Zachman Framework, including the Federal Enterprise Architecture Framework [19].

The Defence community saw the development of the C4ISR, which became the basis of the DoDAF Architecture Framework, with originally (DoDAF1.5) three simple life cycle abstractions (operational, systems/services, technical), and a complex modelling framework (MF), subsequently replaced by eight viewpoints (that are nevertheless aligned with the original three). DoDAF, of which the latest release is v2.02 in 2010 [20], with several offshoots in the defence community (MODAF, DONDAF, NATO AF, etc.).

More recently, the efforts of the Object Management Group (OMG) resulted in the so-called 'Unified Architecture Framework' (UAF)' [21], with the aim of including enterprise architecture in its scope (as opposed to being limited to 'systems architecture'). The claim is that UAF will eventually replace the above defence-related AF variations.

The IT industry also developed its own framework called The Open Group Architecture Framework (TOGAF) [22], which gained popularity with IT consultancies due to its detailed Architecture Development Method (ADM).

Consulting companies, individual researchers, and some vendors developed their own Architecture Framework (AF) versions (not listed here). The variety of proposals appears to owe to AFs being a conceptual structure deemed suitable for organising content for a domain, given typical stakeholders and their concerns, perspectives and viewpoints that determine how these stakeholders prefer to view and organise the answers to their concerns.

The American Heritage Dictionary of the English Language [23] defines a 'framework' as "*a set of assumptions, concepts, values, and practices that constitutes a way of viewing reality.*" An EA framework is therefore a means of sense-making in the complex world of change, in the domain of EA. Similarly, as individual learning is a fundamentally constructivist process, organisations must construct their shared meanings of change-related concepts by building the new concepts of EA into the fabric of their own pre-existing, path-dependent concepts of organisational change.

The original terminology used by the manufacturing community called such constructs 'reference architectures'. However, the internationally accepted terminology has evolved; thus, in line with the above discussion, what ISO 15704/GERAM and its predecessors called a 'Reference Architecture type II', is today called an Enterprise Architecture Framework (AF) (see for example ISO 42010:2011[1] [24]). In today's terminology, GERAM is an AF (thus should perhaps more suitably called Generalised Enterprise Architecture Framework, 'GEAF') – where the origin of the acronym remains only of historical interest.

Notably, recent efforts in the Systems and Software engineering community developed ISO 42020 [25] for 'Architecture Processes' and ISO 42030 [26] for 'Architecture Evaluation', which are now complementary to ISO 15704:2019 and ISO 42010, defining concepts for the processes to develop and to evaluate the Architecture exhibited of an entity of interest. Note the terminological difference: instead of saying 'system of interest' these standards talk about an entity of interest, i) this aligns with ISO 15704's concept of Enterprise Entity, as well as ii) the declared extension of scope, where the entity of interest may not be a 'system', nevertheless has an architecture – such as for example a product line.

Between 2015 and the end of 2019 the concerted effort and collaboration between the ISO TC184/WG1 and ISO/IEC JTC1/SC7/WG42 communities managed to harmonise their respective standards. The ticket to success was the fact that the underlying philosophy behind these communities is similar (with relatively small terminological differences), and it was acknowledged that the user community could benefit from such harmonisation. IFIP WG5.12 members have been participating in both of these standards bodies.

2   A Summary of the Contributions of GERAM to Theory and Practice

2.1   GERAM's Contribution to the Scientific Community

The central problem of EA is how to harmonise and synthesise all the knowledge necessary for understanding, sense-making, leading, managing and executing change in enterprises as complex socio-technical systems of systems. In other words, the role of EA is to create coherency across management levels and activity domains in the enterprise [27]. Therefore, for an AF to qualify as an enterprise AF, its scope must encompass any type of enterprise or constituent entity.

From a scientific point of view, GERAM's important contribution is that it defines a concise set of concepts that can be combined and used to evaluate AFs in terms of completeness of scope and complexity.

---

[1] Note that ISO 42010:2011 is being reviewed (as of July 2021).

GERAM uses the concept of enterprise entity, defined to be any system of interest with socio-technical relevance (this may include systems of interest in the enterprise entity's environment); thus, even the product of the enterprise is seen as an enterprise entity. An enterprise entity may live for a longer period of time, or have limited life span, being dynamically created like a project or a programme; it can also be a single organisation (e.g. a company) or a virtual organisation (virtual enterprise). Certainly, a company is an enterprise entity, but so is a network of companies, a consortium, a government department, even an entire industry: essentially, any undertaking with a shared goal to produce some services, or products, can be considered an enterprise entity.

The constituency of an enterprise entity is usually changing in time: at any one point in time there may be entities joining or leaving, being created, transformed, or decommissioned; in other words an enterprise entity is often a dynamic organisation. For an AF to qualify as an EA framework, the scope of the framework must encompass all enterprise entity types.

The power of GERAM's life cycle generalisation is that the choice between what is the current entity of interest is orthogonal to all other choices. E.g., we can talk about the life cycle of an enterprise or the life cycle of a product in *exactly* the same way. This fundamentally reduces the complexity of architecture-related considerations, because i) there is no need to separately define product life cycle processes, project management processes, production processes and management processes; these are all life cycle processes of the respective entities (product, project, factory, company, etc. as illustrated in Fig. 1), and ii) areas that previously eluded architectural treatment (and needed separate attention) become central elements of enterprise architecture (EA)).

This is illustrated in Fig. 2 by demonstrating that the combination of scope definitions of hardware/software and human/machine implemented functions and processes naturally leads to the inclusion into the architecture's scope of human skill levels, human knowledge, and role-specific communication requirements. As opposed to this, in frameworks lacking the orthogonality property, such considerations need separate metamodel level definitions, leading to excessive complexity (and possible incompleteness).

GERAM as an AF allows a number of elementary differentiations to be made, which can be combined into more powerful concepts as needed. In the GERA MF (which is one of the parts of GERAM), the underlying elementary concepts are derived from pairwise differentiations, mandating the ability to describe:

- human & automated constituents,
- service delivery & management constituents, and
- software & hardware constituents

of any enterprise entity, and the ability to do this over the entire life of the entity.

Furthermore, any combination of these differentiations can be described from the point of view of the *function* (and associated objects processed, such as *information* and *material*), the *resource* performing the function, and the mapping between function and resource (called *organisation*). These differentiations define the scope of *potential* enterprise models, aiming for the scope to be as complete as possible and the framework to remain holistic – i.e., considering enterprise entities in their totality.

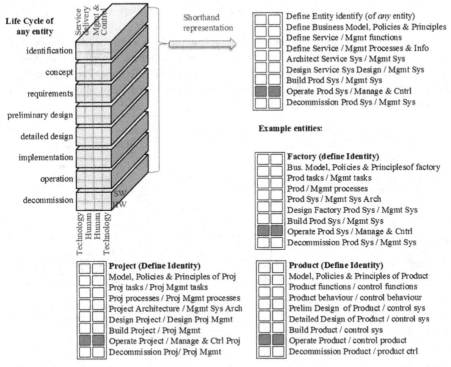

Fig. 1. Life cycle activity types and example of the scope (coverage) of their outcomes for various enterprise entities

According to Ted Williams, when the Purdue Consortium set out to write a methodology for CIM systems development it transpired that separately designing the automated parts of 'material and information processing systems' was too complex a task, and an approach was needed that simultaneously considered the human and automated elements of the enterprise.

If a framework, due to its limited scope, insists on subdividing a complex system-of-systems along a border where there are too many interconnections (such as the human-machine interface), then the designer will have limited ability to reduce apparent complexity through decomposition and modelling of interactions among the system's constituents. Thus, the advice is: '*don't cut it where it is the thickest*' – this was the first impetus behind the development of the Purdue Enterprise Reference Architecture (PERA) [9], leading to the incorporation into the scope of the AF both the human and the automated parts of the enterprise.

Finally, GERA states that descriptions (or *enterprise models*) may be created for an individual entity (called particular *models*), for a type of entity (called '*reference models*' or '*partial models*'), as well as the *models of the languages* used for expressing these models. GERAM calls these latter 'Generic Enterprise Modelling Concepts', as they are essentially *ontologies*, which (in increasing extent of formality) may take the form of terminology definitions in natural language, metamodels, or formal ontological theories.

Note that the term 'partial model' is preferable to the term 'reference model', because a reference model is often associated with the situation where a particular system of interest is a parametric specialisation (instantiation) of the reference. Partial models on the other hand can be model fragments, building blocks, or patterns, allowing modular construction of new types of models.

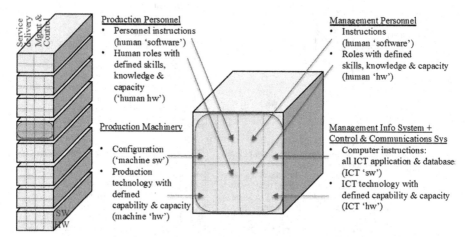

Fig. 2. Orthogonal treatment of 'human or machine' and 'software or hardware' implementation choice preserves scope completeness and leads to complexity reduction: each combination is valid

The above pairwise differentiations in modelling scope can be combined as needed due to their orthogonally to form a large number of model types that *may* be of interest to answer relevant stakeholder concerns about a given enterprise entity.

Thus, instead of creating and prescribing a very long list of model types for every usual type of enterprise entity and typical problem area, and codifying them in the AF, GERAM and its modelling framework GERA allows its user to independently contemplate, and if necessary specify, the problem at hand (as a set of stakeholder concerns), and decide what model types are needed for expressing a solution (that can be represented in various views for the stakeholders – corresponding to their viewpoints from which they consider the entity of interest).

GERA is like a 'bookshelf', with labels similar to the 'Dewey system' used in libraries: 'like' models go on the same shelf. However, even if we pinpoint a given model-type, many kinds of models can still be produced. For example, given a factory workshop as our target enterprise entity (or 'system of interest'), there exist many options to describe the functional requirements of the manufacturing equipment (machine tool hardware). The model may take the simple form of a list of functions, or a set of static process models, or a set of dynamic process models, stochastic or deterministic models, either ignoring or representing cost, etc. The nature of the necessary model is determined by the task at hand, who needs to peruse the model and for what purpose; models are created in response to concerns of stakeholders (as per ISO 42010 [24]).

GERAM's orthogonality of modelling scope definitions may be applied in the development of architecture metamodels, to keep them as simple as possible, or possibly discover hitherto hidden aspects of modelling. For example this was relevant in the efforts [28, 29] to introduce human view elements into the NATO AF (currently version 4).

Many AFs come with an 'associated metamodel', which essentially defines the kinds of facts and relationships that the AF is proposing to cover. However, these 'associated metamodels' are actually generalizations and not a correct view of the roles of metamodels. Given an enterprise entity (a sociotechnical system of systems), the same system may undergo various kinds of change, which in turn determines the stakeholders of that change, and in turn this can determine what is a suitable methodology to address the change. It is then the methodology that dictates (or advises) the kinds of models that may be necessary to build, and this determines the necessary metamodel for the modelling scope at hand. During the life of an enterprise entity multiple methodologies may be used, supported by various metamodels and modelling tools that help the user to create, represent, analyse and share these models.

The upshot of the above consideration is that there is no single enterprise architecting methodology and also there is no single 'optimal', or 'complete' metamodel for enterprise architects. GERAM as an AF defines the fact that in any particular enterprise change case there is an enterprise architecting methodology, which can define the models necessary and codify these in terms of a metamodel, or in an optimal case an ontological theory.

The relevance of this aspect for the EA community is that one needs to develop various methodologies, each for typical types of enterprise change. At the same time enterprise modelling tool vendors need to (in the long run) allow their tools to be extended for various modelling purposes. The enterprise modelling tool landscape is thus predetermined to move into the platform-as-a-product space, where the tool allows the addition, adaptation, extension to the platform (signs of this happening are already present in the current tool vendor arena, but this article is not meant to make comparisons between tools, therefore specific references are omitted).

In addition to the modelling scope, note that an enterprise model's pragmatic information content (i.e., its interpretation by the stakeholders) is also dependent on the model's status [30] in the context of use. This is because one important role of enterprise models is that they are used for communication and agreement among stakeholders (this even includes self-reflection exercised by a single stakeholder). This context of use is best described by the life history of the entity. For example, a model may be interpreted as representing the entity 'as perceived by the analyst', or as the 'agreed view of the AS-IS situation by all stakeholders', or 'as proposed to be', 'as agreed to be', and so on.

The concept of life cycle is fundamental to EA and systems engineering; however, the concept is not well-defined in the majority of EA and systems engineering literature. The following story illustrates this problem.

At a meeting of two Globeman 21 consortium participants at Sanctuary Cove, in 1997, the Japanese and Australian teams were discussing the life cycle of chemical plants, and the life cycle of the project that designs and builds these plants. Each team had its own life cycle representation. The Australian team used the GERAM life cycle model, while the Japanese team used a representation familiar to the project managers in their engineering firm. It soon became apparent that the two teams did not agree. The advocates of the GERAM representation argued that life cycle does not (and should not) represent time, while the Japanese team's model was clearly temporal. During this crucial meeting it became clear that using the same name for such dissimilar concepts is untenable, and the term 'life history' was proposed to refer to how the life of the respective entities unfolds in time.

Shortly after the above events, the IFIP IFAC TF met, and a participant proposed at the end of the meeting that the GERAM life cycle was to be extended with a 're-engineering phase'. However, when at the next TF meeting the life history concept was introduced, it became evident that 're-engineering' is a mere repetition of some already defined life cycle activities: the proposal was dropped, and the life history concept was adopted to be incorporated in the specification of GERAM.

The ISO 15704/GERAM concepts of life cycle and life history deserve discussion, because no other EA framework has made a differentiation between these concepts, with resulting confusion by architecture practitioners. Even ISO 15288:2015 ('Systems and software engineering – System life cycle processes') makes no such differentiation [12].

The GERAM life cycle consists of life cycle *activity types* (or 'phases'), each of which consider the enterprise entity on a different extent of abstraction. These 'phases' are not temporal in nature – if they were, then the term 'cycle' would not be appropriate.

There is a two-way information flow among such life cycle activities: the less the extent of abstraction of the phase, the more concrete detail of the entity is known to the corresponding activity. For example, considering the entity at the 'detailed design' extent of abstraction needs more information than considering the same entity at the 'requirements' extent of abstraction.

The architecture of enterprise entities is usually actively changing: there are elements of the architecture that remain constant over a longer period of time, but many parts are constructed on the fly by configuring short term structures (committees, task forces, projects, etc.), and this configuration activity, at least conceptually speaking, also consists of life cycle activities.

Such self configuration is not necessary for enterprises that have a very stable set of functions to perform, whereupon the structure of resources as built can directly perform the production functions, with perhaps parametric changes.

However, an enterprise may have a less pre-determined structure, and part of the task of operational management is to adaptively configure the dynamic structure (by allocation of resources and establishment of links) necessary to perform the production function.

As opposed to the life cycle, the *life history* of an entity describes how changes to the entity happen in time. The life history of an entity consists of life cycle activity instances, which in turn may form sequences of events (with some parallelism). This timeline of the evolution of an entity may be subdivided into life history stages, and milestones separating such stages can also be defined.

Finally, an important consequence of the concept of life cycle being atemporal is that the GERAM life-cycle concept can be used in two ways: (1) create models to use them in deliberate enterprise engineering activities (where models on various life cycle phases serve for expressing designs and to direct change), and (2) create models on any appropriate life cycle phase, to assess the current situation, or to make sense of *emergent* change, i.e. use models *a posteriori*, to investigate, analyse, understand change that already happened, and use this for decision support.

Even in deliberate, directed change, as-is models are usually derived by first creating detailed design phase models, then creating abstractions of these models at the preliminary design phase, or further, at the requirements phase, or even further, at the concept phase, to elucidate the principles and the explicit business model behind the concept of the current state of the enterprise.

This method of analysis can uncover a model of the current enterprise that represents it on the 'right extent of abstraction' suitable for a strategic change to be contemplated. There is a temptation to simply state that the right extent of abstraction is the extent of abstraction on which stakeholder concerns are expressed. However, this begs the question: are stakeholders expressing their concerns at the right extent of abstraction?

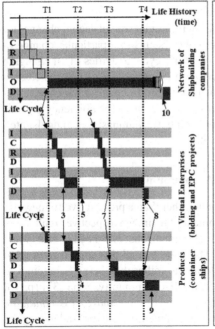

(1) A customer identifies a need for a product. (2) At time T1 the customer contacts the *network broker* and initial negotiations are made. The *broker* informs the *competence manager* about the need. The *competence manager* sets up a **configuration virtual enterprise (VE)** (for bidding purposes). This takes place in the operational phase of the network. An *information and communications manager* is responsible for the set up of the communication system. *Temporary contractors* might be included. The *contract manager* becomes leader of this VE. (3) In the operational phase of the **configuration-VE** the *contract manager* contacts the customer and the *VE-partners* transform the need into a product concept, requirements and a conceptual design. (4) This forms the basis for a quotation at time T2. (5) The **configuration-VE** has completed its tasks and is decommissioned. (6) The customer accepts the quotation, and the *competence manager* sets up a **construction-VE** (for engineering procurement and construction (EPC)). The *contract manager* leads the **construction-VE**. The *inf. and comm. manager* is responsible for the set up of the communication system. *Temporary contractors* might be included. (7) In the operational phase of the **construction-VE**, the product design is finalised and the product is produced, i.e. implemented and deployed. (8) The product is finished at time T4 and delivered to the *customer*, and the **construction-VE** is closed down (decommissioned). (9) After delivery, the customer uses the product, which corresponds to the operational phase of the product life cycle. (A subsequent VE might be responsible for maintenance and service, not shown). (10) For the sake of completeness, the decommissioning of the network is also shown.

Fig. 3. Parallel life histories of systems in a system of systems: each enterprise entity has its own life cycle and life history. (Example of shipbuilding network in the Baltics developed in the frameworks of the Globeman 21 Consortium [31].)

The resolution to this dilemma is that in this sense-making story, the *analysis outcomes* and *stakeholder understanding* of what are the real concerns co-evolve. It is the interaction between the analysis process and the sense-making process through which stakeholders iterate and refine their understanding of the real problems, and that simultaneously arrives at the right extent of abstraction and stakeholder concern formulation.

The difference between these two kinds of change processes (deliberate and emerging) can be visualised as different patterns of life cycle activity instances in the life history of a system. Thus, the life cycle / life history dichotomy allows both researchers and practitioners to discuss deliberate and emergent / organic change within the same framework.

The life cycle of an enterprise entity in GERAM is recursive: when an entity operates, as part of this operation it may perform life cycle activities of other entities (or of itself). An example of this is illustrated in Fig. 3 through a real life example as applied by the Globeman 21 consortium for the creation and operation of a network of shipbuilding companies.

The system of systems concept familiar from systems engineering is naturally represented in GERAM: the system as a whole has its own life history, while constituent systems have their own life history. At any one stage of life of a system of systems, constituent systems appear, evolve, change, and may disappear. Typical such limited-time in existence entities are change programmes and change projects created by them, and other supporting systems may also be ephemeral.

From the methodological perspective, this is an important way of seeing change. By representing the parallel life histories of constituent systems in a particular change of a particular system of systems, one can identify all life cycle activities of all changing constituent systems, resulting in a guide to create a complete list of tasks necessary to orchestrate the change. This is the basis of being able to create a concrete, case-specific methodology and transformation plan [32]. Of course, for efficiency reasons there must exist a library of methodology components (techniques, metamodels, etc.) for each typical life cycle activity type identified.

2.2 The Contribution of GERAM to the EA Community

Given that GERAM is a sense-making instrument rather than a prescriptive framework, it can be used by those who work on the development of their own respective architecture frameworks. ISO 15704 was developed to list requirements that AFs need to satisfy and not be prescriptive about how to achieve this. The logic behind this approach was that the role of the standard was to facilitate development, rather than being an attempt to override the work done by significant groups in the EA community. Saha [33] (p. 16) writes: *"GERAM/ ISO 15704 is an excellent baseline to map and assess candidate architecture frameworks..."* and refers to GERAM as a meta-framework (a language to talk about frameworks), or 'framework of frameworks'.

A number of EA frameworks were analysed and mapped against the ISO 15704 requirements [34, 35]. The conclusion is that, what is often published under the name 'Architecture Framework', is in fact a collection of artefacts that includes an 'AF proper' (as defined in Sect. 1.4) plus a set of artefacts described by that AF. For example, an AF proper may define the concept 'EA methodology', but any such methodology is not part of the AF proper. For a defined type of stakeholder community and typical application, AFs may come bundled with a collection of artefacts, such as architecture description languages (modelling languages), an architecting methodology, a set of reference models, or even a suggested modelling tool. A taxonomy could be built for of any of these;

for example, a factory design methodology may have specialised versions for typical factory types.

Such mappings of AFs against ISO 15704/GERAM requirements have had influence, for example on the release of new versions of DoDAF [36] (p. 3) and [37]) aligning DoDAF terminology to the ISO 15704 and ISO 19439 standards. We believe that similar new applications for AF development could for example contribute to the popular TOGAF framework's newer versions as well, allowing change programmes, and projects to become first class citizens (enterprise entities) in that framework, similar to the way illustrated in Fig. 1.

The content of these artefacts (methodologies, principles, reference models, etc.) is normally not developed by the EA discipline. Thus, a methodology to develop the business model of an enterprise is likely to come from management science, reference models for projects and programmes from the project management discipline, process reference models for IT management from the IS community, and so on.

Prescribing a methodology even for a typical EA problem can quickly become complicated, as the author must prepare advice for all types of situations, contexts, and user skill levels. An alternative is to prescribe a meta-methodology, which is a more economical approach (see Sect. 3.1).

In summary, the EA discipline is (or should be) an interdisciplinary synthesis of the contributions of underlying disciplines. The EA terminology and a theory of EA must be able to describe the interactions among theories, methods, models, and tools developed by these disciplines and how new insights and practices can emerge through such interaction. Thus, EA can be seen as the systems science of change.

For EA researchers, GERAM can also be used as a research framework, with the view of circumscribing the scope of research and formalising the research problem at hand – in other words, to translate the initial informal research question into a formal one [37–40].

2.3 Manufacturing and Engineering Applications

The first industrial application of GERAM was in the Globeman 21 Consortium of approximately 40 industry partners that demonstrated the use of EA principles in a number of applications in the manufacturing industry. The final report of the consortium [41] outlined the most important outcomes as follows:

- The Virtual Enterprise Workbench for World-wide Integration & Development (VIEWBID), providing a company with an integrated set of tools and methods for co-ordinating its global business process for bidding / tender preparation;
- Virtual and Real Information Technologies driven Global Engineering/ Enterprise (VRIDGE) - a virtual enterprise (VE) that carries out the design, procurement, construction, and manufacturing of a chemical plant. This VE facilitated the understanding of global business processes and the investigation of requirements for global product information access and control, as well as of IT infrastructure for VEs.
- GlobOS, that demonstrated a concept of networking among shipyards where pre-qualified partners in the network deliver different generic steel structure assemblies

for the final ship. GlobOS illustrates how facilities, methods and assemblies can be modelled and shared within a network.

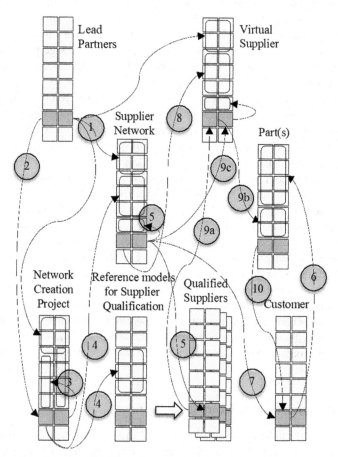

Fig. 4. A Dynamic Business Model of the creation of an Enterprise Network and its Virtual Enterprises (VEs)

The subsequent Globemen consortium of 16 industry and 3 academic partners focused on inter-enterprise collaboration based using global information exchange and control [13, 42]. Globemen demonstrated the applicability of the GERAM framework (specialised by the consortium under the name VERAM) to the creation of global enterprise networks that are capable, on demand, of creating *service* virtual enterprises [31, 38] that provide after-sales service (troubleshooting, turnaround, factory optimisation, etc.) in a transparent way to chemical factories, although each service typically requires the competencies of multiple globally distributed companies.

GERAM has also been applied to support the development of Small and Medium Enterprises (IMMPAC) [43], to design and create the concept of Virtual Industry Cluster

[44], and technological platforms such as PyME CREATIVA [45–47], and to build an EI engineering reference framework and toolbox to improve the design and operations of manufacturing companies [48].

GERAM was the methodological basis for the development of a reference model for Integrated Product and Process development (IPPMD) and which was subsequently applied in multiple industry cases [49]. Three case studies have been published; the first is related to a product transfer for an aeronautical firm to a Mexican manufacturing company. The second case study was implemented in a manufacturing firm to automate a planning process for design and manufacture of an automotive part.

Another case (illustrated in Fig. 4) describes how a Small or Medium Enterprise (SME) created its development process for a new product. Thus, IECOS is a Virtual Supplier integrating qualified suppliers into a network, that according to their website is "an engineering and manufacturing firm that focuses on developing high added value solutions for [...] clients and allies through three different business units: IECOS Supply-, Engineering- and Technology Services". 'IECOS Supply' integrates the capabilities of more than 20 small and medium-sized metal-mechanical and plastics manufacturing companies [50].

Finally GERAM has been used as the theoretical basis to define a reference model to create a sensing, smart and sustainable manufacturing enterprise [51, 52].

2.4 Applications to the Standards Community, Environmental and Emergency Management, and Collaborative Healthcare

The wide applicability of GERAM as an overarching, non-prescriptive ('light-weight', see Sect. 3) AF has allowed its involvement in conjunction with systems thinking and system-of-systems paradigms to address several major challenges faced by society today.

For example, in the standards community, currently there is limited, mainly ad-hoc collaboration between custodian work groups within each technical and scientific committee, causing low awareness of other groups' work and resulting in gaps and overlaps in standards' scope and inconsistencies in standards' glossaries. This makes standards difficult to use together – which is typically expected for any sizeable project. GERAM has been proposed as an essential tool in discovering gaps and overlaps in the areas of relevance and building an intelligent repository underlying an expert system that allows achieving an improved and sustainable interoperability of standards [53].

Environmental management (EM), an increasingly essential aspect of any enterprise or network, is often not properly integrated in the business, resulting in sub-optimal environmental performance and merely minimal compliance with standards. GERAM was used to support the discovery of the areas and extent of EM integration and to ensure that environmental information of adequate quality and detail is promptly delivered to the management to properly support the long and short-term decisional processes [54].

Emergency management is another important field of application in the context of climate change and increasing rate of natural and man-made disasters. Here, GERAM has been used to provide a checklist of participants and aspects required in modelling the present (AS-IS) and desired future (TO-BE) states of emergency management services [55]. This was done with a view to improve the effectiveness and resilience of the command and control and response teams but also to achieve suitable preparedness of the disaster response and management effort participants.

In addition, Noran and Panetto [56] proposed the use of GERAM and systems thinking principles in the lifecycle-centric analysis and design of improvements to healthcare interoperability and collaboration, to meet long term challenges (aging population, patient safety, complexity of services) and improve response to short term, acute challenges (large scale medical emergencies such as pandemics).

Further applications of GERAM continue to emerge, such as enterprise sustainability [57, 58], and in preparedness building for Mergers and Acquisitions [59].

3 'Heavy Weight' vs. 'Light Weight' Architecture Frameworks

3.1 The Complexity Conundrum

Readers following the development of AFs presented above would have noticed the following contradiction:

i) AFs are intended to help simplify the complex and thus sometimes unpredictable and sensitive enterprise change processes ('change' may mean incremental or major change, or the engineering and construction of a green field installation);

ii) Change, including deliberate (engineered and managed), has multiple aspects and numerous stakeholders, with many concerns and relationships; an AF must address all of these to achieve the desired coherency of decision-making and action.

The conundrum lies in the fact that according to the above logic, the 'AF that can address everything' would likely be complex, thus creating unpredictability, whose avoidance was the primary objective in the first place ([58, 60]).

If the AF is too complex for the stakeholders to fully understand, then how can we use it to solve the problem, when it creates another problem of similar nature? The question is: is it possible to have a simple AF as a basis for shared understanding and the development of an approach that can be used to adequately manage the complexity of change?

The objective of leading and managing change cannot be deterministic control, because enterprises operate in an environment capable of producing chaotic, non-deterministic behaviour. An EA methodology should help management navigate this partially determined, partially controllable world, steering change into a future where some important characteristics will hold, without having to predict the exact future trajectory and exact future state. With a vision of the future, management must *channel* change in a desirable direction, and an EA methodology should help achieve this. Part of this channelling is the establishment of change governance (with principles and processes that work in parallel with the change) without *a priori* prescribed sequence of actions.

When members of the Globemen Consortium requested a step-by-step methodology for developing an enterprise network that creates 'Service Virtual Enterprises', they realised that a pragmatically useful generic methodology is too hard to produce, due to the complexity of preparing for all possible cases. They saw, however, that for a fixed set of involved entities (e.g. a leading engineering firm, some representative factory owners, OEM vendors, and typical local service providers) whose life cycle relationships were determined (i.e., which entity should contribute to which life cycle activity of the another), a relatively simple, customised methodology could be defined [32, 61].

Thus, the answer to the dilemma seems to be: rather than bundling prescribed generic methodologies with AFs, use a simple framework and a 'meta-methodology' to adaptively create up-to-date change processes, combining proven methods, techniques and tools of underlying disciplines as necessary.

Some frameworks have a built-in methodology (e.g. TOGAF ADM), but methodology should be tailored to the specific case. Thus, the ADM is a repository of techniques and methods, and a meta-methodology should be used to identify the parts needed for a particular case.

The elements of the simple framework may be described using a (meta) meta-model [62], but care must be taken not to confuse (or mix) with meta-models expressing the semantics of enterprise modelling languages.

According to the same argument we must avoid creating a 'heavy weight' AF by prescribing model deliverables. However, for typical problems one can define a methodology, with associated models and languages.

3.2 Systems Science and Systems Thinking in EA

It is worth illustrating how systems thinking can be applied to locate the need for change and establish the structure of a model that is underlying a meta-methodology.

A typical case is continuous improvement, whereupon someone in the operations notices a problem (on the shop floor or in management) and is searching for a solution by analysing the observed problem and its causes. One can use a systems thinking diagram, or one of the many types of root cause analysis tools, for this to identify the entities involved, those affected, and the location of needed change.

For example, Fig. 5 shows a systems thinking diagram that a lead partner may have used to represent the problem of decreasing orders. The systems thinking diagram identifies the root cause: the SME's limited capability set to fulfil complex orders.

The solution is to create a virtual entity that looks like a medium sized supplier, able to perform complex operations. One way to achieve this is to create a network, in which processes, information flow, planning and scheduling, performance and resource management are coordinated. This needs tactical and possibly strategic information sharing beyond operational interactions, which is only viable if partners are pre-qualified and trusted and they subscribe to the network's operating policies and principles (finances, contracts, technological compatibility, quality and process).

This calls for a tightly regulated network, which in turn can create the desired virtual manufacturing company that looks like a single, well-managed medium sized supplier. This thinking is useful to understand the need for transformation (change, or innovation); subsequently, a *dynamic* business model can be used to represent transformation from the present (AS-IS) to the chosen future (TO-BE).

The change process can be modelled as a 'dynamic business model', a special type of systems thinking diagram of action and outcome used to consider what *may* have to be performed as part of a change. In this model, each entity is represented by its life cycle, and each arrow connects the entity that performs some change activity to the life cycle activity(ies) of the entity being changed. Such diagrams have been used in practice to define complex engineering and change processes; it has been found that despite a seemingly complicated structure, the models created have become a collaborative thinking tool towards defining the scope and location of change.

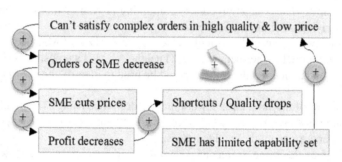

Fig. 5. Systems thinking diagram illustrating why is it hard for SMEs to compete

Figure 4 previously shown is a model of action and outcome leading to the creation of a Virtual Supplier by a network of qualified suppliers. Arrows may stand for generative relationships or operational interactions. A 'generative' arrow represents a relationship expressing that as an entity operates, it contributes to the life cycle activity of another entity. E.g., in Fig. 4, arrow ① between Lead Partners and Network Creation Project represents the fact that Lead Partners' action is to identify the need for, develop the concept of, and define the mandate (which is part of the requirements) of a network creation project. Arrow ② represents an operational interaction, expressing the fact that Lead Partners contribute to the operation of the Network Creation Project.

The Systems Story that accompanies Fig. 4 unfolds like this: the lead partner(s) identify(ies) the entities to be part of the business model, and the concept and mandate of each, and sets up a Network Creation Project (1). Lead partner(s) contribute to this project (2). Project management designs the details of the project and oversees project execution (3). The tasks are to design the supplier network, and a set of reference models (functions, processes, standards, policies and principles etc.) that a qualified member of the network will have to follow (4). Network management builds the network from qualified partners (5).

When a potential customer designs a part (6), leaving some or all detailed design decisions to the supplier, it contacts the network for a quote (7). If successful, the Network Office creates a 'Virtual Supplier' (8), assembled from qualified suppliers compliant with the reference models (4). The selected suppliers contribute to the Virtual Supplier's processes (9a) to perform the detailed design, production and delivery, so as the parts eventually reach the Customer (10). Note that the VE does have its own management function, but its operations are also overseen by the Network Office (9c).

4   Conclusion

4.1   Why is It Necessary to Work on the Future of EA?

Today's enterprises struggle with the number of fragmented models, tools and methods proposed to them by multiple disciplines, and the resulting adoption is less than coherent [27]. We believe that the future of EA is in its ability to develop an interdisciplinary language and theory enabling a concerted and synergistic application of contributions of underlying disciplines (results from management science, systems, industrial, manufacturing and software engineering, IS, Artificial Intelligence, and so on).

GERAM is a valuable *baseline meta-framework* - to discuss the above, to create new theories, schools of thoughts, integration of engineering practices and tools, explanations of how technologies can be part of EA, methodologies for EA implementation, and Partial and Particular models for re-use.

4.2   The Evolution of the Science of EA

EA is an evolving discipline, including and evolving Theory, Framework, Standards, Methodologies, Tools and Models. First and foremost the EA community needs to *continuously improve and enrich the theory of EA* for it to remain relevant and useful. As expressed in Sect. 2.2, *EA should be the systems science of change*. As a consequence, the EA community should:

- Develop a theory and harmonise the contributions of the above disciplines, so that all stakeholders (not only architects) of enterprise change and evolution can use EA as a common language [60].
- Develop recommendations of who and how should *learn this harmonised language*, contribute to *harmonise EA-related international and industry standards*, and continue interpretation and *mapping* of particular frameworks as they develop, in keeping with the common language,
- Extend the theory to cover the *interplay* of *evolution* and *enterprise engineering*, where complexity management plays a crucial role, and extend the scope to include social and ecological systems.

4.3   Emerging Technologies and EA

- Keep demonstrating the usefulness of the EA language and theory by developing commonly understandable *interpretations of existing and new technologies*, as a tool for industry analysts to moderate the 'hype cycle' of new technologies. E.g., one could start with explaining the role in EA in 'big data analytics', 'cloud computing', 'sensing enterprise', 'machine learning', etc.
- *Re-interpret* notable and important *architectural styles*, *schools of thought*, and *reference models* using EA's common language, to make these accessible, comparable and synergistic. This is a very large agenda, which needs the help of underlying disciplines. However, the outcome can be a 'LEGO' of components (models, tools, languages, methodologies) enabling innovation.

- Notable reference models / Reference Architectures exist for service delivery, management & control, or both. The following is an example list of well known ones (with bibliographic references omitted): Service orientation on the IT level and on the Business level, Fractal organisations, Model Driven Architectures to instantiate process oriented organizations, governance models (of IT and of EA), process improvement (Kaizen, CMMI, SPICE, Six Sigma), Reference Architectures for Programme and Project management, etc.

4.4 Applications, Enterprise Integration Engineering and EA

- Continue research on Architecture principles, and conduct and publish architecture evaluations (*cf* ISO 42030), and comparative studies to demonstrate value.
- Publish case studies and solutions to contribute to knowledge of the EA practice, e.g. challenges to introduce EA practice (soft factors, human interactions, change management, interoperability, etc.)
- Enrich the relevance of the discipline by publishing case studies of EA in government defence, petroleum, cement, retail, global companies, health care, etc.
- Develop problem-specific methodologies, arising from *scale* (micro-enterprises, SMEs, global companies) and *type of change* (for implementing new business models, work practices, automation, M&As, new management style, reorganisation, productivity improvement), so as to reflect a relevant sample of typical stakeholder concerns and disseminate solutions to address them.
- There has been decades of debate about 'integration' *vs* 'interoperability' in the domain of Enterprise Architecture. It appears that the debate has never been resolved [3, 63, 64] because the interoperability community never seems to have acknowledged that the goal is still *integration*, not interoperability per se: the latter is only a tool to create, maintain – and if needed re-create in a dynamic fashion – an integrated material and information flow in the enterprise.

4.5 EA Community Building

The community is currently fragmented by *industry* (IT/Systems Engineering, Manufacturing, Public Sector, Defence, Service industries), *nature of enquiry* (scientific / applied), and by *schools of thought*. Communities include academia (IFAC, IFIP, IEEE), Research Groups, Industry Associations & standards bodies (Open Group, Object Management Group, INCOSE, ISO, NIST, DIN), consortia, consulting firms, CIO councils, etc.

These communities have their own conferences or other fora, but there is no forum to bring all of these together. We believe that a revival of the ICEIMT-style conference and workshop series could play a role in creating coherence among the existing 'EA silos'; perhaps EA practice could be used to provide an answer.

Acknowledgements. The authors acknowledge the contributions of the members of IFIP Working Group 5.12 to the development of ISO 15704/GERAM, and especially the tireless efforts of Richard Martin to update GERAM (now 'GERAM-ISO') as part of ISO 15704:2019.

Dedication. This article is dedicated to the memory of Jim Nevins and Ted J. Williams.

References

1. Bernus, P., Noran, O., Molina, A.: Twenty years of the GERAM framework. In: Boje, E., Xia, X. (eds.) Proceedings of 19th IFAC World Congress, Cape Town. IFAC-Papers Online, pp. 3300–3308 (2014)
2. Bernus, P., Noran, O., Molina, A.: Enterprise architecture: twenty years of the GERAM framework. Annu. Rev. Control. **39**, 83–93 (2015)
3. Chen, D.: Framework for enterprise interoperability. In: Archimède, B., Vallespir, B. (eds.) Enterprise Interoperability, pp. 1–18. Wiley, New York (2017)
4. Williams, T.J., et al.: Architectures for integrating manufacturing activities and enterprises. Comput. Ind. Special Issue CIM **24**(2–3), 111–140 (1994)
5. Bernus, P., Nemes, L., Williams, T.J. (eds.): Architectures for Enterprise Integration. IAICT, Springer, Boston (1996). https://doi.org/10.1007/978-0-387-34941-1
6. IEC 62264: Enterprise-Control System Integration. ISO, Geneva (2013)
7. Kosanke, K., Vernadat, F., Zelm, M.: CIMOSA: Enterprise engineering and integration. Comput. Ind. **40**(2–3), 83–97 (1999)
8. Doumeingts, G., Vallespir, B., Chen, D.: GRAI grid decisional modelling. In: Bernus, P., Mertins, K., Schmidt, G. (eds.) Handbook on Architectures of Information Systems, pp. 313–339. Springer, Heidelberg (1998)
9. Williams, T.J.: The Purdue enterprise reference architecture. Comput. Ind. **24**(2), 141–158 (1994)
10. Bernus, P., Nemes, L.: A framework to define a generic enterprise reference architecture and methodology. In: Proceedings of ICARV 1996, vol. 3/3, pp. 88–92. Nanyang Technical University (1994)
11. Bernus, P., Nemes, L.: Computer Integrated Manufacturing Systems, **9**(3), 179–191. (Reprint of Bernus & Nemes (1994)), (1996)
12. ISO 15288: Systems and software engineering – System life cycle processes. ISO, Geneva (2015)
13. Bernus, P., Baltrusch, R., Tølle, M., Vesterager, J.: Better models for agile virtual enterprises – the enterprise and its constituents as hybrid agents . In: Karvoinen, I., et al. (eds.) Global Engineering and manufacturing in Enterprise Networks (Globemen), VTT Symposium Series 224, (9–10 October 2002), pp. 91–103. VTT, Helsinki (2002)
14. ISO 15704: Industrial automation systems – Requirements for enterprise reference architectures and methodologies. ISO, Geneva (2000)
15. IFIP/IFAC Taskforce: The generalised enterprise reference architecture and methodology. In: Handbook on Enterprise Architecture, pp. 22–64. Springer, Cham (2003)
16. ISO 19439: Enterprise integration – Framework for enterprise modelling. ISO, Geneva (2006)
17. ISO 15704: Industrial automation systems – Requirements for enterprise-referencing architectures and methodologies. ISO, Geneva (2019)
18. Zachman, J.: A framework for information systems architecture. IBM Syst. J. **26**(3), 276–292 (1987)
19. FEAF (Federal Chief Information Officers Council): Federal Enterprise Architecture Framework. Version 1.1. (1999)
20. DoD: DoD Architecture Framework Version 2.02. US Department of Defense (2010)
21. OMG: Unified Architecture Framework 1.1. Object Management Group (2020)
22. The Open Group: The Open Group Architecture Framework, v8.1.1; v9.1. The Open Group. (2006, 2011, 2018)
23. The American Heritage Dictionary of the English Language (4th Edition). Houghton Mifflin, Boston (2000, Updated 2009)

24. ISO/IEC/IEEE 42010: Systems and software engineering – Architecture description. ISO, Geneva (2011)
25. ISO/IEC/IEEE 42020: Systems and software engineering – Architecture processes. ISO, Geneva (2019)
26. ISO/IEC/IEEE 42030: Systems and software engineering – Architecture evaluation. ISO, Geneva (2019)
27. Doucet, G., Gøtze, J., Saha, P., Bernard, S.: Coherency management: using enterprise architecture for alignment, agility, and assurance. J. EA **4**(2), 1–12 (2008)
28. Handley, H.A.H., Smillie, R.J.: Architecture framework human view: the NATO approach. Syst. Eng. **11**(2), 156–164 (2008)
29. Handley, H.A.H., Smillie, R.J.: Human view dynamics – the NATO approach. Syst. Eng. **13**(1), 72–79 (2010)
30. Hysom, R.: Enterprise modelling – the readiness of the organisation. In: Bernus, P., Nemes, L., Schmidt, G. (eds.) Handbook on Enterprise Architecture, pp. 373–416. Springer, Heidelberg (2003)
31. Vesterager, J., Bernus, P., Pedersen, J. D., Tølle, M.: The what and why of a virtual enterprise reference architecture. In: E-work and E-commerce. Novel Solutions and Practices for a Global Networked Economy, pp. 846–852. IOS Press, Amsterdam (2001)
32. Noran, O.: Towards a meta-methodology for collaborative networked organisations. In: Camarinha-Matos, L.M. (ed.) PRO-VE 2004. IIFIP, vol. 149, pp. 71–78. Springer, Boston (2004). https://doi.org/10.1007/1-4020-8139-1_8
33. Saha, P. (ed.): A synergistic assessment of the federal enterprise architecture framework against GERAM (ISO15704:2000). In: Handbook of Enterprise Systems Architecture in Practice. IGI Global (2006)
34. Noran, O.: Mapping of individual architecture frameworks. In: Bernus, P., Nemes, L., Schmidt, G. (eds.) Handbook on Enterprise Architecture, pp. 65–210. Springer, Heidelberg (2003)
35. Saha, P.: Analyzing TOGAF from the GERAM Perspective (2004). http://www.opengroup.org/architecture/wp/saha/TOGAF_GERAM_Mapping.htm
36. DoD: DoD Architecture Framework Version 2. US Department of Defense (2009)
37. Chaharsooghi, K., Achachlouei, M.A.: Developing life-cycle phases for the DoDAF using ISO 15704 Annex A (GERAM). Comput. Ind. **62**(3), 253–259 (2011)
38. Vesterager, J., Larsen, L.B., Pedersen, J.D., Tølle, M., Bernus, P.: Use of GERAM as basis for a virtual enterprise framework model. In: Mo, J.P.T., Nemes, L. (eds.) Global Engineering, Manufacturing and Enterprise Networks. ITIFIP, vol. 63, pp. 75–82. Springer, Boston (2001). https://doi.org/10.1007/978-0-387-35412-5_9
39. Noran, O.: Using reference models in enterprise architecture. In: Fettke, P., Loos, P. (eds.) Reference Modelling for Business Systems Analysis, pp. 141–165 Idea Group, Hershey (2007)
40. Magoulas, Th., Hadzic, A., Saarikko, T., Pessi, K.: Alignment in enterprise architecture: investigating the aspects of alignment in architecture approaches. In: Proceedings of 5th European Conference on Information Management and Evaluation, pp. 321–331. Academic Publications Ltd., Reading (2010)
41. Brown, R.H., Syntera, H. (eds): Globeman 21 (Global Mfg. in the 21st Century) Final Report (1999). http://www.ims.org/wp-content/uploads/2011/11/2.4.10.2-Final-Report-GLOBEMAN-21.pdf
42. Karvonen, I., et al. (eds.): Global Engineering and Manufacturing in Enterprise Networks GLOBEMEN. VTT Symposium, vol. 224. VTT Technical Research Centre of Finland, Helsinki (2003). http://www.vtt.fi/inf/pdf/symposiums/2003/S224.pdf
43. Molina, A., Carrasco, R.: Handbook on Enterprise Architecture, pp. 757–778. Springer, Heidelberg (2003)

44. Molina, A., Flores, M.: A virtual enterprise in Mexico: from concepts to practice. J. Intell. Rob. Syst. **26**, 289–302 (1999)

45. Molina, A., Mejía, R., Galeano, N., Najera, T., Velandia, M.: The HUB as an enabling IT strategy to achieve Smart Organizations. In: Mezgar, I. (ed.) Integration of ICT in Smart Organizations. Idea Group, pp. 64–95 (2006)

46. Giraldo, J., Galeano, N., Molina, A.: Virtual organization breeding environment: experiences from its implementation in Mexico. In: Proceedings of 8th IFAC Symposium on Cost Oriented Automation Affordable Automation Systems, La Habana, Cuba (CD Memories) (2007)

47. Nogueira, J.M., Romero, D., Espadas, J., Molina, A.: Leveraging the Zachman framework implementation using action-research methodology – a case study: aligning the enterprise architecture and the business goals. Enterprise Inf. Syst. **7**(1), 100–132 (2013)

48. Vallejo, C., Romero, D., Molina, A.: Enterprise integration engineering reference framework & toolbox. Int J. Prod. Res. **50**(5), 1489–1551 (2011)

49. Pereda, F.J., Molina, A.: Model driven architecture for engineering design and manufacturing. IFAC-Papers Online **6**(1), 400–407 (2013)

50. Molina, A., Velandia, M., Galeano, N.: Virtual enterprise brokerage: a structure driven strategy to achieve build to order supply chains. Int. J. Prod. Res. **45**(7), 3853–3880 (2007)

51. Chavarría-Barrientos, D., Batres, R., Wright, P.K., Molina, A.: A methodology to create a sensing, smart and sustainable manufacturing enterprise. Int. J. Prod. Res. **56**(1–2), 584–603 (2018)

52. Molina, A., Ponce, P., Miranda, J., Cortés-Serrano, D.: Enabling Systems for Intelligent Manufacturing in Industry 4.0. Springer, New York (2021). ISBN 978-3-030-65546-4

53. Noran, O.: Achieving a sustainable interoperability of standards. Annual Rev. Control **36**(2), 327–337 (2012).

54. Noran, O.: Engineering the sustainable business: an enterprise architecture approach. In: Doucet, G., Gotze, J., Saha, P. (eds.), Coherency Management: Architecting the Enterprise for Alignment, Agility, and Assurance. Int. Enterprise Architecture Institute, pp. 179–210 (2009)

55. Noran, O., Bernus, P.: Effective disaster management: an interoperability perspective. In: Meersman, R., Dillon, T., Herrero, P. (eds.) OTM 2011. LNCS, vol. 7046, pp. 112–121. Springer, Heidelberg (2011). https://doi.org/10.1007/978-3-642-25126-9_19

56. Noran, O., Panetto, H.: Modelling a sustainable cooperative healthcare: an interoperability-driven approach. In: Demey, Y.T., Panetto, H. (eds.) OTM 2013. LNCS, vol. 8186, pp. 238–249. Springer, Heidelberg (2013). https://doi.org/10.1007/978-3-642-41033-8_32

57. Franco dos Reis Alves, D., Campos, R., Bernardi de Souza, F.: GERAM: building sustainable enterprises. In: 6th IFAC Conference on Management and Control of Production and Logistics (MCPL13), Fortaleza, Brazil (2013)

58. Kandjani, H., Bernus, P., Nielsen, S.: Enterprise architecture cybernetics and the edge of chaos: sustaining enterprises as complex systems in complex business environments. In: Ralph, H., Sprague Jr. (eds.) Proceedings of HICSS 2013, pp. 3858–3867. IEEE XPlore (2013)

59. Vaniya, N., Bernus, P., Noran, O.: Examining potentials of building M&A preparedness. In: Proceedings of 15th International Conference on Enterprise Information Systems, vol. 3, pp. 201–212. SCITEPRESS, Setubal (2013).

60. Kandjani, H., Bernus, P.: The enterprise architecture body of knowledge as an evolving discipline. In: Maciaszek, L.A., Cuzzocrea, A., Cordeiro, J. (eds.) LNBIP 141, pp. 452–471. Springer, Berlin (2013)

61. Bernus, P., Noran, O., Riedlinger, J.: Using the globemen reference model for virtual enterprise design in after sales service. In: Karvoinen, I. et al. (eds.) Global Engineering and Manufacturing in Enterprise Networks (Globemen), Symposium Series 224, pp. 71–90. VTT, Helsinki (2002)

62. Bernus, P., Noran, O.: A metamodel for enterprise architecture. In: Bernus, P., Doumeingts, G., Fox, M. (eds.) EAI2N 2010. IAICT, vol. 326, pp. 56–65. Springer, Heidelberg (2010). https://doi.org/10.1007/978-3-642-15509-3_6
63. Panetto, H., Whitman, L.: Knowledge engineering for enterprise integration, interoperability and networking: theory and applications. Data Knowl. Eng. **105**, 1–4 (2016)
64. Weichhart, G., Stary, C., Vernadat, F.: Enterprise modelling for interoperable and knowledge-based enterprises. Int. J. Prod. Res. **56**(8), 2818–2840 (2018)

Synthesis of a Composite Imitation Model of the Cognitive Structure of the Ergatic System Operator on the Basis of Conceptual Pattern Technology

Igor Petukhov[1], Liudmila Steshina[1], Andrei Gorokhov[1], Nataliia Vlasova[1], Dimiter Velev[2(⌧)], and Plamena Zlateva[3]

[1] Volga State University of Technology, Yoshkar-Ola, Russia
{petukhoviv,steshinala,gorokhovav,vlasovana}@volgatech.net
[2] University of National and World Economy, Sofia, Bulgaria
dgvelev@unwe.bg
[3] Institute of Robotics, Bulgarian Academy of Sciences, Sofia, Bulgaria
plamzlateva@abv.bg

Abstract. To create effective training programs for operators of ergatic systems, it is necessary to investigate their cognitive structures. A powerful tool for the study of the dynamics of complex systems is simulation. Cognitive structures are considered as compositions of professionally important qualities. The technology of synthesis of a composite simulation model of the cognitive structure of the operator from patterns that implement individual professional-important qualities is proposed.

Keywords: Ergatic system · Human-operator · Cognitive structure · Information technology · Synthesis · Conceptual patterns

1 Introduction

The effectiveness of a person's professional activity depends on his psycho-physiological state and the possibilities of mastering certain types of activity. Therefore, the actual problem is the training of an individual in certain types of professional activity, taking into account the individual characteristics of sensory, cognitive and motor responses [1]. This problem is most acute in the field of professional activity related to human-machine interaction. At present, an integrated approach is being born in the development of human-machine interaction from the standpoint of research and the formation of human cognitive structures.

We will consider the tasks of professional training of a human operator in man-machine systems. Analysis of the literature indicates that the modern concept of providing man-machine "cooperation" is based on the theory of ergatic systems. An ergatic system is a complex control system, of which the human operator is a component, and the

M. Goedicke et al. (Eds.): Advancing Research in Information and Communication Technology,
IFIP AICT 600, pp. 269–285, 2021. https://doi.org/10.1007/978-3-030-81701-5_11

main task is the optimal distribution of functions between the operator and the technical device and their mutual addition [2].

On the other hand, a system in which a human operator or group of operators interacts with a technical device in the process of production of material assets, management and information processing is called a human-machine system [3].

The concepts of "ergatic system" and "man-machine system" are identified in a number of works on ergonomics and engineering psychology. For example, we can find this point of view in the works of V. Mukhin [4], A. M. Bozhok and B. Kh. Draganova [5], V. A. Morozova et al. [6] etc. Other authors have a different meaning in these concepts. Among them are A. A. Piskoppel and L. P. Shchedrovitsky [7], A. P. Pyatibratov and M. Kh. Abdel-wahed [8].

In both cases, one of the objects of the system is a human operator, the need for the presence of which is determined by the following well-known factors:

- the person sets the goal of functioning, both the control object and the operation support system, and manages them to achieve this goal;

- for many reasons, an ergatic system cannot be absolutely reliable, therefore, operator intervention is required to monitor, diagnose and troubleshoot;

- due to the incompleteness and imperfection of our knowledge of all processes in the ergatic system in the external environment, situations may arise that are called algorithmically unsolvable.

According to the research of P. G. Belov [9] more than 60% of the largest incidents of the last century were registered at the last quarter of 20-th century, and 33% of them were in 80th years. At the same time, the damage from accidents, injuries and occupational diseases in the workplace reached 7–10% of the gross national product of industrialized countries.

Analysis of the accident rate at hazardous production facilities shows that the causes of about 70% of accidents are caused by the human factor [10, 11].

The human factor is an even more significant cause of accidents in the event of adverse events (for example, natural disasters) [12].

The above literature review indicates that the modern concept of ensuring the reliability of technogenic objects is based on the theory of ergatic systems.

One of the main goals of this concept is to reduce the likelihood of critical situations and risk zones, providing a mode of sustainable functioning of ergatic systems, which is possible only using a systematic approach to its design in an interdisciplinary research format.

The need to abandon the concept of the analysis of individual operator actions in favor of a model of joint human and machine performance is shown by E. Hollangel [13]. The author emphasizes the need for a comprehensive study of man-machine "co-operation", and not "interaction", as is customary now. The use of a systematic approach was proposed as a methodological basis instead of traditional methods of analysis and reliability assessment [13].

The main procedure for a systematic approach is a decomposition of the operator's professional qualification to the level of professionally important qualities in this context. For effective implementation of professional activity, the operator must have a certain set of professionally important qualities (PIQ) characterizing the physical, anatomical and physiological, mental and personal characteristics of a person, useful or necessary for the rapid and accurate development and solution of his professional tasks.

From the point of view of a systematic approach this set should be corresponded to the goal of the operator activity.

At present, the issues of the relationship between individual PIQs and the success of operator activities in general are not sufficiently studied, questions of developing tools for the intellectual support of managerial decisions on the degree of correspondence of the operator to the position deserve to be asked, there is an incomplete solution to the problem of professional selection and training of operational personnel based on the achievements of modern intelligent technologies.

Therefore, an important task is to study the cognitive structures of the operator in the form of compositions of PIQ, the possibilities of the development of PIQ, taking into account their mutual influence.

2 Research Methods

Modeling of the operator's cognitive structures is used to solve the task with the necessary completeness and versatility to achieve practical results. The features of cognitive structures, primarily their dynamic complexity, complicate the creation of models significantly.

Simulation in such cases allows for the most effective use of the experience and intuition of specialists in the study of complex systems. The development of computing technology led to the appearance in the 1960s of a specialized method of simulation modeling - system dynamics [14]. The method of system dynamics allows for exploring the behavior of complex systems, based on the possibilities of computer simulation. In contrast to the "traditional" methods of computer modeling, system dynamics gives the researcher the tools for modeling in the form of computer-implemented analytic descriptions of system elements and the connections between them.

Initially, the method was known as "industrial dynamics" and was used exclusively to study management problems in production [14]. After some time, this name ceased to correspond to the content, since the application of the method turned out to be much wider. It turned out to be effective for solving other problems, for example, related to urban dynamics, resource management, and the spread of diseases etc. Due to the fact that this method can be used for modeling and studying practically any complex systems, it was called system dynamics [15–17].

System dynamics is aimed at studying not the systems themselves, but the tasks associated with these systems. The main features of such systems is that they are dynamic, contain feedback loops, and their structure is characterized by delays, non-linearity and variability of the causes of complex behavior.

System dynamic models are not able to form their own solution in the form in which it takes place in analytical models, but can only serve as a means to analyze the behavior of the system under conditions that are determined by the experimenter [18].

An important component of system dynamics is the dialogue between the researcher, developer, designer in the modeling process with a complex that implements the model, which allows the most use of the experience and intuition of specialists in the study of real complex systems [19]. This is necessary to control the current results and the ability to adjust the development of the simulated situation in order to obtain new knowledge about the nature of the processes being studied, as well as to train specialists in working with new systems.

On the other hand, system dynamics has a significant limitation—limited modeling accuracy and the impossibility of its a priori estimation (an indirect characteristic of accuracy can be provided by analyzing the model's sensitivity to changes in individual parameters of the systems under study). In addition, developing a good dynamic model is often more expensive than creating analytical models and is time consuming. Nevertheless, system dynamics is one of the most widely used methods for solving the problems of synthesis and analysis of complex systems.

J. Forrester formulated the basic principles of the system dynamics method, which allow him to be considered as a method, despite the absence of a rigorous theoretical justification (14). And although it seems to people with a high mathematical background that system dynamics is a brute force technique, nevertheless, this method is the most common tool in the hands of a scientist involved in the problems of research and management of complex systems. J. D. Sterman refers to Weston's research [20], which examined the 1000 largest US firms in terms of analyzing the suitability of certain methods for in-house planning. The results of this study are shown in Table 1.

Table 1. Methods most commonly used in corpssorate planning

Methods	Frequency of using	Percent
Simulation	60	29
Linear programming	43	21
Theory of scheduling	28	14
Inventory theory	24	12
Nonlinear programming	16	8
Dynamic programming	8	4
Integer programming	7	3
Queueing theory	7	3
Other	12	6

The system dynamics method is based on four principles that determine the effectiveness of the method [14, 15].

The first principle: the dynamics of the behavior of an arbitrarily complex process can be reduced to a change in the values of some "levels", and the changes themselves can be regulated by flows filling or exhausting the levels.

The level accumulates the total amount of the studied "product", which is the result of flows entering and leaving it, the values of which are added or subtracted from the level. System levels fully describe the state of the system at any given time. The values of the levels are the information necessary for making decisions and justifying the control actions on the system. Levels provide the system with inertia and a "memory" of states; they create delays between the inflow and outflow as a cause and effect.

Changes in levels are caused by the corresponding flows.

A level can have a fixed value, or it can be controlled as a function of level values. Also the flow has a direction.

Thus, the totality of levels and flows implementing a model of the dynamics of the behavior of an "arbitrarily complex process" will be a system very similar to a water supply system consisting of various containers and pipes connecting them. But instead of physically simulating the dynamics of the system's behavior with the help of "water supply", it's convenient to use mathematical descriptions of the elements of the system dynamics model for this purpose, and to simulate the processes taking place in the system under study, use numerical methods for integrating these equations.

The concepts of levels and flows are present in many areas of human knowledge. Here are some examples: in mathematics these are integrals and derivatives, in physics these are stable states and transitions, in chemistry these are reagents, reaction products and chemical reactions themselves, in economics these are levels (e.g. welfare) and flows (e.g. labor force), in accounting these are stocks and flows (financial and material), in medicine these are the state of the body and the spread of infection, and so on. This list can be continued for a very long time, which indicates the obviousness of the proposed system dynamics principle proposed by J. Forrester [15].

The second principle: all changes in any system are determined by "feedback loops". The feedback loop is a closed chain of interactions that connects the original action with its result, which changes the characteristics of the surrounding conditions, and which, in turn, are "information" that causes changes.

The third principle: feedback loops in any system are often connected non-linearly. Essentially, this means that information about system levels through feedback indirectly affects levels in a disproportionate and sometimes difficult to predict mode.

The fourth principle: system dynamics is a purely pragmatic apparatus that is able to most adequately reflect the nontrivial behavior of a network of interacting flows and feedbacks. It is advisable to apply it only when traditional approaches are ineffective, when the behavior of objects cannot be accurately mathematically described and only rough estimates are possible.

The widespread use of system dynamics as a method of solving problems in various fields of human activity is becoming increasingly apparent. Therefore, despite the lack of mathematical elegance, system dynamics is one of the most widely used methods used to solve research and control problems.

But the construction of a composite model from them in the case when the object of study is a complex system becomes difficult. Therefore, the main focus of the research was on the search for ways to formalize and automate this process. Conceptual modeling was chosen as a vehicle for this. The conceptual model is used to move from the knowledge of experts to their uniform formal description. After that, a formal synthesis of the system dynamics model becomes possible [21].

The use of conceptual model for the formalization and integration of collective expert knowledge is presented in detail in our research [22].

3 Synthesis of System Dynamics Models Based on Conceptual Patterns Technology

Based on the proposed technology [5], a single conceptual model of the cognitive structure of the operator was obtained, combining the formalized knowledge of an expert group in the form of one or more tree structures, which further provides a formal synthesis of systems dynamics models.

The conceptual model is implemented in the form of a knowledge base consisting of declarative and procedural knowledge [6].

In order to solve the problems formulated, declarative knowledge is highlighted as follows:

– tree of goals of the professional activity of the operator Tr, contains a decomposition of the global goal and the material relations between them, taking into account the view of the problem of each expert;

– the set of patterns A;

– the set of instances of patterns E;

– the directories $V = \{Vk, W\}$.

The set concepts and terms are denoted by V. (The base contains information of domain, for example, different coefficients and constants. The set of norms and constants is denoted W.)

In turn, the goal tree can be formally written as the union of the set of vertices of all decomposition levels and the set of primitives—vertices for which no further splitting is performed:

$$Tr = \overset{n_k}{\underset{k=1}{\cup}} V^k \cup L$$

where k is the hierarchy level,

n_k is the number of vertices of the goal tree at the k-th level of the hierarchy.

$V^k = \overset{m}{\underset{l=1}{\cup}} V_l^{k-1}$ is the set, that is union of the vertices of the lower level, where m is the number of lower vertices for the given vertex.

The set L is the set of primitives of the conceptual model. The selection of these vertices into a separate set is due to the presence of a group of special inference procedures that perform actions only on elements from this set.

The pattern [7] implies a certain structure having a steady-state structure and a set of input, output parameters and initial values. In this paper, the pattern is implemented as a construct in the language of system diagrams.

Formally, a pattern can be represented by the following entry in the language of theory of sets:

$$P = \{St, \; Fn, \; X, \; Y, \; I\},$$

where *St* is the pattern structure, *Fn* is the pattern operation law, *X* is the set of pattern input parameters, *Y* is the set of pattern output parameters, *I* is the set of initial values.

In this paper, the pattern is considered as a "black box" with input and output parameters (Fig. 1).

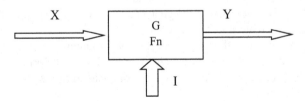

Fig. 1. The formal pattern "black box".

You must distinguish the pattern from the pattern instance. A pattern instance is a filled pattern that contains information not only about the composition and structure of the pattern, but also the specific values of the input, output and initial parameters of the pattern and, in addition, each instance is addressed (corresponds) to one of the primitives of the goal tree.

The declarative knowledge base contains facts that include: a set of pattern, mapped by experts to primitives, the goal tree itself, a set of auxiliary variables, reference books containing textual knowledge about the subject area under study.

Procedural knowledge of experts is implemented in the knowledge base in the form of inference procedures that allow for formalizing the process of synthesizing a dynamic model. The input of the procedures is the declarative knowledge of the knowledge base; the output is obtained fragments of system-dynamic models. Inference procedures are mappings of the structure of the conceptual model to the structure of dynamic models.

The knowledge base contains three groups of inference procedures:

1. Inference procedures that define covering actions for each model template. We will call them matching procedures.

2. Inference procedures that determine the material relationships between patterns in a dynamic model.

3. Inference procedures that determine the informational relationships between patterns in a dynamic model.

By sequentially performing these procedures, we obtain a composite model:

1) The conclusive procedures *D* and *d* determine covered operations for each pattern, i.e. how it (matches) opposites to the primitive of the goal tree.

a) The direct procedure for matching the primitive to the pattern.

The task of this procedure is to cover the primitive of the goal tree of the concept model by pattern, specifically, by instance of pattern.

Let *Tr* be a set of top points of the goal tree of the concept model, $L \subset Tr$ – a set of finite leaves – primitives, then procedure D can be defined as a mapping of the set of primitives to the set of instances.

$$D : L \rightarrow A, \tag{1}$$

what is more, $\forall l_i \in L \exists a_j \in A: f_i = Fn_j, i = \overline{1, m}, j = \overline{1, k}$,

where f_i is the goal of the primitive, Fn_j is the goal of pattern functioning (operation), m is the number of primitives of the goal tree of the conceptual model, k is the number of pattern instances.

That is, for any primitive there is an instance of the pattern covering it, if the law of the functioning of the pattern covers (satisfies) the goal (s) of the primitive.

Thus, the matching process is based on the functional coverage of the primitive goal by pattern $(f_i = Fn_j)$.

b) The procedure for specifying an instance.

To determine this procedure, it is necessary to introduce additional sets:

Let E be a set of all instances in the model, and A is a set of all patterns.

The procedure d can generally be represented as a mapping of multiple patterns to multiple terms and norms.

$$d : D(L) \rightarrow V \cup W, \tag{2}$$

what is more,

$\forall a_i \in A \exists e_j \in E: (\forall s \in St_i \rightarrow v \in V)$ and $(\forall c \in I_i \rightarrow w \in W), i = \overline{1, n}, j = \overline{1, k}$,

where n is the number of patterns in the system, k is the number of instances in the system.

That is, for any pattern from a set of model patterns, there is an instance only when each element of the pattern structure contains a corresponding element of a set of concepts and terms and when each initial value of the pattern is given a value from the norm base - a set of coefficients and constants W.

In other words, the task procedure fills the model patterns with specific content, which is taken from the directories (reference information), thereby creating many model instances.

2) The inference procedure that defines the material relationships between the instances of the patterns.

In this context, material relations are meant the linking of individual instances via the flows. Not only material resources, but also abstract objects can be transmitted through the flows in system dynamics. However, here a fundamental difference from the information connection between the patterns, which will be discussed below, is emphasized.

At this paper, the instance of pattern is the system-dynamic model that has its own structure and content (compound), input and output parameters. The flows are as input and output parameters, which can "inflow/outflow" (to/from), in other words, to be taken and to be provided as parameters to other patterns.

The main purpose of the above proposed withdrawal procedures is the formation of a new "higher level" submodel based on already formed "lower level" submodels in accordance with the hierarchy of goals.

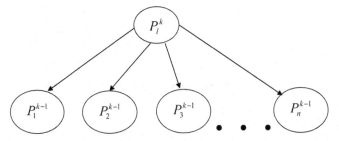

Fig. 2. The fragment of the goal tree.

Graphically, these procedures can be represented as shown in Fig. 2.

Let $P_1^{k-1}, ..., P_n^{k-1}$ are known patterns, h. e., functionally cover the corresponding vertices of the goal tree.

It is necessary to determine the rules for inferencing the sub model from these patterns, which covers parent vertex of the pattern tree P_l^k functionally. Where k is an hierarchy level of the goal tree vertex, $l = 1,...,n_k$, n_k is the number of vertices at the k-th hierarchy level.

In the general case, the parent vertex $P_l^k = \{<P_i^{k-1}, P_j^{k-1}>\}$, that is, represent a set of pairwise ordered pairs of its child vertices. Our task is to determine the binding procedure:

$$P_l^k = \varphi(\bar{P}_l^k) = \varphi(P_1^{k-1}, P_2^{k-1}, \ldots, P_{n_{k-1}}^{k-1}) \tag{3}$$

In the general case, with the requirement that all patterns become instances after they are filled, the procedure φ can be represented as a mapping of a subset of instances to the product of the same subset of itself.

$$\varphi : E_l \rightarrow E_l \times E_l, \text{ where } E_l \subset E, \tag{4}$$

what is more, $\forall e_i \in E_l \exists e_j \in E_l: < e_i, e_j > \in E_l \times E_l, i,j = \overline{1, n_k}$, n_k is the number of patterns in E_l: $(n_k < n)$.

So, scheme of mapping φ_k may be represented as a matrix φ_k ($n_k \times n_k$), rows and columns that match instances of model patterns. The values of the elements of this matrix represent the presence of relationships between existing models of models at the k-th hierarchy level.

Before describing the principles of matrix construction φ_k ($n_k \times n_k$), it is necessary to mention about union types between patterns. Two connection types are considered in this paper.

1. The series connection.

Here the output data, in our case represented by the flows, of one pattern is the input of another (Fig. 3). An explanation should be made here that the case when the input and output data are vectors is considered in the paper. For this reason, for simplicity of constructing the synthesis algorithm, situations are taken into account when the dimensions of the output and input vectors coincide, and the remaining cases are discarded.

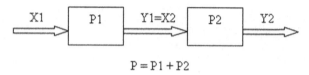

$$P = P1 + P2$$

Fig. 3. The example of a series connection of patterns.

2. The parallel connection.

In this type of union patterns, both patterns are included in the "higher level" model, and their input and output parameters are not connected in any way. In this case, only information relations between two patterns can occur, and the simultaneous modeling of these patterns is implied (Fig. 4).

To define a formal relationship between two patterns, redefine the standard notation for arithmetic operations: + - serial connection, * - parallel connection.

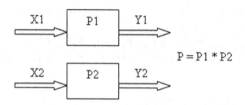

$$P = P1 * P2$$

Fig. 4. The example of parallel connection of patterns.

Therefore, the notation $P = P1 + P2$ means that $\forall y_i \in Y1 \; \exists \; x_j \in X2: y_i = x_j$, $i = 1, \bar{m}, j = \overline{1, n}$, n is the number of input parameters of the pattern $P2$, m is the number of output parameters of $P1$, actually $n = m$ (in this case).

Define the matrix k ($n_k \times n_k$).

$$\varphi_k = \begin{cases} 2, & \text{if } e_i * e_j \\ M_{ij}, & \text{if } e_i + e_j \\ 0, & \text{if } i = j \text{ if no connection between patterns} \end{cases} \tag{5}$$

where $i = 1, j = 1,\ldots, n_k$,

e_i, e_j – instances of patterns k-th level, if parent vertex is $\kappa + 1$ level,

M_{ij} – the matrix of conjugation of the input and output parameters of two copies.

In the trivial case, when each instance is supposed to have one input and output parameter, they do as follows: if there is a serial connection between the patterns, then the current matrix element will be equal to 1.

In the nontrivial case, the element M_{ij} is also a matrix

$$M_{ij} = B_{tp} = \begin{cases} 0, & \text{if } y_t \neq x_p \\ 1, & \text{if } y_t = x_p \end{cases} \tag{6}$$

where $t = 1, p = 1,\ldots, m$, m – the number of input/output parameters of patterns.

Thus, using the procedure described above, the material interconnection of the model patterns is established between themselves, that is, the relationship due to flows.

1) Inference procedures that determine the information relations of the system-dynamic model.

In system-dynamic models, in addition to material relations realized through the flows, information relations are widespread, the main purpose of which is to transmit information about values between model elements during the simulation process.

In the proposed approach, three types of information relations are considered depending on the type of interaction objects: the relationship between the structure elements of two patterns, the relationship between the auxiliary variable and the structure element of the pattern, the relationship between the structure element of the pattern and the auxiliary variable.

a) An inference procedure that defines informational relationships between structural elements of two instances of patterns.

Let $E_l \subset E$ be a subset of the set of model instances and contain instances covering all the child vertices of the parent vertex P_l^k of the goal tree (k is the hierarchy level, l is the vertex index at this level).

There after a mapping

$$\psi : E_l \rightarrow E_l \times E_l, E_l \subset E, \tag{7}$$

moreover $\exists\, e_i \in E_l \exists\, e_j \in E_l$:
$$< e_i, e_j > \in E_l \times E_l, i, j = \overline{(1, n_k)}, n_k \text{ is the number of patterns in } E_l.$$

$$\exists s_p \in St_i \in e_i \exists s_t \in St_j \in e_j :< s_p, s_t > \in St_i \times St_j \subset E_l \times E_l,$$

where $s \in [1; m_i]$ and $p \in [1; m_j]$, m_i and m_j – the number of elements of the structure in instances e_i and e_j respectively.

The first statement says that there is an information connection between two copies of the set E_l, and the second indicates between which elements of the structure of the copies this connection is established.

Consequently, the operator ψ can be represented as a mapping of a subset of the set of instances to the Cartesian product of this set by itself, indicating the elements of the structure of the instances between which an information relation is established in the general case.

The scheme of mapping ψ can be represented as a square matrix $\psi(n_k \times n_k)$, the rows and columns of which correspond to elements of the set E_l. The values of the elements of this matrix are determined by the presence of a connection between the corresponding instances of this set.

$$\psi_{ij} = \begin{cases} B_{ij}, \text{ if } e_i \in E_l \, \exists e_j \in E_l :< e_i, e_j >\in E_l \times E_l, i, j = 1, n_k \\ 0, \text{ if not} \end{cases} \tag{8}$$

In turn, the element B_{ij} of the matrix $\psi\,(n_k \times n_k)$ is also the matrix $B\,(m_i \times m_i)$, where m_i and m_j are the number of structural elements in instances e_i and e_j, respectively. The form of this matrix can be determined as follows:

$$B_{p,t} = \begin{cases} 1, \text{ if } s_p \in St_i \subset e_i \,\exists s_t \in St_j \subset e_j :< s_p, s_t > \in St_i \times St_j \\ 0, \text{ if not} \end{cases} \tag{9}$$

b) The inference procedure that defines the information relations between auxiliary variables and instances of model patterns is defined as the mapping of the set of auxiliary variables Vk obtained by adding expert knowledge about the modeling object to the product of this set with the set of instances of model E_l, which is a subset of the set of all instances of model E.

In the process of practical work on building system dynamic models based on patterns, the fact was revealed that to build an adequate model some patterns are not always enough. For this reason, many auxiliary variables have been introduced into the conceptual model. The main purpose of these objects is to supplement the model built on the basis of patterns with expert comments (estimates).

Let Vk is the set of auxiliary variables of the model, and E_l is the subset of instances of the model, thereafter

$$R1 : \; Vk \;\rightarrow\; Vk \times E_l, \; E_l \subset E \tag{10}$$

moreover, $\forall v_i \in Vk \exists e_j \in E_l :< v_i, e_j > \in Vk \times E_l,$ \qquad (11)

where $i = 1,\ldots,k$, k is the number of auxiliary variables of the model, $j = \overline{1, n_k}$, nk is the number of patterns in El.

Taking into account that each instance has its own internal structure and any element of the structure, i.e. $e_j = \; < St_j, Fn_j, X_j, Y_j, I_j >$, then statement (11) can be written in the following form:

$$\forall v_i \in Vk \exists e_j \in E_1 | \exists s_k \in St_j :< v_i, s_k > \in Vk \times St_j \subset Vk \times E_l \tag{12}$$

The scheme of mapping $R1$ can be represented as a square matrix $R1$ $(k \times n_k)$, the rows of which correspond to elements of the set of auxiliary elements Vk and columns correspond to elements of the set E_l.

The values of the elements of this matrix are determined by the presence of a connection between the corresponding elements of these sets.

$$R1_{ij} = \begin{cases} A_{ij}, \text{ if } v_i \in Vk \; \exists \, e_j \in E_1 :< v_i, e_j > \in Vk \times E_1 \\ 0, \text{ if not} \end{cases} \tag{13}$$

In turn, an element A_{ij} of the matrix $R1$ $(k \times n_k)$ is vector $A\,(m_j)$ also, where m_j is the number of elements of the instance structure e_j. The form of this vector is defined as follows:

$$A_t = \begin{cases} 1, \text{ if } v_i \in Vk \; \exists \, s_t \in St_j \in e_j :< v_i, s_t > \in Vk \times St_j \\ 0, \text{ if not} \end{cases} \tag{14}$$

c) An inference procedure that defines the information links between the elements of the structure of the pattern and auxiliary variables. It is defined as a mapping of the set of instances of the model E_l, which is a subset of the set of all instances of the model E to the product of this set with the set of auxiliary variables of the model Vk.

$$R2 : E_l \rightarrow E_l \times Vk, E_l \subset E \tag{15}$$

$$\text{moreover } \exists e_i \in E_l \exists v_j \in Vk : < e_i, v_j > \in E_l \times Vk, \tag{16}$$

where $i = \overline{1, n_k}$, n_k – the number of patterns in E_l, $j = 1,...,k$, k is the number of auxiliary variables of the model.

Taking in account, that each instance has its own internal structure and any element of the structure can act as a parameter of information communication, i.e. $e_i = < St_i, Fn_i, X_i, Y_i, I_i >$, then statement (16) can be written in the following form:

$$\exists (e_i \in E_l | \exists s_k \in St_i) \exists v_i \in Vk : < s_k, v_i > \in St_j \times Vk \subset E_l \times V_k \tag{17}$$

The scheme of mapping $R2$ can be represented as a square matrix $R2$ ($n_k \times k$), the columns of which correspond to elements of the set of auxiliary elements Vk, and rows correspond to elements of the set E_l. The values of the elements of this matrix are determined by the presence of a connection between the corresponding elements of these sets:

$$R2_{ij} = \begin{cases} C_{ij}, \text{ if } e_i \in E_l \exists v_j \in Vk : < e_i, v_j > \in E_l \times Vk \\ 0, \text{ if not} \end{cases} \tag{18}$$

In turn the element C_{ij} of the matrix $R1$ ($k \times n_k$) is a vector also, where m_i is the number of elements of instance structure e_i. The form of this vector is define as follows:

$$C_t = \begin{cases} 1, \text{ if } s_t \in St_i \in e_i \exists v_j \in Vk : < s_t, v_j > \in St_j \times Vk \\ 0, \text{ if not} \end{cases} \tag{19}$$

Application of the given procedures to the corresponding sets of declarative knowledge provides a formal synthesis of the composition and structure of the dynamic model, adequate to the declarative knowledge of the knowledge base, which is the implementation of the conceptual model of the studied subject area.

4 Evaluation of Accuracy of a Composite Model

A technique for quantifying the accuracy of recurrent dynamic models implemented in instrumental environments using standard integration methods is proposed by Bystrov [7, 8].

The simulation errors considered below are by their nature approximation errors and, at the stage of creating corresponding models, they can be attributed to method errors. As a basic approach to quantifying errors, the method of the reference model was used in the following modification, directly oriented to simulation modeling.

Assuming that:

1. the studied dynamic model M is a precisely known and unambiguously determined composition of relatively independent submodels;

$$M = K\{M_i | i \in I\} \tag{20}$$

2. for each of the M_i sub-models named in paragraph (1), a reference linear recurrent model

$$< M_i; \Delta T_i > \text{ is known, } i \in I;$$

3. the only sources of error for the compositional model under investigation are:

a) deviation of the system-wide time from the elementary cycles of the submodels;
b) the integration method used.

An additional essential assumption for the proposed approach is the assumption about the smoothness of the nominal characteristic function of errors within the real error band of each of the used submodels M_i, $i \in I$. In practice, this assumption allows the real error curves of submodels within the error band to be replaced by the smoothed (in other words, properly filtered) curve.

It should also be noted that the reasons for errors specified in paragraph (3) are additive. The circumstance specified here allows instead of a set of reference models $< M_i; \Delta T_i >$, $i \in I$, for each integration method, simply consider the corresponding cumulative nominal error functions (CNEF).

In the considered method of estimating the methodological error of recurrent dynamic models for the construction of CNEF, linear, parabolic, cubic approximation of functions were used. For each type of approximation, optimization theorems are proved, on the basis of which an analysis of methodological errors is constructed, which made it possible to carry out and substantiate the correctness of the choice of the optimal integration step for composite dynamic models. The statements of the theorems are given below. The proof of the theorems was carried out using the mathematical apparatus and methods of the theory of extreme problems, namely, linear programming, since the problem of studying methodological errors can be reduced to the problem of finding extreme points of the generalized error function of the composite model.

The system time is considered to be a valid value from the interval [0, 1], which is achieved by simple normalization of the values of the elementary cycles of the submodels, i.e. scaling with the coefficient

$$\frac{1}{\max_{i \in I} \Delta T_i}$$

of the set $\{\Delta T_i \,|\, i \in I\}$ characteristic cycles of submodels. In addition, it is further considered $i = \overline{1, 2}$, that this will avoid the need for a detailed account of the "inversion" points for the error curves of the submodels on the set of values of the reduced cycles.

Thus,

$$\frac{1}{\max_{i \in I} \Delta T_i} * \min_{i \in I} \Delta T_i = a \leq b = 1$$

the normalized cycles of submodels, with the corresponding error functions $f_1(t)$ and $f_2(t)$.

Theorem 1. If CNEF $f_i(t)$, $i = \overline{1, 2}$, decomposition elements $\{M_1; M_2\}$ of the dynamic model M are linear with respect to t, then the optimal value ΔT^* of the system time minimizing the error of approximation of M coincides with one of the boundaries of the interval $[a, b]$.

Theorem 2. The pair composition of recurrent dynamic models with the same type of CNEF of the form (21) achieves the smallest approximation error for.

$$\Delta T = \frac{k_1 a + k_2 b}{k_1 + k_2} \text{ and } \begin{cases} f_1(t) = k_1(t - a)^2 \\ f_2(t) = k_2(t - b)^2 \end{cases} \tag{21}$$

Theorem 3: The set of optimal system time values for a pair composition of recurrent dynamic models that have the same type of CNEF type (22) is non-empty and contains at least one point of the set.

$$\begin{cases} \dfrac{(k_1 a - k_2 b) + (b - a)\sqrt{k_1 k_2}}{k_1 - k_2}; \dfrac{(k_1 a - k_2 b) - (b - a)\sqrt{k_1 k_2}}{k_1 - k_2} \end{cases} \text{ and } \\ \begin{cases} f_1(t) = k_1(t - a)^3 \\ f_2(t) = k_2(b - t)^3 \end{cases} \tag{22}$$

Theorems 2 and 3 allow for generalization the results obtained to multiple compositions of recurrent submodels possessing linear CNEF. The empirical method of differentiation of the branches of the CNEF intermediate models can be used as the basis for the formation of the composite error function.

5 Conclusion

For the purpose of studying the cognitive structures of a human operator of ergatic systems, an information technology has been developed for the conceptual synthesis of simulation models (cognitive structures). The technology is based on the use of conceptual modeling. The implementation of the conceptual model in the form of a knowledge base provides for the autonomous use of expert knowledge for the automated synthesis of simulation models. Formal procedures that provide synthesis based on the conceptual model of the corresponding simulation model from a set of patterns. A technique for the quantitative assessment of accuracy is proposed, which makes it possible to optimize the choice of the integration step for composite simulation models built from patterns.

Acknowledgments. The current work reflects the main concept of the International Federation for Information Processing (IFIP) to be the leading multinational, apolitical organization in Information & Communications Technologies and Sciences. The paper emphasizes the goal of IFIP

TC5 – Application of Information Technology - to produce solid scientific results in the field of ITC, combining the efforts of destingushed authors from countries with different political status into an international interdisciplinary research that will contribute to the mankind prosperity.

The reported study was funded by RFBR and NSFB, project number 20–57-18004.

References

1. Petukhov I., Steshina, L., Kurasov, P., Tanryverdiev, I.: Decision support system for assessment of vocational aptitude of man-machine systems operators. In: IEEE 8th International Conference on Intelligent Systems IS 2016, Sofia, Bulgaria, pp. 778–84 (2016)
2. Petukhov, I.V.: Decision support system in assessing the professional suitability of the operator of ergatic systems (for example, transport and technological machines) DSc Thesis (Ufa:USATU), 411 p. (2013)
3. Man-machine system. Soviet encyclopedic dictionary, 1226 p. Sovetskaya Entsyklopedia, Moscow (1980)
4. Mukhin, V. I.: Research of Control Systems. Analysis and Synthesis of Control Systems, 383 p. "Examen", Moscow (2003)
5. Bozhok, A.M., Draganov, B.Kh.: On the ergonomics of agricultural vehicles. Energetika i avtomatika: Electron. Sci. J. 3 (2010). http://www.nbuv.gov.ua/e-journals/eia/2010_3/10b ameav.pdf
6. Morozova, V.A.: The technology of using expert systems for automated control of energy-eco-efficient processes in metallurgy. In: All-Russian Scientific and Practical Conference on Automation Systems in Education, Science and Production, Novokuznetsk, SibGIU, pp. 18–22 (2007)
7. Piskoppel, A.A., Shchedrovitsky, L.P.: 1982 from the "man-machine" system to the "sociotechnical" system. Psychology 3, 15–25 (1982)
8. Pyatibratov, A.P., Abdel-wahed, M.Kh.: Conceptual provisions for assessing the reliability and fault tolerance of a distributed local computer network (DLCN). Univ. Open Educ. Sci. Pract. J. 5, 52–56 (2006)
9. Belov, P.G.: Theoretical Foundations of the Management of Technological Risk. Abstract of DSc, 32 p. STC PS, Moscow (2007)
10. Magid, S.I., Arkhipova, E.N., Muzyka, L.P.: The reliability of personnel is one of the main guarantees of energy security. Reliab. Safety Energy 1, 22–33 (2008)
11. Pulikovsky, K.B.: Priority to the quality of training, vocational training and certification of employees of organizations supervised by Rostekhnadzor. Labor Safety Ind. 728 (2006)
12. Velev, D., Zlateva, P.: Augmented and virtual reality application in disaster preparedness training for society resilience. In: 18th International Multidisciplinary Scientific GeoConference (SGEM 2018), vol. 4.3, pp. 195–202 (2018)
13. Hollangel, E.: Human reliability assessment in context. Nucl. Eng. Technol. 37(2), 159–166 (2005)
14. Forrester, J.W.: Industrial Dynamics, 464 p. Productivity Press, Portland (1961)
15. Forrester, J.W.: Urban Dynamics, 285 p. Productivity Press, Portland (1969)
16. Forrester, J.W., Senge, P.M.: Tests for building confidence in system dynamics models. In: Legasto, A.A. (ed.) System Dynamics, pp. 209–228. North-Holland, Studies in the Management Sciences, New York (1980)
17. Roberts, N., Andersen, D., Deal, R., Garet, M., Shaffer, W.: Introduction to Computer Simulation: A System Dynamics Modeling Approach, 562 p. Productivity Press, Portland (1983)

18. Shannon, R.: Systems Simulation: The Art and Science, 417 p. "Mir", Moscow (1978)
19. Pavlovsky, Y.N.: Course of Lectures: Simulation Models and Systems, 122 p. "Phasis", Moscow (1998)
20. Sterman, J.D.: Business Dynamics: Systems Thinking and Modeling for a Complex Word, 768 p. Irwin/McGraw-Hill, Boston (2000)
21. Gorokhov, A.V.: Synthesis and analysis of models of system dynamics of regional social and economic development. DSc thesis, ISA RAS, Moscow (2003)
22. Gorokhov, A.V., Petukhov, I.V., Steshina, L.A.: The integration technology for collective expert knowledge in the tasks of developing scenarios for vocational guidance and employees' rehabilitation Eurasia. J. Math. Sci. Technol. Educ. **13**(11), 7517–7526 (2017). https://doi.org/10.12973/ejmste/80012

TC 6: Communication Systems

Blockchains and Distributed Ledgers Uncovered: Clarifications, Achievements, and Open Issues

Eder J. Scheid$^{(\boxtimes)}$ ⓘ, Bruno B. Rodrigues ⓘ, Christian Killer ⓘ,
Muriel F. Franco ⓘ, Sina Rafati ⓘ, and Burkhard Stiller ⓘ

Communication Systems Group CSG, Department of Informatics IfI,
University of Zürich UZH, Binzmühlestrasse 14, CH–8050 Zürich, Switzerland
{scheid,rodrigues,killer,franco,rafati,stiller}@ifi.uzh.ch

Abstract. Although the first Blockchain (BC) was proposed about a
decade ago, BC achievements from a technical and functional perspective are measurable, but still face open issues. Since IFIP's Working
Group 6.6 on the "Management of Networks and Distributed System"
investigated BCs in various aspects, this contribution here summarizes
and clarifies key characteristics of BCs and their related approach of Distributed Ledgers (DL).

While many properties are under discussion, the two approaches differ measurably. In turn, the value of BCs and DLs is outlined in combination with selected and exemplified application domains. However, a
set of open issues has been observed, which possibly hinders a practical
operation, *e.g.,* due to excessive expectations, missing interoperability,
wrong scalability promises, or out-of-scope trust assumptions. Thus, the
state-of-the-art in BCs and DLs is clarified and current as well necessary
research steps to follow complement this state.

Keywords: Blockchains · Distributed Ledger · Scalability · Trust

1 Introduction

The International Federation for Information Processing (IFIP) Technical Committee (TC) 6, being focused on the "Communications Systems" broader area,
(*i*) promotes the exchange of knowledge in this field, (*ii*) connects telecommunication users, manufacturers, and providers, and (*iii*) aids standardization bodies
in their efforts. This work is achieved via nine Working Groups (WG) as well
as Special Interest Groups (SIG), the majority of which are concerned either
with specific aspects of communications systems themselves or with the application of communications systems. With its decentralized nature, IFIP TC6 is
the supporter and all WGs operate autonomously, while tackling diverse aspects
of telecommunication, ranging from architectures and protocols for distributed
systems (WG6.1) via network and inter-network architectures (WG6.2), the

© IFIP International Federation for Information Processing 2021
Published by Springer Nature Switzerland AG 2021
M. Goedicke et al. (Eds.): Advancing Research in Information and Communication Technology,
IFIP AICT 600, pp. 289–317, 2021. https://doi.org/10.1007/978-3-030-81701-5_12

performance of communication systems (WG6.3), the management of networks and distributed systems (WG6.6), smart networks (WG6.7), mobile and wireless communications (WG6.8), communications systems for developing countries (WG6.9), photonic networking (WG6.10), communication aspects of the eWorld (WG6.11) to services-oriented systems (WG6.12). In this setting, WG6.6 had selected from 2014 onward the Blockchain (BC) topic as one, which is by itself determines an approach to be managed, resulting in certain security-related outcomes, and which manages data handling in a distributed setting, too, well beyond known approaches' characteristics. Thus, this chapter here discusses key characteristics of BCs and their related approach of a Distributed Ledger (DL), since the two approaches differ measurably.

Since BCs and DLs do provide due to their characteristics suitable means for the management of networks and distributed systems, too, respective umbrella work is performed as well in the context of IFIP by IFIP's TC6 on "Communication Systems", especially within the Working Group (WG) 6.6 on "Management of Networks and Distributed Systems". Thus, since 2017 the IFIP/IEEE Network Operations and Management Symposium (NOMS) [58,63], the IFIP/IEEE International Symposium on Integrated Network Management (IM) [8,57,64], and the International Conference on Network and Service Management (CNSM) [45] included a set of BC- and DL-related keynotes, reviewed papers, and tutorials, which had become part of their respective scientific programs.

1.1 Blockchain History

A bit longer than a decade ago, the Computer Science community was presented with Bitcoin [48], which was, at that time, yet another proposal for electronic cash. However, unlike previous proposals [3,17,65], Bitcoin successfully solved the double-spending problem (*i.e.,* same coin spent twice) in practice and a fully decentralized manner, without the need for a Trusted Third Party (TTP), by combining Peer-to-Peer (P2P) mechanisms, applied cryptography, and time-stamping principles to form an immutable, decentralized, and publicly verifiable ledger of transactions, called *Blockchain* (BC).

Since then, BCs were applied in different areas and use cases [13] due to pseudonymity, low transaction fees, open access, and immutability. Currently, BCs in academia's and public's perception can be observed by more than 9,100 cryptocurrencies listed [20] and over 13,200 BC-related projects registered with versioning control providers [30]. Although time-stamping services existed in the past [33], too, their full decentralization became only possible with an underlying BC, which by itself benefited from earlier developments of a block-based Byzantine storage, applying cryptographic hashes on user data to be stored [46].

The extensive employment of the BC in a wide range of application domains and the exponential growth in popularity has led to the development and research of novel BC platforms [5], with many approaches tackling specific problems of earlier approaches and claiming to solve them. However, not all BC platforms follow the same core principles as the first BC proposal (*i.e.,* Bitcoin) did, as their deployment models, consensus mechanisms, and underlying data structures differ drastically. For example, Ripple [16] restricts the privilege to write blocks to a set of defined nodes, EOS [24] employs a consensus mechanism, where miners are elected and selected based on the number of coins they hold (*i.e.*, their stake), and IOTA [38] implements a Directed Acyclic Graph (DAG) to store transactions. These and many other platforms cannot be considered BCs *per se* but should be defined as Distributed Ledgers (DL).

Both BCs and DLs are evolving currently at a fast pace due to academic research, industrial incentives, and intense funding of projects based on such approaches [35]. However, the differences between BCs and DLs are not easy to grasp and are still fuzzy for users. Although seemingly similar at first glance, BCs and DLs inherently features various advantages and disadvantages, which have to be balanced with the needs of the application area in question. Thus, it is essential to distinguish these two approaches and clarify key differences to users who plan to develop, apply, or invest in projects or companies at the doorstep to employ BCs or DLs in their current operation, *e.g.*, supply-chain [8].

Therefore, this paper contributes besides past work of [9] especially to the clarification of key characteristics of BCs and DLs, while presenting measurable advantages and drawbacks of the two approaches in combination with selected platforms and exemplified application domains. Based on this discernment, the paper (*a*) details those open issues concerning the applicability of BCs and DLs in real life, and (*b*) outlines further research directions to increase their maturity, contributing to the state-of-the-art in this area.

1.2   Paper Structure

The remainder of this paper is organized as follows. First, Sect. 2 explains the necessary background and definitions, and summarizes selected platforms. Second, Sect. 3 clarifies the differences between BCs and DLs, which is followed by Sect. 4 summarizing the value of BCs and DLs. While Sect. 5 discusses open issues, finally, Sect. 6 draws conclusions.

2   Laying the Groundwork—Technical Background

Several concepts, paradigms, and mechanisms build the foundations for BC and DL. Therefore, a concise understanding of major building blocks is required to understand the intricacies of BC and DL, which supports the remainder of this paper. Thus, their description and a set of selected BC implementations and their differences exemplify this understanding.

2.1   Public-Key Cryptography

Public-Key Cryptography (PKC) first emerged to solve the main drawback of symmetric cryptography: the exchange of secret keys [27,66]. Asymmetric cryptography mitigates the key distribution issues by using a public and a private key. These keys are associated in a mathematical way. Knowledge about the public key does not allow one to compute anything about the private key. However, knowing the private key allows unlocking the information encrypted with the public key [66]. In general, PKC relies on the hardness of reversing certain mathematical operations, often referred to as *trapdoors*.

For instance, the resilience of PKC systems (*e.g.,* RSA and ElGamal) stems from the hardness of inverting the exponentiation of prime numbers, often referred to as the Discrete Logarithm problem [66]. PKC is also used to build digital signature schemes. The Digital Signature Algorithm or DSA (often referred to as the Digital Signature Standard, DSS [66], too) preserves the integrity of messages exchanged between two parties. Originally, DSA was designed to work in finite fields. Today, it is common to use it with Elliptic Curves (EC), in which case it is referred to as EC-DSA. The EC variants of DSA run very fast and have smaller footprints as well as key sizes than almost all other signature algorithms [66], which is why EC-DSA is favored in the context of BCs.

Two fundamental processes of BCs make use of PKC: (*i*) Address Generation and (*ii*) Transaction Signing. In (*i*), a valid BC address is generated by using an algorithm based on a public key, which in turn is associated with a private key. In (*ii*), BC transactions are cryptographically signed to guarantee that funds can only be spent by their owners *i.e.,* who know the private key. Figure 1 depicts the generic BC address generation process. The process relies on cryptographic one-way hash functions. These functions take an arbitrary length bit string as input and produce a fixed-length bit string as output. In that context, *one-way* means that it should be computationally infeasible to retrieve the matching input with the usage of a hash digest. Thus, cryptographic hash functions are used to shield the public keys, and only hash digests serve as public identifiers, *i.e.,* BC addresses of the electronic wallet and can thus be used to receive funds. Only users in possession of the corresponding private key can generate authentic BC transactions, which control the funds associated with that wallet. Transactions are validated by verifying the digital signatures.

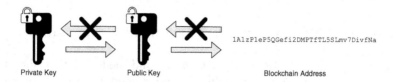

Private Key   Public Key   Blockchain Address

1AlzP1eP5QGefi2DMPTfTL5SLmv7DivfNa

Fig. 1. Address Generation based on Public Keys

Typically, to issue a valid transaction, a user must create a transaction containing the source address (*i.e.,* his/her BC address), the destination BC address, the amount to be transferred, and possibly, the miner fee (*cf.* Sect. 2.2). After this transaction is created, the user must digitally sign it with the corresponding BC address' private key to create a signed, raw transaction, which is broadcast to all computing devices (*i.e.,* peers and their nodes), connected through the Internet, that run applications which implement the BC protocol (*i.e.,* the

BC network). Such a transaction stays in the transaction pool until a miner includes it into a new block. To verify, if the owner of that BC address issued the transaction, anyone could use the public key of that user to confirm that this transaction was not modified by anyone else. Thus, this process provides, in general, the *integrity* and *authenticity* properties of the BC transaction.

2.2 Mining on a Blockchain

The process of validating transactions, adding a new block, solving a crypto puzzle, and minting (*i.e.*, creating) new coins (which are just different terms for the exact same action) in Proof-of-Work (PoW)-based BCs is called "mining" [29]. Mining is performed by dedicated, but not pre-determined nodes in a BC network; these nodes are termed "miners", which store all transactions of that BC, starting from the "genesis block" (*i.e.*, block number 0) to the most recent block. These miners need to maintain this information in order to verify if new transactions are valid or not, which leads to a fully decentralized solution of the double-spending problem (*i.e.*, the same coins spent twice) [48].

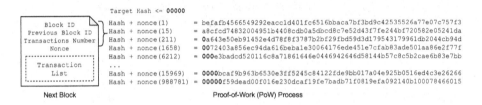

Fig. 2. Hash-based Proof-of-Work (PoW)

For example, in the Bitcoin BC [48] a new block is added to the BC every 10 min by the fastest miner that provided a solution satisfying the crypto puzzle, which resembles a specific form of a hash value of that block with a predefined number of preceding zeros, all based on an agreed-upon hash function. In order to determine this result, a miner must spend significant computational power to calculate this hash values (*cf.* Fig. 2) based on the content of that block proposed (*e.g.*, transactions, headers, and previous block number), and a random number used once (*i.e.*, nonce).

Moreover, miners compete with other miners to find this hash value; thus, the more computational power a miner has, the larger likelihood it has of finding that value. As soon as the miner finds a suitable hash value, it broadcasts the same block, that hash value, and the nonce to the BC network, such that other nodes can verify the correctness of this hash value. This can be performed basically at "no cost", since this verification requires the calculation of this only hash value based on all data known, including the hash function itself. If the hash value is correct, the Bitcoin BC protocol creates an additional transaction containing the reward to that miner, who found this suitable hash value first. Such a reward fee is paid for each successfully persisted block of BC transactions. Since this is an interactive process, it starts all over again once the block is persisted into the chain by taking newly available BC transactions from the mining pool.

2.3   A Few Handful of Blockchain Platforms

Since 2009, more than 9,000 BC platforms, cryptocurrencies, and tokens were proposed [20]. Not all systems proposed so far differ in all dimensions; they may be based on a few dozens of really distinct BC platforms. Thus, systems with the primary goal to offer cryptocurrencies and tokens (in general, an electronic representation of a digital asset) differ from systems, which exploit cryptocurrencies and tokens in an application-specific manner. Therefore, this paper selected such technically different BC platforms that (partially, due to space constraints) represent major BC and DL characteristics, namely Bitcoin, Ethereum, Hyper-Ledger, IOTA, and Bazo (*cf.* Table 1).

Table 1. Platform Comparison

Platform	Type	Data Structure	Consensus	Tps	Notes
Bitcoin	Public	Blocks	PoW	7	First BC proposal
Ethereum	Public	Blocks	PoW	15	Turing-complete Smart Contracts
HyperLedger	Private	Blocks	Many	Variable	Umbrella project: enterprise focused platforms
IOTA	Public	DAG	Own	1,000	IoT BC
BAZO	Experimental	Blocks	PoS	50	Research and experimental BC

Transactions per Second (Tps), Internet-of-Things (IoT)

Bitcoin was originally proposed under the pseudonym "Satoshi Nakamoto" in 2009. This proposal of an experimental cryptocurrency created a fully public and decentralized one, which achieved over time a significant standing due to the disruptive potential of the technical platform on which it is based on, the BC [48]. The conceptual design based on the PoW consensus mechanism (*cf.* Sect. 2.2) providing the guarantee of security and immutability continues up to today as "secure" [28], since no BC-related error or flaw had been discovered.

One of the main factors that contribute to the current success of Bitcoin is the incentive scheme for peers participating in the BC network as miners [48]. Henceforth, incentives do not only ensure that nodes generate valid blocks through the PoW consensus mechanism but also ensure that malicious nodes are not encouraged to assemble more CPU power than all honest nodes. Following the success of Bitcoin, several other cryptocurrencies were created based on Bitcoin's source code [20]. These are typically called *Altcoins*, in which their code includes several modifications in its parameters to tackle different parameters and use cases than

Bitcoin (*e.g.*, block size or creation time). For instance, the Bitcoin protocol has a block time that can be considered too long for some financial applications; thus, certain Altcoins (*e.g.*, Litecoin [41] and Monero [40]) reduce this block creation time, as well as difficulty in PoW hashing competition. Monero, for instance, offers additional security features based on a ring-signature scheme in which transactions can be fully obscured.

Despite the experimental cryptocurrency's success, a performance drawback ensures the security of the PoW model and consensus mechanism [28]. Notably, the resulting large energy consumption by design being generated as an effect of these partial hash collisions, in which several nodes miners participate in a competition to find a suitable hash value above a certain target with X leading zeros, determines only one node as the winner [42]. Additionally, an "unwanted" side effect of these computational demands matures in lower scalability and throughput of the chains in terms of Tps achieved, *e.g.*, 7 Tps in the case of Bitcoin [21]. Thus, if many transactions are submitted at the same time, especially exceeding the storage capacity of a single block, some users' transactions will have to wait until their transactions are appended into a block by a miner, consequently increasing the delay for a confirmation.

Ethereum originated with the intent of creating a public BC platform, where general distributed applications can be built on. The main drivers for such a proposal and the development of Ethereum were the limitations of Bitcoin's scripting language, which does not provide for Turing-completeness or even states. These limitations were solved in Ethereum by relying on (*a*) an account-based BC, which is different from a UTXO model since it modifies the state of an account, and (*b*) an underlying built-in Smart Contract (SC) language (*cf.* Sect. 4.2) providing the capability to developers to write Turing-complete programs, which can operate as SCs [10,75].

Blocks in Ethereum are smaller and are created faster (on average every 14 s) compared to *e.g.*, Bitcoin's block creation time being on average at 10 min. Thus, the overall Ethereum BC size grows faster, too. To alleviate this increase in size, Ethereum implemented apart from full nodes, which store the whole BC data, two other node types: (*i*) fast nodes and (*ii*) light nodes. Fast nodes only store block headers, and light nodes have to rely on full nodes to retrieve blocks when necessary. However, full nodes are always required to perform the mining and execution of SCs. Further, Ethereum's consensus mechanism "ethash" was developed to tackle the danger of centralization imposed by mining pools in Bitcoin [56]. These mining pools exist because the PoW algorithm of Bitcoin can be implemented and performed by Application-Specific Integrated Circuits (ASIC), and miners retrieve block headers from a central pool and perform the PoW on these headers, without needing to maintain the whole BC. Ethash tackles this problem by being more memory-hungry, which is quite expensive in ASICs, and by asking for miners to fetch random blocks, which requires the storage of the entire BC. Nevertheless, "ethash" is based on PoW and, ultimately, is susceptible to centralization, too.

As of today, Ethereum does not scale either, achieving 15 Tps [7], and it is not energy-efficient by relying on PoW consensus mechanisms. However, plans exist to move within Ethereum from PoW to a Proof-of-Stake (PoS) consensus mechanism implementation (*cf.* Sect. 5.4) in the near future [12]. With such a change, sharding can be implemented, which can improve transaction rates by adding clusters of PoS block validators and which contributes to secure the entire Ethereum BC. Thus, the overall energy consumption can be reduced, and the overall scalability can be improved.

HyperLedger (HL) is a cross-industry, open-source project managed by The Linux Foundation. HL includes 14 projects, four are active, and ten are in the "Incubation" phase and not yet ready for full deployment [72]. Thus, this section focus on the four active DL projects by HL:

- *HL Fabric*'s development is mainly driven by IBM, and the initial vision was first described in [1]. HL Fabric supports multiple levels of privacy. Channels enable P2P data sharing, leading to complete data isolation between a set of participants, where each channel a private communication channel between two or more specific network members, enabling confidential transactions. Private data collections enable P2P transactions between authorized participants, keeping data private to a subset of transactors (and potentially regulators/auditors). Private data is only shared P2P, with hashes stored on the BC, offering verifiable evidence to all peers, which can validate transactions. Additionally, an optional Identity Mixer can be deployed to increase the anonymity of transaction submitters.
- *HL Indy* determines an independent project but is commonly associated with "The Sovrin Foundation" [68], which is a public utility for identity, built on top of Indy's codebase. HL Indy's goal is to develop a set of decentralized identity specifications independent of any particular ledger, thus, enabling interoperability across any DL that supports them. HL Indy allows for an identity-based authentication on attributes users are willing to store and share. This can reduce the risks of certain business cases because the data can be kept with the respective user and presented in a way that others can trust and verify the data independently.
- *HL Iroha* was initially developed by Japanese developers for an application-specific BC for a mobile use case. Iroha mainly differs from other DLs, because Iroha offers a novel Byzantine Fault Tolerance (BFT) consensus algorithm called YAC, which specifies a practical decentralized consensus algorithm, guaranteeing the fast finality of transactions with low latency measures. Further, Iroha offers built-in commands as a significant benefit compared to other platforms, since it is straightforward to specify and perform everyday tasks easily, such as creating digital assets, registering accounts, and transferring assets between accounts. Moreover, the narrow focus of Iroha decreases the attack surface, and thus, improves the overall security of the system, since fewer steps may fail or can be exploited. Finally, Iroha is the only DL with robust access control, allowing permissions to be set for all commands, queries, and joining of the network.

– *HL Sawtooth* is similar to Fabric in many aspects, with the main difference that Intel is the company driving the development of Sawtooth, which uses the Proof-of-Elapsed-Time (PoET) consensus mechanism [36]. Thus, depending on Intel's Software Guard Extensions (SGX) leaders are elected to mine blocks based on random wait times. Also, peers have access to all transaction data, unlike in Fabric, where "private" channels can be established.

At this moment, HL Fabric is the most active and prominent HL project. HL Fabric is actively researched and, in theory, able to scale up to 20,000 transactions per second [25]. HL Indy and The Sovrin Foundation are at the forefront of decentralized identifiers, and the paradigm "Privacy-by-Design" seems to be implemented well. In contrast, HL Iroha has a particular and narrow use case, focusing on mobile applications. Finally, HL Sawtooth is the most versatile of active HL projects. The main differences to Fabric cover the PoET consensus mechanism, which allows for a permissioned or permissionless deployment, whereas HL Fabric only allows for a permissioned deployment. However, the dependency on Intel's SGX for that specific consensus mechanism is unfavorable for permissionless settings, since it introduces another TTP, *i.e.,* Intel.

IOTA was developed by the IOTA community and made its public appearance in October 2015, while being supported by the IOTA Foundation. Its major difference from other BCs is that it utilizes a different data structure to store transactions, called the Tangle [55]. In the Tangle each transaction (rather than a block of transactions) references to two previous transactions, forming a complex Web structure known in mathematics as a Directed Acyclic Graph (DAG). The directed feature is needed to ensure that all reference pointers point in the same direction. Acyclicity is demanded because following a path from any transaction and arriving back at the same transaction is not allowed, (*i.e.,* no loops). Moreover, the deployment of a graph suits well, since all reference pointers and transactions form a graph of edges and vertices. Importantly, such a DAG structure allows transactions to be issued simultaneously, asynchronously, and continuously, as opposed to the discrete-time intervals and linear expansion of other BC [38].

By parallelizing transaction issuance and validation, IOTA can achieve a significantly higher transaction throughput at 1,000 Tps [15]. However, the introduction of such parallelization exposes the Tangle to uncontrolled growth attacks, such as parasite chains and splitting [55]. To solve these issues (until the development and testing of mitigation algorithms [37]), IOTA (*a*) introduced the concept of a central "coordinator", which confirms unreferenced transactions every minute, and (*b*) required that new transactions must directly or indirectly reference these confirmed transactions by the "coordinator". Ultimately, securing and controlling the Tangle at the cost of introducing a central entity [37].

In BCs, a bifurcation of roles between the miners and users exist, *i.e.,* interests are opposing (miners want slower transaction confirmation times and collect higher fees, whereas users want higher confirmation time and lower fees). In contrast, the Tangle aligns incentives of all participants equally [38], since every node issuing an IOTA transaction also actively participates in the consensus.

Because there are no miners in the Tangle, transaction validation is an intrinsic part of transaction issuance, and thus, there are no transaction fees. The value which sent is always equal to the value which is received. This approach enables feeless micro and nano-payments, which emerging machine-to-machine communications, *e.g.*, for the Internet-of-Things (IoT), and a sharing economy will require to be able to operate at scale.

BAZO is a research-oriented, experimental BC, with the focus on providing an environment, where researchers and students can experiment with new consensus mechanisms, transaction and account models, sharding schemes, scalability investigations, and novel BC techniques [51]. BAZO's chain-based protocol is developed for simplicity reasons such that the PoS protocol works comparably to the PoW consensus mechanism with a key difference: BAZO designs a throttled PoW algorithm. Since a validator is limited to precisely one hash per second, BAZO defines a semi-synchronous system, such that every node can run on its own local time. If a node attempts to speed up his hashing power, the system detects the malicious node, and suggested blocks are rejected. BAZO chooses validators proportionally to the number of coins that each validator owns.

The basic design concept of the PoS protocol employed in BAZO includes a validator wishing to participate in the staking process, it has to publish a "Stake Transaction" well in advance in order to join the set of validators and he has to fulfill a PoS condition to determine if he or she is eligible to append a block to the BAZO BC. A block must contain information that proves the eligibility of the creator. However, a validator should be invulnerable if he published this information, and a block is considered orphaned in the event of a fork. Thus, a validator's secret information is used to generate publicly verifiable information to prove that the validator is eligible to append a block at height h. BAZO performs at 50 Tps within a network of 20 miners [50]. Research is being conducted on the scalability of BAZO applied sharding mechanisms to deliver a performance spectrum with transaction validations reaching up to 1,000 Tps.

3   A Tale of Two Approaches (BC vs. DL)

In their purest form, BCs act as a decentralized and public ledger, which transparently and immutably record blocks of transactions across a network of computers using a consensus algorithm. Therefore, a BC is, as proposed initially [48], open to all its participants concerning the rights of reading, writing, and participation in the consensus mechanism. A Linked List (LL), however, is a data structure that is traditionally managed by one or more trusted entities holding write permissions. Thus, based on the process of composing new blocks of information (*i.e.*, the consensus mechanism), as well as guarantees of immutability and transparency, it can be stated that although the outcome of a BC and LL is similar, these structures are composed entirely different.

From an abstract point of view, a BC resembles an LL, which defines the abstract data structure, whose instances are interconnected by pointers. Thus, LL-based BC transactions are stored in the form of blocks within this LL by sequentially ordering new blocks (of transactions). However, these are all resemblances of LLs and BCs, since the process of composing a general chain can be very different. *I.e.*, the major differences lie in processes (*a*) of gathering information from the P2P [48] network, (*b*) of assembling information (*i.e.*, transactions) into such an abstract data structure (*i.e.*, blocks), and (*c*) on appending new blocks to the list of blocks (*i.e.*, consensus).

The capacity of a BC to provide a trustworthy, decentralized, and publicly available data storage makes it an interesting opportunity for organizations to increase business agility and to reduce costs by removing intermediaries in distributed applications [59]. However, one crucial aspect of classifying a distributed application as a BC, besides its underlying data structure, is that it should be fully public concerning (*i*) read, (*ii*) write, and (*iii*) consensus participation. Thus, if any of these actions are restricted to selected nodes, such distributed application cannot be classified as a BC, but rather as a DL.

Further, DLs can be classified in different types according to their read and write permissions. Figure 3 depicts quadrants representing a deployment type. The *x*-axis represents the two alternatives write permissions (permissioned or permissionless) and the *y*-axis represents read permissions (public or private). The light gray square represents the definition of a BC, while the dark gray squares represent DLs. Each deployment type is described as follows:

- **Public Permissioned** write permissions are restricted to selected entities, but anyone is able to read from the BC. For example, this deployment type can be used for use cases, where multiple trusted authorities want to publish public data, accessible to anyone, (*e.g.*, publishing hashes of academic certificates).
- **Public Permissionless** are the most prevalent type of BCs. Bitcoin [48], Ethereum [10], and most of their forks are considered to be public permissionless BCs, due to their read and write permissions, as well as the participation in the consensus, which is open to anyone with Internet access. Thus, public permissionless BCs are the standard type of BC deployment, and most cryptocurrencies are implemented as such.
- **Private Permissioned** trust models resemble traditional databases, where read and write permissions are restricted, and consequently, data can only be read by authorized parties. Restricting these permissions creates a hierarchy between participants (*e.g.*, role-based actions), where the main features of a BC (*e.g.*, transparency, immutability, and decentralization) may not be advantageous for a potential application.
- **Private Permissionless** are comparable to public permissionless BCs, but the notion of the reading access control is restricted to a particular (predefined) group or community. Therefore, writing and reading permissions are open to all participating members of such private groups. A dedicated supply chain BC would also act as a possible example since the information exchanged is only readable by its authorized members, but all members can issue transactions without limitations.

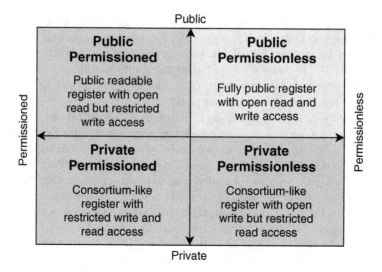

Fig. 3. BC Deployment Types

Therefore, depending on the needs of the application domain, the inherent power of disintermediation can increase trust through transparency among those stakeholders involved. Nonetheless, while BCs have started their widespread adoption within the FinTech domain, many other application areas, use cases, and specific BC types are emerging, too. However, it is crucial to observe that the BC applicability relies on a multitude of different, partially contradicting facets, which are usually determined by dedicated application needs in terms of performance, security, and scalability. They have to be carefully considered in an analysis before the design decision for or against a BC or DL, respectively, can be taken.

While short-term expectations of emerging technical solutions are often over-estimated, BCs are expected to cause a rather evolutionary than revolutionary change, well in contrast to many popular science publications. However with that in mind, BCs may disrupt various industries, not from a technical side, but BCs may also challenge existing business models, business processes, and stakeholder interactions since the full distribution and decentralization allow for the first time an interaction between individual users in a secured, public, and immutable P2P manner without any trusted intermediaries.

4   Blockchains' Suitability and Achievements

Since the BCs proposal in late 2008 as an underlying infrastructure for a cryptocurrency [48] and their later application in several application domains and use cases [13,26,39], the BC concept shows measurably a strong decentralization, transparency, and immutability features. However, for selected use cases concerns raised, whether they require a BC [31,76]. As of today, there is still no clear consensus on such a debate [61]. However, undoubtedly, there are three BC application domains, in which these three features are essential: (*i*) Cryptocurrencies, (*ii*) SCs, and (*iii*) proof-of-existence. Thus, a BC is a perfectly suitable solution to maintain a decentralized, publicly accessible, and append-only ledger.

4.1 Cryptocurrencies and Related Developments

The idea of digital currencies is a concept explored well before the appearance of Bitcoin [48] and summarized as within Fig. 4. Since the idea of creating electronic payment methods arose in the 1960s with the demand to optimize business processes, the system SABRE (Semi-Automated Business Research Environment) by IBM proposed the automation of the booking process of airline tickets by connecting the system directly with a banking credit system [18].

Although SABRE did not propose a digital currency as such, it had been an important milestone for the integration of existing banking systems into the starting digital world. The technical idea of electronic payments was presented in 1983 [18] and proposed a blind signature scheme to automate the payment of services and goods based on privacy standards backed by cryptographic means. The following major requirements for cryptocurrencies were raised:

- **Avoiding double-spending**: to avoid spending of the same coin, which is basically a bit string that could be copied easily, a trusted party is required to be online always. Such a trusted party was also a potential target of attacks.
- **Preserving privacy of transactions**: as transactions were required to be processed and validated by a trusted party, the observation of each transaction of each user has to be prevented.
- **Origin of currency**: related to issues concerned with the creation and value-added of the electronic cash, which impacts directly on the market acceptance and possible applications of a new currency.

DigiCash [17] was presented in 1990 based on this blind signatures scheme [18]. Although not being successful at the time, it was the first electronic currency based on cryptographic standards preventing double-spending and supporting privacy aspects of transactions. With Deutsche Bank and Credit Suisse on board and despite causing an impact on the financial market at the time, the currency did not reach a successful position with the public. The company specialized in digital currency and payment systems operated for a few years only before declaring bankruptcy in 1996.

In the meantime, work on time-stamping digital documents, especially the data and not the medium, was proposed with computationally practical procedures (hash functions and digital signatures), such that it is infeasible for a user either to back-date or to forward-date a time-stamped document [33]. While at the same time, the complete privacy of documents themselves is reached, the approach does not require any record-keeping by the time-stamping service.

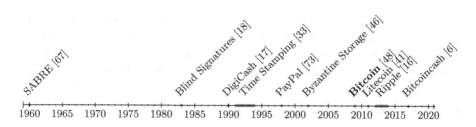

Fig. 4. Timeline of Selected Digital Currencies and Related Developments

The popularity of the Internet, e-commerce, and commercial applications boosted at the turn of the century the increased demand for secure transactions over the Internet and digital currencies [73]. Based on this, PayPal [73] emerged in 1998 as an innovative money transfer service, differing from credit card services. Paypal integrated features to reduce fraud in electronic transactions, such as offering a virtual account, where a customer can add money that could be spent in any currency being converted and deducted from this virtual account.

While cryptographic storage techniques for data had been developed within the'90s, allowing users to keep data secret from non-trusted servers, the multi-user network file system SUNDR (Secure Untrusted Data Repository) focused on the detection of tampering attacks and stale data [46]. Whether or not the server obeys the protocol the ideal and immediate as well as unconditional notice of any misbehavior on the part of the server cannot be reached, however, fork consistency (a weaker form of data integrity) can be proven: if the server delays just one single user from seeing even a single change by another, the two users will never again see one another's changes. This can easily be detected with on-line communications since users own private keys. Thus, SUNDR's virtual nodes contain the file's metadata, the size, and cryptographic hashes of its blocks (the user data), while hash trees are applied to verify a file block's integrity without touching the entire file system. The server stores in addition to the blocks a signed version structure (which includes version data and the i-handle, a single cryptographic hash of the block) for each user and group, including information about operations in progress. SUNDR's practical consistency protocol enables the detection, whether the server has faithfully provided a consistent view of the entire file system to all clients. Thus, SUNDR defines a network file system, whose protocol makes Byzantine file server failures readily detectable—a major prerequisite of a modern's BC functionality.

Until the Bitcoin proposal appeared [48], basically all security approaches deployed preventing double-spending and supporting transaction privacy followed a centralized path, many proposals relying on a TTP as a mediator of online operations. Their similar model compared to fiat currencies, did not trigger a widespread adoption. This was the case of DigiCash [17], which reached a global recognition within financial markets but could not grow its user base to a sufficient size. In contrast, PayPal's innovative financial characteristics, such as virtual wallets and the simplicity of previously complex financial operations (*e.g.,* currency exchange or online payments, marked the beginning of the Fin-Tech area. Bitcoin introduced 2009 a cryptocurrency operating in a fully decentralized manner while being able to respond to concerns raised earlier [48]:

- **Double-spending**: a guarantee of detecting double-spending at any time without a trusted intermediary being involved is reached by the PoW consensus mechanism (*cf.* Sect. 2) deployed. Thus, participants wait for the creation of a certain number of blocks to ensure that a transaction is confirmed on the network, and a comparison against this chain reveals if a coin had been spent twice.
- **Privacy of transactions**: although the transaction history is public and verifiable, all authors of transactions are identified by a public key. Thus, the approach guarantees pseudonymity since it is not easily possible to track the public key to its owner directly.
- **Origin of currency**: the proposed approach seeks to add value to the currency by creating a relative scarcity, (*i.e.,* the number of coins is limited) and by ensuring that efforts to acquire Bitcoin by miners, (*i.e.,* by mining) require an investment in computing power (*cf.* Sect. 2.2).

Despite skepticism in early stages, the Bitcoin work and the underlying public DL, the BC, rose considerable interest due to its dis-intermediation feature, while aligning a balance between anonymity/privacy of users and the transparency of their transactions. As of 2011, several cryptocurrencies for specific purposes emerged based on parametric changes of the Bitcoin source code, *e.g.,* Litecoin [41], and new ones, such as Ripple [16], focused on the integration of banking systems. Public perception was secured at the moment the market capitalization reached 1 billion US$ in Bitcoins in March 2013 [54]. Thus, interest swapped from economic investors (on very shaky grounds) to industry, especially Small- and Medium-sized Enterprises (SME), and academia. The platform enabling Bitcoins to be exchanged safely in a fully distributed manner between unknown stakeholders and without any central element as a mediator, the public BC formed the start of the BC age.

4.2 Smart Contracts

The notion of a SC, as a computerized transaction protocol that executes the terms of a contract agreed between the parties involved, was proposed long before the arrival of BCs [71]. The lack of a decentralized infrastructure providing a suitable dis-intermediation was resolved by BCs, and SCs now became implementable, since BCs outline the perfect distributed environment for their deployment and operation. The goal of an SC is to (*a*) satisfy common contractual conditions as with any regular paper-based contracts, *e.g.,* in terms of payments, liens, confidentiality, or even enforcement, (*b*) reduce malicious and accidental handling, and (*c*) avoid any trusted intermediaries. Thus, the SCs concept is a viable path to automate and ensure agreements reliably and more efficiently than paper-based contracts as of today. Henceforth, as specifically designed from scratch in Ethereum [10], the BC has proven to be a highly appropriate infrastructure for the fully decentralized and transparent execution of a mutual agreement between parties.

Despite Ethereum becoming the first and widely accessible platform that unveiled the entire potential of SCs, Bitcoin also features contracts, however, only in the form of simple scripts for performing transactions, which suite the finality of the application, *i.e.*, a cryptocurrency, in a simple and efficient manner [48]. In contrast, Ethereum proposed a sandbox environment through the Ethereum Virtual Machine (EVM) [10], in which it is possible to execute arbitrary and Turing-complete code directly on-chain, (*i.e.*, allowing for the execution of loops). An EVM defines an environment isolated from the host itself, being precisely the same for all Ethereum nodes (called "Ethereum Clients") in the BC network. A client software, *e.g.*, Geth and Parity, is used for external communications and interactions with the operating system of the host node.

Although many different BCs provide support for the execution of SCs, the majority follows the model determined by Ethereum, in which a sandboxed environment ensures that the execution of the SCs is precisely the same across all nodes of the network. Thus, Fig. 5 illustrates the respective components involved in the creation of an SC in an EVM as well as the deployment steps needed. While the SC is defined in a high-level language, *e.g.*, by applying the Integrated Development Environment (IDE) Remix, it is transformed and interpreted in bytecode, until it is propagated on to the BC network according to the consensus algorithm configured in the EVM. The EVM itself operates on the respective operating system and runs the Ethereum protocol. Thus, the client communicates with the host's operating system to broadcast the transaction containing the bytecode corresponding to the SC, which is crafted into different IP packets and sent to the BC network. The role of the EVM (*i.e.*, the BC's "virtual machine") is crucial, since code must be identical across all Ethereum nodes in the BC network and must comply with well-defined interfaces. Therefore, it is possible to enable flexible support for different clients, which, in turn, can provide different abstraction levels for the development of applications.

A relevant factor for the popularity of general-purpose, decentralized applications (dApps) based on SCs, is the familiarization of developers with high-level SC programming languages and the *modus-operandi* of BC. Following the SC example as shown in Fig. 5, it is possible to create a simple application returning a string the text *hello world* whenever it is called (*cf.* Listing 1). Ethereum provides direct support for its high-level language "Solidity", with a syntax based on JavaScript; however, support for different languages that developers are familiar with exist if that language is compiled into EVM op-codes, which are interpreted and executed by the EVM. Thus, such flexibilization is made possible through such abstraction layer allowing the use of different languages as long as your compiler generates EVM opcodes.

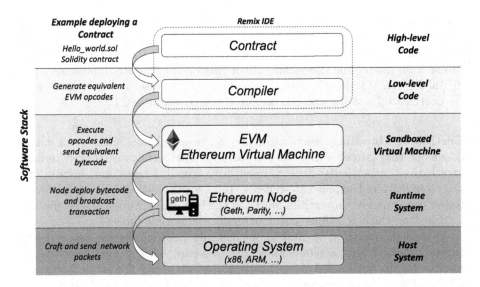

Fig. 5. SC Deployment on the Ethereum Virtual Machine (EVM) [10]

```
1  pragma solidity ^0.4.10;
2  contract HelloContract {
3      string helloWorld;
4      function getHello() public {
5          helloWorld = "Hello World";
6      }
7  }
```

Listing 1. A Simple "Hello World" SC Example in Solidity

Regardless of the high-level language of a SC, the EVM interprets and executes EVM opcodes based on an incentive scheme, the *gas*. Thus, the higher the complexity of an SC is, the higher will be the cost for its deployment and operation, demanding a higher amount of *gas* for its execution. It is important to note that such an incentive scheme is required for BCs, *i.e.,* their permissionless deployments, since anyone with Internet access can participate and, thus, a mechanism is needed to prevent the BC from DoS attacks, either maliciously or just by accident, *i.e.,* an endless loop within an SC. In contrast, for DLs, especially permissioned deployments, such a necessity of incentives may not be needed, since the BC network consists out of permissioned, *i.e.,* pre-selected stakeholders. Once a sufficient amount of *Gas* is provided for the SC's deployment, the EVM generates the bytecode, which is sent to the client.

4.3 Proof-of-Existence and Time-Stamping

One of the significant BC characteristics is data immutability. Once information is inserted and broadcast into the BC, its removal or subsequent alteration becomes practically impossible without the (unlikely) control of the majority of BC network nodes. Therefore, many solutions that require the registration of an event at a certain point in time exploit exactly this BC characteristics to reach an immutable time-stamping of this event, typically represented in a digital format. Within this immutability context, two use cases benefit from it: (*i*) Certificate Handling and (*ii*) Supply Chain Tracking (SCT).

Certificate Handling: certificates play an essential role, since as an official document they attest a fact. In case of academic certificates they determine knowledge in a particular area, are issued by accredited academic institutions, and often delivered on paper to students. To assess the authenticity of certificates today, companies or universities must call the issuing institution to perform this verification, which is a time-consuming and cumbersome process.

Due to the fact that in 2017 about 500 fake doctoral certificates were sold monthly in the US in "diploma mills" [53], a secure, efficient, and decentralized solution for the verification of certificates becomes relevant. Therefore, the role of a BC and its main characteristics indicate that a BC-based proof-of-existence for handling certificates is possible, and several projects follow this path [14,32,60]. In General, hashes of the certificates' PDF documents are immutably stored in the BC, persisted, and signed by the issuing institution with its private key. Thus, the verification process is simplified overall by matching the hash of the currently accessible PDF version of the certificate to the hash stored in the BC by the issuing institution. In addition, such BC-based certificate handling systems tackle the issue of fake certificates from "diploma mills" successfully, since they cannot store certificate hashes in the BC without the institution's private key, in turn, they are not able to issue certificates of counterfeited institutions.

Supply Chain Tracking: there are many use cases deploying Supply Chain Tracking (SCT) systems based on BCs. Since BC and SCT integration supports the persisting of data, their integrity, and, consequently, the establishment of trusted boundaries between different stakeholders for a product's life cycle. Since the production of a particular product encompasses a large number of actions and conditions during its life cycle, collecting throughout a product's supply chain time-stamped quantitative and qualitative data from the process, even including the geo-location of resources or times when certain steps had been performed, adds value beyond financial incentives such as region labels. To collect data required automatically, wireless sensors, IoT devices, and surveillance devices, such as cameras and drones, are integrated. Recent studies, [69], [8], and [4] elaborate on several aspects employing BCs in SCT systems. The key takeaway is that the persistence of the supply chain data tracked within the BCs does seal SCT systems by protecting the data's integrity, however, while the time stamping mechanism and its related undeniable evidence of actions can be proven, the exact values persisted depend on the sensors in use. Supply chain tracking solutions at the enterprise level do include the food industry and many other vendor domains. However, the full decentralization of partially unknown stakeholders within a chain faces pioneer players in this area with challenges.

Even though certificates and SCT determine use cases benefiting from data immutability, modulo the sensor problem as sketched above, there exists an inherent problem with data structures in general concerning the semantics of data stored. Although existing a record that an event occurred at some point in time, it is not possible to verify at the BC's data structure level the semantics of data stored without specific application-level knowledge (*cf.* Sect. 5.3).

5   Missing Pieces and Open Issues

BCs and DLs serve as an ideal infrastructure for select use cases (*cf.* Sect. 4). However, there is still a considerable amount of research required, in order to fully answer the question, which systems could be replaced by a BC- or DL-based approach, such that efficiency gains compared to centralized approaches become measurable. Such efforts include especially (*a*) technical complexity, (*b*) interoperability and openness, (*c*) trust, and (*d*) sustainability, besides pure technical efficiency, manageability including identity management, and operations. The gap of processing sensed data, such as within IoT, and the trust in respectively digitized data will always depend on the calibration and certification of sensors.

5.1   Technical Complexity

The myriad of BC implementations emerging requires that users and companies desiring to adopt a BC —either by integrating it in their solution or creating novel solutions—need to understand the underlying BC technical details, *e.g.*, transaction structure, parameters, transaction signing methods, and address format, of each implementation under consideration. In this context, it is very difficult for non-technical users, *i.e.*, users without prior BC knowledge, to select the most appropriate BC implementation for their use cases. Thus, an approach which directly leads to an increase in the Operational Expenditures (OPEX) of the company is favored over an approach where the company must (*a*) train dedicated personnel or (*b*) hire external consultants to help in the BC selection process. The lack of *"in-house"* capabilities (*i.e.*, skills and understating) was recently highlighted in a global survey by Deloitte [44] as one barrier to more significant investments in BC. Thus, simplifying and abstracting technical details is a crucial challenge to foster the adoption of BCs on a wider scale and to generate valuable investments. An approach to tackle this issue is [63], where a framework to automatically select the best suitable BC for a determined use-case is proposed. In the approach, users define policies that contain information regarding the BC requirements (*e.g.*, minimum Tps, required data size, deployment type, and costs) to store data from different users. The framework then automatically selects the BC that meets the requirements and manages the transactions to the selected BC. Hence, simplifying the complexity of managing data from multiple users in different BCs.

Moreover, besides this company-oriented view, public key and private key concepts (*cf.* Sect. 2.1) are not easy to be understood for non-technical individuals due to their underlying mathematical and computational complexity. This leads to the fact that many cryptocurrency wallets and funds are being managed by central online exchanges, which form a highly profitable target for attackers. Since such central exchanges hold all their clients' funds, the MtGox hack in 2014 was economically successful, 460 million US$ were supposedly stolen [47]. Neither Bitcoin nor Ethereum faced fundamental technical attacks on their protocol and system-internals [19]; most of the attacks targeted external services around these two BCs had been exposed successfully to threats and attacks. Thus, besides BC's highly stable technical dimension, which typically includes the BC protocol, the mining, if applied, and the chain's storage, BCs also require a transparent and straightforward social dimension to be widely accepted as a secure mechanism for handling financial transactions. This does have to involve the BC's ecosystem around the pure BC specification; thus, the technical complexity even grows further.

5.2   Interoperability

As of today, BCs form separated islands of technical solutions, which do not enable a native communication between any two ones. Thus, efforts toward the standardization of BCs and DLs are required and they include international organizations, *e.g.,* International Organization for Standardization (ISO) and the Internet Research Task Force (IRTF), and also focus groups, *e.g.,* ITU Telecommunication Standardization Sector (ITU-T) and Securities Association for Institutional Trade Communication (ISITC) Europe. Standardization are in the process to define a common foundation and set of protocols for a data exchange between BCs and DLs, proving a *de facto* standard for BCs and DLs. Thus, standardization can be viewed as an enabler for interoperability [5,11].

Existing interoperability schemes cover (*i*) a Notary Scheme, (*ii*) Side-chains and Relays, and (*iii*) Hash Locking [11]. Notary schemes introduce one or more trusted entities that verify events in different BCs and provide information to external applications. With the deployment of a notary, applications are not restricted to a single BC platform, technical details of BC interaction can be abstracted, which simplifies the BC integration with legacy systems [62], however, at the cost of the re-introduction of a trusted, this, central entity. In contrast, side-chains and relays propose to maintain a parallel BC, which includes a consensus mechanism, where multiple nodes, *i.e.,* miners, validate events in the different chains and include the blocks into the parallel chain. In this sense, trust can be provided without relying on a central entity. However, it comes at the cost of introducing additional technical complexity to reach interoperability, including the demand for additional storage for the parallel chain. Hash locking allows for an exchange of funds between two different BCs without any intermediary. However, hash locking requires that both BCs support Hashed TimeLock Contracts (HTLC), and these BCs are not able to exchange data or act upon generic events. Thus, a generic, decentralized, efficient, and open interoperability scheme for arbitrary BCs has not been found yet—which is very well visible today in all currently ongoing standardization activities on interoperability.

5.3   Trust Assumptions

BCs as of today can provide the integrity of the *data-at-rest* (data stored in persistent storage) and *data-in-transit* (information flowing over private or public networks), but not of *data-in-use* (active data, which is stored in a non-persistent digital state). The integrity of *data-at-rest* is secured via the consensus mechanism, the full distribution, and hash-based linking, (*i.e.*, immutability). In contrast, the integrity of *data-in-transit* is ensured by the public-private key pairs in use, *e.g.*, one cannot change a transaction already signed without being detected. However, signing a transaction does not mean that the transaction will be accepted or processed, *e.g.*, it can be rejected due to lack of funds or low fees. Further, legit transactions and legit BC traffic might be rerouted to fake nodes with a Border Gateway Protocol (BGP) hijacking attack [2] or by monopolizing connections with eclipse attacks [34].

In terms of *data-in-use*, its trustworthiness depends on the application creating the transaction. Thus, any BC cannot guarantee that data included in the transaction are trustworthy unless the generation process of these data is public, fully electronic, and observable by anyone - the exact case of a cryptocurrency, like Bitcoins. This problem of providing trust in general terms to *data-in-use* is that the input to the BC, if highly depending on IoT environments, originates from physical sensors. As these sensors are susceptible to a myriad of attacks, *e.g.*, node capture, false data injection, spoofing, sibyl attacks, and physical tampering [43], there is no guarantee that the *data-in-use* from IoT sensors is trustworthy, (*i.e.*, was not modified). However, the date and time as well as possibly the geo-location may be trustworthy, since respective control data is based on trustworthy algorithms. Thus, the verification of data from IoT and other sensors and their related integrity must be performed outside the BC before being immutability persisted within the BC.

Overall, a BC can be viewed as an enabler of the "Security Through Publicity" concept, which is defined as *"Acting in public does not guarantee that actions will be correct, but it does provide users with a quantifiable set of information and semantics that enable applications to construct meaningful security mechanisms"* [52]. In this sense, BCs acting as a public and open record of transactions allow for the building of secure systems on top of applications. Users interacting with a BC are acting in public (user interacting with a DL may most likely not fully act in public), which means that their actions (*e.g.*, transactions sent and SC calls), and their data (*e.g.*, account balance) can be verified by any peer or application interested. Of course, this does not guarantee that their behavior or data is correct. However, it provides the guarantee that, following the BC protocol, their actions cannot be forged time- or date-wise or changed otherwise. Hence, reinforcing the statement: BCs serve as a trusted source of information, but solely for information generated within the BC protocol (such as for cryptocurrencies); data generated from external sources may not be trustworthy.

For any SC deployed on a BC, if that is possible, the trust assumptions made are comparable: if the SC code is provided is very basic and simple statements, which can be formally verified, the result of such an SC operation can be trusted. However, SC code potentially belongs to the category of "non-trusted" code, since a formal verification is not attached to an SC such that their integrity could be traced automatically. Note that this relates to the discussion in which the statement "Code is the law" suggests that SCs are final. In the sense of computation of that SC's opcodes, one by one in the given order, this holds true; thus, the result is trustworthy, and any node in the BC network can verify it. However, the programming language-based semantics of this SC are different, since the interpretation of the validity of a certain sequence of functions to be called to be considered right or not being allowed varies. In case these calls violate the intention of the SC, such a situation is much harder, if not impossible in general, to be formalized as the DAO attack [22] on Ethereum shows.

5.4 Sustainability and Consensus Mechanisms

The mining process based on PoW as described in Sect. 2.2 secures the BC network against double-spending. This is achieved by an investment into a larger amount of energy to find the correct solution to the crypto puzzle. As of April 2021, the Bitcoin network consumed 94.92 TWh of energy as estimated by [23], which is comparable to the annual consumption of the entire country of Kazakhstan. Therefore, sustainability concerns arise due the PoW consensus mechanisms in use. To tackle this concern of power consumption and to secure the BC at the same level of security, the validation of transactions may be possible via alternative mining schemes [74]. Among the myriad of alternatives some of them are already deployed in operational and research BCs, such as Proof-of-Stake (PoS) in Bazo, delegated PoS (dPoS) in EOS, and Proof-of-Authority (PoA) in private deployments of Ethereum. Thus, a discussion of respective mechanisms is required to determine the current state-of-the-art.

Proof-of-Stake (PoS): In PoS-based mining the probability of a miner to solve a crypto puzzle depends solely on the number of coins a mining node is willing to put at stake to secure the BC. This is in contrast to PoW, where the probability of a miner to find a solution to the crypto puzzle is related to the amount of computational power it possesses. Therefore, nodes with larger stake are more likely to be chosen to validate transactions and to include a block into the BC compared to nodes holding fewer coins. This main idea of PoS is herewith based on the fact that nodes holding more coins in a BC will contribute to its security, since they have more to lose. In turn, wealthier nodes tend to become wealthier as they verify more blocks more time and collect additional transaction fees.

Since the choice of the next miner is not based on computational power, but on the stake (*i.e.*, wealth), the energy consumption of PoS is negligible compared to PoW [49]. However, a key problem with PoS is the "nothing-at-stake" problem. This arises because nodes potentially can verify concurrently blocks in several branches of the BC. After all, it costs a node nothing to do so, since the stake offered is valid for the entire BC. Thus, with nodes verifying blocks in several branches of the same BC at the same time, such branches show a larger likelihood to be never abandoned, and in turn, no consensus could be reached to which of the chain's branches all nodes have to convert to.

Delegated PoS (dPoS): By adding a democratic process to PoS, dPoS was proposed to solve the "nothing-at-stake" problem. This democratic process defines the selection of nodes that will add blocks to the BC. For dPoS the probability of a node to be selected as the node to persist a block int othe BC depends on (*a*) the wealth staked and (*b*) on the votes provided by other nodes in the BC. Therefore in contrast to PoS, it is not sufficient for a node to have wealth staked, a node must also behave in a manner that ensures a correct and fair overall state of the BC, *e.g.,* by only verifying transactions in a single branch. If a node starts to behave maliciously, other nodes in the BC can remove their votes and place them on another node, which behaves correctly. However, this democratic process comes at a cost, voting for a node might be impacted by financial rewards for other nodes to place their votes for a particular node [70], *i.e.,* buying votes. In practice, the set of verifier nodes in dPoS-based BCs is often restricted to a predefined number, *e.g.,* 21 verifiers in the case of EOS. Thus, while the sustainability argument has seen a relieve of pressure, a possible centralization of mining power in a dPoS-based BC moves in instead.

Proof-of-Authority (PoA): If only a set of "pre-authorized" nodes hold the rights to write a new block into a BC, the developed PoA miming scheme introduces "pre-authorized" nodes. This scheme is often found in DLs, where a selected group of individuals (*i.e.,* organizations, participants, or selected nodes) is allowed to interact with the BC. While this approach relaxes concerns on a higher energy consumption as for PoS, this advantage comes at the cost of a high centralization. Since the number of block verifiers (*i.e.,* miners) is limited and known, they potentially can collude and perform malicious actions, such as censuring transactions or delaying the same.

In summary, Table 2 compares these alternatives described. As the energy consumption lowers, the level of centralization increases. This is due to the fact that whenever a set of trusted participants act to secure the BC, the consensus mechanism can be simplified, *e.g.,* from PoW to PoS or PoA. In contrast, if participants are not known and do not trust each other, any useful consensus mechanism must ensure that it is computationally (*e.g.,* PoW) or financially (*e.g.,* PoS) expensive to propose a new block to be added to that BC. Consequently, academia and industry is engaged in developing and experimenting consensus mechanisms that are both secure and energy-efficient at the same time and could replace PoW-based schemes [74].

Table 2. Non-Exhaustive Comparison of Alternative Consensus Mechanisms

Consensus Mechanism	Key Principle	Energy Consumption	Probability of Centralization
Proof-of-Work (PoW)	Computational power determines chance of adding a block	High	Low
Proof-of-Stake (PoS)	Staked wealth determines the chance of adding a block	Low	Medium
Delegated Proof-of-Stake (dPoS)	Votes by nodes and staked wealth determine the chance of adding a block	Low	Medium
Proof-of-Authority (PoA)	Only a set of authorized nodes are able to add blocks	Low	High

6   Observations and Conclusions

This article provides clarification on two concepts that received high attention over the past decade, namely Blockchains (BC) and Distributed Ledgers (DL). Both BCs and DLs deploy identical technical concepts (*cf.* Sect. 2), especially Peer-to-Peer (P2P) principles, applied strong cryptography, and consensus mechanisms. Overall, BCs and DLs achieve an immutable and distributed record of transactions. However, DLs often rely on a single Trusted Third Party (TTP) or on a consortium of entities (pre-defined stakeholders) to add new transactions and to maintain the ledger. In contrast, BCs offer a fully public and open participation in terms of reads, writes, and consensus mechanisms. Thus, BCs fully remove any intermediaries, thus, any need for TTPs, while still providing a fully decentralized and immutable ledger. While every BC is a DL, not all DLs are BCs. The respective technical details on this distinction were developed in Sect. 3, and respective classification were presented.

As of today, not a single IT system existing was fully replaced by a DL or by a BC. This leads to the conclusion that BCs determine an evolution of databases and linked lists, they do not result in a revolution, since a full replacement of a system or technology did not happen, yet. However, those overall benefits and technical developments, as well as refinements as provided by DLs and BCs (*cf.* Sect. 4), are remarkable since the proposal of Bitcoin in 2009. Moreover, organizational impacts are vast, especially providing in selected instances, *e.g.*, cryptocurrencies, SCs, and time-stamping, an evolution in the way stakeholders interact to reach transparency and traceability of different events and actions. However, the key question to be answered in case of a new development foreseen reads as: "Is a distribution and decentralization of a solution really sensible?" Additionally, for many use cases, the deployment of a DL- or BC-based solution can benefit from those advantages discussed; however, this may come at the cost of an application's inefficiency due to the distributed complexity of a distributed system. Furthermore, incentives and counter-incentivization need to be considered in detail with respect to economic impacts.

In conclusion, by missing a clear definition of the differences between a BC and DL (now being provided above with measurable characteristics, especially with respect to very different trust assumptions on stakeholders involved), a culprit for their inefficient, incomplete, and possibly incorrect deployment combined with misleading expectations may have been found. However, the novelty of these new concepts and their partially "unknown" technical details are possible obstacles as well. A key concern remains in terms of trust assumptions made, because data persisted within a BC are only trustworthy, if they had been generated by an electronically computed algorithm, thus, trust depends in case of IoT applications deploying BCs on the calibration and certification of sensors. Any IoT-driven data, originating from sensors, can only be persisted in a trusted manner with respect to time and geo-location; any further correctness or validity of such data depends on the application and the sensors in use.

Generally, DLs and BCs still require a considerable research effort to optimize technical details, especially lowering technical complexity such that solutions can be integrated easily, defining standards and guidelines for their deployments and interoperability, demystifying trust assumptions, and solving the sustainability question of secure consensus protocols without losing data integrity. These selected research efforts as of IFIP's WG6.6 focus on concepts and protocols, which will need to reach identical maturity levels as known for databases and linked lists. Additionally, probabilities play an important role in BCs and DLs, since many security and consensus mechanisms in a distributed setting are built on probabilities. Thus, hash functions, public-private key pairs, *nonces*, mining power and success, and mining pools do not show a deterministic behavior, which seems to be highly relevant for users and their perceptions in today's societies. However, mathematically proven likelihoods indicate that strong security reached is already accepted within many IT systems of today's use in the FinTech and other domains.

Thus, the question of which IT systems can be (entirely) replaced by a BC- or a DL-based approach or which applications—besides those generating electronically digitally represented values—can benefit in full from these BC and DL advantages outlined, will remain open until answers with many variables to be considered and as addressed above will have been found.

Acknowledgements. This paper was driven by the IFIP WG6.6 involvement of the authors, and thus supported partially by *(a)* the University of Zürich UZH, Switzerland, and *(b)* the European Union's Horizon 2020 Research and Innovation Program under Grant Agreement No. 830927, the CONCORDIA Project.

References

1. Androulaki, E., et al.: Hyperledger Fabric: a distributed operating system for permissioned blockchains. In: ACM EuroSys Conference (EuroSys 2018), pp. 1–15. Porto, Portugal, April 2018
2. Apostolaki, M., Zohar, A., Vanbever, L.: Hijacking bitcoin: routing attacks on cryptocurrencies. In: IEEE Symposium on Security and Privacy (SP 2017), pp. 375–392, San Jose, USA, May 2017

3. Asokan, N., Janson, P.A., Steiner, M., Waidner, M.: The state-of-the-art in electronic payment systems. IEEE Comput. **30**, 28–35 (1997)
4. Banerjee, A.: Blockchain with IoT: applications and use cases for a new paradigm of supply chain driving efficiency and cost. In: Role of Blockchain Technology in IoT Applications, Advances in Computers, vol. 115, pp. 259–292. Elsevier (2019)
5. Belotti, M., Božić, N., Pujolle, G., Secci, S.: A vademecum on blockchain technologies: when, which and how. IEEE Commun. Surv. Tutorials **21**, 3796–3838 (2019)
6. bitcoincash.org: Bitcoin Cash - Peer-to-Peer Electronic Cash (2017). https://www.bitcoincash.org/. Accessed 8 Apr 2021
7. Blockchair: Ethereum Transaction per Second Graph (2021). https://blockchair.com/ethereum/charts/transactions-per-second. Accessed 8 Apr 2021
8. Bocek, T., Rodrigues, B.B., Strasser, T., Stiller, B.: Blockchains everywhere-a use-case of blockchains in the pharma supply-chain. In: IFIP/IEEE Symposium on Integrated Network and Service Management (IM 2017), pp. 772–777. Lisbon, Portugal, May 2017
9. Bocek, T., Stiller, B.: Smart contracts - blockchains in the wings. In: Linnhoff-Popien, C., Schneider, R., Zaddach, M. (eds.) Digital Marketplaces Unleashed, pp. 169–184. Springer, Berlin (2017)
10. Buterin, V.: A Next-Generation Smart Contract and Decentralized Application Platform (2014). https://ethereum.org/en/whitepaper/. Accessed 8 Apr 2021
11. Buterin, V.: Chain Interoperability, September 2016. https://bit.ly/2WH8BM7. Accessed 8 Apr 2021
12. Buterin, V., Reijsbergen, D., Leonardos, S., Piliouras, G.: Incentives in ethereum's hybrid casper protocol. In: IEEE International Conference on Blockchain and Cryptocurrency (ICBC 2019), pp. 236–244. Seoul, South Korea, May 2019
13. Casino, F., Dasaklis, T.K., Patsakis, C.: A systematic literature review of blockchain-based applications: current status, classification and open issues. In: Telematics and Informatics Journal, vol. 36, pp. 55–81. Elsevier, March 2019
14. Castor, A.: Cardano Blockchain's First Use Case: Proof of University Diplomas in Greece, January 2018. https://bit.ly/2DVsrYt. Accessed 8 Apr 2021
15. Chandel, S., Zhang, S., Wu, H.: Using Blockchain in IoT: Is it a Smooth Road Ahead for Real? In: Future of Information and Communication Conference (FICC 2020), pp. 159–171. San Francisco, USA, March 2020
16. Chase, B., MacBrough, E.: Analysis of the XRP Ledger Consensus Protocol (2018). http://arxiv.org/abs/1802.07242. Accessed 8 Apr 2021
17. Chaum, D., Fiat, A., Naor, M.: Untraceable electronic cash. In: IACR Advances in Cryptology (CRYPTO '88), pp. 319–327. Springer-Verlag, Santa Barbara, USA, August 1988
18. Chaum, D.: Blind signatures for untraceable payments. In: Chaum, D., Rivest, R.L., Sherman, A.T. (eds.) Advances in Cryptology, pp. 199–203. Springer, Boston, MA (1983). https://doi.org/10.1007/978-1-4757-0602-4_18
19. Chen, H., Pendleton, M., Njilla, L., Xu, S.: A survey on ethereum systems security: vulnerabilities, attacks, and defenses. ACM Comput. Surv. **53**(3), June 2020
20. CoinMarketCap: Market Capitalizations (2021) https://coinmarketcap.com/. Accessed 8 Apr 2021
21. Croman, K., et al.: On scaling decentralized blockchains. In: International Conference on Financial Cryptography and Data Security (FC 2016), pp. 106–125. Christ Church, Barbados, February 2016
22. Daian, P.: Analysis of the DAO Exploit (2016). https://bit.ly/3ju13GC. Accessed 8 Apr 2021

23. Digiconomist: Bitcoin Energy Consumption Index (2021). https://digiconomist. net/bitcoin-energy-consumption. Accessed 8 Apr 2021
24. EOS.IO: Technical White Paper v2, March 2018. https://bit.ly/3fGmn9k. Accessed 8 Apr 2021
25. Ferris, C.: Does Hyperledger Fabric Perform at Scale? April 2019. https://ibm.co/ 3hkTfov. Accessed 8 Apr 2021
26. Franco, M.F., Scheid, E., Granville, L., Stiller, B.: BRAIN: blockchain-based reverse auction for infrastructure supply in virtual network functions-as-a-service. In: IFIP Networking (Networking 2019), pp. 1–9. Warsaw, Poland, May 2019
27. Garfinkel, S.L.: Public key cryptography. IEEE Comput. **29**, 101–104 (1996)
28. Gervais, A., Karame, G.O., Wüst, K., Glykantzis, V., Ritzdorf, H., Capkun, S.: On the security and performance of proof of work blockchains. In: ACM SIGSAC Conference on Computer and Communications Security (CCS 2016). pp. 3–16. Vienna, Austria, October 2016
29. Ghimire, S., Selvaraj, H.: A survey on bitcoin cryptocurrency and its mining. In: International Conference on Systems Engineering (ICSEng 2018), pp. 1–6. Sydney, Australia (2018)
30. GitHub Inc.: Blockchain - GitHub Topics (2021). https://github.com/topics/ blockchain. Accessed 8 Apr 2021
31. Greenspan, G.: Avoiding the Pointless Blockchain Project (2015). https://bit.ly/ 2Bj8wH3. Accessed 8 Apr 2021
32. Gresch, J., Rodrigues, B., Scheid, E., Kanhere, S.S., Stiller, B.: The proposal of a blockchain-based architecture for transparent certificate handling. In: International Conference on Business Information Systems (BIS 2018), pp. 1–12. Berlin, Germany, July 2018
33. Haber, S., Stornetta, W.S.: How to Time-Stamp a Digital Document. vol. 3, pp. 99–111. Springer, Heidelberg (January 1991)
34. Heilman, E., Kendler, A., Zohar, A., Goldberg, S.: Eclipse attacks on bitcoin's peer-to-peer network. In: USENIX Security Symposium (USENIX Security 15), pp. 129–144. Washington D.C., USA, August 2015
35. ICODATA.io: ICO Funds Raised (2021). https://www.icodata.io/stats/. Accessed 8 Apr 2021
36. Intel Corporation: Proof of Elapsed Time (PoET) (2017). https://bit.ly/2OG1ejJ. Accessed 8 Apr 2021
37. IOTA Foundation: The Coordicide, May 2019. https://bit.ly/3cX1QOO. Accessed 8 Apr 2021
38. IOTA Foundation: IOTA (2021). https://www.iota.org/. Accessed 8 Apr 2021
39. Killer, C., et al.: Provotum: a blockchain-based and end-to-end verifiable remote electronic voting system. In: IEEE 45th Conference on Local Computer Networks (LCN 2020), pp. 1–12. Sidney, Australia, November 2020
40. Kurt, A.M.: Zero to Monero - First Edition (2018). https://bit.ly/3fOpBYC. Accessed 8 Apr 2021
41. Lee, C.: Litecoin - The Cryptocurrency for Payments (2011). https://litecoin.org/. Accessed 8 Apr 2021
42. Lin, I.C., Liao, T.C.: A survey of blockchain security issues and challenges. Int. J. Network Secur. **19**, 653–659 (2017)
43. Lin, J., Yu, W., Zhang, N., Yang, X., Zhang, H., Zhao, W.: A survey on internet of things: architecture, enabling technologies, security and privacy, and applications. IEEE Internet Things J. **4**, 1125–1142 (2017)
44. Pawczuk, L., Rob Massey, J.H.: Deloitte's 2019 Global Blockchain Survey (2019). https://bit.ly/32E67SA. Accessed 8 Apr 2021

45. Mafakheri, B., Subramanya, T., Goratti, L., Riggio, R.: Blockchain-based infrastructure sharing in 5g small cell networks. In: International Conference on Network and Service Management (CNSM 2018), pp. 313–317. Rome, Italy, November 2018
46. Mazières, D., Shasha, D.: Building Secure File Systems out of Byzantine Storage. In: Annual Symposium on Principles of Distributed Computing (PODC 2002), pp. 108–117. Monterey, California (2002)
47. McMillan, R.: The Inside Story of Mt. Gox, Bitcoin's $460 Million Disaster (2014). https://bit.ly/3jqaiaz. Accessed 8 Apr 2021
48. Nakamoto, S.: Bitcoin: A Peer-to-Peer Electronic Cash System (2009). https://bitcoin.org/bitcoin.pdf. Accessed 8 Apr 2021
49. Nguyen, C.T., Hoang, D.T., Nguyen, D.N., Niyato, D., Nguyen, H.T., Dutkiewicz, E.: Proof-of-stake consensus mechanisms for future blockchain networks: fundamentals. IEEE Access. Appl. Opportunities **7**, 85727–85745 (2019)
50. Niya, S.R., Maddaloni, F., Bocek, T., Stiller, B.: Toward scalable blockchains with transaction aggregation. In: ACM Symposium on Applied Computing (SAC 20), pp. 308–315. Brno, Czech Republic (2020)
51. Niya, S.R., Stiller, B.: BAZO: A Proof-of-Stake (PoS) Based Blockchain. Technical report, Zürich, Switzerland, May 2019. https://bit.ly/2G3odoh. Accessed 8 Apr 2021
52. Osterweil, E., Massey, D., Tsendjav, B., Zhang, B., Zhang, L.: Security through publicity. In: 1st USENIX Workshop on Hot Topics in Security (HOTSEC 2006), pp. 13–18. USENIX Association, Vancouver, Canada, August 2006
53. Park, H., Craddock, A.: Diploma Mills: 9 Strategies for Tackling One of Higher Education's Most Wicked Problems (2017). https://bit.ly/2DoEeyu. Accessed 8 Apr 2021
54. Peck, M.E.: Bitcoin Hits $1 Billion (2013). https://bit.ly/39ab6vE. Accessed 8 Apr 2021
55. Popov, S.: The Tangle (2018). https://bit.ly/3bz3KSI. Accessed 8 Apr 2021
56. Ren, L., Ward, P.A.S.: Pooled mining is driving blockchains toward centralized systems. In: International Symposium on Reliable Distributed Systems Workshops (SRDSW 2019), pp. 43–48. Lyon, France, October 2019
57. Rodrigues, B., Eisenring, L., Scheid, E., Bocek, T., Stiller, B.: Evaluating a Blockchain-based Cooperative Defense. In: IFIP/IEEE Symposium on Integrated Network and Service Management (IM 2019), pp. 533–538. Washington DC, USA (April 2019)
58. Rodrigues, B., Scheid, E.J., Stiller, B.: Blockchains in the age of softwarization - hands-on experiences with programming smart contracts and their security pitfalls (Tutorial 1). In: IFIP/IEEE Network Operations and Management Symposium (NOMS 2020). IEEE, Budapest, Hungary, April 2020
59. Rodrigues, B., Bocek, T., Stiller, B.: The use of blockchains: application-driven analysis of applicability. In: Raj, P., Deka, G.C. (eds.) Advances in Computers - Blockchain Technology: Platforms, Tools and Use Cases vol. 111, pp. 163–198. Elsevier (2018)
60. Rodrigues, B., Franco, M.F., Scheid, E.J., Kanhere, S.S., Stiller, B.: A technology-driven overview on blockchain-based academic certificate handling. In: Blockchain Technology Applications in Education, pp. 197–224. IGI Global (2020)
61. Ruoti, S., Kaiser, B., Yerukhimovich, A., Clark, J., Cunningham, R.: Blockchain technology: what is it good for? Commun. ACM **63**(1), 46–53 (2019)
62. Scheid, E.J., Hegnauer, T., Rodrigues, B., Stiller, B.: Bifröst: a modular blockchain interoperability API. In: IEEE Conference on Local Computer Networks (LCN 2019), pp. 332–339. Osnabrück, Germany, October 2019

63. Scheid, E.J., Lakic, D., Rodrigues, B.B., Stiller, B.: PleBeuS: a policy-based blockchain selection framework. In: IEEE/IFIP Network Operations and Management Symposium (NOMS 2020), pp. 1–8. Budapest, Hungary, April 2020

64. Scheid, E.J., Rodrigues, B.B., Granville, L.Z., Stiller, B.: Enabling dynamic SLA compensation using blockchain-based smart contracts. In: IFIP/IEEE Symposium on Integrated Network and Service Management (IM 2019), pp. 53–61. Washington DC, USA, April 2019

65. Simplot-Ryl, I., Traore, I., Everaere, P.: Distributed architectures for electronic cash schemes: a survey. In: International Journal of Parallel, Emergent and Distributed Systems, vol. 24, pp. 243–271. Taylor & Francis, June 2009

66. Smart, N.P.: Cryptography Made Simple. Springer International Publishing (2016)

67. Smith, B.C., Leimkuhler, J.F., Darrow, R.M.: Yield Management at American Airlines. ACM Interfaces **22**(1), 8–31 (1992)

68. Sovrin Foundation: Control Your Digital Identity (2021). https://sovrin.org/. Accessed 8 Apr 2021

69. Stiller, B., Rafati, S., Grossenbacher, S.: Application of Blockchain Technology in the Swiss Food Value Chain (Foodchains Project Report), June 2019. https://bit.ly/3hjxaGX. Accessed 8 Apr 2021

70. Suberg, W.: EOS Node Offers Users Financial Rewards for Votes, Reignites Decentralization Debate (2018). https://bit.ly/2WCrrEc. Accessed 8 Apr 2021

71. Szabo, N.: Formalizing and Securing Relationships on Public Networks. First Monday **2**(9), (September 1997)

72. The Linux Foundation: Hyperledger Wiki (2020). https://wiki.hyperledger.org/. Accessed 8 Apr 2021

73. Trautman, L.J.: E-Commerce, cyber, and electronic payment system risks: lessons from PayPal. UC Davis Bus. LJ **16**, 261–307 (2015)

74. Wang, W., et al.: A survey on consensus mechanisms and mining strategy management in blockchain networks. IEEE Access. **7**, 22328–22370 (2019)

75. Wood, G.: Ethereum: A Secure Decentralised Generalised Transaction Ledger (2020). https://ethereum.github.io/yellowpaper/paper.pdf. Accessed 8 Apr 2021

76. Wüst, K., Gervais, A.: Do you need a blockchain? In: Crypto Valley Conference on Blockchain Technology (CVCBT 2018), pp. 45–54. Zug, Switzerland, November 2018

TC 7: System Modeling and Optimization

IFIP Technical Committee 7: System Modeling and Optimization. A Historical Note

Łukasz Stettner[✉]

Institute of Mathematics of the Polish Academy of Sciences, Sniadeckich 8, 00-656
Warsaw, Poland
stettner@impan.pl

Abstract. Technical Committee 7 of IFIP was created first to establish a bridge
between group of mathematicians and engineers working in modeling and optimization in the east and west countries. With changing world it became an important scientific group stimulating research in modeling and optimization. This note
is trying to summarize activities of the Technical Committee over the last 50 (and
more) years.

Keywords: Optimization · Modeling · Systems

1 Early Years of TC7 and TC7 in Present Time

The idea to create TC7 appeared for the first time during IFIP meeting in 1967 in Rome,
where A.V. Balakrishnan, J. L. Lions and M. Marchuk were thinking about forming
a research coalition devoted to Modeling and Optimization. Officially IFIP TC7 was
founded in 1972 by A.V. Balakrishnan, J. L. Lions and M. Marchuk.

The aims of this Technical Committee were formulated as follows (and there are still
actual):

- To provide an international clearing house for computational as well as related theoretical aspects of optimization problems in diverse areas and to share computing
  experience gained on specific applications,
- To promote the development of necessary high-level theory to meet the needs of
  complex optimization problems and establish cooperation with the international
  Mathematical Union and similar organizations,
- To foster interdisciplinary activity on optimization problems spanning the various
  areas such as Economics (including Business Administration and Management),
  Biomedicine, Meteorology etc., in cooperation with associated international bodies.

Generally at that time it was important to create a research bridge between West and
East. IFIP TC7 for a long time played this role. Geopolitical changes in Europe improved
channels of scientific cooperation and stimulated further development of TC7.

All members of TC7, in particular chairmen had strong impact on its activities.

The list of chairmen of IFIP TC7 looks as follows:

© IFIP International Federation for Information Processing 2021
Published by Springer Nature Switzerland AG 2021
M. Goedicke et al. (Eds.): Advancing Research in Information and Communication Technology,
IFIP AICT 600, pp. 321–329, 2021. https://doi.org/10.1007/978-3-030-81701-5_13

A.V. Balakrishnan, Los Angeles, US 1972–1979
J. Stoer, Würzburg, D 1979–1985
M. Lucertini, Rome, I 1985–1988
P. Thoft-Christensen, Aalborg, DK 1988–1995
P. Kall, Zurich, S 1995–2001
I. Lasiecka, Charlottesville, US 2001–2008
J. Henry, Bordeaux, F 2008–2012
F. Tröltzsch, Berlin, D 2013–2018
Ł. Stettner, Warsaw, PL 2018–

Current list of members of TC7 consists of the chair:

Prof. Dr. Lukasz STETTNER, PL, Polish Academy of Sciences, Institute of Mathematics and two vice chairs: Prof. Dr. Dietmar HÖMBERG, DE, WIAS Weierstraß-Institut and Prof. Irena LASIECKA, ACM, The University of Memphis, Department of Mathematical Sciences as well as (where with * we denote honorary members while with ** the members recommended by TC7):

Barbara Kaltenbacher AT, Philippe Toint BE, Edmundo de Souza e Silva BR, Hector Cancela UY, Jiri Outrata CZ, Josef Stoer* DE, Arnd Rösch** DE, Fredi Tröltzsch* DE, Allan Larsen DK, Josep Casanovas ES, Luis Alberto Fernández** ES, Grégoire Allaire FR, Stefan Scholtes GB, Istvan Maros HU, Maria C. Calzarossa IT, Yongbing Zhang JP, Junho Song KR, Adrie J.M. Beulens NL, Jose Antonio Oliveira PT, Vyacheslav Maksimov RU, Lidija Zadnik Stirn SI.

2 Scope of the Activities of TC7 and Working Groups

Generally speaking the scope of TC7 is two-fold: to foster the theoretical foundation for problems of the TC's concern and, based thereon, to develop or improve corresponding solution methods and their implementations. This broad scope of the TC7 is studied by a number of Working Groups which are involved both in the progress of theoretical research and in the growth of practical needs.

The scope of TC7 consists in computational aspects of optimization problems arising in such areas as Aerospace, Biomedicine, Economics, Meteorology, and Public Services (Health, Environment, Police, Fire, Transportation, etc.).

Some specific examples are:

- on-line and off-line computational techniques in modeling and control of dynamic systems;
- trajectory analysis and computation;
- optimization of decentralized systems (macro-economic systems) and systems with multicriteria;
- optimization of resource allocation in urban systems;
- optimization of pollution-control systems;
- optimization of man-machine systems;
- optimization of power systems operation;
- risk management in particular in mathematical finance and insurance;

- development of machine learning techniques;
- optimization and control under uncertainty.

There are 8 Working Groups being active within TC7, which we list below (in brackets we write year of foundation and the name of the first chair at foundation) with named chairs of them:

WG7.1 Modeling and Simulation (1972, W.A. Karplus, USA), temporarily suspended since 2018
WG7.2 Computational Techniques in Distributed Systems (1973, J.L. Lions, F), Chaired by Lorena Bociu
WG7.3 Computer System Modeling (1973, P.E. Green, USA), Chaired by Mark S. Squillante
WG7.4 Discrete Optimization (1983, M. Padberg, USA), changed in 2014 to Inverse Problems and Imaging, Chaired by Christian Clason
WG7.5 Reliability and Optimization of Structural Systems (1986, P. Thoft-Christensen, DK), Chaired by Junho Song
WG7.6 Optimization-Based Computer-Aided Modeling and Design (1989, H.-J. Sebastian, D), Revised in 1999, Chaired by Janusz Granat
WG7.7 Stochastic Optimization (1989, P. Kall, CH), changed in 2018 to Stochastic Control and Optimization, Chaired by Jan Palczewski
WG7.8 Nonlinear Optimization, (2018, Radu Ioan Bot)

Working groups used to organize workshops and seminars. Periodically they publish proceedings of their activities. We present below the names of the workshops:

Modelling and Optimization of Complex System, IFIP-TC 7 Working Conference Novosibirsk, USSR, 3–9 July, 1978, see [1]
Global Modelling, IFIP-WG 7/1 Working Conference Dubrovnik, Yugoslavia, Sept. 1–5, 1980, see [2]
Advances in Filtering and Optimal Stochastic Control, IFIP-WG 7/1 Working Conference Cocoyoc, Mexico, February 1–6, 1982, see [3]
Recent Advances in System Modelling and Optimization, IFIP-WG 7/1 Working Conference Santiago, Chile, August 27–31, 1984, see [4]
Stochastic Modelling and Filtering, IFIP-WG 7/1 Working Conference Rome, Italy, December 10–14, 1984, see [5]
Control Problems for Systems Described by Partial Differential Equations and Applications, IFIP-WG 7.2 Working Conference Gainesville, Florida, February 3–6, 1986, see [6]
Stochastic Differential Systems, IFIP-WG 7/1 Working Conference Eisenach, GDR, April 6–13, 1986, see [7]
Reliability and Optimization of Structural Systems, IFIP WG 7.5 Working Conference Aalborg, Denmark, May 6–8, 1987, see [8]
Boundary Control and Boundary Variations, IFIP WG 7.2 Conference Nice, France, June 10–13, 1987, see [9]

Control of Partial Differential Equations, IFIP WG 7.2 Working Conference Santiago de Compostela, Spain, July 6–9, 1987, see [10]

Control of Boundaries and Stabilization, IFIP WG 7.2 Conference Clermont Ferrand, France, June 20–23, 1988, see [11]

Stochastic Systems and Optimization, 6th IFIP WG 7.1 Working Conference Warsaw, Poland, September 12–16, 1988, see [12]

Reliability and Optimization of Structural Systems '88, 2nd IFIP WG7.5 Conference London, UK, September 26–28, 1988, see [13]

Modelling and Inverse Problems of Control for Distributed Parameter Systems, IFIP (W.G.7.2)-IIASA Conference, Laxenburg, Austria, July 24–28, 1989, see [14]

Reliability and Optimization of Structural Systems '90, 3rd IFIP WG 7.5 Conference Berkeley, California, USA, March 26–28, 1990, see [15]

Optimal Control of Partial Differential Equations, IFIP WG 7.2 International Conference Irsee, April 9–12, 1990, see [16]

Control Theory of Distributed Parameter Systems and Applications, IFIP WG 7.2 Working Conference Shanghai, China, May 6–9, 1990, see [17]

Boundary Control and Boundary Variation, IFIP WG 7.2 Conference Sophia Antipolis, France, October 15–17, 1990, see [18]

Stochastic Partial Differential Equations and Their Applications, IFIP WG 7/1 International Conference University of North Carolina at Charlotte, NC June 6–8, 1991, see [19]

Reliability and Optimization of Structural Systems '91, 4th IFIP WG 7.5 Conference Munich, Germany, September 11–13, 1991, see [20]

Optimization-Based Computer-Aided Modelling and Design, First Working Conference of the IFIP TC 7.6 Working Group The Hague, The Netherlands, 1991, see [21]

3   General Conferences

One of the main activities of TC7 are general conferences, which in fact started before creation of TC7. The conferences had different names but starting from 1981 it was fixed to System Modeling and Optimization. TC7 general conferences played an important role in research activities. They gathered usually a number of leading specialists. Plenary lectures were delivered by mathematicians and engineers working in theoretical and practical aspects of various applications.

We list below general IFIP conferences, which usually (starting from 7th Conference) are organized every two years.

Colloquium on Methods of Optimization, Novosibirsk, June 1968, see [22]

Computing Methods in Optimization Problems, San Remo, September 1968, see [23]

Symposium on Optimization, Nice June 1969, see [24]

Techniques of optimization : 4th IFIP Colloquium on Optimization Techniques, held at Los Angeles, California on October 19–22, 1971, see [25]

5th Conference on Optimization Techniques Rome 1973, see [26]

Optimization Techniques IFIP Technical Conference Novosibirsk, July 1–7, 1974, see [27]

Optimization Techniques Modeling and Optimization in the Service of Man, 7th IFIP Conference Nice, September 8–12, 1975, see [28]

Optimization Techniques: 8th IFIP Conference on Optimization Techniques, Würzburg, 1977 Sept. 5–9, see [29]

Optimization Techniques: 9th IFIP Conference on Optimization Techniques Warsaw, September 4–8, 1979, see [30]

System Modeling and Optimization, 10th IFIP Conference New York City, USA, August 31–September 4,1981, see [31]

System Modelling and Optimization, 11th IFIP Conference Copenhagen, Denmark, July 25–29, 1983, see [32]

System Modelling and Optimization, 12th IFIP Conference, Budapest, Hungary, September 2–6, 1985, see [33]

System Modelling and Optimization, 13th IFIP Conference Tokyo, Japan, August 31–September 4, 1987, see [34]

System Modelling and Optimization, 14th IFIP-Conference Leipzig, GDR, July 3–7, 1989, see [35]

System Modelling and Optimization, 15th IFIP Conference Zurich, Switzerland, September 2–6, 1991, see [36]

System Modelling and Optimization, 16th IFIP-TC7 Conference, Compiègne, France — July 5–9, 1993, see [37]

System Modelling and Optimization, Seventeenth IFIP TC7 Conference on System Modelling and Optimization, 1995, see [38]

18th annual IFIP TC7 Conference on Systems Modelling and Optimization held in July 1997, see [39]

System Modelling and Optimization Methods, Theory and Applications. 19th IFIP TC7 Conference on System Modelling and Optimization July 12–16, 1999, Cambridge, UK, see [40]

System Modeling and Optimization XX, IFIP TC7 20th Conference on System Modeling and Optimization July 23–27, 2001, Trier, Germany, see [41]

System Modeling and Optimization, 21st IFIP TC7 Conference held in July 21st–25th, 2003, Sophia Antipolis, France, see [42]

Systems, Control, Modeling and Optimization, 22nd IFIP TC7 Conference held from July 18–22, 2005, in Turin, Italy, see [43]

System Modeling and Optimization, 23rd IFIP TC 7 Conference, Cracow, Poland, July 23–27, 2007, see [44]

24th IFIP TC7 Conference, Buenos Aires, Argentina July 27–31, 2009, organizer: Hugo Scolnik,

System Modeling and Optimization, 25th IFIP TC 7 Conference, CSMO 2011, Berlin, Germany, September 12–16, 2011, see [45]

System Modeling and Optimization, 26th IFIP TC 7 Conference, CSMO 2013, Klagenfurt, Austria, September 9–13, 2013, see [46]

System Modeling and Optimization, 27th IFIP TC 7 Conference, CSMO 2015, Sophia Antipolis, France, June 29–July 3, 2015, see [47]

28th IFIP TC 7 Conference on System Modelling and Optimization, Essen, July 23–27, 2018, Org. C. Clason,

29th IFIP TC7 Conference on System Modelling and Optimization, Quito, August 30–Sept. 3, 2021, Org. Juan Carlos de los Reyes, Pedro Merino, Luis Miguel Torres, Tuomo Valkonen.

There was no proceeding of the 24th Conference held in Buenos Aires. Because of the swine flue epidemics the usual attendance of the conference from Europe and North America was under represented and we had relatively small number of participants (about 119). The 28th Conference was primary scheduled in Ankara 2017 but due to unstable political situation it was cancelled and moved in 2018 to Essen. Due to coronavirus pandemic the 29th IFIP Conference in Quito has been postponed to 2021 and will be held online. The 30th Conference will be on July 4th–8th 2022 in Warsaw, to continue general conferences every two years in average.

4 TC7 Future Activities

Modeling and optimization seems to be still important in various applications. Recent interest in machine learning techniques in particular in reinforcement learning and quality learning stimulate applicability of the research works of TC7.

Another area is big data, large scale problems, the problem to find adequate methods as well as sufficiently efficient implementations. Together with an increase of the power of computers we need to develop suitable mathematical tools to handle such problems.

Modeling of coronavirus pandemic is another hot problem in the area of interest of TC7. Consequently there are a lot of to be done in modeling and optimization and therefore we are looking optimistically to the near future.

References

1. Marchuk, G.I. (ed.): Modelling and Optimization of Complex System. Proceedings of the IFIP-TC 7 Working Conference Novosibirsk, USSR, 3–9 July 1978. Lecture Notes in Control and Information Sciences, vol. 18. Springer, Heidelberg (1979). https://doi.org/10.1007/BFb0004146
2. Krčevinac, S. (ed.): Global Modelling. Proceedings of the IFIP-WG 7/1 Working Conference Dubrovnik, Yugoslavia, 1–5 September 1980. Lecture Notes in Control and Information Sciences, vol. 35. Springer, Heidelberg (1981). https://doi.org/10.1007/BFb0006340
3. Fleming, W.H., Gorostiza, L.G. (eds.): Advances in Filtering and Optimal Stochastic Control of the IFIP-WG 7/1 Working Conference. Lecture Notes in Control and Information Sciences, Cocoyoc, Mexico, 1–6 February 1982, vol. 42. Springer, Heidelberg (1982). https://doi.org/10.1007/BFb0004521
4. Luis Contesse, B., Rafael Correa, F., Andrés Weintraub, P. (eds.): Recent Advances in System Modelling and Optimization. Proceedings of the IFIP-WG 7/1 Working Conference. Lecture Notes in Control and Information Sciences, Santiago, Chile, 27–31 August 1984, vol. 87. Springer, Heidelberg (1986). https://doi.org/10.1007/BFb0006773
5. Germani, A. (ed.): Stochastic Modelling and Filtering. Proceedings of the IFIP-WG 7/1 Working Conference. Lecture Notes in Control and Information Sciences, Rome, Italy, 10–14 December 1984, vol. 91. Springer, Heidelberg (1987). https://doi.org/10.1007/BFb0009045

6. Lasiecka, I., Triggiani, R. (eds.): Control Problems for Systems Described by Partial Differential Equations and Applications. Proceedings of the IFIP-WG 7.2 Working Conference. Lecture Notes in Control and Information Sciences, Gainesville, Florida, 3–6 February 1986, vol. 97. Springer, Heidelberg (1987). https://doi.org/10.1007/BFb0038738

7. Engelbert, H.J., Schmidt, W. (eds.): Stochastic Differential Systems. Proceedings of the IFIP-WG 7/1 Working Conference Eisenach, GDR. Lecture Notes in Control and Information Sciences, 6–13 April 1986, vol. 96. Springer, Heidelberg (1987). https://doi.org/10.1007/BFb0038914

8. Thoft-Christensen, P. (ed.): Reliability and Optimization of Structural Systems. Proceedings of the 1st IFIP WG 7.5 Working Conference. Lecture Notes in Engineering, Aalborg, Denmark, 6–8 May 1987, vol. 33, Springer, Heidelberg (1987). https://doi.org/10.1007/978-3-642-83279-6

9. Zolésio, J.P. (ed.): Boundary Control and Boundary Variations. Proceedings of the IFIP WG 7.2 Conference. Lecture Notes in Control and Information Sciences, Nice, France, 10–13 June 1987, vol. 100. Springer, Heidelberg (1988). https://doi.org/10.1007/BFb0041906

10. Bermúdez, A. (ed.): Control of Partial Differential Equations. Proceedings of the IFIP WG 7.2 Working Conference. Lecture Notes in Control and Information Sciences, Santiago de Compostela, Spain, 6–9 July 1987, vol. 114. Springer, Heidelberg (1989). https://doi.org/10.1007/BFb0002574

11. Simon, J. (ed.): Control of Boundaries and Stabilization. Proceedings of the IFIP WG 7.2 Conference. Lecture Notes in Control and Information Sciences, Clermont Ferrand, France, 20–23 June 1988, vol. 125. Springer, Heidelberg (1989). https://doi.org/10.1007/BFb0043348

12. Zabczyk, J. (ed.): Stochastic Systems and Optimization. Proceedings of the 6th IFIP WG 7.1 Working Conference. Lecture Notes in Control and Information Sciences, Warsaw, Poland, 12–16 September 1988, vol. 136. Springer, Heidelberg (1989). https://doi.org/10.1007/BFb0002665

13. Thoft-Christensen, P. (ed.): Reliability and Optimization of Structural Systems. 1988 Proceedings of the 2nd IFIP WG7.5 Conference. Lecture Notes in Engineering. London, UK, 26–28 September 1988, vol. 48. Springer, Heidelberg (1989). https://doi.org/10.1007/978-3-642-83828-6

14. Kurzhanski, A., Lasiecka, I. (eds.): Modelling and Inverse Problems of Control for Distributed Parameter Systems. Proceedings of IFIP (W.G.7.2)-IIASA Conference. Lecture Notes in Control and Information Sciences, Laxenburg, 24–28 Austria July 1989, vol. 154, Springer, Heidelberg (1991). https://doi.org/10.1007/BFb0044477

15. Der Kiureghian, A., Thoft-Christensen, P. (eds.): Reliability and Optimization of Structural Systems '90. Proceedings of the 3rd IFIP WG 7.5 Conference. Lecture Notes in Engineering, Berkeley, California, USA, 26–28 March 1990, vol. 61. Springer, Heidelberg (1991). https://doi.org/10.1007/978-3-642-84362-4

16. Hoffmann, K.-H., Krabs, W. (eds.): Optimal Control of Partial Differential Equations. Proceedings of the IFIP WG 7.2 International Conference. Lecture Notes in Control and Information Sciences, Irsee, 9–12 April 1990, vol. 149, Springer, Heidelberg (1991). https://doi.org/10.1007/BFb0043209

17. Li, X., Yong, J. (eds.): Control Theory of Distributed Parameter Systems and Applications. Proceedings of the IFIP WG 7.2 Working Conference. Lecture Notes in Control and Information Sciences, Shanghai, China, 6–9 May 1990, vol. 159. Springer, Heidelberg (1991). https://doi.org/10.1007/BFb0004431

18. Zolésio, J.P. (ed.): Boundary Control and Boundary Variation. Proceedings of IFIP WG 7.2 Conference. Lecture Notes in Control and Information Sciences, Sophia Antipolis, France, 15–17 October 1990, vol. 178. Springer, Heidelberg (1992). https://doi.org/10.1007/BFb0006683

19. Rozovskii, B.L., Sowers, R.B. (eds.): Stochastic Partial Differential Equations and Their Applications. Proceedings of IFIP WG 7/1 International Conference University of North Carolina. Lecture Notes in Control and Information Sciences, Charlotte, NC, 6–8 June 1991, vol. 176. Springer, Heidelberg (1992). https://doi.org/10.1007/BFb0007313

20. Rackwitz, R., Thoft-Christensen, P. (eds.): Reliability and Optimization of Structural Systems '91. Proceedings of the 4th IFIP WG 7.5 Conference. Lecture Notes in Engineering, Munich, Germany, 11–13 September 1991, vol. 76. Springer, Heidelberg (1992). https://doi.org/10.1007/978-3-642-84753-0

21. Beulens, A.J.M., Sebastian, H.-J. (eds.): Optimization-Based Computer-Aided Modelling and Design. 1991 Proceedings of the 1st Working Conference of the IFIP TC 7.6 Working Group. Lecture Notes in Control and Information Sciences, The Hague, The Netherlands, vol. 174. Springer, Heidelberg (1992). https://doi.org/10.1007/BFb0040130

22. Moiseev, N.N. (ed.): Colloquium on Methods of Optimization. Lecture Notes in Mathematics, Novosibirsk, June 1968, vol. 112. Springer, Heidelberg (1970). https://doi.org/10.1007/BFb0060193

23. Computing Methods in Optimization Problems. Lecture Notes in Operations Research and Mathematical Economics, San Remo, September 1968, vol. 14. Springer, Heidelberg (1969). https://doi.org/10.1007/978-3-642-85974-8

24. Balakrishnan, A.V., Contensou, M., de Veubeke, B.F., Krée, P., Lions, J.L., Moiseev, N.N. (eds.): 1969 Symposium on Optimization. Lecture Notes in Mathematics, Nice, 29 June–5 July 1969, vol. 132. Springer, Heidelberg (1970). https://doi.org/10.1007/BFb0066669

25. Balakrishnan, A.V. (eds.): Techniques of Optimization. 4th IFIP Colloquium on Optimization Techniques, Los Angeles, California, 19–22 October 1971. Academic Press (1971)

26. Conti, R., Ruberti, A. (eds.): 5th Conference on Optimization Techniques. Centure Notes in Computer Science, Rome, vol. 4. Springer, Heidelberg (1973). https://doi.org/10.1007/3-540-06600-4

27. Marchuk, G.I. (ed.): Optimization Techniques. IFIP Technical Conference. Lecture Notes in Computer Science, Novosibirsk, 1–7 July 1974, vol. 27. Springer, Heidelberg (1975). https://doi.org/10.1007/978-3-662-38527-2

28. Cea, J. (ed.): Optimization Techniques Modeling and Optimization in the Service of Man. 7th IFIP Conference. Lecture Notes in Computer Science, Nice, 8–12 September 1975, vol. 40, 41. Springer, Heidelberg (1976). https://doi.org/10.1007/3-540-07622-0

29. Stoer, J. (ed.): Optimization Techniques. Proceedings of the 8th IFIP Conference on Optimization Techniques. Lecture Notes in Control and Information Sciences, Würzburg, 5–9 September 1977, vol. 6. Springer, Heidelberg (1978). https://doi.org/10.1007/BFb0007218

30. Iracki, K., Malanowski, K., Walukiewicz, S. (eds.): Optimization Techniques. Proceedings of the 9th IFIP Conference on Optimization Techniques. Lecture Notes in Control and Information Sciences, Warsaw, 4–8 September 1979, vol. 22, 23. Springer, Heidelberg (1980). https://doi.org/10.1007/BFb0006580

31. Drenick, R.F., Kozin, F. (eds.): System Modeling and Optimization. Proceedings of the 10th IFIP Conference. Lecture Notes in Control and Information Sciences, New York City, USA, 31 August–4 September 1981, vol. 38. Springer, Heidelberg (1982). https://doi.org/10.1007/BFb0006119

32. Thoft-Christensen, P. (ed.): System Modelling and Optimization. Proceedings of the 11th IFIP Conference. Lecture Notes in Control and Information Sciences, Copenhagen, Denmark, 25–29 July 1983, vol. 59. Springer, Heidelberg (1984). https://doi.org/10.1007/BFb0008873

33. Prékopa, A., Szelezsáan, J., Strazicky, B. (eds.): System Modelling and Optimization. Proceedings of 12th IFIP Conference. Lecture Notes in Control and Information Sciences, Budapest, Hungary, 2–6 September 1985, vol. 84. Springer, Heidelberg (1986). https://doi.org/10.1007/BFb0043817

34. Iri, M., Yajima, K. (eds.): System Modelling and Optimization. Proceedings of the 13th IFIP Conference. Lecture Notes in Control and Information Sciences, Tokyo, Japan, 31 August–4 September 1987, vol. 113. Springer, Heidelberg (1988). https://doi.org/10.1007/BFb0042768

35. Sebastian, H.-J., Tammer, K.: System Modelling and Optimization. Proceedings of the 14th IFIP-Conference. Lecture Notes in Control and Information Sciences, Leipzig, GDR, 3–7 July 1989, vol. 143. Springer, Heidelberg (1990). https://doi.org/10.1007/BFb0008351

36. Davisson, L.D., MacFarlane, A.G.J., Kwakernaak, H., Massey, J.L., Tsypkin, Y.Z., Viterbi, A.J., Kall, P. (eds.): System Modelling and Optimization. Proceedings of the 15th IFIP Conference. Lecture Notes in Control and Information Sciences, Zurich, Switzerland, 2–6 September 1991, vol. 180. Springer, Heidelberg (1992). https://doi.org/10.1007/BFb0113266

37. Henry, J., Yvon, J.-P. (eds.): System Modelling and Optimization. Proceedings of the 16th IFIP-TC7 Conference. Lecture Notes in Control and Information Sciences, Compiègne, France, 5–9 July 1993, vol. 197. Springer, Heidelberg (1994). https://doi.org/10.1007/BFb 0035455

38. Dolezal, J., Fidler, J. (eds.): System Modelling and Optimization. 1995 Proceedings of the 17th IFIP TC7 Conference on System Modelling and Optimization. Springer, Heidelberg (1996). https://doi.org/10.1007/978-0-387-34897-1

39. Polis, M.P., Dontchev, A.I., Kall, P., Lasiecka, I., Olbrot, A.W. (eds.): 18th Annual IFIP TC7 Conference on Systems Modelling and Optimization, July 1997. Chapman & Hall/CRC (1999)

40. Powell, M.J.D., Scholtes, S. (eds.): System Modelling and Optimization Methods, Theory and Applications. 19th IFIP TC7 Conference on System Modelling and Optimization, Cambridge, UK, 12–16 July 1999. IFIP Advances in Information and Communication Technology (2000). https://doi.org/10.1007/978-0-387-35514-6

41. Sachs, E.W., Tichatschke, R. (eds.): System Modeling and Optimization XX. IFIP TC7 20th Conference on System Modeling and Optimization. IFIP Advances in Information and Communication Technology, 23–27 July 2001, Trier, Germany (2003). https://doi.org/10.1007/978-0-387-35699-0

42. Cagnol, J., Zolésio, J.-P. (eds.): System Modeling and Optimization. Proceedings of the 21st IFIP TC7 Conference. IFIP Advances in Information and Communication Technology, 21–25 July 2003, Sophia Antipolis, France (2005). https://doi.org/10.1007/b101574

43. Ceragioli, F., Dontchev, A., Furuta, H., Marti, K., Pandolfi, L. (eds.): Systems, Control, Modeling and Optimization. Proceedings of the 22nd IFIP TC7 Conference. IFIP Advances in Information and Communication Technology, Turin, Italy, 18–22 July 2005 (2006). https://doi.org/10.1007/0-387-33882-9

44. Korytowski, A., Malanowski, K., Mitkowski, W., Szymkat, M. (eds.): System Modeling and Optimization. 23rd IFIP TC 7 Conference. IFIP Advances in Information and Communication Technology, Cracow, Poland, 23–27 July 2007 (2009). https://doi.org/10.1007/978-3-642-048 02-9

45. Hömberg, D., Tröltzsch, F. (eds.): System Modeling and Optimization. 25th IFIP TC 7 Conference, CSMO 2011. IFIP Advances in Information and Communication Technology, Berlin, Germany, 12–16 September 2011 (2013). https://doi.org/10.1007/978-3-662-45504-3

46. Pötzsche, C., Heuberger, C., Kaltenbacher, B., Rendl, F (eds.): System Modeling and Optimization. 26th IFIP TC 7 Conference, CSMO 2013. IFIP Advances in Information and Communication Technology, Klagenfurt, Austria, 9–13 September 2013 (2014). https://doi.org/10.1007/978-3-662-45504-3

47. Bociu, L., Désidéri, J.-A., Habbal, A. (eds.): CSMO 2015. IFIP-AICT, vol. 494. Springer, Cham (2016). https://doi.org/10.1007/978-3-319-55795-3

TC 8: Information Systems

5. Information System

The Future of Information Systems in a Post-COVID World by TC8 (Information Systems)

Isabel Ramos[1]([✉]), Dale Mackrell[2], Alta van der Merwe[3], Jan Pries-Heje[4], Jolita Ralyté[5], Janis Stirna[6], John Krogstie[7], Matthew Jones[8], Benjamin Mueller[9], Frédéric Adam[10], Bettina Jaber[11], Edgar Weippl[11], Marijn Janssen[12], Amany Elbanna[13], Banita Lal[14], Pierluigi Plebani[15], Allen C. Johnston[16], and Li Da Xu[17]

[1] University of Minho, Campus de Azurém, Guimarães, Portugal
iramos@dsi.uminho.pt
[2] Institute for Integrated and Intelligent Systems, Griffith University, Brisbane, Australia
d.mackrell@griffith.edu.au
[3] University of Pretoria, Hatfield Campus, Hatfield, South Africa
alta.vdm@up.ac.za
[4] Department of People and Technology, Roskilde Universitet, Roskilde, Denmark
janph@ruc.dk
[5] University of Geneva, Geneva, Switzerland
jolita.ralyte@unige.ch
[6] Stockholm University, Stockholm, Sweden
js@dsv.su.se
[7] Norwegian University of Science and Technology (NTNU), Trondheim, Norway
krogstie@idi.ntnu.no
[8] Cambridge University, Judge Institute of Management Studies, Cambridge, UK
mrj10@cam.ac.uk
[9] University of Lausanne, Lausanne, Switzerland
benjamin.mueller@unil.ch
[10] Cork University Business School, University College, Cork, Republic of Ireland
fadam@ucc.ie
[11] SBA Research, Vienna University of Technology, Vienna, Austria
eweippl@sba-research.org
[12] Faculty of Technology, Policy and Management, Delft University of Technology, Delft, The Netherlands
M.F.W.H.A.Janssen@tudelft.nl
[13] School of Business and Management, Royal Holloway University of London, London, UK
amany.elbanna@rhul.ac.uk
[14] University of Bradford, School of Management, Bradford, UK
b.lall@bradford.ac.uk
[15] Polytechnic University of Milan, Milan, Italy
pierluigi.plebani@polimi.it
[16] Culverhouse College of Business, University of Alabama, Tuscaloosa, USA
ajohnston@cba.ua.edu
[17] IT and Decision Sciences, Old Dominion University, Norfolk, VA, USA
lxu@odu.edu

© IFIP International Federation for Information Processing 2021
Published by Springer Nature Switzerland AG 2021
M. Goedicke et al. (Eds.): Advancing Research in Information and Communication Technology,
IFIP AICT 600, pp. 333–360, 2021. https://doi.org/10.1007/978-3-030-81701-5_14

Abstract. This chapter consists of several sections which contain contributions from members of IFIP Technical Committee 8 (Information Systems). We highlight the accomplishments of Technical Committee 8 (TC8) and its working groups over its 50 years history, and then envisage possible strategies for the future of information systems (IS) in a post-COVID world. This chapter begins with an overall view of the diverse and changing roles of the IS field then moves forward to foresee environmental sustainability and digital glocalization in a post-COVID-19 world. Next, we review the achievements of TC8, the establishment of the working groups within it, and predict what TC8 has to offer into the future. Lastly, we identify the individual working groups of TC8 to detail their activities as important conduits of research and practice in the field of IS over the past 50 years, then imagine the roles of the TC8 working groups in a post-COVID landscape.

Keywords: Information systems · Technology · Society · Organisations · Technical Committee 8

1   Introduction

The call for this chapter has come at an opportune time when we have had a chance to reflect on the recent past and try to imagine post-COVID society where the health of humanity and the health of earth are synchronised. We have had glimpses of this synchronization as nations try to curb economic relationships in attempts to suppress the spread of the COVID-19 virus. This incentive has given us hope that climate change may be slowed if we make efforts to reduce pollution levels in local and global responses. The use of technologies has been instrumental during the COVID-19 pandemic as more citizens work and play online and will continue to dominate the focus of research and practice in the information systems discipline in a post-COVID world.

One perspective on post-COVID society is Society 5.0, defined as "a human-centered society that balances economic advancement with the resolution of social problems by a system that highly integrates cyberspace and physical space" (https://www8.cao.go.jp/cstp/english/society5_0/index.html). It is called Society 5.0 because it follows the hunting society (Society 1.0), agricultural society (Society 2.0), industrial society (Society 3.0), and information society (Society 4.0). In Society 4.0, the common practice is to gather data from physical space via the Web, store it in the Cloud for analysis by humans. While information may be shared, there are limitations. On the other hand, physical space in Society 5.0 is sensor-driven. People, things, and systems are all automatically connected in cyberspace. Analytical results obtained by artificial intelligence (AI) are fed back to physical space. This convergence of cyber and physical space promises new societal awareness and values.

In this chapter, we begin by looking at the role of information systems (IS) with a focus on environmental sustainability and digital glocalization in a post-COVID world. The next section takes us back to the achievements and publications of Technical Committee 8 (TC8) and the working groups within it. It also lets us see what TC8 has to offer into the future. The final section of this chapter recognises the various working groups of TC8 and specifies their activities as important conduits of research and practice in the diverse field of information systems over the past 50 years and moving forward.

2   The Future of the Information Systems Field

For some time now, scientists have been warning about the climate crisis and its growing impacts on the well-being of human populations. The current health crisis is only one of these impacts and other disruptive events are expected in the coming years or decades. This perspective on the near future has brought to the international agenda the need for a more sustainable and equitable global economic model (Oldekop et al. 2020).

In the face of disruptive events on a global scale, there is a need for local economic and social responses coordinated on a global scale. The impacts of future disruptive events will differ from region to region and require action from local communities adjusted to local needs. On the other hand, these local initiatives must clearly contribute to sustainability goals that must be global in order to slow down climate processes that threaten humanity as a whole. This approach, which some authors already call glocalization (Roudometof 2016; 2019), implies concrete focuses of intervention, namely digital globalisation, green economy and local/global governance.

2.1   Digital Globalisation and Sustainability

The concept of digital globalisation refers to a new form of globalisation in a world increasingly aware of its environmental footprint and the danger it poses to the survival of humanity in the medium and long term. The flow of information has been growing in recent decades, ensuring the interconnection of societies and economies at a global level. The global transmission of ideas, knowledge and innovation has enabled a broad participation in the digital economy, adjusting solutions and recommendations to local needs. Governments, citizens and businesses can participate in digital platforms to access globally generated insights and opportunities. Thus, the digital transformation is becoming a central topic of research, education and practice in the area of Information Systems (Vial 2019).

The growing interest in exploring the opportunities offered by technological advances has to be made compatible with the need to guarantee a sustainable development of economies, which ensures that it protects the planet and ensures the well-being of peoples. In other words, the digital transformation of governments and organisations must create environmental, economic and social value (Wessel et al. 2020). The discipline of information systems is called upon to develop insights, approaches and IT solutions that effectively support value creation. It is also called upon to study how available IT technology applications can be used and interconnected effectively to enhance sustainable development.

2.2   The Centrality of Information in Integrating Local and Global Governance

The adequate response to disruptive events requires strong governance, whether at the level of country, city, organisation or information systems. Decision-makers must have the power to make decentralised decisions that allow them to plan and implement the necessary adjustments to the uncertainty and complexity faced at every moment. In addition to this local response, it is necessary to ensure the agility of businesses and communities, promoting their access to the resources they need to deal with the pressure of globalisation and the need to maintain the sustainability of their operations. The threats posed by climate change, environmental decline, water scarcity, overpopulation and misinformation, for example, cannot be adequately addressed with only local efforts (Pappas et al. 2018). They require global collaboration mechanisms that (1) equip nations with the efficiency and agility to respond to global challenges, (2) ensure the solidarity needed to tackle problems that emerge from disruptive events and protect the most vulnerable populations, and (3) make nations and institutions accountable for practices, implemented deliberately or not, which put humanity as a whole at risk.

This interconnection between local and global governance that glocalization requires can only be achieved by the proper management of information flows in an increasingly digital world. The digital transformation of society will change the way we live, interact, learn and work. It has also been amplifying problems related to inequality in internet access, the spread of misinformation, online violence, breaches of privacy, digital warfare, among others. The discipline of information systems is thus called upon to contribute to better management of information and technologies at global and local level (Barnes 2020), including through the production of theories and approaches that support (1) the sharing of information between countries and organisations, (2) the design of engaging digital work environments, (3) the creation of value chains resilient to disruptive events, (4) access to health care at an affordable cost to everyone, (5) the reinforcement of responsible consumption behaviors, (6) the provision of education with a high level of quality, and (7) the construction of a safer and more inclusive society.

2.3   Regional Perspectives in Brief on Glocalization and What Technology is Bringing to the Conversation

At a global level, indications are that the great challenges that need global coordination and local action are associated with economic and climate sustainability, with a particular focus on the continued digitization of the economy and energy efficiency.

With regards to the digital transformation of the economy, Europe is committed to the empowerment and inclusion of citizens, as well as strengthening the capacity of companies to deliver value in the global market. Regarding energy efficiency, the focus is on reducing greenhouse gas emissions and a strong investment in renewable energies (Demertzis et al. 2019). To address the challenges in these two areas, the coming years will bring a significant investment in research, education and innovation. Universities play a crucial role in creating and transferring knowledge essential to strengthening the economy; mechanisms such as science and open innovation will continue to be the pillars of the strengthening of University-Citizen and University-Industry links.

In the United States, these concerns are compounded by the challenges of maintaining its place as the greatest economic and military power. These challenges will bring increasing investment in disruptive technologies and businesses. The desire to reduce dependence on global value chains could reinforce efforts to reintegrate processes and promote regional supplies.

The Asia and Pacific region is very dynamic; the countries of the region show substantial differences in terms of socioeconomic status, physical and population dimensions, and climatic zones. Thus, these countries face similar and/or very different challenges, which makes it even more important to define a glocalized agenda. Some of the common challenges include reducing inequalities across the Asia and Pacific region, improving the environment, stimulating employment, deepening democracy and social cohesion, managing regional and global political and economic relations, among other challenges.

A similar diversity can be seen in Latin America (de Sanfeliú et al. 2020). The countries of that region of the globe are quite different in terms of size, populations and level of development. Although decreasing in the last decade, poverty and inequality are still very present in the region. Corruption is also a serious problem in these countries, limiting their ability to become strong economies. To address these regional challenges, citizens need access to better public services and social justice. The digital transformation of governments can be central to restoring confidence, enabling agile governance and advance smarter regulation.

Africa continues to face serious difficulties in improving living standards across the continent. The dependence on regional institutions for external financing and the difficulty in ensuring continental integration expose the continent to international exploitation and frequent internal conflicts. Informal workers represent 86% of total employment in Africa (Hevia and Neumeyer 2020). This situation highlights the importance of supporting and developing the informal economy, accelerating continental integration, namely through the adoption of transnational technological infrastructures, and ensuring the centrality of food systems. Food systems can benefit greatly from the applications of information technologies, including Internet of Things (IoT) and Artificial Intelligence (AI). Information technologies have allowed the creation of high productivity services and agribusiness. In addition, infotech, biotechnology and fintech may contribute to solving some of the structural problems faced in Africa (Coulibaly 2020).

2.4 IS Research and Education for a Glocalized World

The information systems discipline should reflect this diversity of challenges and technological needs in order to produce knowledge and develop relevant innovations locally, while observing the scientific rigor inherent in a global discipline.

The principles, practices and processes that are widely applicable will naturally be part of IS education and research globally. They allow for the development of sound knowledge and skills required to assist in the digital transformation of organisations and society. Still, the development of knowledge and innovations based on local phenomena with relevance to a particular community, region or country should be encouraged and valued in a glocalized approach to the discipline. The global sharing of knowledge and technologies is fundamental to the development of the IS discipline. However, their application in a way that is sensitive to local conditions is central to address the complexity of innovation systems and, therefore, the continued relevance of the discipline (Martinsons 2016).

3 The Future Role for TC8 Drawn from the Past

Information Systems (IS) emerged as an independent field in the 1960s based on an interest in organisations and people using computers for business processes. From the beginning, most IS research was quite management-oriented and dominated by quantitative research methods. The first major journal focusing on IS was launched in March 1977; Management Information Systems Quarterly (MISQ). The Information Systems research seminar in Scandinavia (IRIS) began in 1978 and is today the oldest IS conference in the world still running every year. The first international conference on Information Systems - ICIS - was held in Philadelphia, USA, in 1981.

Through the eighties, the IS field was characterised by strong growth. Many universities around the world created an institute or a department of IS. In the USA and UK, the majority of IS research was located in business schools. In Europe, IS was often located together with natural sciences or the humanities.

Ahead of this growth, in 1974, the Technical Committee 8 under the International Federation for Information Processing (IFIP) was approved. Shortly afterwards, the first two working groups (WG) were established: WG8.1 Design and Evaluation of Information Systems and WG8.2 Interaction of Information Systems and the Organisation. Hence, from this time TC8 had a dual focus on design and development on one side and on application and utilisation in organisations on the other side. In fact, one could say that this dual perspective on design and use is still the core of TC8.

In the 1980s, and especially after the introduction of the personal computer (PC), Human-Computer Interaction came on the agenda. Many studied the correlation between user friendly IT systems and satisfaction with the same systems. One of the most cited models was the Technology Acceptance Model (TAM) that says that acceptance of new IT depends on the perceived usefulness, the perceived ease of use, and the user acceptance.

In the 1980s, three new TC8 working groups were established, with two of them focusing on specific types of IT systems. In 1981, WG8.3 Decision Support Systems was established. This group focused both on a special kind of systems – decision support – and on a specific business process – decisions. This is still an important task for TC8 to take on when some new technology comes around. For example, for smart cities we can study how they are designed and discuss how and what technology to use. Further, we can look at the business processes within smart cities and how they best utilise new technology to create digital transformation.

The other group initiated in the eighties was WG8.4 Office Systems that a few years later changed their name to WG8.4 E-Business Information Systems, again focusing on new technology in the years where E-business was invented and on how this new technology was applied and utilised. This emphasises that TC8 often has tried to take a leading role when new technology was introduced in businesses and organisations. Typically, TC8 working groups operate through organising working conferences. Often these conferences have set the stage for new and existing research that later after some maturation has become part of mainstream research and practice.

The third group initiated in the eighties was WG8.5 Information Systems in Public Administration. The new thing about this group was that it concentrated on a specific area of society, namely, the public sector.

The 1990s brought increased awareness about IT systems for collaborative support and knowledge management. In 1994, the Association for Information Systems (AIS) was founded as an organisation for academics specializing in information systems. AIS did not seek to interfere with or replace IFIP. In the late 1990s, a wave of internet and web applications led to much interest and research in these areas. In the 1990s, WG8.6 Transfer and Diffusion of Information Technology was approved in 1995. This group combined the two original areas of TC8, design and use, in that it looked at design in the context of the organisational change or implementation of technology.

WG8.7 Informatics in International Business Enterprises became something of a non-starter. No working conferences were held by WG8.7 and the group disappeared after a few years. In 1998, WG8.8 Smart Cards was approved. This group was a bit like 8.3 in that it concentrated on a very specific technology but this time they looked at the use of this specific technology in all kind of business processes. Like WG8.7, WG8.8 is also no longer functioning.

In the new millennium, WG8.9 Enterprise Information Systems was approved in 2005. Again, this group looked at a specific technology that had gained widespread use and researchers discussed the potential. It also provided a critical angle. In 2008, a working group with a shared focus on security was established with TC11. This was WG8.11 Information Systems Security Research. This group had a special purpose in that they were not meeting to present papers published in proceedings by IFIP. Instead, they were meeting with the purpose of writing and improving papers for the very best journals in the field of IS security. Shortly after in 2011, WG8.10 Service-Oriented Systems was established together with TC2 and TC6. Finally, in 2019, the latest working group, WG8.12 Industrial Information Integration was established.

Based on this impressive history, a natural question to ask is how TC8 can inform a strategy for the future? The answer, we believe, is to stick to what TC8 in the past has been good at. First, that could be to maintain the dual focus on design and development on one side and on application and utilisation in organisations on the other side. Second, focusing on new special kinds of Information Systems and the specific business processes. An important example was mentioned in the prior section, digital transformation. Third, TC8 can focus on the use of IS in specific areas of society. For example, in the public sector worldwide there is a growing focus on Smart Cities and Green Sustainability. This can be picked up by an existing working group such as WG8.5 or it can be addressed by a new working group. Time will tell. But no matter what, you will also find TC8 at the forefront of the newest technical development in Information Systems in the future.

4 The TC8 WGs Perspectives

IFIP TC8 was established by the International Federation for Information Processing in 1976 as a Technical Committee dedicated to the field of Information Systems. TC8 aims to promote and encourage the advancement of research and practice of concepts, methods, techniques and issues related to information systems in organisations. TC8 has established eight working groups (WG), the history and activities of which are described below. In addition to the activities of its working groups, TC8 also organises working conferences and publishes books through IFIP. TC8 holds an annual National Representatives meeting.

WG8.1: Design and Evaluation of Information Systems
Established at the creation of TC8 in 1976, WG8.1 is focused on the planning, analysis, design and evaluation of information systems. The aim of the group is threefold:

(1) to define relevant concepts and theories, (2) to develop languages, techniques, tools and methods for applying these concepts and theories, and (3) to develop method engineering approaches for the analysis, construction and evaluation of information systems development methods and tools.

For over forty years the WG8.1 members have contributed to the development and evaluation of modelling languages, techniques, tools and methods for information systems engineering, evolution and assessment. The themes of the conferences and workshops organised reflect the evolution of their research ambitions, from defining the foundations of the field to exploring new trends and shaping new approaches and paradigms. In April 1979, WG8.1 held its first working conference in Oxford on "Formal Models and Practical Tools for Information Systems Design". Then, WG8.1 held two working conferences in 1982, one on each side of the Atlantic. The last of these conferences was the first of a series of so-called CRIS conferences which were collectively part of an in-depth comparative review of information systems methodologies.

The task group FRISCO was established in 1988 with the aim to develop a reference background comprising a consistent and fully coherent system of concepts and a suitable terminology for scientists and professionals in the information systems area. The "Framework of Information System Concepts" (Falkenberg et al. 1998) developed by this group is one of the significant contributions of WG8.1 to the development of a scientific outlook on the field of information systems. The group organised three working conferences on the subject (ISCO1 in 1989, ISCO2 in 1992, ISCO3 in 1995) and published the final report in 1998. The report has initiated an important debate and was a key driver for further research in the field. The ISCO conference series was concluded by ISCO4 in 1999.

The early nineties were marked by the emergence of methods and process models for information systems development. The group held two working conferences on this subject: "Information System Development Process" (Como, Italy 1993) and "Methods and Associated Tools for the Information Systems Life Cycle" (Maastricht, Netherlands 1994). The emergence of Internet technologies has brought new opportunities and challenges to the development of information systems, and was acknowledged with two working conferences: "Information Systems in the WWW Environment" (Beijing, China 1998) and "Engineering Information Systems in the Internet Context" (Kanazava, Japan 2002). The way of building new methods for the development of information systems has evolved from the simple ad-hoc method construction to engineering approaches of situational and domain-specific methods. The working group has been actively involved in the development of method engineering theories, approaches and tools allowing to reach a high degree of flexibility and adaptability of methods. Three method engineering conferences took place: "Method Engineering: Principles of Method Construction and Tool Support" (Atlanta, USA 1996), "Situational Method Engineering: Fundamentals and Experiences" (Geneva, Switzerland 2007), and "Method Engineering: Engineering Methods in the Service-Oriented Context" (Paris, France 2011).

The working conferences were meant to be relatively small and focused. To bring together a larger number of researchers, some of the central people in WG8.1 started in 1989 the CAiSE conference series, which today is an A-level conference with international reach. The longest lasting event of WG8.1, with 25 editions already, is EMMSAD

– a working conference on "Exploring Modeling Methods for Systems Analysis and Development" that all the time has been an associated event to CAiSE conferences. Today EMMSAD invites contributions on a large spectrum of topics, including foundations of modelling and method engineering, methods and modelling approaches for specific fields and purposes (enterprise, business, capability, process, ontology modelling), novel approaches to information systems development, domain specific modelling and various aspects of method evaluation. EMMSAD publishes joint Springer Nature LNBIP proceedings together with the "Business Process Modeling, Development and Support" (BPMDS) working conference. BPMDS has also been a WG8.1 event during the last decade and is associated with CAiSE.

In 2008 WG8.1 established a working conference on the "Practice of Enterprise Modeling" (PoEM). Its mission is to provide a dedicated forum where the use of enterprise modelling in practice is addressed by bringing together researchers, users, and practitioners. PoEM proceedings are published by Springer Nature LNBIP series. PoEM also aims to mix paper presentations with hands-on modelling and discussion sessions. In recent years it has featured accompanying events such as doctoral consortium, Forum of emerging ideas and demos, as well as several workshops. Usually about a quarter of the participants come from industry which makes discussions on emerging challenges as well as new methods and tools particularly insightful. In 2020, the 13th PoEM was organised by Riga Technical University, Latvia and due to the travel restrictions imposed by the pandemic it was held remotely.

WG8.1, drawing from its broad group of members, engages in a multitude of research areas following the group's objectives and focus. The rest of this section discusses some of the emerging trends and areas of concern.

The ongoing digital transformation of all areas has led to the need to involve everyone in organisations and society in the development and evolution of information systems, and thus to the need of representing knowledge of all relevant areas in an understandable way. Although some model-driven approaches such as Model Driven Development are successful in the development and evolution of the technical systems, the possibility of visualising the complete information system as done in enterprise modelling is believed to be even more important in the future.

Since recently many modern IT solutions have started to incorporate Big Data and AI-based solutions and components. This offers many opportunities and brings challenges. A recent survey on expected outcomes from using AI in business were "to improve and/or develop new products and services; achieve cost efficiencies and streamlined business operations, and to accelerate decision-making." (EY 2018). At the same time, AI also raises fundamental concerns regarding its social and economic impact, including ethics, security, privacy and trust. These issues were discussed from the point of view of enterprise modelling at a panel session of PoEM 2019 (reported in Snoeck et al. 2020). A first conclusion from the panel discussion is that, with the advent of AI, the need for traditional data management increases rather than decreases, which makes it more important than ever to include data related aspects in enterprise modelling activities to support the alignment of the business and data-driven solutions. It is important to consider data from a traditional data management perspective, but it is also important to include additional concerns, such as data ownership, ownership of "the original" phenomenon represented by data, i.e. privacy, ethics, biases. Another significant aspect is design for AI – providing foundations for proper data management, by offering means in terms of methods and tools for the design of enterprise-ready AI based solutions. A key aspect of such solutions would be the support for by capturing and analyzing the business motivation and needs for them. Data can also benefit organisational and IS designs and operations. To this end, the emerging development approaches need to make a distinction between "design models" that portray (parts or aspects of) a possible future/desired state of affairs of an enterprise, and "observational models" that portray (parts/aspects of) the current/past affairs of an enterprise and its information systems at runtime.

The future IT landscape will include more and more AI-driven autonomous actors that collaborate with humans. Modern enterprises increasingly involve a hybrid mix of human and digital agents on a large scale, for example, in the context of Industry 4.0. It therefore becomes relevant for emerging methods and tools to embrace lessons learned in the multi-agent systems community.

We also recognise that AI solutions run the risk that over time they turn out to be "digital asbestos" - initially seen as suitable and efficient for the intended purpose, but harmful once the impact and side effects of the application have accumulated. The health hazards of asbestos were discovered only many years later and currently the impact of AI-based solutions has not been studied in depth. Such impact studies should address breadth, i.e. the whole ecosystem in which they operate. Modelling techniques, being a core topic of WG8.1, can be used to better chart out the (potential and materialised) impact of AI. Furthermore, AI solutions need to be designed and implemented in context. This implies, they must comply with the regulations (and ethical norms) of the socio-technical environment in which they set to operate.

The challenging times of a pandemic has led many companies to strengthen their approach to information system portfolio management with an increased emphasis on resilience - the ability to function, to deliver business value, despite adverse circumstances. Due to the ubiquity of IT as a result of the digital transformation, resilience has also been increasingly important independent of the pandemic. Resilience management goes beyond the more traditional areas of concern addressed by cybersecurity because it requires a holistic approach to business and information system design in its context as well as management with respect to often unforeseen changes in the business environment. The complexity of this endeavor is influenced by the high degree of diversity and interconnectedness of the actors involved, which calls for digital ecosystem thinking supported by modelling methods and tools.

WG8.2: The Interaction of Information Systems and the Organisation
WG8.2 was originally established by IFIP in 1977. Over subsequent years, it has played a major role in the methodological and theoretical development of the Information Systems field and in enhancing the field's receptivity to ideas from other social science disciplines. While this may reflect the early contribution of European scholars, especially from Nordic countries, in instituting a distinctive intellectual tradition, over time the group has emerged as a key hub of the international community of IS scholars concerned with the broader social and organisational context of information system development and use. The methodological contribution of WG8.2 was established relatively early

in the group's history, with the 1984 Manchester conference being widely recognised as having played a major part in promoting the acceptance of qualitative methods in IS research. Methods—not exclusively qualitative but also critical, design science, and practice-driven—have remained a core concern of the group with a number of working conferences, in Copenhagen (1990), Philadelphia (1997), Idaho (2001), Manchester (2004), Tampa (2012) and Dublin (2016) adopting a specifically methodological focus.

Although, with the exception of Auckland (2014) and San Francisco (2018), the group's working conferences have generally not predominantly addressed particular theoretical approaches, WG8.2 has been an important venue for early discussion of a number of social theories in the IS field, including Structuration Theory, Actor Network Theory, and Sociomateriality. Members of the group have also been influential in advancing these debates in the IS literature. Reflecting this openness to new theories and perspectives, a number of keynote speakers at WG8.2 conferences have come from other disciplines, including computer science, anthropology and science studies.

This openness, combined with the group's methodological and theoretical heritage, provides an important foundation for addressing the challenges and opportunities posed by the increasing ubiquity, interdependence, and performativity of digital technologies in organisations and society. The hopes and fears evoked by digitalization were specifically explored in the 2018 San Francisco conference under the title of "Living with Monsters" (Aanestad et al. 2018). Issues such as algorithmic decision making and their implications in domains such as predictive policing and automated warfare were discussed. Attention to agency and accountability was identified as priority areas for future research and outreach.

This debate was taken one step further at the 2019 Munich Organisations and Society in Information Systems (OASIS) workshop on post-digitalization (Parmiggiani et al. forthcoming). Group members were invited to consider what will happen once the temporary excitement about digitalization ceases and phenomena currently discussed as digital (e.g. digital innovation, digital transformation, digital business strategy) have become inherently and so naturally digital that they are not discussed separately anymore. While it was evident that there are many different and often conflicting interpretations of post-digitalization, anticipating a future where things being digital is the norm will be crucial to imagine and shape the trajectory of organisations and societies as digitalization becomes ever more pervasive. This is particularly true if research is to help pave the way for a just and inclusive digital future that promotes new forms of organising and novel ways of working, which contribute positively to addressing contemporary economic, societal, and environmental challenges.

Looking forward, we would draw a number of lessons from WG8.2's history and ethos for the future of TC8. First, while the tidal wave of data about organisational and social phenomena that digitalization has unleashed has been viewed in some quarters as meaning that all IS phenomena can, and should, be studied exclusively with quantitative methods, such a loss of methodological diversity in the field should be of concern on a number of grounds. It assumes, for example, that data unproblematically instrument reality—something that qualitative research on practices of data creation can help to interrogate. It treats data as the sufficient cause of phenomena without reference to social and organisational processes that are not well suited to quantification, and it assumes a stability and directionality to the relationship between data and phenomena that is thrown into doubt by the ongoing reconfiguration of organisations, society, and perhaps even humans themselves (Czerski 2012, Introna 2009). Continuing methodological innovation will be needed to enable academia to keep pace with these developments and to address the complexity of emerging phenomena.

Second, and in tandem with methodological advances, there will be a need for new conceptualizations of theory that are responsive to the potential as well as the contingencies of digitalization. Despite predictions of the end of theory—be it because of the ad-hoc analytical capabilities that result from the combination of artificial intelligence with big data or because of the perceived deficiencies of existing conceptualizations and their effects on the discipline (e.g., Avison and Malaurent 2014, Hirschheim 2019)—the WG8.2 tradition provides evidence of its persistent relevance.

Third, genuine inter-disciplinarity (or rather multi-disciplinarity) is needed to enable us to grasp the manifold impacts of digitalization. Comprehending technology not only as an object of engineering skill—obsessed by the technologically possible—but also as a societal, legal, environmental, ethical, and philosophical challenge is necessary to gain rich insight on, explain, and shape the interaction of information systems and organisations (broadly speaking).

WG8.3: Decision Support

The International Federation for Information Processing (IFIP) was founded as a federation of national peak bodies in information processing and technology under the auspices of UNESCO. IFIP established Technical Committee (TC) 8 Information Systems in 1974 in recognition of the maturing nature of Management Information Systems (MIS) as a field of research and practice. The 1970s also saw the establishment of decision support systems as a newly mature area of information systems research, as evidenced by the publication of Gorry and Scott Morton's seminal work in 1971. Consequently, in 1981, IFIP TC8 established WG8.3 on Decision Support Systems (DSS).

The stated aim of IFIP WG8.3 was 'The development of approaches for applying information systems technology to increase the effectiveness of decision-makers in situations where the computer system can support and enhance human judgments in the performance of tasks that have elements which cannot be specified in advance'. The means it proposed to use were 'To improve ways of synthesising and applying relevant work from resource disciplines to practical implementations of systems that enhance decision support capability'. Resource disciplines included information technology, artificial intelligence, cognitive psychology, decision theory, organisational theories, operations research and modelling.

Since its creation, WG8.3 has organised a total of twenty-three international conferences over its thirty-nine years of existence. These events have taken place in Europe, reflecting the distribution of working group members, hosted in 21 different cities and 13 different countries. London (England) and Cork (Ireland) are the only two cities to have hosted two conferences, but several countries have hosted more than one conference and the next event in 2022 promises to bring the conference back to Budapest, where discussions towards the creation of the working group were held all the way back to 1980.

The working group organised its first conference in 1982 and this took place in Austria. The beautiful 'Schloss' buildings of the International Institute for Applied Systems Analysis (IIASA) in Laxenburg, Austria (just south of Vienna) had been selected due to the fact that it was accessible to researchers on either side of what was then known as the 'iron curtain'. A feature of the early days of the working group was to enable the interaction between academics working on different sides of this particular political divide. A bi-annual pattern of conferences was established, each conference planning the theme and location of the next event. The last international conference of the working group was due to be held in 2020 in Wroclaw (Poland) but global events that year and the spread of the COVID-19 virus brought travel restrictions which meant that the conference was in fact held on an on-line platform (quite successfully so, actually). In between 1982 and 2020, 20 bi-annual conferences were held. In addition, there were 3 major conferences outside of the established bi-annual pattern, in 1991, 1993, and 1997 when group members decided to meet on an annual basis. In total, over 750 papers have been published in these 23 events. Over the years, special issues of journals were also published, most of which contain extended versions of the papers published in the official proceedings.

Other outputs of the working group have been identified in the annual reports of the group. For instance, the working group published its own work on the "DSS curriculum" at its conference in Toulouse in 2008 reporting on the work of its 'DSS Curriculum' task force, established two years earlier at the 2006 conference in London.

Over the 23 conferences, 750 papers have been published by nearly a thousand individual authors who represented over 380 institutions from over 50 countries. This is a remarkable accumulated body of knowledge and constitutes a substantial contribution to the discipline of DSS over a very long period and across a variety of sub-topic of the discipline.

Thus, contributing authors come from a wide range of institutions representing many countries. The growth in the geography of contributions is a commendable reflection of the concerted efforts invested by successive officers of the working group to invite new researchers from increasingly diverse horizons into the group, especially since 2002 where the conferences became noticeably larger. Arguably, this might also be explained, at least in part, by the increasing ease with which academics can communicate with each other resulting from the growth in use of the Internet. The significant jump in numbers of papers, authors and institutions is evident in 2002 and 2004. Prior to this time, the conference was comparatively small, with most conferences including less than 40 authors and 20 presented papers, dominated by European authors.

From 2002, a broader range of participants and a higher number of papers were included in the conferences. Analysis of the publication patterns shows three different epochs in the conference history: 1982–2000 with small conferences dominated by European and, to a lesser extent, authors from the United States; 2002–2006 large scale conferences with a larger cross-section of authors from Europe, the USA, Australasia and Asia; and 2008 onwards, with medium scale conferences, and a spread of authors from various regions, albeit dominated by European and Australasian participants. Overall, the working group is now a more diverse, more collaborative community.

Historically, each conference of the working group has had a dedicated theme. These themes have been identified at the successive business meetings of the working group, often proposed by the would-be host of the next conference and accepted by present group members. As is evident in the table below, the themes proposed by successive hosts have alternated between following broad trends within the IS field, towards novel concepts and ideas (e.g. DSS 2.0 – Paris, 2014), and trying to refocus the efforts of the working group on the important core topics of the DSS field (Decision Support Systems: A Decade in Perspective – Noordwijkerhout, 1986). However, irrespective of the stated conference themes, there has been a wide range of recurring topics discussed over the years, some of them thoroughly researched over the entire lifecycle of the working group. These topics represent practical problem areas on the one hand (i.e. what field or activity the problems being supported come from) and decision support aspects (i.e. whether the main question relates to technical or general decision-making issues).

The interest in supported domains and DSS areas has changed considerably over time - yet, at the same time, the group remained focused on support issues related to decision-making. The dichotomy between the focus on decision-making issues on the one hand and technical issues on the other hand is arguably exactly as it should be in a field of inquiry such as DSS, as it reveals a well-balanced dual focus on both the domain of application and the underlying tools and techniques / technology. It is very interesting however to see that the balance between these two focal points has shifted from conference to conference and the equilibrium has been achieved over the complete lifecycle of the working group rather than within each of the conferences.

Generally, in early conferences, working group authors investigated general aspects of decision support, considering both relevant questions of decision-making and issues related to the development aspects of DSS. In later conferences, technical issues became less relevant (with the exception of 2000, where the emergence of Internet-based solutions dominated the conference). On the other hand, general decision-making aspects remained strong over the entire period.

In conclusion, while the most important topics of the conference were about general decision-making and decision support issues, there was a good range of real-life professional and industrial questions covered as well. WG8.3 has made its mark globally in these areas as listed in the table below:

1982 Processes and Tools for Decision Support
1984 Knowledge Representation for Decision Support Systems
1986 Decision Support Systems: A Decade in Perspective
1988 Organisational Decision Support Systems
1990 Environments for Supporting Decision Processes
1991 Support Functionality in the Office Environment
1992 Decision Support Systems: Experiences and Expectations
1993 Decision Support in Public Administration
1994 Decision Support in Organisational Transformation
1996 Implementing Systems for Supporting Management Decisions
1997 Decision Support in Organisational Transformation (reinvestigation based on the 1994 event)
1998 Context Sensitive Decision Support Systems

2000 Decision Support through Knowledge Management
2002 Decision Making and Decision Support in the Internet Age
2004 Decision Support in an Uncertain World
2006 Creativity and Innovation in Decision Making and Decision Support
2008 Collaborative Decision Making: Perspectives and Challenges
2010 Bridging the Socio-technical Gap in Decision Support Systems - Challenges for the Next Decade
2012 Fusing DSS into the Fabric of the Context
2014 DSS 2.0 – Supporting Decision Making with New Technologies
2016 Big Data, Better Decisions, Brighter Future
2018 DSS Research Delivering High Impacts to Business and Society
2020 Toward Enhanced Risk Management, shaping Risk Culture Theory and making Sound Decisions under Pressure

WG8.4: E-Business: Multi-disciplinary Research and Practice

WG8.4 was established in 2001. WG8.4 provides a reference point and a focus for multi-disciplinary research and practice in E-Business Information Systems. The intention is to extend the IFIP community's focus on E-Business to recognise, acknowledge and facilitate research and practice as it crosses the boundaries of IS, organisational, consumer, community, industry and national domains. Where researchers and practitioners focus on specific issues and technologies, for example, smart-card developments, mobile technologies or organisational adoption of IT practices, then that research is more properly located within existing working groups.

In 2017 the International IFIP Cross Domain (CD[1]) Conference for Machine Learning & Knowledge Extraction (MAKE[2]) - CD-MAKE 2020 has been founded as a joint effort of IFIP TC5, IFIP TC12, IFIP WG8.4, IFIP WG8.9 and IFIP WG12.9. CD-MAKE is held annually in conjunction with the International Conference on Availability, Reliability and Security ARES.

The conference is dedicated to offer an international platform for novel ideas and a fresh look on the methodologies to put crazy ideas into business for the benefit of the human. Serendipity is a desired effect and is expected to cross-fertilize methodologies and transfer of algorithmic developments.

Machine learning deals with understanding intelligence for the design and development of algorithms that can learn from data and improve over time. The original definition was "the artificial generation of knowledge from experience". The challenge is to discover relevant structural patterns and/or temporal patterns ("knowledge") in such data, which are often hidden and not accessible to a human. Today, machine learning is the fastest growing technical field, having many application domains, e.g. health, Industry 4.0, recommender systems, speech recognition, autonomous driving, etc. The challenge is in decision making under uncertainty, and probabilistic inference enormously

---

[1] CD stands for Cross-Domain and means the integration and appraisal of different fields and application domains (e.g. health AI, Industry 4.0, etc.) to provide an atmosphere to foster different perspectives and opinions.
[2] MAKE stands for MAchine Learning & Knowledge Extraction.

influenced artificial intelligence and statistical learning. The inverse probability allows to infer unknowns, learn from data and make predictions to support decision making. Whether in social networks, recommender systems, health or Industry 4.0 applications, the increasingly complex data sets require efficient, useful and useable solutions for knowledge discovery and knowledge extraction.

A synergistic combination of methodologies and approaches of two domains offer ideal conditions towards unraveling these challenges and to foster new, efficient and user-friendly machine learning algorithms and knowledge extraction tools: Human-Computer Interaction (HCI) and Knowledge Discovery/Data Mining (KDD), aiming at augmenting human intelligence with computational intelligence and vice versa toward a human-centered AI approach.

Consequently, successful Machine Learning & Knowledge extraction needs a concerted international effort without boundaries, supporting collaborative and integrative cross-disciplinary research between experts from 7 (the magical number seven $\pm$ 0) fields:

1. DATA – Data science (data fusion, preprocessing, mapping, knowledge representation, …),
2. LEARNING – algorithms, contextual adaptation, causal reasoning, transfer learning …
3. VISUALISATION – intelligent interfaces, human-AI interaction, dialogue systems, …
4. PRIVACY – data protection, safety, security, ethics, acceptance and social issues of ML, …
5. NETWORK – graphical models, graph-based ML, Bayesian inference, …
6. TOPOLOGY – geometrical machine learning, topological and manifold learning, …
7. ENTROPY – time and machine learning, entropy-based learning, …

The goal of the CD-MAKE conference is to act as a Catalysator to bring together researchers from these seven areas in a cross-disciplinary manner, to stimulate fresh ideas and to encourage multi-disciplinary problem solving. Since 2017 the conference has taken place in Reggio Calabria, Italy (2017); Hamburg, Germany (2018); Canterbury, UK (2019) and will take place 2020 as a virtual conference. We are happy to announce that CD-MAKE 2021 will take place in Dublin, Ireland.

More information can be found here:

https://ifip84.sba-research.org/index.html

https://cd-make.net/

WG8.5: Information Systems in Public Administration

WG8.5 was approved by TC8 in 1988, and this WG is focused on all aspects of information systems for governments. WG8.5 covers electronic service provisioning, government operations, citizens engagement, democracy, social innovation, and other forms of electronic participation. In the early years, the focus of the working group was on the automation of single systems within a single public organisation. Over time, the emphasis has shifted, and the interoperability between public organisations became a prime focus as more and more public organisations started to collaborate using information systems. Due to all kinds of technological advancements, the scope has been expanded considerably by focusing nowadays on a complete digitalization and transformation of the public sector for public value creation.

Around the year 2000, the name e-government, and more recently the name digital government, was introduced to refer to this domain. This has resulted in the establishment of the annual International e-Government Conference, abbreviated at EGOV, in 2002 by scholars like Roland Traunmüller and Klaus Lenk. Over the subsequent years, IFIP WG8.5 has played a significant role in the automation of government administrative processes, the development of integrated service provisioning, and online forms of participation. This research has resulted in insight for integrated service provisioning, including components for accomplishing this like the only once principle, interoperability frameworks and methods, and citizens and companies are now able to browse to a single website for gaining services from different government organisations without being aware of this.

Over time, more and more emphasis was given to democracy, participation, and engagement using digital means. These developments resulted in 2009 in the first International e-Participation conference, abbreviates as ePart. EGOV and ePart papers are published in the renowned Springer LNCS proceedings, and both conferences are always co-located. In 2018, another conference was merged with EGOV and ePart, e.g., the Conference for E-Democracy and Open Government Conference (CeDEM) expressing the rise of e-democracy. This has resulted in the joint conference on EGOV, which attracts the major researchers in this area. IFIP WG8.5 has developed into a vibrant community with many active members and having as the main highlight the annual EGOV conference.

Over the years, new topics emerged and were embraced like open data, open government, public-private governance and smart government. The IFIP WG8.5 community contributed to the development of effective policies and systems for the opening and use of more data and contributed to accomplishing open government for public sector organisations all over the world. Also, the community contributed to understanding the smart government phenomenon and showing how information systems can be used for the creation of public values.

More recently, numerous subtopics have been introduced into this thriving field, including social innovation (improving the society driven by parties outside the government), transformative government, sustainable government, legal informatics, and algorithmic public decision-making. All are referring to different aspects of ICT in public administration. The many and various topics show the need for understanding the type of information systems within the government context. In-depth knowledge of the public administration field and type of information system is needed to analyse, understand, and design information systems in public administration.

The uniqueness of the WG8.5 is that it concentrates on a specific area of society, namely the public sector. As a domain discipline, insights and areas from other fields are used; however, the very nature prevents the easy translation of theories, methods, and principles. The idiosyncratic nature of governments requires the development of specific theories, methods, and principles. For example, legislation and the translation of legal requirements and rules in information systems is an important aspect in this domain. Therefore, also research in policy-making for the digital world is conducted by this working group. Furthermore, the focus of the public sector is on creating public values and serving the public. Whereas the objectives of for profit-companies are to satisfy their customers, in government all too often, societal trade-offs are needed, and inclusion is an important topic. Information systems should meet public values like accountability, transparency, equal access, fairness, openness, privacy, and so on. Also, the various roles that people can have in our society should be considered. A single person can be a voter, a citizen requesting public services, a data analyst making use of open government data, or even all at the same time.

Public value creation using information systems is a core focus area of the WG8.5. Government structures are shaped by principles founded in legislation like separation of concerns and contain mechanisms for ensuring public accountability and oversight. Information systems and institutional aspects are interlinked in this domain. Furthermore, governments are organised differently per country, which poses limitations to the generalizability. This all requires a deep understanding of the public sector and knowledge about information systems. More and more researchers have entered this very relevant field, but combining these areas remain challenging.

The public sector increasingly relies on Internet of Things (IoT), Artificial Intelligence (AI), (Big) Data Analytics (BDA), Blockchain, 5G, and related technologies to improve and transform the government. WG8.5's methodological and theoretical advances provide an important foundation for addressing emerging topics like sustainable cities in which the government encourages the sustainable use of resources using all kinds of information systems. This is often in close collaboration with companies. Also, the theories for automation and transformation can be used for the domain of computational algorithms for automated decision-making. Automating decisions can have far-reaching consequences to people's lives, harvesting interconnected data about individuals, and has the risk that exclusion, injustice, and privacy violations can happen on a massive scale. The methods and theories developed by WG8.5 ensure adherent to public values, like fairness and openness, are taken into account. The public values perspective is closely related to the ethical implications of the use of new technologies.

The public sector and the public are highly dependent on each other. The research in co-creation and engagement plays an important role in innovating the public sector, improving public service delivery, and providing opportunities for public participation. Society becomes more and more involved in improving the government. Social media is becoming an increasingly important interface between the public sector and the public. In conclusion, digitalization and the government have become integrated over the years. Government phenomena have become inherently digital, and they should not be considered in isolation anymore.

We can draw several lessons from WG8.5's advancement for the future of TC8. Information systems and the public sector should be approached as an integrated whole and should be viewed as a socio-technical phenomenon. Information systems are shaped by their context but also influence the context. Aspect like legislation, institutional structure, and public values should be taken into account when analysing and designing information systems. This results in a multitude of aspects like inclusion, fairness, openness, accountability, privacy, and transparency that play a vital role in making these information systems a success. Many of these aspects sound easy, and most people will agree with the need for adhering to them, but these are hard to put into practice. Hence, dedicated theories and methods are needed which take the nature of the domain into account and are able to help a domain forward. Reductionist approaches are necessary for general insights, but understanding an empirical domain, like the public sector, is needed for ensuring a practical relevance and the ability to relate theory and practice. This requires specific socio-technical theories and methods which take the very nature of a domain into account.

WG8.6: Transfer and Diffusion of Information Technology
The group is focused on diffusion, transfer and implementation of IT. Established in 1994, the first official working conference was on October 1995, at Leangkollen, Oslo, Norway. It was organised by Karlheinz Kautz, Jan Pries-Heje, Tor J Larsen, and Pal Sorgaard. However, in 1993, a formation conference was held in October 10–13, at Champion, PA, in the area also referred to as Seven Springs. The event attracted over 120 academics and practitioners from around the globe. Gordon Davis welcomed the attendees and Priscilla Fowler (Program Chair) opened the event with an overview. Three presentation tracks ran throughout. The format was atypical and allowed for afternoon outdoor activity: scheduled breaks were held from 3:30–6:00 pm so participants might admire the Fall foliage, followed by dinner, and then six working sessions that were held on both evenings. This proceeding was published as: Levine, L. (Ed.). (1994). *Diffusion, Transfer, & Implementation of Information Technology*. Proceedings of the IFIP TC8 Working Conference on Diffusion, Transfer and Implementation of Information Technology. Pittsburgh, Pennsylvania, The Netherlands: North-Holland, Elsevier Science Publishers. Since then, IFIP WG8.6 kept the tradition of being open, inclusive of academics and practitioner and aiming for deep conversations in informal settings.

The first Chair of the IFIP WG8.6 was Priscilla Fowler followed by Karlheinz Kautz, Linda Levine, Deborah Bunker and Yogesh Dwivedi (current chair). The current website for the group is: http://www.ifipwg86.org/. The group mission is centred around fostering understanding and improving research and practice of diffusion, transfer, and implementation of both mature and emerging information technologies and systems in organisations, sectors, and countries. Over the years, its working conference has been held in different countries to foster collaborations and inclusion of different research teams in different universities. The group consistently included members and conference contributors from over 30 countries in Europe, Africa, Middle East, Australia, North America, India, China, Japan, Korea, New Zealand and South East Asia (for detailed analysis, see: Dwivedi et al. 2010 and Kautz et al. 2006). The group encourages diverse methodological approaches and theoretical grounding.

In recent years, the working group's original focus, on technology diffusion and adoption, has been overtaken by myriad technical developments: the social media, mobile computing, cloud computing, agile methods, and so on. The cycle of innovation has sped up, with profound impacts on the way organisations and societies engage with transfer and diffusion of ICT systems within and between organisations, in interactions with customers, and throughout society in general. In 2016, the group discussed the evolution of the field and identified and discussed emerging trends for a new agenda, one that is faithful to the original mission of the group but adapted to today's viral IT diffusion environment. In 2017, the group held a working conference in Guimarães, Portugal on Re-Imagining Diffusion of Information Technology and Systems: Opportunities and Risks. In this conference, diffusion and adoption of emerging technologies such as digital platforms, social media, predictive analytics and e-government platforms were discussed. In 2018, the group organised its working conference in Portsmouth, UK on Smart working, living and organising. The conference aimed to broaden the theoretical base of adoption and diffusion of technology in light of new intelligent systems and technologies and the new challenges they pose to individuals, sectors and society. The debates and discussions on the conference examined how emerging technologies are adopted and appropriated in everyday life and work, and the impact they are exerting. In particular, who is becoming smart, how they are becoming smart and what are they becoming smart about? Who are the "winners and losers" and what role does technology play? How are emerging technologies adopted and appropriated in everyday life and what impact are they exerting? The proceedings were published in Elbanna et al. (2018) and the special issue on Information Systems Frontier was also published based on selected papers from IFIP WG8.6 that were rigorously and competitively reviewed (Elbanna et al. 2020).

The group maintains its focus on theoretical and practical understanding of the adoption of a broad spectrum of information technologies. It continues to update its knowledge base in light of emerging technologies such as AI, predictive analytics, social media, cloud computing, and other emerging technologies. The focus of future events will be on understanding the diffusion and adoption of emerging information technologies and systems (i.e., Artificial Intelligence, Blockchain, Fintech Applications, Internet of Things, Social Media), which are expected to have substantial impact on future social and economic development of society, organisations and individuals. In addition, the group emphasises the importance of inter-disciplinary and multidisciplinary research. Future events will focus on fostering relationships and theoretical and practical links with other disciplines and opportunities for IS researchers to engage and collaborate with other disciplines. Our future conferences will bring together scholars and practitioners from other disciplines for the enrichment of scholarly deliberations on the ICT adoption, usage, impact and potential of emerging technologies.

WG8.9: Enterprise Information Systems

Enterprise Information Systems (EIS) also called Enterprise Systems (ES) or Enterprise Resource Planning (ERP). In the past decades, EIS has emerged as a promising tool used for integrating and extending business processes across the boundaries of business functions at both intra- and inter-organisational levels. This emergence of EIS has been fueled by the global economy and the development in Information and Communications Technology (ICT). The development of ICT and the technological advances in EIS have provided a viable solution to the growing needs of information integration in both manufacturing and service industries, as evidenced by the fact that a growing number of enterprises world-wide have adopted EIS such as Enterprise Resource Planning (ERP), to run their businesses instead of using functional information systems that were previously used for partial functional integration within many industrial organisations.

We have witnessed that, in global economy and in global business operations, there has been a need for EIS such as ERP to integrate extended enterprises in a supply chain environment with the objective of achieving efficiency, competency, and competitiveness. For example, the global operations have forced enterprises such as Dell and Microsoft to adopt ERP in order to take the advantage of a global supply network. Today, not only the large and medium sized companies, but also small companies are quickly learning that a highly integrated EIS is a requirement for the global operation. For instance, business-to-business (B2B) integration generally comprises connections to EIS. EIS has become a basic information processing requirement for many industries. Thus, the ERP market is one of the fastest growing and most profitable areas in the software industry.

It is well recognised that EIS has an important long-term strategic impact on global industrial development. Due to the importance of this subject, there has been a growing demand for research about EIS to provide insights into the issues, challenges, and solutions related to the design, implementation, and management of EIS. In June 2005, at a meeting of the International Federation for Information Processing (IFIP) Technical Committee for Information Systems (TC8) held at Guimarães, Portugal, the committee members intensively discussed the important role played by EIS in the global economy and the innovative and unique characteristics of EIS within the framework of Industrial Information Integration, an emerging scientific sub-discipline. It was decided at this meeting that the IFIP First International Conference on Research and Practical Issues of Enterprise Information Systems (CONFENIS 2006) would be held in 2006 in Vienna, Austria. In August 2006, at the IFIP 2006 World Computer Congress held in Santiago, Chile, the IFIP TC8 WG8.9 Enterprise Information Systems was established. To further respond to the needs of both academicians and practitioners for communicating and publishing their research outcomes on EIS, the science and engineering journal entitled *Enterprise Information Systems,* exclusively devoting to the topic of EIS, was launched in 2007.

Enterprise Information Systems research has become increasingly popular. In EIS research, topics of interest include enterprise engineering, enterprise modelling, enterprise integration, business process management, enterprise architecture and enterprise application integration, information integration and interoperability, service oriented architecture (SOA), etc. Techniques developed in mathematical science, computer science, manufacturing engineering, systems science and engineering, operations management used in the design or operation of enterprise information systems are included.

There are still many challenges and issues that need to be resolved in order for EIS to become more applicable. Designing EIS involves complexity which mainly stems from their high dimensionality and complexity. In recent years, there have been significant developments in this newly emerging technology, as well as actual and potential applications to various industrial sectors. Despite advancements in the field of EIS, both in academia and industry, significant challenges still remain. They need to be dealt with in order to fully realise the potential of EIS. For example, what does Industry 4.0 mean for existing EIS? According to GTAI (2014), Industry 4.0 has sparked a discussion on whether ERP, EIS or ES will establish themselves as the dominant software systems in

Industry 4.0. Although GTAI study (2014) has not given a clear-cut answer on this, it is recognised that as interdisciplinary integration is the essence of Industry 4.0, ERP, EIS or ES will have to address new challenges from Industry 4.0. According to a related study published in 2014, the authors have indicated that IoT and Cyber Physical System (CPS) related technologies have made a large impact on new ICT and future ERP, EIS or ES. In this study, it was predicted that new generation of ERP, EIS or ES will emerge from new ICT with the capacity of CPS (Xu et al. 2014). EIS will continue to embrace cutting-edge technology and techniques and will open up new applications that will impact industrial sectors.

WG8.10: Service Oriented Systems (Joint with WG6.12 and WG2.14)
The role of WG8.10 is organising and promoting a fruitful exchange of information among academics and practitioners within the scope of improving the engineering, further research, and exploitation of service-based systems.

The research community has been considering Service Oriented Computing a relevant topic to be studied for some twenty years. Although most of the initial ideas and proposals are now widely adopted in industry, the evolution of the underlying platforms has required a continuous improvement of the already proposed approaches as well as the definition of new methods and tools. For instance, we started from systems integration based on RPC-like protocols (e.g., SOAP) and architectural styles that allow us to provide better flexibility and scalability (e.g., REST). In the meanwhile, service orientation evolved: it is not only a way to remotely invoke software components using Internet as communication backbone, but it is also the basis of cloud computing where infrastructures, platforms, and services are offered "as a service".

The IFIP WG on Service Oriented Systems, established in 2010, has brought together researchers and practitioners to study the potential of service oriented computing along several directions including, among others, service modeling, service platforms, and methodologies to manage the service life-cycle. Over the last few years, the contribution of the WG members has focused on the latest development of service oriented computing. Most of the contributions of the members have been included in the proceedings of the European Conference on Service-Oriented and Cloud Computing (ESOCC), the flagship conference of the WG. For example, in the recent period, a lot of attention has been devoted to microservice-based architectures and edge/fog computing.

About the former, microservices are gaining more and more momentum in enterprise IT, with IT leading companies (such as Amazon, Netflix and Spotify) already delivering their core businesses through microservice-based solutions. Microservices define an architectural style for developing applications as suites of small and independent (micro)services, each of which is built around a well-defined business capability, running in its own process, and communicating with the other microservices in an application through lightweight mechanisms. Architecting an application with microservices can result in various gains, related to peculiar properties of microservices themselves. These gains include the natural exploitability of patterns while designing an application, the freedom of choosing the technologies and databases for implementing each microservice and its backend, and the native support for fault resilience and CI/CD (Continuous Integration/Continuous Delivery), just to mention some.

At the same time, application developers and operators have to face various open challenges on microservices. For instance, sizing services to match business capability is not easy, as the border among different business capabilities is often blurry. The biggest challenges however come from the highly-distributed nature of microservices, which makes securing an application and controlling accesses a concrete pain. The same applies to testing, especially if wishing to check the overall performance of an application. For the same reasons, monitoring the runtime operation of a microservice-based application is quite complex, as monitoring/logging data is distributed over the various microservices forming an application and needs to be suitably combined. We hence believe that securing, testing and monitoring highly distributed microservice-based applications constitute three concrete challenges for next years' research on service-oriented systems, especially if considered in combination with emerging fog/edge infrastructures (which are distributed, geolocated and mobile, and which feature stringent QoS requirements).

Moving to the edge/fog computing, the impact of the network in the service provisioning/consuming might be relevant especially when a significant amount of data is considered. The typical scenario refers to Industry 4.0 where manufacturing plants are planned to be extensively sensorised, thus able to generate a huge amount of data about the status of machineries, as well as the status of the processes being enacted. To mine useful information from this data, the current approach is to move these data to the cloud where (theoretically) unlimited resources are available to process these data and to return back to the user the results of this analysis. As said, the network could be so impactful that the network latency could return the result of the data with an unacceptable delay. For this reason, fog computing has been proposed to exploit as much as possible the resources at the edge of the network thus to process the data as close as possible to where they are produced. In this way, the amount of data that will be moved to the cloud is reduced. In such a scenario, several challenges must be addressed: how to select which data to process at the edge and which on the cloud; how to ensure the privacy of the data, i.e., the data that cannot leave the premises where they are generated; how to deal with an extremely heterogeneous environment where sensors, smart devices, network devices, as well as cloud resources are involved: and finally, how to manage the dynamicity of a system in which nodes could join and leave the infrastructure without prior notice.

As said, these are just two of the main domains in which the WG community is currently working. For sure, the service orientation will change its skin again in the near future, as the concept of service is so pervasive that needs to be adapted to very different scenarios, and the goal of the WG is to grab the chance to find out new methods and tools to support new cases.

WG8.11: Information Systems Security Research (Joint with WG11.13)

The working group on Information Systems Security Research WG8.11 is a joint working group focused on the creation, dissemination, and preservation of well-formed research about information systems security. Listed under both the International Federation for Information Processing (IFIP) Technical Committee TC8 (Information Systems) (WG8.11) and IFIP TC11 (Security and Privacy Protection) (WG11.13), this working group places a premium on research with highly reliable and validated theory, empirical data, or quantitative/qualitative social scientific methodology. Since its formation in 2008, the working group has focused largely on research on the social, organisational, and managerial challenges pertaining to information security management, including both workplace and home information security. More recently, however, the challenges of interest have mostly centered on behavioral compliance and risk management issues.

Behavioral compliance research is generally focused on the adoption and use of protective security practices by individuals either seeking to benefit themselves or their firms or avoiding negative consequences that result from the non-adoption or misuse of security procedures and methods. Our membership is placed an emphasis on policy related compliance, but other forms of compliance, such as with digital warnings, communicated alerts, and compliance with emerging technical standards have also been examined. A recent working group workshop suggests the behavioral compliance area of study will remain a focus of study for the foreseeable future.

Risk management is the other primary research interest among our membership. The study of risk management by security researchers has mostly been conducted from a normative perspective (Hui et al. 2016) and while our membership has addressed risk management through a variety of frameworks, models, and management techniques, its focus has mostly been on efforts to extend and contextualise the managerial frameworks and theories that help to measure and control risk at the individual level.

Going forward, the IFIP TC8.11/11.13 working group looks to emerging challenges such as neurosecurity (neurophysiological data collection), forensics analysis, and the behavioral analysis of design science treatments that enhance or balance security and privacy tradeoffs. The growing prevalence of advanced persistent threats, blockchain data structures, big data analytics, commercial cyberspace collisions between defensive AI and offensive AI, and quantum computing has presented a new set of organisational and managerial challenges that we are eager to tackle.

WG8.12: Industrial Information Integration
In the first part of the first decade of 2000, the impact of ICT (Information and Communication Technology) on industry has been going beyond the traditional paradigm. It affects industrial processes and production in an unprecedented way. It became more and more clear the emergence of Industrial Integration grew out from a new era of ICT. Due to the strategic importance of the subject, there has been a growing demand for research on Industrial Information Integration to provide insights on issues, challenges, and solutions related to industrial integration.

In 2007, at a European Seminar held in Zurich, a session was dedicated to "Industrial Integration of ICT" aimed at exploring the industrial integration of ICT in manufacturing sector (Abramovici and Filos 2011). In 2008, Fujitsu of Japan challenged the industrialization of IT based on three core technologies: virtualization, automation, and integration (Sagawa and Mitsuhama 2008). Kopar (2008) indicated that information integration become a real challenge, even in NATO. Hua et al. (2008) and Liang et al. (2008) studied the key role played by information integration in industrial information integration and Zajac et al. (2008) studied information integration in manufacturing systems.

Industrial Information Integration encompasses not only information integration, but also hardware and software. Estevez and Marcos (2008) emphasised the integration of tools in engineering process. In 2010, Zuge et al. emphasised the significance of integration of IT with automation technology in information integration. In the same year, Huang (2020) indicated the important role of integration in industrialization and informatization. In 2011, Abramovici and Filos (2011) indicated that emerging ICTs are expected to drive innovations in information processes across the product lifecycle as well as new industrial business models. In 2012, Marinica describes a real case of methodologies and hardware and software systems used to build the road from electrical signal to information. Castillo and Rosario (2012) proposes a generic supervisory and command architecture in which technology and industrial devices have been integrated in a single platform. Such devices include programmable logic controllers, sensors, actuators, image processing, supervisory systems, and robotic manipulation devices. Li et al. (2012) discuss equipment integration for agricultural applications. Narayanan and Haralur (2012) propose seamless integration of network devices.

In 2015, Yue et al. indicated that the development of industrialization and ICT has deeply changed our way of life; in particular, with the emerging Industry 4.0, the integration of cloud technologies and industrial cyber-physical systems (ICPS) becomes increasingly important. Also in 2015, Ministry of Industry and Information Technology of China launched the China Manufacturing 2025 Plan. This 10-year action plan calls for increasing integration of industrialization and information technology. Nine tasks have been identified as priorities, one of them is integrating Information Technology and Industry.

Due to such industrial practice paradigm shift, the new subjects Industrial Integration and Industrial Information Integration have risen, directly resulting in the formal proposal on Industrial Information Integration to IFIP. In June 2019, IFIP TC8 WG8.12, was established, specifically focusing on the Industrial Information Integration. This is the first working group established in IFIP on Industrial Information Integration. In 2016, the journal entitled *Journal of Industrial Information Integration* was launched.

Industrial Information Integration Engineering (IIIE) is a set of foundation concepts, techniques, and technology that facilitate the industrial information integration process; specifically speaking, IIIE comprises methods/techniques for solving complex problems in developing information technology infrastructure for industrial sectors, especially in the aspect of information integration. As an interdisciplinary discipline, IIIE interacts with scientific disciplines such as mathematics, computer science, and engineering disciplines.

In recent years, rapid advances in industrial information integration have spurred tremendous growth in the use of integrated industrial systems (Chen 2016; 2020), so far a variety of techniques have been used for probing IIIE. These techniques include business process management, workflow management, EA/EAI, SOA, IoT, among others. Many applications require a combination of these techniques; this also gives rise to the emergence of IIIE that requires techniques originated from different disciplines. At present, we are at a new breakpoint in the evolution of selected enabling technologies for IIIE.

5   Conclusions

So how do we proceed into the next 50 years? The world at present and the world of the 1970s when TC8 was formed are very different. In economically advanced societies, we are passing beyond the Information Society (Society 4.0) with its information 'pull' mechanisms towards Society 5.0, the essence of which promises to be more cautious and caring locally and more aware globally. Most importantly, we are becoming attuned to the imperative to consider the fragile health of both society and earth, aided by the ready availability of AI-enabled converged information and other emerging technologies.

At the end of Sect. 3, the question was asked "Based on this impressive history, a natural question to ask is how TC8 can inform a strategy for the future?" The answer was given that we should stick to what TC8 has been good at (design and development, application and utilisation in organisations) but not be neglectful of the growing societal and environmental focus on Smart Cities and Green Sustainability. Should these topics and others requiring socio-technical responses in Society 5.0 be picked up by an existing working group or addressed by a new working group? Whatever the answer, TC8 will be found at the forefront of information systems thought leadership in the post-COVID world.

References

Aanestad, M., Mähring, M., Østerlund, C., Riemer, K., Schultze, U.: Living with monsters? In: Schultze, U., Aanestad, M., Mähring, M., Østerlund, C., Riemer, K. (eds.) IS&O 2018. IAICT, vol. 543, pp. 3–12. Springer, Cham (2018). https://doi.org/10.1007/978-3-030-04091-8_1

Abramovici, M., Filos, E.: Industrial integration of ICT: opportunities for international research cooperation under the IMS scheme. J. Intell. Manuf. **22**(5), 717–724 (2011)

Alexandru-Cristian, M.: The road from signal to information. In: Schiopu, P. (ed.) Advanced Topics in Optoelectronics, Microelectronics, and Nanotechnologies VI Proceedings of SPIE, (8411) (2012)

Avison, D., Malaurent, J.: Is theory king? Questioning the theory Fetish in information systems. J. Inf. Technol. **29**(4), 327–336 (2014)

Barnes, S.J.: Information management research and practice in the post-COVID-19 world. Int. J. Inf. Manage. **55**, 102175 (2020)

Castillo, R., Rosario, J.: Supervision and command architecture for automation and robotics platform. In: Proceedings of 2012 IEEE Ninth Electronics, Robotics and Automotive Mechanics Conference, pp. 95–102 (2012)

Chen, Y.: Industrial information integration-A literature review 2006–2015. J. Ind. Inf. Integr. **2**, 30–64 (2016)

Chen, Y.: A survey on industrial information integration 2016–2019. J. Ind. Integr. Manage. **5**(1), 33–163 (2020)

Coulibaly, B.S.: Foresight Africa: top priorities for the continent 2020 to 2030. Africa Growth Initiative Foresight Africa Team. https://www.brookings.edu/multi-chapter-report/foresight-afr ica-top-priorities-for-the-continent-in-2020/. Accessed Nov. 2020

Czerski, P.: My, Dzieci Sieci (We, the Web Kids). In: Dziennik Bałtycki (The Baltic Daily), Gdańsk, Poland (2012)

de Sanfeliú, M. B., Milan, S., Rodríguez, A., de Trigueros, M.: The implementation process of the SDGs: Latin America Regional Survey. http://southernvoice.org/the-implementation-process-of-the-sdgs-latin-america-regional-survey/. Accessed Nov. 2020

Demertzis, M., Sapir, A., Wolff, G.: A strategic agenda for the new EU leadership. Bruegel Policy Brief. https://www.bruegel.org/2019/06/a-strategic-agenda-for-the-new-eu-leadership/. Accessed Nov. 2020

Dwivedi, Y.K., Levine, L., Williams, M.D., Singh, M., Wastell, D.G., Bunker, D.: Toward an understanding of the evolution of IFIP WG 8.6 research. In: Pries-Heje, J., Venable, J., Bunker, D., Russo, N.L., DeGross, J.I. (eds.) Human Benefit through the Diffusion of Information Systems Design Science Research. TDIT 2010. IFIP Advances in Information and Communication Technology, vol. 318, pp.225–242. Springer, Heidelberg (2010). https://doi.org/10.1007/978-3-642-12113-5_14

Elbanna, A.R., Dwivedi, Y.K., Bunker, D., Wastell, D., Wynn, E. (eds.): Smart Working, Living and Organizing. IFIP WG 8.6 International Conference on Transfer and Diffusion of IT 2018, vol. 553. Springer, Heidelberg (2018)

Elbanna, A.R., Dwivedi, Y.K., Bunker, D., Wastell, D.: The search for smartness in working, living and organising: beyond the 'Technomagic.' Inf. Syst. Front. **22**(2), 275–280 (2020)

Estevez, E., Marcos, M.: An approach to use model driven design in industrial automation. In: Proceedings of 2008 IEEE International Conference on Emerging Technologies and Factory Automation, pp. 62–65 (2008)

EY 2018: The Growing Impact of AI on Business. MIT Technology Review (2018). https://www.technologyreview.com/s/611013/the-growing-impact-of-ai-on-business/. Accessed Nov. 2020

Falkenberg, E.D., et al.: A Framework of Information System Concepts (The FRISCO Report). IFIP 1998, ISBN 3-901882-01-4 (1998)

MacDougall, W.: Industries 4.0-Smart Manufacturing for the Future. GTAI (Germany Trade and Invest), Berlin (2014). https://www.bibsonomy.org/bibtex/1380ea22fa34587c62852a49f537b9 13a/flint63 Accessed Nov. 2020

Hevia, C., Neumeyer, P.A.: A perfect storm: COVID-19 in emerging economies. VoxEU CEPR Policy Portal (2020). https://voxeu.org/article/perfect-storm-covid-19-emerging-eco nomies Accessed Nov. 2020

Hirschheim, R.: Against theory: with apologies to Feyerabend. J. Assoc. Inf. Syst. **20**(9), 1340–1357 (2019)

Hua, J., Sun, H., Liang, L., Lei, Z.: The research of manufacturing execution system modeling based on colored Petri nets. In: Proceedings of 2008 2nd International Symposium on Systems and Control in Aerospace and Astronautics, vol. (1–2), pp. 1163–1166 (2008)

Huang, J.: Research on information industry innovation model under the background of integration of industrialization and informatization. In: Proceedings of the 7th International Conference on Innovation and Management, pp. 588–592 (2010)

Hui, K.L., Vance, A., Zhdanov, D.: Securing digital assets. In: Bush, A., Rai, A. (eds.) MIS Quarterly Research Curations. http://misq.org/research-curations, https://doi.org/10.25300/052 72016

Introna, L.D.: Ethics and the speaking of things. Theory Cult. Soc. **26**(4), 25–46 (2009)

Kautz, K., Henriksen, H.Z., Breer-Mortensen, T., Poulsen, H.H.: Information technology diffusion research: an interim balance. In: Baskerville, R., Mathiassen, L., Pries-Heje, J., DeGross, J.L. (eds.) Business Agility and Information Technology Diffusion. IFIF TC8 WG 8.6 International Working Conference, 8–11 May 2006. Springer, Atlanta (2005). https://doi.org/10.1007/0-387-25590-7_2

Kopar, A.: Role of geospatial information and geospatial information application software for security. In: Coskun, H., Cigizoglu, H., Maktav, M. (eds.) Integration of Information for Environmental Security, pp. 229–243 (2008)

Li, J., Ma, C., Wang, J.: Agricultural products quality safety supervision information technology selection and evaluation. In: Liu, Z., Peng, F., Liu, X. (eds.) Advances in Chemical Engineering II PTS 1-4, pp. 550–553 (19521958) (2012)

Liang, T., Li, Q., Hua, J.: The modeling analysis of manufacturing execution system based upon colored Petri net. In: Proceedings of 2008 International Symposium on Intelligent Information Technology Application Workshop IITA 2008 Workshop, pp. 1093–1096 (2008)

Martinsons, M.G.: Research of information systems: from parochial to international, towards global or glocal? Inf. Syst. J. **26**(1), 3–19 (2016)

Narayanan, A., Haralur, G.: New melt-processable thermoplastic polyimides for opto-electrnic applications. In: Krevor, D., Beich, W., Schaub, M., Baumer, S. (eds.) Polymer Optics and Molded Glass Optics: Design, Fabrication, and Materials II, (8489) (2012)

Oldekop, J.A., et al.: COVID-19 and the case for global development. World Dev. **134**, 105044 (2020)

Pappas, I.O., Mikalef, P., Giannakos, M.N., Krogstie, J., Lekakos, G.: Big data and business analytics ecosystems: paving the way towards digital transformation and sustainable societies. IseB **16**(3), 479–491 (2018). https://doi.org/10.1007/s10257-018-0377-z

Parmiggiani, E., Teracino, E.A., Huysman, M., Jones, M., Mueller, B., Mikalsen, M.: OASIS 2019 panel report: a glimpse at the 'Post-Digital'. Commun. Assoc. Inf. Syst. **47**, Article 29 (2020)

Roudometof, V.: Theorizing glocalization: three interpretations. Eur. J. Soc. Theory **19**(3), 391–408 (2016)

Roudometof, V.: Recovering the local: From glocalization to localization. Curr. Sociol. **67**(6), 801–817 (2019)

Sagawa, C., Mitsuhama, G.: Industrialized IT 'Triole' toward datacenter optimization. Fujitsu Sci. Tech. J. **44**(1), 3–8 (2008)

Snoeck, M., Stirna, J., Weigand, H., Proper, H.A.: Panel Discussion: "Artificial Intelligence meets Enterprise Modelling (summary of panel discussion)". PoEM (Forum) 2019, pp. 88–97 (2019). CEUR-WS.org

Vial, G.: Understanding digital transformation: a review and a research agenda. J. Strateg. Inf. Syst. **28**(2), 118–144 (2019)

Wessel, L., Baiyere, A., Ologeanu-Taddei, R., Cha, J., Jensen, T.B.: Unpacking the difference between digital transformation and IT-enabled organisational transformation. J. Assoc. Inf. Syst. **22**, 102–129 (2020)

Xu, L., He, W., Li, S.: Internet of things in industries: a survey. IEEE Trans. Industr. Inf. **10**(4), 2233–2248 (2014)

Yue, X., Cai, H., Yan, H., Zou, C., Zhou, K.: Cloud-assisted industrial cyber-physical systems: an insight. Microprocess. Microsyst. **39**(8), 1262–1270 (2015)

Zajac, J., Chwajol, G.: Towards agent-based manufacturing systems. In: Annals of DAAAM for 2008 and Proceedings of the 19th International DAAAM Symposium, pp. 1541–1542 (2008)

Zuge, Y., Pereira, S., Dias, E.: Enablers and inhibitors of integration between IT and AT. In: Proceedings of the 9th WSEAS International Conference on Signal Processing, Robotics and Automation, pp. 185–191 (2010)

TC 9: ICT and Society

The Impact of *Human Choice and Computers* and *Technical Committee 9* on ICTs and Society: A Critical Sociotechnical Tale

David Kreps[1]([⊠]) [iD] and Gordon Fletcher[2] [iD]

[1] National University of Ireland Galway, Co., Galway, Ireland
david.kreps@nuigalway.ie
[2] University of Salford, Greater Manchester, UK
g.fletcher@salford.ac.uk

Abstract. In this chapter we briefly recount the history of the Human Choice and Computers conference series, and of Technical Committee 9, and show that not only has there been a marked focus, over more than four decades, on a critical and sociotechnical approach to understanding the relationship between ICTs and society, but that HCC and TC9 might be regarded as the original and continuing home of the critical academic voice in ICT. We show this through a textual analysis of the proceedings of the conferences, and through biographical detail concerning the key players involved.

Keywords: Critical · Sociotechnical · IFIP TC9

1 Introduction

What follows is a history of Technical Committee 9 and the Human Choice and Computers conference series, compiled by current TC9 Chair, David Kreps, and HCC12 Co-Chair Gordon Fletcher. To explore this history the authors refer to short histories compiled by predecessors, to obituaries, and to some of the texts published over the many years of TC9's activities. The authors have also used a textual analysis tool to examine the existing corpus of HCC texts, revealing some insightful details of the broader concerns of the many academics over time who have contributed to the activities of TC9.

What emerges from this history, and from the textual analysis, points clearly to TC9 and HCC being the original and continuing home of the critical academic voice in ICT, growing from the isolated thoughts of concerned engineers in the 1970s to the primary and most comprehensive forum where the full range of the concerns of the relationships of ICT and Society can be discussed with a critical perspective.

2 The History of HCC and TC9

Fourteen years after the formation of IFIP, in 1974, the Human Choice and Computers (HCC) conference series – the biennial conference of Technical Committee 9 (TC9) -

© IFIP International Federation for Information Processing 2021
Published by Springer Nature Switzerland AG 2021
M. Goedicke et al. (Eds.): Advancing Research in Information and Communication Technology,
IFIP AICT 600, pp. 363–380, 2021. https://doi.org/10.1007/978-3-030-81701-5_15

began with its first gathering in Vienna. The conference was led by Heinz Zemanek, as the President of IFIP, with the proceedings published in the following year by Mumford and Sackman undertaking duties as the editors [30]. In this first conference, trade unionists, social scientists, and computer technologists all expressed their dismay at being reduced to mere tools of management. The participants notably included Fred Margulies who had foreshadowed much of this concern in a paper on trade unionism at the IFIP World Computer Congress in 1970 [26]. The overarching outcome was a concern over the way they felt people were being forced to use computers in dehumanizing ways. The consensus of the conference, and of Mumford and Sackman's subsequent summary chapter in the proceedings ('International Human Choice and Computers: Conference Retrospect and Prospect' [29]) was that sociotechnical problems, including the use of computer systems, must be solved in ways that include community, national, and especially workers' interests; that, ultimately, humanistic needs must take precedence over technological and economic considerations.

Since that first conference, the HCC series has firmly remained at the cutting edge of innovative and critical thinking about the interface between the social and technology (Fig. 5). The central remit of IFIP's Technical Committee 9 - of which HCC is the flagship conference - is the relationship between computers and society. As Jacques Berleur, Magda Herschui and Lorenz Hilty related in their introduction to the Proceedings of HCC9, "The success of HCC1 was such that IFIP-TC9 henceforth considered it the TC's founding event, if not birthplace. TC9 was conceived in 1976, two years after HCC1." [9].

The founding chair of TC9 was *Calvin C. Gotlieb (1976–1981).* Gotlieb, (known as Kelly) was from the Department of Computer Science at the University of Toronto, Canada. In his keynote, entitled, 'Computers - A Gift of Fire,' to the IFIP Congress in 1980, he said: "As computer technology spreads globally, it begins to behave like other modern technologies in that undesirable side-effects appear. Much more serious than computer effects on privacy are the impacts of microprocessors on industrial employment. Another issue arises out of evidence presented by managers and social scientists that using computers in decision-making can lead to systems which are too rigid and, especially in government, to procedures which failed to meet human needs." [17].

From the outset, then, HCC and TC9 have been focused on the social impacts of computing and not merely the many interfaces that exist between computing and society. This more nuanced perspective also means that HCC and TC9 are among the first sources of sustained consideration of the ethical requirements on computing and information technology professionals. TC9's founding aims (only marginally revised in 2008 and 2009 to include reference to new Working Groups) were: 'To develop understanding of how ICT innovation is associated with change in society'; and 'To influence the shaping of socially responsible and ethical policies and professional practices.' These aims were given application through Gotlieb's legacy in the establishment of the Technical Committee's first two Working Groups, in 1977: WG9.1 on Computers and Work, and WG9.2 on Social Accountability and Computing.

After Gotlieb's six-year tenure ended, the TC9 journey faltered somewhat with two Chairs in two years. ***R. Brotherton (1982–1982)*** and ***Fred Margulies (1983–1983)*** remained in post only from one IFIP General Assembly to the next. Margulies did, however, manage to achieve a fair bit during his time at IFIP. As the Austrian Representative to IFIP, Margulies had supported Zemanek, the President of IBM Austria, to run the first HCC held in Vienna in 1974. He then helped Gottlieb organize HCC2 in Baden (Austria) in 1979 (June 4–8) [28].

With *Harold Sackman (1984–1989)* – co-editor of the HCC1 proceedings - in the Chair a new energy returned to TC9. Sackman staged HCC3 during September 1985 in Stockholm, Sweden. While a new chair had brought new stability to the committee it was a difficult period for the sociotechnical approach associated with TC9. The tension is evident and well-documented in the conference proceedings for HCC3 [36]. The very nature, scope and purpose of the relationship between technology and people were at the heart of an intensely critical and heated debate. In his introduction to the HCC3 proceedings, Sackman took the opportunity to remind an increasingly diverse readership of the ranked list of objectives for TC9 as:

1. Protection of Individual Rights
2. Employment and the Quality of Life
3. International Problem Solving
4. International Studies on Social Impacts
5. Professional Social Accountability
6. Universal Social Benefits
7. Protection of Group and Collective Rights
8. International Planning and Cooperation
9. International Education

To follow on from the challenges presented through the HCC3 conference, Sackman determined to bring better understanding of ethical behavior to the computing profession. In 1988 he began a project "to create an IFIP code of ethics" [6]. This ethical flavor can be recognized in the HCC conferences as a continuing and upwardly trending theme, seen through the more recent conferences (after a decline in HCC7 and HCC8) (Fig. 1). It was to be more than three decades before this project would come to realization. In the same year, Sackman established a new Working Group: WG9.3, with the theme of Home Oriented Informatics and Telematics (and now being reimagined and relaunched as 'Intelligent Communities'). This shift to broader social perspectives is hinted at with the corollary of a declining interest in terms related to professional* (Fig. 2) across the HCC corpus. This declining interest was accelerated in HCC8 and HCC9 with consciously positioned themes around wider viewpoints on the information society.

The energy Sackman had put into TC9 and HCC was then built upon by Klaus Brunnstein (1990–1995), who staged HCC4 in July 1990, in Dublin. The proceedings were edited by Berleur and Drumm [7]. Brunnstein who, as early as 1973, had become "the first European professor for the application of Information Technology, concentrating on education" [38] later became a prominent champion of data security. He was one of the founder members of the Computer Anti-Virus Research Organization (CARO) [14]. As Tommi Uhlemann, from global security specialists ESET, said in his obituary in 2015, "In Germany he'll mostly be remembered for his fight for data protection in the 80's. He played a leading role in having new laws in this field" [39]. During his tenure,

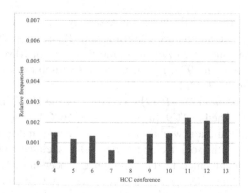

Fig. 1. Frequency of 'ethic*' terms across the HCC corpus

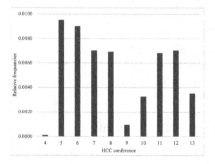

Fig. 2. Frequency of 'professional*' terms across the HCC corpus

Brunnstein formally established Working Group 9.4 on ICTs in Developing Countries. This was a direct response to, and a championing of, Subash Bhatnagar's proposal at the General Assembly in 1989 [37, 39], that followed the launch of the group at a conference in New Delhi in 1988 [11]. At the same time Working Group 9.5 was established with a focus on the social implications of artificial intelligence and virtual worlds.

Collecting together the full HCC4 proceedings reveals expected keywords but the influence of Brunnstein's own personal priorities can also be identified in these keywords (Fig. 3). 'Privacy', 'ethics', 'ethical', 'environmental' and 'sustainable' are all visible but set against the wider perspective on the relationship between 'people' and 'computing'. Keywords such as 'governance', 'process', 'infrastructure' and particularly 'power' indicate that the critical perspective can be found throughout the individual papers in the proceedings.

Pertti Järvinen (1996–1998), who had been TC9 Secretary under Brunnstein, then assumed the chair of TC9 and oversaw delivery of HCC5 in August 1998, in Geneva, Switzerland. The proceedings were edited by Rasmussen, Beardon and Munari [33]. A principal component analysis of the full text of HCC5 reveals the correlation between keywords throughout the proceedings (Fig. 4). The analysis extracts the most used terms and these are then placed closer together when they are more commonly used together. The rising importance of the Internet is an important outlier. 'Society' and 'public'

Fig. 3. HCC4 corpus keywords

strongly evidence another theme as is a cluster linking 'users', 'communication' and 'access' and a further set bringing together 'design', 'human', 'research' and 'university'. The presence of 'research', 'university' and 'conference' as persistent keywords seen across all HCC proceedings reflects levels of self-awareness and the conscious recognition that the researchers in HCC proceedings were in a position of privileged circumstances, looking in on the personal, social and organizational experience of computers and computing. The separation of 'people' and 'data' from other keywords points to their usage in many different contexts. There is a loose indication of the overarching theme for the majority of keywords and the way in which the theme of globalization in this conference was distilled by its contributors.

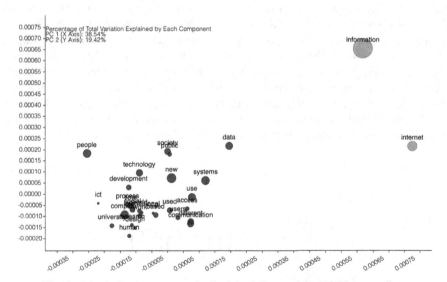

Fig. 4. Principal component analysis of the full text of the HCC5 proceedings

Jacques Berleur (TC9 Chair 1999–2004), a champion of WG9.2, previously an editor of the HCC4 proceedings and a paper contributor to HCC5, then became Chair of TC9 in 1999, with Chrisanthi Avgerou (WG9.4 Chair since 1996) as his Vice-Chair.

Berleur oversaw HCC6 as part of the World Computer Congress in 2002, in Montreal, Canada, co-editing with Klaus Brunnstein [12]. Back in 1988, when Harold Sackman began to champion and progress the development of an IFIP Code of Ethics, Berleur's WG9.2 was the obvious home for such a project, with much attention paid to how it might evolve at the regular Working Group meetings being held at Berleur's home institution, the University of Namur in Belgium. In 1996, Berleur and Brunnstein co-edited a book 'Ethics of Computing: Codes, Spaces for Discussion and Law' as a "Handbook prepared by the IFIP Ethics Task Group" among many other similar outputs that were published during the 1990s [6]. In 2004, at the end of his tenure at the helm of TC9, Berleur's sustained efforts produced the 'Criteria and Procedures for Developing Codes of Ethics or of Conduct' [8]. These criteria were applied in the creation of the Code of Ethics that IFIP adopted, finally, after 32 years of effort, at the 2020 General Assembly.

After Berleur, TC9's leadership moved decisively into the hands of WG9.4, with its former Chair, *Chrisanthi Avgerou (2005–2010)*, moving into the TC9 Chair and then passing it to the South African representative *Jackie Phahlamohlaka (2011–2013)*. By 2005 new working groups WG9.6, on IT Misuse and the Law (jointly with TC11), WG9.7 on History of Computing, and WG9.8 on Women and IT (now Gender, Diversity and ICT), had been formed, and Avgerou oversaw vigorous and enthusiastic chairing of all the Working Groups, revitalizing many of the WG's activities. Avgerou oversaw three Human Choice and Computers conferences: HCC7 [31] in Maribor, Slovenia in September 2006, with the proceedings edited again by Berleur with Nurminen and Impagliazzo [9]; then in September 2008 HCC8 was held in Pretoria, South Africa with proceedings edited by Avgerou herself with Smith and van den Besselaar [1]; and finally HCC9 was held in Brisbane, Australia in September 2010 [10], as part of the World Computer Congress. HCC7 was notable for its memorial to Rob Kling and the proceedings focus on personal reflections as well as consideration to the impact of his body of work. Perhaps the most significant influence on the keywords from the HCC7 proceedings in contrast to previous conferences was the inclusion of Kling's name and the use of the term 'informatics' while many of the remaining words reflect the ongoing development of a critical thinking perspective across HCC scholarship (Fig. 5). Phahlamohlaka then oversaw HCC10 in Amsterdam, Netherlands, September 2012, editing the proceedings with Herscheui, Whitehouse and McIver [18].

Fig. 5. HCC7 Keywords

Chairmanship of TC9 then passed back to the champions of ethics, firstly through former WG 9.2 chair, **Diane Whitehouse (2014–2017)** and then to the current chair, **David Kreps (2018-current)** who had joined WG9.5 in 2008 and became its Chair in 2013.

Whitehouse oversaw two HCCs: HCC11 in Turku, Finland, in July 2014, with the proceedings edited by Kimppa, Whitehouse, Kuusela and Phahlamohlaka [19]; and then HCC12 in Salford, Greater Manchester, UK, in September 2016 with the proceedings edited by Kreps, Fletcher and Griffiths [21]. Working Group 9.10 on ICT Uses in Peace and War was also formed and ratified at this time by Phahlamohlaka and Whitehouse. A belated recognition of the role of ICT in these contexts and acknowledgement of a strong South African team of academics dedicated to the topic.

Kreps, at the time of writing, has overseen three HCCs: HCC12 in 2016; HCC13 in 2018; HCC14 in 2020. He is now overseeing HCC15 for 2022. He has also led the publication of two key critical IFIP Papers.

At the General Assembly in Poznan, Poland, in 2018, Kreps championed the creation of an IFIP Position Paper on E-Waste [24]. This initiative was supported by members of the WG9.2 on Social Accountability and the reformulated WG9.9 on ICT and Sustainable Development. The statement was completed and published as a PDF report on the IFIP website in May 2019.

At the IFIP General Assembly in Kiev, Ukraine, in 2019, Kreps then championed the creation and adoption of an IFIP Code of Ethics. A Task and Finish Group, chaired by Kreps, including the Chair of WG9.2.2 on Frameworks on Ethics of Computing, the Chair of IP3[1], and a representative from the Member Societies Assembly, worked through 2020 to finalize the new Code for its publication launch at IFIP's 60th Birthday Celebration - sadly postponed due to the global COVID-19 pandemic. Thirty-two years after Harold Sackman's stated ambition, nonetheless, the IFIP Code of Ethics has finally come to fruition, adopted by the General Assembly, published, and disseminated widely by IP3. It is also included in this volume.

As well as chairing HCC12, Kreps Chaired HCC13 as part of the World Computer Congress in September 2018 in Poznan, Poland sharing the editing duties of the proceedings with Ess, Leenen and Kimppa [22]. He then co-chaired HCC14 which was set to take place in Tokyo, Japan, in September 2020. However, these plans too fell foul of the pandemic and the Tokyo conference had to be cancelled. The proceedings were still produced with the editing completed by Kreps, Komukai, Gopal, and Ishii [25]. HCC15 in Tokyo is in preparation as this chapter goes to print, with editors Kreps, Davison, Komukai and Ishii. While the setbacks of the pandemic were an unexpected and external marker in TC9 and HCC's history, current indications of the significance of COVID-19's impact on the relationship of people and computing only serves to reinforce the ongoing importance of understanding this complex partnership, and the papers for HCC15 'Human Choice and Digital by Default: Autonomy vs Digital Determination' will no doubt reflect this.

---

[1] IFIP's International Professional Practice Partnership.

3 A Critical Perspective

It is clear that what sets HCC and TC9 apart from other long-standing conference series that focus on information systems or people and technology is the critical perspective that has been its consistent hallmark.

As Avgerou says, in her personal history of her involvement with IFIP [3], "TC9 was, and perhaps continues to be, one of the very few international umbrella forums where the whole range of social issues can be discussed," but there are, today, a great number of specialist fora where academics can discuss and debate particular aspects of the social issues of computing, many of which include a strong critical voice (e.g. ETHICOMP, AoIR, 4S, EASST and others). TC9 - and its flagship conference HCC - remains, however, in many respects both the original (since 1974), and the most wide-reaching and overarching forum for the critical perspective on ICT and Society, as some of its leaders' other publications underline [2, 23, 32]. This critical voice, moreover, brings philosophy into play underpinning its ethical stance [23, 35].

To explore this history, as stated in the introduction, the authors used a textual analysis tool to examine the existing corpus of HCC texts. Initial analysis focused on the prologues, introductions or key introductory chapters of each proceedings. These were analyzed for identifiable trends. HCC6 was not initially included as it could not be located through the UK's interlibrary loan system and HCC11 was not included due to its relatively brief prologue. Using optical character recognition to include the earlier conference introductions, the corpus was then processed through the voyant-tools website [40] to visualize the resulting trends. Figures 8, 9, 10, 12 were all produced in this way using solely the overview of the conference by the editors. After establishing the value of this approach, the entire text of all the conferences from HCC4 onwards - and including the HCC6 conference after obtaining a copy from the publishers - were converted to text and and again examined through the voyant-tools system. This complete corpus proved particularly useful for correspondence (Figs. 5 and 6) and principal components analysis (Fig. 3). Figures 1, 2, 5–7, 11, 13, 15 are all produced from the analysis of the full-text corpus while Figs. 3 and 4 use the full text of just one of the proceedings. Exploration of the corpus for insight is only limited by the constraints of word count.

Correspondence analysis of the HCC corpus (from HCC4 onwards) reveals the consistency of themes over thirty-five years (Fig. 6) with the specific proceedings being positioned relative to the focus and theme of each individual conference (Fig. 7). The blend of people and computing is clearly evident with the specific identification of terms such as 'development', 'work', 'people and 'government' all providing indications of the underlying critical philosophy that informs this large body of work.

Cecez-Kecmanovic [15] identifies critical information systems research as being defined by a socially critical point of view, or, as Klein and Myers put it, IS research "can be classified as critical if the main task is seen as being one of social critique, whereby the restrictive and alienating conditions of the status quo are brought to light" [20]. This view is revealed in Sackman's 1986 list which places the objective most likely to initiate "transformative social change" [15] at the head of the list. Invariably this is reflected as an intertwining of 'social' and 'technology' across the corpus from HCC4. The most identifiable break in this relationship comes with HCC7 when the focus on Rob

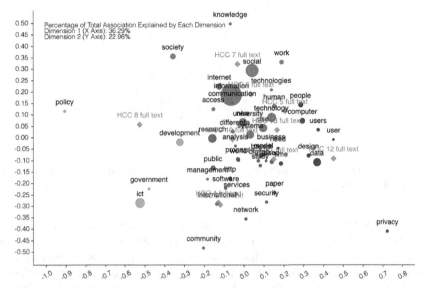

Fig. 6. Correspondence analysis of key terms in the HCC corpus (HCC4 to HCC13)

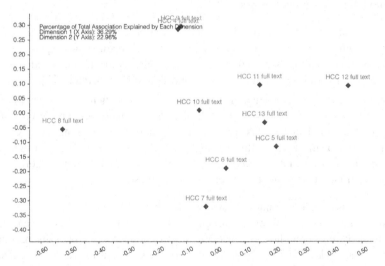

Fig. 7. Correspondence analysis of each HCC proceedings

Kling's work and legacy briefly pushed the balance noticeably in favor of the social over that of technology (Fig. 8). This is as strong an indication as any of Kling's own research emphasis in comparison to the underlying trend of other HCC conference contributors.

McGrath [27] confirmed the distinctiveness of HCC when she cited the proceedings of the first conference in 1974 as a watershed moment in the development of critical information systems thinking. The proceedings, she said, included an encouragement by editors Mumford and Sackman "to engage with the way that computer applications were

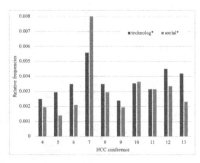

Fig. 8. The intertwined focus of technology and the social across the corpus of the full proceedings from HCC4 onwards

being developed and deployed, and to make the human choices necessary to ensure that democratic values and ideals were preserved for the benefit of everyone" [27]. While Mumford and Sackman probably did not set out consciously to create this theoretical position, the critical focus and variety of challenges presented in the first conference were certainly a product of their time. An almost continuous concern with the position of labor, pressing union issues and the prevailing social theories of the time are peppered throughout the early proceedings of HCC.

> Worker orientation is also possible, and a lot should and will be done. From a certain point on, however, too much adaptation will result in overspecialization and this will rebound back onto the worker in the form of career and position difficulties. Flexibility is a human virtue and should be cultivated [12].

> Our subject, therefore, is a matter far beyond computer sciences. It has to do with sociology, psychology, physiology, with the art of management and government, with democratic decision making as well as legal decision making and even creation of law. It must deal with the large field of problems with which the trade unions are faced. And it extends even into philosophy and religion - if Europe and America do not teach this, Islam certainly does these days [13].

The various threads of what are now recognizable as critical thinking in IS are developed more fully in later conference proceedings. In many cases, it is the small and offhand points made by earlier authors that became the pressing focus for later discussions. For example, Zemanek in 1979 [41] observed, "today we begin to realize how inseparable scientific and human development are." and Margulies' final footnote in 1979 [26] struggled with, "whether we could leave out home computers from our discussions or not - they will probably affect our attitudes towards computers and thereby affect our professional life." Margulies [26] started the first formalizing of the critical thinking perspective of HCC by provocatively entitling his contribution - in a rare moment of editorial reflexivity for any conference - as "Why 'HCC' again?" and by then stating:

> ...technology must not become an end in itself, but has to be seen in the context of man. Throughout history man has developed new means of production in his unceasing endeavor to make work easier and life better, thus at the same time

creating new ways of human cooperation and societal organization. The technology of today also can only be justified by its service to man, by its contribution in improving the quality of life, in providing the chance of self-realization [26].

In all of these early statements, with the benefit of hindsight, it is apparent that, with rapid evolution, adoption and popularization, information technology was pressing nearer and nearer and becoming ever more intimately tied with the human condition. In 1986 Sackman, working amidst the disruption of a fundamental ontological debate, identified major new forthcoming areas of concern for research that included - somewhat prophetically - "home information systems and social networking" and "robotics and artificial intelligence" [36]. While Barnes [4] is regarded as the originator of the term 'social network' this must be one of the first published instances of the term in relation to computers and information technology. This is an even more extraordinary statement when it is placed in the historical context of Dell Computers, the NSFNET (the first major TCP/IP network) and the WELL (the first digital community) all being only one year old in 1986.

With the increasing ubiquity and everyday presence of information technology, more recent HCC conferences have become less focused on work and more concerned with the general human situation including aspects of the personal and of the home (Fig. 9). This does not mean the original concerns of HCC have now somehow disappeared but rather that they have now become supplemented and richer, to incorporate the fuller interplay of public and private (Fig. 10) in ways that were not imagined or possible in the 1970s or 1980s.

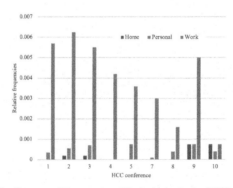

Fig. 9. Home and Personal vs Work through the HCC series.

The spirit of HCC is consequently evident in the link tree of connected terms from the first HCC through to HCC10 held in 2012 (Fig. 11). The juxtaposition and mediating terms are themselves revealing of the intimate relationships between technology and people. "Information", "Human" and "Social" sit at the center of the diagram interlinking all the other concepts. Both "human systems" and "computer systems" are represented as is the classic "man machine" combination. "Human" and "Technology" are only sometimes mediated by the use of "policy" while "society", "technology" and "people" sit in a triangular relationship revealing an interdependence that is acknowledged by

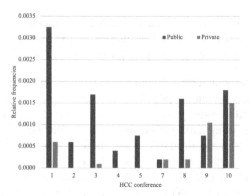

Fig. 10. Public vs Private through the HCC series.

many HCC papers through the years. The entire corpus view of the linked terms from HCC 4 to HCC 13 reveal an even stronger trend (Fig. 12). The six-way linkage of 'new', 'society', 'communication', 'economic', 'policy' and 'systems' predominates heavily and captures the root terms for so many of the recent HCC conference themes and concerns.

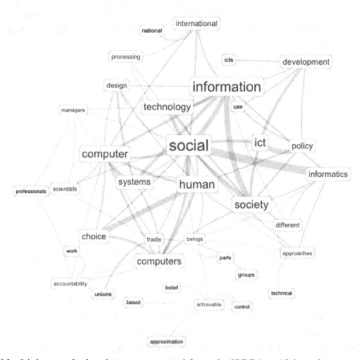

Fig. 11. Link tree of related terms generated from the HCC 1 to 10 introductory corpus.

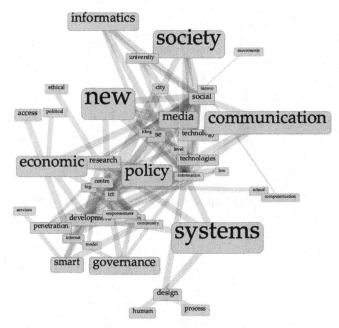

Fig. 12. Link tree of related terms generated from the full HCC4 to HCC 13 corpus

This fluctuating tension echoes the shifting personal emphasis of different TC9 chairs and the choice of conference themes across time appears to reflect a tension between the hardware-orientated concept of "computers" and the more central object in the relationship between technology and people in the form of "information" (Fig. 13). However, across the entire corpus it is clear that contributors to HCC are firmly focused on the role of information in their critical perspectives (Fig. 14). With multiple devices constantly "near us" and "on us" (and soon "in us") the question of what any single computer is doing or how it will be deployed becomes less significant than what "we" will do with the consequent information that is being generated by the many devices now available for us to access, interpret and use.

The predominance of 'information' across the full corpus of HCC papers also parallels an 'ethical' turn for the editors of each proceedings with rising attention commencing from HCC5 [5] (Fig. 15). This editorial trend can also be seen across the full corpus with a generally rising trend since HCC8 (where attention was more fully turned to different social issues) (Fig. 16).

Constantinides et al. [16] might describe this as progress towards the "ends" of Information Systems research. Perhaps, too, this 'turn' can be seen as expressing the gradual shift in the background of those involved in TC9 and HCC from predominantly computing engineers with social concerns, towards information systems academics whose principal background is the social sciences rather than computing [3]. The patterns of critical research, as Richardson and Robertson point out, seem broadly to have settled into a three-part format: insight, critique and transformative redefinition. Insight, "helps to highlight hidden or less obvious aspects of social reality;" critique, "challenges many of

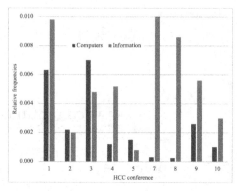

Fig. 13. Timeline of HCC1 to HCC10 proceedings with computers and information reflecting an editorial tension for focus

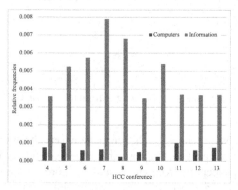

Fig. 14. Timeline of the full corpus of HCC4 to HCC13 with the unambiguous attention on information over computers.

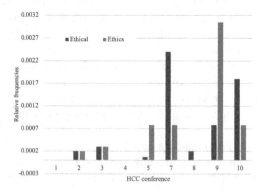

Fig. 15. The rise of ethical and ethics consideration in HCC introductions.

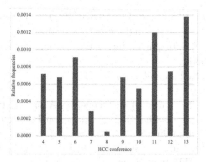

Fig. 16. The pace of the ethical turn across the full corpus of HCC4 to HCC13.

the taken-for-granted assumptions, beliefs, ideologies, discourses;" and transformative redefinition, "is the development of critical, relevant knowledge and practical understanding to facilitate emancipatory change" [34]. This ethical turn over the course of the HCC series, then, is in keeping with the transformative redefinition such critical research engenders. As people are brought into closer constant communication with technology the issues of ethics and the ethical boundaries between "what can be done" and "what should be done" becomes a more pressing and more evident challenge to researchers. As the number of interfaces increases so too do the ethical challenges.

4 Conclusion

As a long-standing conference series dedicated to critical information systems research, HCC has rightly stayed true to its heritage – and the overarching concerns of all those engaged in TC9 and its working groups - by charting the increasing tension between the many possibilities that technology enables, in contrast to what "we" as a society should be doing with these capabilities. The personalities who, over the past decades, have championed these concerns, have all been fundamentally dedicated to these basic questions, whether focused more upon the ethics or upon those - whether socially marginalized in the developed world or located in developing countries - whose needs must not be forgotten, as new technologies evolve, and as our current era of digital determinism unfolds against the backdrop of anthropogenic climate change [23].

References

1. Avgerou, C., Smith, M., van den Besselaar, P.: HCC 2008. Springer, Boston (2008). https://doi.org/10.1007/978-0-387-84822-8_1
2. Avgerou, C.: Information systems in developing countries: a critical research review. J. Inf. Technol. **23**(3), 133–146 (2008)
3. Avgerou, C.: IFIP TC9 Report: 1995–2010 - A personal account. In von Solms and Strous (eds.) 50 Years of IFIP. Springer, Heidelberg (2010)
4. Barnes, J.A.: Class and Committees in a Norwegian Island Parish. Human Relations **7**(1), 39–58 (1954)

5. Beardon, C., Munari, S., Rasmussen, L.: Prologue, In: Rasmussen, L., Beardon, C., Munari, S. (eds.) Computers and Networks in the Age of Globalization, Proceedings of the 5th IFIP-HCC (Human Choice and Computers) International Conference, HCC-5, Kluwer Academic Publishers, Boston (2000)

6. Berleur, J., Brunnstein, K.: Ethics of Computing (1996). http://www.ifip.org/36years/a53berlr. html

7. Berleur, J., Drumm, J. (eds.): Information Technology Assessment: Human Choice and Computers, 4, Proceedings of the Fourth IFIP-TC9 International Conference on Human Choice and Computers (HCC-4), Dublin, July 8–12, 1990, Elsevier, North-Holland, Amsterdam (1991)

8. Berleur, J., et al.: Criteria and Procedures for Developing Codes of Ethics or of Conduct. On behalf of IFIP-SIG9.2.2 IFIP Press, Laxenburg-Austria (2004)

9. Berleur, J., Nurminen, M., lmpagliazzo, J. (eds.): Social Informatics: An Information Society for All? In Remembrance of Rob Kling, Proceedings of the Seventh International Conference on Human Choice and Computers (HCC7), IFIP TC 9, Maribor, Slovenia, September 21–23 (2006)

10. Berleur, J., Hercheui, M.D., Hilty, L.M.: What kind of information society? introduction to the hcc9 conference proceedings. In: Berleur, J., Hercheui, M.D., Hilty, L.M. (eds.) CIP/HCC -2010. IAICT, vol. 328, pp. 3–9. Springer, Heidelberg (2010). https://doi.org/10.1007/978-3-642-15479-9_1

11. Bhatnagar, S.C., Bjorn-Anderson, N. (eds.): Information Technology in Developing Countries. North-Holland, Amsterdam (1990)

12. Brunnstein, K., Berleur, J. (eds): Human Choice and Computers, Issues of Choice and Quality of Life in the Information Society, Proceedings of the IFIP-TC9 HCC-6 Conference, 17th World Computer Congress, Montreal, August 2002, Kluwer Academic Publishers (2002).

13. Bryant, T.: The myth of information society. In: Berleur, J., Drumm, J. (eds.) Information Technology Assessment: Human Choice and Computers, 4, Proceedings of the Fourth IFIP-TC9 International Conference on Human Choice and Computers (HCC-4), Dublin, July 8–12, 1990, Elsevier, North-Holland, Amsterdam (1991)

14. CARO http://www.caro.org/index.html

15. Cecez-Kecmanovic, D.: Doing critical information systems research – arguments for a critical research methodology. Eur. J. Inf. Syst. 20(4), 440–455 (2011)

16. Constantinides, P., Chaisson, M., Introna, L.: The ends of information system research: a pragmatic framework. MIS Q. 36(1), 1–19 (2012)

17. Gottlieb, C.: Computers – A Gift of Fire. Invited Presentation. In: Lavington, S.H. (ed.) Information Processing 80. North-Holland Publishing Company (1980)

18. Hercheui, M.D., Whitehouse, D., McIver, W., Phahlamohlaka, J. (eds.) ICT Critical Infrastructures and Society: 10th International Human Choice and Computers Conference, HCC10 2012, Amsterdam, The Netherlands, September 2012, Proceedings Springer, Heidelberg (2012). https://doi.org/10.1007/978-3-642-33332-3

19. Kimppa, K., Whitehouse, D., Kuusela, T., Phahlamohlaka, J. (eds.): HCC 2014. IAICT, vol. 431. Springer, Heidelberg (2014). https://doi.org/10.1007/978-3-662-44208-1

20. Klein, H.K., Myers, M.D.: A set of principles for conducting and evaluating interpretive field studies in information systems. MIS Q. 23(1), 67–93 (1999)

21. Kreps, D., Fletcher, G., Griffiths, M., (eds.): Technology and Intimacy: Choice or Coercion. 12th IFIP TC9 International Conference on Human Choice and Computers 2016, Salford, UK, September 7–9, 2016, Proceedings Cham, Switzerland: Springer International (2016). https://doi.org/10.1007/978-3-319-44805-3

22. Kreps, D., Ess, C., Leenen, L., Kimppa, K., (eds.): This Changes Everything – ICT and Climate Change: What Can We Do? 13th IFIP TC 9 International Conference on Human Choice and Computers, HCC13 2018, Held at the 24th IFIP World Computer Congress, WCC 2018, Poznan, Poland, September 19–21, 2018, Proceedings Cham, Switzerland: Springer International (2018). https://doi.org/10.1007/978-3-319-99605-9
23. Kreps, D.: Against Nature: The Metaphysics of Information Systems. Routledge, London (2018)
24. Kreps, D., et al.: IFIP Position Paper on E-Waste. Vienna, IFIP (2019)
25. Kreps, D., Komukai, T., Gopal, T.V., Ishii, K., (eds.): 14th IFIP TC9 Human Choice and Computers Conference: Human-Centric Computing in a Data-Driven Society HCC14 2020 Proceedings. Switzerland: Springer International, Cham (2020). https://doi.org/10.1007/978-3-030-62803-1
26. Margulies, F.: Why 'HCC' again? In Mowshowitz, A. (ed) Human Choice and Computers 2, Proceedings of the Second IFIP-TC9 Human Choice and Computers Conference (HCC-2), Baden, Austria, 4–8 June, 1979, Elsevier, North-Holland, Amsterdam (1980)
27. McGrath, K.: Doing critical research in information systems: a case of theory and practice not informing each other. Inf. Syst. J. **15**, 85–101 (2005)
28. Mowshowitz, A. (ed.): Human Choice and Computers 2, Proceedings of the 2nd IFIP-TC9 Human Choice and Computers Conference (HCC2), Baden (Austria), 4–8 June, 1979. Elsevier, North-Holland, Amsterdam (1980)
29. Mumford, E., Sackman, H.: International human choice and computers: conference retrospect and prospect. In: Mumford, E., Sackman, H. (eds.) Human Choice and Computers, Proceedings of the Conference on Human Choice and Computers (HCC-1), Vienna, Austria, April 1–5, 1974, Elsevier, North-Holland, Amsterdam (1975).
30. Mumford, E., Sackman, H. (eds): Human Choice and Computers, Proceedings of the Conference on Human Choice and Computers (HCC-1), Vienna, Austria, April 1–5, 1974, Elsevier, North-Holland, Amsterdam (1975)
31. Nurminen, M., Berleur, J., lmpagliazzo, J.: Preface, in social information: an information society for all? In: Remembrance of Rob Kling, Proceedings of the Seventh International Conference on Human Choice and Computers (HCC7), IFIP TC 9, Maribor, Slovenia, September 21–23 (2006)
32. Patrignani, N., Whitehouse, D.: Slow Tech and ICT. London, Palgrave (2018)
33. Rasmussen, L., Beardon, C., Munari, S. (eds.): Computers and networks in the age of globalization. In: Proceedings of the 5th IFIP-HCC (Human Choice and Computers) International Conference, Geneva, Switzerland, HCC-5, August 25–28, 1998. Kluwer Academic Publishers, Boston (2000)
34. Richardson, H., Robinson, B.: The mysterious case of the missing paradigm: a review of critical information systems research. Inf. Syst. J. **17**(3), 251–270 (2007)
35. Rowe, F.: Being critical is good, but better with philosophy! From digital transformation and values to the future of IS research. Eur. J. Inf. Syst. **27**(3), 380–393 (2018)
36. Sackman, H.: Historical Critique of IFIP TC 9: computer relationships with society. In: Sackman, H. (ed.) Comparative Worldwide National Computer Policies, Proceedings of the 3rd IFIP-TC9 Conference on Human Choice and Computers, Stockholm (HCC-3), Sweden, 2–5 September 1985, Elsevier, North-Holland, Amsterdam (1986)
37. Indian Institute of Management Ahmedabad. http://www.iimahd.ernet.in/~subhash/
38. Virus Bulletin April 1996. https://www.virusbulletin.com/uploads/pdf/magazine/1996/199604-insight-KlausBrunnstein.pdf
39. Threat Radar 2015. https://www.virusradar.com/node/168

40. Voyant-Tools. http://www.voyant-tools.org/
41. Zemanek, H.: Human Choice - a subject of increasing general interest. In: Mowshowitz, A. (ed.) Human Choice and Computers 2, Proceedings of the Second IFIP-TC9 Human Choice and Computers Conference (HCC-2), Baden, Austria, 4–8 June, 1979, Elsevier, North-Holland, Amsterdam (1980)

TC 11: Security and Privacy Protection in Information Processing Systems

Information Security and Privacy – Challenges and Outlook

Steven Furnell[1,2](✉) (iD), Paul Haskell-Dowland[2] (iD), Manish Agrawal[3] (iD),
Richard Baskerville[4] (iD), Anirban Basu[5] (iD), Matt Bishop[6] (iD), Jorge Cuellar[7],
Sara Foresti[8] (iD), Lynn Futcher[9] (iD), Nurit Gal-Oz[10] (iD), Teju Herath[11] (iD),
Christian Damsgaard Jensen[12] (iD), Allen Johnston[13] (iD), Wouter Joosen[14],
Giovanni Livraga[6,9] (iD), Javier Lopez[15] (iD), Stephen Marsh[16], Fabio Martinelli[17],
Fabio Massacci[18] (iD), Aljosa Pasic[19], Stef Schinagl[20] (iD), Abbas Shahim[20],
Kerry-Lynn Thomson[9] (iD), Jaideep Vaidya[21] (iD), Tony Vance[22] (iD),
and Merrill Warkentin[23] (iD)

[1] School of Computer Science, University of Nottingham, Nottingham, UK
steven.furnell@nottingham.ac.uk
[2] School of Science, Edith Cowan University, Joondalup, Australia
[3] University of South Florida, Tampa, USA
[4] Georgia State University, Atlanta, USA
[5] University of Sussex, Brighton, UK
[6] University of California at Davis, Davis, CA, USA
[7] University of Passau, Passau, Germany
[8] Università degli Studi di Milano, Milan, Italy
[9] Nelson Mandela University, Port Elizabeth, South Africa
[10] Sapir Academic College, Ashkelon, Israel
[11] Brock University, St. Catharines, Canada
[12] Technical University of Denmark (DTU), Kongens Lyngby, Denmark
[13] University of Alabama, Tuscaloosa, USA
[14] KU Leuven, Leuven, Belgium
[15] University of Malaga, Malaga, Spain
[16] University of Ontario Institute of Technology, Oshawa, Canada
[17] CNR, Rome, Italy
[18] University of Trento, Trento, Italy
[19] ATOS, Madrid, Spain
[20] VU Amsterdam, Amsterdam, Netherlands
[21] Rutgers University, New Brunswick, USA
[22] Temple University, Philadelphia, USA
[23] Mississippi State University, Starkville, USA

Abstract. The ongoing demand for new and faster technologies continues to leave consumers and business users to face the constant challenge of updating systems and software. This unrelenting pace of technological evolution has not always been matched with a commensurate focus on security and privacy matters. In particular, the obligatory move to embrace cloud and IoT - that frequently result in the collection and analysis of large data lakes has raised challenges for sovereign data protection and privacy legislation where data at rest can change overnight with

© IFIP International Federation for Information Processing 2021
Published by Springer Nature Switzerland AG 2021
M. Goedicke et al. (Eds.): Advancing Research in Information and Communication Technology,
IFIP AICT 600, pp. 383–401, 2021. https://doi.org/10.1007/978-3-030-81701-5_16

mergers and acquisitions of service providers. This chapter examines the role of IFIP Technical Committee 11 (and its 14 underlying Working Groups) in this ever-changing and evolving domain. The discussion provides an outline of key issues in information security when viewed from technical, organisational and human perspectives, which collectively represent the breadth of areas within which TC-11 and its Working Groups are seeking to make contributions. The chapter as a whole gives a clear sense of the challenges involved in achieving and maintaining security and privacy, alongside insights into the ways that they are being tackled within IFIP activities.

Keywords: Information security · Privacy

1 Introduction

Alongside the global adoption and significant growth of information and communication technologies, comes the need to provide protection against potential breaches of security. These may result from deliberate and targeted attacks, as well as from misuse, inadvertent user errors, and system failures. In addition, with the volume and sensitivity of the related data that these systems store and communicate, there is an essential need to consider provisions for ensuring and maintaining privacy [1].

In recognition of these issues, IFIP Technical Committee 11 (TC-11) exists to increase the trustworthiness and general confidence in information processing, as well as to act as a forum for security and privacy protection experts and others professionally active in the field [2]. In parallel with the increasing importance of cyber security issues and concerns, the scope and activity of TC-11 has grown over the years, and at the time of writing encompasses 14 Working Groups, each focusing upon defined areas within the security and privacy landscape [3]. For the purpose of this chapter, each of the groups was asked to outline the challenges that they perceive in the future, resulting in the identification of a range of topical issues that can be broadly classified under the themes of technological, business and organisational, and human challenges. While each of these themes is distinct, this chapter considers how each of these perspectives combine and reflect the function of the Technical Committee while maintaining independent activities within each group. As may be expected, each working group approaches the issues of information security and privacy through the lens of their group role and scope.

After a short introduction to the working groups, this chapter first looks at the technological issues facing the ICT domain with consideration of the significant changes seen in recent years with new technologies and working approaches. The functional issues within organisations are then considered with due regard to policy, procedure and governance as well as a recognition of the changing (often global) legal frameworks in which ICT professionals must now function. Finally, the critical issue of human factors is considered. This is often overlooked but is a vital factor in ICT systems as humans design, implement and use the very systems that are then the cause of many security and privacy concerns.

2 Overview of Technical Committee 11

Technical Committee 11 (formally titled Security and Privacy Protection in Information Processing Systems) was originally established in 1983, and has the overall remit to:

- establish a common frame of reference for security and privacy protection in organizations, professions and the public domain;
- facilitate the exchange of practical experience;
- disseminate information on, and the evaluation of, current and future protective techniques;
- promote security and privacy protection as essential elements of information processing systems;
- clarify the relation between security and privacy protection.

Since its inception, TC-11 has grown to be supported by 14 Working Groups [3] covering a diverse range of security-oriented areas.

2.1 Information Security Management

There is a growing trend for senior business management to be held answerable for the reliable and secure operation of their information systems, as they are for control of their financial aspects. Information Security is, and should always be, an obligation on upper management with appropriate delegated responsibility [4]. Information security professionals and WG 11.1 in particular, should therefore be responsible for the development of all types of tools, mechanisms and methods to support top management in this new responsibility.

2.2 Pervasive Systems Security

Pervasive systems shall be defined to be large scale systems that are comprised of nodes ranging from RFID tags, through embedded systems, to personal mobile devices, interconnected by a mixture of short-range wireless and wide are wired networks. The typical characteristics of a pervasive system are: resource constrained nodes, often physically unreachable or without user interface, whose interconnections often span a large number of administrative domains with conflicting interests. Security of such systems is therefore an emergent property.

2.3 Data and Applications Security and Privacy

IFIP WG 11.3 was formed in 1986 to stimulate activities in both data security and privacy research and in the application of data security and privacy techniques. The goal in forming the working group was to encourage the development of better techniques for stating data security and privacy requirements, for designing, building, and implementing data management systems that satisfy security and privacy requirements, and for assuring that the systems meet their requirements in actual operation.

2.4 Network and Distributed Systems Security

Management in any organization is responsible for the reliable and secure operation of the information systems that support the organization. As inter and intra-organization networking between information systems become the rule as well as the daily operational environment, the scope of concern takes on new aspects and new technical details come into play. Management must not only address the security issues of wholly internal systems together with any networks to which they might be connected, but also must assure that the protective mechanisms installed in them are not accidentally or intentionally thwarted or subverted by other systems with which data exchange connections are established.

2.5 IT Assurance and Audit

The current attention for digitalization and regulatory compliance has significantly changed the way in which IT has been organized, managed and consumed. Given their strict corresponding control objectives, organizations must transparently prove that they act in accordance with the applicable laws and regulations and manage digital risk in a proper fashion. Hence, reasonable assurance with respect to IT is crucial in this case to build confidence whether IT solutions and underlying infrastructures preserve resources, maintain data integrity as well as availability, meet the service levels, satisfy the regulatory requirements and accordingly assist in attaining their goals. For this essential purpose, a number of IT assurance and audit engagements are normally conducted. The aim of the working group is to study and develop detailed knowledge on IT assurance and audit models, standards, processes and techniques to meet the needs of organizations from a wider business perspective.

2.6 Identity Management

The aim of WG11.6 is to promote - through education, research and outreach - the awareness and understanding of issues including identity management applications and methodologies, identity management issues at the national level (including issues of federated and multilateral identity management), and the role and effectiveness of identity management in fighting fraud and other forms of crime [5]. The working group is also specifically interested in biometric technologies that increasingly contribute to the IM landscape, including legal and operational aspects of biometrics, methods and techniques that can help to evaluate and improve the technologies, and their associated impact upon society [6, 7].

2.7 Information Technology: Misuse and the Law

The WG focuses on the relations between IT Misuse, the Law and Society. As "Misuse" depends very much on the point of view and the cultural background of the viewer a very broad understanding of the term "Misuse" turned out to be appropriate. The WG studies technical, organisational, legal and social aspects of information infrastructures and electronic services with regard to their trustworthiness. The emphasis is on legal implications of new technology and vice versa.

2.8   Information Security Education

The aim of WG11.8 is to promote information security education and training in university, government and industry through the encouragement of the development of course models [8]. The WG also aims to establish an international resource center for the exchange of information about education and training in information security and to collect, exchange and disseminate information, relating to information security courses conducted by private organizations for industry [9]. The WG further aims to collect and periodically disseminate an annotated bibliography of information security books, feature articles, reports, and other educational media.

2.9   Digital Forensics

The growth of the Internet and the plethora of technology devices has resulted in more and more information being stored, transmitted and processed in digital form than ever before [10]. At the same time this connectivity is also enabling criminals to act trans-jurisdictionally with ease. Increasingly we are witnessing that a perpetrator of a crime is being brought to justice in one jurisdiction while the digital evidence needed to prosecute the perpetrator residing in other jurisdictions. This requires that all nations have the ability to collect, preserve and examine digital evidence for their own needs as well as for the potential needs of other nations. Digital Forensics is the scientific study of the processes involved in the recovery, preservation and examination of digital evidence, including audio, imaging and communication devices with consideration of forensic evasion techniques [11]. The efforts of the working group in digital forensics strive to discover, define and foster fundamental scientific principles that support the investigation of digital wrongdoings from all perspectives, legal, business and military.

2.10   Critical Infrastructure Protection

The "information infrastructure" – comprising computers, embedded devices, networks and software systems – is vital to day-to-day operations in every sector: agriculture, food, water, public health, emergency services, government, defense, information and telecommunications, energy, transportation, banking and finance, chemicals and hazardous materials, and postal and shipping [12]. Global business and industry, governments, indeed society itself, cannot function effectively if major components of the critical information infrastructure are degraded, disabled or destroyed [13]. Working Group 11.10 on Critical Infrastructure Protection seeks to engage the international information security research community to work together on applying scientific principles and engineering techniques to address current and future problems in information infrastructure protection. In addition to engaging the research community, the WG draws other interested parties (government agencies, infrastructure owners, operators and vendors, and policy makers) in a constructive dialog on critical infrastructure protection.

2.11   Trust Management

The deployment of a global computing infrastructure raises new and difficult security and privacy issues. Global computing allows entities to reason about the trustworthiness of other entities and to make autonomous security decisions on the basis of trust. This requires the development of a computational trust model that enables entities to reason about trust and to verify the security properties of a particular interaction [14]. The global computing infrastructure is highly dynamic with continuously appearing and disappearing entities and services [15]. It is vital that the associated computational trust model is able to incorporate this dynamism and that equally flexible legislative and regulatory frameworks emerge.

2.12   Human Aspects of Information Security and Assurance

Achieving security within information systems is no longer simply a technical problem but increasingly involves the active participation of people in order to securely design, deploy, configure and maintain systems [16]. Whilst the level and sophistication of this interaction may vary; anyone who is engaged with technology, from administrators of the most complex of IT systems to owners of simple devices, all need to make decisions that have an impact on the security and privacy of their device and information. Unfortunately, while people represent a key facet in achieving security, evidence demonstrates that this is often the point of failure [17]. With security now impacting all aspects of society, from the young to old, enterprise organisation to the individual, it is imperative that systems are designed, policies are put in place that assist people in ensuring the security of their systems. It is against this context that Working Group 11.12 aims to contribute.

2.13   Information Systems Security Research

The aim of the working group is the creation, dissemination, and preservation of well-formed research about information systems security. While relevant for advanced practical development, our primary audience consists of researchers in this area. We value research products with highly reliable and validated theory, empirical data, or quantitative/qualitative social scientific methodology.

2.14   Secure Engineering

The Information and Communication Technology (ICT) landscape is continuously changing. We are now witnessing the emergence and consolidation of unprecedented models for service-oriented computing (SOC): Infrastructure as a Service (IaaS), Platform as a Service (PaaS) and Software as a Service (SaaS) [15, 18]. These models have the potential to better adhere to an economy of scale and have already shown their commercial value fostered by key players in the field. Nevertheless, those new models present change of control on the applications that will run on an infrastructure not under the direct control of the business service provider. For business-critical applications this could be difficult to be accepted, when not appropriately managed and secured. These issues are of an urgent practical relevance, not only for academia, but also for industry and governmental organizations [19]. New Internet services will have to be provided in the near future, and security breaches in these services may lead to large financial loss and damaged reputation.

There thus the need and opportunity to organize, integrate and optimize the research on engineering secure services and related software systems to deal effectively with this increased challenge is pertinent and well recognized by the research community and by the industrial one.

3   Technological Issues

The ICT landscape is continuously changing. For example, we have seen the consolidation of models for service-oriented computing (Infrastructure as a Service (IaaS), Platform as a Service (PaaS) and Software as a Service (SaaS)), the increased use of automation, and the emergence of new paradigms such as cloud and the Internet of Things (IoT). However, new developments open up the potential for vulnerability to new threats (or indeed old threats in new guises). As such, some of the consequent challenges are perceived to be:

- maintaining effective cyber defence, as technology and functionality grow faster than security;
- achieving trust in devices specially when they operate remotely;
- security and interoperability of new communication technologies;
- the fact that evidence has moved from being on media in a computer in a single location to existing in myriad locations and forms (e.g. mobile devices, distributed internet-enabled (IoT) electronics, and on corporate controlled servers with server-side processing and storage).

These challenges create fundamental requirements in relation to security engineering, but they also create knock-on implications for issues such as incident handling, response, and forensic investigation, where the scale and complexity of systems calls for new capabilities to maintain effectiveness. Security professionals are also having to address the growing threat to critical infrastructure where industrial control systems (ICS) are connected to operational networks and even to the public Internet [20]. With technology continuing to evolve, the distributed nature of infrastructure will increase and the expansion of autonomous vehicles and increased artificial intelligence/machine learning will all present significant challenges to the security community.

3.1   Securing Applications and Data

Data are today the new oil, as the ability to collect, share, process and analyse data are at the centre of the great advancements we are enjoying in our society. Providing effective techniques for ensuring proper security and privacy is of utmost importance, for both enabling such advancements (as fear of exposure of private information can have detrimental impact on their adoption) as well as enabling their development (as by developing techniques for ensuring data protection can widen the range of scenarios where data can be used).

The evolution of ICT has radically changed our lives, enabling information to be available from anywhere at any time. The growing availability of computational power and network connections at competitive prices facilitates collecting, sharing, processing, and accessing huge amounts of information. Thanks to the wide diffusion of devices collecting information (e.g., IoT devices, smart meters, fitness bands) and of personal devices connected to the network (e.g., smartphones, tablets, laptops), the amount of data generated on a daily basis by companies and final users has grown exponentially and is expected to grow at a continuously increasing rate in the future. Also, the cost of data storage and processing has significantly decreased, enabling the long-term storage and analysis of data and making it accessible when needed. Pictures and videos can be stored in the cloud, analysis performed over huge data collections, third party computational power purchased or leased for heavy elaborations, information collected from sensors spread in the environment where we live, appliances controlled in our houses from a smartphone. These are only a few examples of the advantages of living in a globally interconnected society, where every object is a smart object and anything we need is available from anywhere and at any time.

The advantages of the technological evolution, however, do not come for free as they introduce unprecedented security and privacy risks, due to the increased amount of (possibly sensitive) information collected, stored, and distributed, and to the loss of control of data by their owners when external subjects are involved in the information lifecycle. Users are becoming more and more concerned about their privacy, since collected data can be used to identify individuals and/or infer information that was not intended for disclosure – permission often being provided unknowingly through terse terms and conditions [21]. The location information collected by our phones, the pattern of walking recorded by surveillance cameras, seemingly innocuous information provided when subscribing to a service (e.g., date of birth and city of residence), biometric information used for authentication, are only a few examples of data that can be exploited to identify the person to whom they refer. Sensitive information not intended for disclosure is often collected by devices such as: fitness bands, home assistants, smart home appliances and sensors, social networks, just to mention a few. In all these scenarios, users are not in control over their own data and their privacy is possibly at risk. Indeed, users are often not even aware of the fact that data about themselves are collected and/or cannot control the collection, storage, use, analysis, or deletion of their data [22]. The loss of control is one of the problems slowing the wide adoption of externalized services (cloud, fog, and edge scenarios as well as digital data markets) as an enabling technology for data storage and elaboration. While external providers can be considered reliable for guaranteeing basic security protection (e.g., protection from unauthorized accesses to data and resources by external third parties), they might not be considered trusted for confidentiality (i.e., authorized to know the data content) or for guaranteeing integrity of the data they store or process. Many challenges need to be addressed to guarantee proper security and privacy in the emerging scenarios, including the need to provide confidentiality and integrity of data stored at, shared with, or processed by external parties, while providing needed access and computational functionalities [23]. Advancements in artificial intelligence, which on one side may make the data more exposed and hence user privacy more at risks, can also help in developing better techniques for ensuring protection of information.

The problem of data security and privacy is evolving with technology: the technological evolution provides benefits, but also introduces new vulnerabilities. Data security and privacy in the modern digital society are complex concepts that require attention from several points of views (e.g., legal, social, economic, technological) and raise novel challenges that need to be addressed to enable users to fully enjoy the advantages of technological evolution [17].

3.2 Engineering for Better Security

While the service-Oriented Computing (SOC) models bring significant savings and convenience for organisations and users alike, they also introduce challenges for the security engineering community. These models have the potential to better adhere to an economy of scale and have already shown their commercial value fostered by key players in the field. Nevertheless, those new models present change of control of the applications that will run on an infrastructure not under the direct control of the business service provider. For business-critical applications this could be difficult to be accepted, when not appropriately managed and secured. These issues are of an urgent practical relevance, not only for academia, but also for industry and governmental organizations. New Internet services will have to be provided in the near future, and security breaches in these services may lead to large financial loss and damaged reputation.

There is a need to organize, integrate and optimize research on engineering secure services and related software systems. This challenge is well recognized by the research and industrial communities.

Some of the specific challenges that need to be addressed in security engineering include:

- Security requirements engineering
- Secure Service Architectures and Design
- Security support in programming environments
- Service composition and adaptation
- Runtime verification and enforcement
- Risk and Cost-aware Secure Service Development
- Security assurance and certification
- Quantitative security for assurance

3.3 Investigating the Inevitable

Historically, the focus of digital forensics, incident response and electronic discovery has been on gathering evidentiary trace from desktop computers and small enterprises. While the processes and formalisms remain the same, where the evidence is found, and the volume of evidentiary sources has led to some fundamental challenges. Currently, evidence has moved from being on media in a computer in a single location to existing in mobile devices, internet enabled (IoT) electronics, and on corporate controlled servers with server-side web processing and storage. Additionally, enterprise computing has increased and evolved with data being stored in a myriad of forms in appliances, services, and alternative compute architectures. The digital forensics community needs verifiable and validated capabilities to address these changing computing environments. This is further complicated by the use of service-oriented computing with storage and processing of data moving from on-premise to frequently cloud-based locations. This also introduces complex legal problems with the potential for multi-jurisdictional investigations.

4 Business and Organisational Issues

The current attention for regulatory compliance has visibly changed the way in which IT has been organised and managed. Given their strict corresponding control objectives, organisations must transparently prove that they act in accordance with the applicable laws and regulations. This gives rise to a number of challenges, that collectively span areas such as information security management, audit and governance:

- ensuring adherence to organisational information security policies and procedures;
- transparently proving that organisations are acting in accordance with the applicable laws and regulations;
- better techniques for stating data security and privacy requirements, for designing, building, and implementing data management systems that satisfy security and privacy requirements, and for assuring that the systems meet their requirements in actual operation;

Reasonable assurance with respect to IT is crucial in this case to build confidence whether IT solutions and underlying infrastructures preserve resources, maintain data integrity as well as availability, meet the service levels, satisfy the regulatory requirements and accordingly assist in attaining their goals.

4.1 The Role of Audit and IT Assurance

Today's audit implications are associated with the view on digitalization and the impact of this technology-centric and global phenomenon on the business strategies across the globe. The centre of this digital journey is dominantly filled in by the far-reaching deployment of technology. The intensive use of this evolutionary capability empowers to reinvent business models, improve customer experience, optimize processes and operations, reshape the trade with partners, and more. It is all needed to remain attractive in the modern digital chains, and survive in the current ever-demanding marketplace. It has become a technology-driven environment and business climate that seems not to tolerate low-techs, and appears not to accept the large distances between the traditional physical world and the new digital world any longer. We are entering an age in which the technology defines the bright future, and dictates the way in which we conduct business and how we live our lives.

IT has already become business. This continuously evolving technology forms the beating heart of organizations, and is thus almost a core part of a day-to-day responsibility of average business officials as well as top executives. Their changing view and act for strategizing, steering, transforming, positioning, governing, managing, and running organizations in the digital age calls for a revamped orientation of IT auditing to remain as relevant as before.

A key finding of research among business leaders and Chief Executive Officers (CEOs) with respect to the key business issues facing their organizations was about the new and higher level of risks created by the digital era which are not properly dealt with [24, 25]. This demanding world characterized by a technology-centric perspective requires a broader and more balanced picture of IT auditing that shifts the focus from controlling "around IT" towards the hard-core side of IT, and with the use of IT. The purpose is to concretely discover the technical details about the reality of IT, just the way it is without vagueness. In this challenging context, IT auditing is perceived as an instrument that can provide an independent and objective opinion on the extent to which IT is adequately controlled to ensure that this technology does not affect the risk profile of business practices. In addition, this global discipline can help to address risks and governance concerns so that insight is obtained into the gained degree of trust and acceptance as well as the achieved level of strategic progress and performance.

The demand for IT auditing and control has never been greater. But then, this growing need also implies that a new day has come that imposes to frequently, if not constantly, audit and control through IT and with IT because of the highly ever-increasing level of reliance on technology. However, research in this area is scarce and requires attention to initiate a wide range of studies in this field.

4.2 Establishing Trust in an Untrusted Environment

ICT systems, often known as Supervisory Control and Data Acquisition (SCADA) systems, control our critical infrastructure and are increasingly used to control production of products (known as "Industry 4.0") and services, e.g. through e-Government, Big Data and Cloud Services. IoT and digital communication technologies are forming the fabric of our social interactions through Social Media (SoMe) that have also become the primary source of information and news for many people. In order for humans to live and thrive in this environment, it is essential that they are able to trust the ICT infrastructure on which their existence depends.

Trust management technologies address the problems of how people can build trust in each other across computer networks (inter-personal trust), how people can decide what devices and infrastructure to trust (personal-device trust and infrastructure trust), and how components in computer systems and networks can reason about the trustworthiness of other system components (inter-device trust).

Inter-personal trust is generally based on a combination of personal experience, recommendations from a trusted entity or the reputation of the other party. Personal experience requires the ability to authenticate, or at least recognize, other entities, observe, and record the behaviour of these entities. This implies a study of entity authentication and entity recognition mechanisms, message authentication and authenticated encryption primitives, and mechanisms supported by secure hardware modules, e.g. remote attestation technologies, but also secure and authenticated storage technologies, such as digital signatures and blockchains. Recommendations are authenticated statements regarding one named entity made by another and trusted entity. As such, the technological challenges are very similar to the challenges that arise in building personal experience, e.g. recommendations are commonly carried in digitally signed certificates. The value of recommendations depend on the ability to authenticate the named entity. Reputation systems aggregate behavioural information about a named entity from a multitude of sources. Depending on the reputation system, the behavioural information may be verified and the named entity as well as (some of) the behavioural information providers may be authenticated by the system; the identity of the source of reputation information is not always made available to the users of the reputation system. The success of a reputation system depends on the ability to ignore malicious or incompetent input and the aggregation mechanism, which is typically based on simple heuristics, statistical analysis, machine learning, game theory or other theoretical frameworks.

The aims of trust management, in a business and organisational context, is to support a virtuous circle of formation, distribution, exploitation and evolution of trust in other entities in the system. This means that the many challenges are similar to the challenges outlined above and that trust management technologies may help people decide which businesses or services to rely upon or what information to believe.

Human society is built on trust and people need assurance that the environments, technologies and social relationships that they rely on continue to function in the ways they expect. In particular, the technology (devices and services) that they employ must work to their benefit at a visible and reasonable cost. One societal problem that trust management technologies may help to address is "fake news" (or other forms of fake information).

Trust management is by nature a "horizontal" multi-disciplinary area that brings together communities to support "vertical" areas such as reputation systems, security, identity and access management, social networks, risk and compliance, formal models, legal IT, economics, etc.

5 Human Issues

The human aspect has traditionally, but often unfairly, been portrayed as the weakest link in cybersecurity. Unfortunately, adversaries are indeed likely to target people where they are perceived to be the route to exploitation, and it is also important to ensure that people themselves do not act in ways that introduce avoidable vulnerability. Key areas for attention are considered to include the following:

- the growing volume of threats that explicitly target the human element, such as increasingly sophisticated social engineering and phishing scams;
- major cybersecurity skills gap that needs to be addressed through formalised education;
- addressing resistant user attitude and resistant behaviour to information security by fostering an information security/cybersecurity culture.

Without effective consideration of the human aspect, the overall protection of systems and data will remain sub-optimal. We need to find effective means to support people and help them engage, while at the same time protecting them from the attacks that seek to directly exploit them.

5.1 Addressing the Human Factor

The problem with the focus on human weaknesses is that humans are solely viewed as 'threats' and 'risks' to the organisation. However, it can be argued, that this is only one dimension of the human aspects of cybersecurity and that humans could become the best defence an organisation has to actively defend against cyberattacks. In order to empower employees to become part of the cybersecurity defence of an organisation, there must be a conscious effort to foster an information or cybersecurity culture in an organization [26]. Both sides of the human aspects of cybersecurity, the threats and the defence, should be acknowledged and addressed. Having said that, there are many challenges related to the human aspects of cybersecurity which are discussed below.

Many organisations implement complex technological controls to protect their network perimeter from external threats, as the perception often is that the greatest threats come from attackers outside the organisation. However, insider threats can be particularly dangerous for organisations, as insiders have legitimate access to information systems to accomplish daily tasks. There are typically two broad types of insider threats; malicious users (employees who willfully extract data) and negligent/apathetic users (employees who are careless about cybersecurity).

Malicious users are those who purposefully try to benefit themselves at the organisation's expense or directly damage the organisation. They might steal confidential data, commit financial fraud or sabotage IT systems because they are disgruntled. Malicious insiders are notoriously difficult to identify. However, technological controls, such as behaviour analytics, anomaly detection, threat intelligence and predictive alerts, can be used to attempt to identify and mitigate against malicious users and their actions. Fortunately, for most organisations, malicious users are the exception and not the rule.

However, one of the greatest challenges organisations may face is human error introduced through negligent or apathetic users. Negligent or apathetic users are those who are not aware of or do not realise how important cybersecurity is for an organisation. These users do not appreciate the important role they should play in protecting an organisation from cyberthreats. One of the major challenges with regard to these users is social engineering. Social engineering is the psychological manipulation of users to exploit them into performing actions for, or divulging information to, the attacker. There are a wide variety of social engineering attacks, including, but not limited to; phishing, pretexting, baiting and quid pro quo. Social engineering attacks rely on building trust relationships with targets, and then exploiting these relationships for gain (usually financial).

From a societal point of view, there are a number of cyber vulnerabilities related to both adults and children. Cyberbullying is an online form of traditional bullying where cyberbullies send threatening or humiliating messages to their adolescent victims, and can lead to depression, isolation, illness and, sometimes, suicide.

In addition, social media platforms continue to be very popular ways for people to keep in contact with friends, upload content and share information online. However, there are many privacy concerns related to these social media platforms, for example, many users being unaware of the extent to which their personal information is spread after sharing.

Another societal challenge that is seemingly on the rise is that of fake news. One of the difficulties is that different people have different views of fake news. For many, fake news is seen as it was intended – false information being spread. For others, fake news is seen as anything that goes against their own beliefs or biases. The issue is that, more than making people believe false information, the rise of fake news is making it harder for people to see the truth. In other words, people may become less informed.

Most of these challenges can start being addressed by raising the awareness of both employees and society in general to cyberthreats. The cybersecurity awareness, however, must go further through cybersecurity educational programs to provide a deeper understanding of why cybersecurity is important and the role they should be playing in the defence of their organisation. Often, however, these programs are generic and are not very effective in addressing users and the threats they may be introducing, which may result in people developing the 'it won't happen to me' mindset. Therefore, information and cybersecurity awareness and education programs should be specifically contextualised to become relevant to the audience to ensure they become advocates for information and cybersecurity.

In organisations, for example, as part of management's duties, an organisational vision for cybersecurity should be expressed in policies. These policies should be enforced to assist management in curbing incorrect behaviour in their organisation and, ultimately, change the corporate culture. Transforming the corporate culture, however, takes time and perseverance, as it entails the unlearning of beliefs and changing the attitudes of employees, which can be a painful process [27]. The fostering of an information or cybersecurity culture in an organisation could, ultimately, positively influence the attitude and behaviour of employees towards information and cybersecurity. Although an organisation can never completely eliminate the cybersecurity risk posed by humans, the chances of a breach could be reduced if the cybersecurity education of users is made a priority.

Raising awareness and providing access to educational programs for the general public could also assist in creating a societal cybersecurity culture.

5.2 The Importance of Education

Many organizations, nations, businesses, and individuals are actively seeking to expand their knowledge of, and skills in, cybersecurity. Unfortunately, the amount of misinformation in this area, and the shortage of skilled, knowledgeable cybersecurity practitioners and experts, inhibits the ability to protect information and cyberinfrastructure. Worse, some organizations and individuals do not understand the need to protect themselves, or believe their measures are adequate when in reality they are not. The only cure for this lack of personnel, knowledge and understanding of how to determine and implement measures necessary for protection, is education.

This skills gap requires a multi-faceted solution with a combination of not only formalised education, but also training and awareness programs. It is also important to recognise that for most government departments, organisations and businesses, security is rarely achieved without some impact on performance, usability or cost.

Current estimates indicate that there are about 1 million unfilled cybersecurity positions worldwide, potentially rising to 3.5 million by 2021 [28]. In order to address this rapidly increasing demand for cybersecurity skills, academic institutions worldwide are introducing and adapting courses and programs to teach students about information and cybersecurity. Among the main concerns for academics in computing, however, is what cybersecurity and related topics to cover and to what depth, as most computing courses already cover an expanse of content.

This broad domain encompasses an extensive set of technologies and concepts that can be taught in various ways. Current research in this domain covers both technical aspects (secure programming, network security, offensive security, cryptography, etc.) and human aspects (privacy, social engineering, cyber law, ethics, etc.). In addition, one of the key challenges is to ensure that the methods for teaching and learning in this domain are adapted to suit the specific context. This field is somewhat unique in terms of its cross-cutting multi-disciplinary nature. A further challenge is therefore to inculcate the principles of information and cybersecurity into even the most basic and entry-level courses.

A panel discussion during WISE11 highlighted some of the main challenges of building national cybersecurity workforces. These included how to estimate the size and make-up of national cybersecurity workforces based on needs; how to characterise such workforces; and how to achieve balance between employing organisation's priorities and national needs. During this panel discussion it was also noted that these challenges and the role of educational institutions in addressing the cybersecurity skills gap may differ across nations.

In 2017, a joint task force developed guidelines for undergraduate cybersecurity education programs. The resulting document, the Cybersecurity Curricula 2017 [29], addressed academic aspects of some of these challenges regarding the cybersecurity workforce and skills demand.

Further challenges will include the use of online technologies (for example, MOOCs) to share information and cybersecurity teaching and learning content and how training programs and academic education programs can work together to provide both practical experience and a deeper understanding of why the practical material works. This way, practitioners can adapt their knowledge and experience to circumstances beyond that covered in the training and in their environment, and academics can better understand the problems encountered in practice, and learn how to prevent those problems or handle them.

As noted above, the need for cybersecurity is generally understood. But its practice must be balanced with the cost in financial and human terms, and all too often the latter dominates the need. The need to strike an appropriate balance, and how to do so, will dominate much of the field in the near future.

5.3 The Value of Research

The challenges of behavioral compliance are focused on the adoption and use of protective security practices by individuals seeking to benefit themselves or their firms, or to avoid any negative consequences that may occur from non-adoption or misuse of security procedures and methods. Substantial research efforts have focussed on policy related compliance, but other forms of compliance, such as digital warnings, communicated alerts, and compliance with emerging technical standards have also appeared more recently. It is likely that this area of focus will continue to be of great interest for the foreseeable future.

Another primary challenge of interest is the problem of risk management. As described in the MIS quarterly curation [30], the problem of risk management by security scholars has been mostly approached from a normative lens. Research over the years has addressed risk management through a variety of frameworks, models, and management techniques, with focused efforts made toward the extension and contextualization of managerial frameworks and theories that help to measure and control risk at the individual level.

Moving forward, emerging challenges such as neurosecurity (neurophysiological data collection), forensics analysis, and the behavioral analysis of design science treatments that enhance or balance security and privacy trade-offs will be explored. There is a new scale and scope of organizational and managerial challenges that are created by the growing prevalence of advanced persistent threats, securing blockchain data structures, protecting privacy in big data analytics, and the looming potential of commercial cyberspace collisions between defensive AI and offensive AI, and the cryptanalysis capabilities of quantum computing.

6 Future Opportunities

Many of the areas discussed in the chapter serve to highlight opportunities for future research, and the working group agendas will be shaped accordingly. Space does not permit all of them to be catalogued and explored in this chapter, the magnitude of the challenge can be illustrated by homing in on a single area and looking at the issues that the related working group has identified as requiring attention. To this end, we present an example of some issues from WG11.5 in relation to IT auditing.

Organizations are turning into open and global digital factories that are built around customer experience, speed, agility, mobility, cost, automation, connectivity, and accuracy to drive success. Given this present and future reality, IT auditing can no longer be a profession that suffices with a tick-in-the-box examination without a clear orientation. To provide digital value and capture it we provide a house of IT auditing, Fig. 1. The house of IT auditing includes three main components of IT audit research that we consider the main areas of interest. The first area is concerned with the foundation of the profession: technology (e.g. cloud and digital platforms). It is put right at the center of business models, thereby becoming the beating heart and the base of modern organizations. The second component is related to the strategic pillars linked to the foundational developments: cybersecurity, analytics, and regulatory. Being exposed to serious dangers, data-minded, and subject to laws and regulations are simply accepted as facts of today's life. The third and last component pertains to the professional support that can be provided to make a desired and recognized contribution. It is about the delivery of support in the areas of most need: assurance, advisory, and financial audit.

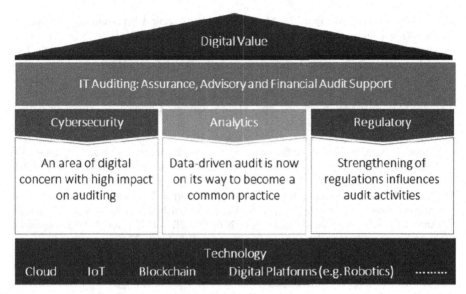

Fig. 1. House of IT auditing.

7 Conclusions

The collective challenges across these areas are considered to be of increasing importance, especially in the context of emerging technologies (e.g. Cloud, IoT) that collect and analyse large data collections, and serve to further amplify the potential for impact in the event of security incidents and breaches. At the same time, there are also potential solutions that can work across the areas, such as the potential for AI technology to defend the human user from malicious hackers, rather than the human trying to recognize malicious intent. This in turn has the potential to serve and support the business objective in terms of effective governance and compliance.

Acknowledgments. We would like to acknowledge the contributions from working group officers and members in addition to the named authors of this chapter. Specifically: Raja Naeem Akram, Kam-Pui Chow, Richard George, Konstantinos Markantonakis, Gilbert Peterson, Damien Sauveron and Sujeet Shenoi.

References

1. OECD: The OECD Privacy Framework (2013). https://www.oecd.org/sti/ieconomy/oecd_privacy_framework.pdf. Accessed 16 Dec 2020
2. IFIP TC11: Aims and Scope (n.d.). https://www.ifiptc11.org/aims-and-scope. Accessed 16 Dec 2020
3. IFIP TC11: Working Groups (n.d.). https://www.ifiptc11.org/working-groups. Accessed 16 Dec 2020

4. Connolly, L., Lang, M., Tygar, D.: Managing employee security behaviour in organisations: the role of cultural factors and individual values. In: Cuppens-Boulahia, N., Cuppens, F., Jajodia, S., Abou El Kalam, A., Sans, T. (eds.) SEC 2014. IAICT, vol. 428, pp. 417–430. Springer, Heidelberg (2014). https://doi.org/10.1007/978-3-642-55415-5_35

5. Wiefling, S., Lo Iacono, L., Dürmuth, M.: Is this really you? An empirical study on risk-based authentication applied in the wild. In: Dhillon, G., Karlsson, F., Hedström, K., Zúquete, A. (eds.) SEC 2019. IAICT, vol. 562, pp. 134–148. Springer, Cham (2019). https://doi.org/10.1007/978-3-030-22312-0_10

6. Giorgi, G., Martinelli, F., Saracino, A., Sheikhalishahi, M.: Walking through the deep: gait analysis for user authentication through deep learning. In: Janczewski, L.J., Kutyłowski, M. (eds.) SEC 2018. IAICT, vol. 529, pp. 62–76. Springer, Cham (2018). https://doi.org/10.1007/978-3-319-99828-2_5

7. Diaz-Tellez, Y.H., Bodanese, E.L., Dimitrakos, T., Turner, M.: Context-aware multifactor authentication based on dynamic pin. In: Cuppens-Boulahia, N., Cuppens, F., Jajodia, S., Abou El Kalam, A., Sans, T. (eds.) SEC 2014. IAICT, vol. 428, pp. 330–338. Springer, Heidelberg (2014). https://doi.org/10.1007/978-3-642-55415-5_27

8. Damopoulos, D., Wetzel, S.: Introducing research into the undergraduate curriculum in cybersecurity. In: Drevin, L., Theocharidou, M. (eds.) WISE 2019. IAICT, vol. 557, pp. 30–42. Springer, Cham (2019). https://doi.org/10.1007/978-3-030-23451-5_3

9. von Solms, S., Marnewick, A.: Identifying security requirements body of knowledge for the security systems engineer. In: Drevin, L., Theocharidou, M. (eds.) WISE 2019. IAICT, vol. 557, pp. 59–71. Springer, Cham (2019). https://doi.org/10.1007/978-3-030-23451-5_5

10. Thing, V.L.L., Chua, Z.-L.: Smartphone volatile memory acquisition for security analysis and forensics investigation. In: Janczewski, L.J., Wolfe, H.B., Shenoi, S. (eds.) SEC 2013. IAICT, vol. 405, pp. 217–230. Springer, Heidelberg (2013). https://doi.org/10.1007/978-3-642-39218-4_17

11. Agarwal, M., Puzis, R., Haj-Yahya, J., Zilberman, P., Elovici, Y.: Anti-forensic = suspicious: detection of stealthy malware that hides its network traffic. In: Janczewski, L.J., Kutyłowski, M. (eds.) SEC 2018. IAICT, vol. 529, pp. 216–230. Springer, Cham (2018). https://doi.org/10.1007/978-3-319-99828-2_16

12. Dupont, G., dos Santos, D.R., Costante, E., den Hartog, J., Etalle, S.: A matter of life and death: analyzing the security of healthcare networks. In: Hölbl, M., Rannenberg, K., Welzer, T. (eds.) SEC 2020. IAICT, vol. 580, pp. 355–369. Springer, Cham (2020). https://doi.org/10.1007/978-3-030-58201-2_24

13. Yoo, H., Ahmed, I.: Control logic injection attacks on industrial control systems. In: Dhillon, G., Karlsson, F., Hedström, K., Zúquete, A. (eds.) SEC 2019. IAICT, vol. 562, pp. 33–48. Springer, Cham (2019). https://doi.org/10.1007/978-3-030-22312-0_3

14. Vossaert, J., Lapon, J., De Decker, B., Naessens, V.: Trusted computing to increase security and privacy in eID authentication. In: Cuppens-Boulahia, N., Cuppens, F., Jajodia, S., Abou El Kalam, A., Sans, T. (eds.) SEC 2014. IAICT, vol. 428, pp. 485–492. Springer, Heidelberg (2014). https://doi.org/10.1007/978-3-642-55415-5_41

15. Eckel, M., Fuchs, A., Repp, J., Springer, M.: Secure attestation of virtualized environments. In: Hölbl, M., Rannenberg, K., Welzer, T. (eds.) SEC 2020. IAICT, vol. 580, pp. 203–216. Springer, Cham (2020). https://doi.org/10.1007/978-3-030-58201-2_14

16. Kitkowska, A., Shulman, Y., Martucci, L.A., Wästlund, E.: Facilitating privacy attitudes and behaviors with affective visual design. In: Hölbl, M., Rannenberg, K., Welzer, T. (eds.) SEC 2020. IAICT, vol. 580, pp. 109–123. Springer, Cham (2020). https://doi.org/10.1007/978-3-030-58201-2_8

17. Simonet, J., Teufel, S.: The influence of organizational, social and personal factors on cyber-security awareness and behaviour of home computer users. In: Dhillon, G., Karlsson, F., Hedström, K., Zúquete, A. (eds.) SEC 2019. IAICT, vol. 562, pp. 194–208. Springer, Cham (2019). https://doi.org/10.1007/978-3-030-22312-0_14

18. Rios, R., Nuñez, D., Lopez, J.: Query privacy in sensing-as-a-service platforms. In: De Capitani di Vimercati, S., Martinelli, F. (eds.) SEC 2017. IAICT, vol. 502, pp. 141–154. Springer, Cham (2017). https://doi.org/10.1007/978-3-319-58469-0_10

19. Chen, W., Lin, Y., Galpin, V., Nigam, V., Lee, M., Aspinall, D.: Formal analysis of sneak-peek: a data centre attack and its mitigations. In: Janczewski, L.J., Kutyłowski, M. (eds.) SEC 2018. IAICT, vol. 529, pp. 307–322. Springer, Cham (2018). https://doi.org/10.1007/978-3-319-99828-2_22

20. Adepu, S., Mathur, A.: Using process invariants to detect cyber attacks on a water treatment system. In: Hoepman, J.-H., Katzenbeisser, S. (eds.) SEC 2016. IAICT, vol. 471, pp. 91–104. Springer, Cham (2016). https://doi.org/10.1007/978-3-319-33630-5_7

21. Drozd, O., Kirrane, S.: Privacy CURE: consent comprehension made easy. In: Hölbl, M., Rannenberg, K., Welzer, T. (eds.) SEC 2020. IAICT, vol. 580, pp. 124–139. Springer, Cham (2020). https://doi.org/10.1007/978-3-030-58201-2_9

22. Paul, N., Tesfay, W.B., Kipker, D.-K., Stelter, M., Pape, S.: Assessing privacy policies of Internet of Things services. In: Janczewski, L.J., Kutyłowski, M. (eds.) SEC 2018. IAICT, vol. 529, pp. 156–169. Springer, Cham (2018). https://doi.org/10.1007/978-3-319-99828-2_12

23. Caelli, W.J., Kwok, L.-F., Longley, D.: Evolving a secure internet. In: Janczewski, L.J., Wolfe, H.B., Shenoi, S. (eds.) SEC 2013. IAICT, vol. 405, pp. 42–54. Springer, Heidelberg (2013). https://doi.org/10.1007/978-3-642-39218-4_4

24. Wheeler J.A.: Top 10 factors for integrated risk management success, Gartner, Inc. (2017). https://www.gartner.com/en/documents/3645368/top-10-factors-for-integrated-risk-management-success. Accessed 16 Dec 2020

25. World Economic Forum (WEF): Digital transformation of industries: digital enterprise. World Economic Forum White Paper (2016). http://reports.weforum.org/digital-transformation/wp-content/blogs.dir/94/mp/files/pages/files/digital-enterprise-narrative-final-january-2016.pdf. Accessed 16 Dec 2020

26. Connolly, L., Lang, M., Tygar, J.D.: Investigation of employee security behaviour: a grounded theory approach. In: Federrath, H., Gollmann, D. (eds.) SEC 2015. IAICT, vol. 455, pp. 283–296. Springer, Cham (2015). https://doi.org/10.1007/978-3-319-18467-8_19

27. Tolah, A., Furnell, S.M., Papadaki, M.: A comprehensive framework for understanding security culture in organizations. In: Drevin, L., Theocharidou, M. (eds.) WISE 2019. IAICT, vol. 557, pp. 143–156. Springer, Cham (2019). https://doi.org/10.1007/978-3-030-23451-5_11

28. Cybersecurity Ventures: Cybersecurity Talent Crunch to Create 3.5 Million Unfilled Jobs Globally By 2021. https://cybersecurityventures.com/jobs/. Accessed 16 Dec 2020

29. CSEC: Cybersecurity Curricula 2017 – Curriculum Guidelines for Post-Secondary Degree Programs in Cybersecurity. Version 1.0 Report 31 December 2017. CSEC2017 Joint Task Force - Association for Computing Machinery (ACM), IEEE Computer Society (IEEE-CS), Association for Information Systems Special Interest Group on Information Security and Privacy (AIS SIGSEC) and International Federation for Information Processing Technical Committee on Information Security Education (IFIP WG 11.8). https://cybered.hosting.acm.org/wp-content/uploads/2018/02/newcover_csec2017.pdf. Accessed 16 Dec 2020

30. Hui, K.L., Vance, A., Zhdanov, D.: Securing Digital Assets. In: Bush, A., Rai, A. (eds.) MIS Quarterly Research Curations (2016). https://doi.org/10.25300/05272016. http://misq.org/research-curations

IFIP General

IFIP Code of Ethics

David Kreps$^{(\boxtimes)}$ (ID)

National University of Ireland, Galway, Ireland
`david.kreps@nuigalway.ie`

Abstract. A short introduction to the creation of the IFIP Code of Ethics, followed by the Code itself.

1 Creating the IFIP Code of Ethics

At the virtual IFIP General Assembly (GA) held 24th September 2020, GA enthusiastically adopted a new IFIP Code of Ethics and Professional Conduct, crowning a project begun in 1988 by then TC9 Chair Harold Sackman[1]. Although countless figures in the world of ICT over the intervening decades contributed to this project, perhaps the names Jacques Berleur and Don Gotterbarn deserve special mention. Berleur and his Working Group 9.2 on Social Accountability worked tirelessly through the 1990s to push the concept of ethical computing, including the creation of IFIP Special Interest Group 9.2.2 on Framework on Ethics of Computing, and producing with members of the group the 'Criteria and Procedures for Developing Codes of Ethics or of Conduct' [1]. Gotterbarn, who had led on the 1999 joint ACM/IEEE-CS Software Engineering Code [2], also led the project to create a revised version of the ACM Code of Ethics that was published in 2018. This revised Code went through many years of consultation and development - consistent with Berleur's criteria and procedures - not just with ACM members but with members of IFIP, IEEE, other national and international bodies and companies all around the world.

Clearly a global code – the conscience of the profession – it struck David Kreps, as the current Chair of TC9, that Sackman's project could at last be completed: that IFIP could adopt this Code of Ethics and bring it to National Computing Societies the world over. Approved by the TC9 Committee meeting in Stockholm in June 2019, Gotterbarn – now Chair of WG9.2.2 – took the proposal to the Working Group who also unanimously supported it. Gotterbarn then joined Kreps, at GA 2019 in Kiev, to propose a Code of Ethics Task & Finish Group, to adapt the ACM Code, and publish it as the IFIP Code of Ethics. GA approved the proposal. Joined by IP3 Chair Moira de Roche, and MSA Representative Margaret Havey, the Code of Ethics Task & Finish Group, led by Kreps, was formally established, and undertook further consultations with Member Societies and with the IFIP Board, over the course of 2020. The group created a new Prologue

---

[1] See the chapter in this volume on the history of HCC and TC9 – a Sociotechnical Tale – for more detail on this decades long project.

© IFIP International Federation for Information Processing 2021
Published by Springer Nature Switzerland AG 2021
M. Goedicke et al. (Eds.): Advancing Research in Information and Communication Technology,
IFIP AICT 600, pp. 405–420, 2021. https://doi.org/10.1007/978-3-030-81701-5_17

contextualising the Code for the IFIP membership, producing the final version adopted at GA2020. That Prologue and the final version of the Code are presented here.

The IFIP Code of Ethics can be adopted in place of, or alongside a Member Society's Code, or Member Societies can modify their Code to include values and guidance in the IFIP Code that is not already included in their own Codes, or they can simply reference it in addition to their own codes.

In the words of Jussi Nissilä, CEO of the Finnish Information Processing Society (TIVIA) "The code has been gone through, line-by-line, by the TIVIA Working Group on Ethics, and no reason to not adopt it was found – on the contrary, the Working Group on Ethics considered it to be culture independent, and suitable for TIVIA, as well as any computing society". Maxine Leslie, Secretariat and Committee Manager at the British Computer Society, likewise, reported that "The BCS Academy of Computing has reviewed the proposed IFIP Code of Ethics and will be pleased to endorse it, finding it a very robust document covering a variety of important and interesting topics." Vicki Hanson, CEO of the ACM, said "As an international member of IFIP, ACM endorses the proposed IFIP Code of Ethics as a common international standard for computing and the profession."

It is a fitting tribute to the work of so many, that – in its 60th anniversary year – IFIP has now formally adopted this international IFIP Code of Ethics, whose creation has spanned many decades and the engagement of countless contributors from around the world.

Reference

1. Berleur, J., et al.: Criteria and procedures for developing codes of ethics or of conduct. In: On behalf of IFIP-SIG9.2.2. IFIP Press, Laxenburg-Austria (2004)
2. Gotterbarn, D., Miller, K., Rogerson, S.: Software engineering code of ethics is approved. Commun. ACM **42**(10), 102–107 (1999). https://doi.org/10.1145/317665.317682

2   IFIP Code of Ethics

Prologue by the IFIP Task and Finish Group.

2.1 Prologue

The purposes and values of a profession, including its commitment to the public good, are expressed by its code of ethics. This Code of Ethics and Professional Conduct expresses the values and reflects the ethics of IFIP's member societies and the wider profession. It is a global statement of the conscience of the ICT profession and clarifies what our profession should strive to be: it is a call to action.

Professional ethics is about what is expected of a professional in a field. As we act, all of us in the ICT Profession must remember that every choice that impacts others is an ethical decision and that those decisions need to be guided by professional ethics.

The competent application of ICT technical skills is necessary for the well-being of contemporary society; our technical skills are important, but how we apply them is what distinguishes us as professionals. Professionals are asked to promote good while working within ethical constraints.

The IFIP Code of Ethics [the Code] provides organizations and governments around the world with a common set of values that should be reflected in codes of ethics for all parts of the ICT profession. The Code promotes the continued development of a global conscience within the ICT sector, providing a common ground for international discourse on professional responsibility.

2.2 Development of the Code

This Code is a response to the degree to which the work of ICT professionals in the 21st-century influences and directs all aspects of society. Our times demand a re-examination and re-statement of the professional responsibilities of ICT practitioners. A clear under-standing of these ethical principles is needed to help guide ICT professional practice to positively contribute to society in ways that minimize unintentional ethical mistakes and maximize ethical opportunities.

IFIP has a long tradition of support for ethical and professional standards. One of IFIP's major responses to this need has been the development and support of the International Professional Practice Partnership (IP3), an international multi-society consortium formed to promote the professionalization of ICT. At its founding meeting in 2008 IFIP's IP3 identified Four Pillars of the ICT Profession. Pillars 1 and 2 focus on professional competence while Pillars 3 and 4 recognize the nature of ICT as employing these skills in service to society. The Four Pillars are about normative ethics - what you should do in any given circumstance. Professional ethics is about what is expected of a professional in a field. This IFIP Code of Ethics is a statement of professional ethics.

IFIP has a Technical Committee on ICT and Society and a Special Interest Group on the Ethics of Computing. The latter was charged with developing a Code of Ethics and Professional Conduct and decided to base this closely on the Code of Ethics prepared by ACM. There are a number of reasons for adapting the ACM Code into an IFIP Code. IFIP was involved in the most recent update of the ACM Code, the objective of which was to define and articulate ICT's professional obligations to the much broader range of stakeholders impacted by modern ICT systems and the requirement for the code to address the intercultural common ethical obligations of its international membership. The development involved extensive worldwide consultation and was consistent with the 1996 IFIP SIG 9.2.2 Framework for Developing a Code of Ethics written under the guidance of the late Jacques Berleur. IFIP was well represented in the transparent multi-year iterative Code development process.

The IFIP Code of Ethics as it finally came together as presented in this publication supports the IP3 Four Pillars. With contributions by IFIP members and the international community. the Code is consistent with the diverse Codes of member societies. It is a global Code created by people from all over the world including members of IFIP.

2.3   The Nature of the Code

Older Codes of Ethics contained specific imperatives or benchmarks which could be used to determine failure to follow a particular Code canon. Codes with fixed benchmarks, however, are of little help in a rapidly changing ICT environment and do not help practitioners make proactive decisions in complex situations. Meeting these needs requires aspirational guidance that can accommodate a rapidly changing profession.

ICT professionals, regardless of where they live and work, have more in common than they think. Different nationalities have diverse cultures, but multinational organizations based on a common profession share significant values to be embodied in a Code, which should articulate the global values of the profession not the differences between cultures. Intercultural global values we have in common establish a discursive ethics on which we can all make decisions.

Those values need to be presented in a reasonably achievable fashion. Instead of fixed rules, the Code therefore is based on an aspirational model setting ethical targets rather than tying an ethical value to the use of a particular technological solution. These ethical markers of professionalism are presented as goals and ideals to which the morally responsible professional practitioner aspires. The Code provides some guidance in decision making in unclear and difficult situations, but it also respects the autonomy of the individual professional. The primary goal in the Code is consistent with the international standards in the IP3 Four Pillars: to establish the Public Good as the primary focus of our profession.

2.4   Structure of the Code

The Code consists of a Preamble that describes the Code and provides some guidance about reasoning with its Principles. The remainder of the Code consists of 25 Principles divided into four sections; each Principle is accompanied by guidance that further explains the Principles and illustrates the application of it to ICT.

The Preamble points to a maxim that should be used to frame any decision made using the Code. Consistent with the IP3 Pillars and most other Codes recognizing ICT's positive public responsibility, "the public good is the paramount consideration." The common conscience of the profession is that our work should contribute to society and human well-being, acknowledging that all people are stakeholders in computing. The Code applies that global principle.

The four sections of the remainder of the Code consist of Principles one should aspire to. Section 1 "General Ethical Principles" contains seven common ethical principles consistent with all professional codes. Section 2 "Professional Responsibilities" provides nine specific ICT professional responsibilities in the light of the general principles of Sect. 1. Section 3 "Professional Leadership Principles" adds seven responsibilities to ICT professionals when they have leadership responsibilities. Each of these Principles is accompanied by some guidance on how that Principle might apply to professional decisions. Putting these Principles in context and relating them to a common ethical foundation helps practitioners understand how these broad Principles apply to their decisions in specific instances and how to incorporate them into their regular practice of the profession. In that way, the Code is a guide to proactive action that helps us, as a profession, to promote good.

The predominant direction of the Code provides guidance for the ICT professional. Only 2 of the 25 Principles deal with compliance. Given the proactive nature of the Code, the compliance section advocates active support for the Code Principles beyond mere compliance. That support includes both a professional's advocacy for the principles and working to correct situations where the principles are not being followed.

2.5 Status

In joining a Technical Committee, Working Group, Special Interest Group, Domain Committee, IP3, or other body or structure of IFIP, members agree to adhere to and support this Code of Ethics.

The IFIP Code of Ethics is compulsory for all serving on the General Assembly or ex-officio members of IFIP.

The IFIP Code of Ethics is not intended to replace Codes specific to Member Societies, which may contain unique points relevant to their cultures. The Code contains elements, however, that might not be included in the Member Society Code. Therefore, the IFIP Code of Ethics can be adopted alongside a Member Society's Code, or Member Societies can modify their Code to include those values and guidance not already included in their own Codes or simply reference it in addition to their own codes.

In this way, when a member of one National Computing Society works in another country, there is a common standard they can appeal to when pursuing development as an ethical professional, making ethically sound decisions when given the opportunity, and when resisting unethical pressures. The Code thereby represents a support for moral courage, encompassing the duty of care and accountability to minimize any adverse impacts as technologies are being integrated into virtually every sector of the economy and society.

2.6 Benefits of the Code

- is consistent with and extends the impact of IP3's Four Pillars
- provides a consistent international statement of ICT values
- is an argument against those who say there are no real ICT standards, but only multiple local policies
- educates the public
- is useful international statement of values.in cross-border judicial discussions
- expresses the intercultural aspects of global ICT
- is a common ground for international discourse on professional responsibility
- adequately reflects the ethics of the profession, and clarifies what that profession should strive to be
- can be used to educate aspiring ICT professionals about their ethical obligations
- can be used to evaluate the consistency of a professional's behavior with the conscience of the profession and the application of appropriate sanctions

2.7 Summary

The Code establishes goals that are valued by the ICT professional to help professionals around the world, describing what brings us together as a profession. It expresses a social contract we have as a professional society, as members of IFIP, a contract describing what we expect of each other and ourselves as members of IFIP. It provides guidance to IFIP members about committing to ethical professional conduct. The Code identifies fundamental considerations for contributing to societal aspirations and human well-being.

3   IFIP Code of Ethics and Professional Conduct

3.1   Preamble

Computing professionals' actions change the world. To act responsibly, they should reflect upon the wider impacts of their work, consistently supporting the public good. This code is adapted from the ACM Code of Ethics and Professional Conduct ("The Code"), which expresses the conscience of the profession.

The Code is designed to inspire and guide the ethical conduct of all computing professionals, including current and aspiring practitioners, instructors, students, influencers, and anyone who uses computing technology in an impactful way. Additionally, the Code serves as a basis for remediation when violations occur. The Code includes principles formulated as statements of responsibility, based on the understanding that the public good is always the primary consideration. Each principle is supplemented by guidelines, which provide explanations to assist computing professionals in understanding and applying the principle.

Section 1 outlines fundamental ethical principles that form the basis for the remainder of the Code. Section 2 addresses additional, more specific considerations of professional responsibility. Section 3 guides individuals who have a leadership role, whether in the workplace or in a volunteer professional capacity. Commitment to ethical conduct is required of every IFIP member, and principles involving compliance with the Code are given in Sect. 4.

The Code as a whole is concerned with how fundamental ethical principles apply to a computing professional's conduct. The Code is not an algorithm for solving ethical problems; rather it serves as a basis for ethical decision-making. When thinking through a particular issue, a computing professional may find that multiple principles should be taken into account, and that different principles will have different relevance to the issue. Questions related to these kinds of issues can best be answered by thoughtful consideration of the fundamental ethical principles, understanding that the public good is the paramount consideration. The entire computing profession benefits when the ethical decision-making process is accountable to and transparent to all stakeholders. Open discussions about ethical issues promote this accountability and transparency.

4   1. General Ethical Principles

A computing professional should...

4.1   1.1 Contribute to Society and to Human Well-Being, Acknowledging that All People Are Stakeholders in Computing

This principle, which concerns the quality of life of all people, affirms an obligation of computing professionals, both individually and collectively, to use their skills for the benefit of society, its members, and the environment surrounding them. This obligation includes promoting fundamental human rights and protecting each individual's right to autonomy. An essential aim of computing professionals is to minimize negative consequences of computing, including threats to health, safety, personal security, and privacy. When the interests of multiple groups conflict, the needs of those less advantaged should be given increased attention and priority.

Computing professionals should consider whether the results of their efforts will respect diversity, will be used in socially responsible ways, will meet social needs, and will be broadly accessible. They are encouraged to actively contribute to society by engaging in pro bono or volunteer work that benefits the public good.

In addition to a safe social environment, human well-being requires a safe natural environment. Therefore, computing professionals should promote environmental sustainability both locally and globally.

4.2   1.2 Avoid Harm

In this document, "harm" means negative consequences, especially when those consequences are significant and unjust. Examples of harm include unjustified physical or mental injury, unjustified destruction or disclosure of information, and unjustified damage to property, reputation, and the environment. This list is not exhaustive.

Well-intended actions, including those that accomplish assigned duties, may lead to harm. When that harm is unintended, those responsible are obliged to undo or mitigate the harm as much as possible. Avoiding harm begins with careful consideration of potential impacts on all those affected by decisions. When harm is an intentional part of the system, those responsible are obligated to ensure that the harm is ethically justified and to minimize unintended harm.

To minimize the possibility of indirectly or unintentionally harming others, computing professionals should follow generally accepted best practices unless there is a compelling ethical reason to do otherwise. Additionally, the consequences of data aggregation and emergent properties of systems should be carefully analyzed. Those involved with pervasive or infrastructure systems should also consider Principle 3.7.

A computing professional has an additional obligation to report any signs of system risks that might result in harm. If leaders do not act to curtail or mitigate such risks, it may be necessary to "blow the whistle" to reduce potential harm. However, capricious or misguided reporting of risks can itself be harmful. Before reporting risks, a computing professional should carefully assess relevant aspects of the situation.

4.3   1.3 Be Honest and Trustworthy

Honesty is an essential component of trustworthiness. A computing professional should be transparent and provide full disclosure of all pertinent system capabilities, limitations, and potential problems to the appropriate parties. Making deliberately false or misleading claims, fabricating or falsifying data, offering or accepting bribes, and other dishonest conduct are violations of the Code.

Computing professionals should be honest about their qualifications, and about any limitations in their competence to complete a task. Computing professionals should be forthright about any circumstances that might lead to either real or perceived conflicts of interest or otherwise tend to undermine the independence of their judgment. Furthermore, commitments should be honored.

Computing professionals should not misrepresent an organization's policies or procedures, and should not speak on behalf of an organization unless authorized to do so.

4.4   1.4 Be Fair and Take Action Not to Discriminate

The values of equality, tolerance, respect for others, and justice govern this principle. Fairness requires that even careful decision processes provide some avenue for redress of grievances.

Computing professionals should foster fair participation of all people, including those of underrepresented groups. Prejudicial discrimination on the basis of age, color, disability, ethnicity, family status, gender identity, labor union membership, military status, nationality, race, religion or belief, sex, sexual orientation, or any other inappropriate factor is an explicit violation of the Code. Harassment, including sexual harassment, bullying, and other abuses of power and authority, is a form of discrimination that, amongst other harms, limits fair access to the virtual and physical spaces where such harassment takes place.

The use of information and technology may cause new, or enhance existing, inequities. Technologies and practices should be as inclusive and accessible as possible and computing professionals should take action to avoid creating systems or technologies that disenfranchise or oppress people. Failure to design for inclusiveness and accessibility may constitute unfair discrimination.

4.5   1.5 Respect the Work Required to Produce New Ideas, Inventions, Creative Works, and Computing Artifacts

Developing new ideas, inventions, creative works, and computing artifacts creates value for society, and those who expend this effort should expect to gain value from their work. Computing professionals should therefore credit the creators of ideas, inventions, work, and artifacts, and respect copyrights, patents, trade secrets, license agreements, and other methods of protecting authors' works.

Both custom and the law recognize that some exceptions to a creator's control of a work are necessary for the public good. Computing professionals should not unduly oppose reasonable uses of their intellectual works. Efforts to help others by contributing time and energy to projects that help society illustrate a positive aspect of this principle. Such efforts include free and open source software and work put into the public domain. Computing professionals should not claim private ownership of work that they or others have shared as public resources.

4.6 1.6 Respect Privacy

The responsibility of respecting privacy applies to computing professionals in a particularly profound way. Technology enables the collection, monitoring, and exchange of personal information quickly, inexpensively, and often without the knowledge of the people affected. Therefore, a computing professional should become conversant in the various definitions and forms of privacy and should understand the rights and responsibilities associated with the collection and use of personal information.

Computing professionals should only use personal information for legitimate ends and without violating the rights of individuals and groups. This requires taking precautions to prevent re-identification of anonymized data or unauthorized data collection, ensuring the accuracy of data, understanding the provenance of the data, and protecting it from unauthorized access and accidental disclosure. Computing professionals should establish transparent policies and procedures that allow individuals to understand what data is being collected and how it is being used, to give informed consent for automatic data collection, and to review, obtain, correct inaccuracies in, and delete their personal data.

Only the minimum amount of personal information necessary should be collected in a system. The retention and disposal periods for that information should be clearly defined, enforced, and communicated to data subjects. Personal information gathered for a specific purpose should not be used for other purposes without the person's consent. Merged data collections can compromise privacy features present in the original collections. Therefore, computing professionals should take special care for privacy when merging data collections.

4.7 1.7 Honor Confidentiality

Computing professionals are often entrusted with confidential information such as trade secrets, client data, nonpublic business strategies, financial information, research data, pre-publication scholarly articles, and patent applications. Computing professionals should protect confidentiality except in cases where it is evidence of the violation of law, of organizational regulations, or of the Code. In these cases, the nature or contents of that information should not be disclosed except to appropriate authorities. A computing professional should consider thoughtfully whether such disclosures are consistent with the Code.

5 2. Professional Responsibilities

A computing professional should...

5.1 2.1 Strive to Achieve High Quality in Both the Processes and Products of Professional Work

Computing professionals should insist on and support high quality work from themselves and from colleagues. The dignity of employers, employees, colleagues, clients, users, and anyone else affected either directly or indirectly by the work should be respected through-out the process. Computing professionals should respect the right of those involved to transparent communication about the project. Professionals should be cognizant of any serious negative consequences affecting any stakeholder that may result from poor quality work and should resist inducements to neglect this responsibility.

5.2   2.2 Maintain High Standards of Professional Competence, Conduct, and Ethical Practice

High quality computing depends on individuals and teams who take personal and group responsibility for acquiring and maintaining professional competence. Professional com-petence starts with technical knowledge and with awareness of the social context in which their work may be deployed. Professional competence also requires skill in com-munication, in reflective analysis, and in recognizing and navigating ethical challenges. Upgrading skills should be an ongoing process and might include independent study, attending conferences or seminars, and other informal or formal education. Professional organizations and employers should encourage and facilitate these activities.

5.3   2.3 Know and Respect Existing Rules Pertaining to Professional Work

"Rules" here include local, regional, national, and international laws and regulations, as well as any policies and procedures of the organizations to which the professional belongs. Computing professionals must abide by these rules unless there is a compelling ethical justification to do otherwise. Rules that are judged unethical should be challenged. A rule may be unethical when it has an inadequate moral basis or causes recognizable harm. A computing professional should consider challenging the rule through existing channels before violating the rule. A computing professional who decides to violate a rule because it is unethical, or for any other reason, must consider potential consequences and accept responsibility for that action.

5.4   2.4 Accept and Provide Appropriate Professional Review

High quality professional work in computing depends on professional review at all stages. Whenever appropriate, computing professionals should seek and utilize peer and stakeholder review. Computing professionals should also provide constructive, critical reviews of others' work.

5.5   2.5 Give Comprehensive and Thorough Evaluations of Computer Systems and Their Impacts, Including Analysis of Possible Risks

Computing professionals are in a position of trust, and therefore have a special respon-sibility to provide objective, credible evaluations and testimony to employers, employ-ees, clients, users, and the public. Computing professionals should strive to be percep-tive, thorough, and objective when evaluating, recommending, and presenting system descriptions and alternatives. Extraordinary care should be taken to identify and mitigate potential risks in machine learning systems. A system for which future risks cannot be reliably predicted requires frequent reassessment of risk as the system evolves in use, or it should not be deployed. Any issues that might result in major risk must be reported to appropriate parties.

5.6   2.6 Perform Work Only in Areas of Competence

A computing professional is responsible for evaluating potential work assignments. This includes evaluating the work's feasibility and advisability, and making a judgment about whether the work assignment is within the professional's areas of competence. If at any time before or during the work assignment the professional identifies a lack of a necessary expertise, they must disclose this to the employer or client. The client or employer may decide to pursue the assignment with the professional after additional time to acquire the necessary competencies, to pursue the assignment with someone else who has the required expertise, or to forgo the assignment. A computing professional's ethical judgment should be the final guide in deciding whether to work on the assignment.

5.7   2.7 Foster Public Awareness and Understanding of Computing, Related Technologies, and Their Consequences

As appropriate to the context and one's abilities, computing professionals should share technical knowledge with the public, foster awareness of computing, and encourage understanding of computing. These communications with the public should be clear, respectful, and welcoming. Important issues include the impacts of computer systems, their limitations, their vulnerabilities, and the opportunities that they present. Additionally, a computing professional should respectfully address inaccurate or misleading information related to computing.

5.8   2.8 Access Computing and Communication Resources Only When Authorized or When Compelled by the Public Good

Individuals and organizations have the right to restrict access to their systems and data so long as the restrictions are consistent with other principles in the Code. Consequently, computing professionals should not access another's computer system, software, or data without a reasonable belief that such an action would be authorized or a compelling belief that it is consistent with the public good. A system being publicly accessible is not sufficient grounds on its own to imply authorization. Under exceptional circumstances a computing professional may use unauthorized access to disrupt or inhibit the functioning of malicious systems; extraordinary precautions must be taken in these instances to avoid harm to others.

5.9   2.9 Design and Implement Systems that Are Robustly and Usably Secure

Breaches of computer security cause harm. Robust security should be a primary consideration when designing and implementing systems. Computing professionals should perform due diligence to ensure the system functions as intended, and take appropriate action to secure resources against accidental and intentional misuse, modification, and denial of service. As threats can arise and change after a system is deployed, computing professionals should integrate mitigation techniques and policies, such as monitoring, patching, and vulnerability reporting. Computing professionals should also take steps to ensure parties affected by data breaches are notified in a timely and clear manner, providing appropriate guidance and remediation.

To ensure the system achieves its intended purpose, security features should be designed to be as intuitive and easy to use as possible. Computing professionals should discourage security precautions that are too confusing, are situationally inappropriate, or otherwise inhibit legitimate use.

In cases where misuse or harm are predictable or unavoidable, the best option may be to not implement the system.

6   3. Professional Leadership Principles

Leadership may either be a formal designation or arise informally from influence over others. In this section, "leader" means any member of an organization or group who has influence, educational responsibilities, or managerial responsibilities. While these principles apply to all computing professionals, leaders bear a heightened responsibility to uphold and promote them, both within and through their organizations.

A computing professional, especially one acting as a leader, should...

6.1   3.1 Ensure that the Public Good is the Central Concern During All Professional Computing Work

People—including users, customers, colleagues, and others affected directly or indirectly—should always be the central concern in computing. The public good should always be an explicit consideration when evaluating tasks associated with research, requirements analysis, design, implementation, testing, validation, deployment, maintenance, retirement, and disposal. Computing professionals should keep this focus no matter which methodologies or techniques they use in their practice.

6.2   3.2 Articulate, Encourage Acceptance of, and Evaluate Fulfillment of Social Responsibilities by Members of the Organization or Group

Technical organizations and groups affect broader society, and their leaders should accept the associated responsibilities. Organizations—through procedures and attitudes oriented toward quality, transparency, and the welfare of society—reduce harm to the public and raise awareness of the influence of technology in our lives. Therefore, leaders should encourage full participation of computing professionals in meeting relevant social responsibilities and discourage tendencies to do otherwise.

6.3   3.3 Manage Personnel and Resources to Enhance the Quality of Working Life

Leaders should ensure that they enhance, not degrade, the quality of working life. Leaders should consider the personal and professional development, accessibility requirements, physical safety, psychological well-being, and human dignity of all workers. Appropriate human-computer ergonomic standards should be used in the workplace.

6.4   3.4 Articulate, Apply, and Support Policies and Processes that Reflect the Principles of the Code

Leaders should pursue clearly defined organizational policies that are consistent with the Code and effectively communicate them to relevant stakeholders. In addition, leaders should encourage and reward compliance with those policies, and take appropriate action when policies are violated. Designing or implementing processes that deliberately or negligently violate, or tend to enable the violation of, the Code's principles is ethically unacceptable.

6.5   3.5 Create Opportunities for Members of the Organization or Group to Grow as Professionals

Educational opportunities are essential for all organization and group members. Leaders should ensure that opportunities are available to computing professionals to help them improve their knowledge and skills in professionalism, in the practice of ethics, and in their technical specialties. These opportunities should include experiences that familiarize computing professionals with the consequences and limitations of particular types of systems. Computing professionals should be fully aware of the dangers of oversimplified approaches, the improbability of anticipating every possible operating condition, the inevitability of software errors, the interactions of systems and their contexts, and other issues related to the complexity of their profession—and thus be confident in taking on responsibilities for the work that they do.

6.6   3.6 Use Care When Modifying or Retiring Systems

Interface changes, the removal of features, and even software updates have an impact on the productivity of users and the quality of their work. Leaders should take care when changing or discontinuing support for system features on which people still depend. Leaders should thoroughly investigate viable alternatives to removing support for a legacy system. If these alternatives are unacceptably risky or impractical, the developer should assist stakeholders' graceful migration from the system to an alternative. Users should be notified of the risks of continued use of the unsupported system long before support ends. Computing professionals should assist system users in monitoring the operational viability of their computing systems, and help them understand that timely replacement of inappropriate or outdated features or entire systems may be needed.

6.7 3.7 Recognize and Take Special Care of Systems that Become Integrated into the Infrastructure of Society

Even the simplest computer systems have the potential to impact all aspects of society when integrated with everyday activities such as commerce, travel, government, healthcare, and education. When organizations and groups develop systems that become an important part of the infrastructure of society, their leaders have an added responsibility to be good stewards of these systems. Part of that stewardship requires establishing policies for fair system access, including for those who may have been excluded. That stewardship also requires that computing professionals monitor the level of integration of their systems into the infrastructure of society. As the level of adoption changes, the ethical responsibilities of the organization or group are likely to change as well. Continual monitoring of how society is using a system will allow the organization or group to remain consistent with their ethical obligations outlined in the Code. When appropriate standards of care do not exist, computing professionals have a duty to ensure they are developed.

7 4. Compliance with the Code

A computing professional should…

7.1 4.1 Uphold, Promote, and Respect the Principles of the Code

The future of computing depends on both technical and ethical excellence. Computing professionals should adhere to the principles of the Code and contribute to improving them. Computing professionals who recognize breaches of the Code should take actions to resolve the ethical issues they recognize, including, when reasonable, expressing their concern to the person or persons thought to be violating the Code.

7.2 4.2 Treat Violations of the Code as Inconsistent with the Values of IFIP and Its Member Societies

Each IFIP member society should encourage and support adherence by all computing professionals regardless of IFIP membership. Individuals in IFIP member societies who recognize a breach of the Code should report the violation to their society, which may result in remedial action as specified in the individual member society's Code of Ethics and Professional Conduct Enforcement Policy.

The Code and guidelines were developed by the ACM Code 2018 Task Force: Executive Committee Don Gotterbarn* (Chair), Bo Brinkman, Catherine Flick*, Michael S Kirkpatrick, Keith Miller, Kate Varansky, and Marty J Wolf. Members: Eve Anderson, Ron Anderson, Amy Bruckman, Karla Carter, Michael Davis, Penny Duquenoy*, Jeremy Epstein, Kai Kimppa*, Lorraine Kisselburgh, Shrawan Kumar, Andrew McGettrick, Natasa Milic-Frayling, Denise Oram*, Simon Rogerson, David Shama, Janice Sipior, Eugene Spafford, and Les Waguespack. The Task Force was organized by the ACM Committee on Professional Ethics. Significant contributions to the Code were also made by the broader international ACM membership, including many IFIP members (marked with *).

This Code may be published without permission as long as it is not changed in any way and it carries the copyright notice.

Copyright (c) 2018 by the Association for Computing Machinery.

8 Contributors

Principle 2.5 stipulates that we should give proper credit to the creators of ideas. In some cases, such as the creation of this Code, that is a difficult task. The Code lists a range of people on organized committees who contributed to the Code, but this does not tell the full story of the many people around the world who thought ethics important enough to take their time and make positive contributions and corrections in the creation of this Code. A brilliant Australian on the executive committee drafted the intellectual property Principle. An anonymous commentator from a company in Italy was the impetus for Principle 2.9 addressing how failure to update systems facilitates the development of ransomware. This contributor was a member of one of the many groups commenting on the Code. The revision and the guidance of the "Harm clause" benefited from an extensive and heartfelt discussion on Twitter, Reddit, and other platforms with some discussants using pseudonyms. Anonymous contribution enables free and open comments but, inevitably, limits giving adequate credit for significant contributions and the countries they were from.

There were a number of task forces organized to respond to each draft, with members from industry and professional societies, some of whom represented subgroups they had organized to comment on the Code drafts rather than their company, country, or professional society; several IFIP members were involved in each of these groups. Taskforce affiliations also included ACM China, Europe, and India; ACM-W; Centre for Computing and Social Responsibility; Center for the Study of Ethics in the Professions; Deutsche Gesellschaft für Informatik; IEEE certification and Professional education; Google; Hoffman Business Ethics Center-Bentley; IFIP TC 9; IFIP WG 9.2; IFIP SIG 9.2.2 Ethical Frameworks; Intel; Microsoft Research; Oracle; Politecnico di Torino; Research Center on Computing and Society; Tata Consultancy Services; Tata Research and Design; and the US Technology Policy Committee.

These contributors represented an international collection of Computer Science, Information Systems, and Software Engineering departments and independent professionals in information systems management and development. Taskforce members were from Australia, Belgium, Canada, China, Denmark, England, Finland, Germany, Greece, India, Italy, Japan, Malaysia, Netherlands, New Zealand, Sweden, and the United States.

8.1 IFIP Task and Finish Group

Constituted at the IFIP General Assembly in Kiev in September 2019, the Task and Finish Group composed and prepared this document between October 2019 and August 2020. It was ratified and adopted at the IFIP General Assembly in September 2020.

Chair: David Kreps. David Kreps is a Philosopher of Information Systems at the National University of Ireland, Galway. He is Chair of IFIP Technical Committee 9 on ICTs and Society and a member of the IFIP Board. David is author of a range of books and papers on the philosophical and ethical aspects of the development of information systems and contemporary digital transformation.

Moira de Roche. Moira de Roche is an independent consultant. She is the Chair of IFIP International Professional Practice Partnership (IP3), and a member of the IFIP board. Moira is a Professional Member and Fellow of IITPSA. She is also a member of ACM. She is convinced that every decision must be viewed through an ethical lens.

Don Gotterbarn. Don Gotterbarn, an evangelist for professional computing, has extensive experience in academe and software systems development. He has spent several decades promoting responsible computing practices including leading the 2018 update of the ACM Code of Ethics and the development of the IEEE/ACM Software Engineering Code of Ethics and Professional Practice.

Margaret Havey. Margaret Havey is a Technical Advisor with Shared Services Canada, the Department responsible for the Government of Canada's ICT Infrastructures. She is a Professional Member and Fellow of CIPS, and is the Canada Country Member Representative to IFIP. Margaret became involved in ICT ethics in the early 2000's drafting a major revision to the CIPS Code of Ethics. She has a special interest in practical ethics.

Author Index

Printed in the United States
by Baker & Taylor Publisher Services